Alvin L. Arnold (J.D., Harvard University) is editor of *Real Estate Review* and Adjunct Professor of Real Estate, New York University. He is also editor of *Mortgage and Real Estate Executives' Report* and has authored or co-authored *The Arnold Encyclopedia of Real Estate*, *Real Estate Law Digest*, and several volumes of *Modern Real Estate and Mortgage Forms* and *Real Estate Review Portfolios*.

Charles H. Wurtzebach (Ph.D., University of Illinois at Urbana—Champaign) is Associate Professor of Real Estate and Finance at the University of Texas at Austin. Dr. Wurtzebach has been active in various executive development programs and has published articles in leading academic and professional journals. He is the president of Southwest Realty Research and Development, Inc., a real estate research and consulting organization.

Mike E. Miles (M.B.A., Stanford University, Ph.D., University of Texas at Austin, and CPA) is Associate Professor of Real Property Economics at the University of North Carolina at Chapel Hill. Dr. Miles is a member of the Finance group concentrating on real estate markets. In this capacity, he teaches at the undergraduate, M.B.A., and Ph.D. levels in several executive development programs. His research has been published in numerous scholarly and professional journals. Prior to his return to academic life, he was associated with Peat, Marwick, Mitchell & Co. and The Alpert Investment Corporation.

Consulting Editor:

Robert O. Harvey (Ph.D., Indiana University) is Professor and Chairman of Real Estate and Regional Science, Southern Methodist University. Dr. Harvey is well known for his activities in real estate education and has taught at Indiana University, University of California at Berkeley, University of Illinois at Urbana—Champaign, and University of Connecticut. He also serves as Educational Consultant to the National Association of Realtors®.

Modern Real Estate

Alvin L. Arnold
Editor, Real Estate Review

Charles H. Wurtzebach
University of Texas at Austin

Mike E. Miles
University of North Carolina at Chapel Hill

Consulting Editor:

Robert O. Harvey
Southern Methodist University

Warren, Gorham & Lamont
BOSTON AND NEW YORK

This book is dedicated to
Nancy, Susan, and Elston

Foreword

T HE author team of Arnold, Wurtzebach, and Miles is synergistic and unique. An impressive combination of academic, journalistic, and professional experience has resulted in an effective entry into this highly competitive textbook area, requiring both authors of recognition and a book of excellence. A balanced blend of the pragmatic and the theoretical has produced a highly adaptable and manageable text. The goal against which all decisions about content were measured was usefulness in real estate decisions.

It is a first-level text appropriate for an individual reader without formal classroom involvement as well as persons in structured classes at any level. The level of a course in which the book is used may be readily adjusted through instructor emphasis and collateral readings, many of which are referenced in the text.

The theme of the book is built around "the game" of real estate. The "game" can take a number of forms, but the goal in any case is "winning." The game most prominently treated calls for winning through maximizing after tax cash flows from real estate investment.

The prose is proper yet worldly. The theoretical foundations of the materials are absolute. The examples reflect the real world of real estate. The directives for analysis and action are correct and clear.

It has been a pleasure for me to counsel, mediate, negotiate, and participate with the authors in the preparation of this book.

ROBERT O. HARVEY

Preface

The past decade has been marked by a significant increase in the recognition given real estate both as a major investment vehicle and as a vital factor in our economy. This recognition, in turn, has led to the acceptance of real estate as an independent field of study requiring both academic preparation and practical experience. Growth in college and university real estate programs evidence this increased attention to real estate as an academic discipline. Educational programs sponsored by various professional real estate associations attest to the vigor with which the industry is promoting formal training both before and during a professional career.

This book is designed for use in introductory real estate courses taught at the college or university level. It will also provide useful background reading for business school graduates entering careers in real estate and related industries without the benefit of formal real estate education. Additionally, individuals entering real-estate-related careers who lack a business background will find *Modern Real Estate* a valuable source of information in a broad range of real estate areas.

As a classroom text, the book assumes previous or concurrent exposure to the standard "core" business courses. Drawing on the student's general business background, the book examines the unique features of real estate with a focus on *action* or *decision-making*. The concentration is on the "why" of decisions and the interrelationship among the key-decision-makers in the industry.

As the real estate business becomes more sophisticated, the real estate professional must make greater efforts to understand the essential workings of all aspects of the industry in order to make correct decisions in his specialized area. For example, the better sales associate is the one who knows real estate financing, law, and construction fundamentals as well as the fine details of real estate marketing. *Modern Real Estate* describes the workings and theoretical underpinnings of the major fields within the real estate industry and clarifies the linkages and relationships among the different fields. In so doing, the book offers a survey of the real estate industry which molds an academic perception with guides for practical decision-making. With this overview, the student may proceed in future study to develop expertise in any of the many specialty areas that make up the real estate industry.

Part I acquaints the student with the *spatial element* and the *interdis-*

ciplinary nature of the real estate industry. The place of real property in the American economic system is traced. The theme or unifying concept of the book is portrayed as the "real estate game." The reader learns the definition of a winner and is introduced to the players and their respective roles in the real estate market place. Working from this macroeconomic introduction, certain theories from regional and urban economics are analyzed to clarify the spatial element in real estate decisions.

Part II introduces the student to the basic concepts of the American legal system and the essentials of real estate law which make up the formal rules of the real estate game. The legal concepts with which the real estate decision-maker deals are explained.

Part III on appraisal is a straightforward presentation of real estate appraisal with an emphasis on what produces *value*. The practical dimension of regional and urban economics is shown in the appraisal process which itself serves as a stepping-stone to the investment section.

Part IV on marketing begins with a brief discussion of the basics of marketing in general and then moves to a consideration of the unique aspects of real estate marketing. The process of marketing the single-family home is distinguished from the marketing and leasing of income properties. Property management and its functions are the subject of a separate chapter. Appendixes describe the National Association of Realtors® and give an overview of brokerage office management.

Part V on finance first reviews the American financial system and identifies the lending institutions which finance real estate. Lender underwriting criteria and loan analysis are presented next, followed by financing mechanics from the borrower's perspective. An appendix to this part deals with the more complex operations of the secondary mortgage market.

Part VI on taxation begins with a brief summary of income and property taxation and emphasizes real estate's tax-favored status. The reader is then introduced to the major provisions of the Internal Revenue Code specifically affecting real estate.

Part VII on investment brings together the previous material in a real estate investment model. The unique features of real estate are highlighted, this time in a risk-return framework. The first chapter in this part reviews the principles of investment analysis. The second chapter develops the discounted cash flow model which is an extension of our original definition of winning the real estate game. The final chapter in the part discusses the various types of real estate investment from a risk-return perspective. The appendix covers more advanced material involving real estate portfolio considerations.

Part VIII's topic is the asset creation side of the real estate industry— real estate development. The description of the development process integrates material from previous parts on law, appraisal, marketing, finance, and investment. The appendix presents a methodology for market and economic feasibility analysis.

Part IX deals with a number of subjects which relate to the real estate industry as a whole. The major issues of public policy—the role of government in real estate—are identified. The importance of personal ethics is discussed. Finally, significant trends likely to have an impact on the industry to the end of the century and beyond are briefly noted.

Compound interest tables, a glossary, and an index provide comprehensive aids in understanding and using the concepts introduced in this book.

The authors are happy to note that both men and women are active and successful in the real estate profession. It is gratifying to note that women are entering the field in increasing numbers. However, if every sentence in this book used "he/she," "him/her," and "his/hers" when referring to the real estate professional, the book would become difficult to read. Therefore, for ease of expression, "he," "his," and "him" are used in this book in their grammatical sense and refer to the female as well as male real estate professional.

Acknowledgments

It would not be possible to recognize and thank all those individuals who have contributed to the development and preparation of this book. Our indebtedness extends to family, former students, and colleagues in academia and business.

However, special recognition and thanks must be given to four people. Robert O. Harvey of Southern Methodist University, as consulting editor on the project, worked closely with us throughout the development of early outlines, manuscript drafts, and final editing, and we greatly appreciate his valuable counsel and contributions. Steven Sears, University of Illinois, Champaign—Urbana, contributed greatly to the secondary mortgage markets appendix. Eugene Simonoff initially brought the authors together and with constant encouragement and unlimited good humor kept the project on schedule. Marie C. Orsini provided outstanding editorial support and somehow kept track of a multitude of manuscript versions. Special thanks go to Tony Gigante for his unfailing patience and expertise in production matters.

We are particularly indebted to the contribution made by the following colleagues who offered insight and suggestions throughout the preparation of this book: James A. Graaskamp, University of Wisconsin—Madison; Michael A. Goldberg, University of British Columbia; William B. Brueggeman, Southern Methodist University; Fred E. Case, University of California, Los Angeles; Kenneth M. Lusht, Pennsylvania State University; Raymond W. Lansford, University of Missouri—Columbia; Wallace F.

Smith, University of California, Berkeley; Howard H. Stevenson, Harvard University; Harold A. Lubell, Assistant Attorney General of New York in charge of the Real Estate Financing Bureau; F. L. Wilson, Jr., Realty Growth Investors, Baltimore, Maryland; and Charles B. Akerson, Akerson Valuation Company, Boston, Massachusetts. Helena R. Frost aided in researching the graphics in this book. We are also grateful to those who helped prepare the manuscript for publication, including Jo Ann Drew, Kathleen Forrest, Nancy Heleman, and Ginger Travis.

A.L.A.
C.H.W.
M.E.M.

January 1980

Contents

VI Taxation

VII Investment

Investment Constraints. ELEMENTS OF INVESTMENT
ANALYSIS. The Accounting Framework. The Time Value of
Money. Two Parts of Real Estate Return. TYPES OF RISK.
Business Risk. Financial Risk. Purchasing Power Risk.
Liquidity Risk. DEFINITIONS OF RISK. Risk as Variance.
Risk of Ruin. Positive Correlation Between Risk and Return.
Risk Aversion. DERIVING THE DISCOUNT RATE. SUMMARY.

Partner.   The Construction Lender.   The Permanent Lender.
The Long-Term Equity Investor.   The Architect.   The
Engineer.   The General Contractor.   Final Users.
Regulators.   Different Risk-Return Perspectives of
Participants.   PRIMARY DECISIONS.   How Should the Site Be
Acquired?   How Expensive Should the Feasibility Study Be?
What Types of Financing Should Be Obtained?.   Who Should
the General Contractor Be?   Should a Major Tenant or Tenants
Be Presigned?   Should the Developer Take in a Joint Venture
Partner?   Should the Developer Presell the Equity to Passive
Investors?   Should an Outside Leasing Agent or Sales Firm Be
Used?   Should an Outside Management Firm Be Employed?
What Government Approvals Will Be Required?   ADDITIONAL
DECISION POINTS.   The Termination Options.   SUMMARY.

IX   Public Policy

INSTITUTIONALIZATION OF THE INDUSTRY.   Development
Financing.   Investment.   Brokerage.   COMPUTERS.
SUMMARY

I
The Analytical Framework

1

The American Real Estate Industry—An Overview

THE REAL ESTATE INDUSTRY is, or can be viewed as, a market-oriented game—a game in the sense that it has players, rules, and a way to determine a winner. Just how this is so is developed throughout this book.

REAL ESTATE AS A MARKETPLACE GAME

Just what is meant by the *real estate game?* In the game context, the winner is the player who ends up with the most chips. In real estate, the chips, using more conventional accounting definitions, are operating cash flows and proceeds from sales.[1] In games, players must act in accordance with previously determined rules. In real estate, a host of formal legal rules and less defined social values limits the real estate professional's actions. Games and the real estate industry both involve different roles for the players, with each having a different strategy in the effort to win. (See **1-1.**).

To play the game, a physical product (e.g., an apartment house) must first be introduced. Then, an estimate must be made of what cash flows it can generate during its life. This estimate must be made in light of the various market factors (e.g., supply of competing apartment units and increases in operating costs) that will impact on the building's operations. Finally, these direct factors must be viewed in light of the *externalities* (i.e., the positive or negative effects of surrounding land parcels). These are associated with the project and an inquiry must be made as to how they affect operating cash flows.[2]

After arriving at an estimate of the future cash flows expected to be generated by the project, the various claims on those cash flows are

---

[1] Of course, there are other measures of success apart from cash flow, and these are discussed later on in the book.

[2] It should be noted that the particular project under consideration will also cause externalities for surrounding properties.

1-1. A WORD ABOUT THE REAL ESTATE MARKETPLACE

The *real estate marketplace* actually consists of a very large number of separate markets, differentiated by (1) geographic location (neighborhood, city, and region, and, in some cases, national or international) and (2) type of real estate (single-family homes, office buildings, industrial properties, etc.). Indeed, since each parcel of property has a unique location which cannot be duplicated, it might almost be said that an infinite number of markets exist.

The real estate marketplaces are the stages on which the players (described in Chapter 2) carry out the activities which constitute the real estate game.

considered. One claim—typically the largest—is that of the lender(s). This player (usually a bank or other financial institution) and its role are studied in considerable detail in this book. Another claimant is the government, which takes a share designated as *taxes*. The rules for determining this share as well as the efforts to minimize it (called *tax shelter*) are also analyzed at length.

Finally, there remains the residual, or equity, cash flow. From a real estate equity investor's standpoint, winning the game is determined by the size of the residual share, the likelihood of receiving it, and the length of time that must elapse before all of it is in hand.[3]

To summarize, the analysis of real estate investment takes the form of a *model* which

- Begins with an operating cash flow which reflects the characteristics of a particular marketplace and the externalities associated with a particular project, and which then
- Deducts claims by lenders, government, and others that have priority over the equity claim, and which
- Ends with a residual cash flow belonging to the equity owner (investor).

REAL ESTATE AS MORE THAN JUST A GAME

It must be stressed that there is *harmony* between playing to win and the successful working of our economy. This is merely another way of stating the basic philosophic premise of Adam Smith in his book, *The Wealth of Nations*. Smith, the eighteenth century English philosopher-

---

[3] This introduction could be approached by presenting real estate as a critical part of the overall economy which, in turn, is vitally important to our lives. Or, this discipline can be seen as a collection of individuals trying to win something for themselves. Both perspectives will be useful, and, hopefully, in the end, there will be a synthesis of the two.

economist, stated that the self-interested dealings of buyers and sellers operating in the marketplace yield the best overall results for society as a whole. The invisible "guiding hand" assures that entrepreneurs working for their own individual benefit will unknowingly also be working to achieve the best possible outcome for the entire society.

Another point to be made about real estate not being just a game is that the players, through their actions, affect a great many important areas of our national life that are not merely "economic." Private development's effect on the physical environment is the most dramatic example; others include the social implications of tax policy, urban and suburban development, and methods of transport. As a result, as is seen in Part IX, society, through government, periodically changes the rules of the game in an effort to assure that the "guiding hand" continues to work—in both economic and noneconomic areas. When the rules are changed, private rights often give way to public rights, and the stresses involved in this "taking" may test the belief in democracy of those individuals who are adversely affected. (See 1-2.)

Philosophy is part of the basis of economics and therefore has a place in the analytical framework of the real estate industry. It is a critical element in building a winning strategy for the real estate game. Without it, one would not be able to understand changing public policy which helps determine the rules of the game.

1-2. AIR TRAFFIC AND PRIVATE PROPERTY

Under English and American common law, ownership of real estate traditionally included ownership of the air space "to the heavens." Consequently, when airplane traffic began early in this century, some landowners sued for damages for invasion of air space (*trespass*). The courts had little difficulty in "reinterpreting" the common law to mean that ownership of air space extended only to a height which the landowner could reasonably anticipate making use of (to put up a building, for example). In this situation, limiting private rights for the benefit of the public seemed wholly justified.

But as years passed, a more serious issue arose. Owners of homes and businesses near airports complained that the noise of arriving and departing airplanes diminished the usability of their property. (In one famous case, the owner of a mink ranch claimed his animals could not breed.) These owners sued for damages.

While most courts have ruled that just as in the above situation, private use must yield to the paramount public right, some cases have gone in favor of the landowner. Factors that courts have considered include: (1) the number of landowners affected (and the consequent burden on the public purse if damages were to be granted), (2) whether property was acquired before or after the noise problem began, and (3) the degree of interference created by the air traffic.

REAL ESTATE DEFINED

Property refers to things and objects capable of ownership—that is, things and objects which can be used, controlled, or disposed of by an owner. *Real property* (and *real estate*, which is treated as synonomous) consists of physical land plus structures and other improvements that are permanently attached.

In a more technical sense, *real property* refers to *the rights, interests, and benefits* inherent in the ownership of real estate. Put another way, one owns not land as such, but a bundle of rights to use and dispose of land and its improvements. Society, through the legislature and the courts, defines the bundle of rights and can change the definitions from time to time. For example, zoning land for residential use eliminates the landowner's right to put a factory on the site. This general subject is discussed in detail in Parts II and IX. At this point, it can be said that property ownership confers the right to receive the cash flow from property subject to any prior claims (e.g., by the government for real estate taxes).

The Volume of Land in the United States

A familiar phrase in real estate is *under all is the land.* That certainly is a literal statement of fact. Just how much land is there in the United States? There are approximately 2.3 billion acres. An acre is 43,560 square feet or 4,840 square yards. A rectangular parcel of land 210 feet by 207 feet is approximately one acre, and there are 640 acres in a square mile. A single-family house in an urban area can be put up on as small a site as one-eighth acre. A large shopping center might take up 40 to 100 acres or more. With several billion acres available, there never has been, nor is there ever likely to be, an absolute shortage of land. However, *well-located* land definitely is in short supply in many places. What makes land well located is a key part of understanding the real estate industry.[4]

In terms of ownership, the federal government owns 33 percent of the total acreage in the United States. (Since a large portion of this land is located in Alaska and other remote areas, the value of federal land is much less than 33 percent of the total.) State and local governments own another 8 percent, with American Indians owning 2 percent. Of the remaining land, 3 percent is classified as urban (i.e., developed or imminently developable land). This leaves 54 percent of the total acreage as privately owned rural land. (See Figure 1-1.)

---

[4] A similar argument can also be made for agricultural land. There is no shortage of land which may legally be farmed but there may be shortages of highly productive land.

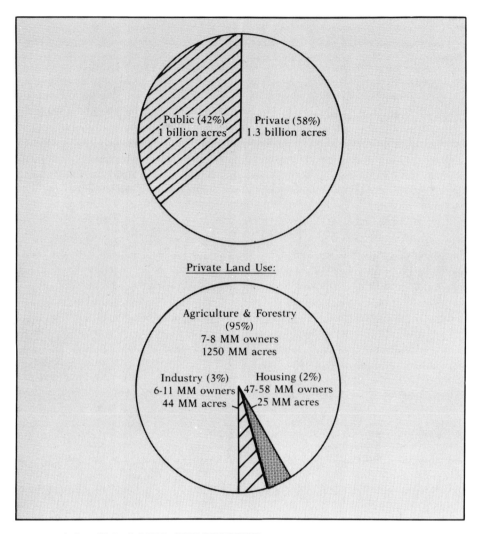

Figure 1-1.   U.S. LAND OWNERSHIP

FEATURES OF THE REAL ESTATE ASSET

The key characteristic of the real estate asset is its association with *land.* All of the features that distinguish real estate from non-real-estate assets flow from this association. These features fall into two main categories: (1) physical and (2) economic.

Physical Features

The physical features of real estate are three:

☐ *Immobility.* Real estate is fixed in location and cannot be moved.[5] Therefore, it is at the mercy of the environment around it. One consequence of real estate's immobility is that real estate markets are primarily local, or, to put it another way, no national market exists for real estate as it does for most manufactured or farm commodities.[6] However, for some properties, the market may be local or international, depending on the use and property rights involved. For example, interests in single-family houses are generally traded locally, while investment interests are often traded in international markets.

☐ *Unique location (heterogeneity).* Because land is immobile, it follows that every single parcel of real estate has a location that cannot be duplicated. Every parcel of real estate, being unique, is therefore heterogeneous or one of a kind. By comparison, commodities, such as grain or coal, or intangibles, such as shares of stock in General Motors Corporation, are exactly alike and are called *fungibles;* it makes no difference to the purchaser which particular one of a group of equal quality he gets.

☐ *Indestructibility.* The third physical feature of land is that, both as a physical asset and as the object of legal interests, it is viewed as indestructible. Land may be mined, eroded, flooded, or desolated; nevertheless, the designated location on the earth's surface remains forever.

Economic Features

Turning next to the economic features of real estate, it can be seen that they generally parallel the physical ones:

☐ *Scarcity.* Since every location is unique, only certain parcels can satisfy the requirements of a particular project or investment. So even though no absolute shortage of land exists in the United States, land for a particular purpose at a particular time and place may be quite scarce. The preference of a purchaser for a particular location is critical in determining the value of real estate. One site, because of its relationship to places of employment, shopping, transportation, schools, and even to the properties immediately surrounding it, can command a much higher price than land with similar physical or topographical features but with a slightly different location.

---

[5] One does hear, from time to time, of homes or other improvements affixed to land being severed and relocated. However, between the time of severance and reattachment, these technically become personal rather than real property.

[6] There is a well-established and active national market for the purchase and sale of mortgages—called the secondary mortgage market—but that is primarily a financial rather than a real estate market.

☐ *Long economic life.* While improvements and additions to land are not indestructible in the sense that land itself is, they do normally have long useful lives. For example, there are homes built at the time of American independence that still are habitable. Of course, they have been remodeled and modernized, with new heating, plumbing, and electrical systems, but the original structure remains. This relative immunity of well-maintained structures against physical deterioration leads to an interesting phenomenom—the fact that buildings rarely fall down but are more often torn down because a new use will make the site more productive and hence more valuable. (This is discussed in greater detail in Part III.)

☐ *Modification.* The economic concept of modification focuses on the impact of development on the total value of a parcel—reflecting the fact that existing or potential future development can have a significant impact upon value. More particularly, it can often be seen that development has a synergistic impact upon property value. For example, the market or investment value of a completed project will normally be greater than the total of the individual costs of the land, labor, and materials necessary to develop the project. Conversely, modification (development) does not guarantee the synergistic value impact. If an incorrect or poor decision is made, the developed value may be well below the cost.

☐ *Situs.* The fourth important economic feature of land is the value placed upon a specific location (situs) by individual or group choices and preferences. Preferring to live in the northwest quadrant of a city or the emerging desire by many to move back to the city rather than out of it, are examples of the situs phenomenon. The result will surely affect the economic value of the site even if identical improvements are available in some other neighborhood or area. As a consequence, land values on one side of town may be twice as high as those elsewhere in the city. In such cases, the economic difference can only be attributed to varying user tastes and preferences.

REAL ESTATE AND THE GENERAL ECONOMY

Before moving to a further study of the real estate industry itself (or, as economists say, a microanalysis), real estate should be viewed as part of the overall economic life of the nation.

Gross National Product

One way to do this is to look at gross national product (GNP)—the value of all goods and services produced in the country. GNP is now running about $2 trillion a year—roughly $10,000 per person. Of this total, individuals consume about 63 percent, the government purchases another 21 percent, and the private sector invests 15 to 16 percent. This reinvestment must be noted because it determines the nation's productive capacity in the future. Private investment *first* must be sufficient to provide for replacement of existing depreciated assets and *second* must provide for new investments if the nation's productive capacity is to improve (i.e., if society's wealth is to increase).

From a real estate standpoint, it is interesting to note that over half of annual domestic private investment is in real property assets, and over half of this (one-quarter of the total) is in residential housing. Remember that these figures do not include governmental investment in real property. In short, the investment factor in GNP is a key figure, and real estate is the largest component of gross private domestic investment.

National Income

A second way to get a feel for the relative importance of the real estate industry is to look at national income. *National income* is essentially GNP minus depreciation and indirect business taxes. The different components of national income are:

- *Compensation of employees*, which represents about 77 percent of the total and has been increasing over the past two decades.
- *Corporate profit*, which today represents about 8 percent of GNP and has been decreasing over the past two decades.
- *Proprietors' income*, which represents about 7 percent of the total and has also been decreasing.
- *Rent*, which is about 2 percent and decreasing.
- *Interest*, which is about 6 percent and increasing.

The relationship between the last two items is interesting. Two decades ago, rent was nearly three times interest, whereas today interest is three to four times rent. Why has this happened? One reason is that interest rates have risen more rapidly than rents (and there are several causes for this). Another is that over the past quarter-century borrowed capital has increased as a percentage of the total financing for real estate investment. For both reasons, more of total cash flow is going to lenders. This means lenders have gradually been obtaining a more active voice in decision-making in the real estate industry.

Employment

Another way to come to grips with the scope of the real estate industry is to look at national employment figures. Approximately 78 million non-farm workers were employed in the United States in the late 1970s. Of these, about 1 million were classified as being in the real estate business, with another 4 million being employed in construction, which, for the purposes of this book, is part of the real estate industry. Thus, about 6 percent of nonfarm employment is represented by real estate. This is an impressive figure and indicates that the creation of new jobs is one reason why government at all levels is continually interested in new construction of real estate projects.

An interesting sidelight to the total employment figures deals with the number of people actively marketing real estate. In 1969, less than 100,000 persons were entitled to be designated Realtors® (a designation limited to members who have satisfied specified requirements of the National Association of Realtors® (NAR®) the leading real estate trade association in the United States).[7] This figure has risen to over 700,000. This tremendous rise in the number of people involved in the service functions associated with real property illustrates the extraordinary growth in real estate transactions in that period as well as the increased interest in real estate by people throughout the country.

Importance for Decision-Making

Why are such matters of macroeconomics important to microlevel decision-making? Even though the real estate game is primarily played in a series of local markets, the industry is always and sometimes dramatically affected by national economic conditions. The extent of this impact varies from market to market, whether defined by geography or property type. Certainly, the price of construction materials is set by national conditions; so is the price of money (interest), and this often is the most important cost of all. Labor tends to be more of a localized phenomenon (because people really are not as mobile as many economics texts assume), but nevertheless remains subject to trends within the national economy. Witness recent regional population shifts to the Southeast and Sun Belt.

Real estate also has a significant impact *on* the macroeconomy. The construction industry, in its broadest definition (which includes the construction of industrial plants, highways, and other public facilities as well as homes and commercial properties), is larger than any other industry, accounting for almost 10 percent of the GNP. (In dollar terms, about $164 billion of new construction was completed in 1979.) The real estate industry is a major source of employment, a voracious user of capital, and, insofar as housing is concerned, a provider of one of the basic necessities of life. Consequently, government at all levels has assumed a major role in real estate.

Since the Housing Act of 1948, which set forth the goal of "a decent home and suitable living environment for all Americans," the federal

---

[7] In the early 1970's, sales associates became eligible for the title Realtor® Associate. Accordingly, the Realtor® ranks increased immediately by about 450,000 and then grew more gradually to the present figure in excess of 700,000.

government has been an active, even aggressive, player in the real estate game. A major cabinet-level department, the U.S. Department of Housing and Urban Development (HUD), is totally devoted to real estate issues, with many other departments devoting a significant portion of their time to real estate. Further, local governments are even more involved in real estate matters from land use regulation to real property taxation. The multifaceted role of government in real estate is developed throughout this book until, in Part IX, the logic behind governmental involvement is studied so that future changes in its role can be anticipated.

REAL ESTATE AND THE NATIONAL WEALTH

If the real estate market has gamelike characteristics and the goal is to maximize the residual value to the equity holder, then, in a long-term sense, the object really is to maximize wealth. In this regard, it is interesting to look at some national wealth statistics as part of our effort to get a proper feel for the role of real estate in the national economy. (See Tables 1-1 and 1-2.)

Total national wealth, recent figures show, amounts to about $9 trillion. Of this, one-fourth (about $2.2 trillion) represents the 55 million

Table 1-1. CHANGE IN WEALTH INSTRUMENTS: 1967 TO 1975 (in billions of dollars)

TYPE OF ASSET	CURRENT DOLLARS		CONSTANT (1958) DOLLARS	
	1967	1975	1967	1975
Total tangible assets	2,679.5	5,587.6	2,152.6	2,772.1
Total reproducible assets	2,088.6	4,302.8	1,765.4	2,299.3
Structures [1]	1,215.9	2,555.3	958.1	1,187.3
Nonfarm	1,203.8	2,534.4	948.0	1,176.2
Residential [2]	425.7	952.9	337.9	440.1
Public nonresidential	356.2	745.4	281.1	318.7
Institutional	50.8	125.6	37.3	47.7
Other priv. nonresidential	371.1	710.5	291.7	369.7
Residential-rental	170.5	350.7	134.9	162.8
Farm structures	12.1	20.9	10.1	11.1
Equipment	541.6	1,040.3	502.4	713.4
Priv. business and public equip.	315.9	543.7	277.4	358.6
Consumer durables	225.7	496.6	225.0	354.8
Inventories	331.1	707.2	304.9	398.6
Private farm	27.7	43.9	26.4	31.4
Private nonfarm	268.3	555.8	244.9	314.0
Public	35.1	107.5	33.6	53.2
Land	590.9	1,284.8	387.2	472.8
Private farm	152.7	336.2	88.3	87.0
Private nonfarm	302.4	705.6	201.5	258.5
Public	135.8	243.0	97.4	127.3

SOURCE: U.S. Bureau of the Census, *Statistical Abstract of the United States: 1978* (99th ed.) (Washington, D.C.: U.S. Government Printing Office, 1978), p. 478.

Table 1-2. COMPONENTS OF PERSONAL WEALTH BY ASSET: 1958-1972 (in billions of dollars)

ASSET	1958 Value of gross personal assets held by—			1958 Percent held by—		1972 Value of gross personal assets held by—			1972 Percent held by—	
	All persons	Top ½ percent of all	Top 1 percent of all	Top ½ percent of all	Top 1 percent of all	All persons	Top ½ percent of all	Top 1 percent of all	Top ½ percent of all	Top 1 percent of all
Total assets	1,625.1	332.0	414.4	20.4	25.5	4,344.4	822.4	1,046.9	18.9	24.1
Real estate	621.5	62.5	93.9	10.1	15.1	1,492.6	150.9	225.0	10.1	15.1
Corporate stock	264.1	175.9	199.2	66.6	75.4	870.9	429.3	491.7	49.3	56.5
Bonds	87.0	31.3	36.0	36.0	41.4	158.0	82.5	94.8	52.2	60.0
Cash	216.0	22.5	32.8	10.4	15.2	748.8	63.6	101.2	8.5	13.5
Debt instruments	43.7	12.5	16.3	28.6	37.3	77.5	30.3	40.8	39.1	52.7
Life insurance	79.9	7.5	11.3	9.4	14.1	143.0	6.2	10.0	4.3	7.0
Trusts	30.3	25.8	27.9	85.1	92.1	99.4	80.3	89.4	80.8	89.9
Miscellaneous	312.9	19.8	24.9	6.3	7.9	853.6	59.5	83.3	6.8	9.8
Liabilities	227.4	29.2	38.3	12.9	16.8	808.5	100.7	131.0	12.5	16.2
Net worth	1,396.7	302.8	376.1	21.7	26.9	3,535.9	721.7	915.9	20.4	25.9
Number of persons, mil.	(X)	.87	1.74	(X)	(X)	(X)	1.04	2.09	(X)	(X)

SOURCE: U.S. Bureau of the Census, *Statistical Abstract of the United States: 1978* (99th ed.) (Washington, D.C.: U.S. Government Printing Office, 1978), p. 478.

single-family homes in the nation. This sum, in turn, is made up of $700 billion in mortgages and $1.5 trillion in homeowner equity.[8]

Wealth can be defined as the money value of a person's possessions or rights in personal and real property. (The concept of *national wealth* is somewhat different since it includes publicly owned property as well.) Wealth, being money value, can be described as a function of three elements:

- The expected income stream from the property rights.
- The riskiness or likelihood of receiving the expected income stream.
- The timing of the expected income stream.

Put another way, in determining a person's wealth, a discount (for risk and for the time value of money) must be applied to the expected income. These relationships are developed more fully in Part VII, but it is appropriate to remember that the value of the equity (residual) interest in real estate is a function of these three elements.

Looking at personal assets today (including stocks, bonds, and savings), one finds that the value of real estate is nearly double the value of all common stock. This represents a dramatic change within the past decade or so since in 1969 the value of all corporate stocks and bonds was approximately equal to the value of all real estate claims. Much of this shift of value toward real estate was due to the decline in common stock prices during the rapid inflation experienced during the period. (See Table 1-2).

[8] *NAR ® Press Release* (1979).

REAL ESTATE DEMAND AND SUPPLY

Returning from the world of macroeconomics, it should be understood that the equity investor's return primarily depends on the price which can be obtained for the product sold, which is *space*—more accurately, space-over-time with certain associated services. For example, the indoor tennis club sells space per hour, the motel, space per day, and the apartment building, space per month or year (all of these being designated as rental space). The home builder, on the other hand, sells space subject to no time limit.

The price that can be charged for space is a function of the same three elements that set any other type of price: (1) demand, (2) supply, and (3) public policy restraints.

Demand

Only *effective demand* is relevant to use. That is, potential users of proposed space not only must exist, but they must have the purchasing power to acquire (through purchase, lease, or whatever) the desired space over time plus associated services. This is true of demand for any product.

But real estate is more complicated because it is *both* a capital good and a consumer good. For-sale housing (a single-family house or condominium or cooperative unit) is a consumer good—it is sold directly to the occupant-user. It is also the largest investment asset of many homeowners. Most other kinds of real estate—income properties—are owned by investors who then sell space (via a lease or other means) to the final consumer. It may be said that the entire building is a capital good, intended to produce income, while the individual units of space within are the consumer goods, intended for actual occupancy and use.

In the final analysis, real estate will be profitable only to the extent the space available is occupied and paid for, whether outright (through purchase) or from period to period (through rent). Thus, a developer should make careful market studies to ascertain the probable extent of effective demand for the space when it is expected to be ready. This is not always done properly. One trouble with market studies can be that four developers simultaneously identify a demand for, say a 100-unit project, and each builds a project so that 400 units swamp the market. Real estate market analysis is far from a precise science, as is discussed in Part VIII.

Supply

The key to analyzing supply is the ability of a constructed asset to satisfy needs—that is, attention must be paid to the utility derived from

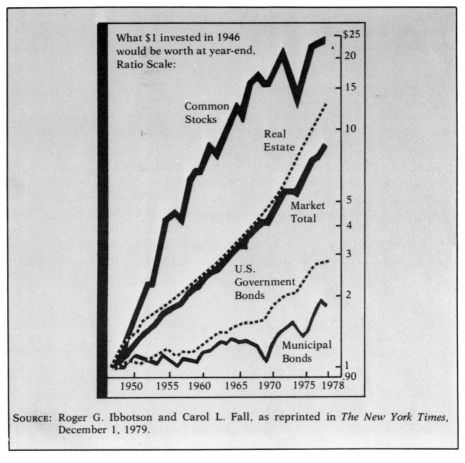

What $1 invested in 1946 would be worth at year-end, Ratio Scale:

Common Stocks

Real Estate

Market Total

U.S. Government Bonds

Municipal Bonds

SOURCE: Roger G. Ibbotson and Carol L. Fall, as reprinted in *The New York Times*, December 1, 1979.

Figure 1-2. HOW SELECTED INVESTMENTS HAVE FARED

the asset. Three special factors are involved when supply of real estate is discussed: (1) time, (2) place, and (3) substitution.

☐ *Time.* The long construction period for real estate means that supply often lags behind demand. This affects the marketplace in both expansionary and contracting phases of the business cycle. During periods of expansion, supply lag means that demand is unsatisfied so prices and rentals rise. During periods of contraction, supply lag (the inability of producers to stop work on a project under construction) results in an oversupply of space. For-sale units remain unsold, and vacancies in rental properties are high.

☐ *Place.* As already noted, one of the unique characteristics of real estate is its fixed location. New supply can only be created by (1) new construction or (2) substitution at the particular location; it cannot be transferred from elsewhere (as, for example, oil, grain, or capital may be).

☐ *Substitution.* To some degree, one kind of real estate may be converted to another in order to meet shifts in demand. For example, the demand for owned (compared to rented) residential units has been quite high in recent years as individuals seek to take advantage of the considerable tax benefits of home ownership, as well as its ability (so far) to appreciate in step with inflation. This has resulted in the conversion of rental apartments to condominiums in many parts of the country. An even more striking example is the conversion of unused commercial or loft space in many cities into residential properties due to the increased effective demand for housing. Substitution often meets with obstacles in the form of zoning laws, building codes, and tenant-protection legislation. Such legislation often seeks to slow down the conversion of rental properties to condominiums in the interests of tenants who may lack the capital to purchase their residential units.

Public Policy Restraints

In addition to basic supply and demand considerations, a third factor is important in real estate pricing. This is the restraint on new development and redevelopment by government regulation, which expresses public policy. The regulation of land development in the interest of environmental protection is a good example.

Much regulation on the local level, while purportedly aimed at protecting the environment, may actually seek to slow down or even prevent growth in order to preserve the style of living preferred by the existing residents. Whatever the motive, these restraints can effectively limit additions to supply. This usually results in higher prices.

In the interests of providing adequate housing for those otherwise unable to afford it, government at all levels has made available a large number of programs to subsidize, insure, or directly finance new and rehabilitated housing. In addition, the government plays a vital role in providing the necessary infrastructure (roads, sewer and water facilities, schools, etc.) that are the necessary preliminary to new development. The relationship among the government's roles as regulator, supplier, and user of real estate as well as the policy implications of the government's role—what types of activities should be encouraged and who should pay the cost—are discussed further in Parts VI and IX.

PERCEPTIONS, EXPECTATIONS, AND PSYCHIC INCOME

Real estate is different from most other economic assets both in the way people perceive it and in what they expect of it. A few thoughts on these subjects round out this introductory overview of the real estate industry.

Perceptions

Consider first the question of home ownership. One's home always represents both an investment and a use; home ownership gives one shelter, status, and an investment. But in the past few years, the investment aspect of home ownership has become much more important. Clearly, this has been due to the effectiveness of private homes as an inflation hedge. (See **1-3.**)

For the past several years, home prices have been increasing at the rate of 10 to 15 percent a year, significantly faster than the general rate of inflation and offering a much better return to the individual investor than other common forms of investment. This is one reason why home buyers are willing to pay ever larger portions of their total income to carry a house. Until fairly recently, it was taken as an article of faith by many lenders that no more than 25 percent of a family's income should go for

1-3. HOW AMERICANS THINK ABOUT HOUSING

A 1979 survey of over 300,000 homeowners confirms what most commentators say: The single-family house occupies a preeminent role in American life, and upgrading one's home is one of the most important avenues of social mobility. Some key findings of the survey are:

☐ Not surprisingly, 97 percent feel their home is a good investment. Only 26 percent say they must make significant sacrifices in other areas to maintain their present home.

☐ If a move were contemplated, the most important consideration for 42 percent would be a more energy-efficient house, while 35 percent want more land and 26 percent want a bigger house. Only 9 percent would be interested in less expensive housing or in a low-tax neighborhood. And, a surprisingly low one percent mentioned a new development house.

☐ Even though 63 percent of owners do not consider their home a financial burden, 87 percent think the single-family home is being priced out of the reach of the average American family (perhaps indicating that few of us think of ourselves as average).

☐ In a 1972 survey, 22 percent said that an apartment in a comparable neighborhood would be as good a place to raise children as a single-family house. Despite the rising costs of home ownership, this figure rose only to 26 percent in the current survey, indicating the overwhelming preference of Americans for the single-family house.

housing or rental costs. This rule has become obsolete, at least in connection with home ownership. This is true even though more women than ever are entering the work force and their pay is now counted as part of the family income.

A study of housing costs by the U.S. League of Savings Associations indicated that throughout the United States, 38 percent of all homeowners spend more than 25 percent of their income to carry their own homes. Home ownership costs generally are considered to include: (1) mortgage payments covering interest and amortization, (2) real estate taxes, and (3) insurance premiums. While it is true that in older European societies, even greater proportions of total income are spent on shelter, nevertheless the sharp upsurge in housing costs in the United States is a source of concern to many analysts.[9]

Investors in income property also have experienced a change in their perception of real estate. In the 1960s and the early 1970s, tax ramifications dominated many investment decisions. The game then was as much or more tax shelter as it was real estate. More recently, economic feasibility and prospective value appreciation have assumed the forefront of investment considerations. This shift has been caused primarily by two factors: (1) tax reform and (2) inflation.

Expectations

It seems fair to say that most people expect continued appreciation in real estate values. As already noted, this is a prime reason for the increased desire for home ownership by the general public. The same expectation on the part of income property investors can be inferred from their willingness to buy property at prices that permit them to realize a relatively small annual cash flow. On the other hand, "no tree grows to the sky."

For example, it seems difficult to believe that farmland prices can continue to rise as rapidly in the future without a concomitant rise in prices received by farmers. In other words, expectations of continued price increases works only for a while; the point finally comes when investors see that there is no longer economic logic behind the price increases and prices cease rising and either stabilize or decline.

Another way of stating this is to say that the "greater fool" theory of investing works only for a limited time. Under this theory, investors justify purchases at a high price because subsequent resales can be made to an even greater fool at an even higher price. Ultimately, when no greater fool can be found, prices stop rising.

---

[9] Note that utility costs have also been increasing in recent years, and this is another cost associated with home ownership.

Psychic Income

It is clear that satisfaction derived from the ownership of real estate is often nonpecuniary in nature. Examples of such psychic income abound in the marketplace. In the housing sector, this phenomenon is known as "keeping up with the Joneses" or expressed as "pride of ownership." Such utility derived from ownership certainly represents a return to homeowners and, as such, affects the price they are willing to pay. Investors, too, derive psychic income from their ownership share (however small) in a prestigious building such as the Empire State Building in New York City. Users may pay a premium rent for the "right address," whether residential or commercial.

SUMMARY

The general overview in this chapter forms the basis of a decision-making framework which is completed in the next two chapters. This overview has identified all of the key concepts to be developed in more depth throughout the book in the course of carrying out two objectives: (1) describing how the real estate industry operates and (2) analyzing the decision-making process utilized by the major participants.

The emphasis throughout is on understanding why real estate players play the way they do, why real estate institutions function as they do, and why the real estate markets price assets as they do. Thus, purely descriptive material is kept to a minimum, while examples and illustrations are drawn from real life to highlight the practical considerations that affect decision-making. In Part IX, policy issues touched on elsewhere in the book are discussed, and the book concludes with a consideration of what changes in the real estate industry are desirable and what can reasonably be anticipated in light of political realities.

IMPORTANT TERMS

Department of Housing and
  Urban Development
  (HUD)
externalities
gross national product (GNP)
heterogeneity
immobility
market

National Association of Realtors®
national income
national wealth
psychic income
real estate market
real property
tax shelter
time value of money

REVIEW QUESTIONS

1-1. Differentiate between real and personal property.

1-2. Why can it be said that although there is no absolute shortage of land in the United States, good properties are hard to locate?

1-3. List and define the key physical and economic characteristics of land.

1-4. Relate the importance of the real estate industry to our economy in terms of the GNP.

1-5. Discuss the recent trends in the value of real estate as compared to the value of corporate stock.

1-6. Why should real estate analysts focus on effective demand when analyzing a real estate market?

1-7. How might the concept of psychic income affect an owner's valuation of a single-family dwelling?

1-8. What are operating cash flows?

1-9. To what can real estate supply lag be attributed?

1-10. How can real estate be both a capital and a consumer asset?

2
Marketplace Individuals and Institutions

A KEY PART OF our analytical framework for real estate decision-making is an understanding of the players in the marketplace and their motivations. The real estate markets are the stages on which the market-oriented game described in Chapter 1 is played out. Who, then, are the players who participate in the various real estate markets, which, in turn, have such a pronounced influence on the national economy and life-styles in general?

To answer this question, the players must be identified, and the reasons why they participate in the marketplace the way they do must be given. Throughout this introduction to the real estate industry, *why* is the key question. It is the key to understanding the descriptive material and further the key to projecting changes in the future.

The framework of judging winners based on residual value is implicitly a forward-looking or futuristic framework. First, a project which is expected to have a long life in a fixed location must be chosen. Then, a projection of probable future events which will affect operating cash flows and consequently residual value must be made. When these are completed, the individual players in the marketplace and their role in the creation of cash flows should be clear. The process also will show how the players affect the "bottom line" and what compensation they expect in return for their efforts.

THE PARTICIPANTS

There are several broad categories of participants, each including both individuals and institutions:

- *The users*, those demand-oriented consumers, including owner-occupants, tenants, and investors.
- *The suppliers*, including construction workers, architects, engineers, and surveyors.

- *Federal, state, and local government,* along with their respective agencies, and the courts, which are the final arbitrators among the participants.
- *Associated professionals,* independent of users, suppliers, and government but critical to the operation of the real estate markets.

An examination of these categories and several of their subcategories reveals the inherent interrelation of all of the players.

THE USERS

On the demand side of the pricing equation are the users of real property. The users enjoy the benefits which are in essence the socially defined rights conveyed in real property ownership. (See 2-1.)

Users are represented by both owner-occupants and tenants. They include (1) individuals, (2) private and public institutions, and (3) governmental units. Furthermore, their motivation or need for real estate services varies considerably. Investors are also critical to demand as intermediaries seeking an outlet for their funds and a return which is a function of users' demand for space (i.e., the rent which the property can command).

Owner-Occupants

Owner-occupants include, first of all, *homeowners,* both primary residence owners and owners of secondary homes. As noted in Chapter 1, a home has come to be seen as more than simply a way to provide shelter. It expresses aspects of personal ego and social status, as evidenced through psychic income, as well as serving as an investment. Also classified as owner-occupants are *business owners,* both proprietary and corporate. These individuals and institutions often own the offices, shops, and plants in which they produce and market the nation's goods and services. *Government* itself, at the federal, state, and local levels, as well as supporting agencies, very often owns its own offices. And, finally, within the owner-occupant category are *churches and other civic groups* that own not only their primary structure, but other property used in some way to further the goals of the particular group. Each of these groups can be further stratified by income level as well as social and cultural background.

Tenants

While roughly two-thirds of the nation's residential stock is owner-occupied, tenants represent a very significant factor on the user, or de-

2-1. POPULATION AND LONG-TERM DEMAND TRENDS

Ultimately, all real estate demand is related to people. It is people who use real estate for living, working, storing goods, recreation, and, finally, interment. So when demand for real estate is discussed, insight can be gained by initially looking at population trends.

The last detailed census in 1970 showed a population of 203 million in the United States. An interim census in 1975 showed 10 million more Americans. In 1980, this number is probably nearer to 222 million (exact figures are not available for some time after the census). And by 1990, about 244 million people are likely to inhabit our nation, an increase of about 10 percent in the period from 1980 to 1990.

To illustrate how the population profile affects real estate, consider the 20- to 29-year age group. The group included 31 million people in 1970, jumps to 40 million in 1980, and should decline slightly to 38 million by 1990. (These projections are not in doubt since this age group already exists.)

Why the big jump between 1970 and 1980? This age group reflects the baby boom that occurred after World War II, particularly in the five-year period from 1950 to 1955. Since it is this age group which normally forms most new households, its members constitute the main demand for apartment units and first-time houses.

Consequently, it has not been surprising that the decade of the 1970s has been very strong for residential building. During the decade of the 1980s, this age group will not grow and so will not generate any increased demand (although the 30- to 39-year age group, also important in home buying, will increase substantially in numbers in this coming decade).

Consider next the very sharp growth in the 65-year-and-over group throughout the entire twenty-year period. Senior citizens will grow by 24 percent in the first decade and by 20 percent in the second. This is one reason why real estate developers anticipate sharply rising demand for retirement communities and congregate-housing facilities (i.e., with central dining rooms) as well as for medical and nursing facilities. And to the extent members of this age group live in their own homes, the demand will be for small and compact housing units near public transportation and with easy access to shopping and recreational facilities.

Not only does the total number of space users along with their age (and consequently their desires) change over time, but they may also move geographically. The recent past has shown migration tendencies toward the Sun Belt as well as an increased willingness to decentralize manufacturing operations.

mand, side. Single- and multifamily rental housing is the largest component of the housing stock in larger metropolitan areas, particularly in older cities. There are also business tenants, both large and small, proprietary and corporate, which lease rather than own. In many cases, government is also a tenant rather than an owner. A consideration of leisure activities demonstrates that almost the entire population at some time has been a tenant of a hotel, motel, or vacation unit.

Investors

Directly connected with user-oriented demand is investor demand. The connection is direct because investors are looking for cash flow from their investments, and the cash flow from any real estate project is a function of user demand. However, to understand the operations of the various real estate markets, it is important to look at investors initially as a separate group.

Investors are represented by individuals and institutions which provide the capital necessary for the purchase or development of a particular real estate project. They may take the position of either an equity investor or a lender. In either case, the funds they provide contribute to actualizing the effective demand for specific types of real estate projects.

☐ *Individuals.* Within this investor group are individuals investing in rental property as well as raw land. While initially their portfolios may be rather small, there have been numerous cases of the use of creative financing, knowledge, and personal drive to amass large fortunes through real estate investment. In addition to individuals, investor groups provide both equity and debt capital. Such investor groups spread risk and allow for the concentration of large-scale amounts of equity capital. In this way, larger properties can be acquired and managed centrally, taking advantage of tax laws to minimize the taxable income of the participants in the investor group.

☐ *Corporations.* Corporate users can also be considered investors. Corporations have come to own real property, not only in order to provide the space they need for their primary activity, but also to provide for corporate growth planning and, in some cases, to take advantage of the pure investment attractiveness offered by real property.

☐ *Institutional lenders.* In addition to the business corporation, there are certain types of institutional investors. Even in a strictly lending posture, commercial banks, savings and loans, life insurance companies, and pension funds regard the loans they make on real estate as investment assets. Certainly, such loans show up as assets on these institutions' books.[1] By providing long-term financing, institutional lenders help satisfy effective demand. Without long-term financing, effective demand would be limited to user's equity, and many of the needs of today's tenants would not be met.[2]

---

[1] These institutions also take equity positions through both direct ownership and participations in pooled or commingled funds.

[2] In the interrelated real estate marketplace, it is inappropriate to discuss investors without considering the potentially major impact of foreign investment in certain American real estate markets. This topic is discussed in Chapter 24.

THE SUPPLIERS

In the context of the overall importance of the real estate market, it is relevant to note that almost every facet of one's life-style is influenced by how real property is developed and used. In other words, the demands of the users, as satisfied by the suppliers, have a pronounced impact not only in the immediate future, but also in the distant future.

John Portman discusses the need for the supply side to produce space which is oriented to the individual and the satisfaction of that individual's needs. This concept of satisfaction goes beyond a purely spatial dimension to consideration of the individual's psychological well-being.

On the supply side, the key characteristic of the real estate industry is the relatively long lead time required for supply to adjust to demand. This is because of the nature of the construction process. The response time is considerable even when construction is completed on schedule. Add to this the nature of development, which includes delays related to weather problems, material and labor shortages, strikes, and governmental regulatory action, and the response time can become even longer.

Developers, Surveyors, Architects, and Engineers

The developer is the prime mover of the supply side functioning as the quarterback of the development process. He is the entrepreneur who puts together the various input factors required to satisfy user effective demand. The first professionals used by the developers are the surveyors, who are involved not only in defining the land originally acquired by the developers, but also later in the process by locating the improvements on that land in a manner suitable for construction. Next comes the architects, who design the project to meet the specifications laid out in a general form by the developers. Given the physical constraints of the particular site as identified by the surveyors, the architect in many cases will go beyond the design role and become involved in the construction supervision process. (See Figure 2-1.) As part of the design function, the architects will typically employ engineering experts. The engineers will be responsible for assuring the structural soundness of the project designed by the architect.

Collectively, the surveyors, architects, and engineers provide the plans and specifications which translate the developers' requests into a usable plan for the general contractor. Note that, on large projects, the architectural supervision role has often been transferred to a construction manager, whose function is explained in greater detail in Part VIII.

General Contractors and Subcontractors

The focal point of the 4-million-worker construction industry must now be considered. This is the general contractor (GC). GCs can range in size

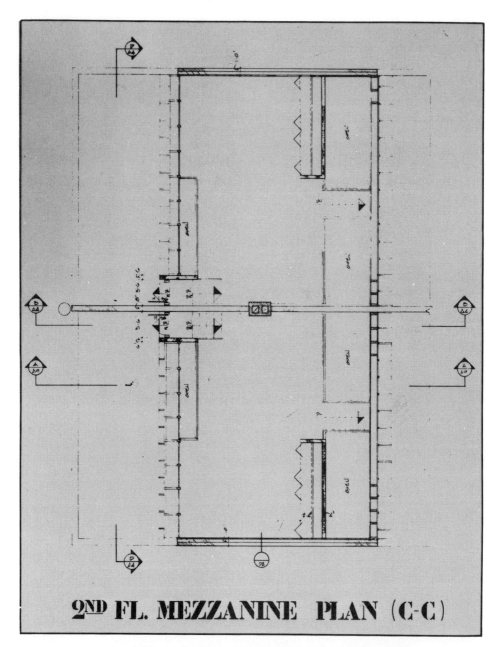

2ND FL. MEZZANINE PLAN (C-C)

Figure 2-1.   EXCERPTS FROM ARCHITECT'S PLANS AND SPECIFICATIONS

DEMOLITION

The existing building now located on the site shall be completely demolished, down to grade, including all foundation walls, piers, etc. The entire existing cellar slab shall be removed to allow for new underground piping and foundations.

Site Work, Excavation and Backfill

1. Excavate for new construction including foundation walls, underpinning, etc.
2. Excavate for site work, utilities and landscaping.
3. Excavate for new oil tanks if required.
4. Clear and grub for new top soil and seeding.
5. Remove existing pavements and other obstructions as required.
6. Backfill where required.
7. Regrade yards for proper drainage and serviceability.

Landscaping

1. Provide new trees, shrubs, staking, top soil, fertilizer.
2. Provide seeding of all lawn areas.

Fences

1. Provide new railings, fences and gates as per drawings.

Pavements

1. Provide new street pavement, curbs, and sidewalks as required by the drawings and in accordance with the Department of Highways.
2. Provide new on site pavements, service areas, yard walks, etc. as per drawings.
3. Replace missing or badly damaged concrete curbs and sidewalks as per drawings.

Miscellaneous Site Work

1. Provide on site lighting.
2. Provide concrete site work including ramps, walls, planters, footings for fences, steps, ramps, etc.

STRUCTURAL EXCAVATION AND CONCRETE

Excavation

1. General earth and rock excavation to 1'-0" below sub-grade slab elevation.
2. Trench excavation for column footings, elevator and mechanical pits.
3. Underpinning as required for adjacent structures.
4. Sheeting and shoring as shown.
5. Pumping as necessary for installation of foundation concrete.

Courtesy of Architects Design Group, New York, New York

Figure 2-1. EXCERPTS FROM ARCHITECT'S PLANS AND SPECIFICATIONS (continued)

from the giants who command national and even international reputations, such as Brown and Root, to individual home builders, who perform the same function on a smaller scale.

The GC's function is one of grouping and coordinating the activities of the workers who actually build each different segment of a particular project. The typical real estate construction job would involve the following:

- One set of subcontractors doing the excavation work.
- Another set of subcontractors doing the concrete work.
- A rough carpentry group.
- An interior group.
- Roofers.
- Assorted suppliers of mechanical appliances which become fixtures in the completed structure.

It is the GC's job to schedule each of these tasks so that the workers arrive on the site and accomplish the various tasks in such a manner that the overall work flow is completed efficiently and on schedule. It is also the GC's job to see that the subcontractors arrive on site when needed with a clear description of what they are to do.

The GC signs a contract with the developer to build the project according to the plans and specifications of the architect. The work is then subcontracted to different construction workers or construction companies, who perform the actual construction tasks. In some instances, especially with larger firms, the general contractor will specialize in one or more construction task and subcontract the rest.

THE GOVERNMENT

As is stressed throughout this study of the real estate industry, government is a key factor. At this point, it is appropriate to note the role of government as a partner to the industry in providing the total package of benefits offered by real estate development. Government at all levels affects the value and use of land almost as much as developers do. Federal, state, and local governments do this by providing the infrastructure—the roads, utilities, etc.—which complement constructed property. The decisions of governments on the extent and location of supporting infrastructure have a very great influence on the nature and scope of development. (See 2-2.)

2-2. DRAWBACKS OF GOVERNMENT'S INVOLVEMENT

A major problem is associated with the government's role in real estate. Unlike the private developer, there is no explicit personal liability associated with government decisions. This does not suggest that errors made in the government sector are cost-free. The absence of personal liability means that the cost of honest mistakes made in the public sector is borne by society in general. This is not the case in the private sector, where the cost of errors is more likely to be borne primarily by the individual responsible for the error. This can lead to suboptimal decision-making and costly time delays by government personnel.

Federal Government

The federal government is a tremendously important factor in real estate markets, first of all because it owns one-third of the total acreage in the fifty states. In addition, federal facilities—particularly military installations—have a dramatic impact on the nature of surrounding development. This impact can be identified by the effect of federal facilities on the economic base of the community in which they are located. Such elements as housing patterns, commercial services, and entertainment represent areas on which the impact is most visible.

The federal government also has a series of regulatory programs, most notably in the environmental area, which affect private development. One result of such programs has been an increase in the time and cost associated with planning a development and obtaining federal government approval. The federal government also subsidizes, both directly and indirectly, many types of real estate development. In addition, there are a series of federal government programs which support and finance a state government role in land use planning.

State Government

The state government, often in conjunction with the federal government, provides a good deal of the regional infrastructure necessary for real property development. State government also handles the location of state government facilities (such as prisons, universities, and office buildings) which have a significant impact on development in given regions.

State governments have traditionally passed most of their regulatory role on to local governments through local government enabling statutes. However, this can vary considerably from state to state. In some instances (notably California), state governments have implemented a significant amount of legislation affecting real estate development, while in others (for example, Texas), relatively little legislation has emerged. Throughout the last decade, a trend toward greater land use planning at the state level has developed.

Local Government

Local government is tremendously important because it is local government which has the power—or which most often uses the power—to tax real property. Further, through the power of eminent domain, local government can condemn land for public use. Also, local governments are the government unit most likely to exercise the police powers (the power of government to preserve the health and well-being of the citizenry) through zoning, subdivision ordinances, and building codes. Master plans or growth management plans have recently been developed by many local governments in an effort to respond to urban growth. Local government is also responsible for record-keeping, which, as seen in Part II, is a tremendously important function. And, as mentioned at the federal and state levels, the provision of infrastructure is a key role of local government as is facility location.

Just as in the private sector, each of these government functions is carried out by individuals. The number of government sector real-estate-related careers has grown as the functions of government have expanded. In Part IX, there is a closer and more detailed discussion of working with, in, and for the government.

The Courts

The courts have come to play an increasingly important role in real estate markets as the final arbitrators of disputes. Essentially, the courts refuse to allow one individual or institution to unduly burden the property of another. This concept, which evolved over several centuries in both English and American law, has lead to the development of certain pre-planning activities designed to avoid the heavy cost of later litigation. Such preplanning is the basis for zoning and subdivision ordinances, both of which have become key instruments of local government regulation. In Part II, the focus is on law and the courts' recent interpretations of the law as they constitute the rules of the game in the real estate industry.

ASSOCIATED PROFESSIONALS

Working with users, suppliers, and government are a host of associated professionals who make possible the activities which occur in the various real estate markets. These professionals provide services which make up an important part of the actual day-to-day activity in the real estate market. In most instances, they provide staff support and input for users, suppliers, and government. As such, the role of the associated professional is to assist in policy formulation and decision making. They do not generally make line decisions but surely have a significant affect on what decisions are ultimately made and implemented.

Attorneys

The legal profession plays a key role in the support of real estate decision-makers with many attorneys specializing in real-estate-related matters. From initial contract negotiation through title transfer and courtroom representation, attorneys have a significant impact on real estate decision-making. In the area of contract negotiations, attorneys are called on to prepare contracts which satisfy the requirements of buyers and sellers. After contract terms have been agreed on, the attorney is responsible for putting together the documentation which defines the property rights being conveyed and sees to it that the transaction is properly recorded in the public record. When disputes requiring court action occur, the real estate attorney represents the different individuals and institutions in the courtroom.

Title Examiners

Closely associated with the work of real estate attorneys are title abstract and title insurance companies. The professionals in these companies provide a vital service to the real estate industry. Each time real property is transferred, the title must be thoroughly examined for any defects or encumbrances. An abstract of title provides a chronology of all previous transactions and all possible encumbrances. Title insurance also involves an examination of history of the title but goes a step further by insuring the quality of the title against defects.

Nearly all real estate transactions now require either an attorney's examination of the abstract of title (as provided by the abstract company) or title insurance (which requires the title company to perform a similar examination). In the latter case, the title company then serves as an insurance agent offering insurance against the possibility that title may eventually be proved defective. If the owner is subsequently forced out of the property because of title defects, he may recover the purchase price from the title company. (This process is explained in greater detail in Parts II and IV.)

Land Planners

Planning is an integral part of the real estate decision-making process. As already indicated, government units rely on planning as a mechanism for implementing a broad range of government policy considerations. As such, planners go beyond simple location and growth issues and must deal with a complex set of market constraints. These market constraints affect the land planner because users, suppliers, and the public sector may not reach a consensus on the goals of land planning. With this in mind, the land planner, as well as all other participants in the process, must recognize that market equilibrium is only reached when each of the three groups is satisfied.

In the private sector, planners are utilized extensively by developers in designing for large areas and related transportation systems. (Architects are traditionally concerned with constructed space, while land planners deal with site design of multistructure projects.) Again, private sector planners must also operate within a market over which they have limited control. The truly successful land planner is able to satisfy user needs and at the same time create a plan which satisfies all developmental, legal, and political constraints. It is only when the land planner satisfies the requirements of the user, the supplier, and the public sector that market demand is truly satisfied. (See Figure 2-2.)

Marketing Agents

The marketing function within the real estate industry is a very exciting and dynamic field. Marketing ranges from the sale of a single-family home to leasing large commercial developments. As is seen in Part IV, the selling of a single-family home is by no means simple. The various functions performed by the marketing agent can be tremendously important to the user and the developer. In the leasing of a major commercial structure such as the Sears Tower in Chicago, the complexity of the marketing function almost defies imagination.

Professionals involved in the marketing function range from salespersons to brokers with various levels of professionalism and expertise required at each level. It should be stressed at this point that marketing affects every phase of the real estate industry and is, in fact, the connecting link in this industry. (The major role that marketing professionals play within the real estate industry is discussed in some depth in Part IV.)

Property Managers

Closely associated with the marketing function is the property management function. Property managers range from the graduate student with a 50-percent-off rent deal managing a seven-unit apartment house in Eugene, Oregon to the individual charged with operating the Bank of America Tower in San Francisco. In real property, the user is demanding space over time with certain associated services. It is the property manager's function to see to it that those services are provided and the physical

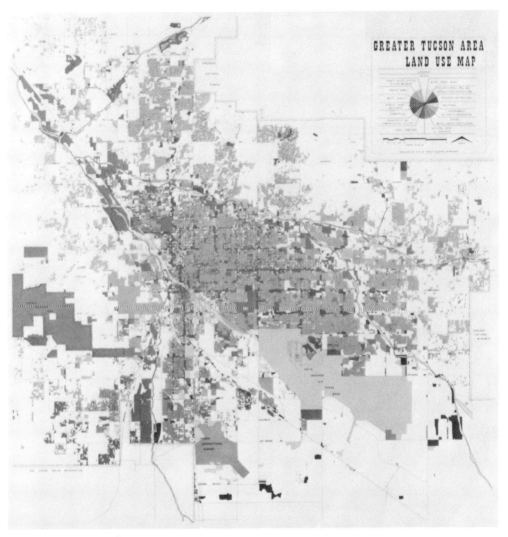

Courtesy of Tucson Planning Commission, Tucson, Arizona.

Figure 2-2.   LAND USE PLAN—TUCSON, ARIZONA

space properly maintained. In the case of the Bank of America Tower, the engineering skills and the personnel management skills required are enormous. As is true in all the groups of associated professionals, property managers have their own set of professional designations based on training programs offered by their national associations.

As a career opportunity, property management is emerging as one of the more attractive fields within the real estate industry. Effective property management is very important to all participants in the real estate marketplace. To the user group, property managers see to it that the services stipulated in the lease are adequately delivered. To the investor, the property manager sees to it that rents are kept at a competitive level, rent is collected, operating expenses paid, and the property properly maintained. Lenders view quality property management as an important aspect of their interests since the value of the mortgaged property can be enhanced and maintained by aggressive management.

Appraisers

Real estate appraisers render value opinions which are used as an integral source of information by many participants in the real estate marketplace. Lenders utilize appraisals when evaluating loan applications. Insurance companies settle property loss claims with the aid of appraisals. Local governments establish real estate tax assessments with the aid of appraisal techniques. Local, state, and federal governments utilize appraisals to estimate the value of condemned property. Courts frequently call on appraisers to attest to property value estimates within the context of legal proceedings.

Fee appraisers are generally independent entrepreneurs who provide an opinion of value for a client for a predetermined fee. *Staff appraisers*, on the other hand, are generally salaried employees of financial or government institutions who appraise only property involved in their employers' business dealings. (The role of the appraiser and the various appraisal techniques are the focus of the discussion presented in Part III.)

Consultants

Real estate consultants provide a broad range of counseling services to many of the participants in the real estate industry. These would include investment analysis advice, financial packaging, and estate planning services.

In a relatively new area, consultants are acting as government relations specialists. These individuals represent developers and investors who must interact closely with government units in their day-to-day business. By understanding both the perspective of the public and private sectors, the government relations specialist provides a needed link between producers and government. Finally, such consultants can provide valuable input to the public sector as their planning and growth management policies develop.

Accountants

The accounting profession is vitally concerned with activities in the real estate marketplace. Market value problems are a continual source of challenge to auditors rendering an opinion on a firm's financial statements. In particular, construction audits or audits of companies who have ongoing construction projects are particularly difficult, as is noted in Part VIII.

An associated specialist within the real estate accounting profession is the tax specialist. This specialization has developed as a result of real estate's position as a tax favored investment vehicle. The myriad and ever-changing real estate tax environment requires users and investors to call frequently on tax accounting specialists when making real estate decisions.

Insurance Agents

The insurance industry is also heavily involved in real property. The largest portion of fire and casualty policies is written on real property. In addition, liability insurance is becoming increasingly important to the real estate owner. Finally, on the financial side, mortgage insurance is possible, both through government-related agencies and through private companies.

Lenders

Because of the extensive financing required by many real estate projects, lenders play a vital role in the industry. The purchase of developed property usually relies on some form of institutional financing which represents from 75 to 95 percent of the purchase price. (See 2-3.) In essence, the lender is the major source of financing for the real estate project. The benefit stream (i.e., the cash flows generated by a project) is divided between the lender and the equity investor.

In many cases, the distinction between lender and equity investor is becoming increasingly blurred, as is discussed in Part VII. Traditionally, the lender takes a prior position and a lower fixed return with more safety. The equity investor receives the residual which is a potentially higher return but is also a riskier return because of the prior claim of the lender.

Within the American monetary system, there are a series of financial intermediaries, all performing different lending functions based on their own sources of credit. In other words, within the financial marketplace, there are lenders who specialize in certain types of real estate loans based primarily on their perceived expertise, risk tolerance, source of funds, and government regulation.

2-3. DEBT FINANCING

All stages of the development and ownership process generally have debt financing associated with them. This might lead one to identify financing as a factor controlling real estate decisions. However, although the availability and cost of financing can be the pivotal factor in affecting real estate decisions, financing should not be viewed as *the* most important factor in the decision process.

Many developers and investors erroneously overestimated the importance of financing during the 1973-75 recession. In many instances, the importance of financing was stressed while the actual economic viability of a project was virtually ignored. All participants in the real estate industry should recognize that the economic viability of a project is much more important than the project's financing. Without economic success, the financing becomes a burden and, in many instances, failure follows.

☐ *Commercial banks.* The largest of the lenders are the commercial banks, which specialize in short-term loans since their primary sources of credit are short-term in nature. Consequently, commercial banks emphasize construction loans in their real estate portfolios.

☐ *Savings and loans.* While commercial banks are the largest financial intermediary, the largest source of credit for the real estate industry has been savings and loan associations. Savings and loans vary from the small, conservative, single-unit associations in rural areas to the very active and aggressive multi-unit associations, particularly some of those on the West Coast. Since savings and loan associations rely heavily on more stable savings accounts, they have traditionally made longer term loans on real estate projects.

☐ *Mutual savings banks.* Mutual savings banks have been a significant factor in the northeastern United States. Although they have traditionally concentrated in limited geographical areas, mutual savings banks have recently expanded their lending area outside the Northeast. They function much like savings and loans but with slightly greater flexibility.

☐ *Life insurance companies.* Another important source of long-term mortgage financing are life insurance companies. Concentrating their lending in the area of large commercial properties, life insurance companies have greater flexibility in lending than the commercial banks or savings and loans.

☐ *Mortgage banker.* A related mortgage loan originator is the mortgage banker who provides loans similar to those provided by savings and loan associations and mutual savings banks. However, the mortgage banker has a distinct role in the financial markets. Unlike other long-term lenders, the mortgage banker is not a depository source of funds but rather a middleman who makes and then sells loans, usually to one of the sources above or through one of the secondary mortgage market operations which are described in detail in Appendix 12A.

☐ *Other lenders.* In addition to these firms or financial institutions, other individuals and institutions make loans on real estate projects. *Seller financing,* which is simply a loan by the individual selling the property, is very common in the real estate industry. The *government,* to facilitate certain government goals, also make loans. *Pension funds* have at times been involved directly in real estate lending (although sometimes very unsuccessfully as in the case of the Teamsters Central States Pension Fund).[3] *Investment bankers* have also become interested in the field. In fact, investment bankers have been a primary route, along with commercial banks, for channeling foreign investment into American real property. Finally, it should be noted that *real estate investment trusts* (REITs) are a type of lending entity whose legislated purpose is specifically to make loans on (or to purchase) real property. While the REITs are no longer highly active in the lending field, their story helps explain the crash in the real estate market between 1972 and 1975.

More detail on the operations of each of these lenders is provided in Part V.

SUMMARY

The real estate marketplace gathers together a wide variety of individuals, institutions, and governmental units with varying resources, skills, and objectives. In view of the enormous importance of real estate in the political, economic, and social life of the nation, this is not surprising. The real estate decision-maker must have a clear understanding of the demand and supply considerations arising from the relationships among these groups which affect real estate markets. It is only when all participant roles in the marketplace are viewed in their proper perspective that effective analysis for real estate decisions can occur. (See **2-4.**)

---

[3] Most pension funds invest in real estate through life insurance companies or commercial bank trust departments.

2-4. REAL ESTATE EDUCATION

No overview of the participants in the real estate marketplace would be complete without a brief discussion of real estate education and management decision-making in the real estate industry. The recent past has seen tremendous growth in interest in real estate education. This is due to a series of factors which include the prosperity of the industry and the increasing complexity of the real estate decision-making process. Additionally, license regulation and related private sector designations have become more prevalent and more rigorous in the recent past, increasing the demand of those in the industry for higher levels of education.

Finally, and possibly most importantly, the nation has come to realize that its physical resources are not inexhaustible or indestructible.

This last factor implies a need to relate use and development of real property assets with the general goals of the society as a whole. Or, alternatively stated, real estate decision-making involves certain externalities which must be monitored to assure that the individual pursuing his enlightened self-interest (winning the game) is functioning in a manner consistent with the general well-being of society as a whole.

The response to the recent growth and interest in real estate education has come from several groups of institutions. Universities have offered undergraduate, masters, and doctoral programs in the real estate field. Colleges have moved toward undergraduate programs, or at least elective courses, focusing on the real estate industry. In many cases, community colleges now offer two-year associate degree programs in real estate. In addition to these full-time academic programs, the same institutions have provided a series of continuing education offerings to help those already engaged in the industry improve and develop their skills.

Professional associations have also been very active in promoting real estate education. The National Association of Realtors®, the Mortgage Bankers Association, the American Banking Association, and many other groups have been active in this area. Finally, certain proprietary schools have arisen to teach specific subjects within the industry. (Such schools are most significant in the brokerage licensing field.)

IMPORTANT TERMS

appraiser
architect
broker
consultant
developer
disintermediation
general contractor (GC)
infrastructure

insurance agent
institutional lender
land planner
property manager
real estate investment trust (REIT)
subcontractor
surveyor
title examiner

REVIEW QUESTIONS

2-1. What are the four categories of real estate participants?

2-2. How might land planning conflict with development?

2-3. What is the overriding motivation for all participants in the real estate game?

2-4. What factors cause real estate to adjust slowly to changes in demand?

2-5. Discuss the function of general contractors and subcontractors in terms of the supply of real estate.

2-6. Why must government be viewed as a partner to the real estate industry in the area of real estate development?

2-7. What is the role of the court system as it affects the supply of real estate?

2-8. How much of the nation's residential housing stock is owner-occupied?

2-9. Complete a population profile for the census tract you live in.

2-10. Name four types of real estate lenders and identify their areas of specialization.

3
Regional and Urban Economics

As already noted, the primary distinguishing characteristic of real property is its fixed and unique location (i.e., its spatial dimension). The value of real estate, improved or unimproved, is significantly affected by its immediate physical environment as well as by the economic activity which occurs on or around it. Conversely, an automobile or a share of common stock is movable rather than fixed; hence, its value is not affected by location.

The relationship of real estate to its physical environment is the subject of regional and urban economics. Put another way, regional and urban economics deal with the application of economic concepts in (1) a regional and (2) an urban context; it is economics with a spatial dimension.

REGIONAL ECONOMICS

An understanding of regional economics should help provide an understanding of how real estate acquires, retains, and loses value. It can be said that the value of a parcel of improved real estate is affected by activity occurring on the site itself (*the use effect*) as well as from activity occurring in the vicinity of the site (*the location effect*). In the case of vacant land, the use effect arises not from actual current use but from potential future use.

One important difference between use and location effects is the degree of control the landowner can exercise with respect to it. Use effect is subject to the owner's control, except to the extent use is restricted by private agreement or public regulation. By comparison, location effect, or the impact of the surrounding physical and economic environment on the site, is an *exogenous* factor, not usually subject to the control of the owner; the owner can respond to the effect but not change it. Still, the proper response to the location effect can have an important bearing on land value. For example, identifying a market need consistent with activities surrounding a site may enable the site to be put to its highest and best (and hence most profitable) use.

In real property analysis, physical, economic, and political relationships do matter. Distance, geography, and topography all are important, as is climate. Soils are of crucial importance in agriculture and extractive industries; their load-bearing capacity and related characteristics are relevant whenever construction is contemplated. The man-made environment (e.g., roads, airports, and railroads) as well as political boundaries have a very significant influence on land use and value.

Surrounding economic activity may well be the single most important determinant in setting land value and influencing land use decisions. This is so because land *values* depend on land *use*, and the uses in demand for housing, commercial, and industrial real estate almost always involve land close to economic activity. (See Figure 3-1.) It follows that changes in economic activity can significantly affect land use decisions. For example, the construction of the Alaskan pipeline represented a major stimulus to the economic activity of affected regions in that state. The resulting impact upon land use decisions and value also was significant. On the other hand, the closing of a manufacturing plant or a military base can have a devastating impact upon surrounding property values.

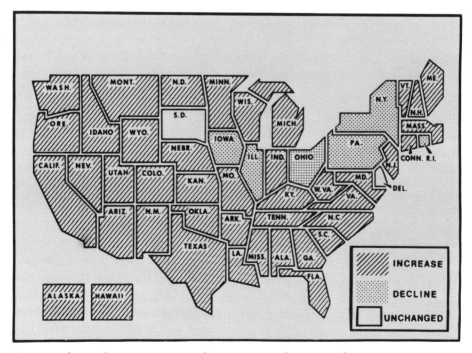

Courtesy of United Press International, Inc., New York, New York.

**Figure 3-1.   U.S. POPULATION MAP SHOWING RECENT
INCREASED GROWTH IN SOUTH AND WEST**

There are exceptions to the simple proximity of economic activity stimulating land use and land value, but they are the result of special circumstances. Thus, a gold mine has value, even though it is located in the midst of a desert, because its use value arises from the mineral deposits there. A resort located in an exotic and inaccessible area also has value precisely because it is not near other activities. Here, the use effect derives from the very isolation of the location.

Beyond the direct physical and economic factors of a particular region, cultural characteristics also may be significant. Clearly, residents of the San Francisco Bay area find a quality of life in that area which arises from more than the purely physical characteristics of the region and which induces them to pay more for real estate than could be justified by strictly economic measures.

Pragmatic Origin

Regional economics is distinguished by its pragmatic origin—that is, its concepts have grown from practical experience and what individuals have seen around them. *Regional economics* may be defined as a discipline devoted to explaining dynamic economic activity within a spatial context.

Regional growth analyses, or *models*, were first used to help determine where certain public services should be provided by government. Inherent in these early models was a political element; cultural and noneconomic factors were considered along with the physical characteristics of the particular region. Subsequently, industrial location models were developed and were even more pragmatic. These were used by regional economists to assist businesses seeking optimal locations for new facilities. The products of these private-sector studies were *location pro formas*. These location pro formas can be viewed as a type of regional economic study with a business orientation.

Interdisciplinary Flavor

As should be clear from its definition, regional economics is not limited to a mechanistic "balance sheet" description of a particular region at one moment in time. Politics, social factors, and cultural amenities all will have a long-term impact upon a region. Since the real estate asset is fixed in location with improvements having a long economic life, regional changes eventually will affect the residual cash flow of the individual real estate project. Therefore, the interdisciplinary approach of regional economics is consistent with our analytical framework which considers all influences on the residual cash flow. Unlike Parker Brothers' popular real estate game Monopoly®, players in the real world real estate game must consider a complex and dynamic set of social factors as well as immediate cash flows.

Importance of Regional Economics

From what has been already said, it should be clear why the analyst must carefully examine all surrounding influences when seeking to determine the value of real property. In particular, attention should be paid to expected future trends in light of the long life of the real estate improvement and the inability to move real estate to a different location. (See Figure 3-2.)

For example, the regional analyst will seek to identify *external economies* (benefits) that arise because like-kind and supporting facilities are near to the property in question. This factor is referred to as *benefits from agglomeration*. The analyst also will note *external diseconomies*—that is, negative influences—from the nearness of dissimilar activities or uses which are not compatible with the property in question. Both these positive and negative factors will have an effect on the cash flow of income properties and the sales prices of owner-occupied single-family homes.

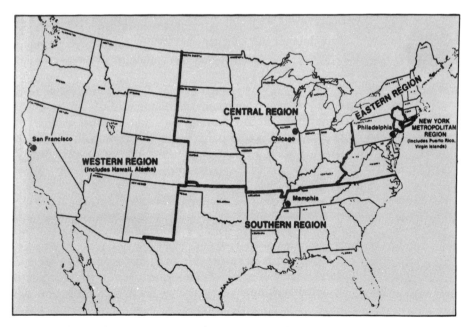

Courtesy of United Press International, Inc., New York, New York.

Figure 3-2.   U.S. REGIONAL MAP

THEORIES OF REGIONAL GROWTH

Although this book focuses on the real estate industry rather than regional or urban economics, a brief introduction to the major planning theories that have evolved over the past 150 years will cast light on the sources of real estate value.

Von Thünen: Highest and Best Use

Johann von Thünen is often cited as one of the first regional economists. His *Isolated State* (1826) sought to explain agricultural locations in Germany and became the first serious attempt to incorporate the spatial element in pragmatic economic thought.

Von Thünen assumed a central town as the sole market center, surrounded by a flat featureless homogeneous plain with no transportation advantages (save distance) and of equal fertility. The wilderness at the edge of this market area could be cultivated if necessary, and farmers tried to maximize profits in the context of a given demand and fixed coefficients (costs) of production. These assumptions (which clearly are never met in real life situations) led to an explanation of land use by a rent gradient which put high-intensity crops (density of yield per acre) near the center along with higher-priced crops and crops necessitating heavier transportation costs. His work first gave expression to what has become the *highest-and-best-use principle*—namely, that land use will be economically determined in the marketplace by the ability of user groups to pay rent for the land. In an agricultural setting, this involves (1) yield per acre, (2) price of crops, and (3) cost of transporting the crops.

Weber: Business Location Decisions

Alfred Weber, in his *Location of Industry* (1909), transferred many of von Thünen's ideas to a consideration of business location decisions. To von Thünen's assumptions, he added scattered "deposits" of natural resources and labor. His results extended earlier work by showing that businesses locate to minimize both transportation costs to market and the transportation cost of moving the factors of production (materials and labor) to the plant site.

Losch: Spatial Element of Consumer Demand

August Losch, in the *Economics of Location* (1939), assumed uniform population distribution (consumers) and showed that the market penetration of a firm (based solely on price) can be explained by the spatial element. In other words, the plant located closest to the consumer would be able to offer that consumer the lowest price due to lower transportation costs and therefore dominate the market. This was a twist on Weber, moving from one market center to describe demand as well as supply on a spatial basis.

Hoover: The Role of Institutional Factors

Edgar M. Hoover, in his *Regional Economics* (1948), moved beyond a consideration of direct costs and incorporated *institutional factors* in his regional analysis. He noticed that political boundaries were important and opened the door for consideration of all the cultural and psychological characteristics of a region as well.

Isard: A Format for Decision-Making

In *Location and Space Economy* (1956), Walter Isard borrowed from previous writers and refined their ideas into a straightforward format for industrial location. He postulated that industries would make location decisions based on the costs, revenues, and personal factors associated with alternative locations. Under costs, he focused on transfer of inputs, transfer of outputs, and such local costs as available labor and utilities. In the revenue area, he talked about market control through location. Finally, under personal factors, he included the whole spectrum of interdisciplinary concerns about life-style in a particular location. (See Figure 3-3.)

Our goal is to use Isard's format to move beyond the restrictive assumptions of earlier writers while still drawing useful material from their insights. The key considerations noted above seem obvious with hindsight (even though they are often very difficult to apply and reduce to dollars and cents). However, throughout the book, examples are noted of serious errors resulting from a failure to fully integrate these simple concepts in the analysis of real estate projects. Note at this juncture that Isard's format is forward-looking. The "why" must be put into the past so that it may help us predict the future.

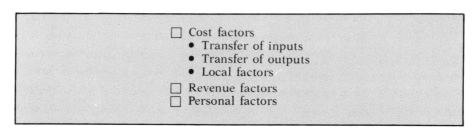

☐ Cost factors
  • Transfer of inputs
  • Transfer of outputs
  • Local factors
☐ Revenue factors
☐ Personal factors

Figure 3-3. THE ISARD FORMAT

ANALYTICAL TOOLS FROM REGIONAL GROWTH THEORIES

Over the years, some practical tools for analysis have been developed from the theories about regional growth that were previously sketched. While the results obtained from using these tools are often imprecise, they do emphasize the key factors which should influence the decision-maker in real estate and urban planning.

The Export Base Multiplier

The export base multiplier is used to project the number of new jobs that will be generated by certain types of new industry that locate within the region. The multiplier is arrived at as follows. All outputs in the region are divided into *basic* and *service* categories. Essentially, all goods and services which are sold outside the region (*exports*) are considered basic, and all others are considered in the service category. The *multiplier* is simply the ratio of jobs (or income) in the whole region (service plus basic) to jobs (or income) in the basic industries. When a new export industry moves to the region, the number of jobs generated there will be a product of the number of jobs in the new industry times the multiplier.

This is a very quick and easy approach and is often the basis of "chamber of commerce" estimates. However, the method is certainly not without faults. The multiplier is a crude measure and changes over time. Classification of basic industries is difficult, and an unusual base year will distort the results. Finally, on a more theoretical basis, this approach is flawed because clearly the world economy grows with no exports—so why must the regional economy have exports to have growth?

Export base projections are common in the real estate markets and can be both interesting and informative. However, they are generally not suited to serve as the sole basis for estimating market demand in a more refined real estate analysis.

Location Quotient

Beyond the export base multiplier, there are several other common short-cut classification aids. Variations of the location quotient express a region's percentage of jobs in any given industry as the numerator of a ratio whose denominator is the national percentage of jobs in the given industry. Thus, regions with location quotients greater than one are said to reflect concentrations of the particular activity, and their local economies will be more affected by the fortunes of the particular industry. For example, California would have a high location quotient for aerospace activities, while Ohio would have a low location quotient for oil exploration. An example of a location quotient formula is:

$$\text{Location quotient} = \frac{\% \text{ of region's jobs in industry}}{\% \text{ of nation's jobs in industry}}$$

Shift Share

Shift share analysis is a similar approach to analyzing a region's growth. In it, the region's industry is measured by two standards:

☐ *Industry mix.* For each regional industry, the location quotient is determined in the manner just described. The industry's national growth rate also is established. The region will have a favorable "mix" if its industries with location quotients greater than one are also fast-growing nationally. The region, in other words, has more than its share of employees in industries that are growing rapidly.

☐ *Competition.* Here, a ratio is established for each regional industry between the region's growth rate in that industry and the nation's growth rate in the industry. The region will enjoy a favorable competitive position in any industry in which its growth is more rapid than the national growth. The shift share technique is a quick way to look at a region and analyze the characteristics of its growth. Like the location quotient and export base multiplier, it is a useful tool but is not the primary element in a complete market analysis.

Input/Output Analysis

Input/output analysis is a matrix (tabular) approach to understanding a regional economy. The rows and columns of the various tables have identical headings representing the major industries in the region plus an export category. After a series of transition matrices, the final input/output matrix shows how an additional dollar spent in any one industry will affect sales in each of the other industries.

Input/output tables (matrices) can be very useful in anticipating derivative regional growth, but they suffer from certain data limitations. First, the information is suspect because of possible deficiencies in collection procedures and (more important to the real estate analyst who uses the past only to predict the future), the data are usually several years old before they are published.

PROJECTING TRENDS

The theories of regional growth discussed in the early part of this chapter are descriptive in nature. The tools previously described represent an attempt to move beyond description to prediction. Unfortunately, they are usually too simplistic to be more than a starting point in serious real estate analysis. Still, these theories provide a useful framework for analysis. As a determination of why real estate markets operate in a particular way, such theories' descriptive natures can provide a useful check or safeguard. To be successful, this historically determined framework must be expanded to encompass dynamic considerations based on the "why" of past experience in order to protect future residual cash flows as the model requires.

URBAN ECONOMICS

Regional economic considerations introduce the importance of the spatial element from a regional economic perspective. To complete the analytical framework, a move must be made from regional considerations to the more micro world of urban economic analysis. The concern is still for the real estate asset, which is uniquely defined by its particular location. Now, however, one more step will be taken, and an examination of the location not just within the region, but within an urban area, will be made. Analysis of real estate decisions requires that the analysis be brought down to a specific site. It is appropriate to begin at the regional level, but the intracity dynamics must also be understood to complete the analysis.

Definition of a City

What is a city? A *city* may be defined initially as a group of people; it is also certainly a government and the set of laws by which that government operates. More than this, it is a group of services provided by the government for the people who make up the city. Closely linked to this service function is the government's role as a taxing authority. Through the government's taxing authority, the people provide the resources necessary to finance the group of services rendered by the city.

Remember that real estate is an interdisciplinary area; thus, the city may be thought of as a kind of social and cultural concentration as well. These nonphysical elements must be understood as well as more precisely defined government boundaries and related service areas if the delineation of particular real estate markets is to be appreciated. Recall that the various real estate markets are defined by both (1) product type (office space, single-family residential, etc.) and (2) geographic area. First, in the regional section, markets are classified geographically. Then, in this portion of the analytical framework, the emphasis is on urban dynamics.

Refer back at this time to the earlier part of this chapter and the discussion of the proper use of regional and urban economics in real estate analysis. Remember the descriptive theories of regional growth, the development of certain tools from these theories, and based on these tools, the forward-looking approach to location analysis. Note that within regions, urban concentrations develop. It is now time to study these urban concentrations and try to establish the "whys" behind urban growth patterns. Again, by understanding the "whys'" an accurate projection of what will go on around a real estate site in the future can be made. Given the real estate project's long life and the significant possibility of positive and/or negative externalities, projection of urban growth patterns is a key element in successful real estate analysis.

DESCRIPTIVE URBAN MODELS

Following the same pattern used in the study of regional economics, the "whys" of urban dynamics are begun by examining the historic evolution of descriptive urban models.

Concentric Circle Theory

In *The Growth of the City* (1925), Ernest Burgess suggested a concentric circle theory to describe urban growth patterns. Remember that Burgess was writing in the early twenties, and at that time, what he saw in most cities was a clearly distinguishable central core. He labeled this core the *central business district (CBD)* and postulated that it typically contained large office buildings, well-established retail stores, government buildings, etc.

This CBD was the most intensively used space and therefore the most valuable land in the city. Around this CBD spreading out equally in all directions, he saw a second circular area, which he labeled the *zone of transition*. Located in this area were some low-income dwelling units, some nightclubs, some light manufacturing, and the commercial activities which could not justify space in the CBD. Moving out to a third concentric circle, Burgess saw a *zone for worker homes*. These were the workers who worked in the manufacturing areas in the zone of transition as well as the CBD. Very often, these were large older homes which over time had been converted to multifamily units. They were not the slums seen in parts of the zone of transition, yet they were clearly lower- or working-class dwelling units. A fourth concentric zone included *the middle-class and some high-income units*. Here, Burgess saw the very wealthy and the middle class in both single- and multifamily homes. Even at this early date, he started to notice some entertainment and some commercial establishments appearing in this zone near higher-income consumer groups. The fifth and final circle in Burgess's theory was the *commuter zone*. It was comprised of scattered dwelling units for workers who were willing to commute long distances for the privileges of less-urbanized living. (See Figure 3-4.)

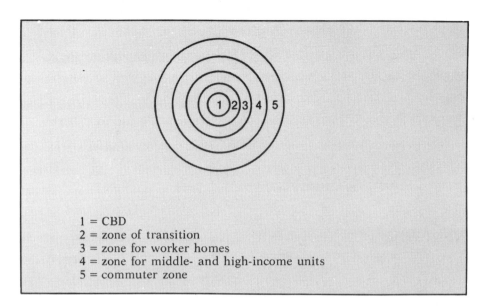

1 = CBD
2 = zone of transition
3 = zone for worker homes
4 = zone for middle- and high-income units
5 = commuter zone

Figure 3-4. CONCENTRIC CIRCLE THEORY

Axial Theory

In 1925, Burgess's concentric circle theory seemed a reasonable description of many urban concentrations. However, soon after his publication, several other authors began to describe what has come to be known as the *axial theory of urban growth.* The axial theory is a direct takeoff on Burgess but picks up on a key factor affecting urban growth which Burgess ignored: transportation axes or arteries.

The axial theory begins, as did Burgess's concentric circle theory, with a CBD, which is still the most intensively used land, the most valuable land, and the land supporting the largest buildings. Here again, around the CBD are several zones. Depending on the particular author's interpretation, these zones parallel to a greater or lesser degree Burgess's zones. In other words, beyond the CBD, there is a transition zone which encompasses light manufacturing operations and some worker housing. Beyond this comes the rest of the worker homes and eventually upper-class homes, subdivisions for the middle class, and finally a commuter zone. What distinguishes the axial theory from the concentric circle theory is that these zones do not radiate in concentric circles from the CBD. It is not *distance* to the CBD that is the key but rather *commuting time* to the CBD. Thus, the axial theory develops growth patterns around the major transportation arteries to the CBD. Remember that in the 1930s and 1940s, most workers did not own cars and commuted to their jobs on public transportation. Therefore, the development beyond the CBD tended to

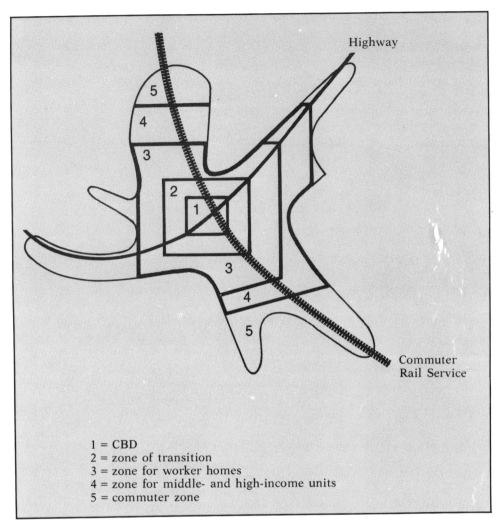

Figure 3-5. AXIAL THEORY

cluster around the sources of existing transportation. The axial theory, by focusing on transportation, was a logical and useful extension of the concentric circle theory. (See Figure 3-5.)

Sector Theory

In the 1930s, Homer Hoyt developed what is known as the *sector theory*. This theory attempts to explain residential concentrations around the CBD. When studying residential concentrations, Hoyt was the first to notice that the pattern of activity within the CBD in some cities was changing dramatically. Essentially, Hoyt noted that various groups in the social order tended to be segregated into rather definite areas according to their self-perceived social status. Naturally, there were several exceptions to this rule, but it is something which the casual observer would clearly note in most areas. In other words, where the axial theory stated that like-income groups would locate like-commuting times from the CBD, Hoyt said that this was not the total picture. Cultural as well as economic factors would result in clustering at logical distances from major transportation routes. Quite naturally, higher-income groups lived in homes which command the highest prices, and lower-income groups lived in lower-priced dwelling units.

In Hoyt's work, the lower-priced units were located near the CBD and tended to expand out from the central city as the city grew. For Hoyt, the key principle of American cities (distinguishing them from most European cities) was that the American cities grew by new building taking place at the periphery rather than in the CBD. Based on this observation, Hoyt began to notice what he termed a *hollow shell effect* in certain central cities. Up to this time, the CBD had always been the most valuable area within the city. Consequently, the property constructed on the land in this area was generally the most valuable property in the city. However, during this period of history, the pattern was changing. For several reasons, certain areas within the central city were beginning to decay. Money was being spent at the periphery; the wealthy were moving out. As they moved out, the lower-income groups were moving into lower-middle-class neighborhoods; the lower-middle class moved into the middle-class homes; and the middle class moved into the upper-middle-class homes. All this resulted in a filtering effect, and in the CBD, a decayed or hollow shell was left. (See Figure 3-6).

Multiple Nuclei Theory

In the 1940s Chauncey D. Harris and Edward L. Ullman developed a new twist on the sector theory. Their *multiple nuclei approach* consisted of describing new urban centers within the residential concentrations created by the purchasing power and job requirements of those living in the residential area. In other words, as homogeneous income groups clustered together, certain services were demanded and mini-CBDs developed to provide those services. Certain groups profited economically from locating together outside the urban core, and coupled with many social factors, this outside activity collectively caused the CBD to lose its position as the sole focal point within the urban concentration. Several smaller focal points, or *nuclei*, developed in the residential areas surrounding the old CBD, which was itself now partially decaying. (See Figure 3-7.)

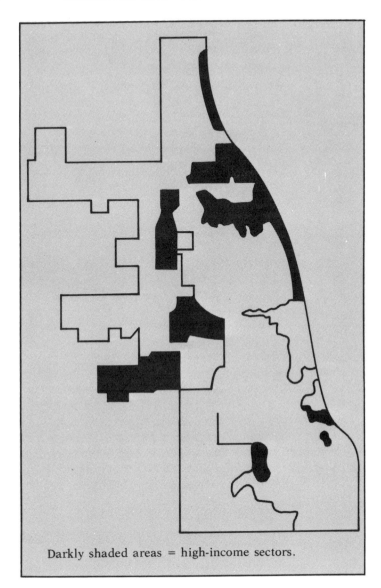

Darkly shaded areas = high-income sectors.

Figure 3-6. SECTOR THEORY

SUMMING UP WITH AN EXAMPLE

All four of these theories are logical. In fact, using hindsight, their supposed insights now appear quite obvious. Nevertheless, very useful conclusions from these simple descriptive urban models can still be drawn.

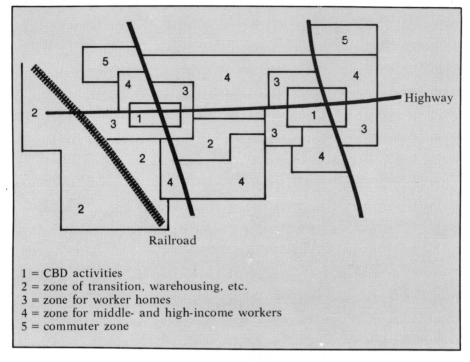

Figure 3-7. **MULTIPLE NUCLEI THEORY**

For example, the Dallas-Fort Worth area in the early 1970s was a hotbed of land speculation. The two Texas cities are approximately 30 miles apart, and it seemed logical to assume that they would eventually grow together to be one city. (See Figure 3-8.) This had happened before in the Boston-Washington, D.C. corridor. The prevailing forecast was for this same phenomenon to happen in this rapidly growing southwestern area.

The Dallas-Fort Worth airport (when constructed, the largest in the world) was located between the two cities. The Texas Rangers and Dallas Cowboys both located their respective baseball and football stadiums at intermediate points between the two cities. Major recreational facilities, such as Six Flags Over Texas, located in the area. In the small municipalities which controlled the area, development enthusiasm seemed unbounded. Syndicators bought parcels of land and (through investment packages which will be described later in this book) made these parcels particularly attractive to potential investors. The syndicators were able to organize partnerships to buy from other partnerships and sell to still other partnerships, with each group recognizing tremendous profits (at least on paper).

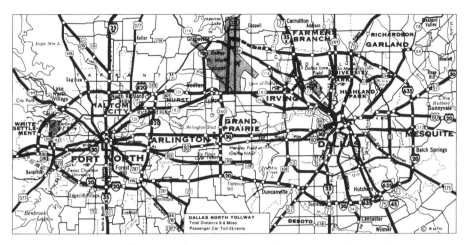

Courtesy of Rand McNally Road Atlas (New York and Chicago: Rand McNally & Company, 1979), p. 93.

Figure 3-8.   DALLAS-FORT WORTH, TEXAS MAP

In mid-1970, as the real estate industry experienced a severe slow-down, these land ventures fell on difficult times. Foreclosures "fell through" several layers of partnerships. What happened was that one partnership would foreclose the property (taking it over by bidding it in at the foreclosure auction) when the group to which it had sold defaulted on its note. The result was that the partnership would itself lose the land when it could not pay its own note to the partnership which had originally sold it the land.

How could the simple urban models just described have helped avert the Dallas-Fort Worth fiasco? If one remembers the seemingly simplistic concentric circle theory, one would realize that for Dallas and Fort Worth to grow together into a city whose center was located midway between the two existing cities, a population concentration greater than the City of New York would be required. Certainly, all the land between the two cities would not be developed in the near future. Looking to the axial theory and growth in transportation patterns for an explanation, one would still realize there was still an incredible abundance of land. Using the sector theory, one would have noticed that only certain parts or sectors of this land would be developed with high-income property, which would, in turn, generate high land values and consequently high profits for land investors. The multiple nuclei theory takes this one step further and suggests that there would only be certain smaller commercial concentrations within the residential concentrations between these two cities. While these four theories seem quite simple, millions and millions of dollars would have been saved, had investors been reflective enough to use logical insights derived from these descriptive models to understand the real estate markets in which they were investing.

By 1975, the bubble had burst, the chain letter had ended, and economic logic again came to dominate land pricing. With the return to economically justifiable prices, many speculators were wiped out. While particular real estate markets may in some sense feed on themselves (relying on the "greater fool" theory), the sophisticated analyst realizes that in the long run, prices must be economically justified.

WHY CITIES GROW

Historic descriptive models are useful only as aids in predicting the future. In the example of Dallas-Fort Worth, the results clearly suggest that the serious analyst should go beyond these models and ask "why" cities grow. Harry Richardson, in this classic text *Regional Economics*, cites several possible hypotheses. He begins with Walter Christaller's *central place theory*, which postulates that a city grows because of the demand for services from what Christaller termed the *hinterland* or surrounding areas. Christaller developed a hexagonal model which is not totally unlike Von Thunen's model described earlier. Different sizes of cities could be explained, according to Christaller, by the size of the area they serviced. Certain goods have to be supplied at fairly local levels; grocery stores would be an example. Other services could be supplied by more distant and more concentrated urban areas. The types of services involved here would include universities, manufacturing plants, etc. Cities such as New York could be explained as providing a set of financial services to the nation as a whole.

Christaller's approach was a starting point, and Richardson goes on to examine other theories. The *economic base theory* (discussed earlier in the regional economics section) can also be used to describe urban growth. A *human ecological approach* explains city growth based on various needs for human interaction. A takeoff on this is the *information theory*. The information theory postulates that cities grow in order to provide information flows (certainly New York City is again a good example). There are even theories which argue that cities grow to a certain minimum size, and once they hit this size, growth is locked in a ratchet-like manner.

Some combination of these theories must be used to explain why cities grow the way they do and why we have competition for location within a city. What will this competition do to the price of land and to the development of surrounding land parcels?

There is no complete model to offer as a substitute for the "why" theories previously suggested. However, there are additional factors which quite clearly affect the way cities grow.

OTHER FACTORS IN URBAN DYNAMICS

The story of cities—their origin, growth, and decline—is a fascinating one, combining, as it does, elements of geography, trade, sociology, economics, and culture. History itself can influence urban dynamics. Certainly, both Boston and Philadelphia offer clear evidence of how historic areas can significantly influence urban-development patterns.

Legend also can be a factor. At a certain point in time, critical events may transpire which cause residents to believe that one part of a city is superior to another. Legend has it that when Stephen F. Austin's troops were camped on the Colorado River during the war with Mexico, a group of his troops became ill with a highly contagious disease. To isolate these troops, he sent them south of the river and successfully avoided contaminating the entire army. Ever since then, the city (which has come to be known as Austin, Texas) has had its more expensive development north of the river. The city of Austin is not alone in having a northwest orientation.

The majority of American cities tend to develop the more expensive residential communities on the northern and western sides. Jacksonville, Florida; Tulsa, Oklahoma; Charlotte, North Carolina; Tampa, Florida; Charlestown, South Carolina; Dayton, Ohio; and St. Louis, Missouri are notable exceptions, but there is a certain tradition which says that northwest is best. This may well be irrational legend. Or, this may be because in the Northeast the prevailing winds came from the north. As the original American cities developed, with industry in the CBD, the prevailing winds kept any unpleasant odors away from the northern part of town. Whatever explanation seems most believable (or enjoyable), legend and tradition play a part in the real estate industry. (See Figure 3-9.)

Certainly, changing racial and ethnic patterns are important in understanding urban dynamics. Filtering, whereby better homes are continually filtering down to owners with lower incomes, with the very wealthy building new homes and so triggering the process, can affect urban dynamics. Racial patterns are slightly different. Racial and ethnic concentrations can create some of the more beautiful and more interesting sections of a city. On the other hand, changing racial and ethnic patterns have been identified by some as the causes of the growth of slums and blight in previously healthy neighborhoods.

Migration is also a very important element in many cities. In faster-growing sections of the country, particularly in the Southwest and West, migration to the region explains a large part of the growth of certain cities. If migration can be tied to particular industries and jobs in those industries, then in some sense residential development and consequent commercial activities can be explained. In other cities, especially port or border ones, migration is significantly composed of illegal aliens, and real

Boston, Massachusetts

Los Angeles, California

Courtesy of United Press International, Inc., New York, New York.

Figure 3-9. SELECTED U.S. URBAN CONCENTRATIONS

St. Louis, Missouri

Houston, Texas

Bozeman, Montana

Figure 3-9. SELECTED U.S. URBAN CONCENTRATIONS (continued)

estate markets adapt to provide the services which this group is able to support financially.

The list of considerations in this interdisciplinary field is almost endless. A growing awareness of the importance of energy makes certain areas more attractive than others. In fact, as the price of gasoline rises, locations with easier access to mass transit increase in attractiveness relative to areas serviced by the private automobile. Crime is also a factor, particularly after some of the precedent-setting landlord liability cases in the Washington, D.C. courts.[1] The changing concept of the modern family, unmarried couples living together, higher divorce rates, smaller families, and later families all have a dramatic impact on real estate development. Technological change is important, as are new patterns of leisure-time use, population growth, social ideals, quality of television, air conditioning, and even changing weather patterns. Adding increasing complexity to the analysis is the *accelerating rate of change*. Remember that the real estate asset has a long economic life in a fixed location. The faster the rate of change, the more important consideration of future trends becomes to the real estate analyst. It is only after analyzing all of the relevant market factors that projections of residual cash flows can be made. (Remember, the microdefinition of winning is tied directly to projected cash flows.)

HOW TO USE REGIONAL AND URBAN ECONOMICS

For the real estate analyst, the study of regional and urban economics must be put into the proper perspective. This requires that the topics and ideas presented throughout this chapter be evaluated on the basis of how such theory can assist the real estate decision-maker. Clearly, regional and urban development affects the marketplace and, as such, is not itself at issue. However, applying or using theory in the analysis of a *specific localized* real estate market is another matter. What the analyst needs is to be able to draw analogies from regional and urban economic theory which help explain activity, current and future, occurring in a specific market.

Descriptive Theories

Regional and urban economic theories are important to the real estate analyst because such theories firmly fix the spatial dimension of the real estate marketplace. This *spatial dimension concept* includes the impact of

---

[1] These decisions are discussed in greater detail in Part IX. They involve holding the landlord liable to the tenant for crimes where only the landlord was able to effectively provide security, such as a security guard for an apartment building in a high crime area.

many factors upon a particular site. Employment opportunities, transportation, public services, climate, entertainment, and educational facilities are a few of the factors which affect the evaluation of a particular site by the marketplace. These factors determine how the site fits into the surrounding regional and urban economic scenes. Demand for (and hence value of) a particular site can be critically related to how it fits into the spatial setting. This includes both how the site is affected by surrounding activity (location effect) and how the site itself (use effect) affects surrounding activity.

For example, the development of a regional economy can be highly affected by climate. In the case of Florida, land use decisions are materially affected by climatical characteristics. The growth and development of a tourism-dominated economic base is largely a function of the climate. Consequently, land use decisions are significantly affected by how the site fits into economic activity of the area. Beachfront property would be more valuable than some central city areas, for example.

Another example of how the site affects surrounding uses within the spatial context can be exemplified by the impact of regional shopping centers. When such a center is developed, it serves as a magnet for many other uses (e.g., office and light commercial development). The opportunity to take advantage of the traffic generated by the center can make other developments feasible, whereas without the presence of the shopping center they could not be justified.

Location Analysis

Relationships suggested by regional and urban economic theories have been relied upon in the development of quantitative tools which are useful in location analysis. Some of these tools (e.g., export base multipliers, location quotients, and shift share analysis) can be used by the real estate analyst to project future economic activity in an area. As markets change, it is important to be able to forecast future trends and these tools can give a quick first approximation.

For example, the location of a new manufacturing plant may have considerably more impact on an area than merely an increase in employment. The type of employees required makes a great deal of difference. If local skills satisfy the new labor demand, the effect on the economy will be considerably different than if new skills must be attracted to the community. In the prior case, unemployment would fall, some shifting might occur in the housing market, and the demand for city services would be only slightly affected. If new skills in employees are required by the new manufacturing plant, the resulting in-migration would increase the demand for housing and city services, but the level of unemployment might not be materially affected.

Governmental Policy Decisions

Based on regional development patterns, certain urban concentrations develop. As cities grow and change, many government policy decisions must also be made. These policy decisions can materially affect land use decisions and future growth. Since real estate decisions are highly influenced by government policy, it is critical that real estate analysts recognize the dynamic role of government as regional and urban economic considerations change.

Descriptive urban models can be useful in identifying the forces which shape the internal structure of cities. This structure refers not only to the spatial development of cities, but also to their social, political, and cultural characteristics. The real estate analyst can utilize urban models in understanding and anticipating governmental policy as it relates to city growth and development, for hopefully, government policy-makers are using the same models.

SUMMARY

The fixed location and long economic life of improved real estate represents unique asset characteristics. Location fixes a site within a regional and/or urban market. Long economic life of improvements necessitates a clear understanding of dynamic market factors affecting a site over the long run. As a result, the spatial characteristics of the real estate market plus specific site improvements define or identify specific markets. The market of a particular site can be examined in terms of how the site affects surrounding parcels (use effect) and how surrounding activity affects the site (location effect). As all markets are somewhat different, the real estate analyst must understand the region and the city in order to develop a coherent framework for real estate analysis.

Regional and urban economics provide useful tools for focusing upon the important spatial element of real estate markets. The pragmatic origin and development of regional and urban economic theory provide tools which the real estate analyst can use to evaluate the location effect. This requires an interdisciplinary approach which accurately evaluates both positive and negative externalities. Evaluation of the impact of these externalities is important in projecting residual cash flows over time for any particular project.

Finally, it is important to remember that the real estate market is governed by a set of socially defined rules. It is important to recognize that the rules of the game can be changed if society's best interest is not being served. Local, state, and federal government policy decisions represent the mechanism society has chosen to implement such change. Therefore, in developing an analytical framework for the analysis of real estate decisions, regional and urban economic considerations must be evaluated within the context of a dynamic marketplace and society's best interest.

In this regard, what are appropriate public policy goals? Should government support (1) maximization of business profits, (2) maximization of real incomes, (3) improvement in the quality of life, and/or (4) redistribution of income (wealth)? Are these possible goals inherently contradictory? Remember these questions. They are explored more fully in Part IX.

At this point, the basic analytical framework is in place. It includes a residual cash flow model (Chapter 1) which takes into account the interactions of the motivations and aspirations of all the different players (Chapter 2), with the primary focus on the spatial element (Chapter 3). Now, law (Part II), appraisal (Part III), marketing (Part IV), finance (Part V), and taxation (Part VI) are examined in detail. These are important facets of the general framework which comes together in the discussion on investment (Part VII).

IMPORTANT TERMS

axial theory
central business district
  (CBD)
city
concentric circle theory
exogenous
export base multiplier
external diseconomies
external economies

highest and best use
input/output
  analysis
location effect
location quotient
regional economics
sector theory
shift share technique
urban economics

REVIEW QUESTIONS

3-1. Why can regional and urban economics be called economics with a spatial dimension?

3-2. What is the difference between the use effect and the location effect as they affect the value of a site?

3-3. In reference to the export base multiplier, how is the output of a region divided between basic and service categories?

3-4. Name three identifying features of a city.

3-5. How did the axial theory expand on the concentric circle theory of urban land development?

3-6. Explain the sector theory.

3-7. How can legend play a role in the pattern of a city's development?

3-8. Briefly discuss von Thünen's explanation of agricultural locations.

3-9. What are the basic differences between regional and urban economics?

3-10. What are the possible uses of a descriptive urban model?

The Legal Environment

4

Ownership of Real Estate Interests

In Part I, real estate is viewed in an economic context. The central question is how value in real estate is created. The conclusion is that the key element in valuing real estate is its location. More precisely, real estate has value because of the uses to which it can be put, and its location is the critical element in determining those uses.

Now the question of use is approached from a different perspective by inquiring into the mechanics by which interests in land can be created and transferred. These are the formal rules of the game and, consequently, an important part of the framework for decision analysis.

Real estate law is discussed not from the point of view of the attorney, because that is not the focus of this book, but rather with two other objectives in mind:

- To introduce basic concepts relating to land ownership and transfer in order to have the background necessary to negotiate a transaction or to make a decision as to the use or disposition of real estate.
- To illustrate some of the unique investment advantages of real estate—in particular, the ability to permit different kinds of interests to be created in the identical parcel and so to tailormake investment "positions" to meet demands of the various participants in the investment process.

As the subjects in this chapter and the next are discussed, it will be apparent that the features that make real estate a unique asset—its fixed location and its long life—also are the critical elements in determining its legal characteristics.

MEANING AND OBJECTIVES OF LAW

While there is no totally adequate definition of *law*, it has been variously defined as what is right, as social planning, as custom, and in several related fashions. The objectives of law are somewhat clearer. One is to keep the peace. Beyond this, the law also seeks to influence and enforce certain standards of conduct. Some might call this maintaining the status quo, but a more appropriate concept would be the facilitation of orderly change. Promoting social justice, facilitating planning, and protecting the general economic well-being are also logical objectives of the law.

Sources of Law

There are several sources of the body of laws which today make the rules of the game in the real estate industry. Among them are:

- The U.S. Constitution, the supreme law of the land.
- The constitutions of the various states.
- Federal and state legislation.
- Federal administrative agencies, such as the Environmental Protection Agency (EPA), Federal Trade Commission (FTC), Federal Communication Commission (FCC), and Securities and Exchange Commission (SEC), and comparable state agencies.
- Common law (i.e., prior judicial decisions interpreted as the law of the land).
- Treaties, executive orders, and other less well-known sources.

A unique feature of the American legal system involves the dual judicial process (i.e., parallel federal court and state court systems). The significance of the dual system is that the final judgment on certain issues is rendered by the highest court of a state rather than by the U.S. Supreme Court.

PHYSICAL INTERESTS

The title of this chapter—*"Ownership of Real Estate Interests"*—reflects the three parts into which the chapter is divided. The real estate itself is examined first to determine what precisely is owned. Next, an inquiry is made as to the different types of interests (in the legal sense) that can exist in a parcel of real estate. The final inquiry relates to the kinds of entities that are utilized in owning interests in real estate.

First to be examined is the real estate itself. Real estate consists of land plus whatever grows on the land or is permanently attached to the land. But, in addition, real estate includes all of the space *above* and *below* the surface of the earth.

Ownership of land thus includes:

- Above-surface space (i.e., air space) extending from the surface of the earth to an infinite point in space.
- Subsurface space within an area circumscribed by lines drawn from the surface boundaries of the land to the center of the earth (the space forming an inverted cone).

So a parcel of real estate really consists of three different physical levels: (1) surface, (2) subsurface, and (3) air space. Each of these may be utilized or occupied separately from the others. For example, *X* may start out by "owning" Blackacre, a parcel of real estate, and then may transfer to *Y* ownership of the space beneath the surface of Blackacre (i.e., the subsurface rights) and then may transfer to *Z* ownership of the space above the surface of Blackacre (i.e., the air space).

Air Space

One of the most dramatic examples of air space rights is the Pan Am building in New York City. The Penn Central Railroad originally owned the real estate; it utilized the subsurface to run trains and the surface (plus air space just above) for Grand Central Terminal. All of the remaining air space was leased for 99 years to the company that owns the Pan Am office tower. A necessary part of the lease of the air space included "support rights," consisting of columns sunk into the ground on which the air space building rests.

Subsurface Rights

Subsurface rights normally involve the right to remove minerals, such as coal, oil, or gas, or to put something in the ground, such as a pipeline. The general rule is that the owner of land may remove anything from it, subject to governmental regulation with respect to zoning and mining practices (such as laws which bar strip mining). In addition, common law recognizes that a landowner may excavate land but not to the point of depriving adjacent property of its natural support (which might cause buildings on those properties to collapse).

LEGAL INTERESTS

Real property—that is, the physical entity itself—is comprised of the three separate facets of surface, subsurface, and air space. One may have an ownership interest in any one of these, in two out of three, or in all three. But of just what does ownership consist?

Ownership as a Bundle of Rights

In Anglo-American law, real estate ownership is most often viewed as consisting of a "bundle of rights." This includes the rights of (1) possession, (2) control, (3) enjoyment, and (4) disposition:

- The *right of possession* refers to occupancy and includes the right to keep out all others.
- The *right of control* deals with the right to physically alter the property.
- The *right of enjoyment* protects the current owner from interference by past owners or others.
- The *right of disposition* permits conveyance of all or part of one's bundle of rights to others.

All these rights are subject to limitation or restriction by governmental action. (See Part IX for a discussion of zoning.) They also are subject to restrictions created or agreed to by prior owners that are binding on their successors. For example, owners in a residential community may desire that no parcel of land shall be used in the future for a commercial enterprise. Provided they comply with the legal rules, they can restrict future use of the land within reasonable limits.

The bundle of rights that constitute real estate ownership can be divided in a surprising number of ways. In general, these rights can be classified into two major categories: (1) ownership (freehold) rights and (2) possessory (leasehold) rights. A third category covers certain nonpossessory uses of real estate. (See Figure 4-1.) In the paragraphs that follow, these three general categories are described.

FREEHOLD ESTATES

Freehold (ownership) estates represent the highest quality of rights associated with real property under our legal system. In general, the holder of such an estate may exercise the full bundle of rights that relate to real property, subject always to overriding public policy as expressed in statute law, court decisions, and governmental regulation. The freehold category includes three significant types of estates: (1) fee simple, (2) defeasible fees, and (3) life estates.

Fee Simple Absolute

The most straightforward estate in land is known as the *fee simple absolute* or *fee simple*, and is often referred to simply as a *fee*. Fee simple ownership represents the most complete form of private property own-

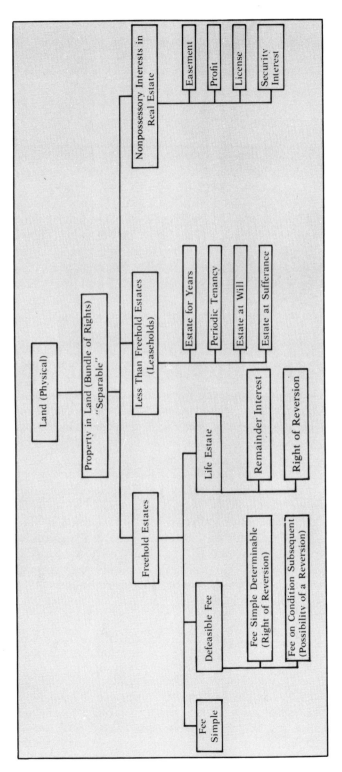

Figure 4-1.   ESTATE IN LAND

ership recognized by our law. A fee simple interest creates an absolute and complete right of ownership for an unlimited duration of time with an unconditional right of disposition and use (i.e., the complete bundle of rights). Consequently, fee simple ownership is the most preferred interest in land.

Defeasible Fees

A special kind of freehold interest, seen only infrequently today, is the defeasible fee. In plain terms, this is a fee simple interest subject to certain conditions which, if not met, will cause the owner to lose the property. The origin of defeasible fees goes back to the early English common law when land was virtually the sole significant source of wealth. By tying up land with defeasible fees (and other devices), large landholders sought to insure that the land would remain in certain uses or "within the family" for generations to come—which, in fact, has been the case. This is the reason why some English peers today still hold vast acreages in the United Kingdom.

Two kinds of defeasible fees are: (1) fee simple determinable and (2) fee on condition subsequent.

☐ *Fee simple determinable.* This is fee simple ownership which automatically will terminate and revert back to the grantor (original fee holder) or the grantor's heirs on the happening of a stated condition. Such a fee is usually expressed by a conveyance "to *X* and *X*'s heirs *so long as they use the property for Y purpose.*" The restrictive condition associated with a fee simple determinable interest essentially limits the right of control and subsequent disposition of the real estate.

An actual example a few years ago involved land which had been conveyed to the local municipality "so long as the land is used as a railroad station." Presumably, the grantor wished to provide a desirable site for the local commuter railroad line and wanted to insure that the land would not be used for any other purpose. With changing times, the railroad discontinued service to the community, and the municipality sought to sell the land. At that point, about ninety years after the grant, the heirs of the original grantor were able to regain the land on the basis that the condition of use was no longer met.

☐ *Fee on condition subsequent.* Just as with a fee simple determinable, a fee on condition subsequent creates an ownership interest that can be lost on the happening of a stated event or condition. The typical phrasing in a conveyance of such a fee would be "to *X* and *X*'s heirs *on the condition that they use the property for Y purpose.*"

As in the case of a fee simple determinable, it is clear from such a conveyance that the bundle of rights associated with fee ownership is limited. What is the difference between these two types of defeasible fees? In essence, it is a matter of the precise manner whereby title can be lost by the owner who fails to comply with the condition. The grantor of a fee simple determinable automatically regains ownership on the stated event, whereas the grantor of a fee on condition subsequent must initiate action to recover ownership.

Even though defeasible fees may still be created, they are extremely unusual and regarded with disfavor by the courts because they are *restraints on alienability.* They limit the transferability of real estate, since one would be reluctant to buy a defeasible fee because of the risk of forfeiture if the condition to title were ever violated. ˙

Why do courts care about the free transferability of real estate? The answer is that the economic as well as the social development of the country would be hindered if many parcels of real estate were tied up with ancient restrictions that prevented the most productive use of the property in today's world. Consider the parcel of real estate, referred to above, that could only be used as a railroad station even though no railroad continued to serve the community.[1]

Life Estates

The life estate is an extremely common form of freehold estate. In a life estate, the grantor conveys the fee simple interest to a grantee (usually a spouse or other family member) for a period measured by the lifetime of the grantee (or sometimes by the life of a third party). After the measuring lifetime has expired, title to the property automatically will go to another person specified by the grantor. (See **4-1.**)

This subsequent interest is called a *remainder* (because it is what remains after the life interest expires) and the person who ultimately will receive it is called the *remainderman.* The person holding the life estate is the *life tenant,* a term that can be confusing since it has nothing to do with a lease. The life tenant may treat the property in all respects as an owner in fee simple would, subject only to two restrictions:

☐ *The life tenant must maintain the property in reasonably good condition in order to protect the interests of the remainderman.* For example, an apartment project cannot be permitted to deteriorate to the point where it becomes uninhabitable. Any act or omission by the life tenant which does permanent injury to the property or unreasonably changes its character or value constitutes *waste* and may be enjoined (prohibited) by a court following legal action by the remainderman.

---

[1] In older books, the fee tail is also mentioned at this point. Under a fee tail, which has been abolished in the United States, the property was always inherited by the elder male child. This feudal concept clearly would be detrimental to a "market" economy.

4-1. DOWER AND CURTESY RIGHTS

Life estates were the first form of social security. When a landowner died in feudal England, his wife automatically received a one-third interest in all of his real estate, whether or not such an interest was specifically conveyed to her by will. In this way, the community was assured that widows would not become a burden on the community. The life estate in feudal England was known as the *dower interest*, and the widow holding such interest was known as a *dowager*, a term which has come to mean an elderly lady of means. Under certain circumstances, a widower also had certain rights in his wife's estate. This was known as the *right of curtesy*. The rights of dower and curtesy have been abolished in the United States and in most states have been replaced by a *statutory interest* or *statutory share*. This statutory interest consists of the right by the surviving spouse to claim an interest in the deceased spouse's estate even though the spouse was left out of the will. For example, in New York State, the surviving spouse is entitled to receive a one-third interest in all of the property (real and personal) owned by the deceased at his or her death. However, the surviving spouse must elect either the statutory share *or* the legacy (if any) provided in the decedent's will. However, a statutory share does not extend to property legitimately transferred by the decedent during his or her lifetime; thus it is still possible for a surviving spouse to end up with nothing.

☐ *Life tenants may convey the interest to a third party but can convey no more than such interest.* Thus, if a husband dies, leaving his wife a life estate, she may sell only her life estate. Since the duration of her estate is completely unknown and indeed may end the next day, it is not likely that anyone would pay a great deal for such an estate. For this reason, life estates are normally not used in commercial transactions.[2]

LEASEHOLD ESTATES

Whereas a freehold interest conveys *ownership*, a leasehold estate conveys *possession*. A leasehold interest is created by a lease, which is usually in writing but is sometimes oral. A lease is a unique form of

---

[2] Several states, such as Florida, have created a homestead right. By this right, a surviving spouse is entitled to a life estate in the couple's residence if title was held by the deceased spouse at his or her death and regardless of any other disposition provided by will.

instrument because it is both a *conveyance* (i.e., it transfers the right to possession of real estate) and a *contract* (i.e., it creates rights and duties between the landlord and the tenant).

A primary feature of leasehold interests is that they are for a definite term. Consequently, it is convenient to categorize leasehold interests according to their duration (see Figure 4-1). The four categories are:

- Estate for years.
- Estate from period to period.
- Estate at will.
- Estate at sufferance.

Estate for Years

By far the most common type of leasehold interest is the estate for years. This type includes all leases with a fixed term—whether a residential lease for one year or a ground lease for 99 years. An estate for years will expire automatically at the end of the period designated, at which time the tenant's right of possession ends and possession reverts to the landlord. The lease, however, may grant renewal options to the tenant which, if properly exercised, will continue the leasehold for another designated term.

Estate From Period to Period

This type of leasehold estate, also very common, is most often used for residential and small commercial properties. It is created whenever the lease specifies the amount of rent for a designated period but does not state a specified term for the lease.

For example, if a lease provides that rent shall be paid at the rate of $100 per month, a *month-to-month tenancy* is created. The tenant is entitled to possession and is obligated to pay rent until either landlord or tenant gives notice of intention to terminate the lease. The time of such notice and the form in which it must be given are usually determined by statute (e.g., either party may terminate the lease on thirty days' written notice, delivered personally or sent by certified mail to the other). Since this type of estate cannot assure the tenant of possession for any lengthy period, it is not normally used where a tenant, such as a retailer, must spend substantial sums to prepare the premises for use.

Estate at Will

An estate at will (or tenancy at will) is created by an oral agreement between landlord and tenant to the effect that the tenant may occupy the premises so long as it is convenient for both parties. Estates at will can create problems for both parties since no written instrument specifies the amount of rent or the rights or responsibilities of either party.

Estate at Sufferance

This rather unusual form of leasehold estate exists when a leasehold interest, whether for years, period to period, or at will, expires or terminates without the tenant vacating the property. In other words, the tenant continues to hold the premises at the sufferance of the landlord; hence, another term for this estate is a *holdover tenancy.*

In theory, such a tenant may be dispossessed at any time by the landlord. However, as in the case of an estate by will, a prior period of notice may have to be given by the landlord.

Separating the Bundle of Rights

At this point, an important observation about leasehold interests should be made. When a leasehold interest is created, it represents a current *separation* of the bundle of rights that makes up ownership of real estate. The separation is into a fee interest (the interest of the landlord, also called the *lessor*) and a leasehold interest (the interest of the tenant, also called the *lessee*).

Therefore, whenever a transaction involves a leasehold, it means that a double interest exists in the property. The tenant has the right to possession of the property, subject to the terms of the lease and for the duration specified in the lease. The landlord retains all of the other ownership rights plus the right to regain possession when the lease expires (the *right of reversion*).

The ability to divide real estate into a fee and leasehold interest offers enormous flexibility in putting together a transaction between several parties. Probably the greatest master of the technique of "slicing up" a parcel of real estate into various interests was the late William Zeckendorf, Sr. At different times, Zeckendorf referred to his technique as the *Hawaiian technique* (he claimed he thought of it while fishing in that state) or the *pineapple technique* (the initial single ownership interest in a parcel of land could be sliced up into a number of interests, just as a pineapple could be sliced into a number of sections). Whatever he called it, Zeckendorf was able to create complicated real estate interests that resulted in developments that otherwise would never have been built. A notable example is the United Nations Plaza building adjacent to the United Nations in New York City. In this development, three different fee interests plus a leasehold interest plus five mortgage interests were carved out of a single parcel of land. (See 4-2 for a description of how it was done.)

4-2. UNITED NATIONS PLAZA BUILDING—NEW YORK CITY

In midtown New York City, next to the United Nations, stands a single structure that consists of a six-story office building on top of which rise two 32-story residential towers. Begun in 1964, the project is a classic illustration of the late William Zeckendorf's *pineapple technique*. The project was originated by Zeckendorf's company, Webb & Knapp, but when it began its slide into bankruptcy, development was taken over by Alcoa Associates, a joint venture between Alcoa and Canadian interests.

The best way to visualize the various interests created in the building is to follow the transactions as they occurred:

☐ *Three fee interests.* The developer (Associates) originally owned the property in fee simple. The first step it took illustrates the fundamental operating principle that Zeckendorf followed, which was to minimize or eliminate entirely the need for any of his own cash in the transaction. Associates created two cooperative housing corporations, each to own one of the 32-story towers to be constructed above the office building. Associates then sold a fee simple interest in air space to each cooperative corporation. At that point, three separate fee interests had been created in the parcel of real estate. The price received for the two air space parcels was $38 million.

☐ *Leasehold interest.* To further reduce its cash requirements, Associates sold its fee interest (consisting of the land plus sufficient air space for the office building) to Equitable Life Assurance Society for $12 million. Simultaneously, Associates leased back the identical space from Equitable for a term of 999 years. This transaction is known as a *sale-leaseback.*

☐ *Leasehold mortgage.* Associates then obtained a loan of $3.5 million from Equitable secured by Associates' leasehold interest. This type of loan is called a *leasehold mortgage.* How could the leasehold interest be security for a loan? Associates anticipated making a substantial profit from the difference between the rent it would collect from office tenants and the rental (the *ground rent*) it would have to pay Equitable. This flow of income (anticipated for 999 years) was adequate security for a 27-year loan.

☐ *Four fee mortgages.* Since it was not likely that the cooperative apartment units could be sold without substantial financing, Equitable agreed to provide first mortgage financing to each of the cooperative corporations, while Associates agreed to provide financing secured by second mortgages.

☐ *Total of nine interests.* A total of nine different interests were created. Of these, three were fee interests, one was a leasehold interest, and five were security (mortgage) interests, consisting of a leasehold mortgage, two first fee mortgages, and two second fee mortgages (all of the fee mortgages covering the air space fee interests owned by the cooperative corporations). Associates raised a total of $53.5 million by selling off the two air space fee interests and mortgaging its leasehold interest. This probably came close to paying for the original land cost plus the cost of putting up the 6-story office building. Associates ended up (for very little cash investment) holding a 999-year leasehold of an office building in the heart of New York City.

NONPOSSESSORY INTERESTS

The two major types of interests in real estate just discussed are freehold (ownership) interests and leasehold (possessory) interests. A third category includes interests and rights to utilize land which, as a group, may be designated *nonpossessory* interests or rights—that is, none of these rises to the "dignity" of an interest that carries with it ownership or possession. The three common types are: (1) easements, (2) profits, and (3) licenses (see Figure 4-1).

Easements

An easement is an interest in real estate that gives the holder the right to use but not to possess the real estate. A common form of an easement is a right of way—that is, the right to cross over the land of another. Another is the electric utility or telephone easement, which permits a utility company to place poles at designated points on the land and run wires between them. Since an easement involves some restriction or limitation of the right of ownership, land subject to an easement is said to be *burdened* with an easement, and, to some extent, its value may be diminished.

There are several types of easements, generally distinguished by the manner in which they are created:

☐ *Express easement.* An express easement is created by a writing executed by the owner of the *servient tenement* (the property subject to the easement). The writing may be called a *grant of easement* or similar title.

☐ *Easement appurtenant.* Consider two plots of land adjacent to one another. The deed, or document of title, to lot *A* gives its owner the right to cross over lot *B* in order to reach a public highway. In this situation, ownership of *A* (called the *dominant tenement*) includes as one of the bundle of rights of ownership an easement appurtenant (i.e., an easement that accompanies ownership). *B*, which is burdened by the right of way, is the *servient tenement;* it is subject to an obligation that may or may not reduce its value in any significant way, depending on the location of the right of way and the use to which *B* is being put.

An easement appurtenant, being a part of the bundle of rights of ownership, is not a personal right but attaches to the land (the legal phrase is *runs with the land*) and so is conveyed to subsequent owners of the dominant tenement.

☐ *Easement in gross.* Real estate may be subject to an easement which is unconnected with any other parcel of land, that is, an easement that is personal to the individual or institution benefiting from it.

Electric utility and telephone easements would be an example. Other types of commercial easements in gross are railroad and pipeline rights of way.

☐ *Implied easement.* Such an easement arises when the owner of a tract of land subjects one part of the tract to an easement (such as a right of way) that benefits the other part and then conveys one or both parts of the tract to other parties so that divided ownership results. In such case, common law holds that an implied easement arises in favor of the *dominant tenement* and burdens the *servient tenement.*

☐ *Easement by necessity.* This is a special form of implied easement and arises when the owner of a tract subdivides or separates a part of the tract so that the severed part has no access to the outside world except across the balance of the tract. Under such circumstances and in order to permit the productive use of the isolated land, common law implies the right of way across the grantor's land to a public highway. Some states provide by statute that the owner of land lacking access to a public way may petition the courts to have a *cartway* condemned for his use. Again, the purpose is to encourage the development and use of land for the benefit of society in general.

☐ *Easement by prescription.* This type of easement arises when a stranger (i.e., one without ownership or possessory right) makes use of land for a prescribed period of time (e.g., ten years) and does so openly and without pretense of having the true owner's consent. Under such circumstances, the use which was originally adverse (against the interest of the owner) may ripen into an easement which is recognized by law. This is similar to the process of acquiring title to land by adverse possession (discussed at page 103). An example of a prescriptive easement would be extended use by one neighbor of another neighbor's driveway, with the first neighbor openly claiming the "right" to such use.

Profits

A profit in land (technically known as a *profit à prendre*) is the right to take a portion of the soil or timber or remove subsurface minerals, oil, or gas in land owned by someone else. A profit represents an interest in real property and it must be in writing. The distinction between a profit and an easement is that the latter merely permits use of the property, while the former involves a removal of part of the land. A profit also is to be distinguished from a gas and oil or mineral *lease*. These require the lessee to pay a royalty to the landowner calculated on the amount of natural resource taken.

License

A license is the right to go on land owned by another for a specific purpose. A license in most cases is merely a revocable privilege granted by the owner to another and does not represent an interest in real estate. Almost everyone frequently is a licensee. Whenever a ticket is purchased to attend a sports or other event in a stadium or hall, the individual is purchasing a license. Similarly, if the privilege of hunting or fishing on the lands of another is given, whether or not for a consideration, the hunter or fisherman is a licensee.

Security Interests

A final type of nonpossessory interest in real estate is the security interest (i.e., the interest of one holding a mortgage). Security interests are discussed in detail in Chapter 13. At this point, note only that the holder of a mortgage has a legal interest in real estate, but it will not develop into possession or ownership unless a default occurs under the terms of the mortgage (e.g., nonpayment of an installment when due), at which point the mortgage holder can exercise its rights to foreclose against the property. (The foreclosure procedure is covered in Part V.)

FORMS OF OWNERSHIP

At this point, it should be clear that:

- The physical entity that is real estate is really made up of three different elements: (1) surface rights, (2) subsurface rights, and (3) air space (called the *physical interests in real estate*).
- A variety of "shares" may be held in each of these physical interests in real estate, including: (1) ownership shares, (2) possessory shares, and (3) nonpossessory shares (called *legal interests in real estate*).

The topic of ownership—the third part of the three-part formula—set out at the beginning of this chapter is now introduced. There are five ways in which ownership may be held in a legal interest in real estate:

- Single ownership.
- Tenancy in common.
- Joint tenancy with right of survivorship.
- Tenancy by the entirety.
- Community property.

The four latter types of ownership are known generally by the term *concurrent ownership* (i.e., ownership by more than one person).

Dividing the Bundle of Rights

The various forms of ownership discussed in this chapter can be used to effectively *divide* the bundle of rights. That is, more than one party or entity may share the entire bundle or a portion thereof. Any true co-ownership means that a legal interest in the property is owned by more than one party. Obviously, it is neither necessary nor always desirable for equal (e.g., 50-50) division of the bundle of rights to occur. (See Figure 4-2.)

Tenancy in Common

The tenancy in common is the most frequently used form of concurrent ownership. When two or more persons hold as tenants in common (the term *tenants* as used here has nothing to do with a lease or leasehold interest), each has an undivided interest in the entire property to the extent of his ownership share.

For example, three tenants in common will each own a one-third undivided share in the entire property rather than each owning a specified one-third portion of the property. While normally each tenant in common has the same share as his co-tenants, this need not necessarily be the case; one of three co-tenants may own a 40 percent undivided share, with each of the others owning 30 percent shares.

Each tenant in common may sell, mortgage, or give away his interest during his life or transfer it at death, just as if the entire property were owned in single ownership. Each tenant in common's right to possession of the property is subject to the rights of his co-tenants. Each has the right to an accounting of rents and profits (when the property produces income), and each is entitled to reimbursement by the others of monies expended by him for necessary maintenance, repair, property taxes, and other expenses.[3] Any such reimbursement will be proportionate to each tenant's interest.

Joint Tenancy

A joint tenancy is the same as a tenancy in common—with one very significant difference. The difference is the *right of survivorship*, which

---

[3] Since each tenant in common owns an undivided interest in the property, difficult problems may arise when they disagree among themselves and wish to go their separate ways. Any tenant in common is entitled to begin a legal proceeding called an *action for partition*. If the property cannot be equitably divided, the court will order it to be sold, with the proceeds to be divided among the co-tenants according to their interests.

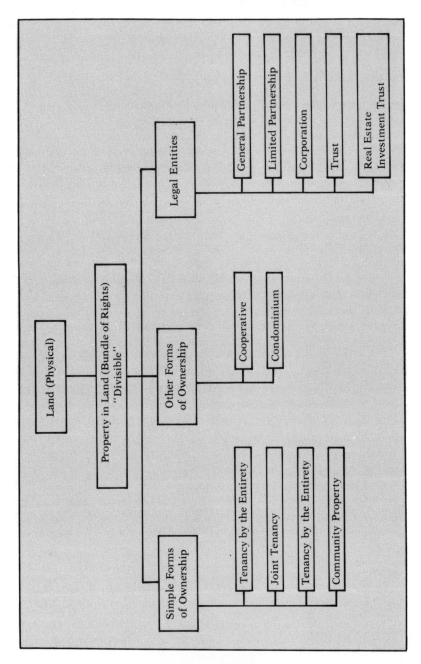

Figure 4-2.   FORMS OF OWNERSHIP

means that if any joint tenant dies, his interest automatically passes in equal shares to the remaining joint tenants.

For example, if *A* and *B* are joint tenants and *A* dies, title to his one-half undivided share automatically goes to *B*, who thereby becomes the sole owner of the property. If three joint tenants had owned the property and one died, each of the two survivors would take one-half of the deceased joint tenant's interest.

Since the survivorship feature runs contrary to the traditional pattern of devise and descent (inheritance), those wishing to enter into a joint tenancy must clearly specify this intent at the time they take title. Otherwise, a tenancy in common is presumed.

While a joint tenant cannot devise his interest by will (since it passes automatically on death), he can sell or give away his interest during his lifetime, thus changing the joint tenancy to a tenancy in common.

Tenancy by the Entirety

A tenancy by the entirety is a joint tenancy between husband and wife. The tenancy carries with it the same right of survivorship as a joint tenancy so that, on the death of either spouse, the survivor takes the entire estate. Unlike a joint tenancy, however, neither spouse can convey any part of the property during their joint lives unless the other spouse joins in the conveyance. In many states, any conveyance to a husband and wife is presumed to create a tenancy by the entirety. Thus, tenancy by the entirety acts to protect the rights of a surviving spouse in property owned during the marriage.

Property held under tenancy by the entirety is not subject to levy by creditors of only one of the owners. This feature was designed to protect the family from the business failures of one of the spouses. In the event the owners are divorced, the tenancy is destroyed and the divorced spouses become tenants in common. Just as in the case of a joint tenancy, on the death of a tenant by the entirety, the entire value of the property is included in his or her estate unless it can be shown that a part was contributed by the surviving spouse.

Community Property

The three types of concurrent ownership just described—tenancy in common, joint tenancy, and tenancy by the entirety—are derivations of English common law. The type of ownership, known as *community property*, by contrast, derives from Spanish or French law and is now recognized by statute in eight states:

- Arizona.
- California.

- Idaho.
- Louisiana.
- Nevada.
- New Mexico.
- Texas.
- Washington.

In these states, each spouse is an equal co-owner of all the property acquired during the existence of the marriage as a result of the joint efforts of the spouses, and there is a presumption that all the property of husband and wife is community property. However, the spouses can, by mutual consent, convert community property into the separate property of either spouse.

Property is not considered community property if it was owned by either spouse before the marriage or acquired by either spouse during the marriage by gift, inheritance, or will. Community property statutes sometimes also provide that one-half the earnings of either spouse during the existence of the marriage belongs to the other spouse. This rule has been the basis of some celebrated proceedings between both married and unmarried couples in recent years.

On the death of a spouse *intestate* (i.e., the state of leaving no will), the surviving spouse may or may not take all of the community property, depending on the statute of the particular state. Divorce ordinarily destroys the community property status, and, pending a divorce, separation agreements involving property settlements, and reservations with respect to the future earnings of one or both spouses, usually are made.

The effect of community property is similar (although the legal form is very different) to tenancy by the entirety. Both serve to protect the interest of the "uninformed" spouse. To assure a good conveyance, it is often necessary for both husband and wife to sign the deed in community property states and both signatures are always required when the selling interest is owned by a tenancy by the entirety.

TWO SPECIAL FORMS OF OWNERSHIP

In addition to the ownership forms just described, two special types of ownership interests exist in real estate. These are the condominium and the cooperative corporation.

Condominiums

As with community property, the condominium concept does not derive from English common law. Rather, it dates back over 4,000 years to

Roman law, from which it has become a part of the civil law followed by most countries in Western Europe and South America. Although introduced into our country as early as 1952 (in Puerto Rico), statutes authorizing condominium ownership now have been passed by every state and the District of Columbia.

Condominium (*co-dominion*) means joint ownership and control, as distinguished from sole ownership and control. In a condominium project, each unit (e.g., apartment) is individually owned, while the common elements of the building (e.g., lobby, corridors, exterior walls) are jointly owned. While by far most condominium projects are residential, the concept has been extended to commercial, industrial, and recreational projects.

To create a condominium, the owners of the property must file a declaration of condominium (or master deed) with the local land records office. The declaration includes a detailed description of the individual units in the property and of the common areas which may be used by all of the owners. The declaration also sets forth the percentage of ownership that attaches to each individual unit. This percentage establishes the voting rights of each unit owner and each owner's contribution to the operating expenses of the property.

Each owner of a condominium unit may sell or mortgage his unit as he sees fit. Property taxes are levied on each unit rather than on the entire project. The condominium unit owners constitute an owners' association and elect a board of directors, which is responsible for the day-to-day running of the condominium project.

Cooperative Housing Corporations

The essential element of a cooperative housing corporation (cooperative) is that ownership is in a corporation, the shares of which are divided among several persons, each of whom is entitled to lease a portion of the space by virtue of his ownership interest—that is, ownership and the right to lease and use the space are inseparable. Typically, a residential building is acquired by a corporation organized as a cooperative (as distinguished from a business corporation organized for profit). Each share (or specified group of shares) in the corporation carries with it the right to lease and use a designated apartment. Each shareholder executes a *proprietary lease* with the corporation which is similar to a standard lease and pursuant to which the tenant-owner may occupy the designated unit.

Just as with a condominium, the cooperative project is run by a board of directors. Unlike a condominium, the project has a single owner—the cooperative corporation—which may mortgage the property (thus automatically providing financing for each apartment owner). The property is a single parcel for purposes of real estate taxation and the taxes paid by the corporation are allocated among the various unit owners, as are all of the common area and maintenance expenses of the building. Each owner then pays a monthly assessment (equivalent to rent) to cover the operation expenses and necessary repairs and replacements.

Difference Between Condominiums and Cooperatives

A significant difference between a condominium and cooperative lies in the possible "snowball" effect if an individual owner defaults. In the case of a cooperative, default by a tenant-shareholder means that his portion of real estate taxes, mortgage debt service, and common area expense must be assumed by the remaining owners. If a number of tenant-shareholders default, the burden on the remaining owners becomes correspondingly heavier and a snowball effect may be created, causing more and more tenants to default. Precisely this kind of situation happened during the 1930s depression, causing many cooperatives to fail.

By contrast, a condominium unit owner is responsible for his own mortgage financing and real estate taxes on the unit owned. Consequently, in the event of a default by a single unit owner, only that owner's share of operating expenses (but not taxes or debt service) must be assumed by the remaining owners. As a result, a "snowball" is much less likely to occur in a condominium project—one obvious reason for the popularity of this form of ownership.

VEHICLES FOR OWNING INTERESTS

It is at this point that the three-part division of ownership indicated at the beginning of the chapter ends. That is, there has been a discussion of physical interests in real estate, legal interests in real estate, and forms of ownership of real estate. Now the discussion moves to the different ownership vehicles that may be utilized but that are not unique to real estate, being available for ownership of any kind of property. These vehicles provide added flexibility in the areas of financing the property and tax planning. The five types to be briefly mentioned at this point are:

- The general partnership.
- The limited partnership.
- The corporation.
- The trust.
- The real estate investment trust (REIT).

Two frequently used terms in real estate investing, *syndicate* and *joint venture*, are omitted here. In fact, the term *syndicate* does not refer to a specific type of ownership but rather to the concept of multiple ownership itself. Both terms simply refer to a group of people who have joined together to invest in or own real estate.

General Partnership

The general partnership is a form of business organization in which two or more persons are associated as co-owners in a continuing relationship for the purpose of carrying on a common enterprise or business for a profit. An agreement of partnership (also called *articles of partnership*) defines the rights and obligations of each partner and sets forth how profits and losses are to be shared. Unlike a corporation, a general partnership requires no formal legal action or charter from the state in order to function. Once organized, however, a partnership must operate in accordance with legal rules that in most states follow a model known as the Uniform Partnership Act.

In the ownership or operation of real estate, a partnership has one overriding advantage over the business corporation. The partnership is not considered a tax entity apart from its members. Consequently, the income tax consequences of real estate operations carried on by the partnership are passed through directly to the individual partners. Many real estate investments are so set up that "tax losses" are generated which can be used to offset taxable income, even though the investment does not generate a cash loss. Since a partnership is not a separate tax entity, tax losses on real estate owned by a partnership can be "passed through" to the individual partners; if a corporation is the owner, no pass-through can occur since the corporation is an independent tax entity.

A second reason why a general partnership is sometimes used is that each general partner is entitled to an equal voice in partnership affairs, in the absence of an agreement to the contrary. This assures each participant of a right to join in the management of the investment. However, because all partners must agree to decisions in a general partnership, this type of ownership vehicle is most suitable for relatively small and intimate groups of investors who are confident of their ability to work together.

The major disadvantage of the general partnership is that each partner is personally liable for the partnership debts (i.e., all of a partner's assets may be reached by a creditor of the partnership in the event the partnership assets are not sufficient). For this reason, too, the general partnership is normally used only by a small group of investors known to each other.

A joint venture is essentially a general partnership organized to carry on a particular transaction (rather than a series of transactions or a continuing business).

Limited Partnership

A limited partnership is a special type of partnership. It is composed of one or more general partners who manage the partnership affairs and one or more limited partners who are passive investors, do not actively participate in the management of partnership affairs and who, as a consequence, may legally limit their liability to the amount of cash actually invested (or which they specifically promise to provide in the event they are called upon to do so). By comparison, the general partner must assume full and unlimited personal liability for partnership debts.

The limited partnership is the most common form of organization used for real estate syndications since it combines for the limited partners the limited legal liability offered by the corporate form of organization with the tax advantages of the partnership form (i.e., the pass-through of losses). By using a limited partnership, a real estate professional may join the financial resources of outside investors with his own skills and resources and at the same time concentrate management in his own hands.

A limited partnership is formed by a written agreement of partnership pursuant to a state statute. Most statutes are patterned after a model known as the Uniform Limited Partnership Act. Whereas a general partnership is an entity recognized by common law and therefore can come into existence independent of any statute, a limited partnership is a "creature of statute" and will not be given legal recognition unless an appropriate certificate of limited partnership has been filed with the appropriate state authority.

Corporation

A corporation is a separate legal entity—an artificial person—created in accordance with the laws of a particular state (the federal government not having the power to create business corporations). Thus, the corporation is an entity entirely distinct from its shareholders. Its charter may provide that it shall have a perpetual life, and it operates through a board of directors elected by the shareholders. The major advantage of, and the original purpose for, the corporate form was to limit each shareholder's liability to the amount of his capital investment; a secondary purpose was to make shareholder interests freely transferable by means of assignable corporate shares. Both of these features made corporations useful for aggregating investment capital.

The major disadvantage in using a corporation to own real estate is that the corporation is recognized as an independent entity for tax purposes. Thus, tax losses from corporately owned real estate may not be passed through to the individual shareholders but may be utilized only by the corporation itself. Since it may not have any other income against which the losses may be offset, the losses may be of no use. On the other hand, if the corporate real estate produces net income, a problem of double taxation must be faced. The corporation first must pay a corporate income tax on its net income. Then, to the extent the income is distributed in the form of dividends, the shareholders must pay a personal income tax on such income. In the case of a small, closely owned corporation (known as a *close corporation*), the problem of double taxation often can be avoided by distributing corporate income to the shareholders in the form of salaries or other compensation. In this situation, the corporation may deduct the cost of such salaries and thus reduce its own income, although the shareholder-employees will be taxed on the income they receive.

Trust

A trust is a legal relationship by which (1) a trustee holds legal title to property (real estate or otherwise) with the responsibility of administering the property and distributing the income for the benefit of (2) a beneficiary who holds beneficial or equitable title.

A trust is a common means of holding property for the benefit of members of a family, particularly the spouse or children of a decedent. However, a trust need not be set up by will (a testamentary trust) but may be set up during the lifetime of the donor (an inter vivos trust—one between living persons). A trust is an extremely flexible instrument and, for that reason, is one of the most frequently used vehicles for controlling personal wealth, which today is more often in the form of securities than real estate.

Real Estate Investment Trust

A special form of trust ownership is the REIT, which is wholly a creature of the Internal Revenue Code. REITs were set up as a parallel form of investment vehicle to common stock mutual funds, to permit small investors to invest in a diversified portfolio of real estate just as they could in a portfolio of common stocks in a mutual fund.

The major tax benefit of a REIT is that, so long as it distributes at least 95 percent of its net income to its shareholder-beneficiaries, it need not pay any income tax (although the individual shareholders must pay a tax on the dividends received). Thus, the problem of double taxation is eliminated. REITs are strictly limited by statute to the types of operations they may conduct. (More detail on REITs is provided in Parts V and VI.)

SUMMARY

The contents of this chapter should have amply demonstrated that it is no simple matter to answer the question, "Who owns the parcel of real estate known as 150 Main Street?" Three parallel lines of investigation must be followed to provide an adequate answer:

☐ *First*, one must determine if the physical real estate at 150 Main Street has been separated into different types of physical interests—that is, whether there has been a severance of air rights, surface rights, or subsurface rights or whether the physical interest remains a unified one.

☐ *Second*, one must determine if there is a single legal interest in the real estate (i.e., a fee simple absolute) or whether there has been a separation of legal interests, either between a present and future fee interest, or between a fee and leasehold interest, or by creation of a nonpossessory interest such as an easement or license, or any possible combination of the foregoing.

☐ *Finally*, one must determine whether each legal interest in each physical interest in the real estate is owned by a single person (*in severalty*) or divided through some concurrent ownership form. Additionally, different ownership vehicles are possible whether the real estate is owned in severalty or in some concurrent ownership form.

IMPORTANT TERMS

air space
bundle of rights
close corporation
community property
concurrent ownership
condominium
contract
cooperative
co-ownership
defeasible fee
easement
estate at will
estate from
    period to period
fee simple absolute

ground rent
intestate
joint tenancy
leasehold estate
lessee
lessor
life tenant
nonpossessory interest
partnership
remainderman
security interest
syndicate
tenancy by the entirety
tenancy in common
trust

REVIEW QUESTIONS

4-1. How are the bundle of rights both separable and divisible?
4-2. What physical interests in real estate can be owned?
4-3. Differentiate between a defeasible fee and a fee simple interest in real estate.
4-4. Why are defeasible fees generally looked on with disfavor by the courts?

4-5. If you were granted a life estate, what would be the extent of your ownership rights in terms of the bundle of rights?

4-6. What type of leasehold interest could be referred to as a month-to-month lease?

4-7. List and define two examples of nonpossessory interests in real estate.

4-8. What might be the advantages of a joint tenancy ownership over a tenancy in common?

4-9. Differentiate between tenancy by the entireties and community property.

4-10. List the advantages of a limited partnership over a corporation in owning income-producing property.

5
Transferring Real Estate Interests

T HE PRECEDING CHAPTER discusses the various ways in which legal interests in real estate (the bundle of rights) are both separable and divisible. It is worth mentioning again that the virtually infinite number of combinations that can be created among these different factors makes real estate an extremely flexible form of investment. It may seem strange that this is so since real estate as an entity is permanent and immobile. Actually, it is precisely because land has perpetual life and fixed location (and great economic value) that makes feasible the various legal interests that can exist simultaneously in a single parcel.

In this chapter, a number of "nuts and bolts" matters concerning the mechanics of transferring interests in real estate are discussed. The subjects of this chapter normally lie in the domain of the real estate counsel (lawyer) when real estate transfers occur. Nonetheless, the terminology and procedures must be understood for at least two reasons. The first is that some of these procedures are, in fact, usable as investment techniques. For example, the use of an option to tie up land pending future events that will determine a course of action is a much more efficient use of capital resources than would an outright contract to buy the land. The second reason for understanding of the concepts in this chapter is that in negotiating a transfer, the existence of certain legal risks or limitations will affect the terms and price of a transaction.

This chapter deals with three major subjects:

☐ *The concept of title.* The bundle of rights involved in ownership is defined, and the extent to which such rights can be limited by governmental action or private agreement is explained.

☐ *Methods of transferring title.* The various ways, both voluntary or involuntary, by which title passes from one person to another is explained.

☐ *Method of transferring possession.* The lease agreement, by which separate fee and leasehold interests are created, is explained.

THE CONCEPT OF TITLE

The term *title* is virtually synonymous with *ownership*. When used without limitation, title implies the highest degree of ownership that may exist—that is, ownership in fee simple absolute. Title may also be used in a more restricted sense, to indicate a form of ownership that is limited in duration or extent. For example, one owning a life estate or holding a fee simple determinable interest also has title, but it is subject to the limitations inherent in these types of fee interests.

Title is ownership, and ownership is a bundle of rights. But of precisely what do these rights consist? The four key rights of ownership were identified in Chapter 4: (1) possession, (2) control, (3) enjoyment, and (4) disposition.

Private Limitations on Title

The bundle of rights that makes up title is never absolute. *First* and most basic, title may be limited or restricted because of the existence of other types of legal interests in the property—for example, future fee interests (remainders), leasehold interests, or easements.

Second, limitations may arise through *restrictive covenants* imposed by prior owners of the land that bind all successive owners. Such a restrictive covenant (which usually is written into the deed which conveys title) may cover such matters as the (1) minimum size of lot into which a tract may be divided (e.g., one-acre lots), (2) setback requirements (i.e., the number of feet from the property line which cannot be built on), and (3) uses to which the property may be put (e.g., residential only). Restrictive covenants may be terminated by the unanimous agreement of the property owners who benefit by the covenant or through their acquiescence in repeated violations of the covenant by a number of owners over a period of time. When courts are called on to interpret or enforce restrictive covenants, they tend to resolve all doubts against restrictions because of the fundamental social policy in favor of the free and unrestricted use of land.

Third, a type of limitation on title and ownership arises under the *law of nuisance*. Nuisance, as a legal concept, refers to the use of one's property in such a manner as to cause injury to an adjacent landowner. Conducting a manufacturing process on one's land that creates noxious fumes or odors or operating a motorcycle track in a residential area are examples of legal nuisances that may be subject to being enjoined (barred) by a court of law.[1]

---

[1] A special application of the nuisance concept is the doctrine of *attractive nuisance*. This holds a landowner responsible for injury to children who may enter on the property and suffer injury as the result of a feature of the property that is both attractive and dangerous. An unfenced swimming pool is perhaps the most common example. Here, the law imposes a restraint on the use of property in the interests of the safety of others.

Public Limitations on Title

Other limitations on title or ownership arise from an overriding public interest. Such public controls generally fall into three groups: (1) property taxation, (2) police power, and (3) eminent domain.

☐ *Property taxation.* Levying a tax on real estate was one of the earliest methods of public finance. It remains today the primary source of funds for local government. The process of property taxation is discussed in more detail in Chapter 15. Unpaid property taxes constitute a lien (claim) against the real estate, and take priority over any private liens.[2]

☐ *Police power.* Police power constitutes the inherent power of a sovereign to enact laws which promote the public health, morals, safety, and general welfare. Under our system of government, each state exercises police powers.

While laws enacted under the police power can be very broad, they are not entirely without limitation. Under both federal and state constitutions, such laws must be nondiscriminatory and must operate in a uniform manner. The police power of a state may be delegated to its political subdivisions (e.g., county, city, or other municipality). For the real estate owner or developer, the most significant police powers are those which

- Regulate the use of land through zoning and subdivision ordinances.
- Create local building codes or standards.
- Seek to limit pollution by environmental controls (which may limit or bar the development of real estate).
- License professionals operating in the real estate industry.

An important point to note is that exercise of the police power does not impose an obligation upon the state or local government to compensate the landowner for any loss of value—unlike a taking under eminent domain, discussed next. Thus, in many cases, it becomes critical to determine at what point the police power ends and the right of eminent domain begins.

For example, if the state bars *any* development of land in the interests of environmental control, so that the owner is unable to realize an economic return on his investment, has there been a legitimate exercise of the police power or a taking requiring compensation? As is seen in Part IX, this issue remains one of the major areas of controversy in the field of real estate law.

☐ *Eminent domain.* The most extensive public limitation on title or ownership is the right to take private property for public use through the

---

[2] A particular type of property tax is the *special assessment*, which is levied by a municipality against property within a specific neighborhood in order to pay for a local improvement (pavements, sewers, street lights), that is intended to benefit only the properties within the area rather than the entire community.

exercise of the power of eminent domain. This taking is known as a *condemnation;* whenever it occurs, the owner is entitled, by constitutional requirement, to proper compensation. This usually is based on the property's appraised value on the date of taking. Examples of public purposes for which property may be taken include construction of highways, schools, and parks.

At this point, it should also be noted that government strongly influences land use decisions through the provision of public facilities (economic infrastructure). The location of roads, utilities, and the like probably has a more significant impact on land use than all of the public restraints previously noted.

Examining and Insuring Title

What title is and what limitations may exist with respect to title have been discussed up to this point. The question remains of how title to a parcel of real estate can be verified or established. This question usually arises at the time property is sold; the buyer will not be willing to pay over the purchase price unless the buyer is assured that the seller's title is in fact what it is represented to be in the contract of sale. Normally, the buyer of real estate is entitled to receive *good and marketable title.* Such a title

   ☐ *Can be traced from the present owner backwards in time through a series of previous owners until a point is reached at which the property was transferred from a sovereign government, the ultimate owner of all land.* This will be either the federal government, a state government, King George III of England, or, in Louisiana or Texas, a French or Spanish sovereign.

   ☐ *Is not subject to any defects or limitation except those specified in the contract of sale.* The contract normally specifies all known limitations on ownership—for example, utility easements, use restrictions, and the like. Since these limitations on title are beyond the power of the seller to eliminate, the buyer must accept them or decline to enter into the contract.

The buyer of real estate normally will verify or establish title by utilizing the services of (1) an attorney, (2) a title abstract company, and/or (3) a title insurance company to examine the land records to ascertain whether a good and marketable title can be conveyed.

The result of the examination will be an *abstract of title,* which provides a history of title to the property and lists all restrictions and limitations. In addition to those already mentioned (limited fee interest in the seller, restrictive covenants, etc.), these may include (1) tax liens (for unpaid property or income taxes), (2) mortgages, or (3) other claims. Additionally, *mechanic's liens* (claims by persons who have performed work on the property and who have not been paid) may exist. Mechanic's liens can be particularly troublesome since they may be filed after the work is done but are effective, when filed, as of the date the work began. Like problems with adverse possession, the potential of mechanic's liens forces the examiner to physically examine the property as well as study the abstract.

The buyer will carefully compare the abstract of title to the title promised by the contract. If the comparison reveals defects, claims, or limitations not specified in the contract, the buyer will not be required to go through with the transaction.

It is possible that a mistake may be made in preparing the abstract of title or a defect in the title of the present owner may not be discoverable (e.g., a forgery in an earlier deed). To obtain protection against such mistakes or undiscoverable defects in title, the buyer may obtain title insurance from a *title insurance company*. Such insurance provides coverage against any loss to the buyer in the event title to the property is lost or limited for a reason not known at the time the buyer acquired his title.[3] The lending institution that provides the buyer with financing normally will require that its loan be protected by title insurance. (See **5-1.**)

Land Description and Measurement

Title and ownership and what they include have been discussed. A moment should be spent discussing how to measure the physical space to

5-1. WHEN INSURING TITLE PAID OFF

The Easton Manor Motel in Easton, Maryland was purchased in the mid-1970s by B. He thought he had acquired title to all of the buildings and the entire parking lot. Within a year, the true owner of a substantial portion of the parking lot served notice that Easton Manor could no longer use this area.

The reduction in parking area meant that the motel failed to meet local zoning requirements. (Zoning ordinances often require that certain amounts of parking accompany constructed space). B had both a deed and title insurance policy to the property, including the entire parking lot area, but obviously a mistake had been made somewhere in the chain of title.

Without the entire parking lot, B might be forced to close. He made a claim under his title policy. The title insurance company bought the portion of the parking lot not owned by B and conveyed it to him without cost. If B had not had the insurance, the cost of the additional land would have significantly reduced the attractiveness of the investment.

[3] Title insurance differs in one major respect from all other types of insurance. It provides coverage against loss due to a cause which has already occurred (e.g., a prior forgery). All other insurance provides coverage against loss due to a future cause. This is one reason why payment for title insurance is by a single premium paid at the time of closing. It is important to note that title insurance protects the insured against loss only to the extent of the policy. If land is bought for $20,000 ($20,000 obtained in title insurance), and then a home for $80,000 is built, in the event of faulty title, the insurance pays only $20,000, not $100,000.

Table 5-1. TABLE OF LAND MEASUREMENTS

Linear Measure		Square Measure	
9.92 inches =	1 link	30¼ square yards =	1 square rod
25 links =	16½ feet	16 square rods =	1 square chain
25 links =	1 rod	1 square rod =	272.25 square feet
100 links =	1 chain	1 square chain =	4,356 square feet
16.5 feet =	1 rod	4,840 square yards =	1 acre
5.5 yards =	1 rod	640 acres =	1 square mile
4 rods =	100 links	1 section =	1 square mile
66 feet =	1 chain	1 township =	36 square miles
80 chains =	1 mile	1 township =	6 miles square
320 rods =	1 mile		
5,280 feet =	1 mile		
1,760 yards =	1 mile		
5,280 feet =	1 mile		
1,760 yards =	1 mile		

An Acre Is:

- 43,560 square feet
- 165 feet × 264 feet
- 198 feet × 220 feet
- 5,280 feet × 8.25 feet
- 2,640 feet × 16.50 feet
- 1,320 feet × 33 feet
- 660 feet × 66 feet
- 330 feet × 132 feet
- 160 square rods
- 208 feet 8.5 inches square or
- 208.71033 feet square
- any rectangular tract, the product of the length and width of which totals 43,560 square feet

which title is held. How does a buyer determine precisely how much land is being purchased? How does an owner determine precisely what the boundaries are so that the extent of his exclusive rights of possession are known?

Land typically is described by surface measurements, with the property rights extending downward like an inverted cone to the center of the earth and upwards "to the heavens." (See Table 5-1.) Surface measurements are usually by one of two means:

- Metes and bounds.
- Government survey.

☐ *Metes and bounds.* By this method, certain boundary points are measured by physical features or markers (called *monuments*)—for example, the bed of a brook or "the old oak tree." Boundaries are then drawn by lines connecting these monuments which are described by degrees of latitude and longitude (called *bearings*).

This type of land measurement is common in the eastern states. In the case of developed areas, the monuments usually are public streets or highways. In the case of a subdivision or built-up area, where a *plat* (a plan or chart of an area) has been recorded, specific parcels of property within the plat may be identified by *lot* and *block*. (See Figure 5-1.)

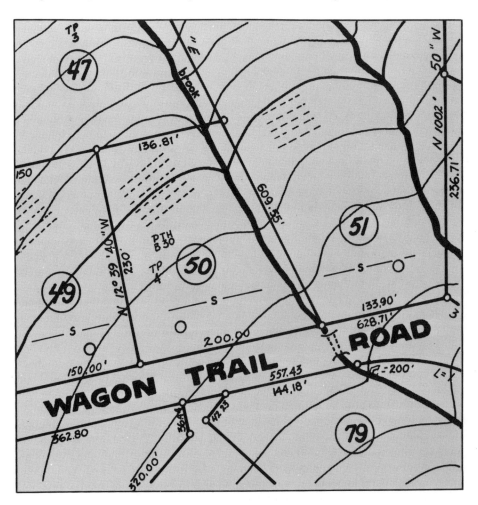

Courtesy of Dutchess County Clerk's Office, Poughkeepsie, New York.

Figure 5-1. EXCERPT FROM METES AND BOUNDS SURVEY—DUTCHESS COUNTY, NEW YORK

☐ *Government survey.* The government (or rectangular) survey is the typical method of measurement in the western United States. A grid is imposed on a map of the land, with the north and south lines called *meridians* and the east and west lines called *parallels.* A single square in the grid, known as a *tract,* is 24 miles square and is composed of 16 townships. A township is 6 miles square (36 square miles) and is made up of 36 sections. Each section is one mile square and is divided for platting purposes, as shown in Figure 5-2.

The map or description that shows the precise boundaries of land is called a *survey.* A survey may also show slope (topography), the precise location of any improvements on the site as well as the location of any easements, rights of way, encroachments by adjacent structures, and other physical features of the site. Surveyors, real estate professionals trained in the science of land measurement, prepare surveys. (See **5-2.**)

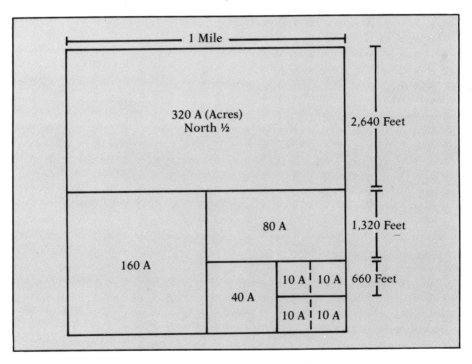

Figure 5-2. A SECTION OF LAND (640 ACRES)

TRANSFERRING TITLE

One of the fundamental rights associated with ownership of real estate is the right to transfer title to others. This right of transfer is absolute. It is

5-2. WATER RIGHTS

Water rights vary from the East Coast to the West Coast. On the East Coast, there are court-made law and *riparian rights.* Essentially, one riparian owner cannot take water out of a watershed, and the rights of each owner are qualified by the rights of the other riparian owners. On the West Coast and in other western states, legislative law holds with the rule of *prior appropriation.* Remember that many of these areas were developed first as mining claims where the right to use the water was tremendously important. In prior appropriation areas, the first user has priority, and there are permit systems allowing individuals to take water out of a watershed and deprive other riparian owners of the use of the water.

subject only to the rule that one cannot convey that which is not owned (so that a person holding a life estate can convey only that interest and no more) and subject to statutory restrictions on the ownership of real estate.

Title to real property may be transferred in one of seven ways:

- Purchase and sale.
- Gift.
- Inheritance.
- Foreclosure or tax sale.
- Adverse possession.
- Escheat.
- Eminent domain.

The first four of these are normally evidenced by a deed (or will), while the latter three are not.

Purchase and Sale

By far the greatest number of property transfers are by sale for a consideration (price). Unlike the sale of personal property, the sale of real estate involves a rather complex process that may extend anywhere from thirty days to six months or more.

The reason for the complexity of the real estate transfer process is not, as one might think, primarily because of the large capital investment normally required, although this is certainly part of the reason. A more important reason relates to one of the unique features of real property: *its permanence.* A new automobile or a new oil tanker, when it comes from the hands of the manufacturer, has no history. It has not been possible, except perhaps in rare cases, for other claims to attach to the property or for any restrictions on the title to the property to have come into being.

But, as already seen, the matter is quite different in real estate. Every parcel of property does have a history—of transfers, financing, improvement and claims of one kind or another. Consequently, a period of time must elapse to permit a buyer to properly examine the title to determine whether clear and marketable title can be conveyed by the seller. In addition, outside financing normally must be arranged, and this, too, takes time.

The essentials of the real estate sale process may be summarized as follows:

☐ *With respect to a designated parcel of land*, a buyer makes the seller an offer of purchase, or the seller makes the buyer an offer of sale. This is often done through the use of real estate brokers. (The brokerage process is discussed in Chapter 9.)

☐ *If the offer by one party is accepted by the other*, a meeting of the minds has occurred, which is evidenced by a written contract of sale. The contract is the crucial element in the real estate sale process, and it is discussed later in this chapter.

☐ *After the contract of sale is signed*, a period of time (the *contract period*) normally elapses before the actual transfer of title (the *title closing*). During this period, certain preclosing activities occur. The two most important are done by the buyer: (1) examination of title to be sure the seller can convey what has been promised (discussed earlier) and (2) the arranging of any financing. In addition, a property survey may be necessary, and the seller must take any necessary steps to be sure the property conforms to the conditions set forth in the contract (e.g., that it be free of any tenants, that it be in good repair, etc.).

☐ *The contract of sale normally will set a closing date*, at which time the buyer receives a deed evidencing title to the property in exchange for which the agreed-on price is paid to the seller. If the buyer has arranged financing, the lender or a representative may also be present at the closing to transfer the loan proceeds to the seller as part of the sales price. In consideration of the loan, the lender will receive a mortgage executed by the buyer whereby the property becomes security for the loan.

The type of closing just described, in which the parties meet together to exchange instruments of conveyance and consideration, is the form usually followed in the eastern United States. In many western states, title is transferred by an *escrow closing*. A third party, such as a trust company or title company, is designated as an escrow holder and the deed, consideration, loan proceeds, note, and mortgage as well as other necessary instruments are deposited with it as they are prepared or become available. When all of the conditions of the contract of sale have been complied with, the escrow holder will redistribute the deposited instruments and cash to the appropriate parties and thus end the closing process.

Gifts

The two essential elements of a gift are the intention by the donor to make a gift and delivery of the property constituting the gift. When the property itself is not capable of being physically delivered, such as real estate, delivery is made by means of a deed.

Inheritance

Second only to purchase and sale, the most common method of transferring title to real estate is as a result of the owner's death. The general term to describe such transfer is *inheritance,* which includes both a transfer by last will and testament (called a *devise*) or a transfer by the laws of intestacy—that is, where no will has been executed so that the owner dies intestate (called *descent and distribution*).

The subject of inheritance is a complex one that does not primarily concern us in this book. A few brief observations, however, will sum up the key points that should be remembered:

☐ *Certain types of legal interests automatically expire at the death of the holder,* and, consequently, no transfer takes place. For example, a life estate measured by the holder's life expires by its own terms. In addition, an easement or license which is personal to the holder also does not survive the holder's death.

☐ *Legal interests held in concurrent ownership,* where a right of survivorship exists, pass automatically to the surviving owner and thus are unaffected by the provisions of the decedent's will or by state laws regarding descent and distribution. The two types of concurrent ownership which involve this right of survivorship are: (1) joint tenancies and (2) tenancies by the entirety.

☐ *Apart from these two exceptions,* legal interests in real estate may be transferred by will in any way and to whichever persons the decedent wishes. The single most important exception to this rule is that in many states, a surviving spouse, for whom no adequate provision has been made in the will, may *elect against the will* and claim a statutory share, frequently one-third of all of the personal and real property in the estate. Property passing by will carries with it all of the rights and privileges as well as all of the liens and encumbrances that existed prior to the death of the owner.

☐ *When a decedent has made no will and so dies intestate,* property will *descend and be distributed* among the legal heirs of the decedent in accordance with the laws of the particular state in which the property is located. In general, these statutes provide that the property will be distributed among spouse and children if they survive and, if not, among collateral family members (*e.g.* parents, brothers and sisters, and nephews and nieces).

Foreclosure Sale or Tax Sale

A transfer of title to real estate as a result of a mortgage foreclosure or failure to pay real estate taxes is an involuntary form of transfer—that is, against the will of the owner. A mortgage foreclosure is one of the remedies of a mortgage holder (*mortgagee*) in the event the property owner (*mortgagor*) fails to pay installments when due or fails to comply with other provisions of the mortgage instrument.

In general, two types of foreclosure are utilized in the United States: (1) foreclosure by action and sale and (2) foreclosure under power of sale. When the secured interest is evidenced by a mortgage, a court action is commenced by the mortgagee resulting in a decree of foreclosure and an order by the court that the real estate be sold upon proper notice to the mortgagor and to the public. When the secured interest is evidenced by a deed of trust, no court action is needed and the lender or his agent may conduct a sale (provided proper notice is given to the public) at which the mortgaged property is sold. (Both situations are covered in Part V.) The intention in both cases is to realize a price as close as possible to the fair market value of the property. The proceeds of the sale are applied first to payment of the mortgage debt (together with unpaid interests and costs), with the balance going to the property owner (or junior creditors, if any).

Sometimes, in order to avoid the expense and publicity involved in a foreclosure sale, a defaulting mortgagor will convey the property to the mortgagee by a *deed in lieu of foreclosure,* in consideration of which the mortgagee will cancel the balance of the debt.

In the case of a failure by a property owner to pay real estate taxes for a prescribed period, usually several years, the municipality may file a tax lien against the property and enforce the lien by conducting a tax sale. Again, notice to the public is required so that some assurance exists that a price close to the fair market value is realized. Unpaid taxes are satisfied from the sale proceeds with the balance going to the property owner or to discharge outstanding mortgages.

Adverse Possession

An unusual method of acquiring title to real estate is by adverse possession. This doctrine has its roots in the very early history of the English common law. An individual may obtain a valid title to a parcel of real estate by openly occupying the land and representing himself as its owner for a period of years. This period was 21 years under English law but now varies from state to state.

For example, suppose *A* begins to farm a tract of land under honest presumption of ownership—perhaps because it is adjacent to land which *A* *does* own or because *A* has a deed which appears to be genuine but which in fact has a forged signature. *A* farms the land, pays taxes on it, and presents himself as the owner for the period of years which the law of the state requires to obtain title by adverse possession. At the end of that period of time, *A* will have legal title to the land. If *B*, the true owner, then presents himself and seeks to eject *A*, *A* will have a good defense to the action.

If *A* wants to have a document establishing his title, he will have to bring a special type of legal proceeding—called an *action to quiet title*. The essence of this proceeding is publication of notice setting forth *A*'s claim to title and notification to every individual who may have any claim to the land, as determined by an examination of pertinent legal records. If the court then finds that *A* has met the statutory requirement—generally stated as open, hostile, continuous, and notorious possession for the statutory period—then *A* will have the judgment declaring him to be the owner of the land.

Note that adverse possession is the fee equivalent to a prescriptive easement. In both cases, the rights of one person are taken by another. The original justification for such statutes lies in the belief that the land should be productive for someone and that after a long period of time an occupant claiming ownership should not be evicted in favor of the previously absent owner. In most states, the statutory period is shorter if the occupant has a logical reason to believe that he is the owner (he is then said to be holding under *color of title*) than if he is simply trying to take what he has no reason to believe is his. Further, the statutory period will not "run" in many states under some conditions—for example, if the owner is a minor, insane, or in the military.

Escheat

An even more unusual method of acquiring title to land is by escheat. Under this doctrine, if the owner of real estate dies without leaving a will disposing of the real estate and there are no heirs to inherit the property under the laws of descent and distribution, the state obtains title to the property. In other words, the state is the final "heir" to all real estate that is privately owned.

The doctrine of escheat also arose under English common law and was an expression of the feudal concept that all land ultimately was owned by the king. Even though the feudal system of land ownership has long since been replaced by what is known as the *allodial system* (under which land can be owned absolutely), the doctrine of escheat remains as a vestige of the concept of feudal tenure.

Eminent Domain

The power of eminent domain has already been referred to. Again, it is the power of government to take private property for public purposes and represents another way that property rights may be transferred.[4]

CONTRACTS OF SALE

The contract of sale (also known as a *sales contract, agreement of sale,* and by a variety of other names) is the key instrument executed when real estate is purchased and sold. The contract states the conditions under which the property will be transferred and the rights and duties of each party during the contract period.

Once having signed the contract, a party is legally bound by it unless the other party consents to a change. While the contract of sale does not itself transfer title—this being the function of the deed—it is extremely rare for any real estate transaction to be consummated without a written contract.

Elements of a Contract

A contract is essentially an exchange of promises or an exchange of a promise (by one party) for performance of an act (by the other party). All contracts—whether for transfers of real estate, brokerage services or any other purpose—can be classified in certain ways and have certain essential elements[5]:

---

[4] Compensation must be paid not only for land actually taken or utilized but also for damages resulting from the taking. The two types of such damage are *severance damage* and *consequential damage. Severance damage* occurs when only a portion of property is taken. As a result, the remaining portion may lose much of its value, perhaps because it has a distorted or unusual shape, or is not large enough to permit an economic use, or has lost access to a highway or other desired location. In all of these cases, the property owner must be compensated not only for the property actually taken but also for the loss of value to the remaining property. *Consequential damage* is suffered when property of one owner is taken by the government, and, as a result, damage is suffered by an adjoining owner. For example, property *A* is taken for a public use, as a result of which flooding occurs on adjacent property *B*. The owner of property *B* may be in a position to claim consequential damages for the taking.

[5] Contracts can be classified as: (1) bilateral and (2) unilateral.

By far the most common type, a *bilateral* contract, is one in which promises are exchanged. For example, *A* says to *B*, "I will pay you $10,000 for 150 Main Street." *B* says to *A* "I agree." This example is of an *oral* bilateral contract. If the promises were reduced to writing, it would be a *written* bilateral contract. Furthermore, it is an *express* contract because the promises are spelled out in words (whether spoken or written). There are circumstances where promises can be inferred by circumstances or by the actions of the parties. Such an *implied* contract is just as

☐ *Mutual agreement.* A contract requires a "meeting of the minds" by the parties concerning the substance of the agreement. This mutual agreement is normally manifested by the procedure of *offer* and *acceptance.*

An *offer* is a statement by one party of willingness to enter into a contractual arrangement. An offer must (1) be definite and certain, (2) define the precise subject matter of the proposed contract, and (3) be communicated by the offeror (the one making the offer) to the offeree (the recipient of the offer).

Once an offer has been received by the offeree, it remains open and capable of being accepted until (1) it expires by its own terms, (2) the offeree rejects it, or (3) the offeror revokes it. An offer also can be canceled by the destruction of the subject matter (as where a building is destroyed by fire) or by circumstances which make the proposed contract illegal.

Acceptance of an offer occurs when the offeree, by word or deed, clearly manifests his intention to accept. The acceptance must (1) be positive and unequivocal, (2) conform precisely to the terms of the offer, and (3) be communicated to the offeror within the permissible time period.

An offeree may neither accept nor reject an offer but instead may make a *counteroffer.* Then, it is up to the original offeror to decide to accept, reject, or make yet another counteroffer. And so the procedure will continue until a final rejection or acceptance has taken place.

☐ *Reality of assent.* The assent of a party is real when it is given freely and with full knowledge of the circumstances affecting the agreement. When assent is not freely given, the contract may be invalid (i.e., not binding), depending on the cause. Four such causes are fraud, mistake, duress, and undue influence.

Fraud is the intentional misrepresentation of a material fact in order to induce another to part with something of value. It clearly indicates an absence of real assent by the defrauded party. To constitute fraud, there must be a misrepresentation of a fact, not merely an opinion (so-called *puffing*). The misrepresentation also must be material (i.e., significant or substantial), and it must be made with the intention that the other party rely on it to his detriment.

Mistake may or may not be a ground for holding a contract invalid. Mistakes of law (i.e., not understanding the legal consequences of an action) normally are not enough to excuse someone from complying with a contract. Mistakes of fact (e.g., how much acreage is included in a parcel of land) may or may not justify a cancellation (*rescission*) of a contract, de-

---

enforceable as an express contract, although it is much harder to prove. It is difficult to visualize a situation where an implied contract to sell land could arise.

A *unilateral* contract involves the exchange of a promise for an actual performance of an act. For example, *A* says to *B*, "I will pay you $50 if you will pace off the boundaries of this land." *B* says nothing but proceeds to perform the requested act. Upon *B*'s performance, a binding unilateral contract has been entered into and *A* must pay *B* $50.

pending on how material the mistake is and whether the other party should have realized a mistake was being made.

Duress is the obtaining of consent by the use of force.

Undue influence is the use of improper or excessive persuasion by one in a confidential relationship to another.

☐ *Legal capacity to contract.* A valid contract also requires that each party have the legal capacity to enter into a contractual relationship. *Legal capacity* means the ability to reason and understand the significance of an agreement.

Minors (children under the age of 18 or 21, depending on the particular state) generally lack legal capacity to enter into a contract except for contracts for necessaries (e.g., contracts or purchases of food, medicine, clothing, etc.). Essential housing is usually considered a necessity as well, and so a minor may be held liable for the reasonable value of residential property occupied by the minor. If the contract is not for a necessity, the minor has the right to disaffirm the contract on reaching majority. This type of contract is called *voidable* because it is considered to be valid until the minor takes steps to disaffirm his obligations.

Insane, incompetent, and at times intoxicated persons are not legally competent to enter into a contract. Until fairly recently, married women often lacked the right to own real estate as well as to exercise other legal rights. But by enactment of laws protecting married women's rights in virtually all states, these common law disabilities have been eliminated so that a married woman now occupies the same legal status as her husband.

☐ *Consideration.* Consideration for a promise or for performance is that which is given in exchange for it. The concept of consideration is fundamental to the Anglo-American idea of a contractual relationship. Except in rare instances, a promise unsupported by consideration from the other party cannot be enforced.

In general terms, consideration can include anything that constitutes a detriment to the *promisor* (the one making a promise) or a benefit to the *promisee* (the one to whom the promise is made). If *A* promises to pay *B* $10, that is consideration because *B* benefits. If *A* promises to refrain from doing something which is otherwise a matter of right (such as putting a building of more than six stories on his land), that also is consideration. It is important to note that the law does not look to the adequacy of the consideration but merely whether consideration was actually bargained for. Thus, past consideration (payment for an obligation already owed) cannot be consideration for a new contract. Similarly, illusory promises are not good consideration.

☐ *Legality of the transaction.* A contract will be enforceable only if the purpose is legal. A contract to buy or sell real property for an illegal purpose (e.g., gambling in a state which bars this activity) would be void and unenforceable.

☐ *Contract in writing.* A final requirement for certain types of contracts is that they must be in writing in order to be enforceable. This requirement originally was imposed by an English statute, the *Statute of Frauds*, enacted in 1677. Its purpose was to prevent many fraudulent claims that were based on alleged oral promises or agreements. All American states have statutes modeled after the original Statute of Frauds, and they are known by that name. For the purposes here, the two significant types of agreements to which statutes of frauds apply are:

- All contracts for the sale and purchase of real estate.
- All leases of real estate for a term exceeding a specified period (more than one year in most states).

Note that the statute of frauds will be satisfied so long as the person against whom the contract is sought to be enforced has signed it. It is not necessary that the person seeking to enforce the contract has signed it.

Generally, the writing must contain the following information:

- The identity of the parties.
- The identification of the subject matter of the contract.
- The consideration.

The writing need not be designated a contract. Any written memorandum will suffice to satisfy the statute, provided it contains the requisite information.[6]

Key Provisions of the Contract

With this general background in mind, the major provisions in a typical real estate contract are now reviewed. (Sometimes an option agreement precedes the contract of sale—see 5-3.) Preparation of a contract is normally the work of an attorney. However, the real estate decision-maker should have sufficient background to understand the substance of an

---

[6] An important exception to the writing requirement of the statute of frauds is that an oral contract can be enforced where substantial *part performance* has occurred. While the various states do not agree on precisely what constitutes substantial part performance, the acts most commonly relied on in the case of real estate are: (1) total or part payment of the purchase price, (2) delivery of possession of the property to the buyer, and (3) improvements made on the property by the buyer. The reason these acts make a writing unnecessary is that it is unlikely that any of these acts would be performed if the parties had not reached a contractual agreement concerning sale of the property.

5-3. USING OPTIONS

An *option* is the right to buy, lease, or sell a particular parcel of real estate to or from another at a specified price within a designated period. The most common type of option is the *option to purchase.* For example, Mr. *S* (the optionor) promises Mr. *J* (the optionee) that Mr. *J* may elect within the next thirty days to buy the property known as 150 Main Street from Mr. *S* at a price of $10,000. Mr. *J* pays Mr. *S* cash or other consideration to bind the agreement; in this arrangement, the cash might equal one or 2 percent of the sales price.

If Mr. *J* decides not to buy the property within thirty days, Mr. *S* keeps the consideration for his willingness to keep the offer open (and the property off the market) for that time. If Mr. *J* decides to buy the property within thirty days, the parties then enter into a contract of sale. The cash paid for the option sometimes is credited against the purchase price and sometimes is not.

agreement and be alert to possible business or investment decisions that must be made in connection with certain provisions:

☐ *Date of agreement.* The agreement should be dated because some provisions may contain time periods which refer to the date of execution of the contract. In addition, some states require real estate contracts to be dated.

☐ *Names and capacity of parties.* The parties should be identified by name and, if other than individuals, by type of organization (e.g., corporation or partnership).[7]

☐ *Description of property and interest conveyed.* Any description of the property is sufficient, provided it in fact accurately defines the parcel of real estate being conveyed. If the seller has less than a fee simple interest, this should be specified.

☐ *Consideration and manner of payment.* In most cases, the consideration paid for the real estate will be money. When money is the consideration, it normally will be paid in two installments: (1) the escrow or down payment (frequently, 10 percent of the total price); and (2) the balance at the closing of title. To the extent that the buyer takes over an existing

---

[7] In any case where an individual party is not acting on his own behalf (e.g., an agent for a principal or an individual for an organization), such individual should establish his authority to act. An agent can bind his principal in a real estate contract only when the agent's authority is in writing. A general partner has the authority to bind the partnership, but it must be clear that he is, in fact, a general partner. A corporate officer may bind the corporation if he has actual authority or apparent authority (i.e., circumstance make it appear as if he has authority). To be on the safe side, however, a corporate officer should produce a resolution of the board of directors authorizing the purchase or sale.

mortgage on the property, the cash to be paid will be reduced by that amount.

☐ *Conditions of sale.* Frequently, the sale will be subject to specified conditions, with one party (usually the buyer) or both parties entitled to cancel the contract if the conditions are not satisfied.

☐ *State of title; type of deed.* Since no title is "perfect," the contract will specify precisely what defects and limitations the buyer is obligated to accept. In addition, the form of deed will be specified.

☐ *Personal property.* Frequently, a sale of real property is accompanied by the sale of related personal property, such as the furnishings in a motel or the carpets and blinds in a private home. A list of personal property to be conveyed should be attached to the contract.

☐ *Risk of loss.* During the contract period (between the signing of the contract and the closing of title), the property might be destroyed or damaged by fire or other cause. Who bears the risk of loss? Most states have a statute which spells out where the risk lies (usually on the seller). If the parties wish a different result, the contract should so provide. (Note that the party assuming the risk can be protected by purchasing insurance.)

☐ *Date and place of closing of title.* The contract will often specify the date and place when the actual closing of title will take place. This should be set far enough ahead so that reasonable time is given for the performance of any conditions that must be satisfied. Normally, either party is entitled to one (or possibly several) adjournments of the closing. However, if the contract specifies that *time is of the essence,* then it is understood that the closing date is firm and no adjournment will be permitted without penalty to the delaying party.

☐ *Default provisions.* In practice, real estate contracts normally contain provisions covering possible defaults by either party. In the case of a default by the buyer, the contract may provide that the seller is entitled to keep the down payment as liquidated damages but has no further claim against the buyer for the balance of the purchase price. On the other hand, in the event of a default by the seller, the buyer may be entitled only to receive back any down payment (plus reimbursement for certain specified expenses, such as a title examination) and have no further remedy against the seller.[8]

---

[8] In the case of a contract for the purchase of real estate, a default by the purchaser normally will consist of his failure to pay the full purchase price at the time set for the closing of title. In such event and absent any contrary provision in the contract, the seller may sell the real estate elsewhere and seek damages against the defaulting purchaser equal to the difference between the contract price and the price received by the seller in the substitute transac-

In any case, the contract should clearly state the intent of the parties with regard to default.

☐ *Signatures.* Finally, the contract must be signed by all parties to it. Recall that under the statute of frauds, the contract will not be enforced against one who has not executed it.

It is worth repeating that the real estate contract of sale is the most important instrument in a real estate transaction because it establishes the framework in which the transaction will take place. While both statutory law and common law do provide a set of rules for settling disputes between parties to a real estate agreement, most of these can be overridden by a provision in the contract itself. So it is up to the real estate decision-maker and his professional counsel to be sure that the contract achieves the desired objectives and provides protection against possible risks.

DEEDS AND THEIR RECORDATION

In virtually all cases, title is evidenced by a written instrument called a *deed.* Three questions to be answered about deeds are:

- What makes a deed valid?
- What are the various types of deeds?
- Why are deeds recorded?

Elements of a Valid Deed

A deed must (1) be in writing, (2) identify the person or persons to whom title is conveyed (the grantee or grantees), (3) identify the property being conveyed, and (4) be signed by the person or persons making the conveyance (the grantor or grantors).

If more than one grantee is named, the nature of their concurrent ownership should be specified (e.g., tenants in common or joint tenants with right of survivorship). The grantees must be legally capable of holding title, while the grantors must have the legal capacity to convey title and if they are doing so on behalf of an artificial person, such as a corporation or partnership, they must have the authority to act on its behalf.

tion. If the seller defaults, by being unable or unwilling to convey title to the real estate in the form set forth in the contract, the purchaser (absent any provision in the contract to the contrary) normally is in a position to seek specific performance of the contract—that is, the purchaser may seek a judgment by a court requiring the seller to convey the contracted real estate. The purchaser is not limited to an action for money damages because every parcel of real estate is deemed unique by virtue of its unique location, and thus, monetary damages do not always represent adequate compensation to the purchaser.

☐ *Words of conveyance.* The deed must contain words of conveyance—that is, language that makes clear the intention to transfer title. An example is "the said grantor does hereby grant and convey to the said grantee. . . ."

☐ *Consideration.* In addition, common law required the deed to recite the payment of consideration, although the amount was irrelevant. While many states have passed laws eliminating this requirement, most deeds do use language such as "in consideration of one dollar in hand paid, the receipt and sufficiency whereof is hereby acknowledged. . . ." The parties will not wish to specify the exact purchase price since the deed almost always will be recorded and thus open to public view.

☐ *Delivery.* Finally, a deed must be delivered in order for the transfer of title to be effective. The most common form of delivery is directly to the grantee. But delivery may be effective if the deed is given to an agent of the grantee, is given to the local records office for recording, or otherwise is transferred under circumstances making clear the grantor's intention to complete the transaction. However, when a grantor signs a deed and then retains possession of it, no transfer of title has occurred.

Types of Deeds

Deeds come in several different categories. The key distinction among them relates to the precise responsibilities which the grantor assumes in connection with the conveyance. These responsibilities are called *warranties*. A warranty combines a representation that a certain state of facts is true and the responsibility to make good any damages if the facts turn out to be otherwise.

☐ *General warranty deed.* This deed includes the broadest warranties by the grantor and so would be most preferred by the grantee. While the precise warranties in such a deed depend upon the law of the particular state, generally a warranty deed usually contains four basic covenants:

- The *covenant of seisin,* by which the grantor represents that he, in fact, owns the property.
- The *covenant of the right to convey,* by which the grantor represents that no obstacle exists to a transfer of the property.
- The *covenant against encumbrances* (i.e., a representation that no claims exist against the property other than those specified in the deed or contract).
- The *covenant of quiet enjoyment,* by which the grantor represents that no person with a superior right to the property can interfere with the grantee's use or possession of the property.

☐ *Special warranty deed.* This is exactly the same as a general warranty deed with one important distinction: The grantor will be liable for breach of warranty only if the cause arose through the grantor's own act or during his period of ownership. The grantor thus disclaims any responsibility for defects that arose before he became the owner. A special warranty deed is commonly given by a bank trust department. The bank wishes to avoid responsibility for any defects that originated prior to the bank's ownership (as trustee). (See Figure 5-3.)

THIS INDENTURE, made the .... day of ...., 19...., between .... party of the first part, and .... party of the second part,

WITNESSETH, that the party of the first part, in consideration of Ten Dollars and other valuable consideration paid by the party of the second part, does hereby grant and release unto the party of the second part, the heirs or successors and assigns of the party of the second part forever:

All that certain plot, piece or parcel of land, with the buildings and improvements thereon erected, situate, lying and being in the [*insert description*].

This CONVEYANCE is made and accepted subject to an indebtedness secured by a mortgage upon said premises held by ...., which said mortgage was recorded [*insert recording data*] and upon which there remains unpaid the aggregate principal sum of .... with interest from ...., at the rate of .... percent per annum, which said mortgage debt the party of the second part hereby executes and acknowledges this instrument for the purpose of complying with the provisions of [*set forth any pertinent statute*].

The premises conveyed hereunder are subject to a purchase money mortgage intended to be recorded simultaneously herewith.

(2) Together with all right, title and interest, if any, of the party of the first part in and to any streets and roads abutting the above described premises to the center lines thereof; Together with the appurtenances and all the estate and rights of the party of the first part in and to said premises; to have and to hold the premises herein granted unto the party of the second part, the heirs or successors and assigns of the party of the second part forever.

(3) And the part of the first part covenants that the party of the first part has not done or suffered anything whereby the said premises have been encumbered in any way whatever, except as aforesaid.

The word "party" shall be construed as if it read "parties" whenever the sense of this indenture so requires.

IN WITNESS WHEREOF, the party of the first part has duly executed this deed the day and year first above written.

....
Grantor

....
Grantee

Figure 5-3. **SPECIAL WARRANTY DEED**

☐ *Quitclaim deed.* While this deed, too, can effectively convey title, it is normally used as a means of surrendering a claim to property that may or may not be valid. In effect, the grantor under a quitclaim deed says: "I don't know if I own this property, but if I do, I convey to you whatever rights I may have." This type of deed is also used to correct an error made in an earlier conveyance.[9]

Recording Deeds

As noted previously, title effectively passes to the grantee once the deed has been delivered to and accepted by the grantee. In practice, however, the grantee will take one further step—and is well advised to take it as quickly as possible. This step is to bring the deed to the local land records office and have it "recorded." A photostat is made of the deed and is filed in a record book which is tied to an indexing system so that ownership claims become public knowledge. By thus making it relatively easy for title holders to be identified, the recording system is considered to "put the world on notice" that the property described in the recorded deed is owned by the individual named there (the owner of record).

Most recording statutes generally have the following features:

- They do not affect the validity of the deed between the grantor and grantee; they merely determine the outcome if more than one deed is given to the same property.
- The deed cannot be recorded until it is acknowledged—that is, the person signing the deed must acknowledge his signature before a notary public or commissioner of deeds.
- Whether the deed itself or a memorandum of deed is recorded, sufficient information must be placed on record so that the parties and the property can be identified.

Constructive Notice   Not only deeds but mortgages, leases, contracts of sale, mechanic's and tax liens, assignments, restrictive covenants, and other matters pertaining to land may be recorded. In this way, protection against fraudulent acts is afforded to anyone having an interest in real estate since anyone dealing with land is deemed to know any fact which has been spread upon the public record. A person is said to have *constructive notice* of such information, whether or not the person has

---

[9] In addition to the categories just distinguished, deeds are often known by the name or authority of the person executing them. Thus, an *executor's deed* is made by the executor of an estate (and the grantee is put on notice that he must be sure of the executor's authority to make the conveyance). A *sheriff's deed* conveys property sold at a sheriff's sale following foreclosure proceedings while a tax deed follows a forced sale for failure to pay real estate taxes. The term *judicial deed* is often used to describe any deed from a sale resulting from a judicial proceeding. Most of these deeds are without covenants, but this is not invariably so.

actual notice of it. Again, all of these recorded instruments become part of the abstract (history) of title.

The history of recording statutes is an interesting one but can only be briefly given here. Under early law, the rule was "first in time, first in right." If *T* sold property to *D* on Monday and then sold the same property (fraudulently, of course) to *H* on Wednesday, *D* had the better title. To reduce the possibility of this type of situation arising, recording statutes were passed—the first one in this country being a 1640 law in the Massachusetts Bay Colony. Over the years, all states have passed recording statutes which differ in certain significant ways. Most statutes say that "first to record, first in right." So, in the above example, if *H* (the second grantee) raced to the courthouse ahead of *D* and recorded a deed first, *H* would keep the property. (*D*, of course, would have a claim against *T* if *T* could be found.) Therefore, this statute is called a *race-type statute*.

Another type says that if the first grantee fails to record before the second conveyance is made and the second grantee did not know of the first conveyance, the second grantee is the title holder. Thus, in the example, if *D* failed to record the deed before Wednesday, when the second conveyance was made to *H* and *H* was ignorant of the deed to *D*, *H* is the title holder. This type of statute, called a *notice-type statute*, again penalizes the original grantee if he fails to act promptly.

TRANSFERRING POSSESSION: THE LEASE

The previous several sections have discussed the various procedures in connection with the transfer of *title* to real estate (i.e., conveyance of a freehold estate). Now the procedure involved in transferring *possession* in real estate—that is, the creation of a leasehold estate—is considered.

The instrument used in this process, the lease, is unique in that it is both a conveyance (because it effectively transfers the right to possession to real estate) and a contract (because it sets forth the continuing rights and duties of landlord and tenant). In other words, a lease combines within itself both of the functions performed, in the case of a transfer of title, by the contract of sale and the deed. The reason for this is that, in the case of a transfer of title, the contract of sale sets forth the rights and duties of the parties only during the contract period. Once the closing of title takes place and the deed is executed and delivered, the contract falls by the wayside and most or all of its provisions become irrelevant. (Lawyers say that the "contract merges with the deed.")

In the case of a lease, however, a continuing relationship exists between landlord and tenant. Therefore, it makes sense to combine in a single instrument the transfer of the right to possession as well as a statement of all of the rights and duties of the parties during the whole of the lease term.

The lease should be in writing for several reasons. *First,* a written lease helps avoid misunderstandings. It is much easier to recall the specific understanding on a particular point when a lease is in writing. *Second,* a lease should be in writing to be legally enforceable. In most states, leases for over a certain period will be enforced by the courts only if they are evidenced in writing. (See Figure 5-4.)

The requirements of a valid lease include:

- Names and signatures of legally competent parties.
- Description of premises.
- Amount of rent.
- Term of the lease.
- Commencement and expiration dates.
- Rights and obligations of the parties during the lease term.

A typical lease will include provisions covering the following matters: What areas are to be maintained by the landlord and which by the tenant? Who will pay utilities? Who will pay for property insurance and property taxes? It is possible that, as these costs increase, the tenant will bear the increase (an *escalation clause*). What improvements and alterations does the tenant have the right to make? Will the tenant be allowed to assign or sublet the premises? What happens in the event that the tenant cannot pay? What happens if the property is condemned by the government under eminent domain? What happens at the end of the lease period? Does the tenant have the right to assign or sublease the premises? If so, at what price and under what terms? (See 5-4.)

Changing Concept of Leases

The concept of a lease has changed in an interesting and dramatic way in the past twenty years. For centuries, a lease was always regarded by the courts and legislatures as primarily a conveyance, with the contractual aspect purely secondary. As a result, a very dim view was taken of tenant efforts to hold back rent when landlords failed to carry out their obligations, such as providing heat in the wintertime.

The courts' view was that rent was the consideration for the conveyance of the right to possession. Consequently, the rent had to be paid regardless of the landlord's failure to perform his contractual duties. The reason for this seemingly harsh view was that leases originally were primarily for farm-land, where the farmer operated as a totally independent businessman, putting up his own house and farming the land as an entrepreneur. Quite a difference from a tenant in a studio apartment in a 25-story apartment house.

However, in the past two decades, a very sharp shift has taken place toward emphasizing the contractual aspects of the lease. This is the legal

THIS LEASE made the .... day of ...., 19........, between .... (hereinafter called the "Landlord"), and ...., a .... corporation, having its principal office at ...., ... (hereinafter called the WITNESSETH: "Tenant").

THAT THE Landlord hereby leases to the Tenant, and the Tenant hereby hires and takes from the Landlord the following described premises: [*description*] being more particularly shown on the plan attached hereto and made a part hereof, located at ...., in the City of ...., State of ....

[Use]

TO BE USED and occupied by the Tenant for offices, sales, display, storage, service, repair, and use of Tenant's products and equipment, engineering, education, and training of Tenant's customers and employees, parking of cars, and all other uses incidental and related thereto, and, without limitation, for other lawful business and commercial purposes;

[Terms]

For a term of ...., to commence on completion of the work to be performed by Landlord in accordance with Article ...., hereof, the target date for which is ...., subject to extension as may be hereinafter provided. If the term commences on a date other than the first of the month, it shall terminate .... years from the last day of the month in which it commenced. If the term commences on the first day of a month, it shall terminate .... years from the last day of the preceding month. The parties shall enter into a supplemental agreement setting forth the commencement and termination dates of the term.

THIS LEASE is made upon the following terms and conditions, which the Landlord and Tenant covenant and agree to keep and perform:

[Rent]

(1) The Tenant shall pay the annual rent of $..............., payable in monthly installments in advance of $..............., one each on the first day of every calendar-month during the term. Rent for any period of less than one month shall be apportioned. The Tenant will pay the rent to .... at .... or to such other person or at such other place as the Landlord may designate in writing.

[Preparation for Occupancy]

(2) Prior to the commencement of the term, the Landlord, at its own cost and expense and to Tenant's reasonable satisfaction, shall alter and fit up the premises for occupancy by Tenant in accordance with layout plans to be provided by Tenant and in accordance with the Specifications set forth in Exhibit ...., attached hereto and made a part hereof.

The Tenant shall have at least .... days prior to the commencement of the term to install its equipment and furnishings and to perform such other work in the premises preparatory to its occupancy as Tenant may desire.

Accordingly, the Landlord shall notify Tenant when Landlord's alteration and construction work in the premises has advanced sufficiently to permit Tenant to install its equipment and furnishings and to commence such other Tenant work. The obligation to pay rent shall not commence until all work to be done by the Landlord as set forth in the aforesaid plans and specifications is completed in a good workmanship manner, in compliance with law, and a certificate of occupancy has been issued by the government stating that the premises may lawfully be occupied.

Figure 5-4. EXCERPT FROM OFFICE LEASE

5-4. TYPES OF RENTAL PAYMENTS

To a businessman or investor, the rent provisions of a lease are important. Types and manner of rental payments are limited only by the ingenuity of real estate professionals. The most common types are these:

☐ *Gross rental (gross lease).* This is rental that covers operating expenses as well as the landlord's profit. Under a gross lease, the landlord, not the tenant, pays the costs of operating the premises. An apartment house lease is an example.

☐ *Net rental (net lease).* This is a rental which represents the landlord's return on his investment and does not include operating expenses, which are paid by the tenant separately. The net lease is typically used in commercial leases of free-standing premises (e.g., a building occupied by a single retail tenant such as a supermarket). The tenant pays all operating expenses, often including real estate taxes (net lease), in addition to the net rental.

☐ *Flat (fixed) rental.* This is a rental that is fixed and unchanging throughout the lease term. At one time, flat rentals were common even for long-term commercial leases, but because of recent inflation, these are now rather uncommon. An apartment house lease typically calls for a fixed rental since the term is usually short.

☐ *Graduated rental.* A graduated rent is one that moves up or down in a series of steps during the lease term. A step-up rental involves an increase at each stage. A step-down rental involves a decrease in each stage.

☐ *Escalator (index) rental.* This type of rental moves up or down in accordance with an outside standard (e.g., the consumer price index) or an inside standard (e.g., operating costs of the particular property). Rental escalation has now become very common in office and commercial leases as a means of shielding the landlord against the effects of rapid inflation. Escalation clauses are also beginning to appear in apartment leases.

☐ *Percentage rental.* This is an extremely common form of rental payment in retail store leases. The tenant normally pays a minimum fixed rent plus an additional rent equal to a percentage of sales over a fixed amount. The tenant's gross sales rather than net profits is almost always used as a standard in order to avoid disputes about how net profits are to be determined. In addition, gross sales are more likely to keep pace with inflation than are net profits. Consequently, a percentage rental based on sales is a better inflation hedge for the landlord than is one based on profits.

rationale for such phenomena as *rent strikes,* where tenants hold back rent payments until landlords perform in accordance with the lease. In a broader context, this has been part of the consumer revolution that has seen the passage of a number of important statutes at both the federal and state level which seek to protect the rights of purchasers and users of property.

SUMMARY

The material contained in this and the prior chapter constitutes the legal rules by which the real estate game is played. It is extremely important that the real estate decision-maker have knowledge of this legal environment. One need not be a legal expert, but one must possess a sufficient legal background to know the right questions to ask, be abl to negotiate business aspects of a transaction successfully, and use the services of legal counsel effectively.

In this chapter, the "nuts and bolts" of real estate conveyancing and leasing were discussed. Among the 7 methods described, the real estate contract of sale prescribing a transfer by deed is by far the most important method by which title to real estate is transferred. When it comes to transferring possession rather than title, the key instrument is the lease, which, in recent years, has been viewed more as a contract than a conveyance, with resulting greater rights for the tenant than was true in early days.

IMPORTANT TERMS

abstract of title
adverse possession
agreement of sale
allodial system
condemnation
consideration
deed
default
devise
escheat
foreclosure
government survey
legal capacity
marketable title

mechanic's lien
metes and bounds
mortgagee
mortgagor
option
percentage rental
police power
promisor
promisee
rescission
restrictive covenant
statute of frauds
title

REVIEW QUESTIONS

5-1. List and define the four public limitations on title.
5-2. How can a restrictive covenant be used to limit private property rights?
5-3. What are the requirements for a good and marketable title?
5-4. Why can mechanic's liens be particularly troublesome in regard to an abstract of title?
5-5. Differentiate between the metes and bounds and the government survey method of land description and measurement.
5-6. How can a claimant acquire ownership through adverse possession?
5-7. List and define the essential elements necessary in a valid contract to convey real estate.

5-8. What is the impact of the statute of frauds on the conveyance of real estate ownership?

5-9. Under what circumstances might a quitclaim deed be used to convey real estate?

5-10. Discuss the practical implications of viewing leases as both a conveyance and a contract.

Valuation and the Appraisal Process

6

Principles of Valuation

IN PART I, real estate is described in economic terms and the features which make it desirable as a commodity in the marketplace are identified. Recall that the unique features of a parcel of real estate are its location and its perpetual life (the latter with respect to the land rather than the improvements). In Part II, specific ownership in real estate is defined. In this part, a close look is taken at the subject of real estate valuation and answers are sought to two particular questions:

- Can the specific elements or factors which contribute to the value of a parcel of real estate be identified?
- What methods are used to arrive at a valuation figure for a parcel of real estate (the process known as *appraisal*)?

This chapter deals generally with the answers to the first question, while the succeeding two chapters discuss the three traditional appraisal methods used in the valuation process (i.e., the market data, cost, and income methods). At the outset, it should be emphasized that the concept of value is a complex one since values will differ depending on the assumptions of the person making the valuation and the context in which the appraisal is made. Owners of real estate, using different assumptions, have been known to argue *simultaneously* for a higher valuation (in a condemnation proceeding to determine the compensation to be paid by the municipality) and for a lower valuation (in a tax-reduction proceeding, in which the owner seeks to lower the assessment placed on the property).

Still, there are a number of empirical rules that have been sufficiently tested by experience so that they are entitled to be called concepts or principles of valuation. These concepts are discussed later on in this chapter after some preliminary matters are disposed of.

REASONS FOR AN APPRAISAL

An appraisal is an opinion of value based upon an analysis of the factors influencing value. An appraisal may be sought for a number of different reasons, as discussed below.

Property Taxes

Perhaps the most common reason for appraisals is to prepare assessment rolls in connection with the levying of property taxes. These taxes are based on the current fair market value of real estate within the taxing district.

Loan Purposes

Probably the next most frequent use of an appraisal is to establish the value of a parcel of real estate which is to serve as collateral for a loan. Either because of statutory restriction or internal policy, a lending institution normally will not lend in excess of a specified percentage of value (called the *loan-to-value ratio*).

For example, a lender may be unwilling to lend more than 75 percent of the appraised value of an office building. Alternatively, some lenders may be willing to lend a higher percentage of value, provided the borrower is willing to pay a somewhat higher interest rate to compensate for the extra risk. In either situation, an independent determination of value is necessary.

Other Purposes

Appraisals are frequently required by insurance companies in connection with the adjustment of a loss resulting from fire or other casualty. When private property is taken under the power of eminent domain and the municipality and owner are unable to agree on what is fair compensation, testimony by appraisers is a crucial element in the condemnation proceeding to determine the amount to be paid for the real estate.

When a person dies owning real estate, an appraisal normally is required in connection with the determination of estate tax. Separation or divorce agreements frequently require appraisal of property owned by either or both spouses. In some ground leases, where vacant land is leased for a long period of time to a developer who builds an improvement, the ground rental may be subject to adjustment at periodic intervals based upon a reappraisal of the land. And, in many sales transactions, the purchaser seeks an independent appraisal as an aid to determining the price to be paid.

CONCEPTS OF VALUE

Two principal types of value have come to be identified over the years: (1) value in use and (2) value in exchange. *Value in use* refers to the value a commodity may have even in the absence of interaction between buyers and sellers in a marketplace. For example, a college hangout may generate a tremendous cash flow because of its reputation as a "watering hole," not because of the demand for space. Value in use is considered to be subjective in nature in that it is determined without reliance upon exposure in a marketplace. *Value in exchange* assumes that a commodity is traded in a marketplace and, for that reason may be measured objectively in terms of value. It is an estimate of this latter value that is sought in most real estate appraisals.

Characteristics of Value

Real property values are affected by four characteristics. All are necessary, in varying degrees, for value to be present, and none alone is sufficient to create value. The four characteristics are: (1) utility, (2) scarcity, (3) effective demand, and (4) transferability.

☐ *Utility.* Utility can be viewed as the ability of a good or service—in this case, real property—to satisfy a need. The degree to which a property satisfies particular needs is highly affected by the characteristics of the property and the purpose for which it is being used.

☐ *Scarcity.* Scarcity refers to the relative availability of a particular good or commodity. In the case of real property, the value characteristic of scarcity is probably more affected by the state of building technology and by location than mere quantity. Land need not be scarce in an absolute sense in order to have value, but its value is highly affected by the scarcity of certain property types (uses) within a given area.

☐ *Effective demand.* In order for real property to have value, effective demand for the property must exist. As noted in Part I, effective demand is the desire (need) for an economic good coupled with the buying power or ability to pay for that good. Desire alone is not sufficient; many people would like to live in a $200,000 house, but few are likely to have the ability to pay for such a house.

☐ *Transferability.* Transferability refers to the absence of legal constraints on the owner's right to sell or convey his property rights to another. If the legal interest associated with the ownership of real property cannot be conveyed, its value in exchange will be nonexistent, whatever its value in use to the owner.

Forces Affecting Values

Real estate will have value provided it is useful, scarce, and transferable, and provided there is an effective demand for it. In general, four primary "forces" exist that influence real estate values: (1) physical, (2) economic, (3) social, and (4) governmental. Together, they interact and create the environment and the marketplace within which real property is owned, used, and transferred.

☐ *Physical forces.* The physical forces which influence real property site values include location, size, shape, area, frontage, topsoil, drainage, contour, topography, vegetation, accessibility, utilities, climate, and view. The values of structures are determined by construction quality, design, adaptability, and harmony with their surroundings. Each of these physical characteristics can play a major role in determining how a particular parcel may be utilized. The use to which a parcel is put, in turn, materially affects the benefits which accrue to the owner and thus the property's value.

☐ *Economic forces.* Economic forces influencing the value of real property reflect how the property interacts or fits within the economy of the region and neighborhood. Such factors as community income, the availability and terms of mortgage credit, price levels, tax rates, and labor supply represent economic forces affecting property values.

☐ *Social forces.* Social forces such as attitudes toward household formation (living alone or with others, having children, etc.), population trends, neighborhood character, architectural design, and utility have an impact on value. Unlike physical and economic forces, social forces are more subjective in nature and therefore are sometimes difficult to interpret.

☐ *Governmental forces.* Governmental forces include the impact of local, state, and federal governments and are collectively referred to as *public policy.* Examples of governmental forces which affect value include zoning and building codes, real property taxation, public housing, and police and fire protection. The role or impact of governmental decisions on market value cannot be ignored.

All of these forces are dynamic or changing over time—even the physical forces. The framework in this book is forward-looking, requiring the decision-maker to estimate the impact of these forces over the life of the subject property.

VALUE, PRICE, AND COST

The terms *value, price,* and *cost* are frequently used in relation to real estate decision-making. As far as real estate appraisal is concerned, it is of critical importance that these terms be differentiated. Value, price, and cost involve different concepts, and the real estate decision-maker should use these terms only within the context of their proper definition.

Value

Using the objective definition of value (i.e., value in exchange), *value* can be defined as the power of a good or service to command other goods or services in the marketplace. In a very simple barter economy, value can be determined by following this definition literally. For example, *A* may offer a dozen bananas in the market and see what response he receives from *B* who may offer him goods or services in exchange.

In our modern economy, the process of determining value is somewhat more complicated. When talking about a *capital asset* (i.e., something that produces income, such as ownership of an office building), it is common to define value as the *present worth of the future cash flow.* If the office building is expected to produce $100 of cash flow every year in perpetuity, the value of the office building will be equal to the value today of the right to receive these future annual cash flows.

While this financial concept of value is more useful than the simple definition just given, it has some weaknesses when applied to real estate. Two are that (1) not all property generates a periodic cash flow (e.g., raw land) and (2) some benefits associated with property ownership are non-pecuniary in nature (e.g., the benefits of living in one's own home). So real property value might be defined as the present worth of all future benefits.

Price

Price is the amount of money that is actually paid, asked, or offered for a good or service. As such, price represents one person's estimate of value in terms of money. Such an estimate may be greater than, equal to, or less than the "objective value" of the good or service in question.

In real estate transactions, one of the major factors that causes the price of a particular parcel to differ from its objective value is the type of financing that may be available. A property that is worth $X on the assumption that customary financing will be available might well be worth as much as $X plus $Y if the seller is willing to take back a mortgage equal to the full price so that the buyer need put up no cash equity at all. In addition, price may vary from value because of the lack of negotiating skills by either buyer or seller, because of unwarranted optimism by the buyer or pessimism by the seller, or because either party is operating under unusual constraints.

A good example of the last is the urgency felt by many foreigners to move capital out of their own country to the United States. The United States is regarded as one of the most stable societies in the world and one that continues to offer opportunities to private capital. In such circumstances, a buyer may be willing to pay a price above the value that may be put upon the property by an independent appraisal. One might say that, in this situation, the value in use exceeds the objective value. The same would be true of the old family home or the dilapidated but still popular college beer joint.

Cost

The cost of a particular commodity is a historical figure, a price paid in the past. A property's cost may have little or no affect on its value today.

Value, price, and cost might possibly be equal for a new property, but this would be the exception rather than the rule. Value in exchange or objective valuation requires the interaction of buyers and sellers. Therefore, the forces at work in the marketplace which influence value and the characteristics of value previously discussed must be understood in order to develop an appropriate model for real property valuation. Clearly, the decision-maker must know value in order to avoid paying too much for an existing property or building a new property which cannot be cost-justified.

THE TEN CONCEPTS OF VALUE

On the basis of many years of experience, appraisers have developed certain principles of value which represent a crystalization of their understanding of how the real estate marketplace operates. The brief descriptions of the concepts that follow are drawn from *The Appraisal of Real Estate*, a publication of the American Institute of Real Estate Appraisers.[1]

Substitution

This key concept states that when two parcels of property have the same utility, the property offered at the lower price will sell first. This concept is crucial in two of the three appraisal approaches. In the *market data approach* (in which properties are compared), one issue is whether, in fact, the various properties have the same utility. In the *cost approach*, the concept of substitution explains why a buyer would not pay more for an existing improvement on real property than the cost to the buyer to build such improvement new.

Anticipation

This concept embodies a point of view that is obvious enough. An estimate of value should always be based upon future expectations (anticipation) rather than past performance.

This is not to say that the past may not be a good forecaster of the future or that the past financial history of an investment should not be studied carefully. The concept is intended to emphasize that because of the antici-

---

[1] *The Appraisal of Real Estate* (7th ed.; New York: American Institute of Real Estate Appraisers, 1978).

pated long life of improved real estate, the appraiser must never forget that the concern is with future productivity and not simply with historic data.

In the recent past, many apartment house investments turned out badly due to sharp increases in fuel costs which, because leases did not so provide, could not be passed along directly to tenants. This turned positive cash flows into losses. Perhaps the sharp increases could not have been anticipated. Nevertheless, this is a dramatic illustration of the importance of anticipating and projecting regional and urban trends, as discussed in Chapter 3.

Change

This concept is, in one sense, merely a specific application of the concept of anticipation. The emphasis here is on the identification of trends which affect the subject property and which will cause foreseeable consequences.

For example, the *concept of regression* says that the value of a superior property in a neighborhood will be adversely affected by surrounding inferior properties. The *concept of progression* states the reverse: An inferior property will benefit by its location in a superior neighborhood.

Competition and Excess Profit

This concept expresses a principle of a free enterprise system: Abnormal profits cannot be expected to continue indefinitely into the future. In other words, unless monopoly profit is protected by unique location, governmental regulation, or some other factor, competition will be generated that in time will reduce the abnormal profit from the subject property to a normal range. For example, the first hotel with a glass elevator attracted a flood of customers and, for a time, generated extraordinary cash flows. However, once competition picked up the idea and built similar elevators, the cash flows were reduced to a more normal level.

Since every parcel of real estate has a unique location, it would seem that the concept of competition has little application. However, the uniqueness of real estate is a relative concept. A residence occupying the only waterfront site within miles indeed is unique and will command a monopoly price. More commonly, the prime commercial or retail location in a city (called the *100 percent location*) will be sufficiently extensive to accommodate several buildings and so permit competition. Even the major traffic intersection in a city will have four corners which normally can be developed (although, even here, one corner will probably be superior to the others because of traffic and pedestrian flow). The real estate decision-maker using the income approach to value projects abnormal profits to continue into the future only until competition can be expected to cause a change in supply.

Increasing and Decreasing Returns

This concept simply restates the law of *diminishing marginal utility*. It says, in effect, that in any given case, a certain optimum combination exists of (1) land, (2) labor, (3) capital, and (4) entrepreneurship. If any one of these four factors of production is increasingly applied in the particular case, diminishing percentage returns to that factor eventually will be experienced.

For example, a commercial site at the edge of town may be capable of returning a small but positive cash flow to the owner if developed with a small retail store. If the owner were to invest additional capital and build a ten-story office building on the same site, the positive return would disappear and be replaced with a negative cash flow because additional rental revenues would be far less than the increasing costs of operation and financing. Thus, diminishing returns are eventually experienced as a result of increased capital investment. (Naturally, over a period of years, as the community expands, more extensive improvement may become justified.)

Contribution

This concept is an application of the one just discussed, relating to marginal utility. The concept of contribution says that changes in an existing improvement or in a portion of an improvement can only be justified in a financial sense if the increase in cash flow represents a fair return on the additional investment.

For example, suppose the owner of an office building is considering replacing the manned elevators with automatic ones. There will be an initial capital investment, but once the change is made, operating expenses will decline because fewer employees will be needed. The concept of contribution addresses the impact on value of increasing the net operating income (NOI) relative to the cost to do so.

Surplus Productivity and Balance

Of the four factors of production, land is assumed to be the last one to be paid. This is so because it plays a passive role, and a return must first be paid to the other three factors—capital, labor, and entrepreneurship—in order to induce them to utilize the land. Consequently, the return to land is *surplus productivity*, in the sense that it is the residual return after payments to the other three factors. The concept of surplus productivity underlies the land residual approach to valuation.

Related to the concept of surplus productivity is the concept of *balance*, which says that the overall return will be highest (and, consequently, the return on the land will be highest) when the optimum balance is struck among the various factors of production.

For example, consider the case of a man and wife who operate a fast-food restaurant as a "mom and pop" operation. They purchase the land, construct the improvements, and work twelve hours a day, seven days a week. At the end of their first year in operation, they have a nice profit. But what is earning a return?

☐ *First*, the couple must pay themselves salaries for their labor as well as some return for the entrepreneurial risk they have assumed.

☐ *Second*, a portion of the profit must be set aside as a return *of* investment (representing the depreciation of the improvements) and an additional portion properly represents a return *on* the investment in the improvements.

☐ *Finally*, the balance, if indeed anything is left, represents a return on the capital invested in the land. At times, it may turn out that there is *no* surplus productivity and that the land in that particular use is in fact earning no return at all.

Conformity

Maximum value accrues to a parcel when a reasonable degree of social and economic homogeneity are present in a neighborhood. This is not to say that monotonous uniformity is rewarded above all else. Rather, it illustrates the sector theory of urban growth (see Chapter 3) and the fact that economic or psychological benefits arise from the grouping of reasonably similar activities. Zoning laws are a partial recognition of this concept.

Supply and Demand

In a completely free economy, the interaction of supply and demand would be the sole determinant of value. In our partially free economy, governmental influences are often as important in establishing a complete pricing model. In any case, demand must be backed by purchasing power in order to be effective, and supply must provide utility satisfaction in order to attract effective demand.

Highest and Best Use

The best-known and most-quoted principle of real estate valuation is that of highest and best use, a concept which can be traced back to Johann von Thünen, whose theories are briefly noted in Chapter 3. The essence of this concept is that land is valued on the basis of the use which, at the time the appraisal is made, is likely to produce the greatest return. Put another way, the highest and best use of land is the use which produces, according to the concept of surplus productivity and balance, the highest residual return to the land. The highest and best use must be legally, physically, and economically logical over the foreseeable future and must take into consideration all relevant elements of risk.

The highest and best use of a parcel of land is likely to change over time. A retail site away from the central business district (CBD) may be only suitable today for a small grocery store. However, if the city grows in that direction, the highest and best use of the site will change, justifying increasingly large structures as time passes.[2]

THE MEANING OF MARKET VALUE

To this point, an attempt has been made to isolate the various aspects of value and to distinguish value from such other related concepts as cost and price. For the remainder of the chapter, the focus is on the actual process by which an appraiser arrives at a figure which is a conclusion about value.

First, just what the final appraisal figure represents must be defined. What can be used as a working definition of *value*? Depending on the reason for the appraisal, the definition may vary. It is possible that an appraiser may be asked to estimate *going concern value* (the value of a business that anticipates continuing in operation), *liquidation value* (the value of the separate assets of a business that is being terminated), or *insurable value*. Most frequently, however, the appraiser seeks to determine *market value*.

Market value is defined as

> the highest price estimated in terms of money which a property will bring if exposed for sale in the open market allowing a reasonable time to find a purchaser who buys with knowledge of all the uses to which it is adapted and for which it is capable of being used.[3]

Recall that value exists when a scarce good satisfies the needs of those able to trade other resources to obtain the particular good. This definition of market value, though, goes beyond the straightforward economic definition. It is the highest price estimated in terms of money. *In terms of money* means cash, not trades, and includes a normal amount of debt financing at a market interest rate. This is an important distinction in real property because the purchase of real property usually involves financing. Particularly advantageous financing terms included in the offer to sell can

---

[2] On the other hand, an additional factor must be included in the highest and best use equation in the case of land already developed. That extra factor is the cost of demolishing the existing improvement. Thus, the highest and best use of vacant land might be a 20-story office building. But if the land already is improved with a 10-story building, the cost of demolishing the existing structure may be so great that the highest and best use (from the point of view of return on investment) remains the present use rather than a taller building.

[3] American Institute of Real Estate Appraisers, *op. cit.*

affect the sales price of the property. Consequently, the appraiser seeking to determine market value typically estimates value based on the most likely (or a market-determined) debt level and interest rate.

The phrase *reasonable time* is a reference to the fact that real property is not a perfectly liquid asset and that to obtain the highest price may require more than a few days or a few weeks, depending on the particular type of property. Finally, in the analytical framework and the land bubble example in the Dallas-Fort Worth area in Chapter 3, note that an appraisal is an estimate of the *present worth* of future benefits or interest. As long as this definition is kept in mind, the appraiser avoids being caught in a speculative abberation.

As the three approaches to value are explored, the possibility of being caught in a market where the greater-fool theory is alive and rampant is lessened if reflection is made on the underlying economic logic supporting a market value conclusion.

THE APPRAISAL PROCESS

The steps in the appraisal process can now be outlined. This process is not merely the technical agenda followed only by a professional appraiser. It is the analytic process that any experienced investor will go through when looking at properties.

The Six Steps

The formal appraisal process consists of six steps as illustrated in Figure 6-1:

- Definition of the problem and the objective.
- Preliminary survey and appraisal plan.
- Data collection and analysis.
- Application of the three appraisal approaches.
- Reconciliation of the three estimates of value.
- Final estimate of value.

Definition of the Problem and the Objective

As Figure 6-1 indicates, defining the appraisal problem involves five items which collectively set the stage for the actual appraisal:

☐ *The particular parcel of real estate must be identified,* using one of the forms of legal description previously discussed.

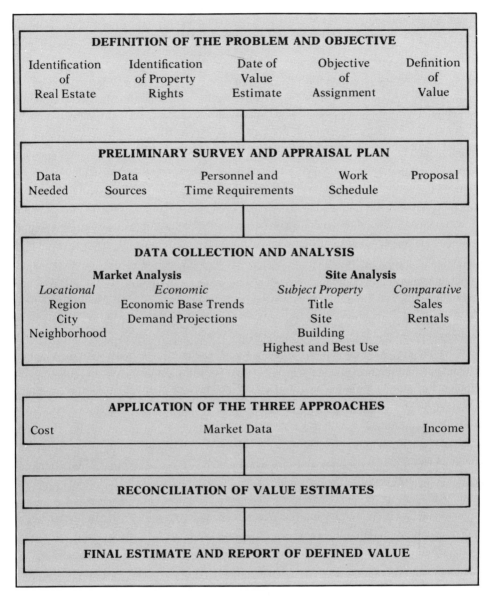

Figure 6-1. THE APPRAISAL PROCESS

☐ *Then, the particular legal rights or estates to be appraised must be identified.* Is the appraiser to value a fee interest, a life estate, or a long term leasehold?

☐ *The date of valuation also is important,* since an appraisal describes and values real estate as of a precise moment in time. This is a particularly crucial factor in condemnation proceedings, since the land taken is valued as of the date of taking. (Consider the importance of setting the date of valuation in connection with recent Indian claims for compensation for land taken many generations ago.)

☐ *Finally, a clear understanding must exist both as to the purpose of the appraisal and the type of value sought.* It has been indicated here that market value is normally the standard of value, but, on occasion, the issue may be the rental value of property, the liquidation value of a business, etc.

Preliminary Survey and Appraisal Plan

The preliminary survey and appraisal plan constitute the logistics of the appraisal process. The appraiser defines the data which will be needed and the sources of that data. Based on this information, personnel needs are estimated, a time schedule established, and, in a more complex appraisal, a formal flow chart of the activities is prepared.

Data Collection and Analysis

All relevant data affecting a property are considered in a sound appraisal. The pool of information generally will fall into two categories: (1) that relating to the environment in which the particular property is located (market analysis) and (2) that relating to the property itself (site analysis).

☐ *Market analysis.* In the first category social, economic, and political characteristics of the region, city, and neighborhood are included. Remembering the principle of anticipation, the appraiser will concentrate on the identification of trends that are expected to continue in the future. A continuing question will be how data about the past relates to a projection of the expected economic life of a particular property.

☐ *Site analysis.* The second category of data involves the property itself. The physical site is inspected and the improvements are examined to determine the extent of depreciation and the ability of the improvement to carry out its present or intended use. The highest and best use of the property is ascertained.

In the case of vacant land, the appraiser is free to consider any reasonably potential use. In the case of property already improved, the appraiser must be instructed as to whether the property is to be evaluated in terms of its existing improvement or whether a demolition would be considered if an alternate use were more desirable.

The appraiser also will seek complete financial and operating information about the property, as well as comparative market information. "Comparables" are used in all three approaches to value. Depending on the nature of the subject property, comparable property information includes sales data, rental rates, and operating expense figures as well as physical and locational characteristics of properties used in the comparison process. (A detailed description of feasibility analysis and the component market study is presented in Part VII.)

Applying the Three Appraisal Approaches

It should now be apparent that property appraisal is an art, not a science. An estimate of value is never spoken of as a scientific fact, but rather as an opinion.

Because of this, an appraiser normally will not follow a single path toward a value conclusion. Over the years, three separate approaches have been developed: (1) the cost method, (2) the market data (or market comparison) method, and (3) the capitalization of income method.

Each of these approaches is discussed in some detail in the following chapters. At this point, only the essence of each method is noted:

☐ *The cost approach* relies on the principle of substitution. It says that one should pay no more for an existing building than an amount equal to the cost of replacement.

☐ *The market data approach* also relies on the principle of substitution, saying that a property is worth approximately the same as another property offering similar utility (a similar stream of benefits).

☐ *The income approach* states the value of property is the present worth of future cash flows which the property is expected to generate (e.g., a property is worth X times its annual net or gross operating income).

Reconciling Estimates of Value

The fifth step in the appraisal process involves a reconciliation of the value estimates derived from the three different approaches to value. The reconciliation is *not* an average of the three results. Depending on the nature of the property and the objective of the appraisal, one approach will appear to be more appropriate than another. Experienced appraisers will meld the results of the three approaches. (See **6-1.**)

Final Estimate of Value

The end of the appraisal process is an estimate of value of the property as of a particular date. Normally, the professional appraiser will write a formal appraisal report setting forth the six steps just described. This report

6-1. RECONCILIATION IS NOT ADDITION

An investor in Ann Arbor, Michigan hired an appraiser to evaluate two adjoining tracts of land which were offered for sale at an aggregate price of $3 million. The appraiser, relying on the market data and land residual approaches (a variation of the income capitalization method) ended up with an estimate of $2.5 million for the two tracts.

The investor mistakenly assumed that the market data approach was used on one tract and the land residual approach on the other, giving a *combined* value of $5 million for the two tracts. He snapped up the properties at the asking price, believing he had a bargain, but eventually regretted that he had not more fully understood the appraisal process.

is the justification and evidence of the final opinion of value rendered by the appraiser.

SUMMARY

Appraisal involves the formulation of an opinion of value—most often an opinion of market value. This opinion is derived by analyzing the forces influencing value and utilizing the ten concepts of value and the appraisal process described in this chapter.

Even the income approach to value does not represent an objective assessment, but rather a subjective estimate made by the appraiser. Appraisal is a way to approach value which includes all of the market and property considerations which are part of our framework for analysis. However, the appraisal process is geared to a market consensus and not to the unique situation of an individual investor. In later chapters, a more individualized and flexible approach to investment analysis is presented.

IMPORTANT TERMS

anticipation
appraisal
conformity
contribution
cost approach
diminishing marginal utility
effective demand
excess profit
going concern value
income approach

increasing and decreasing returns
insurable value
liquidation value
market data approach
market value
100 percent location
progression
regression
scarcity
substitution

supply and demand   utility
surplus productivity   value

REVIEW QUESTIONS

6-1. How might an appraisal designed to estimate market value differ from one designed to estimate value for fire insurance purposes?

6-2. Assume you are interested in buying a property and discover the owner has a life estate interest. How might this discovery affect your offering price?

6-3. What are the critical differences among value, price, and cost with respect to their use in real estate decision-making?

6-4. How might the concept of increasing and decreasing returns affect the value of a 1,000-acre mobile home park?

6-5. Define market value as it should apply to real estate appraisal.

6-6. What is meant by the term *highest and best use* as it is applied to real estate?

6-7. Why is the date of valuation crucial when appraising condemned property (eminent domain)?

6-8. What should be included in the site analysis portion of the appraisal process?

6-9. Would you maintain that an estimate of market value is an opinion or fact? Why?

6-10. How should the three estimates of value be reconciled to result in a final estimate of value?

7

The Market Data Approach and the Cost Approach

THE BASIC CONCEPTS of value described in the previous chapter find concrete expression in the three approaches to value: the market data approach, the cost approach, and the income approach. The first two, discussed in this chapter, correspond more or less closely to practices most people follow in making judgments about any kinds of value. The third method, the income approach, requires a more detailed explanation, to which Chapter 8 is devoted.

THE MARKET DATA APPROACH

Of the three basic approaches to value, the market data (or market comparison) approach is most easily grasped by the newcomer to real estate because it is related to the comparison shopping done when purchasing a new automobile, a new suit, or products in the local supermarket.

The theory of comparable sales analysis is based on the assumption that the market value of a property (the *subject property*) bears a close relationship to the prices of similar properties that have recently changed hands. Since no one property is exactly like another and since the passage of time affects values (including the value of the dollar), the goal is to find properties that resemble the subject property *as closely as possible* and then to make appropriate adjustments to reflect whatever differences exist (including those relating to the time and terms of sale).

It is apparent that the market data approach lends itself best to situations where very similar properties are bought and sold on a relatively frequent basis. Single-family dwellings and raw land often represent such markets, and it is with such properties that the market data approach is most successful. (See Figure 7-1.)

Courtesy of United Press International, Inc., New York, New York.

Figure 7-1. ROW OF HOUSES—DOUGLASTON, NEW YORK

STEPS IN THE MARKET DATA APPROACH

A straightforward outline of the steps involved in the market data approach is as follows:

- First, comparable properties which recently have traded hands are located.

- Second, the key features or characteristics of the subject and the comparable properties are identified.
- Third, the sales price of each comparable property is "adjusted" to reflect the differences between the comparable property and the subject property. (In effect, the price the purchaser of the comparable property would have paid for the subject property is estimated, considering the differences between them.)
- Fourth, a judgment about the market value of the subject property is reached through a consolidation process which weighs the adjusted prices of the comparable properties.

Finding Comparables

The first step in applying the market data approach is finding comparable properties.[1] The reliability of the market data approach is a direct function of the comparable sales used in the analysis.

Suppose *A* is seeking to value a three-bedroom, two-bath, all-brick home at 411 Yorktown Street. *A* discovers that five other three-bedroom, two-bath, all-brick homes on similar lots located on Yorktown have sold in the past three months for $47,500. It is not hard to come to the conclusion that the value of the subject property is very close to $47,500. On the other hand, a ranch house, located in Montana, with twelve bedrooms and one bath which is 30 miles from the nearest house, is more difficult to evaluate by the market data approach.

Not surprisingly, nearly all appraisals fall somewhere between these two extremes. The task of the appraiser or analyst is to find similar properties *whose sales terms can be verified* to use as comparables in judging the market value of the subject property. In choosing comparables, the appraiser must have a clear idea in mind of what constitutes an acceptable comparable. In addition, the characteristics of the comparable that differ from the subject property must be identifiable and they must be of a kind that can be "priced" with a reasonable degree of certainty.[2] Under normal circumstances, it is desirable that four to seven comparable properties be located. (See **7-1.**)

Remember that property differences can be either positive or negative. That is, each comparable property normally will have some features that make it worth more than the subject property and have some deficiencies that make it worth less.

---

[1] This is actually part of the data collection and analysis that makes up stage three of the overall appraisal process, as described in the last chapter.

[2] A property with unique historical or cultural associations, or with sole access to an adjacent body of water, normally will not be a suitable comparable.

7-1. CHOOSING VALID COMPARABLES

"They're Having a Sale in Orlando, Florida and What They're Selling is Orlando." This story was reported in *The Wall Street Journal* on March 14, 1975. The Orlando area experienced significant over-building during the 1974-1975 period, and some people feel that a misuse of the market data approach was largely responsible. In the *Journal* article, Robert N. Gardner, an executive with Condev Corporation, a real estate development firm, says:

> We were so busy building apartments that everyone was unaware that a lot of people who were in the apartments were construction workers who were coming in to build more new apartments. No one knew what anyone else was doing and the real estate development trusts were throwing money in every direction.

What happened was that many properties used as comparables in appraisals were tenanted by transient construction workers or were owned (as condominium units) by speculators holding for resale. As soon as demand showed signs of turning down, the cycle reversed and the result for Orlando investors was a very drastic drop in occupancy ratios.

Identifying Characteristics of Value

The appraiser or analyst must next identify the key characteristics of the subject and the comparable properties that determine its value. On this basis, the appraiser will determine which properties are comparable to the subject and then check the comparables for additional characteristics which affect their value. These characteristics can be divided into two broad classifications: (1) property characteristics and (2) nonproperty characteristics.

☐ *Property characteristics.* The property characteristics are essentially physical items. The significant ones are (1) location, (2) size of the land parcel, (3) size of constructed space, (4) type of construction, and (5) quality of construction. The terrain of the site, the design, age, and condition of the improvement, and the interior configuration, are also relevant items. In the case of a residence, consideration should be given to such outdoor amenities as tennis courts and swimming pools as well as for special features of the house, such as fireplaces, elaborate interior features, or any other major element of difference between the subject property and the comparable property.

☐ *Nonproperty characteristics.* In addition to physical characteristics, certain nonproperty characteristics are important in utilizing the market data approach. Key nonproperty characteristics include:

☐ *Verified sales price.* Since the market approach adjusts comparable selling prices to make them similar to the subject, this method relies heavily on a verified sales price. In most cases, verification is based on information provided by real estate brokers and other appraisers.

☐ *Date of sale.* The elapsed time since a comparable property has been sold may be important if either the national or local economy has been experiencing significant inflation. In recent years, rapid inflation has created a situation where elapsed time of as little as six months has pushed the current market value of the comparable property several percent above its sales price.

☐ *Financing terms.* Since real property is usually purchased with the use of borrowed funds, the financing terms are particularly important. A property which has unusually attractive financing will command a better price than an identical property without such financing.

Consider again the example of the home on Yorktown Road. If the subject home was financed with a 7 percent interest rate loan which could be assumed (taken over) by a new purchaser despite much higher current rates, while the comparable homes had 11 percent loans of equivalent amounts, then the prices of the latter properties would have to be adjusted to reflect the less advantageous financing.

☐ *Unusual conditions of sale.* Finally, any special conditions of sale must be taken into account. This is particularly important in sales that are not at *arm's length* (i.e., sales between persons who are not strangers to one another, as by a father to a daughter or between business associates).

For example, if a condition of one particular sale was that the seller could continue to use the property for six months without payment of any rent or if the property was to be repaired by the seller subsequent to the sale, then these items must be accounted for in the adjustment process. (See 7-2.)

Adjusting the Prices of Comparable Properties

The next step is to adjust the prices of the comparable properties to reflect the differences between each of them and the subject property. Where the comparable property lacks an element of value possessed by the subject property, then the value of that particular element is *added* to the sales price of the comparable. Where the comparable has a feature which is not present in the subject property, the value of the feature is *subtracted* from the sales price of the comparable.

By this process, the subject property is given a value (vis-à-vis each comparable) so that, in theory at least, the person who bought the compa-

7-2. COMPARABLES USED IN THE MARKET APPROACH
(see Table 7-1)

Subject property: The subject property is a single-family dwelling located at 5811 Pine Street. It has 1,800 square feet, three bedrooms, two baths, two-car garage, two living areas, no pool, central air and heat, no fireplace, above-average landscaping, and a fully fenced yard. The lot is 75 feet by 150 feet.

Comparable 1: Located on a 75 foot by 175 foot lot, two blocks from the subject, this comparable has 1,900 square feet, three bedrooms, two and one-half baths, two-car garage, two living areas, no pool, central air and heat, a fireplace, good landscaping, and a fully fenced yard. It sold nine months ago for $131,000 with market financing.

Comparable 2: Located across the street from the subject, this comparable is on a 75 foot by 150 foot lot and has 1,800 square feet, three bedrooms, two baths, two-car garage, two living areas, no pool, central air and heat, no fireplace, poor landscaping, and a fully fenced yard. This comparable sold last week for $116,000—cash.

Comparable 3: This comparable is located six blocks from the subject on a 65 foot by 125 foot lot near a major expressway. It has only 1,600 square feet, three bedrooms, one bath, two-car garage, a single living area, no pool, central air and heat, no fireplace, excellent landscaping, and a fully fenced yard. Comparable 3 sold fourteen months ago for $96,000 with market financing.

Comparable 4: Located on an 85 foot by 175 foot busy corner lot, one block from the subject, comparable three has 1,850 square feet, three bedrooms, two baths, two-car garage, one living area, no pool, central heat but not air conditioning, a fireplace, above-average landscaping, and an unfenced yard. It sold for $114,000 last month with market financing.

Comparable 5: This comparable, on a 75 foot by 150 foot lot located three blocks from the subject, has 2,000 square feet, four bedrooms, two baths, a two-car garage, two living areas, a pool, central air and heat, a fireplace, above-average landscaping, and a fully fenced yard. It sold three months ago for $125,000 with market financing.

rable property would have been willing to buy the subject property at the given value. (See 7-3.)

The actual adjustments can be made by (1) unit of comparison (e.g., an adjustment per square foot), (2) dollar adjustments (e.g., a lump-sum adjustment for a fireplace or central air conditioning), or (3) a percentage adjustment. The percentage adjustment is particularly useful in handling differences in location. For example, a property on one street may be 2 to 5 percent more valuable than property on another street which has less prestige, ease of access, or some other particular attribute. (See Table 7-1.)

Reaching a Correlation of Value

The final step in the market data approach is to reach an opinion of value for the subject property based upon the adjusted sales prices of all the

7-3. MARKET COMPARABLE ADJUSTMENTS (see Table 7-1)

Date of sale: Values in the subject neighborhood have been increasing by one percent per month.

Financing terms: Comparable 2 was sold for cash, and hence, the sales price was deemed to have suffered.

Location: Comparable 3 has been penalized due to nearness to the expressway and comparable 4 for the busy corner.

Size: Comparables 1 and 5 are penalized for being larger than the subject, while comparables 2 and 4 were adjusted upward due to smaller size.

Number of bedrooms: Comparable 5 was adjusted downward because of the fourth bedroom.

Number of bathrooms: Comparable 1 was penalized for the extra half-bath, while comparable 2 was adjusted upward for lacking a full two baths.

Living areas: Comparables 3 and 4 were adjusted upward for lacking a second living area.

Pool: Comparable 5 was penalized for a pool which the subject lacks.

Central air and heat: Lacking air conditioning resulted in a downward adjustment for comparable 4.

Fireplace: Comparables 1, 4, and 5 all have fireplaces which the subject lacks and they were consequently penalized for the overimprovement.

Fence: Comparable 4 was adjusted upward for lacking a fence.

comparables. Most professional appraisers eliminate any sales prices that vary widely from the others in the group. They do so on the assumption that some element of comparison has been missed or that these particular properties have unique features which make them inappropriate to be used as comparables.

The remaining adjusted sales prices are evaluated and correlated to produce a final indication of market value of the subject property. In the correlation process, the appraiser may give more emphasis to those properties which most closely resemble the subject property.

THE COST APPROACH

The cost approach to value states that the worth of a property is roughly equal to (1) the cost of reproducing the property minus (2) a figure that approximates the amount of value of the property that has been "used up" in the course of its life (i.e., a figure representing its lessened productivity). In short, a property is worth its reproduction cost minus accrued depreciation. By comparison, the market data approach states that the worth of a property is equal to the price an informed purchaser would pay for it; the income approach says that the worth of a property is equal to the present value of the anticipated stream of future benefits.

Table 7-1. THE MARKET DATA GRID

The grid format is an excellent way to display data collected under the market data approach. The information below is derived from data set out in 7-2 as adjusted for all the reasons given in 7-3.

	Subject	1	2	3	4	5
Nonproperty characteristics:						
Sales price	—	$131,000	$116,000	$ 96,000	$114,000	$145,000
Date of sale	—	11,790	—	2,880	1,140	4,350
Financing terms	Market	—	11,600	—	—	—
Conditions of sale	Normal	—	—	—	—	—
Property characteristics:						
Location	5811 Pine Street	—	—	11,520	10,000	—
Lot size	75 × 150	(5,000)	—	(8,000)	(9,600)	—
Structure size (square feet):	18,000	(4,000)	—	8,000	2,000	(8,000)
Number of bedrooms	3	—	—	—	—	(3,000)
Number of bathrooms	2	(1,000)	—	2,000	—	—
Garage	2	—	—	—	—	—
Living areas	2	—	—	2,000	2,000	—
Pool	No	—	—	—	—	(12,000)
Central air conditioning and heating	Yes	—	—	—	—	—
Fireplace	No	(1,500)	—	—	(1,500)	(1,500)
Landscaping	Above average	500	1,500	(750)	1,500	—
Fence	Yes	—	—	—	1,500	—
Adjusted sales price:	—	$131,790	$129,100	$113,650	$121,040	$124,850
Indicated market value of subject:	$126,600					

After close examination of the comparables, the indicated market value of the subject was determined by averaging the adjusted sales prices of comparables 1, 2, 4, and 5. Comparable 3 was ignored because of its location, which was interpreted to be in an outlying area compared to the subject property.

Principles of Value

While the definition of the cost approach given in the previous paragraph is not controversial in a theoretical sense, the application of this method can be very controversial indeed. Some of the controversies are indicated in the course of this chapter. Several of the ten principles of value set forth in Chapter 6 are involved in the cost approach, particularly the principles of anticipation, substitution, change, increasing and decreasing returns, and highest and best use.

STEPS IN THE COST APPROACH TO VALUE

Four steps are involved in the cost approach to value:

- First, an estimate is made of the cost to reproduce the existing improvements.
- Second, an estimate is made of the dollar amount of accrued depreciation that has occurred during the life of the improvements. The accrued depreciation is deducted from reproduction costs to show the depreciated cost of the improvements.
- Third, the estimated value of the land (site value) is arrived at using the market data approach.
- Fourth, an opinion of value is arrived at by adding the site value to the depreciated cost of the improvements.

REPRODUCTION AND REPLACEMENT COST

An important distinction exists between reproduction cost and replacement cost. *Reproduction cost* refers to the cost at today's prices to build an exact replica of the structure being valued. Reproduction cost assumes that the same quantity and quality of material and labor is utilized as when the structure actually was built. In short, reproduction denotes the same structure in replica. By comparison, replacement cost denotes the cost of replacing an existing building with one of equal utility although the same materials or the same design may not be used, reflecting changes in technology, design, building techniques, and cost.

Reproduction Cost New

Although it might appear that replacement cost should be used in the cost approach to value, the concept of *reproduction cost new* represents the true theoretical foundation for the cost approach because it relates directly to the accrued depreciation that is estimated in the next step in the process. Consequently, most of the discussion that follows is designed to estimate reproduction cost new. While this estimate of reproduction cost must reflect *all* ingredients of cost to the typical purchaser, there are several alternative methods of cost estimation. Generally, an appraiser or analyst will either use one of these methods or use one of several published construction cost services.

Trade Breakdown or Builder's Method

The trade breakdown or builder's method of estimating reproduction cost is the recommended method when preparing the demonstration appraisal report required for designation by the American Society of Real Estate Appraisers (ASREA). This method most nearly represents the thinking of residential building contractors and can readily be understood by both appraiser and investor. The method does require a knowledge of the major components of the structure. (Certainly, a working knowledge of structural components is fundamental to the entire appraisal process.)

In the trade breakdown or builder's method,

- Direct costs (labor, materials, equipment, and subcontractors' fees) are added to
- Indirect costs (financing charges, selling costs, insurance premiums, permit and license fees, survey costs, architectural and legal fees, and builder's profit and overhead) to arrive at
- Estimated reproduction cost new of the improvements on the site.

Quantity Survey Method

A more elaborate approach to estimating reproduction cost involves a complete building cost estimate by a contractor involved in the particular kind of construction in the area. The quantity survey method requires a complete itemization of all prices for materials, equipment, and labor, plus a complete list of all overhead items plus profit. The cost of such an estimate, however, normally exceeds that which an investor or purchaser is willing to pay, and so this method is not used frequently.

Comparative Unit Method

A much more simplified approach is the comparative unit method. Here, an estimate of reproduction cost per square foot is derived by dividing the total known cost of similar structures by the total square footage of those structures. The resulting standard or comparative unit of cost is then applied to the subject property. This approach is acceptable only for preliminary or cursory appraisals rather than in-depth analyses.

Construction Cost Services

Published cost services provide estimates of reproduction cost for typical structures and are useful time-saving devices. These services also provide localized indices to take into consideration varying costs throughout the country. One such cost service is the Dodge Cost Calculator, published by McGraw-Hill. The services identify the costs of the major components of structures and provide adjustments for inflation and for different geographic areas of the country. (See Table 7-2.)

ESTIMATING ACCRUED DEPRECIATION

The concept of depreciation is pervasive in real estate. It is meant here as an appraisal or valuation concept, and it is met again in later chapters as an accounting concept and then as a tax concept. As used here, *depreciation* refers to reduction in the value of buildings or improvements as a result of physical, functional, or economic factors.[3]

Accrued depreciation is a measure of the loss in utility of the subject property in its present condition, from all forms of depreciation, as compared with its condition as a totally new improvement representing the highest and best use of the site. To the extent that improved real estate loses utility (i.e., suffers depreciation), it has suffered a decline in value from its *reproduction cost new.* Therefore, after the accrued depreciation suffered by an improved parcel of real estate is estimated, the amount of such depreciation is subtracted from reproduction cost new to arrive at the present depreciated cost of the improvements.

The appraisal process recognizes 3 different types of depreciation: (1) physical depreciation, (2) functional depreciation (functional obsolescence), and (3) economic or locational depreciation (economic obsolescence).

Physical Depreciation

Physical depreciation is the kind of "using up" of an improvement that is easiest to understand. It is the loss of value suffered by improvements

---

[3] Land does not depreciate in an appraisal, accounting, or tax sense. The reason is that land has perpetual life, and the "bundle of rights" that constitute the legal concept of ownership also goes on forever.

Table 7-2. REPLACEMENT COST

Reproduction Cost

Simplified Computation From Dodge Building Cost Calculator

5811 Pine Street
Los Angeles, California

Single Family, Two Story (basement and air conditioning)—Good Quality
Masonry Wall—1,800 Square Feet

Cleveland, Ohio—January 1, 19X9

☐ *Direct Costs:*

1. Base cost based on characteristics above and
   picture below—$17.05

2. Multiply base cost by floor area (1,800 sq. ft.) $ 36,690

3. Additions
   a. Basement (block not finished)   3.35/sq. ft.
   b. Air conditioning   1.25/sq. ft.
                                           4.60/sq. ft. × 1,800   9,880

4. Total cost $ 46,570

5. Multiplier (local building cost multiplier—Cleveland, Ohio
   —October 1, 19X9 through March 31, 19X8)   1.987

   Hard Cost Total (Site Preparation, Labor, Materials, $ 92,535
   Architects and Engineers' Fees, Supervisory and
   Administration, Permits, and Insurance)

☐ *Indirect Costs:*

Construction Interest (12% for
3 months, equal draws)   2%

   Closing Costs:
   Loan and legal   3%
   Commission   4%   7%
                                           9% × $92,535 $ 8,328

Total reproduction costs $100,863

resulting from wear and tear, disintegration, and the action of the elements.
All man-made improvements suffer physical depreciation, although it may
be very gradual, particularly in the early years of use.

☐ *Curable physical depreciation.* Physical depreciation may either be
curable or *incurable.* Curable physical depreciation is also known as *deferred maintenance,* because the primary cause of such depreciation is the

failure of the owner to maintain the property on an ongoing basis. Such depreciation is called curable because the cost of eliminating or correcting it is less than or equal to the value that will be added to the property as a result. Most items of "normal" maintenance come under this heading.

Examples of curable physical depreciation include replacing broken windows, painting the exterior and interior of the house, and cleaning and making minor replacements to the furnace. In all of these cases, the cost to cure is relatively small and is undoubtedly justified (in an economic sense). (See Table 7-3.)

☐ *Incurable physical depreciation.* The other type of physical depreciation is that which is incurable. The term *incurable* does not refer to the impossibility of curing the defect, since virtually any physical defect can be repaired or replaced, but to the lack of economic justification in doing so. Physical depreciation is considered incurable if the cost to cure or correct the physical defect is greater than the value that will be added to the property as a result. For example, it would be illogical to replace a five-year old roof which was capable of lasting another ten years. However, the five-year old roof is less valuable than a brand new roof. (See Table 7-4.)

Functional Depreciation (Functional Obsolescence)

Functional depreciation is the loss of value suffered by real estate because buildings or improvements do not provide the same utility, or do so less efficiently, than would a new structure. Functional depreciation represents the impact of changes in building technology and consumer tastes and preferences on the value of improvements.

Another term for such depreciation is *obsolescence.* Just as with physical depreciation, functional obsolescence may either be curable or incurable. And again, the use of these terms does not refer to the absolute ability to cure but rather to the economic justification.

☐ *Curable functional obsolescence.* A good example of this is a modern kitchen in a residence. Many individuals will not buy an old house with a

Table 7-3. CURABLE PHYSICAL DEPRECIATION

5811 Pine Street Los Angeles, California	
1. Crayon on walls—children's bedroom: paint room	$125
2. Broken tile—kitchen: replace	65
3. Torn screen—playroom: replace	40
Total physical curable depreciation	$230

Table 7-4. INCURABLE PHYSICAL DEPRECIATION

	5811 Pine Street Los Angeles, California				
Short-Lived Items	Cost (Part of Hard Construc- tion Cost)	Original Expected Life (Years)	Remaining Expected Life (Years)	Per- centage Depre- ciation	Depre- ciation
Roof	$ 4,000	12	9	25	$1,000
Heating and air conditioning	8,500	15	12	20	1,700
Water and plumbing	3,500	20	16	20	700
Interiors (compos- ite to simplify presentation)	17,000	6	5	16.6	2,833
Total short-lived items	$33,000				$6,233
Long-lived items ($100,863 − 33,000)	$67,863	60	57	5	3,393
Total incurable physical depreciation					$9,626

kitchen that has not been modernized or will reduce their offer by the cost of a new kitchen. Consequently, the owner of a house who installs a new kitchen might well anticipate recouping the investment upon sale. Other examples of curable functional depreciation include lack of air conditioning in office or commercial space, and outmoded store fronts.

The amount of curable functional depreciation from which a property suffers is equal to

- The cost to cure, minus
- Physical depreciation previously deducted.

The reason for this second step is that, in the appraisal process, the physical depreciation of the particular component has already been deducted. In order to avoid double counting, this depreciation factor must be netted out from the computations. Note that if replacement cost rather than reproduction cost is used, functional obsolescence may be neglected. However, the result will not be as precise. (See Table 7-5.)

☐ *Incurable functional obsolescence.* Incurable functional obsolescence is, again, a measure of the reduced ability of a structure, or one of its components, to perform with the same utility as when new. The cost of

Table 7-5. CURABLE FUNCTIONAL OBSOLESCENCE

5811 Pine Street Los Angeles, California	
No electric outlet in second bath	—
Cost to install	$150.00
Note: Since this item is new, no netting of previously taken physical depreciation is required.	

curing or correcting the defect, however, is more than the value increment that would result. Consequently, the depreciation is deemed incurable.

For example, a four-story private residence which might otherwise be suitable for a multitenant building has a large, winding staircase which, in a modern structure, would be replaced by an elevator. The cost of installing one, however, is not justified by the value added to the property. An office building built many years ago with high ceilings and wide corridors offers amenities which cannot be provided today because of high costs and is another example of incurable obsolescence. The owner of such a building probably would decide against lowering the ceilings and narrowing the corridors in order to create more rental space because the additional rental income would not represent a satisfactory return on the additional investment that would be required. Note that in both of these cases, the presence of incurable depreciation does not mean that the property is not a good investment. It may well be so, provided the price reflects the depreciation which acts to reduce the future flow of income.

To approximate the amount of incurable functional obsolescence, the appraiser or analyst most often relies on the income approach to value. An estimate is made of the lower rent that the improvement will command due to the incurable depreciation, and this rent loss is capitalized by a process that is explained in the next chapter dealing with the income approach to value. (See Table 7-6.)

Economic or Locational Depreciation

The final form of depreciation is termed economic or locational depreciation (sometimes known as *economic obsolescence*). It is a measure of the diminished utility, and hence diminished value, of improved real estate due to negative environmental forces in the surrounding area. It directly reflects the importance of the spatial element (location) in real estate valuation.

Note the significant difference between this type of depreciation and the other two. In the case of physical and functional depreciation, the loss of

Table 7-6. INCURABLE FUNCTIONAL OBSOLESCENCE

5811 Pine Street Los Angeles, California	
No built-in dishwasher (and no kitchen location suitable)	—
Cost measure—estimate of lost value	$500.00

value arose from the condition of the subject property itself, whereas in economic depreciation, the loss of utility arises because of the relationship of the subject property to its surroundings. It is obvious that economic or locational depreciation is almost always incurable since the property owner is not in a position to control conditions external to the property. (See 7-4.)

As in the case of the other types of incurable obsolescence, economic loss is approximated by setting a value on (capitalizing) the lessened rent that can be anticipated because of the negative economic factors. For example, a zoning change may permit commercial or industrial uses in a formerly residential neighborhood, with the result that an apartment building must drop its rentals to attract tenants.

7-4. INSTANT ECONOMIC OBSOLESCENCE: THE TIME FACTOR

In 1974, a very astute group, Baltimore Real Estate Investors, formed a partnership to invest in the planned Botzlor-Emory Warehouse. The partnership borrowed funds and constructed a high-quality warehouse as planned. According to the cost approach to value, the warehouse was worth $2.7 million. Once completed, the investment partnership found that they could not lease the warehouse at rental levels sufficient to justify what they thought to be the fair value, the $2.7 million cost. The building had legitimately cost that amount and being new, there was no physical deterioration, either curable or incurable. Further, the group had researched the warehouse market and the Botzlor-Emory Warehouse showed no signs of either curable or incurable functional obsolescence.

Where had the group made a mistake? They had valued the site at its highest and best use, which they took to be a warehouse. In the long run, the site *was* best suited to be a warehouse, but the market would not absorb the additional warehouse space for some years. Consequently, to value the project using the cost approach to value, the group should have shown a value reduction to reflect the fact that the space could not be fully occupied for the first few years of the project's existence—that is, there should have been recognition of economic obsolescence to reflect the fact that the site could not for a number of years support a warehouse.

Note: The example shows that pro forma appraisals of planned projects can be more difficult than appraisals of existing properties.

Determining Depreciated Cost

After completion of the two initial steps in the cost approach, the total accrued depreciation arising from all three types of depreciation is added up and that figure is subtracted from reproduction cost new. The resulting figure is the present depreciated cost of the improvements on the land.

The problem of valuing the land, which so far has not been considered, remains to be solved.

VALUING THE SITE

Since the cost approach cannot be used to value land, one of two other methods is utilized. The most common method is the *market data approach*, which is discussed earlier in the chapter. In other words, the appraiser or analyst asks the question, "What have comparable undeveloped parcels of property sold for in this approximate location in the recent past?" It is also possible to use a variation of the income approach to value, called the *land residual approach*. (This is explained in some detail in Chapter 8.) Essentially, it involves dividing the projected cash flows from a completed structure between the building to be constructed and the land. Then, the income stream attributable to the land is capitalized to obtain a valuation for the site.

It should be more and more evident that the three approaches to value are closely interrelated, and all deal with identical data, similar logic, and, in many cases, the same mechanics.

OPINION OF VALUE

The opinion of value is the fourth and final step in the cost approach. In the second step, accrued depreciation is subtracted from reproduction cost new to yield the present depreciated cost of the improvements. Now the value of the site is added, which is determined in accordance with one of the methods just described, to arrive at an estimate of value for the entire parcel.

The cost approach to value is most reliable when a property is relatively new and accurate estimates of construction costs can be made. Further, a newly improved property will normally have suffered less depreciation, particularly of the functional and economic types which are the most difficult to measure. (See Table 7-7.)

Table 7-7. COST APPROACH: VALUE CONCLUSION

Reproduction cost		$100,863
Depreciation:		
Physical curable	230	
Physical incurable	9,626	
Functional curable	150	
Functional incurable	500	
Economic (none)	-0-	(10,506)
Site value (market data approach)		26,000
Total		$116,357
Rounded		$116,400

SUMMARY

The market data approach is the most sensible method of estimating market value. Even to the experienced appraiser, it often seems the most logical approach when sufficient data can be obtained. It is the approach used most heavily in appraisals of single-family homes and raw land.

The steps involved in the market data approach include the (1) location of comparable properties, (2) identification of value characteristics, (3) adjustment of differences in value characteristics, and (4) final correlation of value. Each of these steps requires a knowledge of the sources of data and experience in making value judgments.

Any value conclusion reached by the market data approach should be carefully cross-checked. One way of doing so is by looking at the underlying economics. Specifically, in the case of the valuation of a single-family home, if the rent that could be obtained from a tenant does not justify the value under the market data approach, then any excess value must be sustained as arising from the "psychic income" associated with home ownership. In the case of raw land evaluation, beware when the land residual approach to value gives a significantly lower value conclusion than does the market approach. You may end up being the greater fool.

The cost approach to value relies on several of the basic principles set out in Chapter 6. Perhaps the most obvious one is the principle of substitution, which states that a property's value will be no greater than the cost to reproduce the improvements in order to produce the same stream of utility. That is, no one will pay more for existing property than would be necessary for new construction on a comparable site. Thus, the cost approach is sometimes useful in setting a ceiling on value.

Under the cost approach, reproduction cost new of the improvements less all elements of accrued depreciation is added to the site value to obtain an estimate of total value. The cost approach is most reliable when accurate construction cost figures are available and little depreciation is involved. The approach is very often used for valuing new properties which do not produce income and have few comparables—in other words, in situations where the market data and income approach are difficult to apply.

Appendix 8A offers sufficient data for the reader to test his understanding of all three approaches to value.

IMPORTANT TERMS

builder's method
comparables
comparative unit method
construction cost services
cost approach
deferred maintenance
depreciation
economic or locational
  depreciation

functional depreciation
  (obsolescence)
land residual approach
physical depreciation
quantity survey method
replacement cost
reproduction cost
subject property
trade breakdown method

REVIEW QUESTIONS

7-1. When implementing the market data approach, on what basis should an appraiser identify comparable properties?

7-2. What are the most common nonproperty characteristics of a single-family comparable?

7-3. How might the actual adjustments in the market data approach be carried out?

7-4. If a father sold a property to his daughter just before his death, how should the reported sales price be adjusted in the market data approach?

7-5. What real estate property types might be most accurately appraised using the market data approach?

7-6. Differentiate between the concepts of reproduction cost new and replacement cost as they are used in the cost approach.

7-7. Outline the general steps in the cost approach to value.

7-8. What methods might an appraiser utilize to estimate reproduction cost new?

7-9. Discuss the differences between curable and incurable physical depreciation.

7-10. Since the market data approach is normally relied on in valuing the site in the cost approach, what important property characteristics might be utilized?

8

The Income Approach and Valuation Conclusion

THE KEY TO understanding the income approach to valuing real estate lies in understanding the relationship between a stream of income and value. In essence, an investor who buys real estate (or stocks, bonds, or other income-producing property) really is buying a *future flow of income*—that is, a future stream of benefits. If this is so, it follows that the present value of a parcel of property can be ascertained by

- Determining the amount, certainty, and length of time of such future flow of income.
- Placing a dollar valuation on the future flow of income—by, as appraisers say, applying an appropriate capitalization rate.

The process can be stated more precisely as follows:

The market value (V) of property equals its stabilized net operating income (NOI) divided by an appropriate market capitalization rate (R), or V = NOI/R.

While the logic of using the income approach for appraising income-producing property is impeccable, a great deal of talent and experience is required in estimating stabilized NOI. This is the "true" earning capacity of the property uninfluenced by extraordinary or nonrecurring factors. In addition, there are several subtleties involved in deriving the appropriate capitalization rate. These matters are discussed in greater detail in this chapter.

THE CONCEPT OF STABILIZED NET OPERATING INCOME

One of the major difficulties in real estate financial analysis is the lack of uniform terminology. Sometimes, the same term has different meanings; sometimes, several terms are used to refer to the same thing. In this book, financial terms are given very specific meanings, and it is important, when using other sources or analyzing particular real estate transactions to be sure that the same terms are similarly defined.

Net Operating Income

One of the most frequently used terms in real estate financial analysis is NOI. This is defined as the balance of cash remaining after deducting the operating expenses of a property from the gross income generated by the property.

There are two important points to remember about NOI:

- In determining NOI, debt service on any existing or projected mortgages is ignored, since NOI is intended to demonstrate the earning capacity of the real estate exclusive of any financing.
- In determining NOI, depreciation deductions and any other purely bookkeeping deductions are ignored; only cash expenses for operating the property are considered.

☐ *Gross rental receipts.* The first step in deriving NOI is to estimate gross rental receipts (GRR). (See Table 8-1.) GRR reflects the appraiser's estimate of what rental income would be if the property were 100 percent occupied for an entire twelve-month period. In deriving GRR, the appraiser relies on three major sources: (1) the records of the subject property, (2) comparables, and (3) trends in the marketplace. (See Chapter 3.) The property records (preferably signed leases and audited financial statements) will indicate the present rent roll and the total rent currently being received. However, rents currently being paid under existing leases (called *contract rents*) may not represent *market rents*. The latter may be

Table 8-1. DERIVING NET OPERATING INCOME

1. Gross rental receipts
+ Nonrental income
Gross possible income
2. Gross possible income
− Vacancy and credit loss
Gross effective income
3. Gross effective income
− Operating expenses
Net operating income

higher or lower than the former since market conditions may have changed since the leases were signed and rents were fixed. It is necessary, therefore, to determine the current market rental value of the space in the subject property.

Where the contract rent and market rent differ, the appraiser must decide which to use in the projected operating statement. If tenants have very short-term leases, it is likely that, within a fairly brief period, contract rents will move up or down toward current market rents as the current leases expire. On the other hand, if the building is occupied by a single tenant who has a lease for 25 or 50 years, current market rentals mean little in evaluating the future rental stream. Usually, since lease terms fall somewhere between these extremes, the analyst prepares a *lease expiration schedule,* showing when each lease expires, and constructs a future rental stream to reflect these expirations. As mentioned earlier, the figure for GRR will include the rental expected from *all* space in the building, whether or not it is vacant at the present time. A provision for vacancies is introduced later on in the calculation of NOI.

☐ *Gross possible income.* After arriving at a figure for GRR, the analyst must ascertain any additional income earned from sources other than rent. Examples of these are: (1) automatic washers and dryers in the laundry room, (2) vending machines, (3) parking fees, (4) swimming pool, and (5) other amenity fees. The GRR plus other income represents the property's gross possible income (GPI).

☐ *Gross effective income.* The next step in determining NOI is to calculate the gross effective income (GEI), which is arrived at by substracting from GPI a figure representing vacancy and collection (or credit) loss. The vacancy expense, which is calculated as a percentage of GRR (frequently ranging between 5 and 10 percent of GRR) reflects the experience of the subject property or of comparable properties in the area, and projected trends in the marketplace.

Collection loss expense, also expressed as a percentage of GRR, reflects unpaid rent as well as bad checks. Subtracting vacancy and collection loss from GPI results in GEI.

☐ *Operating expenses.* The final step in calculating NOI involves the estimation and deduction of operating expenses. As already noted, these are expenses directly related to the operation and maintenance of the property. They do not include debt service or depreciation. Typical operating expenses include:

- Real estate taxes (not last year's but next year's).
- Payroll.
- Maintenance and repair (M&R).

- Fire and hazard insurance premiums.
- Utility costs.
- Management fees.
- Supplies.
- Replacement reserve.

After deducting operating expenses from gross effective income, the resulting figure is NOI.

Stabilized Net Operating Income

The initial derivation of an NOI figure will be based on the financial records of the property. Since the focus here is not on an historical record but a projection of future income, it is necessary to exclude unusual or nonrecurring items of income and expense as well as eliminate distortions that may have been introduced into the financial statements, inadvertently or otherwise, by the present owner. The result is a stabilized NOI figure, often called *stabilized net*.

The purpose of the stabilization process is to show, to the extent possible, the true future earning power of the property. One traditional approach to reaching a stabilized NOI figure is to simply average income and expenses for the past several years. Thus, for example, a five-year average would be shown as five-year stabilized net.

During a period of rapid inflation or significant economic change, however, this approach may not be adequate. A better way to arrive at a stabilized NOI is to analyze the operating statement for the past two or three years, make appropriate adjustments, and then further adjust the figures to reflect foreseeable future changes (e.g., a proposed increase in the property tax rate.) (See 8-1.)

There are several ways in which a property's current NOI, as shown on its financial statement, can diverge from the property's true stabilized NOI. Among these are: (1) lease concessions, (2) deferred maintenance, (3) needed capital improvements, and (4) inadequate reserves, which are discussed below:

☐ *Lease concessions.* An owner's financial statement may accurately show GRR currently being collected. However, in order to fill up a new building or survive a period of market weakness, the owner may have granted rent concessions which have not yet been fulfilled. For example, every tenant may be entitled to one rent-free month for each year of the lease. Some tenants may have step-down renewal options, giving them the right to renew at a lower rental in the future. In these unusual cases, future rental income will be less than at first appears.

☐ *Deferred maintenance.* A property may show a healthy NOI along with a very low figure for maintenance and repair. It may turn out that the

8-1. INCONSISTENT REVENUE AND EXPENSE ESTIMATES

In 1971, a major East Coast financial institution made a construction loan on the Brandywine Apartments to be built in East Lansing, Michigan. In convincing the institution to make the construction loan, the developer showed a projected value based on the income approach to value. At the date he made the loan request (1974), he was careful to document his expense projections. In fact, they were the exact expenses for a similar apartment project in East Lansing in 1973.

The developer then projected income for the first year of operations, 1975. He subtracted the 1973 expenses from the 1975 income to arrive at the NOI figure, which was capitalized to determine value. Once the project was completed, the developer sought permanent financing. Potential permanent lenders used the income approach to determine the value of the collateral. They did not, however, make the mistake of using next year's revenues with last year's expenses.

Consequently, their value projection involved lower NOI and a lower overall project value.

With this lower value, they were not willing to make a loan large enough to cover the entire construction loan made by the East Coast lender. With no possibility of getting out of the Brandywine project except by partial payment plus a second lien position, the East Coast lender reluctantly took back a second mortgage.

Simple errors (in this case the construction lender's failure to fully analyze the original appraisal) can be costly.

building suffers from deferred maintenance (which is identified in Chapter 7 as a form of physical depreciation). Here, the true return from the property is not only less than appears, but, also, a new owner must spend additional funds to restore the property to optimum operating condition.

☐ *Needed capital improvements.* The owner may have postponed making needed capital improvements. While this inadequacy will not be reflected in the operating statement as such, it does mean that a new purchaser will be required to provide additional capital for the necessary improvements, thus reducing the return on his investment.

☐ *Inadequate replacement reserves.* When personal property is a significant factor, as in the case of motels, adequate cash reserves should be maintained to replace short-lived items (e.g., furniture, carpets, etc.). Once again, to the extent that reserves are inadequate, the indicated NOI is too high, and, in addition, the new owner will have to build up the reserves as soon as he takes title.

DERIVING A CAPITALIZATION RATE

Having arrived at a stabilized NOI figure for the property in question, the appraiser has accomplished the first step in applying the income approach to value. The second step is calculating the appropriate capitalization rate. *Capitalization* is the process of converting a future income stream into a present value. The capitalization rate is the percentage by which the future income stream is divided to arrive at a single figure that represents present value. For example, a capitalization rate of 10 percent applied to an annual income of $1,000 gives a capital value of $10,000 ($1,000 ÷ 0.10 = $10,000).

Capitalization rates vary among particular types of investments and from one period of time to another. Higher capitalization rates (expressed as a percentage) are utilized when NOI is more speculative or when abnormal inflation is anticipated. The converse is also true. Lower capitalization rates are utilized for projects generating a more secure NOI or when significant inflation is not anticipated.

Important factors in choosing a capitalization rate include:

- Type of property (e.g., apartment building, office building, etc.).
- Location (in the main business district, a few feet may make one location better than another).
- Age (the older the building, the less future income can be derived from it in its present state).
- Quality of the tenancies (e.g., a long-term lease usually means more secure NOI than a short-term lease).

Four Elements of a Capitalization Rate

From a theoretical standpoint, the capitalization rate has four separate elements:

- Real return.
- Inflation premium.
- Risk premium.
- Recapture premium.

☐ *Real return.* A person invests capital only if there will be compensation for deferring immediate consumption. Even if the investment involves no risk and even if the price level remains stable, the return will still be sought. Thus, the central element in any return calculation is the real return.

The real return required by investors and lenders can be estimated by looking at the historic relationship between risk-free government bonds and the rate of inflation over the past two decades. Various researchers have put this difference (i.e., the real return) at 2 to 3 percent annually.

☐ *Inflation premium.* Investors have come to expect a decline in the value of the dollar over time—that is, they assume an inflationary economy. Expecting inflation, the investor requires the return from any pro-spective investment to go beyond the real return and give an additional return to compensate for inflation. Put another way and perhaps more logically, the investor wants to receive back the number of dollars that gives the same purchasing power as the dollars he originally invested. In a period of inflation, this requires more dollars to be returned than were invested. Then, a real return, in addition, is required.

When an analyst or appraiser is constructing a capitalization rate, a judgment must be made as to the expected rate of inflation during the holding period of the asset which is being valued. Obviously, this may be an extremely difficult judgment to make. One guideline in estimating the combined real return and inflation premium expected by investors is the current rate on Treasury bonds having a maturity equal to the projected holding period of the subject property. Treasury bonds are used because the return on such bonds is made up almost wholly of the required real return plus inflation premium (i.e., there is virtually no risk except the risk of underestimating inflation). Subtracting 2 to 3 percent (real return) from this Treasury rate gives the composite market expectation about inflation.

☐ *Risk premium.* Unlike Treasury bonds, real estate projects carry risk, which may be substantial. The investor recognizes this risk and requires compensation for it through a return higher than that paid on riskless or lower-risk investments.

Just how large the risk premium should be is the subject of endless professional and academic debate. This topic is discussed and a straight-forward approach to choosing a risk premium is suggested in Chapter 18. At this point, it is appropriate to say that the riskier the project, the higher the risk premium and consequently the higher the capitalization rate.[1]

☐ *Recapture premium.* If an investment were to produce income in perpetuity, the three elements already mentioned would be sufficient to make up the capitalization rate. While improved real estate usually has a long economic life, it cannot have an infinite life.[2] Consequently, the investor requires not only a return *on* invested capital (the first three factors above) but also a return *of* invested capital. Thus, an element representing recapture of investment must be included in the capitalization rate.

The recapture premium can be calculated using either the straight line or sinking fund method. If, for example, a project is expected to last 50 years, then the straight line recapture premium (calculated with respect to

---

[1] It should be noted that the sum of the real return, the inflation premium, and the risk premium are often referred to as the discount rate or the rate of return on capital.

[2] The *land* element in a property investment does have perpetual life, but the improvements will depreciate over a longer or shorter period of time.

the value of the improvements) would be 2 percent a year (50 × 2 percent = 100 percent over the economic life).

A more theoretically acceptable approach is to use a *sinking fund concept*. This concept introduces the element of interest that will be earned on the capital recouped each year during the period. Thus, the investor can receive something less than 2 percent each year and still recover an entire investment over the 50-year period because interest will be earned (or some other return) on the money received in years 1, 2, 3, etc., compounded up to year 50.

The major distinction between the straight line and sinking fund methods is that under the former, reinvestment is *not* assumed. In the latter, reinvestment of the recaptured capital is assumed to produce a return, which can be calculated in one of several different ways. (See Table 8-2.)

Table 8-2.   RECAPTURE PREMIUM: STRAIGHT LINE VERSUS SINKING FUND

Note the impact of using the straight line method or the sinking fund method on the capitalization rate. Assume a 30-year economic life:

	Straight Line (%)	Sinking Fund (%)
Real return	2.0	2.0
Inflation premium	6.0	6.0
Risk premium	2.0	2.0
Recapture premium	3.3	0.6
Capitalization rate	13.3	10.6

OTHER WAYS TO DEVELOP A CAPITALIZATION RATE

Two Alternative Approaches

Several other theories about the components making up a capitalization rate have been developed. Two of the better-known are mentioned here so that they may become familiar.

☐ *Band of investment approach.* One well-known approach is called the *band of investment approach.* This is a direct analogy to the weighted average cost of capital concept used in corporate finance. In the band of investment approach, the appraiser or analyst calculates the most proba-

Table 8-3. BAND OF INVESTMENT APPROACH

Debt	75% of total value
Interest cost	9½%
Equity	25% of total
Equity rate	11%

$$0.75 \times 0.095 = 0.07125$$
$$0.25 \times 0.11 = 0.02750$$
$$\text{Capitalization rate} = 0.09875 \text{ or } 9.875\%$$

ble mortgage interest rate that will be utilized for financing the property as well as the rate of return that is sought to be earned on the equity investment. Each of the rates is weighted by the proportion of total value they represent to determine the capitalization rate. In a typical case, the mortgage rate might account for 75 percent of the total value (this being a common loan-to-value ratio), while the equity rate would represent 25 percent of the investment. (See Table 8-3.)

☐ *Built-up method.* Another approach is the *built-up method*, which estimates a safe return (e.g., a return equal to that on Treasury bonds) and then adds to the safe return additional increments to compensate the real estate investor for (1) risk, (2) illiquidity (since real estate is much more difficult to dispose of than is a Treasury bond), and (3) management (since real estate carries a management burden which the real estate investor must either assume or pay for).

While these and several other approaches have validity and can add to an understanding of the valuation process, they do not lay out the theoretical components of the capitalization rate as clearly as the four-part method suggested above. (See Table 8-4.)

Table 8-4. BUILT-UP METHOD

Risk	3%
Illiquidity	4
Management	4
Capitalization rate	11%

Using Comparables

In the world of the practicing appraiser, the capitalization rate often is derived from the marketplace by using a comparable sales approach. In other words, the appraiser finds sales of similar properties. For these properties, the stabilized income and the sales price are determined.

Based on these, the capitalization rate is calculated. For example, if a sales price of $100,000 is associated with a $10,000 NOI, the capitalization rate is 10 percent ($\frac{\$10,000}{\$100,000}$ = 10%). Thus, in a manner similar to the market data approach, an appropriate overall capitalization rate for the particular type of property is derived from the marketplace. However, while this is a practical way to calculate the capitalization rate, it should always be checked by the theoretical approach suggested above in an effort to justify the market value on an economic basis. (See Table 8-5.)

Table 8-5. INCOME APPROACH TO VALUE

5811 Pine Street Los Angeles, California		
Expected rent per month: (from comparable rents in the neighborhood)		$625
Capitalization rate: Theoretical		
Real return	2%	
Inflation premium	6½%	
Risk premium	1%	
Recapture (sinking fund)	½%	
	10%	
From comparable sales of rental property		
Average sales price	126,600	
Average annual rent	7,500	
Rent/price	5.92%	
Value:		
Theoretical capitalization rate (625 × 12 months) ÷ 10%		$ 75,000
Market capitalization rate (625 × 12 months) ÷ 5.92%		$126,689
Rounded opinion		$126,700

* Note again that in the case of a single-family home, psychic income and social status are important considerations and might lead to a result where the market-data-determined value exceeded the rent-justified price under the income method.

Gross Income Multiplier Approach

The gross income multiplier (GIM) is a rule of thumb method of arriving at an indication of value. It involves multiplying gross rental income (rather than NOI) by a factor which varies according to the type of property and its location.

For example, an apartment building in a particular neighborhood may be valued at "6 times annual gross." Thus, if its GRR for one year amounts to $100,000, the value would be taken as $600,000. This approach also can be used to establish a rule of thumb rental for a private home where fair market value is known. For example, the monthly rental of a private home in a particular area might be set at one percent of the fair market value. Thus, if the value is $60,000 (established by the market data approach), the rental would be $600 per month.

As with all rules of thumb, the multiplier method should be used with caution, if at all. If all properties of a particular type had similar operating expenses and were identical in all respects except for the amount of rental income, the multiplier approach could be used with confidence. Obviously, this is not often the case, and the danger in the use of this approach is that unique features of the particular building being considered, whether good or bad, are not given proper weight.

Tax Considerations

It is important to note that a capitalization rate determined from the marketplace embodies a particular set of tax considerations, which reflects the tax position of whatever type of investor dominates the particular market. Obviously, these tax considerations may not be that of a specific investor who is seeking to evaluate a property. So while it is appropriate for an appraiser seeking a value which has general validity to use a market-established capitalization rate, the person about to make a decision in a particular investment situation should always develop an investment model incorporating income tax considerations, as is discussed in Part VII.

MORE SOPHISTICATED APPLICATIONS OF THE INCOME METHOD

The essence of the income method, as described in the preceding pages, is to establish NOI, identify the appropriate capitalization rate, and arrive at a value by dividing the first by the second. In actual practice, the income method is somewhat more complicated and has a number of variations. Three of these variations, known collectively as the *residual appraisal approach*, are:

- The building residual approach.
- The land residual approach.
- The property residual approach.

All of these share a single feature that distinguishes them from the simple income approach previously described. In each of them, the value of one element in the investment formula is known, and the value of another (the *residual* or leftover factor) is sought.

Building Residual Approach

In the building residual technique, the land value is known (as determined by the market data approach), and the object is to find the value of the improvements on the land.

To illustrate, suppose a projected office building is expected to generate $56,000 of NOI. The land is to be purchased for $100,000. The appraiser determines the market demands a return on investment of 10 percent on the total investment. Thus, of the total $56,000 NOI, $10,000 (10 percent of $100,000) is assigned to the land. (Since land does not depreciate, no recapture premium is necessary.) The balance of $46,000 is assumed to come from the building to be put on the land. With respect to the building, the market also wants an annual 2 percent return *of* investment (assuming a 50-year life using straight line recapture). Thus, the total annual return on the improvements is set at 12 percent. Knowing this and allocating $46,000 of NOI to the improvements, it can easily be calculated that the improvements value is $383,000. (See Table 8-6.)

Table 8-6. BUILDING RESIDUAL APPROACH (LAND VALUE GIVEN)

NOI	$ 56,000
Less: income attributable to land ($100,000 × 0.10)	10,000
Income attributable to building	$ 46,000
Building value ($46,000 ÷ 0.12)	383,333
Plus: land value	100,000
Market value	$483,333
Approximation	$483,000

Land Residual Approach

A more common situation than the one just described is where the cost of construction is known or can be estimated with reasonable accuracy and the object is to determine the value of the raw land. Here, the land residual approach is used. It can be illustrated by merely reversing the figures in the first example. (See Table 8-7.)

Table 8-7. LAND RESIDUAL APPROACH (BUILDING VALUE GIVEN)

NOI	$ 56,000
Less: income attributable to building ($383,333 × 0.12)	46,000
Income attributable to land	$ 10,000
Value of land ($100,000 = $10,000 ÷ 0.10)	100,000
Plus: building value	383,333
Market value	$483,333
Approximation	$483,000

The building and land residual approaches also can be used to estimate the market value of already improved properties. They will be used whenever the appraiser or analyst has determined, by some other method (e.g., market comparisons), the value of either component and desires to develop a value for the other.

Property Residual Approach

In using the property residual technique, the appraiser or analyst need not allocate the total NOI between the land and the building. The object here is to derive the value of the whole property after deducting a known factor representing recapture of the investment in the improvements.

Referring back to the previous example, if an NOI of $56,000 is known or can be calculated from improved property, an annual 2 percent recapture rate for the improvements is assumed, and the investor wants an overall 10 percent return on investment, the value of the entire property can also be calculated. (See Table 8-8.)

Table 8-8. PROPERTY RESIDUAL APPROACH

NOI	$ 56,000
Less: recapture (2% a year of $383,333 building value)	7,666
Annual income attributable to property (land and building)	$ 48,334
Property market value capitalized at 10%	$483,340
Approximation	$483,000

Recognizing Appreciation or Diminution of Value

One of the most basic problems with the simple formula $V = NOI/R$ as well as with all of the variations mentioned so far is the failure to account for appreciation or diminution of value in the property over the assumed period of ownership. In periods of rapid price changes, this can be an important factor in an investor's calculations. Witness the past decade of rapid inflation, during which real estate in general has risen sharply in price. Even though future value changes obviously are speculative, is there a way to consider them in an estimate of value?

There is such a method, representing a more sophisticated twist on the income approach to value. It is known as the *Ellwood technique,* named after the late L.W. (Pete) Ellwood, one of the deans of the appraisal profession. While this technique goes beyond the scope of the investigation in this book, one should be aware that the Ellwood tables do account for appreciation and diminution of value as well as for loan amortization. Still, even the Ellwood tables leave something to be desired in terms of their treatment of the time value of money and the special tax considerations applicable to individual investors.

SUMMARY

In this chapter, the simplified formula for the income approach to value was analyzed. Further, some of the more sophisticated variations used by professional appraisers and analysts were mentioned. The two key elements noted were: (1) estimation of stabilized NOI income and (2) selection of the appropriate capitalization rate. Both require experience and knowledge. The ability to accurately estimate NOI is the real test of one's familiarity with the market.

Of the three approaches to value, the income approach is the most similar to the analytical framework for determining the "winner of the game." However, remember that the income approach, as well as the two others, are generalized estimates of value, as distinguished from a value conclusion that is relevant to a particular investor who must judge an investment in the context of his own financial, tax, and investment circumstances.

When reviewing the three approaches to value, remember that step 5 in the appraisal process (as described in Chapter 6) is the *reconciliation* of the various value conclusions reached. The professional appraiser or analyst rarely *averages* the three conclusions. For any particular appraisal, one approach may be more appropriate than another and so deserving of more weight. (Table 8-9 illustrates a value conclusion based upon a reconciliation of the various approaches.)

The cost approach is useful in valuing properties which do not generate measurable income and have few comparables (e.g., the new city library). The market data approach is most useful when a substantial number of truly comparable properties can be located. The income ap-

Table 8-9. VALUE CONCLUSION

5811 Pine Street Los Angeles, California	
Cost approach	$122,400
Market data approach	126,600
Income approach	126,700
Conclusion relying primarily on the market data approach	126,000

proach is most logical when evaluating income-producing property, for here the investor is really buying a future flow of income.

The most difficult part is estimating NOI; it may be more of an art than a science. Appendix 8A shows the application of the appraisal techniques presented in the foregoing chapters to arrive at a value conclusion.

APPENDIX 8A

Appraisal Case

Given the information below, estimate the appraised market value of the described property by utilizing:

- The cost approach.
- The market approach.
- The income approach.

THE SOUTHHILLS GARDEN OFFICE*
RIVER CITY, TEXAS

Improvement Analysis

The subject property is located at the east corner of Southhills Drive and Bart Lane. The tract contains a total of approximately 22,692 sq. ft. or approximately 0.52 acre. The site is basically rectangular in shape and appears to be flat and level with adequate drainage. Adjacent land uses are

---

* The authors wish to express their thanks to James A. Baker for assistance in developing this case.

Mitchell Junior High School across Bart Lane to the northwest, a dental office to the northeast, additional office space to the southeast, and service stations located to the southwest and west across Southhills Drive and Bart Lane. The site has approximately 175 feet of frontage on Bart Lane and 104.87 feet of frontage on Southhills Drive exclusive of the corner curve with a radius of 15 feet.

A check of the HUD flood hazard maps for this area revealed that the subject property is not influenced by such a detrimental condition. All public utilities are available with water and sewer mains running along Bart Lane and Southhills Drive. Electricity and gas are supplied by River City and Southern Union Gas Company, respectively. Adequate fire plugs and fire protection are available to the area, and trash collection is available from the city as well as from commercial trash collection services.

As related to this office by the Building Inspection Department of River City, the subject tract is zoned "LR"—Local Retail, first height and area. The "LR"—Local Retail designation permits a variety of uses, including those permitted in single and multi-family classifications, "O"—Office zoning districts, banks, barber shops, cafeterias, restaurants, camera shops, drugstores, wearing apparel shops, gasoline service stations, grocery stores, etc. Based upon our physical inspection of the subject property and available plats, there appear to be no easements which adversely affect the tract. The site is not considered to suffer from any adverse influences and is assumed to be free and clear of all other encroachments and encumbrances.

The subject site is presently improved with three individual structures, hereafter referred to as building A, building B, and building C. A was just recently completed. The subject is legally described as Lot 1, block B, Baker Subdivision, Section 9, River City, Travell County, Texas, locally known as 3630 Southhills Drive. B and C were constructed ten years ago according to the Tax Department of River City. A physical inspection of the three structures was made on February 26, and the facts and figures pertaining to that are presented below.

A is said to have been constructed on a 4 inch monolithic and reinforced concrete slab foundation. According to the plans, there are to be four covered parking spaces on the first floor or ground level of the structure. In addition, the first level of the structure contains a garage or small warehouse of approximately 472 square feet at the east end of A. On inspection, this warehouse was found to have exterior walls of stone veneer covering standard sheathing. The interior of this space consists of unfinished stud walls and ceiling with the concrete slabs serving as its floor.

The second story of A is being partitioned for single-tenant occupancy office space. The interior finish is to consist of carpet in all offices with sheet vinyl in the restrooms and vinyl and fabric wallcovering. Lighting in the offices is to consist of tract lighting. There appears to be adequate fenestration (light) in the building using a combination of sliding and fixed double glazed aluminum windows. The exterior of the second floor is rough sawn cedar siding and is to be painted to match the two existing buildings, B and C. According to the plans, the gross building area upstairs is roughly 1,541 square feet with a covered balcony of 240 square feet. A plan of the stairs leading to the second story indicate that these cover an area of approximately 88 square feet. The building contains two air-conditioning units which are located to accommodate the east-west orientation of the structure.

B is ten years old and is basically a rectangular structure with exterior walls of painted redwood siding. The interior walls of the structure are also of redwood siding and floors are covered with commercial grade carpet. The ceiling is covered with acoustical tiles and perhaps needs some replacements. Heating in the building is accommodated by a forced air gas furnace and cooling is provided by one central air-conditioning unit. According to measurements, the gross building area is approximately 1104 square feet with a covered entry porch of approximately 72 square feet. The truss roof of the building is covered in cedar shakes.

C is a structure also covered primarily in redwood siding and is covered with a combination of built up tar and gravel roofs and truss roofs covered in cedar shakes. The interior of the space also makes use of some of the original redwood interior finishes although some of it has been finished with relatively high grades of wallpaper and sheet vinyl as leasehold improvements. The floors are covered in good to very good grades of commercial carpeting, as the present tenant is an interior decorator. Like *B*, the windows in *C* are primarily fixed (i.e., do not open) and there appears to be an abundance of single pane glass throughout the structure. Heating is provided by forced air from each of two gas fired furnaces and cooling is provided by two central air-conditioning units. Like *B*, *C* contains only one restroom. According to measurements and calculations, the gross area of the building is 1,219 square feet with a covered porch of 48 square feet.

On completion of the proposed remodeling, the subject property should contain approximately 10,000 square feet of asphalt paving and should be striped for parking 26 cars on-site. This is considered more than adequate and in conformity with the current city code. It is assumed that all electrical and plumbing work and material in the building presently under construction will meet the current code requirements of River City. All utilities are available to the site including underground electricity.

LAND COMPARABLES

Comparable 1

This sale transpired three years ago on November 24 and was purchased by the Heavenly Body Protestant Church from J.J. Walker, Executor, *et al.* The reported consideration for this tract was $261,350 or $1.20 per square foot. The tract consists of five acres, being fairly flat and level with good accessibility and commercial exposure. The site was vacant at the time of sale, and it was purchased for the construction of a church. The zoning at the time of the sale was LR—Local Retail, First Height and Area. The tract is located on the west corner of Highland Drive and Stork Avenue. Although somewhat larger than the subject site, it is felt to be similar in terms of corner influence.

Comparable 2

This transaction took place on May 14 five years ago. The site contains 14,646 square feet and is located at the south corner of Stork Avenue and Highland Drive. The site was vacant at the time of sale and has been subsequently improved with a Stop & Spend Food Store. The grantor was G. Brown and Associates, and the grantee was International Convenience Stores, Inc. The reported consideration for the tract was $64,000. The site was zoned LR—Local Retail, First Height and Area, and is felt to be comparable to the subject in terms of size; however, the site is felt to be slightly superior to the subject property due to its more heavily trafficked location.

Comparable 3

This sale occurred four years ago on April 23 and was purchased by Janet Fahar. The reported consideration for this site was $36,000. This tract is rectangular in shape and contains 11,240 square feet of land. The site was vacant at the time of sale, however, it is currently improved with a Doctors' Clinic. The zoning at the time of sale was LR—Local Retail, First Height and Area. The tract is located near the east intersection of Stork and Highland Drive along the southwest line of Stork Avenue.

Comparable 4

This transaction took place two years ago on May 19 and involved a tract measuring 21,380 square feet or approximately 0.4908 acres. This tract is irregular in shape as it "wraps" around the existing self service gasoline station which is located at the east intersection of Springs Road and Highland Drive. It has approximately 93 feet of frontage on the southeast line of Highland Drive and approximately 40 feet of frontage on the northwest line of Springs Road. The reported consideration for this tract was $58,000 in cash. However, the net usable area of this tract would consist of approximately 19,600 square feet, as approximately 1,780 square feet was given back to the grantor via a perpetual access easement. In addition, the buyer of the tract was required to construct a retaining wall along the north property line which amounted to approximately $12,075 of additional site improvements. This property was vacant at the time of sale and zoned LR—Local Retail, 1st Height and Area. It has been subsequently improved with an office/retail center which contains approximately 5,168 square feet of building area.

Comparable 5

This transaction took place in the fall five years ago. The tract involved 36,575 square feet of land located at the east corner of Highland Drive and Springs Road. The reported consideration was $135,000 cash. The property was vacant at the time of sale and zoned LR—Local Retail, First Height and Area; it is presently improved with a self-service gasoline station and was purchased for this intended use.

IMPROVEMENT COMPARABLES

Comparable A

Date:	September three years ago.
Location:	12701 Rosewood Boulevard.
Legal description:	10,905 square feet of land being lot 4A, Resub of lot 4, White Subdivision, Williams County, Texas.
Consideration:	$78,000 (cash) plus a $8,000 note Total = $86,000 or $39.38 per square feet of gross building area.
Land size:	87.5 feet × 119 feet.
Improvements and remarks:	This tract is improved with a one-story 2,184 square feet office building of which 2,100 square feet was rentable. Brick veneer construction three years old and 21 parking spaces. The building was rented at the time of sale at approximately $0.45 per square foot but is now all owner occupied. It was in good condition at the time of sale and was purchased by two real estate brokers.
GIM:	7.20.
NOI:	$7,950 (projected at market rents and 95 percent occupancy).
Overall capitalization rate:	9.24 percent.

Comparable B

Date:	October two years ago.
Location:	4019 Springs Road (south line of Springs Road, between Pac Highway and Highland).
Legal description:	1.06 acres out of the Mitchell Survey, River City, Travell County, Texas.
Consideration:	$160,000 or $47.63 per square feet of gross building area.

Land size:	1.06 acres (245 feet × 200 feet approximately).
Improvements and remarks:	These improvements consist of a concrete block and brick veneer building constructed in 1966. The building was built for dual medical occupancy and has somewhat of a similar floor plan to that of the subject (i.e., mirror of each). The building was in average condition at the time of sale, and the consideration did take into account the fact that the improvements were legal, but not conforming to the *A* zoning—Residential. The new owners do understand that they will not be able to add on to the existing structure without prior approval from the City by way of a special variance. Also, the sale was stimulated by a divorce of the grantor, and the terms might have been a bit more favorable for the grantees (i.e., $120,000 new loan plus $30,000, second lien carried by the grantor). Improvements = 3,359 square feet.
GIM:	8.79 (estimated on 95 percent occupancy at contract rent).
NOI:	$15,800 (at economic rents and 95 percent occupancy).
Overall capitalization rate:	9.9 percent (projected as above).

Comparable C

Date:	March two years ago.
Location:	Creek Boulevard between Anderson Road and Stork Avenue.
Legal description:	Lot 2, North Medical Addition, River City, Travell County, Texas.
Consideration:	$400,000 or $37.93 per square feet of gross building area; assumption of an existing note; $120,000 cash to the loan.
Land size:	315 feet × 175 feet or 55,265 square feet.
Improvements and remarks:	These improvements were constructed in 1970 and consist of an "L"-shaped brick veneer and wood frame medical clinic containing approximately 10,547 square feet. The building was 100 percent occupied by several doctors and a pharmacy subject to ten-year leases originated in 1970. The leases were averaging around $0.45 per square feet per month with the tenants be-

ing responsible for all utilities except trash. The gross rentals totaled $56,730 annually with the landlord paying taxes ($7,900), insurance ($1,700), maintenance and reserves ($1,900), and management ($3,000). Conversations with the new owner revealed the cash on cash return was approximately 13 percent. The new owner has spent between $15,000 to $18,000 remodeling the air-conditioning system and installing a new sprinkler system, but the building was in good condition at the time of sale.

GIM:	7.05.
NOI:	$46,873 ($40,100 after reserves and maintenance allowance).
Overall capitalization rate:	11.72 percent (10 percent after reserves and maintenance).

Comparable D

Date:	January two years ago.
Location:	7800 Creek Boulevard.
Consideration:	$570,000 or $35.86 per square feet of gross building area.
Site:	Irregularly shaped tract containing 3.65 acres; 442 feet frontage on Anderson Road, 508 feet frontage on Creek; building to land ratio is 1:2.02; on-site parking for approximately 450 cars.
Improvements and remarks:	This is a two-story masonry building, built four years ago; a gross building area of 158,957 square feet, modern construction, with central heat and air conditioning, carpet, in good condition at date of sale, with a net rentable area of 135,000 square feet. The above transaction involved an actual sale; however, the seller did retain a management contract on the building. Presently the building is 100 percent leased with rentals ranging from $6.00 to $9.00 per square foot/year with all bills being paid by the owner. Also, this contract was contingent upon the buyer occupying approximately 25 percent of the available space within the building.
GIM:	8.14 (estimated).
NOI:	$55,000 (projected at economic rents and 95 percent occupancy).
Overall capitalization rate:	9.7 percent.

Comparable E

Date:	March four years ago.
Location:	32nd and LBJ Highway, 1025 East 32nd.
Legal description:	13,800 square feet out of City Block 23, River City, Travell County, Texas.
Consideration:	$140,000 or $50.60 per square foot.
Land size:	100 feet × 138 feet.
Improvements and remarks:	These improvements involve a one-story brick veneer medical building originally constructed twelve years ago. This building was in good condition, and the sale involved a leaseback with the rental being structured against 10 percent of the total sales price and the lessee is the grantor. The lease is $1,400 per month or approximately $0.50 per square foot on a triple net basis. Improvements = 2,767 square feet.
GIM:	8.33.
NOI:	$16,800.
Overall capitalization rate:	12 percent.

Comparable F

Date:	February three years ago.
Location:	406 East 11th Street.
Consideration:	$300,000 or $41.99 per square foot of gross building area.
Site:	Rectangular inside tract containing 14,839 square feet; sloping terrain; minor landscaping; fronts major artery; building to land ratio is 1:2.
Improvements and remarks:	A twenty-year-old owner-occupied two-story masonry building built in 1957; contains approximately 7,144 square feet of modern construction; central heat and air; carpet; paved parking for fifteen cars; average condition at date of sale.
GIM:	8.73 (estimated on $0.40 per square foot net rent).
NOI:	$34,300.
Overall capitalization rate:	11.4 percent.

RENT COMPARABLES

Rent Comparable 1

Oval Square has been completed in the last year, located just east of the intersection of Highland Drive and Springs Road. This is an office-retail strip with a new rentable area of approximately 5,100 square feet. Last year at this time, the retail tenants in this space were generally renting from $0.55 to $0.65 per square foot per month or $6.60 to $7.80 per square foot per year on a triple net basis (i.e., tenant paying pro rata share of all expenses) with the landlord being responsible for management and exterior building maintenance only. The office space within this center was leased for $0.55 per square foot on a triple net basis. All leases are designed on a triple net basis for a period of ten years, with two or three five-year options. These rentals are all against a 4 to 5 percent of gross sales (i.e., the tenant pays whichever figure is larger) on the retail space with no percentage rental on the office portion. In addition to this rental, a common area maintenance fee of $0.15 per square foot per year is assessed for the upkeep and maintenance of such areas as parking, exterior lighting for the center, and water for exterior use (i.e., upkeep of the center's landscaping).

Rent Comparable 2

Construction on Greybeard Center was just recently completed, with the developer revealing that it was approximately 60 percent preleased one year before completion. This center contains approximately 18,600 square feet of office space, approximately 15,000 square feet of retail space, and approximately 6,700 square feet of restaurant space. The leasing agent revealed that the office space rents from $0.60 to $0.65 per square foot per month for approximately 1,000 square feet; retail space will rent from $0.47 to $0.55 per square foot for 1,000 to 3,750 square feet; and the restaurant space has been leased for $0.83 per square foot per month on a fifteen-year lease, with two options open for negotiation. The office space is leased on five- to ten-year terms, with the retail space all being ten-year leases. The retail tenants are responsible for all utilities except for area lighting, along with a prorata share of taxes and insurance. The office leases are structured on a gross basis with lessor providing utilities, janitorial, and taxes and insurance for the base year.

Rent Comparable 3

Creek Office Building is located at 8705 Creek Boulevard. This building involves a two-story, garden office building that has a gross building area of 25,630 square feet with a net rentable area of 24,256 square feet. Talks with the owner-manager early last year indicated that the rents were ranging from $0.575 per square foot to $0.625 per square foot, depending upon the amount of space rented and terms of the lease. A recent conversation with the leasing agent indicated that most rentals at present are at $0.65 per square foot on one-year terms, with longer leases tied to the consumer price index. This space is leased from 350 square feet to 1,400 square feet, with the average tenant having approximately 800 square feet. The lessor pays all utilities and expenses. The building is well insulated but does have a lot of glass, and the majority of the exterior is masonry.

Rent Comparable 4

Construction of the Springs Office Park building was completed about six months ago and talks with the developer revealed that it was approximately 50 percent preleased six months before completion. This is a two-story, masonry office building containing approximately 16,776 square feet. The leasing agent revealed that the office space presently rents from $0.50 to $0.71 per square foot per month, with the tenants being responsible for all utilities. Also, there is a pass-through of about $0.015 per square foot per month in order to provide coverage for exterior maintenance, area lighting, project sign, etc., along with a pro rata share of janitorial service. These leases range from one to two years for leased area ranging from 387 square feet to 2,765 square feet. A discussion with the leasing agent indicated that utilities run from $0.04 to $0.07 per square foot in this solar-heated building.

Rent Comparable 5

Shamrock Office Building is located at 8301 Balcony Drive, northeast of the subject site. This property was completed five years ago and has approximately 62,842 square feet of net rentable area. This office park involves a one-story building, which is presently near 100 percent occupancy and in the summer of last year was rented from $0.50 to $0.65 per square foot, with the average leases running approximately $0.56 per square foot. Most of this office space is rented on one- to two-year leases, with the lessor paying all utilities and expenses. However, the manager revealed that most new leases are on three to five-year terms at $0.65 per square foot per month. The amount of space rented will range from 600 square feet to 5,000 square feet, with the amount of rent paid depending on the lease terms and conditions of business. This building is also masonry with an approximate ground area of 70,000 square feet, with on-site parking for approximately 400 cars.

Rent Comparable Operating Expenses

A summary of the operating expenses of the rent comparables revealed operating expense ratios ranging from 25 to 30 percent of GRR. In such cases, the landlord was generally responsible for real estate taxes (14 to 16 percent), maintenance (3 to 5 percent), management (5 to 7 percent), and property insurance (3 to 5 percent).

IMPORTANT TERMS

band of investment approach
building residual approach
built-up method
capital improvement
capitalization
contract rent
deferred maintenance
gross effective income (GEI)
gross income multiplier approach
gross possible income (GPI)
gross rental receipts (GRR)
Ellwood technique

inflation premium
lease concession
lease expiration schedule
market rent
net operating income (NOI)
operating expenses
property residual approach
real return
recapture premium
replacement reserve
risk premium
stabilized net operating income

REVIEW QUESTIONS

8-1. What is the distinction between gross rental receipts and gross effective income?

8-2. Why should an appraiser make sure stabilized NOI is being used in the income approach?

8-3. How would the existence of long-term leases affect the capitalization rate associated with an office building?

8-4. Differentiate between a return *on* capital and a return *of* capital.

8-5. From a theoretical point of view, why might the sinking fund method of calculating the recapture premium be more acceptable than the straight line method?

8-6. How is the gross income multiplier used to estimate market value?

8-7. When must the appraiser make sure he uses the market rent when appraising an income property?

8-8. How will the preparation of a lease expiration schedule aid the appraiser in accurately estimating an appropriate stabilized NOI?

8-9. Should management fees be included in the operating expense statement when management responsibility is being assumed by the property owner?

8-10. Why might an appraiser find the interest earned on U.S. Treasury bonds helpful in estimating a capitalization rate?

IV
Marketing, Brokerage, and Management

9
Marketing

T HE MARKETING FUNCTION, broadly defined, is the process of anticipating society's needs and producing or distributing goods and services to satisfy those needs. For the average business, it boils down to, "It's not worth anything if it can't be sold."

In real estate, the product sold is space (over time with certain services). The person who buys or rents space either wants to use it (e.g., a family buying a house or a retailer renting a store) or wants to hold it as an investment and lease it out to others to use (e.g., an investment group buying an office building).

In this part, some general concepts involved in marketing real estate are introduced, and some techniques used to market particular types of properties are considered. Other aspects of the broad marketing function are discussed in appropriate chapters throughout the book, particularly demand analysis in Part VIII. In Chapter 10, the mechanics of brokerage are covered (drawing heavily on the legal framework for a real estate conveyance as depicted in Chapter 5). Finally, Chapter 11 deals with ongoing management, operation, and the service element associated with the use of real estate.

What is discussed in this chapter is the subject of how buyers and sellers, or landlords and tenants, are brought together—the linkages in our study of the real estate industry.

TYPES OF MARKETING STUDIES

It is appropriate at this point to summarize the different steps of the entire marketing function. They are described below in terms of the various studies utilized in the real estate industry:

- Market study.
- Feasibility study.
- Marketing study.

Market Study

A *market study* typically analyzes general market demand for a single type of real estate product (e.g., apartments, shopping centers, or office buildings) within certain geographic bounds. The study considers both the present and future demand for the particular type of land use as well as the present and future supply of competitive facilities. A study of the demand for office space in downtown Detroit would be considered a market study.

The final product of the market study is an *absorption schedule*. This schedule lists the expected demand for new product over time (e.g., 2 million square feet of office space annually) as well as the expected price range (e.g., rental at $12 or $15 per square foot).

Feasibility Study

The feasibility study seeks to determine whether a *specific* real estate project or program can actually be carried out successfully in a financial or investment sense. Thus, feasibility studies nearly always involve computing likely rates of return on investment (ROI) for a particular use planned for the land. A project can be marketable but not feasible. For example, the absorption schedule might indicate that a particular amount of square footage proposed to be developed at a given site might be rented quickly at certain rental levels. However, the construction costs, the time lag, and all other costs involved in purchasing and developing the site might reduce profitability below acceptable investment return levels. Both market and feasibility studies are considered in detail in Part VIII, which covers real estate development.

Marketing Study

The final step, when the choice of use has been made and the development has begun, is the marketing study. This is a plan, with detailed methods and techniques, for selling or leasing the space. This stage in the overall marketing process is the focus of this chapter.

Marketing of for-sale properties, such as single-family homes or condominium units, occurs within a fixed time period (anywhere from ninety days to three years), since once the properties are sold, the developer or previous owner is usually out of the picture. By comparison, marketing of rental properties is a continuing process. In the case of motels, hotels, and other "hospitality facilities," marketing is done continuously since space must be sold each day.

ELEMENTS OF A MARKETING PLAN

A marketing plan or marketing strategy may be an elaborate blueprint for the sale of millions of dollars worth of homes, condominiums, or commercial space over a period of years involving the expenditure of hundreds of thousands of dollars. At the other extreme, it may be prepared by a property owner who scratches some ideas on the back of an envelope. But all of these marketing plans should have some elements in common:

☐ *First,* marketing strategy involves defining the objective. Is the goal to rent a single-family house, sell 150 projected homes in a new subdivision, lease apartments in a new building, or sell a distressed property that is on the verge of bankruptcy?

☐ *Second,* is the goal strictly profit maximization, or does the decision-maker have a residual interest in the long-term success (including the social aspects) of the project?

☐ *Third,* the potential pool of tenants or buyers must be identified. This is a refinement of the market absorption schedule previously described. The primary market can be the immediate neighborhood, urban area, state, or entire nation (as in the case of sales of building lots or raw land in a western or southern resort area). This process of market segmentation is critical for the rest of the marketing plan because the plan is largely a function of the needs, desires, and characteristics of the defined market segment.

☐ *Fourth,* a list of the marketing techniques that are available must be compiled. These techniques may include the following:

- A sign at the property, often the only marketing aid needed when demand is very high.
- Classified or space advertisements in local newspapers.
- Billboards.
- Printed brochures.
- Radio or television time.
- Direct mail.
- "Cold" canvasing (i.e., contacting all the individuals in a neighborhood by telephone or door-to-door solicitation).

Financial Resources and Sales or Leasing Schedules

In choosing the particular marketing techniques to be utilized, the seller or his agent must bear two important considerations in mind. One is the financial resources available for marketing. The other is the sales or leasing schedule, which is necessary for the project to succeed financially. This last consideration, relevant only in the case of a large marketing program and partially determined by the absorption study referred to earlier in this chapter, is simply the rate at which the particular property for sale or lease can be marketed in a given locality (e.g., six single-family homes in a specific subdivision can be sold each month).

The sales or leasing schedule is important because the longer it takes to market the properties, the higher will be such carrying costs as interest, real estate taxes, and selling costs. Aggressive marketing can usually increase the absorption rate somewhat. However, basic factors determining demand will put limits on any increase, at least in the absence of substantial price concessions which the developer will seek to avoid, except in extreme cases.

SELLING THE PROPERTY

One question frequently asked is, "Can personal selling be taught?" Undoubtedly, certain natural gifts can make a person a very effective seller. However, these gifts alone are rarely enough; also essential is a knowledge of the product, the user, and the market as well as familiarity with the selling techniques appropriate for the product. This entire book is about the product and its market. Here, the focus is on specific techniques for marketing different types of real estate.

RESIDENTIAL PROPERTIES

The overwhelming percentage of marketing transactions involve the sale or rental of residential space, whether single-family houses (see Figure 9-1), condominiums, or apartment units.

New Single-Family Houses

Each year, around one million new single-family homes are built in the United States. While in any given year sales may be somewhat above or below the number of starts, it is obvious that a tremendous merchandising effort must be put forth by developers each year to dispose of their inventory.

Except in times of abnormal demand, a large-scale advertising campaign must be mounted, and many prospective purchasers must be attracted to the development to be interviewed and see the model homes.

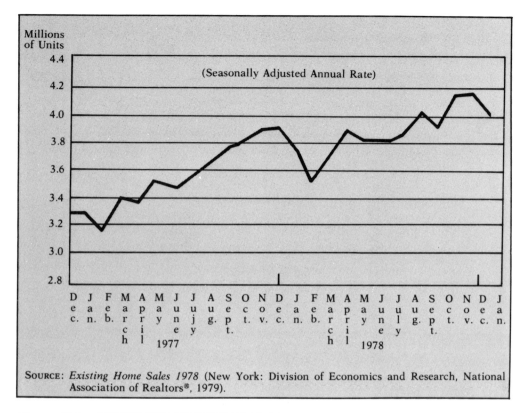

Millions of Units

(Seasonally Adjusted Annual Rate)

SOURCE: *Existing Home Sales 1978* (New York: Division of Economics and Research, National Association of Realtors®, 1979).

Figure 9-1. EXISTING SINGLE-FAMILY HOME SALES FOR THE UNITED STATES

Even here, the differences between selling real estate and selling other kinds of property are evident in two particular respects.

☐ *First,* even the most interested prospect frequently will require a fair amount of personal attention by the broker or salesperson in order to create that atmosphere of confidence necessary to induce the purchaser to enter into what undoubtedly will be one of the largest transactions of his lifetime.

☐ *Second,* a purchaser must be "qualified"—that is, he must have sufficient resources for the down payment and a credit rating that will justify a first mortgage loan that will represent 80 percent or more of the total price.

Success in merchandising new homes often depends in large part on the ability of the broker or salesperson to analyze the space needs as well as the financial position of the purchaser and to put together a purchase that will convince both the purchaser and the lender that acquisition of this home by this buyer makes good sense.

Resales of Single-Family Houses

While a large number of new homes is sold each year, the number of annual resales of existing homes is even larger. For example, in 1978, 3.9 million resale transactions took place, a 9 percent increase over the previous year. In dollar terms, the volume of resale activity in 1978 amounted to $217 billion, 27 percent above the year earlier total. (See Figures 9-1 and 9-2.)

The rapid rise in dollar volume as compared to the number of resales is explained by the rise in the median sales price of a single-family home. This jumped from $42,900 in 1977 to $48,700 in 1978. The great majority of these transactions are consummated through real estate brok-

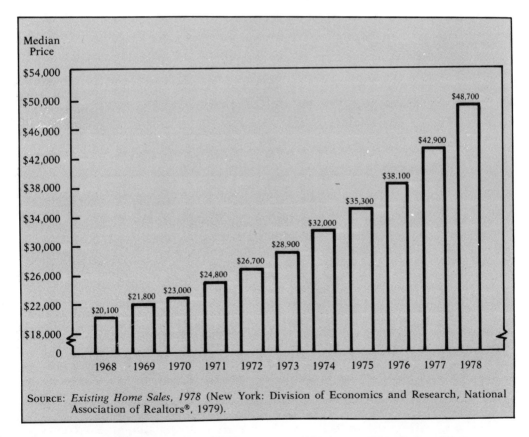

SOURCE: *Existing Home Sales, 1978* (New York: Division of Economics and Research, National Association of Realtors®, 1979).

Figure 9-2. MEDIAN SALES PRICE OF EXISTING SINGLE-FAMILY HOMES FOR THE UNITED STATES

ers, who earn their major source of commissions in this type of marketing. Unlike the sale of a large number of homes in a residential subdivision, the sale of an existing house calls for a much more personal relationship between agent and owner, if only because listings of existing houses are more varied than those in a single new subdivision.

Role of the Agent   Once a house is "for sale," the role of the agent generally can be divided into three different stages:

☐ *Preparing the house for sale.* Often, the first step for the broker to take is to persuade the owner to offer the house at a price close to its estimated market value. Many owners, perhaps understandably, consider their house more valuable than it really is, and it may require several weeks of little or no activity to convince the owner that the asking price is unrealistic.

The agent also will inspect the property and suggest necessary repairs and such cosmetic improvements as mowing the lawn and painting the outside of the house. The agent will be interested only in curable physical and functional depreciation, as discussed in Chapter 7, because these expenditures can be justified by the anticipated increase in the sale price.

Next, the agent will establish all the terms and conditions of the offer to sell. These include:

- What the price is.
- Whether any existing financing may be taken over by the buyer.
- Whether the seller is willing to provide any financing by a purchase money mortgage.
- Which appliances and other personal property go with the property.
- What the amount of the agent's compensation is.
- What the date of occupancy is.

☐ *Marketing the house.* The agent then proceeds to market the property. A "for sale" sign may be put on the property and a classified ad may be placed in the local newspaper. (See **9-1.**) The agent may hold an "open house," with the property open for inspection by potential buyers with the agent or an associate on the premises.

☐ *Negotiating the sale.* Only rarely will the prospect accept the seller's offer as stated. A certain degree of serious negotiation takes place most often over the price but also over other items such as (1) the personal property to accompany the sale, (2) the date of closing (the seller often wishing to delay until a new residence can be found while the buyer may be eager to take occupancy prior to the beginning of the school year or because the buyer's residence already has been sold), and (3) whether the seller will guarantee that the plumbing, heating, and electrical systems are in good working order or will repair them, if not.

9-1. WHAT SHOULD A CLASSIFIED ADVERTISEMENT CONTAIN?

The National Association of Realtors® National Marketing Institute, an affiliate of the National Association of Realtors®, reports that buyers say they want to read about the following in a residential property advertisement:

Information	Percentage
Geographic area	67
Price and terms	66
Number of bedrooms	58
Condition of property	55
Convenience to schools	52
Convenience to shopping	45
Convenience to churches	45
Number and size of closets	42
Size of lot	38
Number of bathrooms	36
Taxes	34

It is here that the agent or salesperson must tread a narrow line. The agent's primary loyalty is to the seller, who is the agent's principal. But, at the same time, the agent must create a feeling of confidence and even confidentiality with the purchaser. In addition, the agent must be careful to avoid making statements to the purchaser that go beyond mere "puffing" (sales talk) and become representations of fact. If the facts turn out to be otherwise, the agent may become liable for misrepresentations.

On the successful execution of a sales contract, the agent will often assist the purchaser in obtaining financing through a local lender and will continue to act as an intermediary between the parties during the contract period. Finally, the agent follows up with both buyer and seller after the closing to handle potential problems and develop referral business.

Condominium Projects

The rapid growth of condominiums as a form of housing is due to the fact that they combine the status of ownership and tax advantages with "maintenance-free living." Cooperative ownership, in those areas of the nation where it is popular, offers some of the same advantages.

Marketing both of these types of housing is essentially the same as marketing new single-family homes. The major difference is that the condominium buyer is often much less aware of the legal aspects of condominium living. Therefore, it is important that the agent or salesperson make clear that the owner of a condominium unit has a close relationship with co-owners, because of the joint ownership of common areas and the need to manage the entire project in the interests of all.

Apartment Rentals

The final major category of marketing residential space is the leasing of units in rental buildings. Since this is often the function of the property manager, discussion of this form of marketing is deferred until Chapter 11.

INCOME PROPERTIES

Marketing income properties involves two quite different types of transactions. The first is the *sale* of an income property (office building, apartment building, or shopping center, etc.) to investors who expect to hold the property for rental income or to space users who prefer to buy rather than rent space needed to carry on their trade or business. The other type of transaction is *rental* of space in an income property, almost always to space users such as business tenants, retail operations or service firms.

Sales

The purchaser of an income property typically is more sophisticated than the single-family buyer, and tax consequences become much more important in this type of transaction. And since the market for income properties—particularly large ones—is much smaller than for residential ones, the income property agent often will use a "rifle approach" rather than a "shotgun approach" in seeking out prospects. Still, the basic principles of marketing apply just as well to the sale of a multi-million-dollar office building or shopping center as they do to the sale of a single-family home.

Types of Purchaser   Purchasers of income properties can be grouped into three general categories. The first is the individual or small business firm seeking a property for use in a trade or business. The agent performs much the same function in this type of transaction as in the sale of a residential property except that a much more detailed knowledge of the buyer is usually required.

Next is the institutional purchaser seeking to develop a portfolio of income properties. Examples of this type of purchaser include: (1) life insurance companies, with large real estate equity interests as well as mortgage portfolios, (2) real estate investment trusts (REITs), which hold real estate just as mutual funds hold common stocks, (3) large public partnerships, which syndicate interests in real estate to hundreds or even thousands of individual investors, and (4) pension funds, although their expanding real estate assets still represent a minute portion of their total capital.

These clients are generally looking for relatively safe investments and often are more interested in cash flow than tax shelter. Here, the agent must know the client's needs and present the transaction in a fairly sophisticated manner. These institutions are generally conservative and typically use agents whose personal manner corresponds to this conservative bias.

Finally, and falling somewhere between the first two categories, are individuals and smaller syndicates which are made up of a number of investors, frequently local professionals and businessmen, who wish to own one or more properties for investment purposes. Frequently, the agent himself may be a member of such a syndicate, sometimes acting as the general partner responsible for choosing and managing the properties of the syndicate. In such situations, tax considerations are often very important. Some of the clients will be very sophisticated in financial affairs, while others will be relatively naïve, and the agent must present the transaction accordingly.[1]

Rentals

Marketing strategies to rent space in an income property will depend largely upon the type of tenant that is required. (See ███9-2███) When retail space is sought to be leased, the broker must determine the kinds of retail operations that might be suitable and make an effort to contact or locate business concerns within the area that might be interested in moving or expanding to a new location.

In the case of an office property, the prospective market is much broader since an office tenant is much less likely to require a precise location than a retail operation. Put another way, office space is much more *fungible* than retail space, where even a difference of a few feet may be important. In the office building situation, the quality of the constructed space is more likely to be able to offset a locational disadvantage. The retailer, conversely, demands a location which is convenient (in every sense of the word) to trade clients.

SPECIAL PROPERTIES

Some types of property, because they require special know-how on the agent's part or because only a limited market exists for the property, are handled by specialists. The selling fee or commission in these situations

---

[1] In the recent past, various efforts have been made to establish a real estate exchange similar to the stock exchanges. One such exchange is the American Real Estate Exchange (AMREX). AMREX conducts sessions in various cities around the country at which information about various properties is flashed on screens around the room. An interested purchaser then goes to a table on the exchange floor where he is put in touch with the seller with whom private negotiations may take place.

9-2. LOCATING PROSPECTIVE TENANTS

The agent can use a variety of techniques to develop a pool of prospective tenants:

☐ *Door-to-door canvas.* Representatives of the developer may seek to contact personally every office tenant in every building around a new project, seeking any indications of interest in new space.

☐ *Telephone canvas.* Alternatively, the agent may, by using a reverse telephone directory, call every office tenant within the vicinity. If the call evinces any interest by the prospect, a follow-up meeting is arranged.

☐ *Distant prospects.* Demand for space also may come from areas outside the local market. This requires that the successful agent have extensive contacts that can be utilized for this type of marketing.

☐ *Letter of intent.* A prospect who shows any interest in new space is asked to sign a letter of intent which states, in effect, that "I have some interest in X square feet at $\$Y$ per square foot, and I sign this letter with the understanding that it is in no way legally or morally binding." The purpose of the letter is twofold: (1) The prospect has made some commitment, however minimal, toward considering a move when the space is available, and (2) these letters constitute some evidence of demand for space which may have some effect in connection with negotiations to obtain financing for the project.

☐ *The space study.* When a letter of intent has been obtained, the agent may offer to make a study of the prospect's current space. The objective is to present both the prospect and the developer with a clear picture of the space requirements and so make negotiations more fruitful for both sides.

often is negotiated for each particular transaction in recognition of the marketing expertise required and because of the extra time, effort, and expense usually involved. Some of the specialized areas are discussed below.

Vacation Homes and Building Lots

The second-home market has experienced periods of extremely rapid growth. Many second-home projects are sold in the same manner as any residential subdivision. However, because resort areas draw on a much larger market area (perhaps the entire nation), advertisements in national or regional media often are used. More significantly, buyer motivation usually is a combination of personal (vacation) use and investment for potential appreciation in value. Consequently, in this type of selling, the educational function of the agent is very important.[2]

---

[2] An even more specialized type of selling is required when "time sharing" is utilized.

Farms and Ranches

Farm and ranch brokerage is an important specialty because of the large amount of farm and ranch property in the United States and its importance in the overall economy. Such subjects as agricultural productivity, the cattle cycle, water rights, and pasture rights must be understood by the agent. Marketing can be expensive as properties are not clustered together in an urban area. Showing a farm prospect takes considerable time and getting to the second farm to be shown may take even longer.

Distressed Properties

This term is used to describe a for-sale project in which the developer is having difficulty with sales or any income property which is failing to show a positive cash flow or which has already been foreclosed by an unpaid lender. The object in such cases is either to sell the property as quickly as possible or mount a crash effort to fill up vacant space and put the property in the black. (See 9-3.)

Agents dealing with distressed properties often need special skills, particularly in mass merchandising techniques. For example, an auction is sometimes used to dispose of unsold units in a condominium; while buyers may obtain bargains, the ending of the developer's carrying charges for construction loan interest and real estate taxes may be his best alternative. Legal skills also are important both in dealing with foreclosure and handling disgruntled tenants.

SUMMARY

The composite market function in the real estate industry is very broad, ranging from preliminary market research and feasibility studies to "face to face" dealings with the purchaser. In this chapter, marketing has been discussed in a general way, with the intention being to introduce the major concepts and considerations in this area.

While the sales functions vary widely depending on the type of property, all require that the effective broker or salesperson have a good overall understanding of the product, an in-depth knowledge of the marketplace, and a good feeling for the objectives of the prospective purchaser.

Under this system, one may purchase a specific "time slice" (e.g., the first two weeks in July) instead of buying the entire unit. Thus, a single unit may have as many as 25 different owners (with two weeks set aside each year for maintenance and repair).

The great advantage of a time share is the much smaller investment required. In addition, several exchange services are available whereby the owner of a time share may exchange it for a stay at a different resort which is a member of the service.

9-3.　MARKETING DISTRESSED PROPERTIES

Here are three actual examples of how creative thinking can help a property in trouble:

☐ *Lower carrying costs.* An agent was asked to suggest ways of saving a condominium project that was selling at the rate of three units per month, with overhead and carrying charges gradually wiping out the builder's equity. Applying the principle that the buyer worries more about carrying costs than ultimate price, the agent increased the price by $2,000 and cut the mortgage interest rate to 7 percent. This jumped unit sales to 10 per month, an absorption rate that enabled the lender to get out whole.

☐ *Equity buildup.* In another case, a consultant was retained by a lender worried about slow sales in a new condominium. Believing that the problem lay in the 20 percent down re- quirement, the consultant suggested that buyers be permitted to take possession upon signing a contract, paying only a monthly charge equal to debt service under the mortgage. However, the initial monthly payments went toward the required 20 percent down payment; usually this required some time after which the permanent loan was funded and the monthly charge went to service the loan. During the buildup period, the developers paid the real estate taxes and the maintenance fees. As a result the condominium was a success.

☐ *Redesign units.* In yet another case, a three-bedroom townhouse project was drawing interest from young families and singles who found the units too large. A wall was removed, turning two bedrooms into a large bedroom suite. The project sold out at the same price within six weeks.

A specific discussion follows in Chapter 10 of brokerage and the mechanics of the marketing of real estate (i.e., selling space over time with certain services).

IMPORTANT TERMS

absorption
　schedule
feasibility study
fungible

market study
marketing study
"puffing"
time sharing

REVIEW QUESTIONS

9-1.　What specific information is provided by an absorption schedule?

9-2.　What is the critical difference between a market study and a feasibility study?

9-3.　As an agent representing a seller, how might you advise your client as to presale fix-ups and repairs?

9-4.　Why might the purchaser of an income property for investment purposes be more sophisticated than a single-family dwelling buyer?

9-5. Would you expect a retail tenant or an office tenant to be more concerned about the *exact* location when moving or expanding? Why?

9-6. What factors might affect a marketing campaign for vacation homes?

9-7. How might the concept of "time sharing" be utilized in marketing resort property?

9-8. List and explain the major elements of a marketing plan.

9-9. Identify some of the important information you would recommend be included in a classified ad for a single-family dwelling.

9-10. Why might an agent find it necessary to explain the legal ramifications of condominiums when selling property in that ownership form?

10

Brokerage

T HUS FAR, the accent in Part IV has been primarily on establishing a conceptual framework for understanding the marketing of real estate. In this chapter, *people* are the focus—either the principals (buyers and sellers) in real estate transactions or their agents (brokers and associated salespersons).

Of the various players in the real estate game, the one with the central role and the one whose function and relationships require the most explanation is the real estate broker. This chapter is devoted to a discussion of how the brokerage function is carried out.

HOW REAL ESTATE IS MARKETED

The term *marketing process* refers to the methods used to enable, assist, or encourage the sale of property and goods in the marketplace. (This follows directly from the marketing study outlined in the preceding chapter.) If marketing methods are examined strictly in terms of the people involved, three different methods of transactions can be identified:

☐ *Sales between principals directly.* Mail order sales by companies selling their own products are the most important example of sales between principals in the general economy. In the real estate industry, sales between the seller and the buyer directly are fairly common in the resale of private homes. Residential real estate advertisements frequently specify "for sale by owner" or "principals only." Another area of direct selling in real estate is by developers of residential or resort projects who use an in-house sales staff.

☐ *Sales by dealers.* This is by far the most common form of commercial transaction found in the general economy. A *dealer* performs an intermediary role between the producer of goods and the final consumer. In contrast to a broker, a dealer acquires title to goods to be sold. Most retailers are dealers. When it comes to big-ticket items, the automobile industry is the prime example of dealer-controlled commerce. Dealer sales in real estate are less common.

☐ *Sales by brokers.* A broker is an intermediary or middleman who brings together buyers and sellers of the same commodity or product and who receives a commission for services. The distinction between a broker and a dealer is that the broker does not have title to the brokered goods or property. In real estate, brokers play the major marketing role.

Suitability of Brokerage for Real Estate Transactions

Why is the method of brokerage so suitable for real estate? The reasons lie in the nature of the real estate asset.[1]

☐ *High cost.* Because a parcel of real estate generally costs a great deal to acquire, it is not feasible to sell most real estate through a dealer system. This would involve purchase by a dealer of a portfolio of real estate assets, that would then be held for resale at a profit. In practice, the cost of carrying the inventory would be too high.[2]

☐ *Unique asset.* Again, the uniqueness of real estate is an important consideration. Because of this, a parcel of property often must be seen or described to a very large number of people before a buyer for that precise parcel can be found. The property owner usually cannot sell the property personally for lack of a list of prospects or an office to which new prospects will be drawn. Brokers have both.

The one major exception to the uniqueness of real estate is illustrated by mass-developed building lots on vacant land, and large residential subdivisions with a single builder constructing new homes that are practically alike. And it is precisely these types of real estate sales that are often done directly between buyer and seller rather than through brokers.

---

[1] Note that this enumeration parallels the discussion of the unique aspects of real estate in the analytical framework developed in Part I.

[2] The one occasion when a dealership role often is assumed is when a lender acquires properties following defaults under mortgage loans. In these situations, the involuntary dealer normally is anxious to dispose of the properties as quickly as possible. Indeed, national banks which acquire properties through foreclosure proceedings are required by regulatory agencies to dispose of the property within a fixed period of time. Such property is listed separately on the bank's financial statement.

Another example of a dealer-type transaction is the residential trade-in program occasionally utilized by the real estate brokers to encourage resales. Under these programs, the broker agrees to purchase the present residence of a person seeking a new home—usually a more expensive one to which he is "trading up." The broker normally will not take title to the old house until after it has been listed with the broker and offered on the market for a specified period of time (e.g., ninety days).

☐ *Need for financing.* Most real estate purchases are financed in large part by third-party loans, typically from institutional lenders. Particularly in the residential market, the real estate broker performs an important function in keeping track of lending sources (usually local banks or savings associations) and knowing their particular requirements for mortgage loans.

☐ *Complex and difficult market.* Because of the uniqueness of every parcel of real estate, its high cost, its varied uses, and the need for outside financing in most cases, the marketing process is complex and difficult. Every transaction requires time-consuming face-to-face negotiation, as well as an understanding of legal documents, financial statements, etc. A trained broker is in a position to provide the needed assistance to buyers as well as sellers. An important point to note is that the broker usually knows the prices of all recent sales in the neighborhood, and so is able to judge the value of the present property by applying the market data approach.

DEFINING BROKERAGE

Just what is a broker? One statutory definition is that a *broker* is anyone "who, acting for a valuable consideration, sells, buys, rents or exchanges real estate or, in fact, attempts to do any of these things." Each of the fifty states has a statute requiring any person who performs a real estate brokerage function to obtain a license from the state prior to receiving any commission or fee. The rigor of the licensing requirements varies dramatically, ranging from states such as California and Texas, with very strong licensing laws, to some others where licensing is little more than a formality. (See 10-1.)

Licenses usually are of two types: (1) the broker's license and (2) the salesperson's license. The broker's license permits the holder to carry on any brokerage activities independently. The salesperson's license permits the holder to render brokerage services only in association with a fully licensed broker. In such cases, the commission is paid to the broker who then divides the commission with the salesperson.[3] Consequently, the typical brokerage office involves one or more brokers who are principals in the firm together with a group of salespersons who work either as employees or more frequently as independent contractors.[4] (Management of the brokerage office is discussed in Appendix 10A.)

---

[3] A broker cannot legally split a commission with an unlicensed person.

[4] The term *Realtor*® is often used synonymously with *real estate broker.* This is a misuse of the term *Realtor* which is a trademark designation for persons who are members of the National Association of Realtors® (NAR®), the leading brokerage association in the United States (described in more detail in Appendix 10B).

10-1.   REAL ESTATE LICENSING EXAMINATIONS

The various states set their own requirements for obtaining a real estate broker's or salesperson's license. The applicant normally must pass a written examination and must have completed a specified course of study and/or a period of employment in a brokerage office.

In 1970, a movement began to develop a professionally prepared uniform examination that could be offered by any state. This examination, known as the *Real Estate Licensing Examination* (RELE), is administered by the Educational Testing Service (ETS) in Princeton, New Jersey and is now used by over half of the licensing jurisdictions in the United States.

The uniform test comes in two different versions: (1) for salesperson license candidates and (2) for broker license candidates. A separate portion of the RELE, known as the *State Test*, covers the laws, regulations, and practices unique to each jurisdiction and so differs in each case.

Even though a state uses the RELE, it still sets its own prelicensing requirements. For example, the applicant may be required to have a minimum number of hours of real estate instruction from a qualified school.

Certain categories of individuals are exempt from the licensing requirements. While these vary among the states, the most common include:

- Individuals acting on their own behalf.
- Attorneys acting in the course of their law practice.
- Court-appointed administrators, executors, or trustees.
- Public officials in the course of their official duties.
- Employees of regulated utilities acting in the course of the firm's business.

The Broker as Agent

In describing the legal position of the broker vis-à-vis the other parties to the transaction, the key term is *agent*. An *agent* is one who represents or acts for another person, called the *principal*, in dealing with third parties.

The agent is in a *fiduciary relationship* with a principal. An agent acts only with the principal's consent and is subject to his direction and control. Whatever business a person can transact for himself may be delegated by him to an agent.

Agents generally fall into two classes:

- *Special agents* are authorized to perform one or more specific acts for the principal and no others. Real estate brokers normally are special agents.
- *General agents* are authorized to conduct all the business, or a series of transactions, for the principal within stipulated limits.

Creation of an agency generally is governed by the principles of contract law and may arise by written or oral agreement. However, most state statutes of frauds require the agent's authority to be in writing if a real estate contract or lease is involved. Less frequently, an agency relationship can be created by circumstances which give the agent justified reasons for believing the principal has created an agency. This is called *implied agency*. Finally, even when no express or implied agency actually exists, there may be an *apparent agency*. An apparent agency is created when the principal, by words or acts, gives third parties reason to believe that they may rely on someone as the agent of the principal.

An agency may be terminated by (1) expiration of the written agreement establishing the agency, (2) mutual consent of principal and agent, (3) revocation by the principal (except in certain cases where the agent has an interest in the transaction), or (4) operation of law, such as the death, insanity, or bankruptcy of either the principal or agent.

The obligations of the principal in the agency relationship are many. Among them are:

- Compensate the agent for services rendered.
- Reimburse the agent for expenses incurred.
- Indemnify the agent for certain losses and liabilities incurred in the course of the agency.

The agent's chief duties are:

- Loyalty to his principal.
- Obedience to the principal's instructions.
- Care in the performance of his duties.
- Accountability for the principal's money or property.
- Full disclosure to the principal of all material facts relevant to the purpose of the agency. (See 10-2.)

The specific methods for establishing the agent-principal relationship in real estate are discussed next.

LISTING AGREEMENTS

A *listing agreement* is often referred to simply as a *listing*. It represents a contractual relationship between the seller of property, who is the principal, and a real estate broker, who is the agent.

Approximately half the fifty states impose a requirement (as part of their statutes of frauds) that a broker may not sue for an unpaid commission unless the agreement is in writing. In the remaining states, an oral

10-2. THE FIDUCIARY RELATIONSHIP

A real estate broker is a fiduciary—that is, in a relationship of trust and confidence with his principal. As a consequence, the broker assumes obligations which are not present in the normal arm's-length business relationship.

Brokers have been held to have *breached* the fiduciary relationship to their clients for the following activities:

☐ *Secret profits.* If the broker stands to make any profit other than his commission, he must disclose the source of that profit to his principal or forfeit his commission, lose his profits, or be forced to pay both compensatory and punitive damages.

☐ *Undisclosed purchase for own account.* A broker must avoid an undisclosed dual agency for another or action for his own account. This might occur when a broker locates a property he feels is underpriced, buys it and immediately sells it to an unsuspecting buyer-client for a profit.

☐ *Failure to disclose an offer.* A broker may be liable in damages if he fails to inform the seller of an offer to buy regardless of whether the broker profited from the concealment.

A broker must also disclose to his principal any knowledge that a prospective purchaser may be willing to offer better terms than the submitted offer reflects.

☐ *Failure to disclose material information.* The broker must disclose all material matters within his knowledge. For instance, he must reveal any knowledge concerning recent sales of surrounding land, and whether the seller could obtain a greater profit by subdividing his property.

agreement is enforceable; however, it is a good idea to always have a written agreement to lessen the chance that a misunderstanding can arise on either side.

A listing agreement normally will contain the following particulars:

- Names of the parties.
- Services to be performed by the broker (e.g., obtaining a buyer or tenant for the principal's property).
- Description of the property.
- Seller's asking price and other material terms of the sale.
- Amount of commission and terms on which it is to be paid.
- Duration of the agreement.
- Type of listing.
- Signatures of the parties.

Types of Listings

Three types of listing agreements generally are utilized in the real estate industry: (1) open, (2) exclusive agency, and (3) exclusive right to sell.

□ *Open listing.* Under an open listing, the owner of property notifies the broker that it is being offered for sale at a specified price. It is understood that the broker will be entitled to a commission if—in a classic phrase used in the brokerage business—the broker procures a purchaser *ready, willing, and able* to purchase the property on the terms specified by the seller.

Generally, the courts have held that a ready, willing, and able buyer does not have to be one who accepts every condition laid down by the seller, since it is normal to anticipate that a certain amount of good-faith bargaining will take place once a basic agreement as to price has occurred. It is conceivable that a broker may become entitled to a commission, having procured a ready, willing, and able buyer, even though no contract of sale, for any reason, ultimately is signed. To avoid this possibility, some sellers insist that the broker agree in advance that the commission will not by payable *unless and until* a contract of sale is signed or title to the property passes to the buyer.

The open listing agreement is an example of a *unilateral contract.* The consideration for the seller's promise to pay a commission is the performance by the broker of the requested service: procuring a buyer. Until the service has been performed, the seller is free to revoke an offer to pay a commission. The offer cannot, however, be revoked under conditions amounting to fraud. Such a situation is where the seller rejects a buyer introduced by the broker, revokes the listing, and then begins negotiations with the same buyer.

The seller also may list the property with many different brokers or sell the property directly since no liability to pay a commission will arise until a broker actually produces a buyer, at which point the remaining listings will be revoked.

□ *Exclusive agency.* By this type of listing, one broker is given an *exclusive* on the property and the seller agrees that if any other broker procures a buyer, the exclusive broker nevertheless will receive a commission. Thus, the seller can retain another broker only at the risk of paying a double commission. The seller, however, can sell the property personally without paying a commission to the exclusive broker.

An exclusive agency listing is a *bilateral*, rather than a unilateral, *contract*—that is, promises are exchanged, with the broker's promise considered to be an agreement to devote time and effort to selling the property. Consequently, the seller cannot revoke the listing at will and should have the agreement specify a term (frequently, ninety days). If the agreement fails to specify a term, the law assumes a *reasonable period*, which means that ultimately a court may have to be called upon to decide when the listing ends.

A seller normally will agree to an exclusive agency for a property that is likely to be difficult to sell because of its location or condition or when

10-3. COMMISSION SPLITS

Assume that a 7 percent commission is earned on the sale of a $100,000 home, so that the total commission is $7,000. If the home had been sold through a multiple listing service by a broker other than the listing broker, the commission must be divided between them.

Assume further, for the sake of simplicity, the split is 50-50, so that each broker receives $3,500. Within each firm, a further division may take place between the salesperson who listed/sold the property and the broker for whom the salesperson works. Usually this split is set forth in an agreement between the salesperson and the broker.

If this split also is 50-50, then each salesperson (who either obtained the listing or brought about the sale) receives $1,750 (one-quarter of the commission), while each broker receives the same amount.

The broker's share must cover the cost of office operations, including rent, secretarial costs, and advertising. In addition, if the broker is a member of one of the franchise chains now operating, such as Century 21, Red Carpet, Homes for Living, or Electronic Realty Associates, a portion of the broker's share of the commission must go to the parent organization.

there is a dearth of buyers. In these cases, an effective selling job by the broker may require vigorous efforts to find prospects as well as expenses for advertising, the preparation of brochures, and the like. A broker, understandably, will be reluctant to expend time and incur costs without the protection of an exclusive agency.

☐ *Exclusive right to sell.* This type of listing is exactly the same as an exclusive agency with one important exception: Even if the seller finds a buyer directly, a commission will be payable to the exclusive broker. Most courts will not recognize the existence of an exclusive right of sale unless the agreement specifically sets forth the broker's right to be paid under any circumstances.

An exclusive right to sell is sometimes required in order to use a multiple listing service. In such cases, where brokers share listings, the selling agent needs to be assured of compensation when working through a subagency agreement with the listing broker. (See 10-4.)

Multiple Listing Service

A multiple listing service (MLS) differs from the three types of listing just described. MLS is the pooling of listings by a group of sales agents. In the most common situation, agents negotiate exclusive right to sell listings and then notify a central service group of the listings. This central service group periodically disseminates information about all listings available in the market. In this manner, any agent through subagency agreements can sell the listing of any other agent and be assured a portion of the commis-

10-4. PROTECTING THE BROKER

> Seller Donahoe gave broker Calka an exclusive right of sale providing:
>
> ☐ The seller would refer any *prospective purchaser* of whom he had knowledge during the term of the listing to the broker;
>
> ☐ In the event of sale by the seller during the term of the listing or within twelve months thereafter to any person with whom the broker negotiated during the term, a commission would be payable.
>
> During the listing period, Vollmar approached the seller, Donahoe, and asked if it was his farm that was up for sale and the selling price. When told that it was $130,000, he stated he would not pay that much for a farm. However, he told Donahoe to contact him if Calka didn't sell the farm. Donahoe never advised Calka of this prospective purchaser. One day after the expiration of the listing, Donahoe and Vollmar reached an agreement at a price of $110,000. Calka then sued for his commission.
>
> A Michigan court held that when Donahoe promised to refer any prospective purchaser to Calka, he was bound to do so. The court said that a "prospective purchaser" is not necessarily one who is willing to pay the asking price. He may be one who wants to bargain. The broker was entitled to negotiate with him in his efforts to make the sale. The failure of the seller to advise the broker of Vollmar's inquiry was a breach of the contract. Since the subsequent sale was consummated within the twelve-month period stated in the contract, Calka would then have been entitled to his commission. The seller was required to pay Calka his commission.

sion as specified in the information disseminated. From the seller's perspective, MLS provides for wider exposure of the property than would be possible using a single broker. (See Figure 10-1 and **10-3.**)

Objectives of the Sales Agent

The vast majority of MLSs are sponsored by local real estate boards and tend to be dominated by residential listings. The sales agent wants not only an exclusive right to sell but also an exclusive right to sell a listing which *will* sell and consequently generate a commission. In this regard, price, terms, and seller motivation make up the listing triangle. Essentially, the more competitive the price, the longer the term of the listing (the amount of time in which the agent has a right to receive a commission for finding a buyer) and the higher the seller's motivation, the more likely the listing will generate a commission for the listing agent. If the sales agent spends time and money marketing a particular listing which expires without a sale, the agent loses both time and money.

Obtaining Listings

The job of the listing agent is first to gain the confidence of the seller. The agent must then establish what can be done for the seller in marketing

RESIDENTIAL FORM

73508	Add 3405 Suncrest Drive			**$** 69,500	
Legal Lot		Block E	Buckingham Ridge	Section 2	
Bdrm. 3 or 4*	Baths 2	FPA No	Age 3 Yrs.	1st Lien $	
LR 1 Den 1	Zoned A	Lot 70 x 180		Type CV P 397.00	
Sep.Din. N	Liv.Din.	Faces E	Corner No	Yrs.Left 27 Int. 9%	
Trees s	Sewage c	Street P	Pool Yes	Mortgagee Franklin Savings	
Const. Stone	Found. S	Blks. to Bus 1	Fence Privacy	Com't.Amt. $	
Stories 1	Roof C			Type	
Floors C/T	LD No	Elem.Pleasant Hill		How Sell C, A, CV	
Air Cond. C	Heat C	Jr. Travis Hts.		Owner Carry No	
Garage 2	C/P	Hi Sch. Crockett		Title Evid. TP at S	
Wash Conn. Yes	DW Yes	TAX-City 279.65		Trans. Fee	
Dryer Gx E	DSP Yes	Sch. 380.70		Area 6 WD	
FP in SLA	R BI	St.&C.		How Show CF-LB	

Remarks Large, nicely landscaped lot with a 16' x 32' above ground pool*.
Study off living room can be 4th bedroom. Beamed front room and master
bedroom. Covered patio.

Occupant	Ph.	Key	Poss. Closing
Owner		Ph.	
Listor		Ph.	
REALTOR		Ph.	

Figure 10-1. SAMPLE OF A MULTIPLE LISTING

the property. The agent must show that it is good business to deal with an agent. Finally, the seller must be motivated to act—that is, to sign a listing agreement.

Once the listing is obtained, the property must be sold. This requires a knowledge of the consumer's buying process.

THE BUYING PROCESS

The effective sales agent must know the customer, including where the customer is in the buying process—whether he is merely a shopper or a ready buyer. The buying process can be described in four general stages:

☐ *The first stage is the client-awareness stage.* Here, a general need is perceived by the client, but heavy pressure is not warranted on the part of the sales agent.

☐ *The second stage finds the client in the market and actively gathering information.* Here, the role of the effective salesperson is to provide that information and, in the process of providing that information, become established as a credible source.

☐ *The third stage is a decision-oriented stage.* Here, the client is ready to buy, and it is incumbent on the sales agent to provide the product, motivate the client to action, and close the transaction.

☐ *The final stage is the post-purchase period.* Here, the sales agent must follow up to assure that the client is receiving the level of satisfaction expected when the purchase decision was made. Follow up is essential for the salesperson to develop a good referral system which is one of the keys to longevity in real estate sales.

At this point, the reader should recall the particular functions performed by the listing and the selling broker. This will be useful in judging the adequacy of broker compensation as well as in understanding the closing, the next two topics discussed here.

COMPENSATING THE BROKER

The broker is usually paid a commission based upon some percentage of the final sales price (or total rentals in the case of a lease). To understand the commission arrangement adequately, three questions must be answered:

- Who pays the commission?
- How much is the commission?
- When is the commission paid?

Payment of the Brokerage Commission

In the great majority of cases, the owner (seller) of the property retains the broker and has the obligation to pay the brokerage commission. It may sometimes happen, however, that the buyer enters into an agreement with the broker and promises to pay a commission. This might occur where the buyer is eager to obtain a particular parcel of property which is not currently on the market or where the buyer is seeking an unusual and difficult-to-find property.

The Amount of the Broker's Commission

For many years, local real estate boards published a schedule of recommended commission rates for various types of transactions. Beginning in the 1970s, a series of federal antitrust complaints and legal proceedings resulted in the withdrawal of such schedules. Consequently, principals may feel more free today to negotiate commissions than in the past.

As a matter of practice, many sellers tend to accept the "going rate" in the community. The commission rate today usually ranges between 5 and 7 percent in the case of residential properties. The same range may apply to income properties up to a specified amount of the sales price (say, the first $100,000), declining in stages as the price increases. A 10 percent or higher rate may apply to raw land where the purchase price is typically lower.

In income-producing, as distinguished from single-family residential, transactions, the commission often is directly related to the specific services rendered by the broker. The more valuable the broker's services, the higher the commission.

When dealing with brokers, remember that a broker must invest a good deal of time and effort in many transactions that never close and for which the broker receives no commission. Consequently, it becomes easier to understand the occasional "quick deal" that brings an immediate commission to the broker. Furthermore, the gross commission must often be divided among several different people, with each only receiving a small share of the total, some of whom will have incurred significant out-of-pocket expenses. At the same time, a hard-working and aggressive individual can earn a great deal of money as a broker.

When the Broker's Commission Is Paid

In the absence of a specific agreement, the broker is legally entitled to a commission upon procuring a ready, willing, and able purchaser, even though no final transfer of title ever occurs. It is obvious that interpreting "ready, willing, and able" in such situations can lead to disputes and litigation.

To avoid this type of controversy, most principals and brokers prefer to spell out in a written agreement the precise conditions on which, and the time when, the commission will be paid. For example, the agreement may provide that the commission will not be payable if title does not pass for any reason whatsoever. This is the language most favorable to the seller. The broker may object that if the transaction fails because of the willful default of the seller, the broker should not lose the commission, and the language may be amended accordingly. Other variations of the basic language can narrow or enlarge the possibility that the seller may have to pay a commission, notwithstanding failure of the transaction. Still, in most cases, the broker is not paid until a successful closing is held.

THE CLOSING

At the end of the third stage in the buying process, the sales contract is executed. After financing and other arrangements are made and title is checked (see Chapter 5), the participants meet for the closing. The typical single-family closing requires all of the following individuals. They will not all be at the closing, but all must perform a function prior to conclusion of a successful closing[5]:

Participant	*Closing Functions*
Lawyer	May handle closing Drafts deed, note, mortgage, etc. Checks title records Records deed, note, etc., after closing
Title company	May handle all four functions attributed to the lawyer depending on the state Issues an insurance policy guaranteeing title
Lender	Checks buyer's credit Requires title check and/or title insurance Discloses cost of financing to the buyer Requires an appraisal to establish the value of the collateral (home) Makes the loan

---

[5] A single-family home example is chosen because of its familiarity. Clearly, large commercial closings are considerably more complex.

Participant	*Closing Functions*
Listing broker	Obtains property listing from seller
Selling broker	Produces buyer and assists in negotiations
Appraiser	Provides an estimate of the collateral's value for the lender May assist the buyer or the seller in setting the price
Surveyor	Assures no encroachments (i.e., that the subject buildings and no others are located on the land described in the contract of sale)
Inspectors	Inspectors may be used to assure that the roof, mechanical systems, etc., are in working order before the closing

This collection of individuals brings together all of the figures necessary to prepare the closing documents. The required data include the purchase amount, loan amount, loan charges, escrow included with the purchase offer, commission, handling of property taxes and insurance, lawyers' fees, title insurance, appraisal costs, survey costs, recording fees, tax stamps, and various other items depending on the state in which the transaction takes place. All of these items go together to determine how much, including financing, the buyer has to pay, and how much, after repayment of his obligations, the seller gets to keep. In order to get a feel for the handling of each of these different items, a sample closing is described below. (See 10-5 and 10-6.)

With all the different items involved, as demonstrated in 10-5 and 10-6, not all closings go smoothly. In fact, a recurring nightmare of the sales agent is the closing that does not close. (As already noted, although the sales agent is legally entitled to the commission for having produced a buyer ready, willing, and able to buy, the agent typically does not receive the commission in practice unless the transaction closes.) In the example in 10-7, potential closing problems are listed. Working through the "why" behind each of these problems as well as the resolutions of the problems will serve as an excellent summary of the brokerage function and much of the legal material in Part II.

SUMMARY

The brokerage process is particularly suited for real estate transactions. Some reasons for this are the cost of real estate, its unique features as an investment asset, the need for financing, and the complex and difficult nature of the real estate market. Because of the importance of the brokerage function and the role of the broker as a fiduciary, all states require real estate brokers and salespersons to be licensed.

10-5. CLOSING EXAMPLE

You have had the dubious good fortune to list Mr. and Mrs. Verytight's home. A competitor has found a buyer, and you bring the offer to purchase to the Verytights. After courteously offering you one-half glass of flat beer, Mrs. Verytight wants to know exactly how much cash everyone will receive, assuming they accept the offer and the closing goes according to schedule. The listing contract and offer to purchase provide the following information.

- The buyer claims to be ready, willing, and able to buy the Verytights' property.
- The closing is scheduled to take place at Last Hope Savings and Loan at 9:00 A.M. on March 5.
- Mr. Stuffy is the attorney who will represent the Verytights.
- Hold-On Title Guarantee Company will provide the title insurance and the contract calls for the "survey exception clause" to be deleted.
- Buyer is authorized to inspect the property on March 4.
- The stated purchase price is $50,000 and the buyers have made the purchase contingent on receiving an 80 percent loan at market rates.
- The Verytights bought a 3-year fire insurance policy costing $600 on January 1, which will be transferred to the buyers.
- All of the kitchen appliances, the curtains, drapes and lawn mower are included in the sale.
- In the prior year, city property taxes came to $480 while county taxes were $150.
- A special assessment of $60 was made, on January 31 of this year, against the property to support a nearby recreational area. The assessment is payable $12 a year at the end of each year for the next five years.
- All utilities will be cut off by the Verytights on March 5.
- The Verytights owed $32,150 on a 9 percent first lien as of the end of February when they made their last payment.
- The buyer is expected to get a 9 percent loan and pay one point origination fee at closing.
- The deed preparation will cost $20 and the recordation $2.50. The sales commission is 6 percent which will be split evenly between the selling and listing broker.
- The earnest money deposit of $500 is being held by the selling broker.
- The actual prorations will be based on a 360-day year and a 30-day month.
- The title insurance will cost $150.
- The appraisal will cost $100.
- The survey will cost $75.
- All costs are to be paid by the customary party.

Before arriving at the Last Hope Savings and Loan, please prepare a closing statement based on the assumptions above (see **10-6**) as well as a list of potential problems that might be encountered.

Brokers and clients are in the relationship of agent and principal and, thus, each has specific duties and obligations toward the other. The most important are loyalty in representing a principal's interest and strict compliance with the instructions of the principal.

The relationship between a broker and client is established by a real estate listing agreement. The agreement may take one of three forms: open listing, exclusive agency, and exclusive right of sale. In addition, brokers have established multiple listing services to assure the widest distribution of information among themselves of properties on the market.

Compensation of the real estate broker is usually in the form of a

10-6. BUYER AND SELLER CLOSING STATEMENT FROM 10-5

Seller's Closing Statement	Debit	Credit	Buyer's Closing Statement	Debit	Credit
Purchase price		$50,000.00	Purchase price	$50,000.00	
Loan retired	$32,150.00		Lien assumed		$40,000.00
Prorations:			Prorations:		
Interest*	32.15		Property taxes*		112.00
Insurance**		564.45	Insurance**	564.45	
Special assess-			Special assess-		
ment***	2.13		ment***		2.13
Property tax†	112.00		Cash charges and		
Other charges:			credits:		
Buyers deed	20.00		Loan origination	500.00	
Revenue stamps	25.00		Appraisal	100.00	
Commission‡	3,000.00		Survey	75.00	
	$35,341.28	$50,564.45	Title insurance	150.00	
Balance due			Deed recordation	2.50	
seller		$15,223.17	Earnest money		500.00
				$51,391.95	$40,614.13
			Balance due from		
			buyer		$10,777.82

* $4/30 \times \dfrac{1}{12} \times \$32,150 \times 9\% =$ $32.15. This interest and the remaining principal balance will be paid to the appropriate lienholder.

** $\$600 - (64 \times \dfrac{1}{360} \times \dfrac{1}{3} \times 600) =$ $564.45. The Verytights get credit for the unused portion of the insurance policy.

*** $64 \times \dfrac{1}{360} \times \$12 = \$2.13$. The Verytights must pay their portion of the assessment which will be paid by the new owner (buyer) on December 31.

† $\$630 \times \dfrac{64}{360} = \$112$.

‡ 1,500 to listing broker and 1,500 selling broker.

* $\$630 \times \dfrac{64}{360} = \$112.00$.

** $(200 \times \dfrac{296}{360} + 400 =$ $564.45.

*** $12 \times \dfrac{64}{360} = \$2.13$.

commission, payable either when the broker produces a purchaser ready, willing and able to buy the listed property, or when title to the property passes to a purchaser. In either case, the seller normally pays the commission. The commission frequently must be divided among several parties, including the listing broker, the selling broker, and the salespersons working for them who may have actually listed or sold the property.

The real estate conveyance culminates in the closing. Here, legal requirements (see Part II) are a significant part of the marketing process. Understanding the adjustments described in 10-5 and 10-6, as well as the problems listed in 10-7, will result in an understanding of the important linkages in the real estate marketing process.

10-7. POTENTIAL CLOSING PROBLEMS

☐ The buyer may request an adjournment but the seller may refuse because the contract specifies "time is of the essence."

☐ The buyer may tender a personal (rather than a certified or bank) check in payment of the price.

☐ The survey may reveal an apparent right-of-way easement over the land.

☐ A search of the land records may reveal materialmen's and laborer's liens as well as unpaid taxes.

☐ The buyer's inspection may show the following:

• Apparent occupancy by persons claiming to be tenants or owners by adverse possession.
• Violations of the local building code.
• Evidence of new construction.

☐ The appraised value may be insufficient to support the loan requested by the buyer.

☐ The seller may wish to remain in occupancy for two weeks following the closing.

☐ The building may not be empty of furnishings or not "broom clean."

APPENDIX 10A

Brokerage Office Management

Management in the broadest sense involves company success through the coordination and judicious use of employees and business associates. The real estate broker who seeks to create a brokerage firm is looking for synergy—the creation of an organization which has a total product greater than the sum of the individual results if each acted alone. If this synergy is not achieved, the brokerage office will not be a success. The broker must have the leadership ability to bring the agents of the firm into a profitable relationship.

MANAGEMENT FUNDAMENTALS

The broker is very much concerned with the distinction between *authority* and *responsibility*. When delegating office functions, the broker must be careful to see that responsibility is coupled with authority. The manager must also be careful to manage and not attempt to do everything himself. The broker managing an office cannot make every sale, but may assist others in making sales. Likewise, the broker cannot write every advertisement or answer every telephone call. The owner-broker achieves success and profitability through other people. Finally, *consistency* is a key. Erratic behavior may yield individual success, but it is seldom the way to lead an organization.

The major management functions in any line of business are:

- Planning.
- Coordinating.
- Analyzing.
- Controlling.
- Directing.

Planning involves establishing the what, when, where, who, and how objectives. From a real estate perspective, this involves forecasting and analyzing the market. Regional and urban economics are used to develop trends on which expectations can be developed. Based on the estimate of market demand, the broker must coordinate individuals who are capable of offering to clients the combination of services demanded. This involves creating an organization, which must be constantly analyzed. How can it be made more effective? How can new markets be developed and existing markets exploited more fully? Finally, the manager is concerned with control and direction. From a control standpoint, the broker is concerned not only with cash management and control of operating expenses, but with the quality of the service being rendered by the agents. The broker must be close enough to the agents to offer constructive criticism and to assure quality control.

Since the manager seeks to direct and oversee the organization, performing routine tasks is inadvisable. The manager must handle the exceptional situation and devise a system to permit routine brokerage office functions to be carried out with minimal supervision. Different management functions must be ranked by importance. The broker will focus on the most critical elements in achieving success. In the real estate brokerage business, one critical element is client service. The successful real estate broker will manage an organization which collectively knows the market and translates that knowledge into useful service for clients.

THE PERSONNEL QUESTION

From a personnel perspective, managing a brokerage office involves establishing job descriptions, recruiting, and training. The *job description* is an important element in any company, and it is often overlooked in brokerage office management. Not every sales agent is identical. Different agents specialize in different markets. There must be someone in the office to type contracts. Someone has to be responsible for signs and advertising. If the total office is to achieve the synergy necessary for profitable operations, the brokerage office manager must be careful to identify each job involved.

Recruiting

Based on job descriptions, recruiting is undertaken. People are the assets of the brokerage firm. They must be chosen to perform certain functions so that overall synergy is achieved. This is not to say that people must be squeezed into boxes on an organizational chart. Rather, different individuals have different talents, and the successful brokerage operation must blend these talents. Ten superlative salespeople may not be as successful as a group as three superlative salespeople, two secretaries, a manager, an advertising expert, and three solid detail people.

Training

In most real estate brokerage situations, training is not as formal as one might find in, say, commercial banking. While several organizations, particularly the National Association of Realtors® (NAR®) and its affiliated state associations offer numerous courses, the level of training in real estate brokerage has not reached that of many other professions. Consequently, the brokerage office manager must provide considerable in-office training. This is one of the ways that the broker contributes to the development of the sales agents. Certainly, part of the training involves learning by doing and by watching the broker. However, sales meetings, training in sales techniques, and formal direction of the sales force are all important.

Directing the Sales Force

There are several possible *leadership styles* which can be successful in real estate brokerage management. The particular style chosen should be the one which fits the nature and skills of the individual broker. However, certain general considerations should be mentioned. Real estate sales people face tremendous emotional swings. They often receive the big dollar but also suffer the big "near miss." Further, most successful sales personnel do not work well in the kind of structured environment that exists in a large corporation. Consequently, the leadership style of the individual must be adapted to the real estate salesperson and his particular image and ego needs.

Goal Setting

It is the responsibility of the broker to set specific goals for both the company and the individual. These goals must be compatible among sales agents within the firm. They must also be realistic in the sense that they are possible for the agent to achieve. They should be high enough so that the broker will be comfortable with that level of performance and so that the compensation payable to the individual sales agents meets their income expectations.

COMMUNICATION

Communications are an important part of management. The broker achieves through the salespersons. This requires communication of all the management items discussed in this appendix. The salespersons achieve by serving clients and this again requires communication.

In most real estate brokerage operations, paperwork tends to be a last priority. This can often cause significant problems internally as well as externally. The final product of the agent's work is an executed contract. The same attention should be paid to internal details such as the employment agreement which specifies the commission split between the broker and the sales agent, as well as the cost items to be borne by the office, and those which are the responsibility of the sales agent. What dollar value of advertising will the agent be allowed? How often is he expected to have "phone duty"?[1] When these items are in writing, internal disagreements can be avoided.

BEHAVIOR MODIFICATION

The broker-manager is responsible for reinforcing positive behavior and, in some cases, for behavior modification. When the agent does well, a show of appreciation is appropriate. Recognition in the form of "salesperson of the week," special lunches, and free trips are important incentives to the individuals who are involved in the selling function. In terms of behavior modification, the broker seeks not only the most effective salesperson in an immediate dollar sense, but salespersons who reflect well on the company as a whole. A $30,000 car may cause the client to wonder if he is not overpaying for the broker's services. On the other hand, ragged bluejeans and dirty office space usually do not create the atmosphere in which a relationship of confidence can develop. Such an atmosphere is crucial to closing the real estate transaction.

CONTROL

In order to handle the evaluation and control function, the manager must know who is responsible. He must know what listings a firm has, how active they are, which agents are bringing in new clients, and how much each of the agents is contributing to the overhead of the office. Control not only requires cash accountability, but also an informal feedback mechanism so that the broker can always stay close to the sales agents. Selling is a very personal business, and real estate is no exception. In the case of brokerage office management, control is as much a personal attribute as an accounting system.

---

[1] Phone duty involves responding to telephone questions generated by the office's various forms of advertising. Phone duty gives the agent the opportunity to meet clients. However, no one ever made money answering the phone. Most agents would prefer to have someone else answer the phone and give them the client. This is not collectively possible, and it is the broker's function to be sure that the telephone is utilized to the greatest advantage of the office as a whole.

SALES MEETINGS

The broker is responsible for sales meetings—a critical time for the brokerage office. It is then that information both on clients and available property is shared. The broker can make the meeting work in the sense of keeping it on track and making it time-efficient. If the broker fails to do so, he is wasting both personal time and the agent's time. Motivation is critical in sales meetings. Further, it is essential that the agent feel that he has taken something away from every sales meeting which will help sell property. For example, the agent must have new client leads, new information about property, or a new way to put these two things together. It is the function of the manager to assure that things happen.

ADVERTISING

The brokerage office manager is responsible for assuring the effectiveness of the firm's promotion and advertising campaigns. In this regard, advertising is used to position the firm—that is, the firm is differentiated in such a manner that possible clients see the firm as able to meet their needs. Advertising is used to create an image of the firm (trade names, logos, etc.) which is consistent over the long run with the market segment the firm is trying to satisfy.

In the real estate business, newspaper advertising is the most common medium. There are good ads and bad ads. Some ads may be good in certain situations and bad in other situations. If the firm has more listings than it can handle, it will write very specific ads drawing in clients interested only in a particular listing. On the other hand, if the firm is short of listings (i.e., if it has time to work with less-directed clients), then the advertising will be more general, such as "well-built, well-priced, three-bedroom, two-bath home in nice section of town." This type of ad is designed to bring in certain potential clients. Even simple newspaper advertising must be designed both to the market segment and the particular condition of the firm.

Major brokerage operations are also moving to radio and television to create a particular image in the public's eye. In addition to such formal media, the free lunch is also heavily used in the real estate business. The free lunch idea is more than a drink for a potential client. Office parties can be used to motivate the sales staff and to introduce the staff to potential clients. Press releases, announcement letters, and other less direct advertising appeals come under the general heading of the free lunch. In total, all of the promotion and advertising of the firm should be directed at its selected markets. Further, this promotion and advertising should be designed in a consistent manner to achieve the desired image of the firm.

CONCLUSION

The broker is the planner and the problem-solver. In this role, the broker should be both technically competent and a good judge of people. A defined system consistent with the firm's mission should be established. Then when sales agents have problems, the successful broker solves those problems within the system. At the same time, the broker leads by personal example. Finally, the broker imparts enthusiasm to all of the agents in the office.

By planning, solving problems, leading, and imparting enthusiasm, the broker fulfills the general management functions described in this appendix. Real estate sales are unique because the real estate asset is unique. In the long run, the successful firm will be the well-managed firm, the firm that develops market expertise and marketing methods that satisfy the public's needs.

APPENDIX 10B

National Association of Realtors®

The real estate industry has a number of associations, operating at national, state, and local levels, which seek to promote high standards of conduct and to protect the interests of the public. By far the largest and best known of these is the National Association of Realtors® (NAR®), at one time known as the National Association of Real Estate Boards (NAREB).

The membership of NAR® consists of Realtors® and Realtor®-Associates and includes among its members real estate brokers, property managers, appraisers, and salespersons working in all areas of the real estate industry.

The NAR® functions through state and local real estate boards. The term Realtor®, which was adopted by the Association in 1916 to identify its members, is a federally registered collective trademark. Only active real estate brokers admitted to membership in state and local NAR® boards are permitted to use the trademark. Salespersons are admitted to Realtor®-Associate active status.

The NAR® consists of a national office, fifty state associations, and more than 1,600 local boards. Its members subscribe to a strict code of ethics established by the Association (set forth in Appendix 10C). The national board provides educational programs in various real estate specialities, public relations work, and research and legislative activities.

The national association authorizes the state associations to issue a certificate and the designation GRI (Graduate, Realtor®'s Institute) to those members who have demonstrated competency in the course material of the GRI program. The purpose of the program is to educate and train persons to function effectively in the residential real estate brokerage business in which the primary activity is brokering single-family homes and in which occasional opportunities arise in auxiliary activities such as leasing and managing, and the sale of simple investment, commercial and industrial units.

The NAR® has a number of affiliates (designated as Societies, Institutes, and Councils) which represent specialized activities in the real estate profession. These affiliates are briefly described below.

American Institute of Real Estate Appraisers (AIREA)

Purpose: Conducts educational programs, publishes materials, and promotes research on real estate appraisal.

Designations conferred: MAI (Member, Appraisal Institute), RM (Residential Member).

Requirements: MAI requires a combination of experience and education, as well as written and oral examinations on course work and performance on demonstration appraisals. RM requirements follow along the same line but are less rigorous.

American Society of Real Estate Counselors (ASREC)

Purpose: Conducts educational programs for counselors and advisors on real estate problems.

Designation conferred: CRE (Counselor of Real Estate).

Requirements: Strict requirements as to experience, education, and professionalism. A minimum of ten years' experience prior to application is required.

Farm and Land Institute (FLI)

Purpose: To bring together specialists in the sale, development, planning, management, and syndication of land and to establish professional standards through educational programs for members.

Designation conferred: AFLM (Accredited Farm and Land Member). This designation was formerly known as Accredited Farm and Land Broker but was changed in 1975.

Requirements: AFLM requires a set number of points to be earned according to a scale established by the institute based on experience, education, and completion of written and oral examinations.

International Real Estate Federation (IREF), American Chapter

Purpose: To promote understanding of real estate among those involved in the real estate business throughout the world.

Designation conferred: None.

Requirements: Invitation to join based on membership in a local board of Realtors® and a demonstrated interest in real estate on an international level.

Institute of Real Estate Management (IREM)

Purpose: To professionalize members involved in all elements of property management through standards of practice, ethical considerations, and educational programs.

Designations conferred: CPM (Certified Property Manager), AMO (Accredited Management Organization), ARM (Accredited Resident Manager).

Requirements: All designations are awarded by the institute according to a point system based on experience, education, and examinations.

Realtors National Marketing Institute (RNMI)

Purpose: To provide educational programs for Realtors® in the area of commercial and investment properties, residential sales, and real estate office administration.

Designations conferred: CRB (Certified Residential Broker), CCIM (Certified Commercial and Investment Member), CRS (Certified Residential Specialist).

Requirements: Designation awards based on requirements of experience, education, and completion of a GRI program.

Society of Industrial Realtors (SIR)

Purpose: To provide educational opportunities for Realtors® working with industrial property transactions.

Designation conferred: SIR (Society of Industrial Realtors).

Requirements: Ethical, educational, and experience requirements must be met prior to receiving the designation.

Real Estate Securities and Syndication Institute (RESSI)

Purpose: To provide educational opportunities in the field of marketing securities and syndication of real estate.

Designation conferred: CRSS (Certified Real Estate Securities Sponsor), CRSM (Certified Real Estate Securities Marketer).

Requirements: Membership open to Realtors® with an interest in the area of syndication or real estate securities.

Women's Council of Realtors

Purpose: To provide educational programs, training, and publications for women realtors® whose primary interest is in residential brokerage.

Designation conferred: None.

Requirements: An interest in furthering the role of women in real estate brokerage.

APPENDIX 10C

National Association of Realtors® Code of Ethics

Preamble

Under all is the land. Upon its wise utilization and widely allocated ownership depend the survival and growth of free institutions and of our civilization. The REALTOR® should recognize that the interests of the nation and its citizens require the highest and best use of the land and the widest distribution of land ownership. They require the creation of adequate housing, the building of functioning cities, the development of productive industries and farms, and the preservation of a healthful environment.

Such interests impose obligations beyond those of ordinary commerce. They impose grave social responsibility and a patriotic duty to which the REALTOR® should dedicate himself, and for which he should be diligent in preparing himself. The REALTOR®, therefore, is zealous to maintain and improve the standards of his calling and shares with his fellow-REALTORS® a common responsibility for its integrity and honor. The term REALTOR® has come to connote competency, fairness, and high integrity resulting from adherence to a lofty ideal of moral conduct in business relations. No inducement of profit and no instruction from clients ever can justify departure from this ideal.

In the interpretation of his obligation, a REALTOR® can take no safer guide than that which has been handed down through the centuries, embodied in the Golden Rule, "Whatsoever ye would that men should do to you, do ye even so to them."

Accepting this standard as his own, every REALTOR® pledges himself to observe its spirit in all of his activities and to conduct his business in accordance with the tenets set forth below.

Article 1

The REALTOR® should keep himself informed on matters affecting real estate in his community, the state, and nation so that he may be able to contribute responsibly to public thinking on such matters.

Article 2

In justice to those who place their interests in his care, the REALTOR® should endeavor always to be informed regarding laws, proposed legislation, governmental regulations, public policies, and current market conditions in order to be in a position to advise his clients properly.

Article 3

It is the duty of the REALTOR® to protect the public against fraud, misrepresentation, and unethical practices in real estate transactions. He should endeavor to eliminate in his community any practices which could be damaging to the public or bring discredit to the real estate profession. The REALTOR® should assist the governmental agency charged with regulating the practices of brokers and salesmen in his state.

Article 4

The REALTOR® should seek no unfair advantage over other REALTORS® and should conduct his business so as to avoid controversies with other REALTORS®.

Article 5

In the best interests of society, of his associates, and his own business, the REALTOR® should willingly share with other REALTORS® the lessons of his experience and study for the benefit of the public, and should be loyal to the Board of REALTORS® of his community and active in its work.

Article 6

To prevent dissension and misunderstanding and to assure better service to the owner, the REALTOR® should urge the exclusive listing of property unless contrary to the best interest of the owner.

Article 7

In accepting employment as an agent, the REALTOR® pledges himself to protect and promote the interests of the client. This obligation of absolute fidelity to the client's interests is primary, but it does not relieve the REALTOR® of the obligation to treat fairly all parties to the transaction.

Article 8

The REALTOR® shall not accept compensation from more than one party, even if permitted by law, without the full knowledge of all parties to the transaction.

Article 9

The REALTOR® shall avoid exaggeration, misrepresentation, or concealment of pertinent facts. He has an affirmative obligation to discover adverse factors that a reasonably competent and diligent investigation would disclose.

Article 10

The REALTOR® shall not deny equal professional services to any person for reasons of race, creed, sex, or country of national origin. The

REALTOR® shall not be a party to any plan or agreement to discriminate against a person or persons on the basis of race, creed, sex, or country of national origin.

Article 11

A REALTOR® is expected to provide a level of competent service in keeping with the Standards of Practice in those fields in which the REALTOR® customarily engages.

The REALTOR® shall not undertake to provide specialized professional services concerning a type of property or service that is outside his field of competence unless he engages the assistance of one who is competent on such types of property or service, or unless the facts are fully disclosed to the client. Any person engaged to provide such assistance shall be so identified to the client and his contribution to the assignment should be set forth.

The REALTOR® shall refer to the Standards of Practice of the National Association as to the degree of competence that a client has a right to expect the REALTOR® to possess, taking into consideration the complexity of the problem, the availability of expert assistance, and the opportunities for experience available to the REALTOR®.

Article 12

The REALTOR® shall not undertake to provide professional services concerning a property or its value where he has a present or contemplated interest unless such interest is specifically disclosed to all affected parties.

Article 13

The REALTOR® shall not acquire an interest in or buy for himself, any member of his immediate family, his firm or any member thereof, or any entity in which he has a substantial ownership interest, property listed with him, without making the true position known to the listing owner. In selling property owned by himself, or in which he has any interest, the REALTOR® shall reveal the facts of his ownership or interest to the purchaser.

Article 14

In the event of a controversy between REALTORS® associated with different firms, arising out of their relationship as REALTORS®, the REALTORS® shall submit the dispute to arbitration in accordance with the regulations of their board or boards rather than litigate the matter.

Article 15

If a REALTOR® is charged with unethical practice or is asked to present evidence in any disciplinary proceeding or investigation, he shall place all pertinent facts before the proper tribunal of the member board or affiliated institute, society, or council of which he is a member.

Article 16

When acting as agent, the REALTOR® shall not accept any commission, rebate, or profit on expenditures made for his principal-owner, without the principal's knowledge and consent.

Article 17

The REALTOR® shall not engage in activities that constitute the unauthorized practice of law and shall recommend that legal counsel be obtained when the interest of any party to the transaction requires it.

Article 18

The REALTOR® shall keep in a special account in an appropriate financial institution, separated from his own funds, monies coming into his possession in trust for other persons, such as escrows, trust funds, clients' monies, and other like items.

Article 19

The REALTOR® shall be careful at all times to present a true picture in his advertising and representations to the public. He shall neither advertise without disclosing his name nor permit any person associated with him to use individual names or telephone numbers, unless such person's connection with the REALTOR® is obvious in the advertisement.

Article 20

The REALTOR®, for the protection of all parties, shall see that financial obligations and commitments regarding real estate transactions are in writing, expressing the exact agreement of the parties. A copy of each agreement shall be furnished to each party upon his signing such agreement.

Article 21

The REALTOR® shall not engage in any practice or take any action inconsistent with the agency of another REALTOR®.

Article 22

In the sale of property which is exclusively listed with a REALTOR®, the REALTOR® shall utilize the services of other brokers upon mutually agreed upon terms when it is in the best interests of the client.

Negotiations concerning property which is listed exclusively shall be carried on with the listing broker, not with the owner, except with the consent of the listing broker.

Article 23

The REALTOR® shall not publicly disparage the business practice of a competitor nor volunteer an opinion of a competitor's transaction. If his opinion is sought and if the REALTOR® deems it appropriate to respond, such opinion shall be rendered with strict professional integrity and courtesy.

Article 24

The REALTOR® shall not directly or indirectly solicit the services or affiliation of an employee or independent contractor in the organization of another REALTOR® without prior notice to said REALTOR®

> **NOTE:** Where the word REALTOR® is used in this Code and Preamble, it shall be deemed to include REALTOR®-ASSOCIATE. Pronouns shall be considered to include REALTORS® and REALTOR®-ASSOCIATES of both genders.

The Code of Ethics was adopted in 1913. Amended at the Annual Convention in 1924, 1928, 1950, 1951, 1952, 1955, 1956, 1961, 1962, and 1974.

IMPORTANT TERMS

agent
bilateral contract
broker's license
dealer
exclusive agency
exclusive right
　to sell
fiduciary
general agent
lender
listing
listing broker

multiple listing service (MLS)
open listing
principal
Real Estate Licensing Examination
　(RELE)
"ready, willing, and able"
salesperson's license
selling broker
special agent
surveyor
title company
unilateral contract

REVIEW QUESTIONS

10-1. Why does the marketing of real estate tend to rely on sales by brokers?

10-2. Compare and contrast special and general agents. Of what type would you expect a real estate broker to be?

10-3. What is the nature of the relationship between a broker and a sponsored salesperson?

10-4. What is the broker's role as an agent of the principal?

10-5. How might an implied agency between a broker and principal be created?

10-6. What is the purpose of a real estate listing agreement?

10-7. How might participation in a multiple listing service enhance a broker's ability to successfully market a property?

10-8. When is a broker's commission earned? When is it usually paid?

10-9. How is the level or size of a real estate commission determined?

10-10. Under what circumstances might a listing salesperson receive a relatively small portion of a real estate commission?

11

Management

THE PRODUCT OR "good" produced by the real estate industry is *space over time*. Whenever the user of the space over time is a party other than the owner, the owner may also provide some services (utilities, maintenance, or security) as part of the agreement, in exchange for which the user of the property pays a rental or fee.

Property management is the name given to the function of providing services to the property user and of maintaining the property and collecting rents to which the owner is entitled. The management function usually is performed by owners themselves in the case of small properties. For larger properties or when owners live at a distance, the function normally is performed by a property manager, either an individual or a management firm.

Property management is very possibly the most underrated function within the real estate industry. (See **11-1.**) This might seem strange, since running a multi-million-dollar investment which serves the needs of hundreds or even thousands of people is a highly challenging task, requiring training, experience, and the ability to understand a wide variety of people and institutions. In fact, the emphasis in the real estate industry

11-1. THE IMPORTANCE OF MANAGEMENT

The classic mistake of the stock and bond investor moving into real estate involves underestimating the importance of management. Very often, a $3 million apartment complex will be run by a resident manager who makes $10,000 a year. The investor who hires this level of management would never consider paying such a salary to the president of a $3 million company, but some investors have the feeling that real estate manages itself.

Once constructed in a fixed location, the single most important controllable variable in the real estate project is operating management. A San Francisco real estate broker recently noticed a project which was on the market for $1 million. He knew how the property had been managed in the past and that the million dollar valuation was based on a capitalization of historic income figures. He borrowed money to buy the property, renegotiated certain leases, established more efficient operating procedures and in six months, sold the property for $1.4 million. His contribution was simply to recognize that management is important.

has been on the "permanent" elements of the investment—good location, sound construction, inexpensive long-term financing—rather than on the day-to-day operation of the property. It sometimes seems as if the property owner, having made a very large investment in a permanent structure, assumes that the property will run itself with a minumum amount of supervision.

This concept of property management is gradually changing. (See 11-2.) The most important reason is the increasing recognition by owners that good property management is the major controllable variable influencing residual cash flow. It is true that both rentals and operating expenses are primarily affected by market forces beyond the control of any single property owner (witness the recent sharp rise in energy costs). But it is also a fact that comparable properties within the same city or neighborhood often show wide variances in rental income and operating costs. In these cases, analysis frequently reveals that "higher than market" operating expenses and "lower than average" net rental levels are due to inadequate property management.

11-2. MANAGEMENT ASSOCIATIONS

A number of professional and trade organizations exist in the field of real property management. The leading ones are:

□ *Institute of Real Estate Management (IREM).* IREM is an affiliate of the National Association of Realtors®. Individuals who seek to join must meet education and experience requirements. IREM offers two designations that are widely recognized in the real estate industry. A qualified individual may become a Certified Property Manager (CPM) or Accredited Property Manager (APM), while a qualified management firm may be awarded the designation of Accredited Management Organization (AMO).

□ *Building Owners and Managers Institute.* Operated by Building Owners and Managers Association International, the institute offers to those who successfully complete its management courses the professional designation of Real Property Administrator (RPA). The Building Owners and Managers Institute specializes in office building management.

□ *International Council of Shopping Centers (ICSC).* ICSC specializes in retail property management and awards the designation of Certified Shopping Center Manager (CSCM) to those individuals who attend a series of courses and pass an examination.

THE MANAGEMENT CONTRACT

The property manager is the professional who provides management to the owner. The specific responsibilities of the property manager should be outlined in the contract between the manager and the owner. An important aspect of such a contract is that it establishes an agency relationship between the manager and the owner. This agency relationship empowers the manager to perform management duties with the assurance that as long as the duties are performed satisfactorily, the owner is legally bound by, and responsible for, the actions of the manager. As a result, it is important that the management contract is carefully written and lists the responsibilities and authority of the manager. The management contract will specify all the details involved with provision of the services associated with a particular space and should include the following essential information:

☐ *Management services.* The manager is to be responsible for the physical condition of the property by preventing avoidable depreciation and tending to maintenance needs. The manager also is charged with collecting rent and other payments due the owner, providing utility and other services to the property users, and the hiring of employees and outside firms as necessary.

☐ *Management employees.* The agreement may specify the number of employees and the job descriptions of each. The manager is to be responsible for the acts of each employee at the property site. Persons who handle money may need to be bonded.

☐ *Authorized expenditures.* Expenditures by the manager should be limited to specified periodic charges, except in case of emergency. This protects the owner against large outlays without his knowledge or consent.

☐ *Record-keeping and notification.* The agent often is expected to prepare an annual operating budget for each calendar or fiscal year and maintain financial records as the year progresses. The agent should inform the owner by a specified date each month of all collections and disbursements for the most recent period and should remit any balance due the owner.

☐ *Insurance coverage.* Insuring real property is a complex task that requires continuing supervision and review, to be sure both that premiums are paid and that coverages are updated to meet changing conditions. The agent's responsibility in this area should be spelled out.

☐ *Advertising and promotion.* Different properties require different degrees and types of advertising, and the management agreement should specify the agent's duties in this regard. At the very least, the agent should have a basic obligation to advertise vacancies and display signs. Often, the agent for a rental property handles the entire leasing function.

☐ *Duration of the contract.* It is not a good idea to contract for an unspecified period. A definite period should be stipulated, with the contract then to continue until terminated by either party or extended for a defined period.

☐ *Management fee.* A property manager frequently works on a commission basis (e.g., 5 percent of gross income collected). However, a fixed fee may be payable, particularly when the management services require a relatively predictable amount of time (e.g., maintaining property records) and where an incentive for extraordinary effort is not deemed necessary by the owner. On the other hand, a service such as finding new tenants is one that calls for the exercise of discretion and good judgment, and may involve intensive efforts. For this type of work, a leasing commission frequently is paid to the manager over and above the regular management fee. In addition, the manager may be entitled to fringe benefits and expense reimbursements.

THE BUDGET

The management contract is typically tied directly to an *operating budget.* The budget is a pro forma of expected revenues and expenses. The budget is used by the equity owner to estimate cash flows to be generated from the investment and as a performance measure for the property manager.

Budgets are usually derived by estimating revenues and expenses from comparables. (This directly parallels the market data approach, discussed in Chapter 7.) In addition to general market data, the professional property manager will have built an extensive data base of rents and operating expenses from the local marketplace. As an operating professional, the property manager will be sure that this source of data is current and easily adaptable to the most common types of development in the area. (Note that the property manager is an excellent source of information when establishing an investment pro forma.)

The property manager, in conjunction with the owner, must go beyond comparable data and incorporate expected trends in the marketplace. These trends are estimated from analysis of regional and urban economic data as explained in the appraisal section. Extrapolating trends, along with the use of comparables, allows the property manager to develop a budget which will provide the equity owner a reasonable basis for estimating cash flows. An accurate budget is essential if the equity owner is to be able to make effective decisions concerning the investment.

The budget is also critical to the equity owner in terms of evaluating the property manager's performance. As previously stated, the budget is tied to the management contract. Very often, the compensation of the property manager (described in the management contract) is on an incentive basis. In other words, if the property manager "makes budget" or exceeds budget, then the compensation is adjusted accordingly. Since management is the largest controllable variable in an existing property, it is critical that the equity owner be able to effectively analyze the performance of the property manager.

PROPERTY MANAGEMENT FUNCTIONS

Rent Collection

The property manager's first function is the collection task. ˥enants must pay minimum rent and possibly percentage rents and expens⸱ items as provided for in the lease. When tenants do not pay on time, i⸱ is the responsibility of the property manager to safeguard the owner's interests and collect revenues in the most expeditious manner possible.

Tenant Relations

Once rent has been collected, the property manager has responsibility for ongoing operations. First, these include, tenant relations. As in any business, it is important to satisfy the customer. The property manager is in a better position to do this if he knows the tenants' general needs and is periodically in personal contact with all of the tenants.

Operating rules will be defined in the lease; however, there are always gray areas in enforcing certain operating rules. For example, in a regional shopping center, how loud can the music be played by a record store? Can a tenant have handbills distributed to shoppers? How late must stores remain open before Christmas? All of the general management functions come into play here as the property manager, working under the basic rules established in the lease, seeks to satisfy all tenants' desires for space over time with certain services.

Personnel

Depending on its size, a property may require one or many employees for purposes of maintenance, security, etc. The property manager is the one to determine employment requirements and recruit prospective employees. In addition, the manager normally will handle employment contracts and will supervise, and, where necessary, discharge employees who fail to perform satisfactorily.

The management contract must specify who is to pay the resident employees (including the resident manager). In some cases, the resident manager is on the property manager's payroll and is therefore an additional cost to the property manager. In other cases, the resident manager is paid out of the operating cash flows of the project. In the latter case, one would expect a lower level of compensation to the property manager since fewer expenses would be incurred. (See 11-3.)

11-3.   WHAT IS A RESIDENT MANAGER?

Many individuals begin a career in property management by becoming the "on site" or "resident" manager. For all practical purposes, the two terms are synonymous.

A resident manager is an employee who oversees and administers the day-to-day building affairs in accordance with direction from the property manager or owner. Resident managers, in general, have the greatest amount of day-to-day contact with the building(s)' tenants. They also usually spend the greatest amount of time on the premises of the property. They may or may not supervise a maintenance staff, but they are directly responsible for managing the physical upkeep and maintenance of the property, as well as often leasing vacant units and collecting rents.

It is essential that resident managers possess a congenial personality and a well-kept appearance. In most cases, they act as ambassadors of the management company, and are usually the first, if not the only, company representative a prospective or current tenant deals with face to face.

SOURCE: The Institute of Real Estate Management (1979).

Maintenance Schedules

The property manager is responsible for establishment of the maintenance schedule. This involves not only custodial services but also, for example, provisions for snow removal in those regions requiring it. In a larger property, one or more engineers will be required for ongoing operation. It is the responsibility of the property manager to see to it that these individuals perform in a consistent and coordinated manner. The property manager is also responsible for inventory control, including making certain that cleaning supplies and any other necessary items are available when needed. (Note that in a major hotel situation, inventory control involves furniture, food, liquor, and so forth.)

Security

Security has become an increasingly important function of the property manager. The increase both in personal and property crime has made security precautions a top demand by many tenants, whether residential, office, or commercial. In addition, legislation and court decisions in many states have increased the liability of a landlord for injury or property loss suffered by a tenant resulting from inadequate safety precautions or failure to repair doors, windows, or other points of access into the building or into rental units. The property manager must seek to minimize the risks of crime while at the same time keeping operating cost increases under control.

Property Insurance

Adequately insuring a property at the minimum cost is an important duty of the property manager. This requires the manager to keep up to date about the many types of insurance coverages available and to recommend appropriate insurers for the property. (This latter function is often performed by an insurance broker who deals with the property manager or directly with the owner.) Finally, the property manager must investigate all accidents or claims for damages and see to it that reports are filed promptly with the insurer.

Payment of Expenses; Books and Records

The property manager must see to it that operating expenses, real estate taxes, and mortgage payments are made when due. Depending on the particular arrangement, the manager may be authorized to sign checks or may merely prepare a list of payments for the owner's attention. The manager also will keep financial records of income and outlays and will work with the accountant retained by the owner in the preparation of annual financial statements and tax returns. The manager also will be responsible for preparing reports required by governmental authorities.

Showing and Renting Space

Although marketing real estate is a function distinct from managing it, the two often are combined in the hands of the property manager. This is particularly true in the case of apartment properties where the manager actually on the site (the resident manager) usually shows vacant apartments and handles lease negotiations. Because of the importance of the leasing function and the expertise and special effort required for successful leasing, the manager often receives a leasing commission over and above his regular management fee. The leasing function can be classified into three steps, all or some of which may be performed by the property manager:

☐ *Set rental levels.* One of the most important functions of the property manager may be to establish a lease schedule that will maximize the rental income over time from the property. To do this, the manager must (1) keep current information on rentals in comparable buildings, (2) tolerate a certain percentage of vacant space (since a fully occupied building may be evidence of unduly low rentals), and (3) vary rentals among the various space units in the building to reflect the relative advantages and disadvantages of each. For example, space on higher floors usually commands a premium over that on middle floors due to a better view.

☐ *Solicit prospects.* The second step in the leasing process is to advertise space in appropriate media (whether billboards, newspapers, radio, or television) and show space to prospective tenants. This latter function, often performed in a perfunctory way, should more properly be regarded as the time for an intensive personal selling effort on the part of the leasing agent. To do this properly, the leasing agent must not only be familiar with every detail of the property being shown but also should ascertain the precise needs and desires of the prospect.

☐ *Negotiate and execute leases.* Finally, the property manager will be involved, to a greater or lesser extent, in the negotiation and execution of the lease. In the case of an apartment project, where standard form leases are used and little negotiation normally occurs, the manager may perform the entire process. On the other hand, a long-term lease of several floors in a major office building will require the efforts of legal counsel and the owner, too. Even here, however, the property manager plays an important preliminary role because of his initial contacts with the tenant.

If the property manager is successful in enforcing rules of operation, does a good job of re-leasing (if this is part of his contract), has effective maintenance and security schedules, does a good job of inventory control, manages his employees well, efficiently handles collections, and keeps good accounting records, then he has done all that he possibly could to assure that the anticipated budget will be achieved—market conditions allowing, he should "make the budget." The owner will receive the expected cash flow, and the property manager will be compensated as specified in the management contract.[1]

PROPERTIES REQUIRING MANAGEMENT

Residential

To the extent that property management involves tenant relations, the greatest challenge is presented by residential properties. The space leased by the residential tenant is "home," where the tenant and other family

---

[1] As in most budget situations, the manager can often play accounting games to improve performance in one period at the expense of performance in another. Well-written management contracts, budgets, and leases help to reduce management flexibility in this area. As is described in Chapter 23, personal ethics are also important in making this system work.

members spend a substantial amount of their free time and the rent for which may represent the tenant's largest single financial obligation. Consequently, the residential tenant expects a well-run property, with services and utilities available as promised, at rentals which are kept as low as possible because, among other things, residential rentals are not tax-deductible as are business rentals. On the other side of the coin, one or two bad tenants in a project can be a continuing source of vexation to the property manager and to the other tenants.

Finally, the relatively short term of a residential lease means that the property manager is under continual pressure to maintain a high renewal rate in order to avoid vacated premises which must be repainted, repaired, and re-leased in as short a time as possible. A property that is theoretically fully rented may nevertheless lose a substantial amount of rental income if turnover is very high and more than a few weeks elapse before each new tenant moves in.

Among the types of residential properties are: (1) apartments, (2) condominiums and cooperatives, and (3) single-family homes.

☐ *Apartments.* Special management difficulties involved with apartment managers are often the result of the varied backgrounds of the tenants. The personal relationship between management and tenant can be crucial in maintaining high occupancy. Turnover of tenants results in higher operating expenses and lower rentals collected. Offering fair rents and responding to tenants' needs (e.g., maintenance and repairs) are often the most important variables in successful apartment management.

☐ *Condominiums and cooperatives.* The management of condominium and cooperative housing projects also presents some special problems. Although the general nature of the work to be done is very similar to that in other rental projects, the manager is dealing with a large number of owners (who may act like tenants) rather than with a single owner. Consequently, the manager sometimes is caught between owners arguing for major repairs and owners seeking to hold down their expenses which ultimately fund the repairs sought by the other owners.

☐ *Single-family homes.* The least involved form of residential management is that in connection with the rental of single-family homes. The owner may have moved away for business or other reasons with the intention of returning at a later date to occupy the house, or may be holding the property as an investment. In either case, the owner retains a local agent to collect rent, pay real estate taxes and debt service, and handle any problems that may arise. This type of management is frequently performed by real estate brokers, who charge a fee equal to a percentage of each month's rent.

Office Buildings

The property manager of an office building must be familiar with rather more complex lease provisions than those used for residential properties. For example, the office building tenant is very much aware of paying a rental measured by the square foot, and so the measurement of space becomes an important consideration. Different measures of renting space are used and must be familiar to the building manager. One frequently used measure is *rentable area* or *rentable space*.[2] In addition, escalation and cost-of-living clauses are common in office building leases and frequently become a subject for negotiation with the tenant.

In handling leasing, the property manager must bear in mind that the value of an office building is directly related to three interlocking elements: (1) the rental rate per square foot, (2) the quality of the tenancies, and (3) the length of the leases. The higher the rental rate, the higher the gross income. The more prestigious the tenant and the better its credit rating, the more assured is the owner that rents will be paid. And the longer the lease term, the lower the risk of vacancies and turnover problems in the future.

In office building management, service is particularly important. The property manager is responsible for assuring that space satisfies user demands (e.g., that elevator service, cleaning schedules, security, and maintenance are adequate). To many office tenants, the amount of rent is secondary to the efficient provision of these services.

Retail Complexes

For larger retail complexes and particularly for shopping centers, the property management function is extremely important:

☐ *First*, maintenance of the property itself requires substantial work. Each day, large numbers of shoppers visit the premises, generating a great deal of rubbish and causing much wear and tear to the improvements. In addition, daily security is an important consideration.

☐ *Second*, the property manager must keep alert to possibilities of making the premises more attractive and to the need to renovate and modernize selling areas. The fierce competition for retail business means that constant efforts must be made to have customers return as often as possible. In addition, whenever new tenants lease space, an extensive renovation may be required to make the particular premises appropriate for the new use.

---

[2] In the case of a single-tenancy floor, rentable area is the amount of space computed by measuring to the inside finish of permanent outer-building walls and excluding stairs, elevator shafts, pipe shafts, and utility rooms not actually available to the tenant but without any deduction for columns and projections necessary to the building.

☐ *Third,* the property manager performs an important function in obtaining a proper tenant "mix" for the retail complex. Too much competition among similar uses may mean business failures for the tenants and a negative cash flow for the landlord. Ideally, the various tenants should complement each other so that a shopper coming to one store will find related products or services in adjacent stores.

☐ *Finally,* since retail leases frequently contain percentage rental provisions under which the landlord is entitled to additional rental based upon a percentage of gross sales over a specified minimum, the property manager must be prepared to negotiate the most favorable terms for the owner and also must insure that percentage rentals are paid as they become due.

Industrial

A more specialized type of management is involved with industrial property—that is, improved real estate used primarily for the purpose of manufacturing or warehousing and which may also include a limited amount of office space. Much industrial property is either built or altered to meet the specific needs of a tenant who normally will be expected to sign a long-term lease (e.g., twenty years) to enable the landlord to recover the special costs involved. Such special-purpose buildings may involve a minimal amount of management by the landlord since the property is frequently leased on a net basis, with the tenant being responsible for all operating expenses, possibly including real estate taxes and insurance. On the other hand, some types of warehouse space are let on relatively short terms since bare space is the subject of the lease. In this type of situation, the landlord may be responsible for maintenance and repair and also must anticipate the need to market the space at frequent intervals. In such situations, a property management function must be performed either by the owner or managing agent.

Hotels and Motels

It is not possible in an introductory text to deal at length with the management activities involved in hotel and motel properties. In the hospitality industry, the service function is the most crucial. In many cases, convention business is relied on as a major source of revenue. As a result, hotel and motel management includes food service and entertainment as well as the typical property management functions.

In addition, the lease period is extremely short. In many motels, the usual stay is for one night. This means that each room must be re-leased every day—a formidable task indeed. Consequently, management is an even more important element for successful investment.

SUMMARY

Property management often can make a significant difference in the net cash flow from income property and consequently is an important variable when analyzing a property. The management contract is the key document defining the relationship between the managing agent and the property owner-principal. By virtue of the contract, the property manager acts as the owner's agent in satisfying the service demands of users (who lease space over time) and in seeing to it that the users perform their lease obligations, most notably the prompt payment of rent.

The property management function varies widely in its complexity and in the time demands made of the manager. At one extreme, management of a single-family residence is least time-consuming and complex and is often combined with the real estate brokerage function. At the other, property management in a large shopping center or office building is a full-time occupation. In hotels and motels, the service element is critically important, and consequently makes good management even more valuable.

IMPORTANT TERMS

Building Owners and
   Managers Association International
escalation clause
Institute of Real Estate
   Management (IREM)
International Council of Shopping Centers

maintenance schedule
management contract
operating budget
property management
rentable area
resident manager

REVIEW QUESTIONS

11-1. Why has property management tended to be the most underrated function within the real estate industry?

11-2. What is the role of the management contract in specifying the relationship between the owner and the manager?

11-3. How are most property management fees determined?

11-4. List and discuss four important functions of the property manager.

11-5. What types of conflicts might arise between owners and managers of residential condominiums?

11-6. How might rentable area be computed in the case of a single-tenancy floor of an office building?

11-7. Why is the tenant mix critically important to the successful management of a shopping center?

11-8. Would the lease associated with special purpose industrial property tend to be long or short term?

11-9. List and discuss some of the management activities associated with hotels and motels.

11-10. What special considerations apply to management of retail properties?

V
Financing

12

The Financial System and Real Estate Finance

REAL ESTATE FINANCE is approached here from three perspectives. First, in this chapter, the macroeconomic perspective is considered. The overall economic picture developed in Chapter 1 is expanded to include a description of the financial intermediaries that make real estate investment and development possible. The government's role in real estate finance is also considered, with extensive detail on mortgage insurance and secondary mortgage markets provided in Appendix 12A. Chapter 13 presents the lender's perspective. Who makes what types of loans and why? Finally, in Chapter 14, the effect of financing on equity (or residual) cash flows is examined. Thus, financing is integrated into the game analogy as a prior claim on cash flow affecting both the absolute return to equity and the riskiness of that return.

ELEMENTS OF A FINANCIAL SYSTEM

A financial system, as the term is used here, exists only in an economy in which there is a surplus of production over consumption. The surplus—called *capital*—can be thought of as excess funds available for investment.

The role of the financial system is to gather or mobilize capital from many small (and some large) savers and allocate that capital to individuals and organizations who need it for investment and who are prepared to pay for it. The intermediaries or middlemen between the savers and the borrowers are financial institutions and intermediaries. Their activities in gathering and allocating capital make up the financial markets. (See Figure 12-1.)

Within the financial marketplace, priorities for fund allocation are on the basis of a pricing structure expressed in terms of interest rates. The range of interest rates at any given time is determined by the supply of and

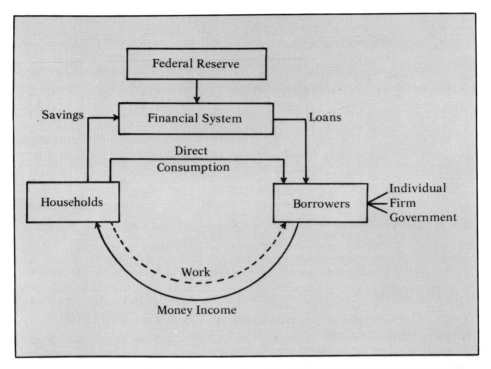

Figure 12-1.   FLOW OF FUNDS THROUGH THE FINANCIAL SYSTEM

demand for funds within certain categories. These usually are classified according to the risks assumed by the lender.

All interest rates are affected very significantly by the degree of inflation or deflation in the general economy. Put another way, if inflation is running at a high rate, a larger "inflation premium" will be built into all interest rates to reflect the erosion of capital, because of the loss of its purchasing power over the term of the loan.

Savers of Capital

The financial system receives its input of capital from those who generate excess funds. The most obvious group of savers are individuals and households who receive income for their employment and from previous investments. They, in turn, dispose of their income in one of two ways: (1) through direct consumption (including income taxes) and/or (2) savings.

A second source of saved capital is the business firm which does not expend its entire cash flow in outlays for business operations or in the form of dividends but retains some earnings for financing needs. Both these types of savers contribute a steady stream of capital into the financial markets, which then flows to borrowers either directly or through financial intermediaries.

Borrowers of Capital

Borrowers in the financial system run the gamut from an individual who seeks a personal loan of $1,000 to the U.S. Government which borrows billions of dollars each year. The real estate industry relies heavily on the financial system for debt financing because of its absolute size and because it utilizes far more debt in proportion to equity than most other industries.

There are two reasons for the heavy use of debt. First, the real estate investor normally wishes to finance acquisitions with as much debt as possible because the investor is thus enabled to acquire larger and better-quality properties and because debt financing may create desirable financial leverage and tax advantages, increasing the owner's return. (See Chapters 14 and 15.) Second, lenders are willing to make loans amounting to a very large percentage of a property's value because well-located and well-maintained real estate—immovable and long-lived—is perhaps the finest form of loan collateral. The strong reliance of the real estate industry upon debt financing makes the industry particularly susceptible to changes in the cost and availability of loan funds.

Financial Intermediaries

When a Treasury note is purchased directly from a Federal Reserve Bank, the government is borrowing directly from the saver without any financial middleman. Similarly, when the seller of a single-family home takes the buyer's mortgage note for a portion of the purchase price (a purchase money mortgage), no intermediary is involved. But these cases are exceptions to the general rule that financial markets normally involve a *financial intermediary* channeling savings into investment uses.

Some of the more important financial intermediaries in the real estate industry are:

- Commercial banks (CBs).
- Savings and loan associations (S&Ls).
- Mutual savings banks (MSBs).
- Life insurance companies (LICs).
- Real estate investment trusts (REITs).
- Pension funds.
- Credit unions.
- Federal and state agencies (to the extent they make direct loans rather than insure or guarantee loans made by other lenders).

Together, they control an enormous pool of capital which they invest in the form of loans. In this endeavor, each intermediary seeks to make those types of loans which are compatible with the kinds of capital they raise.

Financial Markets

Loans are originated (created) in a variety of ways and in a variety of places, all known as the *primary financial market*. A business firm which raises capital by selling newly issued securities to the general public is raising capital in the primary market. So is the U.S. Government when it sells a new issue of Treasury bonds. And so is an S&L when it agrees to finance the purchase of a home with a first mortgage loan. In all of these cases, new debt is being created.

Once debt has been originated, units of such debt, represented by bonds, notes, and mortgages, etc., may be traded in the *secondary financial markets*. The major secondary markets (for both common stock and bonds) include the (1) New York Stock and Bond Exchanges, (2) American Stock and Bond Exchanges, (3) regional exchanges, and (4) over-the-counter (OTC) markets. Short-term debt instruments—such as the U.S. Treasury bills and commercial paper issued by large corporations—are traded in the *money market*, which is a conceptual, rather than a geographic, designation.

In the real estate industry until quite recently, only a limited secondary market activity existed for debt instruments—that is, mortgages—or equity interests. In recent years, however, a very active *secondary mortgage market* has developed. This has had the effect of broadening the capital pool for financing real estate since, for the first time, many new types of savers and financial intermediaries are in a position to invest (lend) in real estate. Additionally, many traditional real estate lenders are able to do more real estate lending because of the liquidity provided by the secondary mortgage market. (This subject is discussed in detail in Appendix 12A.)

The Government's Regulatory Role

A number of federal agencies are closely involved with the financial system and the financial markets. Their objectives may generally be described as the enhancement of an orderly financial system which promotes overall economic growth without unduly restricting individual freedom. The major federal agencies are:

☐ *Federal Reserve System.* This is the central banking system of the United States, which is charged with overall monetary policy and related commercial bank regulation. While an extensive discussion of the Federal Reserve System goes beyond the scope of this book, the reader should remember that Federal Reserve policy affects both the overall money supply and the rules under which financial intermediaries operate. The Federal Reserve System has a significant effect on the real estate industry in that its monetary policy often influences the cost and availability of credit.

☐ *Federal Deposit Insurance Corporation (FDIC).* This independent executive agency, originally established in 1933, has the function of insuring the deposits of all commercial banks entitled to federal deposit insurance. The FDIC insures deposits up to $40,000 per account. The agency also has examination and supervisory powers over insured banks.

☐ *Comptroller of the Currency.* This office was created in 1863 as a part of the national banking system. Its most important functions relate to the organization, regulation, and liquidation of national banks.

☐ *Federal Home Loan Bank System (FHLBS).* This system was established in 1932 to provide a permanent system of reserve credit banks for eligible thrift institutions, such as S&Ls, engaged in long-term home mortgage financing. Over the years, its functions have expanded to the point where it now constitutes a number of separate federal agencies and federally sponsored organizations. The central agency in the group remains the Federal Home Loan Bank Board (FHLBB). It supervises twelve Federal Home Loan Banks, each located in one of the twelve regions into which the nation is divided. Savings associations holding 98 percent of the assets of the industry belong to the FHLBS.

One of the FHLBB's major functions is to provide supplemental mortgage credit (liquidity) by advancing funds to its members to assist them in meeting heavy or unexpected withdrawals. In addition, the FHLBB charters federal savings associations and has jurisdiction over state savings associations that are members of its affiliated agency, the Federal Savings and Loan Insurance Corporation (FSLIC). Another affiliated agency, the Federal Home Loan Mortgage Corporation (FHLMC), provides liquidity through secondary mortgage market operators, as described in Appendix 12A.

LENDING INSTITUTIONS

Financial institutions generally specialize in one or more areas of real estate finance. In order to obtain the best loan, the borrower must know the type of institution which prefers the type of loan he is seeking. (See Table 12-1.)

As the different loan originators are examined, the following must be kept in mind:

☐ *Institutions prefer loans which fit well with their liability structure* —that is, loans that have similar maturities to their source of funds. (See 12-1.)

Table 12-1. MORTGAGE ACTIVITY OF BANKS, INSURANCE COMPANIES, AND SAVINGS AND LOAN ASSOCIATIONS: 1950-1977

[In billions of dollars. Loans outstanding are as of end of year. Bank data include Puerto Rico; savings and loan data include Puerto Rico and Guam. See *Historical Statistics, Colonial Times to 1970,* series N 266-267, X 836-839, and X 911]

ITEM	1950	1960	1965	1970	1972	1973	1974	1975	1976	1977
Commercial banks:										
Loans outstanding	13.7	28.8	49.7	73.3	99.3	119.1	132.1	136.2	151.3	176.7
Nonfarm residential	10.4	20.4	32.4	45.6	62.8	74.9	82.4	82.9	94.3	110.0
FHA-insured	(NA)	5.9	7.7	7.9	8.5	8.2	7.2	6.3	5.6	(NA)
VA-guaranteed	(NA)	2.9	2.7	2.6	3.2	3.3	3.2	3.1	3.0	(NA)
Conventional	(NA)	11.7	22.0	35.1	51.1	63.4	72.0	73.5	85.7	(NA)
Other nonfarm	2.3	6.8	14.4	23.3	31.8	38.7	43.7	46.9	50.3	58.7
Farm	1.0	1.6	2.9	4.4	4.8	5.4	6.0	6.4	6.7	8.0
Mutual savings banks:										
Loans acquired	2.5	4.4	8.7	5.9	12.9	13.3	8.7	9.4	11.9	(NA)
Loans outstanding	8.3	26.9	44.6	57.9	67.6	73.2	74.9	77.2	81.6	88.0
Nonfarm residential	7.1	24.3	40.1	49.9	57.1	61.1	62.1	63.8	67.3	72.8
FHA-insured	1.6	7.1	13.8	16.1	16.0	15.5	14.8	14.4	14.6	(NA)
VA-guaranteed	1.5	9.0	11.4	12.0	12.6	12.9	12.7	12.4	12.3	(NA)
Conventional	4.0	8.2	14.9	21.8	28.5	32.7	34.6	37.0	40.4	(NA)
Other nonfarm	1.2	2.6	4.5	7.9	10.4	12.0	12.7	13.3	14.3	15.2
Life insurance companies:										
Loans acquired	4.9	6.1	11.1	7.2	8.7	11.5	11.4	9.6	9.7	13.6
Nonfarm	4.5	5.6	10.0	6.9	8.0	10.5	10.4	8.5	8.2	11.1
Farm	.4	.5	1.1	.3	.7	1.0	1.0	1.1	1.5	2.5
Loans outstanding	16.1	41.8	60.0	74.4	76.9	81.4	86.2	89.2	91.6	96.8
Nonfarm	14.8	38.8	55.2	68.7	71.3	75.4	79.9	82.4	84.1	87.9
FHA-insured	4.6	9.0	12.1	11.4	10.0	9.2	8.5	7.9	7.3	6.6
VA-guaranteed	2.0	6.9	6.3	5.4	4.7	4.4	4.2	3.9	3.6	3.3
Other	8.2	22.9	36.8	51.9	56.6	61.8	67.2	70.6	73.2	78.0
Farm	1.3	3.0	4.8	5.6	5.7	6.0	6.3	6.8	7.5	8.8
Savings and loan assns.:										
Loans made	5.2	14.3	24.2	21.4	51.4	49.5	39.0	55.0	78.8	(NA)
Loans outstanding	13.7	60.1	110.3	150.3	206.2	231.7	249.3	278.6	323.0	381.2
FHA-insured	1.0	3.5	5.1	10.2	15.4	15.1	14.5	16.5	14.7	(NA)
VA-guaranteed	3.0	7.2	6.4	8.5	13.5	14.7	15.3	14.0	16.6	(NA)
Conventional	9.8	49.3	98.8	131.7	177.3	202.0	219.4	248.0	291.7	(NA)

Source: Board of Governors of the Federal Reserve System. Current data in *Federal Reserve Bulletin,* monthly.

□ *The institution's self-image* as well as its management's attitude are important.

□ *Regulation* has an important effect on the portfolios of financial institutions. These regulations range from ceilings on loan-to-value ratios to the allowable percentage of certain types of loans in the institution's portfolio.

□ *The institution's contact with,* and *knowledge of, the particular real estate markets* affects the types of loans being made. Each institution's lending policy is largely a function of the segment of the industry it understands.

12-1. THE COST OF FUNDS

The prospective borrower must not only know the potential lender's different source of funds but should also be aware of the cost of those funds. For example, the CB has three primary sources of funds: demand deposits, time deposits, and certificates of deposit. REITs, on the other hand, are financed (in addition to the beneficial shares or equity) primarily by short-term bank debt. Therefore, the CB's average cost of funds, including the less expensive demand and time deposits, is lower than that of the real estate investment trust. Therefore, the commercial bank is thus better able to make lower interest rate (and lower risk) loans and still make a profit.

SOURCES OF FINANCING

Individuals

Individuals can provide both equity and debt financing. As lenders, individuals can make loans directly or through financial intermediaries. In the latter case, the individual can place money with an institution, such as an S&L or commercial bank. The institution then aggregates several individual savers' deposits and originates loans which fit with the nature (risk and maturity) of the deposits. Individuals can also buy direct financial claims in the financial markets (e.g., Government National Mortgage Association Pass-Throughs, as discussed in Appendix 12A).

Commercial Banks

CBs are the largest financial intermediary in the American financial system. The CBs are regulated by federal and/or state governmental agencies and are the primary means by which the Federal Reserve carries out its responsibilities for monitoring the nation's money supply. Federally chartered CBs are required to belong to the Federal Reserve System and to the Federal Deposit Insurance Corporation. In terms of mortgage loans, related regulations limit loan-to-value ratios and limit real estate loans to a certain percent of savings or equity capital. As a result, mortgage loans make up only about 15 to 17 percent of most commercial banks' portfolios. (A notable exception would be Hawaiian CBs, where mortgage loans dominate the portfolio.) It should be noted that the large amounts of short-term construction and land development loans found in CB portfolios are not included as real estate loans for regulatory purposes.

Traditionally, the CBs' sources of funds are dominated by short-term savings deposits and checking accounts. Consequently, their assets are concentrated in shorter-term loans to businesses for operations and receivables financing.[1] Consumer loans are primarily represented by automobile and personal loans. In the area of real estate loans, commercial banks emphasize construction and development loans and less frequently make long-term loans.

Savings and Loan Associations

S&Ls are not as large in total assets as CBs. However, their loans are concentrated in the real estate industry, and they are the nation's largest mortgage lender. S&Ls draw on savings accounts and certificates as their primary source of funds. They are regulated by the Federal Home Loan Bank Board (FHLBB) and/or state agencies which regulate such factors as the types of loans they can make, the maximum interest rates they can pay on savings accounts, and geographical lending limits. Since savings accounts (time deposits) are more stable than demand deposits, S&Ls have traditionally made longer-term loans, primarily single-family mortgages in their local market.[2]

Even with time deposits, however, S&Ls have found that during certain periods of the economic cycle, they experience a heavy outflow of deposits. This *disintermediation* causes serious problems for the management of the S&Ls. To reduce the impact of disintermediation on the real estate industry, S&Ls have recently been given certain new market alternatives. They have been allowed to issue short-term money market certificates with rates tied to those available on short-term U.S. Treasury bills—that is, at higher rates of interest than are allowed on savings accounts. Thus, the S&Ls are still able to acquire funds during high interest rate periods.

However, money market certificates offer only a partial solution to disintermediation. The major reason is that many existing depositors immediately switch to the new, higher-yielding certificates—thus placing the S&L in the unfortunate position of paying higher rates for existing deposits (liabilities) while their existing loans (assets) continue to yield the same rate of interest as before. Obviously, paying more for funds than they receive on loans is not a viable long-term strategy for S&Ls.[3]

---

[1] Bank holding companies have grown both in size and scope in recent years. Through these holding companies, commercial banks are able to offer borrowers a range of service which goes beyond the services traditionally provided by smaller commercial banks. Consequently, the nation's money center bank holding companies are able to offer the full spectrum of real estate financing.

[2] It should be noted that some S&Ls, particularly on the West Coast, are large and very aggressive lenders, which go well beyond the traditional savings and loan role. These S&Ls make development loans and also joint venture subdivision development with land developers.

[3] The 1971 Hunt Commission report and the subsequent FINE study both suggested significant reforms in the nation's monetary system. Significantly, this commission recommended that S&Ls and commercial banks be allowed to compete more directly. In other words, it suggested that the consumer would benefit if regulations were eased so that these

Mutual Savings Banks

MSBs are very similar to S&Ls. Savings banks exist only in twenty states, all but two—Oregon and Washington—in the Northeast and Middle Atlantic regions. Savings banks originally developed to encourage thrift among working people in the nineteenth century. At that time, the primary population centers were in the northeastern part of the United States. Population growth in other parts of the country coincided with the development of the S&L, which now dominates most of the country.

Mutual savings banks are regulated in ways similar to the S&Ls. The term *mutual* indicates that savings banks are owned and operated by their depositors and are managed by a board of trustees. They are nonprofit institutions. S&Ls, by comparison, may be either mutual or stock—that is, owned by depositors or by shareholders.

Life Insurance Companies

LICs function to provide financial security through life insurance to their policy holders. The premiums they collect are used largely to maintain reserves from which benefits are paid. These reserves constitute large pools of capital which must be invested. Since the inflows of funds—as well as the demands on these funds—are fairly stable over time, the LICs can make long-term mortgage loans. In fact, LICs are the major long-term lenders on many commercial and industrial properties. These loans have maturity structures similar to single-family loans, but there is neither mortgage insurance nor an active secondary market (i.e., there is less liquidity). Also, unlike CBs and S&Ls, LICs are not geographically dispersed throughout the nation; rather, they are concentrated in certain centers. Therefore, they cannot afford to make a large number of small loans throughout the nation. This again is logically reflected in an asset structure which consists primarily of larger long-term commercial loans.[4]

Real Estate Investment Trusts

REITs were established legislatively in the early 1960s. They are essentially corporations which pay no corporate taxes if they follow fairly strict investment regulations. Recognizing the large capital necessary to make real estate investments and the limited resources of the small inves-

---

financial intermediaries could operate in each other's traditional sphere of influence. Some of the commission's regulations have been enacted, and more will probably come. Hence, in the future, more similarity in the types of loans made by S&Ls and commercial banks can be expected.

[4] Life insurance companies do hold substantial portfolios of single-family mortgages loans, but they typically are originated and are serviced by mortgage bankers whose position is explained shortly.

tor, Congress saw REITs as a way to group small investors so that they could take advantage of the benefits of real estate investments.

REITs sell beneficial shares which are traded on the stock markets much like corporate common stock. In the past, many of them chose to leverage their position by borrowing short-term from commercial banks. These short-term loans were thought to be safe for the bank because of the cushion created by the equity capital as well as by the diversity of loans or equity interests held by the trusts (the trust's assets). The exact make-up of a REIT's portfolio varies, depending on the management philosophy of the trustees. Some of the trusts are very conservative, making only first lien loans on fully leased high-grade properties while others, seeking higher returns, are involved in much riskier land development and second lien financing. (See 12-2.)

Pension funds

Some pension funds have also become active in real estate lending. In fact, through commingled real estate funds operated by CBs or LICs, more and more pension funds are finding real estate investment attractive. Pension funds have their own set of regulations, and when operating through CBs or LICs, a second set of regulations is imposed.

The pension funds' liability structure is somewhat similar to the LIC in that their obligations are actuarily determinable and inflows of funds are fairly stable. Consequently, they would be expected to make similar types of loans. However, since most pension funds have usually used others (CBs or LICs) to manage their money, they have not emphasized real estate loans to the extent that LICs have. Pension funds can be expected to become larger real estate lenders in the future.

Mortgage Bankers

Another major originator of mortgage loans is the mortgage banker.[5] The mortgage banker differs significantly from the other lenders in that it is not a depository source of funds. The mortgage banker typically makes loans and then resells these loans to a permanent lender. Its function is to originate loans in particular markets where certain permanent lenders cannot operate efficiently. The most common example is found in single-family lending with LICs serving as the final lender. Remember that the LIC is not located in the local market as is the S&L; therefore, it needs someone to originate the loans and to service the loans (collect principal, interest, insurance, and tax payments). The mortgage banker serves this function.

---

[5] An expanded discussion of the role of the mortgage bankers is presented in Appendix 12A on secondary mortgage markets.

12-2. HOW REITs FELL INTO TROUBLE

Many REITs borrowed short-term, hoping that financial leverage would improve the return to their equity holders. They borrowed from the CBs at rates varying with prime. The most adventurous of them then made construction loans also tied to prime, but at four and five points over prime. It looked like a money tree, and the REITs quickly became the darlings of Wall Street. Upside financial leverage meant even greater percentage returns to equity.

However, by 1974, real estate development was in serious trouble. The REITs found that they had the weakest loans. Since they charged the highest rates, developers with better projects went to a lower cost source of financing. The high-cost REIT loans were taken by developers involved in riskier projects. During the recession, demand for space was seriously curtailed. At the same time, serious supply shortages arose because of the Arab oil embargo. Further, sources of long-term credit (which would be used to pay off the short-term construction loans) dried up as significant disintermediation was experienced in the real estate financial markets. All of these factors, collectively, made developers unable to repay loans made by the REITs.

What had looked like a money tree turned out to be a money sink. When developers were unable to pay, the REITs had difficulty repaying their loans to CBs. On the one hand, the REITs could not afford to leave a project half-finished; and on the other, they could not find the money to complete them. As the REITs scrambled for cash to complete what had now become unfortunate development experiences, the banks tightened the credit reins. After a substantial grace period (a period of time to solve their own financial problems), the REITs came to recognize that the collateral for their loans—that is, the partially completed development projects—were in many cases not worth as much as the debt owed the REITs or the REITs corresponding obligations to the commercial banks. Over the past few years, many of the REITs have tried to trade their development and construction loans to CBs for debt reductions and generally have tried to work themselves out of the real estate lending business.

Essentially, the mortgage banker borrows from a CB through what is referred to as a warehousing line of credit and uses these funds to originate individual mortgage loans. Once a package of mortgage loans has been originated, this entire package is sold to an institutional investor such as a life insurance company. The package of loans is a large enough investment for the LIC to be interested, and the mortgage banker will continue to service these loans, eliminating the need for the life insurance company to have a local office. The mortgage banker earns a fee for originating the loan and charges a fee to service the loan for the life insurance company. The origination fee typically represents one percent of the mortgage amount while the servicing fee will normally run from one-fourth to one-half of one percent of the outstanding loan balance.

Mortgage bankers should not be confused with mortgage brokers. Mortgage brokers help only to originate loans and do not service them. Most mortgage brokers bring large commercial borrowers and lenders together and are not active in the single-family mortgage market; they receive an origination fee for bringing the borrower and lender together.

Government

In addition to the private institutions mentioned above, the federal government plays a significant role in real estate finance. As already noted, the Federal Reserve and the Federal Home Loan Bank Board have significant regulatory responsibilities and provide credit to various loan originators. In addition, the federal government and its agencies also make direct loans through such agencies as the Federal Land Banks and the Federal Housing Administration (FHA).

FACILITATING GOVERNMENT ROLES IN REAL ESTATE FINANCE

Mortgage Insurance Programs

A special feature of real estate debt financing is the availability of mortgage insurance to protect lenders against losses due to defaulted loans. Mortgage protection is available through one of two government programs (FHA loan insurance or VA loan guarantees) or from private mortgage insurers.[6]

All of the programs insure single-family home loans; the FHA programs extend to multifamily units as well as single-family homes. The basic objective in all cases is to encourage private lenders to make loans that otherwise might be rejected because the applicant failed to meet normal credit standards. The borrower (home buyer) pays for the insurance either in a lump sum at the closing or as a fractional percent added to the periodic interest.

Liquidity and the Secondary Market

The mortgage lender is also concerned with the liquidity of its loans. Even if loans are safe (i.e., the collateral/borrower characteristics and mortgage insurance are sufficient to guarantee that the lender will not lose principal), it is still possible for the lender to experience a liquidity problem. When financial institutions experience an outflow of deposits, they must be able to liquidate assets to meet the claims of their depositors or policy holders (sources of funds). The liquidity needs of the various financial intermediaries will vary based on the volatility of their fund sources. For example, CBs have greater liquidity needs than LICs.

---

[6] The use of private mortgage insurance allows regulated financial intermediaries to go beyond the standard 75 to 80 percent loan-to-value ceiling.

To meet these liquidity needs, certain government agencies have been established. Among these are the Federal National Mortgage Association (FNMA or Fannie Mae), the Government National Mortgage Association (GNMA or Ginnie Mae), and the Federal Home Loan Mortgage Corporation (FHLMC or Freddie Mac). These government and quasi-government agencies provide or facilitate a secondary mortgage market where mortgage loan originators may sell loans when liquidity needs arise. In addition to these agencies, stockbrokers are active in marketing related debt instruments and some of these instruments are now traded in the futures and options markets. (For a full discussion of the secondary mortgage markets as well as the various forms of insurance which facilitate their operation, see Appendix 12A.)

CONSUMER PROTECTION

In the 1960s, consumer groups in the United States began a major effort aimed at educating consumers in economic and commercial affairs and the passage of legislation to protect consumers from fraud. This movement, called by some the "consumer revolution," has had a major impact on business transactions in this country. One example has already been indicated. In the discussion of real estate leases in Chapter 5, it was pointed out that courts have been moving toward a view of leases as contracts rather than conveyances because the former characterization provides greater protection for tenants.

In the area of real estate finance, two significant federal statutes reflect the movement toward greater consumer protection. They are the Truth in Lending Act and the Real Estate Settlement Procedures Act.

Truth in Lending Act

In 1969, Congress passed an omnibus statute known as the Consumer Credit Protection Act (CCPA). Title I is the Truth in Lending (TiL) Act. It requires lenders to make advance disclosure to borrowers of the amount and type of finance charges incurred in connection with the loan being made. (See ▮12-3▮ for a description of Title VI of the CCPA, commonly known as the Equal Credit Opportunity Act.)

TiL applies only to consumer loans, real estate, or otherwise. A lender making a residential mortgage loan must prepare a *TiL statement*, showing all finance charges incurred by the borrower, and must furnish the statement to the borrower before a contractual relationship is established between borrower and lender.

When the loan is a first mortgage on a single-family dwelling, the key disclosure is the *annual percentage rate* (APR), which is the effective annual

12-3. EQUAL CREDIT OPPORTUNITY ACT

In addition to the TiL Act, the CCPA also contains, as Title VI, the Equal Credit Opportunity Act (ECOA). This prohibits discrimination in lending on the basis of sex, marital status, age, race, color, religion, national origin, or receipt by the applicant of public assistance.

Lenders must also consider permanent part-time earnings in evaluating an application for credit (sometimes an important consideration when a mortgage loan is being sought). The law prescribes in detail what questions may be asked or are prohibited on loan application forms.

The law is administered by the Federal Reserve Board, which has issued Regulation B to implement the law.

interest cost of the loan. The *finance charge* includes interest, loan fees, FHA mortgage insurance fees, and discount points.

Real Estate Settlement Procedures Act

While the TiL Act affects all types of consumer loans, the Real Estate Settlement Procedures Act (RESPA) is aimed specifically at the real estate loan closing (settlement) process. The original 1974 statute aroused strong opposition in the industry because of its complex and time-consuming requirements. Recognizing that there was some validity to these objections, Congress amended the Act in 1976 to make it a more workable piece of legislation.

In essence, RESPA applies to first mortgage loans on single- to four-family residences where the lender is "federally related"—that is the lender is subject to federal regulation or is a member of a federal program, such as the one insuring deposits. The practical effect is to include the great majority of residential mortgage lenders in the United States.

RESPA is both a disclosure law and a regulatory law. In the disclosure area, it requires the lender to prepare a closing statement at least one day prior to the loan closing and permit the borrower to inspect it. This statement must disclose the amount of all known loan closing costs. The closing statement itself must follow a uniform statement prescribed by HUD. In addition, the borrower must be given a booklet titled *Settlement Costs* at the time of loan application.

In its regulatory aspect, RESPA restricts the amount of escrow deposits which may be required by the lender as part of the monthly mortgage installment. (The use of escrows is described in more detail in the following chapter.) In addition, kickbacks and unearned fees are prohibited. In the past, some lenders paid fees to third parties referring loan applicants, and these fees were passed along in the form of higher loan costs to the borrower.

THE FINANCING CYCLE

This macroeconomic overview of the real estate financing process concludes by classifying real estate loans according to the time the loan is made, along a sequence that begins with the acquisition of raw land and ends with a fully developed property ready for use or sale. The object of this discussion is threefold:

- To demonstrate the importance of financing at every stage of the real estate development process.
- To indicate how different sources of financing specialize in particular stages.
- To illustrate how loans at each stage are tailored, in their terms and interest rates, to reflect the particular lender risks at each stage.

Land Acquisition

The most common feature of land acquisition financing is the absence of institutional lenders. Institutions generally consider risk to be in inverse proportion to the cash flow from the property, since they consider the primary source of loan repayment to be the property itself. (See **12-4.**) Since raw land generates no cash flow, loans to finance its acquisition are considered the most risky and frequently are avoided altogether or limited to a small percentage of an institution's loans, either as a matter of legal restriction or internal policy.

A significant source of financing is a purchase money mortgage taken back by the seller of the land. In this particular situation, the financing is

12-4. RAW LAND FINANCING

Since land acquisition financing is relatively unavailable and costly, the developer often must have recourse to equity financing. One obvious source is the developer's own assets. Another frequent approach is to raise cash by a sale of interests to outside investors in a limited partnership in which the developer is the general partner.

The developer may avoid the need for any significant financing by entering into a joint venture with the landowner directly. The landowner contributes the land, and the developer contributes expertise and whatever small amount of cash is needed for preliminary expenses.

Yet another approach is to acquire the land under a long-term ground lease. This substitutes for an initial large capital outlay the obligation to pay a continuing ground rental for the term of the lease, which may run 99 years or more.

extended because the seller often has no alternative if a buyer is to be found.

Land Development

Land development refers to the process of preparing raw land for the construction of improvements. The process includes grading of land where necessary, obtaining rezoning if required, and the installation of utilities, sewers, streets, and sidewalks. Although developed land (in the sense used here) creates no more cash flow than does raw land, it is nevertheless one step closer to the ultimate use and thus is somewhat easier to finance. Most development loans represent a first lien on the property, they are short term in nature, and the interest charged is usually tied to commercial banks' prime lending rate (3 to 4 points above prime).

Development loans are usually made separately from construction loans when the raw land must be subdivided into smaller tracts or lots. The proceeds are dispersed in draws as the development progresses. The lender will allow release of specified tracts (lots) from the overall mortgage as development proceeds and the individual lots are sold to builders. When tracts or lots are released, the borrower must make a payment to the lender in exchange for the release. This *release price*, as it is called, is generally 10 to 20 percent greater than the proportional principal and interest associated with the released tract. This insures the lender of repayment with the sale of the choice lots and defers the developer's receipt of most of the profit until the development has been nearly sold out.

Construction

Real estate construction finance is a specialized process in which the commercial banks play a dominant role. (At one time, REITs were a major factor in the construction lending field, but this is no longer true.) The funds provided by the construction loan are used to pay for construction materials, labor, overhead, and related costs. The real estate is the collateral for the loan. Sometimes, the developer is required to post additional collateral, such as other real estate, securities, or possibly third-party guarantees.

Construction loans usually run from six months to two years, and, unlike most other types of loans, the actual loan funds are disbursed in stages (or draws) as construction proceeds. For example, 20 percent of the loan might be drawn down when the foundation is laid, the next 20 percent when the walls are put up, and so forth. In this way, the construction lender is assured that construction funds are being used for the intended purpose and no other and that, in the event of a default, the value of the property will (hopefully) have been increased in an amount equal to the construction loan disbursements.

Construction lending is considered hazardous because construction itself is a risky form of real estate activity, subject to numerous natural, economic, and political pitfalls. Therefore, the lender's return on construction loans is at the high end of the interest range. Typically, the borrower (developer) pays an initial loan fee plus an interest rate on funds drawn down that will be several points above the prime rate. Interest is accrued only on funds actually advanced.

Permanent Loan Commitment   The source of repayment of the construction loan is the permanent loan. The construction lender, being a short-term lender, is often unwilling to contemplate the possibility that no permanent financing may be available when the construction is complete. To prevent this possibility, the construction lender usually requires the developer to obtain a *permanent loan commitment* as a condition to obtaining the construction loan. The commitment is an agreement by another lender (such as an S&L or LIC) to make the permanent loan provided the building is constructed in accordance with approved plans and specifications.

This permanent loan commitment is often known as a *takeout commitment*, because it is the means whereby the construction lender will be taken out of the transaction when construction is completed.

Ownership and Use

The final stage in the real estate cycle begins when the property is put to use either by the owner or by tenants who have leased space. Now a lender can anticipate a long period of cash flow from the property to service a loan and so it is at this point that a long-term (permanent) loan can be funded.

In most cases, a lender will already have committed itself to make the permanent loan. The developer needs only to provide to the permanent lender evidence of satisfactory completion and the loan is disbursed (funded), most or all of it being used to pay off the construction lender.

Sometimes, the permanent loan commitment will require not only that the improvements be completed but also that a minimum rental level be achieved before the full amount of the permanent loan is funded.

Such a *rental achievement requirement* might provide that upon completion of the improvement, 70 percent of the permanent loan will be disbursed, with the balance of the permanent loan to be disbursed once 80 percent of the building is rented.

A loan containing this type of clause is called a *floor-to-ceiling loan*, since it is disbursed in two stages. The purpose of the clause is to assure the lender that sufficient cash flow is forthcoming to service the loan before the entire amount is disbursed.

Gap Financing   Suppose the construction lender has insisted on a permanent (takeout) loan commitment equal to the full amount of the construction loan. If the best the developer can do is obtain a floor-to-ceiling loan, with the ceiling equal to the construction financing, a gap will exist if only the floor amount of the permanent loan is funded at the completion of construction.

To close this gap, the developer must obtain an additional loan commitment to provide *gap financing.* By this commitment, another lender agrees to provide a permanent second mortgage in the event the full amount of the permanent first mortgage is not advanced when construction is completed. As with most second mortgages, such an agreement will be quite costly in terms of both interest and origination fees.

This is merely one example of the many financing variations that have been developed in the industry to meet specific situations. The varieties of financing techniques rival, if not exceed, the combinations of real estate interests that were discussed in Chapter 4.

Permanent financing of a newly completed real estate project is likely to go through a number of different modifications over the life of the project. The types of modifications include many and varied possibilities. Among the more common possibilities are:

☐ *Liquidation.* The loan may be gradually amortized (paid off) during its term, eventually being liquidated in its entirety, at which point the owner's equity interest will equal the full market value of the property. This is likely to happen only in the case of single-family homes since with most investment real estate, owners desire a fairly high level of debt financing both to minimize their own cash investment and (where possible) to create desirable financial leverage.

☐ *Refinancing.* Prior to the maturity of the original mortgage, the owner may (1) renegotiate its terms with the original lender, (2) increase the loan amount, or (3) pay off the existing mortgage and obtain a new mortgage. All of these are known by the term *loan refinancing.* In general, refinancing is done for one of three reasons: (1) to increase the property's sale potential by making the financing more attractive to a buyer, (2) to generate tax-free cash for the owner by increasing the existing debt, or (3) to decrease the existing debt so as to reduce the monthly debt service and so increase the cash flow to the owner.

☐ *Prepayment.* In many cases, the owner of the property will sell it before the existing mortgage has been paid off. In such event, the lender may call the loan or the new owner may wish to pay off the existing mortgage and arrange new financing.

SUMMARY

A diverse group of financial intermediaries is involved in real estate lending. Government is not only a lender, but a regulatory insurer and secondary mortgage market facilitator as well. The various lenders make different types of loans (different both in type of property and duration) based on their sources of funds, location, expertise, and regulatory constraints. Lender specialization can be evidenced by their varying participation in the real estate financing cycle.

APPENDIX 12A

The Secondary Mortgage Markets: Structure and Participants

INTRODUCTION

The secondary mortgage market is the arena in which previously originated mortgage loans are bought and sold. It is important to the real estate decision-maker because opportunities for resale have a significant influence on what types of loans lenders choose to originate.

The mortgage loan originator is always concerned with the safety of the loan. Certainly the physical property itself provides good collateral for a loan. However, this does not mean that lenders feel perfectly safe with a 100 percent loan-to-value ratio loan. Appraised values are not always perfect; properties may be physically damaged or decline in value due to a general deterioration of the neighborhood. Further, many of those who desire to borrow funds to buy real property do not have ideal borrower characteristics (i.e., personal wealth, job stability, etc.).

In response to this need for safety, several mortgage insurance programs have been developed. As described below, these programs guarantee or insure either the entire principal amount or the riskiest portion of the principal amount. With mortgage insurance, the lender has negligible long-term risk.

The lender also faces certain liquidity problems, and secondary mortgage markets developed in response to this second lender concern. Previously originated loans are both bought and sold in secondary mortgage markets. The consequent liquidity provided the mortgage loan originator, when coupled with the safety provided by mortgage insurance, makes possible higher loan-to-value ratio loans for a greater number of icans. In fact, more individuals own their own homes in the U.S. than in any other nation.[1]

MORTGAGE INSURANCE AND GUARANTEES

The federal government, through the Federal Housing Administration (FHA) and the Veterans Administration (VA), has greatly facilitated operation of a viable secondary mortgage market by increasing the safety of mortgage lending. Indirectly, federal mortgage insurance programs have had a significant spillover affect on original lending terms, actual building plans, and uniform loan documentation.

In regard to lending terms, the FHA and VA provide underwriting guidelines to mortgage loan originators. This allows loan originators to package many loans while maintaining an acceptable level of quality. Building requirements as established by the FHA and VA contribute to standardization in the area of construction quality. This has a tendency to upgrade the quality of the mortgage collateral. The requirement of uniform loan documentation enhances the marketability of such mortgages. These specifications provide for a great deal of homogeneity among such loans. This homogeneity, in turn, makes mortgages associated with the FHA and VA programs marketable throughout the United States.

The Federal Housing Administration

The Federal Housing Administration was created by the National Housing Act of 1934. This Act has been amended several times and currently charges the FHA with the following major objectives:

- To operate housing loan insurance programs designed to encourage improvement in housing standards and conditions.
- To facilitate sound home financing on reasonable terms.
- To exert a stabilizing influence in the mortgage market.

The FHA is not a direct lender of mortgage funds. Neither does it plan or build homes. It does, however, affect both lending terms and building plans as well as a selection of housing sites by underwriting conditions. Lenders, borrowers, and the property involved must meet specified qualifications before an FHA insured loan can be originated.

Currently, the majority of FHA-insured loans are originated under either Section 203(b) or Section 245 of the National Housing Act. The 203(b) program covers single-family insured loans where the loan limits,

---

[1] In other words, in the U.S., higher loan-to-value ratio loans for longer terms are possible for a greater portion of the population than in any other major country. This is true not only because of the strength of the U.S. economy and U.S. financial markets, but also because of the governmental and private initiatives discussed in this appendix.

as a percentage of appraised value, are 97 percent on the first $25,000 and 95 percent on the remainder up to a maximum which is set by the Secretary of the U.S. Department of Housing and Urban Development (HUD).

The Section 245 program covers graduated payment mortgages (as opposed to level payment mortgages). Currently, five plans exist, each of which provides for a different rate of increase in the annual payment over the first five years of the loan. The maximum interest rate for these loans is also initially established by the Secretary of HUD.

Setting maximum interest rates does, at times, produce a divergence between FHA and conventional lending rates. As a result, it is often necessary that the seller of the property being financed by FHA-insured loans pay discount points to the lender as an inducement to make the loan at the FHA rate.[2]

In the case of default, the lender is entitled to receive from the FHA debentures equivalent to the amount of the debt then unpaid. The interest and principal payments on the debentures are fully guaranteed by the U.S. Government. The interest rate on such debentures is a function of the government's cost of money. Such obligations generally mature in three years.

The Veterans Administration

Created in 1944, the VA is authorized to aid veterans in securing financing for houses. Guaranteed loans may be made to veterans of World War II or the Korean conflict who have served on active duty for ninety days or more. In addition, other veterans in active service for over 180 days may also qualify as well as widows of veterans who died in service or as a result of service-connected disabilities. Finally, wives of members of the armed forces who have been listed as missing in action or prisoners of war for ninety days or more are also eligible.

The VA guarantee is an absolute guarantee in which the VA becomes liable for the amount of the existing guarantee on default. The guarantee has always been based on a percentage of the loan with a maximum amount fixed by law. The percentage adheres to the loan as the debt is decreased by payments or increased by unpaid interest. At the present time, the mortgage guarantee ceiling is 60 percent of the loan amount or $25,000, whichever is greater.[3] Any person, firm, association, corporation, or state or federal agency can be an eligible lender under VA legislation. (The VA also provides insurance, but the magnitude of such insured loans is not significant.)

---

[2] The question as to who (buyer or seller) actually pays the points is debatable. Even though FHA regulations do not allow the buyer to pay the points directly, the seller will often pass on the points to the buyer in the form of a higher price.

[3] If the borrower becomes delinquent, the lender may file a claim with the VA. The VA may elect to make good the amount of the delinquency, bringing the loan current again or pay the amount of the guarantee. Any payments made by the VA to the lender under such circumstances do not, however, reduce the borrower's obligation and the mortgagor then owes the VA for this unpaid portion.

Private Mortgage Insurers

Prior to the provision of mortgage insurance by the government in the 1930s, the field was exclusively occupied by private companies. Under the impact of the Depression, these firms either failed or otherwise ceased operations. From the Depression period until 1957, mortgage insurance and guarantee underwriting was done almost exclusively by the FHA and the VA.

In 1957, the Mortgage Guaranty Insurance Corporation (MGIC) was organized and licensed by the Wisconsin Commissioner of Insurance. Since that time, fourteen additional private insurers have begun operations. These fourteen mortgage insurance companies have been approved by the FNMA and the FHLMC as qualified insurers, making their guarantees acceptable in the secondary conventional loan market[4] and their guarantees are accepted by the different regulatory bodies supervising the mortgage loan originators. (See 12A-1.)

When foreclosure is necessary, the policy holder (lender) must first secure title to the real property covering the loans. Once the claim is filed, the MIC can settle in one of two ways:

- Accept title to the real property and pay the insured lender the full amount of the claim.
- Pay the percentage of coverage selected and paid for by the insured and have no further liability under the policy.

Arguments for Private Mortgage Insurance

Unlike the FHA (which offers insurance up to one hundred percent of the principal amount) or the VA (which provides a guarantee of $25,000 of the loan), the mortgage insurance companies (MICs) offer insurance coverage up to a maximum of 20 to 25 percent of the loan amount, depending upon the loan-to-value ratio and the coverage desired by the lender. (This is the top or most risky portion of the loan.) This feature has enabled the MICs to offer their insurance at a lower cost than the FHA and VA programs.

In addition, private insurance coverage can be canceled by the is the top or most risky portion of the loan.) The feature has enabled the reduced via monthly payments and inflation (which increase the value of the collateral). Conversely, the insurance/guarantee granted by the FHA/VA is generally carried for the life of the loan.

Furthermore, the MICs insure loans which are made at the prevailing market rate. The FHA and VA, on the other hand, impose ceilings or maximum rates allowed on loans they insure/guarantee. This can result in discount points being charged to the seller.

Finally, the MICs leave the determination of acceptable standards of risk selection to their approved lenders, thus leaving borrower selection more in the lender's hand. The FHA and VA supply their lenders with

---

[4] A "conventional loan" is a non-government-insured loan. In order to make greater than 75 to 80 percent loan-to-value ratio loans, most loan originators are required to have either governmental or private mortgage insurance.

12A-1. MEMBERS OF THE MORTGAGE INSURANCE COMPANIES OF AMERICA (MICA)

The following are members of the Mortgage Insurance Companies of America:
- American Mortgage Insurance Company
- Commercial Credit Mortgage Insurance Company
- Commonwealth Mortgage Assurance Company
- Continental Mortgage Insurance Company
- Foremost Guaranty Corporation
- Home Guaranty Insurance Corporation
- Investors Mortgage Insurance Company
- Liberty Mortgage Insurance Corporation
- Mortgage Guaranty Insurance Corporation
- PMI Mortgage Insurance Company
- Republic Mortgage Insurance Company
- Secura Insurance Company
- Ticor Mortgage Insurance Company
- United Guaranty Corporation

standards for the selection of insurable/guaranteeable loans as well as borrowers. As a result of this (and other factors), the paper work on government-insured loans substantially exceeds that required on privately insured loans.

The proportion of total mortgage insurance in force supplied by the MICs has grown steadily since 1957. As can be seen in Figure 12A-1, by 1976, the MICs insurance in force comprised about 49 percent of the total.

Year	FHA/VA Insurance	MICA* Insurance	MGIC Insurance
1955	$ 39.9	$ 0	$ 0
1960	56.4	.3	.3
1965	73.1	3.6	2.6
1970	97.3	7.3	5.1
1971	105.2	9.6	6.3
1972	113.0	17.5	11.0
1973	116.2	27.4	17.1
1974	121.3	33.5	20.2
1975	127.1	39.9	22.6
1976	133.5	49.3	27.4

* Mortgage Insurance Companies of America—total of fourteen companies.

Figure 12A-1. FHA/VA AND MICs—INSURANCE IN FORCE (BILLIONS OF DOLLARS)

THE MORTGAGE BANKER AND THE SECONDARY MORTGAGE MARKET

As this discussion proceeds from a consideration of mortgage insurance to a focus on the overall secondary mortgage market, it is useful to look again at the function of the mortgage banker. While the opportunities for secondary market involvement noted below are available to most financial institutions, it is only the mortgage banker who relies on these sources exclusively. Each of the other financial institutions has depository funds of some sort which serve as its primary source of funding. The mortgage banker is the entrepreneur who operates without depository funds. Therefore, the mortgage banker will be used to illustrate utilization of the different secondary market alternatives.

The mortgage banker profits through the successful management of five different cash flows. These are:

☐ *Mortgage loan originations.* The loan origination process, often called *loan production,* involves certain costs to the mortgage banker. To offset these costs, a loan origination fee is usually charged to the borrower at the closing, typically one percent of the loan amount.

☐ *Warehousing operations.* As noted in the preceding chapter, the mortgage banker borrows short-term from a commercial bank while accumulating mortgage loans. Once the package of loans is accumulated, the mortgage banker then sells the entire package. During the period of time that the banker is accumulating loans, interest is paid to the commercial bank for the short-term funds and at the same time collected on the mortgage loans originated but not yet sold. The difference between the interest paid the commercial bank (short-term) and the interest received on the mortgage loans (long-term) is termed the warehousing profit (or loss).

☐ *Servicing activities.* Once the loans have been sold to a permanent lender, the mortgage banker typically continues to service the loan. In other words, the mortgage banker collects the periodic principal, interest, insurance, and tax payments and forwards them to the permanent lender, insurer, and government, respectively. The mortgage banker charges a fee for this servicing. Such revenue is the major profit item for most large mortgage bankers.

☐ *Float.* As part of the servicing activity, the mortgage banker accumulates funds prior to sending them on to the permanent lender. Depending on who the permanent lender is, the mortgage banker may accumulate principal and interest payments for a few days up to a month. In addition, the mortgage banker will accumulate property tax and insurance (fire and casualty) payments for a period of time before actually paying the local government or the insurance company. There is a definite value to these bank balances which the mortgage banker can trade off against the interest cost of the short-term loan from the commercial bank.

☐ *Marketing.* The mortgage banker may experience a gain or loss when the package of loans is sold to the final lender. If market interest rates rise between the date of origination and the date of sale, then the loans the mortgage banker is selling are less attractive and must be discounted (i.e., sold at a loss). On the other hand, if market interest rates fall, then the mortgage banker's loans will sell at a premium (i.e., a gain on sale).

The mortgage banker seeks to maximize positive cash flows from the five sources noted above, subject to certain constraints. The first constraint is an *overall volume restriction.* No more loans can be originated and held than can be financed through equity or line of credit sources. The mortgage banker must originate and sell loans in a cycle since the absolute amount of loans which can be held in the portfolio is limited.

The second constraint involves *interest risks.* During the period when the mortgage banker is holding long-term loans, fluctuations in mortgage interest rates might very well occur. As noted above, if market interest rates go up during this period, the loans the mortgage banker is holding will become less valuable and a "marketing" loss will be experienced on disposition. The mortgage banker will not usually wish to be exposed to an unlimited amount of interest rate risk. As we will see, several of the secondary market alternatives make it possible for the mortgage banker to pass on this risk, but at a definite cost.

The Secondary Mortgage Market

The mortgage banker seeks to maximize cash flows, particularly servicing subject to the constraints mentioned above. Traditionally, this meant maximizing loan originations (and thus eventual servicing fees) in the local area and selling them to a permanent lender, most often a life insurance company. This traditional process, even with mortgage insurance, was not successful in moving the desired level of funds into the real estate industry. Consequently, the public sector has established alternative methods of secondary mortgage market financing. In fact, the secondary mortgage market is one of the major successes of federal government involvement in the real estate industry.

MARKET MAKERS IN THE SECONDARY MORTGAGE MARKET

The Federal National Mortgage Association

History and Current Organization   In the 1930s, as an aftermath to the Depression, attempts were made by Congress to induce private capital to form national mortgage associations to provide a secondary market for insured mortgages. Failing in its efforts, Congress authorized the Reconstruction Finance Corporation (RFC) to form a subsidiary which was known as the Federal National Mortgage Association (FNMA or "Fannie Mae").

Starting with an initial capitalization of $10 million, the FNMA's original purposes were to

- Establish a market for the purchase and sale of first mortgages insured by the FHA covering newly constructed houses or housing projects.
- Facilitate the construction and financing of economically sound rental housing projects or groups of houses for rent or sale through direct lending on FHA-insured mortgages.
- Make FNMA bonds or debentures available to institutional investors. (This was the source of the financing necessary to achieve the first two purposes, above.)

In 1950, the FNMA was transferred from the RFC to the Housing and Finance Agency. This move enabled the FNMA's activities to be more closely coordinated with the Federal Home Loan Bank Board (FHLBB) as well as with the FHA.

In 1954, the FNMA was rechartered by Congress and commissioned with three separate and distinct activities:

- Secondary market operations in federally insured and guaranteed mortgages.
- Management and liquidating functions (i.e., the management and liquidation of the loans which FNMA had purchased up to that time).
- Special assistance programs (i.e., subsidy programs which the federal government might initiate from time to time).

FNMA was to be administered as though it were a separate corporation with its own assets, liabilities, and borrowing ability.

A major objective of the Charter Act of 1954 was to establish a procedure whereby the FNMA would be transformed over time into a privately owned and managed organization. With the passage of the Housing and Urban Development Act of 1968, the assets and liabilities of the secondary market operations were transferred to a private corporation—also known as the Federal National Mortgage Association. As a result, the FNMA is now a government-sponsored corporation owned solely by private investors.

The remaining functions of the "old" FNMA (sanctioned under the Charter Act) remained in HUD. To carry out these duties, the Government National Mortgage Association (GNMA or "Ginnie Mae") was created.

Today, the FNMA is largely run by its board of directors consisting of fifteen members—one-third appointed annually by the President of the United States with the remainder chosen by the common stockholders. Of those chosen by the President, at least one appointee must be from each of the home building, mortgage lending, and real estate industries.

Authorized Activities   Sections 302, 303, and 304 of the FNMA Charter Act describe the principal activities empowered in FNMA with respect to its secondary market operations:

Purchase and Sale Operations   The first and primary authorized activity has to do with FNMA provision of funds in the secondary market. FNMA, under Section 302(b), is authorized to purchase, sell, or otherwise deal in government-guaranteed or -insured securities. Since 1970, with the passage of the Emergency Home Finance Act, FNMA also has the authority to deal in mortgages not federally insured or guaranteed (i.e., conventional mortgages). FNMA, however, is not permitted to purchase such mortgages if the outstanding principal balances of the mortgages at the time of the purchase exceeds 80 percent of the value of the underlying property, unless

- The seller retains a participation of not less than 15 percent in the mortgage, or
- For such period and under such circumstances as the FNMA may require, the seller agrees to repurchase or replace the mortgage in the event of default, or
- That portion of the unpaid principal balance of the mortgage which is in excess of 80 percent is guaranteed or insured by a qualified insurer as determined by FNMA. (i.e., a private mortgage insurer).

Financing Operations   Section 304 of the Charter Act allows FNMA to finance its secondary market operations via the issuance of securities. One such financing instrument available to FNMA is the issuance of *general obligations*. The aggregate amount of such obligations outstanding at any point in time is not allowed to exceed fifteen times the sum of the capital, capital surplus, general surplus, reserves, and undistributed earnings of FNMA. Such general obligations are *not* guaranteed by the U.S. Government.

FNMA and the Mortgage Banker

As mentioned in the section describing the risk-shifting activities of the mortgage banker, the FNMA can be used by the mortgage banker in a risk-expected/return format. The first and most obvious use involves the FNMA Free-Market System auction. Successful bidders in these auctions obtain commitments from the FNMA to purchase packages of mortgages at any time during a four-month period.[5]

To use the auction, mortgage loan originators must be approved and buy stock in FNMA. At the biweekly auction, the loan originators (sellers) make sealed offers to sell certain amounts (up to five bids of up to $3

---

[5] The Free-Market System auction is divided into FHA/VA and conventional components. There is also a twelve-month convertible standby commitment as well as a noncompetitive section of the auction.

million each are allowed) at specific yields. FNMA then determines which bids it will accept (i.e., offer commitments on). Since the mortgage banker seeks a marketing profit, he wants to bid the lowest possible yield. However, the lower the bid, the less the chance that it will be accepted by FNMA.

Such commitments, if obtained, enable the banker to do several things. First, the commitment acts as a hedge by allowing the banker to "lock in" a guaranteed sales price on the mortgage loan portfolio. If market rates rise, the mortgage banker can deliver against the commitment at the yield established at the date the commitment was issued. In addition, should market interest rates fall, the mortgage banker can renege on his commitment (delivery is optional, not mandatory, even though the commitment has been issued and is binding on the FNMA). Therefore, the upside return is unrestricted by the optional commitment, while the downside is hedged.

In addition, the commitments provide the banker with the assurance that the funds will be available, if the banker needs them, to cover promised loans to home buyers (borrowers) as well as to clear up any outstanding bank loans or to originate any new loans. Since these funds are obtained only if the commitment is "exercised" (i.e., the loans are sold to the FNMA), a systematic approach combining loan origination, optimal bidding, and commitment exercise strategy is necessary if such endeavors are to be as profitable as possible.

The Government National Mortgage Association

History and Current Organization   The GNMA is a government corporation comprising a section of HUD. All powers and duties of GNMA are vested in the Secretary of Housing and Urban Development. The Secretary is authorized to determine the general policies, administrative affairs, and officer appointments. (see Figure 12A-2.) Created through Title III of the Federal National Mortgage Association Charger Act of 1968, GNMA is empowered with three functions:

	GNMA	Aaa
First-quarter 1978	8.60%	8.45%
1977	8.04	8.02
1976	8.17	8.43
1975	8.52	8.83
1974	8.72	8.57
SOURCE: Board of Governors of the Federal Reserve System, "Mortgages," *Federal Reserve Bulletin* (Washington, D.C.: U.S. Government Printing Office, 1974-1978).		

Figure 12A-2.   COMPARISON OF GNMA AND Aaa CORPORATE BOND YIELDS (the rates indicated represent the average net yield received by the investor for the period indicated)

- The special assistance function (old FNMA subsidy function now expanded).
- The management and liquidation of GNMA's own mortgage portfolio (this portfolio was originally obtained from the FNMA in 1968; the GMNA differs from the FNMA and the FHLMC in that it does not accumulate a portfolio of mortgages—that is, mortgages purchased by the GNMA are generally resold within a year).
- The guaranteeing of specified securities collateralized by specific pools of mortgages (pass-throughs).

Mortgage-Backed Securities Function   Under Section 306(g), of the Charter Act, GNMA is authorized "to guarantee the timely payment of principal and interest" on long-term securities backed by self-liquidating pools of mortgages. Currently, only pools comprised of FHA-insured or VA-guaranteed mortgages qualify as collateral for such securities.

The pass-through security is a very popular form of mortgage loan financing. (To date, over 85 percent of the outstanding pass-throughs have been issued by mortgage bankers and thrift institutions.) Each certificate represents a share in a pool of FHA and/or VA mortgages. The pass-through comes in two forms: (1) standard and (2) modified.

Under the standard alternative, the total interest and principal collections are "passed through" to the certificate holders on a monthly basis. Any mortgage delinquencies are immediately replaced in the pool. The standard plan has not enjoyed the same popularity as the modified plan; hence, it is not frequently issued.

The modified pass-through is by far the most popular of all the mortgage-backed securities. With these securities, the investor can have the interest and principal collections passed through less frequently than monthly (perhaps quarterly, semiannually, etc.). Again, principal and interest payments are passed through to the certificate holders, whether or not the corresponding mortgage payments are received. Furthermore, mortgage delinquencies are replaced by the issuer via mortgage reserve pools.

All of the mortgage-backed securities have several common characteristics. First, each instrument bears interest at a rate less than the rate borne by the supporting mortgage pool. This provides the issuer with a differential to cover the administrative costs and guarantee risks. Substantial reinvestment risk exists, however, if mortgages are liquidated (by the mortgagor) prior to maturity. This "cuts off" the interest stream which provides payments to the security holders. If interest rates have fallen since issuance, the investor may not be able to reinvest the prepayments from the loan payoff at a rate commensurate with the certificate rate.[6]

---

[6] Many home loans pay off before the stated maturity, as the houses are sold, refinanced, destroyed by fire and not replaced, etc. Since the exact timing of such early repayments is a function of many things (particularly interest rates and home prices), it is difficult to estimate the exact life of the GNMA security. Remember, principal payments are "passed through" as received.

The reader should ponder how this situation effects the yield calculation (for the GNMA security holder) as described in Chapter 13.

In any event, if interest or principal collections from the mortgagors are insufficient to meet the security payments, GNMA unconditionally guarantees the prompt payment of interest and principal to the security holders should the security issuer be unable to do so. (Through the issuance of GNMA securities, the issuer has pledged the underlying mortgages as collateral to GNMA.) Thus, such securities are more than general obligations of the issuer (supported by the mortgages themselves) in the sense that GNMA guarantees the interest and principal payments. (The mortgages are also either insured by the FHA or are VA-guaranteed, with the GNMA guarantee adding the "timeliness" element.) As far as the issuer is concerned, the issuance of such guaranteed securities is the practical equivalent of the sale with recourse of the underlying mortgages to GNMA and retention of a servicing contract. Remember that servicing is the major profit item.

The significance of the mortgage-backed security cannot be understated. It may be one of the most innovative ideas in recent security market history. Prior to the introduction of such securities, the mortgage insurers provided the necessary standardization of mortgage loans. Through their rigid requirements, they provided the necessary grading that was essential for the marketing of mortgage loans in the secondary market. The mortgage-backed security goes one step further by providing the investor with a financial instrument which is both inexpensive to maintain and easily marketable. Hence, the trend toward pooling mortgages and issuing a self-liquidating security should continue. These securities serve not only to bring additional investors into the market (by providing them with a means of converting an illiquid investment—the mortgage loan—into a marketable security), but they also provide the issuers (i.e., mortgage bankers) with immediate funds for additional mortgage lending while at the same time providing a source of servicing revenue.

GNMA and the Mortgage Banker

Commitments from GNMA security dealers come in two forms: (1) mandatory and (2) optional. The arrangements for delivery usually call for completion of the pool and issuance of the securities at some point in the future. Typically, the mortgage banker arranges for the GNMA guarantee, and then, while originating the loans, negotiates an arrangement with New York (or other money center) securities dealers to market the pass-through interests. The risk shifting as well as financing possibilities for the mortgage banker paralleled those described in the FNMA section, except that negotiation with a securities dealer replaces the competitive auction.[7]

The Federal Home Loan Mortgage Corporation

History and Current Organization   Created by Title III of the Emergency Home Finance Act of 1970, the FHLMC is a corporate entity whose

---

[7] In the 1980's there will be both an active futures and an options market in GNMA securities.

designed purpose is to serve as a secondary market facility for real estate mortgages under the sponsorship of the Federal Home Loan Bank System (FHLBS). It assists in the development and maintenance of a secondary market in conventional (not FHA-insured or VA-guaranteed) residential mortgage loans.

As such, the FHLMC views its responsibilities as threefold:

- To circulate funds from capital surplus geographical areas to capital deficit areas.
- To develop new sources of funds during periods of credit stringency.
- To develop new financing instruments to aid in the development of the private secondary mortgage market.

The FHLMC is controlled by a board of directors whose members are appointed by the President of the United States, with the advice and consent of the U.S. Senate for terms of four years.

Authorized Activities   The FHLMC's authorized activities come largely under the jurisdiction of the Emergency Home Finance Act of 1970. Its operations fall into two general categories:

- Purchase and sale operations.
- Financing operations.

Purchase and Sale Operations   All whole loans or loan participations purchased by the FHLMC must meet certain standards as set forth in the Act. First, the FHLMC deals almost exclusively in conventional, rather than FHA or VA, mortgages. In doing so, the FHLMC is confined in its purchases to those obligations secured by first mortgages. In addition, the outstanding principal balance of such conventional mortgages (at the time of purchase) is not allowed to exceed 80 percent of the value of the underlying property unless

- The seller retains a participation interest in the mortgage of not less than 10 percent.
- Or, the seller agrees for such period and under such circumstances as the FHLMC may prescribe to repurchase or replace the mortgage obligations in the event of default.
- Or, the portion of the unpaid principal balance of the mortgage obligation which is in excess of 80 percent is insured by a qualified mortgage insurer as determined by the FHLMC. (See Figure 12A-3.)

The FHLMC may purchase mortgages from any Federal Home Loan Bank, the Federal Savings and Loan Corporation, any member of the FHLBS, any other financial institution (the deposits of which are insured by an agency of the United States), and from certain financial institutions (the deposits of which are insured under state law). Legislation, prepared

	FNMA	GNMA	FHLMC
Commitments issued	$10,894,000	$ 1,926,452	$5,501,000
Mortgages purchased	4,784,000	927,516	4,116,007
Mortgages sold	81,629	2,079,182	5,441,000
Mortgage-backed securities outstanding	469,223	41,663,000	6,764,000
Mortgage loan portfolio	34,376,527	—	3,110,000

SOURCE: Federal National Mortgage Association, *Annual Report for 1977* (Washington, D.C.: U.S. Government Printing Office, 1978); The Mortgage Corporation, *Annual Report for 1977* (Washington, D.C.: U.S. Government Printing Office, 1978); Government National Mortgage Association: *GNMA Annual Report 1977* (Washington, D.C.: U.S. Government Printing Office, 1978).

Figure 12A-3. FHMA, GNMA, AND FHLMC—COMPARING THEIR MAJOR ACTIVITIES FOR FISCAL YEAR 1977 (in thousands)

in 1978[8] would also enable qualified mortgage companies to sell (and hence service) mortgages to the FHLMC. (Although mortgage bankers have not traditionally been permitted to deal *directly* with the FHLMC, many utilize the placement alternatives provided by the FHLMC through their parent commercial bank holding companies.) Loan purchase commitments are issued via a weekly auction similar to the FNMA auction.

Financing Operations   One of the principal methods of financing afforded the FHLMC is through direct borrowing from the FHLBS. The loan obtained from it is required, however, to be secured by the mortgages purchased by the FHLMC.

In addition, the FHLMC is permitted to issue its own general obligations backed or secured by mortgage pools and guaranteed by the GNMA. The FHLMC *now* employs two principal methods of financing its secondary market operations. The two financial instruments are:

- Guaranteed mortgage certificate (GMC).
- Mortgage participation certificate (PC).

□ *The guaranteed mortgage certificate.* The GMC represents undivided interests in mortgages, either whole loans or participations. Certificate holders are allowed to receive, pro rata, interest collected by the trustee on the mortgages and interim investments of principal and interest (up to the certificate rate). Any interest earned in excess of the certificate rate is paid by the trustee to the FHLMC as compensation for its guarantee and its services under the trust indenture.

---

[8] Housing and Community Development Amendments of 1978, Conference Report No. 1161, 95th Cong., 2nd Sess. (1978).

The FHLMC unconditionally guarantees the certificate holder's payment by the mortgagors of the interest on the mortgages to the extent of the certificate rate. The trustee, on receiving mortgage interest and principal payments, forwards the principal and interest due to the certificate holders. Interest is payable semiannually, whereas principal payments are forwarded annually.

The trustee is allowed to make short-term investments of mortgage interest and principal receipts, pending payments due the GMC holders. If the interest received and earned is less than the certificate rate, then the FHLMC unconditionally warrants a return equal to that rate.

In addition, the FHLMC unconditionally guarantees collection of the mortgage principal payments. Insufficient collections result in the FHLMC paying the deficiency to the trustee. In this event, the FHLMC is deemed to have made a purchase and thus has a vested interest in the mortgages.

Most GMCs typically have repurchase agreements giving the holder the right to sell his certificate back to the FHLMC. To do so, the holder must give thirty days' notice of his intention.

☐ *The mortgage participation certificate.* The PC also represents an undivided interest in mortgages whether the instruments be whole loans or participations. The mortgages backing the securities are specified conventional mortgages underwritten and owned by the FHLMC.

Interest and principal payments received by the FHLMC from the mortgages are passed through monthly (as received) to the certificate holders. In addition, any mortgage prepayments received by the FHLMC are also passed on to the PC holders.

The FHLMC unconditionally guarantees the timely payment of interest (up to the certificate rate) to the PC purchasers. If mortgage interest receipts are insufficient, the FHLMC makes up the difference.

Furthermore, the FHLMC unconditionally guarantees collection of the mortgage principal payments. The FHLMC reimburses the certificate holders for the deficiency and, as such, acquires an interest in the mortgages.

FHLMC and the Mortgage Banker

The FHLMC represents still another opportunity for the mortgage banker to adjust his risk-expected return position. Through the FHLMC commitment programs, the mortgage banker can minimize his exposure to interest rate risk as well as have the assurance that funds will be available to meet liquidity needs. Thus, the FHLMC purchase commitments represent alternatives comparable to the FNMA and the GNMA. The auctions held by the FHLMC, however, are only for conventional mortgage loans.

THE PRIVATELY GUARANTEED MORTGAGE LOAN PACKAGE SECURITY

The newest financial instrument in the mortgage market is the privately guaranteed security (PG), one that is now being issued by some of the larger financial institutions notably the Bank of America). Mortgage bankers and thrift institutions have been issuing GNMA-guaranteed securities for many years, but the privately guaranteed claim represents a new endeavor.

These securities do not represent the obligation of any governmental agency, nor are they guaranteed by any governmental agency. The securities represent an undivided interest in a pool of conventional mortgages originated and serviced by the issuing financial institution. The underlying mortgage loans may be either whole loans or participations.

Interest and principal payments received by the issuer are passed through monthly (as they are received from the mortgagors) to the certificate holders. Any mortgage prepayments are generally passed on to the PG holders in the month following their receipt.

Usually the underlying mortgages are insured by private mortgage insurers, somewhat reducing the exposure of the issuing institution. Generally, only the very large financial institutions are thought to be able to issue such securities, for investor confidence is very important to the success of the offering. The issuer unconditionally guarantees the prompt payment of the interest and principal payments to the PG holders. If mortgage collections are insufficient, the issuer reimburses the trustee for the necessary amount and, as such, acquires an interest in the underlying mortgages.

The pool of underlying mortgages has the same general characteristics of those pools backing GNMA- and FHLMC-guaranteed securities. The mortgages in any pool bear similar interest rates, cover the same types of dwelling, and have approximately the same maturity. However, PGs are sufficiently new and have such a low volume outstanding that generalizations are difficult.

SUMMARY

As evidenced by the volume of institutional material presented in this appendix, the secondary mortgage market has come a long way since the days of the correspondent system. The new FNMA, GNMA, FHLMC, and PG initiatives have opened up a new world to the mortgage banker. Together, these new devices provide the mortgage banker with a menu of placement alternatives.

Whether these alternatives individually or collectively will be totally effective in providing the level of financing necessary to assure satisfaction of the goal of the decent home and suitable living environment for every American is as yet an unanswered question. It is quite clear that the system is more efficient than it was in 1934.[9] It is equally clear that the secondary market is an important reason why it is easier for an American to own a home than for citizens of any other major nation.

---

[9] The reader might ask, "Is it a good thing to channel an ever increasing percentage of aggregate savings into housing finance? How is inflation affected?"

IMPORTANT TERMS

annual percentage rate (APR)
capital
commercial bank (CB)
disintermediation
Equal Credit Opportunity Act (ECOA)
finance charge
financial intermediary
floor-to-ceiling loan
gap financing
inflation premium
life insurance company (LIC)
liquidity
money market

mortgage banker
mutual savings bank (MSB)
pension fund
permanent loan commitment
primary financial market
real estate investment trust
  (REIT)
release price
rental achievement requirement
savings and loan association
secondary mortgage market
takeout commitment
Truth in Lending Act (TiL)

REVIEW QUESTIONS

12-1. What is the role of financial intermediaries in bringing together savers and borrowers in the financial system?

12-2. Of what importance is the secondary mortgage market to real estate finance?

12-3. When evaluating financial institutions, how might you expect them to attempt to match their sources of funds (liabilities) with their uses (assets)?

12-4. What has been the principal role of commercial banks in real estate lending?

12-5. What factors distinguish a mortgage banker from a mortgage broker?

12-6. How does the provision of mortgage insurance, private or government-sponsored, reduce the risk to real estate lenders?

12-7. What has been the thrust of consumer protection in the area of real estate lending?

12-8. Why doesn't the financing of raw land usually include a financial institution?

12-9. How does the repayment pattern of development loans differ from construction loans?

12-10. What is the purpose of a rental achievement requirement in a permanent loan commitment?

13

Mortgage Underwriting: The Lender's Perspective

THE MORTGAGE LENDER should be viewed as a special kind of real estate investor, one having a claim that is senior to the claim of the equity investor who is the primary focus of our real estate decision-making framework. As an investor, the lender wants to earn a return consisting of three elements:

- Real return (i.e., compensation for deferred consumption).
- Inflation premium (i.e., compensation for the declining value of the dollar).
- Risk premium (i.e., compensation for the possibility that the loan may not be repaid as agreed to).

The real return, as noted in Chapter 9, is an essentially unchanging rate, perhaps 2 to 3 percent annually. Changes in the level of interest rates are a result of changes in the other two factors. Just as noted in the derivation of a discount rate for use in the income approach to value, the inflation premium will move up and down in accordance with inflationary trends in the economy and will, in general, affect all loans of similar maturity equally. The risk premium, on the other hand, is a function of the safety and liquidity of the particular loan. The better the collateral (the higher the quality of the real property asset) and the wealthier the borrower (assuming personal liability on the note), the lower will be the risk premium demanded by the lender. Mortgage underwriting essentially is the process whereby a lender analyzes a loan to determine the degree of risk involved—that is, the likelihood that interest and principal payments on the loan will not be made promptly and that the loan eventually may not be repaid. Within the class of loans the lender wishes to make, the interest rate charged will rise or the loan-to-value ratio will decline with the perceived riskiness of the loan.

Mortgage underwriting decisions are generally made on the basis of a set of guidelines which the lender has designed for use in evaluating individual mortgage loan applications. The specifics of such guidelines vary from one type of property to another and among the various types of lending institutions. In general, several major underwriting considerations must be examined.

MAJOR UNDERWRITING CONSIDERATIONS

In evaluating a mortgage loan, the lender will concentrate on certain key considerations, whether the loan is on a residential or commercial property. These are briefly described below.

First Lien Position and Good Title

Since the loan will be secured by a particular property, the lender must be sure the borrower has good title to the real estate. This will involve an examination of title as described in Chapter 5. In addition, the lender's security interest (in the form of a mortgage or deed of trust) normally must be a first lien (e.g., have first priority in the event of a default by the borrower.) This, also can be confirmed by a title examination which will reveal the existence of any outstanding claims or liens against the property.

Regional and Urban Economics

After an evaluation of legal title, the mortgage lender will be interested in the region's general economic health, as well as the particular urban area's development pattern. Both of these factors were important in the establishment of our analytical framework, and the lender's perspective is identical to the perspective we developed in the opening chapters. In essence, the lender looks at regional and urban economic conditions as a means of evaluating the strength of the location of the subject property over the term of the loan.

The Property and the Borrower

Next, the lender will consider an appraisal of the specific property, calculating the proposed loan-to-value ratio and the debt coverage ratios described in detail later on in the chapter. The lender will also examine the borrower's own financial position. In the case of owner-occupied property, the borrower's income and assets are a crucial factor in determining the amount of the loan the lender will be willing to make. Even when income-producing property secures the loan, borrower characteristics remain important, for if the lender is forced to foreclose and the property fails to sell at a price high enough to pay off the remaining amount on the note, the lender will seek a *deficiency judgment* against the borrower for the difference. Once obtained, this judgment is only good if the borrower has resources which may be attached.

Safety and Liquidity

In general, lenders prefer safer loans. In line with our definition of winning, lenders prefer not only higher interest rates, but lower risk associated with the loan. In lending, two important elements are safety of principal and liquidity.

☐ *Safety of principal.* There is a chance that the lender will not get the principal back. This can occur if the borrower fails to repay the loan. In the case of real estate finance, if such a default occurs, the lender can foreclose and force the sale of the financed property.

Mortgage insurance is not the only form of insurance available to protect the lender's interest. In Chapter 5, it is noted that title insurance is also available and that it can protect the lender from loss due to a previously undiscovered superior claim (i.e., to a loss resulting from title problems). Fire and casualty insurance are available to protect the collateral against the elements. Finally, the lender may require the borrower to take out mortgage life insurance which will pay off the note in the event of the borrower's death.

☐ *Liquidity.* There is a chance that the lender's source of funds may require repayment before the lender's loans (assets) mature. As already seen, the *secondary mortgage market* is a partial answer to this problem.

Other things being equal, lenders are more attracted to insured loans for which there is an active secondary market.

Lender Portfolio Considerations

Lenders must look beyond specific loan characteristics to overall portfolio considerations. If loans are diversified, both by location and by property type, less risk exists in the overall portfolio. However, it is not always easy to diversify either by property type or geographically, because real estate markets are both local in character and inefficient in nature. This means that market expertise is required in order to make a successful loan, and expertise by its nature, normally is localized. Therefore, full diversification often requires more expertise than is possessed by the lender.

Other portfolio considerations involve loan terms. The lender will not want all or a substantial percentage of its loans maturing at the same time, since this will create problems of reinvestment. The lender will be concerned with balancing the terms of its loans (assets) with the sources of its funds (liabilities) as discussed in the previous chapter. The lender will seek a portfolio of loans which fit with the institution's sources of funds and the stability of those sources.

MORTGAGES AND DEEDS OF TRUST

A loan made to finance the acquisition or construction of real estate normally is secured by the real estate itself. Whenever a loan has real estate as collateral, the loan is called a *mortgage* or a *deed of trust* depending on the particular state in which the loan is made. The function of both types of instrument is the same. The way each type of instrument carries out the function is somewhat different, as is explained below.

Although the terms mortgage and deed of trust imply that only a single instrument is executed, in fact, there are two. One is a promissory note, whereby the borrower expressly contracts to repay the loan principal together with interest at a specified rate. The other is the instrument which makes the real estate security for the note. It is the latter instrument that, properly speaking, is either the mortgage or deed of trust.

Security Interest

As pointed out in Chapter 4, a mortgage creates a *security interest* in real estate. The mortgagee (lender) has no right to possess or use the real estate by virtue of the mortgage. In "title theory" states, the mortgage is viewed as more than just a lien. The title to the mortgaged property is in the name of the lender. This distinction, however, is not of practical significance. In lien theory states, the mortgage simply creates a *lien* (claim) on the real estate to secure the repayment of a debt. In such states, the title is in the name of the borrower. Once the debt is repaid, the lien is canceled or discharged.

When a mortgage or deed of trust has been executed and delivered to the lender, it should immediately be recorded in the local records office. By so doing, the lender gives public notice of its lien on the real estate and so retains priority against subsequent purchasers or claimants.

Distinctions Between the Mortgage and Deed of Trust

The mortgage is the instrument which gives the lender the legal right to force foreclosure when the note is not paid. The mortgage is therefore tied to the note and specific to the particular piece of property serving as collateral. The foreclosure procedure involves posting notice and eventually an auction sale. The exact mechanics of foreclosure vary from jurisdiction to jurisdiction and usually require the use of legal counsel.

In many areas, a note and a deed of trust are used as a substitute instrument for the note and mortgage just described. Basically, this is a combination instrument which facilitates the foreclosure procedure. The borrower deeds the property to a trustee, who holds the deed until the note is paid. In the event of default on the note, the trustee can more easily sell the property at auction.

ELEMENTS OF THE MORTGAGE AND DEED OF TRUST

The mortgage or deed of trust usually is a lengthy document which sets forth the various obligations of the borrower, both with respect to the loan and with respect to the real estate which acts as security. The major elements included are:

- The parties.
- Loan amount and repayment.
- Interest rate.
- Description of property.
- Priority of mortgage.
- Prepayment clause.
- Due on sale clause.
- Escrow provision.
- Condition of property.
- Default clause.
- Foreclosure.
- Personal liability.

☐ *The parties.* The mortgage is a two-party instrument, with the borrower (who gives or executes the mortgage) called the *mortgagor,* and the lender (who takes the mortgage as security) called the *mortgagee.*

When a deed of trust is used, three parties are involved. The borrower is known as the *trustor,* a third party (usually a trust company or attorney) is the *trustee,* and the lender is the *beneficiary.* In effect, title to the trust deed is split into legal title and equitable title. Whereas the mortgagee in the case of a mortgage holds both kinds of title, in a deed of trust, the legal title is held by a trustee who acts on behalf of the lender who owns the equitable title. The trustee will transfer the security instrument back to the borrower when the debt has been repaid or, alternatively, will act to protect the lender in the event of a default under the terms of the trust deed.

☐ *Loan amount and repayment.* The note sets forth the amount of the loan and the manner in which it will be repaid.

☐ *Interest rate.* The note sets forth the contract rate of interest and the manner in which interest is to be paid.

☐ *Description of property.* The real property that is to secure the loan must be precisely described. The legal description and the local address will meet this requirement. If the mortgagor's interest in the real estate is other than that of a fee simple, the exact nature of the interest should be spelled out.

☐ *Priority of mortgage.* It is possible for an owner to execute several mortgages on the same piece of property, each securing a debt to a different lender. In the absence of any agreement among the lenders themselves, the priority of the mortgages is determined by the date of execution and recordation. The mortgage first executed and recorded is the *first* or *senior* mortgage. All others are *junior* loans, being designated as the second mortgage, third mortgage, etc.

☐ *Prepayment clause.* An important clause in any note is that permitting prepayment of the loan under specific terms and conditions. For example, an income property loan might provide that no prepayment may be made for the initial ten years (lock-in period), with prepayment permitted thereafter at a penalty of 2 percent of the outstanding loan principal. In the case of home mortgages, the borrower frequently is given the right to prepay a portion of the loan (e.g., 20 percent) any year without penalty, with any additional prepayment permitted only upon payment of a penalty.

☐ *Due on sale clause.* The due on sale clause is a relatively recent innovation, having come into general use only since the mid-1970s. Found in the note, the purpose of the clause is to permit the lender to *call the loan* (accelerate the maturity date) in the event the buyer sells the property.

☐ *Escrow provision.* It is common for the borrower to be required to pay to the lender each month approximately one-twelfth of the annual amount necessary to pay real estate taxes and insurance premiums. Then, the lender makes the payments directly to the taxing authority or insurance company when bills are rendered. Such payments are known as *escrow payments*, because the lender is obligated to hold them separate and apart from its other funds and use them only for the purpose specified.

☐ *Condition of property.* The borrower is obligated to (1) maintain the property in good repair, (2) not demolish any improvements without the permission of the lender, and, in general, (3) not permit the occurrence of "waste." Waste constitutes acts or omissions by the owner of real estate which injures it to the detriment of the mortgage lender which relies on the property as security.

☐ *Default clause.* The default clause normally specifies a number of *events of default,* which might include (1) failure to pay interest and principal when due, (2) failure to pay real estate taxes and insurance premiums, and (3) failure to keep the property in good repair. In virtually all cases, the mortgagor is given a period of time within which to cure the default (e.g., thirty days in the case of a failure to pay interest and principal when due).

If a default is not cured by the mortgagor within the permissible period, the mortgagee has the right to accelerate the payment of the entire loan principal.

☐ *Foreclosure.* Foreclosure is the legal process by which a mortgagee may have property sold at a public sale in order to raise cash to pay off a debt due the mortgagee. Two types of foreclosure are common in the United States. *Foreclosure by action and sale* is associated with the mortgage, while a *foreclosure by power of sale* is associated with the deed of trust.

In both types, the property securing the loan is sold to the highest bidder at a public sale. The proceeds of sale are applied first to the payment of the unpaid mortgage debt plus unpaid interest and court costs, and second to the mortgagor (or any creditor).

☐ *Personal liability.* In most kinds of loans the lender wants the borrower to be personally liable for the loan. Personal liability means that the borrower (individual or business entity) agrees that all of the borrower's assets stand behind the loan and that, in the event of a default, the lender may through appropriate legal action claim those assets.

A mortgage loan without personal liability is known as a *nonrecourse loan,* because the lender agrees it will seek no recourse against the borrower personally if the debt is unpaid.

ALTERNATIVE SECURITY AGREEMENTS

There are a number of variations on the basic mortgage (deed of trust) which may be useful in particular lending situations. They are briefly described below.

☐ *Blanket mortgage.* This is the name given to a mortgage that covers several properties or which covers a single tract of land which is to be subdivided into individual building lots. In the latter case, the developer pledges the entire tract as collateral for the blanket first mortgage. As the lots are subdivided and sold either to builders or to homeowners, the lender releases the sold lots from the lien of the mortgage in exchange for a partial repayment of the loan. The amount of the repayment, the "release price," is generally 10 to 20 percent above the portion of the loan that would be allocable to the released lot on a strictly pro rata basis to maintain the integrity of the remaining collateral.

☐ *Open-end mortgage.* The open-end mortgage is so named because the lender may advance additional funds in the future secured by the original mortgage which thus has an "open end." This type of mortgage is most frequently used in connection with construction loans which are funded as the work progresses. Its major purpose is to eliminate the cost of additional paperwork in the event of a subsequent loan and to prevent subsequent disbursements from being viewed as second mortgages.

☐ *Package mortgage.* This term has two different meanings in real estate finance:

- A package loan may combine two separate loans into a single loan transaction. An example of this would be as follows: A lender may extend a construction loan to a developer and agree that, upon completion of construction, the loan will automatically be converted into a long-term mortgage. The developer then need negotiate only with a single lender and usually pay only a single set of closing costs.
- A package loan also may be a mortgage loan in which the collateral includes not only real estate but other items normally considered personal property (with the result that the loan can be in a larger amount than otherwise). This type of loan is used to permit a borrower to obtain maximum financing; the additional collateral may include such items as refrigerator, washer, dryer, stove, carpeting, drapery, etc.

☐ *Purchase money mortgage.* This type of mortgage is one taken by a seller from a buyer in lieu of purchase money. That is, the seller helps finance the purchase. This type of mortgage may or may not be a first mortgage, depending on whether the property is subject to an existing mortgage. (See 13-1.)

☐ *Participation mortgage.* In the case of a large-scale development, a single lender may be unable or unwilling to provide all of the necessary financing. A participation mortgage can be used to bring two or more lenders together to share in the loan. The terms of the participation are set

13-1. PURCHASE MONEY MORTGAGE TO REDUCE BUYER'S EQUITY

An important function of the purchase money mortgage may be to close the gap between the sales price and the balance of an existing mortgage which the buyer wishes to take over. For example, the seller may have purchased the property ten years earlier for a price of $50,000 and obtained a $40,000 mortgage. Now, the value of the property may have doubled to $100,000, while the mortgage has been amortized down to $30,000, so that the current equity is $70,000. If the first mortgage carries a low interest rate, a buyer will wish to keep the mortgage but is likely to have trouble raising $70,000 in cash. In this kind of situation, the seller may be willing to take back a second lien purchase money mortgage for, say, $35,000, with the loan to run for a certain number of years. The cash down payment has been cut in half and the new owner gets to keep the first mortgage which is at lower than current interest rates.

forth in an agreement signed by all of the lenders. Each lender is assigned a designated portion of the loan, including a commensurate portion of the collateral, and will receive that portion of the debt service as paid. Frequently, the originating ("lead") lender receives a fee for servicing the loan on behalf of the entire group.

☐ *Wraparound mortgage.* A wraparound mortgage is a second mortgage that "wraps around" or includes an existing first mortgage. The face amount of the wraparound mortgage loan is equal to the balance of the existing first mortgage plus the amount of the new (second) mortgage. The wraparound loan typically calls for a higher interest rate on the entire loan than is payable on the existing first mortgage; so the wraparound lender is able to realize a very high return on the new money advanced. (See 13-2.) In addition, the wraparound provides an easy way for the second lien holder to be sure the first lien holder is paid out of the proceeds of the wraparound loan payment.

LOAN AMORTIZATION ALTERNATIVES

In the discussion of loan underwriting, the manner in which loan principal and interest will be repaid comes next. These two items together constitute the *debt service.*

The question of debt service is of crucial importance to the borrower because it will absorb the largest portion of the cash flow from the property. Since both borrower and lender look to the property's cash flow to provide the funds to service the loan, the amount of the debt service often is a determining factor in setting the amount of the loan itself. Naturally,

13-2. PROFITING ON WRAPAROUNDS

Assume the owner of a property subject to a $1 million first mortgage at 7 percent interest requires an additional $200,000 in financing. Current market mortgage rates are 9 percent and the first mortgagee is unwilling or unable to refinance the mortgage and increase the loan. Prepayment of the first mortgage is either barred or subject to heavy penalties. Since the first lien is at a desirable interest rate, the owner goes to a different lender and negotiates a wraparound loan which works as follows:

- The new lender advances $200,000 in cash.
- The owner executes a promissory note in favor of the new lender in the face amount of $1.2 million (total of the first mortgage and the new financing).
- Interest rate on the $1.2 million note is 8 percent.

- The owner pays the new lender debt service on the entire $1.2 million loan, the latter then forwarding to the first lender the debt service on the first mortgage.

The new lender ends up receiving a return of 13 percent on his $200,000. The *upside leverage* results because the new lender is receiving (1) 8 percent on the $200,000 actually advanced plus (2) the one-percent difference between the 8 percent now being received on the existing $1 million loan and the 7 percent that must be paid to the old lender. At the same time, the owner of the property is able to keep alive the existing first mortgage with its desirable 7 percent interest rate. Consequently, the new owner has obtained the desired total financing at the cost of 8 percent, which is lower than the current market rate of 9 percent.

higher interest rates mean higher debt service (other things equal), but the term of the loan is also important. The shorter the term, the faster the principal must be repaid and consequently the higher the debt service and vice versa.

From the point of view of loan amortization, real estate mortgages fall into three categories:

- No amortization (interest-only or standing) loans.
- Partially amortized (balloon) loans.
- Fully amortizing (self-liquidating) loans.

☐ *Interest-only or standing loan.* A standing loan calls for no amortization during its term—interest only is paid. The entire principal becomes due on maturity. From the borrower's point of view, standing loans have one significant advantage. Since no part of the cash flow need be set aside for loan reduction, the periodic residual cash flow to the borrower from the property is increased.

The disadvantage of a standing loan is that the borrower may be unable to pay the full principal when the loan matures. This may happen either because the value of the location has deteriorated, the property has deteriorated, or financing is not readily available precluding sale or refinancing.

☐ *Balloon loan.* A partially amortized or balloon loan calls for some but not complete repayment of principal during the loan term. At maturity, the borrower will have a substantial sum (balloon) still to be repaid. A balloon loan represents a compromise between a standing loan, which maximizes cash flow to the borrower but increases the risk of principal nonpayment, and a fully amortizing loan (to be discussed next), with its opposite result.

In a typical loan situation, a borrower may apply for a mortgage loan in a specified amount for a specified term (say, twenty-five years), with the loan to be fully amortized over its life. The loan request is based upon the maximum amount of annual debt service that can be paid while still permitting the borrower to realize a residual cash flow from the property in an amount sufficient to warrant the investment.

The lender may agree to the amount of annual debt service but not want to be committed for 25 years. In this situation, the parties may agree that the loan will have a ten- or fifteen-year maturity, with periodic debt service on a 25-year amortization basis.

☐ *Self-liquidating loan.* A self-liquidating or fully amortized loan is the type of financing usually used for residential mortgages in the United States. In this type of payment, the constant periodic payments are in amounts slightly larger than the interest due at that time. The excess amount goes toward reduction of the loan so that, at the time the loan matures, the entire principal has been paid.

As time goes by, the borrower is building up additional equity in the property and the lender is obtaining an additional "cushion" against loss in the event of a default. (The lender's "cushion" grows only when market value of the property remains stable or increases, and not if the market value decreases.) (See **13-3.**)

INCOME PROPERTY LOAN ANALYSIS

Two particular distinctions can be noted when comparing the underwriting of income property loans and residential loans. First, the terms of a residential mortgage are fairly standardized while the terms of income property loans are generally much more flexible and open to negotiation. Second, the relative emphasis placed upon borrower and property analysis is reversed. Whereas in a residential loan the credit of the borrower is the paramount consideration, it is the property that constitutes the main security for an income property loan. The reason is that an income prop-

13-3. GRADUATED PAYMENT MORTGAGE

A relatively recent innovation in home mortgages has been the *graduated payment mortgage* (GPM) or *flexible payment mortgage* (FPM). Each of these creates a variable-payment schedule in order to reduce payments in the early years when the borrower's income is low. The early payments may be in the amount of the interest due so that the loan is standing during this period or may be less than the interest due so that a portion of the interest accrues and is added to the outstanding principal.

In later years, the payments are increased sufficiently to pay the accrued interest and make up for the missed amortization in the early years. This insures that the loan liquidates at maturity. The main purpose of this type of loan is to allow young persons in the early stages of their earning careers to qualify for home loans.

For example, the loan may provide that only interest be payable during the first five years, with payments during the balance of the loan term being at a higher constant rate sufficient to pay off the loan at maturity. Alternatively, a thirty-year loan term might be divided into five six-year periods with different constant payments during each period. Presumably, each payment steps up to reflect the borrower's increased income. (As noted in Appendix 12A, the FHA has five approved graduated payment plans.)

erty, by definition, will generate cash flow and this will be the primary means of paying the debt service on the loan.

Property Analysis

The lender will base the underwriting decision upon a complete real estate feasibility analysis. Such an analysis includes both a market study and an economic study. The market study focuses on these factors:

☐ *Market area.* The market area (e.g., for a shopping center) usually is measured in terms of the amount of people living or working within a specified distance from the site; the area is highly affected by location, competition, use, and project size.

☐ *Demand.* Demand is a function of both economic and demographic factors. These include not only number of people but income trends, migration patterns, age distribution, employment opportunities, and similar factors.

☐ *Supply.* Supply will be analyzed by examining existing and projected competition, and the existence of alternative uses to the one projected (e.g., a condominium project is normally not directly competitive with rental use but may be so depending on prices, vacancy rates, etc.).

An economic study builds on the information gathered in the market study in order to estimate potential rental income and operating expenses. Once these pro forma figures have been developed, certain ratios normally are utilized to test the soundness of the proposed loan.

The Mortgage Loan Constant

The lender will analyze the proposed financing from the perspective of risk and return. Lender return consists of interest and principal repayment. Interest represents a return *on* the lender's investment while principal repayment represents a return *of* the investment capital. This return is represented by the debt service and is a function of the contract rate of interest and the maturity of the loan.

These two factors result in a *mortgage constant (K)* which represents the amount of debt service, expressed as a percent of the original loan, necessary to pay the contract rate of interest and the entire principal in equal periodic installments over the term of the loan. K is usually expressed as the percentage of the original principal which will be paid *annually* in monthly installments. Thus, the debt service represents an annuity paid over the life of the loan. Each periodic payment consists of two parts: (1) interest for the preceding period on the outstanding amount of the loan at the beginning of the period and (2) partial payment of principal (amortization). (See Table 13-1.)

Table 13-1.   HOW TO DETERMINE MORTGAGE LOAN CONSTANT

What must a borrower pay each year on a $40,000 loan at 8.5% annual interest if the loan is to be amortized over 25 years?

I. Annual mortgage loan constant (from the Compound Interest Tables):
   A. Loan amount = $40,000
   B. Interest rate (annual) = 8.5%
   C. Loan term = 25 years
   D. Mortgage constant factor (page 514 column 6 = 0.097712)
   E. Annual debt service ($40,000 × 0.097712) = $3,908.48

What would the *monthly* debt service be?

II. Annual mortgage loan constant (from the Compound Interest Tables):
   A. Loan amount = $40,000.00
   B. Interest rate (monthly) = .708%
   C. Loan term = 25 years or 300 months
   D. Factor (page 514 column 6) = 0.008052
   E. Monthly debt service ($40,000 × 0.008052) = $322.08

Note: The twelve monthly payments are less than the one annual payment as the borrower is reducing the principal in twelve steps during the year and thus pays less total interest (322.08 × 12 = $3864.96 < $3908.48).

In the early years of a level constant amortizing loan, the largest proportion of the periodic payment is interest. However, as the loan principal is gradually reduced while the periodic payment remains constant, the amount of interest declines (since interest is calculated only on the outstanding balance). At the same time, the portion of the total payment going to amortize the loan principal gradually increases.

Without a full amortization schedule, the interest and principal component's of any year's constant payment can be determined if the *mortgage loan constant* is known. This calculation is shown in Table 13-2.

Note in Tables 13-1 and 13-2 that changes in either the term (repayment period) or the interest rate will change the mortgage loan constant.

If the term remains the same, then

- The higher the interest rate, the higher the constant.
- The lower the interest rate, the lower the constant.

If the interest rate remains the same, then

- The longer the repayment period, the lower the constant.
- The shorter the repayment period, the higher the constant.

Table 13-2. THIRD-YEAR INTEREST CALCULATION

How much interest will the borrower pay in the third year on a $40,000, 8.5% interest, 25-year amortizing loan?

I. Mortgage loan constant:
   A. Loan amount = $40,000
   B. Mortgage constant factor (page 514 column 6) = 0.097712
   C. Annual debt service = $3,908.48

II. Third-year interest:
   A. First-year interest = $40,000 × 8.5% = $3,400
      First-year principal = $3,908.48 − $3,400 = $508.48
   B. Principal in the second year = $40,000 − $508.48 = $39,491.52
      Second-year interest = $39,491.52 × 8.5% = $3,356.78
      Second-year principal = $3,908.48 − $3,356.78 = $551.70
   C. Principal in the third year = $39,491.52 − $551.70 = $38,939.82
      Third-year interest = $38,939.82 × 8.5% = $3,309.88

Effective Yield

The true or effective yield to the lender can be calculated using the Compound Interest Tables at the end of the book, as shown in Tables 13-3

Table 13-3. YIELD CALCULATION

A borrower has requested a $1,000,000 loan at 9.5% for twenty years on a small motel which is expected to have an annual *net* operating income of $150,000 and is appraised at $1,200,000. The borrower has agreed to pay a two-point origination fee. What is the lender's effective yield?

I. Mortgage loan constant:

  A. Term = 20 years
  B. Interest = 9.5% annually
  C. Mortgage constant factor (page 518 column 6) = 0.113477
  D. Annual debt service ($1,000,000 × 0.113477) = $113,477

II. Yield:

  A. Cash advanced by lender = $1,000,000 − $20,000* = $980,000
  B. Annual debt service = $113,477
  C. Term = 20 years
  D. Factor ($980,000 ÷ $113,477) = 8.63611
  E. Yield determination

    1. Check each page in the Compound Interest Tables looking at column 5 (present value of an annuity) on the 20-year row.
    2. The 10% page 520 shows an approximately equal factor of 8.513564. Therefore, the effective yield of this loan is approximately 10%.

  * Two-point origination fee.

and 13-4. It should be noted that the effective yield to the lender is also the effective *cost* to the borrower. (See 13-4.)

Loan-to-Value Ratio

The loan-to-value ratio (LTVR) is an expression of the safety of the principal of the loan based on the value of the collateral. The LTVR is calculated as follows:

$$LTVR = \frac{\text{Loan amount}}{\text{Project value}}$$

In the yield calculation example, the loan to value ratio is:

$$LTVR = \frac{\$1,000,000}{\$1,200,000} = 83.3\%$$

The lower the LTV, the lower the risk to the lender since in the case of default there would exist a greater gap between the outstanding loan balance and project value. However, it must be noted that overvaluing the project can give the lender a false sense of security.

Table 13-4.   YIELD CALCULATION WITH KICKER INTEREST

In the motel example in Table 13-3, assume that the lender will also receive 2% of *gross* income above $200,000. This "kicker interest" is estimated to be about $18,000 per year. What is the effective yield including the kicker interest?

A. Cash advanced by lender = $980,000
B. Annual debt service plus kicker interest = $113,477 + $18,000 = $131,477
C. Factor = $980,000 ÷ $131,477 = 7.4537
D. Again, searching the tables in the 20-year row, the factor for 12% (page 522 column 5) is approximately equal 7.46944. Therefore, the expected yield is about 12%.

13-4.   VARIABLE RATE MORTGAGE

Variable rate mortgages (VRM) have been recently introduced as an alternative to the traditional fully amortized constant payment mortgage. The interest rate charged on a VRM is not fixed throughout the term of the loan but rather is tied to a market index such as the prime interest rate or rate on long-term government bonds. As a result, the interest rate on a VRM rises and falls over the term of the loan in response to changes in the market index. The benefits associated with a VRM are generally intended to include:

☐ *To allow or encourage continued borrowing during high interest rate periods.* Since a VRM is tied to a market interest rate index, should rates fall during the term of the loan, so would the interest associated with the VRM. Consequently, borrowers may not hesitate to borrow during high interest rate periods and risk being "locked in" to the high rates. Conversely, should market rates rise, so would the interest rate associated with the VRM.

☐ *To protect lenders from interest rate risk and consequently to allow them to exclude an inflation premium when determining the original rate associated with a VRM.* When rates rise in the market, the lender's portfolio return will rise, and when rates fall, their return will fall.

☐ *In addition to lower original interest rates, VRM borrowers are relieved of prepayment privilege clauses and are charged a lower origination fee.*

A decision must be made indicating how the periodic payments will be altered when the market index fluctuates. This can be done in one of three ways: (1) increase or decrease the monthly payment, (2) lengthen or shorten the term of the loan, and (3) raise or lower the principal balance owed and keep the term constant resulting in a balloon payment or a refund at maturity. Changing the monthly payment is the most common with the number of changes per year limited to one or two and the interest rate change limited to a maximum of 2 percent.

Debt Coverage Ratio

In addition to calculating the yield received for money lent and the safety of principal, lenders wish to measure the risk associated with receiving the return. The debt coverage ratio (DCR) helps the lender to evaluate the riskiness of an income property loan. It measures the "buffer" or "cushion" between the NOI and the debt service. The debt coverage ratio is calculated as follows:

$$DCR = \frac{NOI}{\text{Debt service}}$$

In the yield calculation example in Table 13-4, the debt coverage ratio is:

$$DCR = \frac{\$150,000}{\$113,477} = 1.32$$

For an average motel project, a lender will be looking for a debt coverage ratio of approximately 1.30 to 1.5. Consequently, most lenders would view this loan as of average risk. Generally, the lower the debt coverage ratio, the higher the risk to the lender and vice versa.

The Maximum Loan Amount

The maximum loan a lender would be willing to provide can be determined by examining the relationship between the NOI, desired DCR (assumed here to be 1.5), and the mortgage constant (K). The relationship can be expressed as:

$$\text{Maximum loan} = \frac{NOI}{K} \div \text{desired } DCR$$

Given the example above, the maximum loan would be:

$$\text{Maximum loan} = \frac{\$150,000}{0.1135} \div 1.5 = \$881,057$$

Clearly, the request for a $1 million loan does not meet the lender's hypothesized standards. Why? First, the borrowers want a relatively high loan to value ratio loan, 83.3 percent (for reasons that are examined in Chapter 14). Second, motels are relatively risky and lenders demand relatively high DCRs (i.e., 1.3 to 1.5). This lender has opted to be on the high side of that range (1.5) because of its own portfolio situation. Would a lender seeking a 1.3 DCR make this loan? The answer to this question is yes as can be demonstrated by calculating the maximum loan amount using the 1.3 DCR.

$$\text{Maximum loan} = \frac{\$150,000}{0.1135} \div 1.3 = \$1,016,600$$

This clearly demonstrates the importance of accurately evaluating the risk associated with a particular loan. By changing the required DCR the lender can change the accept/reject decision associated with a loan application even though the project's NOI and the terms of the loan (K) have not been changed.

Operating Expense Ratio

The lender will be concerned with the relationship between the operating expenses and gross rental receipts. Depending on the property type and market, the lender will establish a guideline operating expense ratio (OER). This ratio shows operating expenses as a percentage of gross rental receipts and should not exceed some maximum (25 to 45 percent).

Break-Even Ratio

Sometimes referred to as the *default ratio,* the break-even ratio (BER) indicates the percentage of gross possible income that must be collected in order to meet the operating expenses and debt service. The ratio is calculated by dividing the total operating expenses *plus* debt service by the gross possible income. Lenders ordinarily establish some maximum allowable percentage from 80-85 percent.

Loan Terms

The lender is also concerned with other terms of its loans. Can the borrower prepay; if so, is there a prepayment penalty involved? The lender experiences certain costs in loan origination and expects to receive a return over the term of the loan to cover these origination costs (their costs usually exceed the loan origination fee). Additionally, if a loan is repaid early, the lender must reinvest the same funds and experience the origination costs again. Finally, if interest rates drop, an existing loan made at a higher interest rate is very attractive to the lender. And in the case of prepayment, the lender would have to reinvest at a lower rate of interest.

Consequently, the lender will typically want some form of compensation if the loan is to be prepaid at an early date. Lenders call this compensation a prepayment privilege and it is usually expressed as a percentage of the outstanding loan balance at the time of repayment. (In many states there are significant legal restrictions on the size and duration of prepayment penalties on some loans.)

Lenders are adversely affected if interest rates rise after they have made a long-term loan. As partial protection against such occurrences, lenders often ask for *escalation clauses* in the loan agreement. An escalation clause states that if the original borrower (owner) sells the property and the new owner assumes the loan, the lender has the right, at that time, to renegotiate the interest rate. Escalation clauses protect the lender to some extent against rises in long-term interest rates.

The real estate decision-maker should be clear on the difference between an escalation clause and an acceleration clause. The *acceleration clause* is a clause which states that when certain periodic payments are missed (default occurs), the entire face amount of the note is due, thus facilitating the foreclosure procedure. This should be carefully distinguished from the escalation clause described above.

Lenders also may want restrictions on the operation of the project, guaranteed levels of maintenance, and insurance, and probably the personal liability of the borrower for all or a proportion of the loan amount. (See 13-5.)

13-5. THE FINE PRINT IN A LOAN AGREEMENT

The developer of Presidential Towers in Wilmington, Delaware was constructing the third tower. He negotiated a $4 million construction loan from a large real estate investment trust with the tower serving as collateral for the loan. The developer actually borrowed only $1 million under the construction loan, choosing to raise the balance from less expensive unsecured sources. When the project was approximately 90 percent complete, the unsecured creditors pressed for payment and the developer sought to borrow the final $3 million from the trust according to the original loan agreement. However, the loan agreement had a clause which provided that the trust was obligated to lend only according to a certain time schedule.

As the developer had not met the completion schedule, the trust refused to loan the additional $3 million. They now felt the project could not justify the original loan figure. This caused the developer to have to renegotiate the overall project financing in an atmosphere where potential lenders were well aware of his difficult situation.

Not reading all of a loan agreement can cause minor problems to become major problems and result in a decision-maker ending up "over a barrel."

Analysis of the Borrower

The lender's analysis of the borrower concentrates on the borrower's past investment history and credit. The borrower's "track record" and reputation are a vital part of the analysis. A series of successful projects insures, at the very least, a very careful scrutiny of the loan application, while past failures significantly reduce the chances for approval. The borrower's credit standing will be based upon a credit report and current financial statements. Where available, a Dun & Bradstreet (D&B) report will be obtained. Finally, the lender will evaluate the project in light of current business conditions. In the case of new construction, where the lead time may be several years, the lender will make some effort to anticipate where the business cycle will be when the building is ready for rental. It is extremely common in the real estate industry for enthusiastic developers, at the height of a boom, to plan new buildings which will be ready to receive tenants just when the boom has peaked and vacancy rates are beginning to rise.

RESIDENTIAL LOAN ANALYSIS

In the course of analyzing a residential mortgage loan application (see Figure 13-1), the lender must make decisions in three interrelated areas. If the underwriting process reveals significant problems or weaknesses in any one of the areas, the loan is likely to be rejected. The three areas are: (1) property analysis, (2) loan analysis, and (3) borrower analysis.

Property Analysis

Although the residential lender looks primarily to the credit of the borrower when reaching the loan decision, the real estate which will be the collateral for the loan is obviously also of great importance. Lenders rely primarily upon an appraisal as the source of information for the property analysis.

The estimated market value of the property is critical to the lender's decision as to the size of the loan. The LTVR will be a percentage of either the appraised value *or* the purchase price of the property, whichever is *lower*. The difference between the loan amount and the price to be paid by the borrower represents the equity to be put in the property.

Loan Analysis

In determining the terms of a proposed loan, the lender will consider both its own requirements and the needs of the borrower. The key terms in a residential mortgage loan are briefly discussed in the following paragraphs:

☐ *Loan-to-value ratio.* The amount of a residential mortgage loan typically is expressed as a percentage of the property's market value at the time the loan is made. This percentage is commonly referred to as the loan-to-value ratio. The ratio for residential mortgages can range anywhere from 50 percent to 95 percent of market value. In any given case, the ratio is a function of several factors:

• The lender's supply of loanable funds.

The undersigned hereby applies to _____ BANK and TRUST COMPANY, _____, for a loan of the amount and upon the terms hereinafter set forth, said loan to be secured by a first mortgage upon the real estate hereinafter described.

_____   _____
Applicant's full name   Full name of wife or husband

Property located at _____ (Street) _____ (City)
Amount of Loan: $_____ for _____ years at _____ per cent interest per annum.
Payments of $_____ monthly.
Is the purpose of the loan to finance the acquisition or construction of a dwelling in which you reside or expect to reside? _____
If not, will the first mortgage secure property which you use or expect to use as your principal residence?

_____
If not answered above, please state the purpose of the loan _____

_____
Is the property now mortgaged? _____ If so, to whom? _____
_____ Address _____
Is the property now occupied by owner or rented? _____
Title now stands in the name of _____
Dimensions of land _____ feet front, by depth of _____ feet,
area _____ square feet
Description of buildings (frame or brick, dwellings, store, etc.) _____

No. of stories high _____ No. of rooms _____ Baths _____ Year in which Building erected _____
Cost of property $ _____

Utilities		Roof		Heating System		Fuel		
Water	[ ]	Non-combust. shingles	[ ]	Hot Air	[ ]	Coal	[ ]	No. of
Elec.	[ ]	Wood shingles	[ ]	Hot Water	[ ]	Gas	[ ]	Heaters
Gas	[ ]	Tar and Gravel	[ ]	Steam	[ ]	Oil	[ ]	
Sewer	[ ]	Slate	[ ]			Elec.	[ ]	_____

Assessed Value 19 _____   Applicant's Valuation 19 _____
Land $_____   Land $_____
Buildings $_____   Buildings $_____
Total $_____   Total $_____
Remarks _____

The undersigned understands that the title of the above described real estate is to be examined and the necessary papers are to be prepared and recorded by the attorney for the mortgagee Bank, all at the expense of the undersigned, and that the closing of the loan is contingent among other things upon the title of the real estate being satisfactory to the Bank. The undersigned agrees to pay the expenses incurred by the Bank in having the title examined and the property inspected, whether this application is accepted or rejected.

Figure 13-1.   RESIDENTIAL MORTGAGE LOAN APPLICATION

- The borrower's ability or willingness to provide equity.
- Limitations on LTVRs set by the particular lender or by regulatory agencies to which it is subject.

□ *Rate of interest.* The rate of interest charged on a residential mortgage loan is a function of current market conditions, LTVR, term of the loan, and financial condition of the borrower. Of these, current market conditions are the most important factor since the lender cannot charge much more or it will lose out to competitors and it will not charge much less since it would be unnecessarily sacrificing profit. A lender will sometimes offer loans with different LTVRs and different terms; the higher the former and the longer the latter. The greater the risk assumed by the lender the higher will be the interest rate. The type of residential property being financed also will be considered by the lender. Typically, condominium loans have a slightly higher interest rate (perhaps one-eighth to one-fourth percent) than do detached single-family dwellings. Other considerations affecting the interest rate include the age and physical condition of the property and the financial condition of the borrower; however, a lender often will prefer to decline the loan rather than to charge an interest premium to compensate for the extra risk.

□ *Term to maturity.* The loan term may range anywhere from 20 to 30 years, with the shorter terms customarily utilized for older buildings. The general rule to be observed in any loan, residential or otherwise, is that the term should not exceed the remaining economic life of the improvements.

□ *Origination and closing costs.* Origination and closing costs fall into two categories. First, they include actual out-of-pocket expenses which must be paid by the borrower for a property survey, title insurance, mortgage recording fees and the like. The second, frequently known as an *origination fee*, is an "up front" amount, equal to one or two percent of the loan, paid to the lender for compensation of overhead costs associated with underwriting the loan. Generally, this latter fee is considered a form of interest when calculating the maximum rate that may be charged under usury statutes; the borrower also may treat it as a tax deductible item for federal income tax purposes.

□ *Mortgage insurance.* We have already discussed the subject of mortgage insurance in Appendix 12A. In the case of an FHA-insured mortgage, the lender is completely protected against loss in the event of default and in consequence, the FHA sets an interest ceiling which is somewhat below that for conventional loans. To finance the FHA insurance program, a mortgage insurance premium (MIP) equal to one-half percent of the loan principal is added to the interest rate.

Private mortgage insurance (PMI) is frequently required on conventional loans when the LTVR is in excess of 80 percent. PMI, unlike FHA insurance, usually covers only the top 15 percent of the mortgage. Thus, if a 95 percent LTV ratio loan is foreclosed upon and sold at a price equal to 80 percent of the original appraised value, the private mortgage insurer will pay the lender the additional 15 percent and the lender will suffer no actual loss. The cost of a private mortgage insurance policy runs about one-quarter of one percent of the loan amount.

Borrower Analysis

In residential loan underwriting, primary emphasis is placed on the borrower's ability to repay the loan, whereas in income property lending, the real estate itself is the primary security. The residential lender will concentrate upon three areas in reaching a decision about the borrower's credit standing.

☐ *Ability to pay.* A borrower's financial capacity is evaluated by examining the quality and quantity of income available to meet debt service requirements. Quality of income refers to the stability of the income stream—how likely is it that the borrower will become unemployed or lose the assets which provide him with income. Certain kinds of employment are very stable, for example, professional work and government employment, while other jobs are much less certain, for example, commission salespersons (such as real estate brokers), seasonal workers, and self-employed business persons.

A more difficult question arises when a borrower has more than one source of income. At one time, the income provided by a working wife was discounted by lenders because of the possibility that the wife might leave her job to bear children. However, this latter consideration has been made irrelevant by passage of the Equal Credit Opportunity Act (ECOA). ECOA prohibits a lender from discounting the quality of income because of the borrower's age, sex, national origin, marital status, race, color, religion, or the fact that the borrower's income is derived from welfare or public assistance payments.

☐ *Income ratios.* Income ratios are used by lenders to relate the borrower's ability to make the loan's monthly payments. Income ratios express in percentage terms how much of the borrower's monthly income must be devoted to debt service if the requested loan is granted. The debt service is assumed to include payments covering principal amortization, interest, taxes, and insurance premiums, and so is referred to as PITI (an acronym made up of the first letters of each word). The ratios are used as guidelines only and do not constitute the sole basis for evaluating a loan application.

When a conventional (non-FHA or -VA) home mortgage is being sought, lenders concentrate on four guidelines in their underwriting process: Two income ratios and two multipliers. The first income ratio, which is now in a state of transition, holds that the monthly PITI payment may not exceed 25 or 30 percent of the monthly gross income. The second income ratio requires that PITI *plus* monthly installment payments covering other debts (e.g., automobile, credit cards) should not exceed one-third of the monthly gross income.

With respect to FHA-insured mortgage loans, underwriting guidelines emphasize two income ratios; these are referred to as the 35 percent rule and the 50 percent rule. The 35 percent rule stipulates that total housing expense (PITI plus monthly utilities and maintenance) should not exceed 35 percent of *net effective income*—that is, gross income less federal income taxes, or what is more generally known as "take home pay." The 50 percent rule states that total monthly obligations should not exceed 50 percent of net effective income. Total monthly obligations include total housing expense plus installment payments on other debt obligations plus withholding for state income taxes plus social security (F.I.C.A.) payments.

☐ *Credit analysis.* The final element to be examined is the borrower's credit standing or reputation. The question here is whether the credit history of the applicant raises any question about the applicant's commitment to discharge his obligations. The lender, with the applicant's permission, will contact a credit bureau for a credit report. The report lists the status of the applicant's various credit accounts, both past and present. The type of each account (open, installment, or revolving) and source of credit (bank, credit card, department store) will be listed. The applicant's customary payment pattern will be rated on a scale that ranges from "pays as agreed" to "turned over to a collection agency."

SUMMARY

Lenders consider numerous items when evaluating a loan proposal: their own position, the property itself, the security agreement, and the relationship of the loan requested to the projected net operating income of the property or the borrower's income. The real estate decision-maker must understand the lender's perspective if he is to obtain the best possible financing for any given project.

IMPORTANT TERMS

acceleration clause
amortization
balloon loan
blanket mortgage
break-even ratio (BER)
debt coverage ratio (DCR)
debt service
deed of trust

deficiency judgment
flexible payment mortgage
lien
loan-to-value ratio (LTVR)
mortgage
mortgage constant
open-end mortgage
operating expense ratio (OER)

package mortgage
participation mortgage
promissory note
purchase money mortgage
security interest

self-liquidating loan
standing loan
variable rate mortgage
wraparound mortgage

REVIEW QUESTIONS

13-1. List and define the basic lender objectives in the area of real estate finance.

13-2. How might the physical condition of a property affect a lender's evaluation of a proposed financial package?

13-3. Differentiate between a mortgage and a deed of trust.

13-4. What are the differences between a blanket mortgage and package mortgage?

13-5. How might a purchase money mortgage be used to reduce the down payment required for the purchase of an existing single-family dwelling?

13-6. Under what circumstances might a wraparound mortgage represent an attractive real estate financing alternative?

13-7. List 2 ways to reduce the mortgage constant.

13-8. How does the payment of an origination fee affect the effective cost of a real estate loan? Why?

13-9. What factors would a lender consider in evaluating the riskiness of an income property loan?

13-10. Relate the maximum loan formula to the yield and safety requirements of a real estate lender.

14

Financing Mechanics: The Borrower's Perspective

IT IS IMPORTANT to remember that financing divides the claims on a property's cash flow. In cases where a project does not normally generate a cash flow (e.g., an owner-occupied single-family dwelling), the owner makes the payments and the property's financing establishes the priority of rights in the case of default. All of the costs of the project must be financed either through debt, or equity, or some combination thereof.

DEBT AND EQUITY FINANCING

When discussing financing, the entire right-hand side of the balance sheet, both debt and equity, is referred to. The different financial instruments simply divide the cash flow generated by the left-hand side of the balance sheet (assets) among the different sources of funds represented by the right hand side of the balance sheet. Each of the different suppliers of funds is willing to face certain risks and expects commensurate returns.

As shown in Figure 14-1, the net operating income (NOI) is essentially shared by the sources of financing. Consequently, they are competing for the available NOI. In order to convince the sources of financing to participate—that is, invest in the project—they must feel that they are receiving a return which is commensurate with their risk. It is important

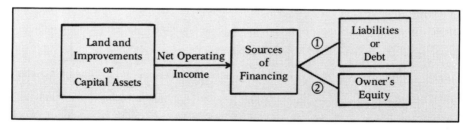

Figure 14-1. HOW NET OPERATING INCOME IS SHARED

that the sources of debt and equity financing understand one another's investment requirements because both sets of requirements must be satisfied for the project to be financed.

It is also important to note that the NOI available to meet the cost of financing the project is limited by the marketplace. This means that an equity investor cannot increase his rate of return by arbitrarily increasing rents or reducing operating expenses. (This presumes a property already efficiently managed.)

In the last chapter, the lender's perspective in financing real estate was examined. Now, the borrower's perspective will be discussed.

The Before-Tax Cash Flow Statement

Since the sources of financing share the NOI, it is appropriate at this point to discuss how the decision is made as to which source—debt or equity—gets how much of the NOI. Essentially, both sources view themselves as investors. As such, they establish, independently of one another, minimum investment criteria. Their major goal is to balance the risk they assume with the return they expect. For the sake of simplicity, the source of debt financing is referred to as the lender and the source of equity as the investor.

The following pro forma cash flow statement shown in Table 14-1 will be used in presenting the lender's and equity investor's investment criteria. Assume that a twenty-unit existing apartment house has fifteen two-bedroom units ($250 monthly rent) and five one-bedroom units ($200 monthly rent). Vending income equals $2 per month per unit. Market analysis indicates a vacancy and credit loss of 6 percent of gross possible income (GPI) and operating expenses of 38 percent of GPI. Asking price is $357,600 and a mortgage loan of $260,000 (73 percent of the purchase price) is available at nine and three-fourths percent interest for 25 years.

Table 14-1. CASH FLOW PRO FORMA

Gross rental receipts:	$57,000
15 units × $250 month × 12 months	
5 units × $200 month × 12 months	
Plus: Other income	
$2 unit × 20 units × 12 months	480
Gross potential income:	$57,480
Less: vacancy and credit loss (6% of GPI)	(3,449)
Gross effective income:	$54,031
Less: operating expenses (38% of GPI)	(21,842)
Net operating income:	$32,189
Less: debt service	(27,820)
Before-tax equity cash flow	$ 4,369

Annual debt service on the mortgage is $27,820. The equity investment is $97,600. The before-tax cash flow is then $4,369.

Before analyzing the effect of the lender's prior claim on the residual equity claim, it is appropriate to review a concept which was introduced in Chapter 1 and has been inherent in most of the subsequent discussions.

Time Value of Money

When determining the value of a particular cash flow to be received in the future, the real estate decision-maker must take into consideration the time value of money. The theory of the time value of money states simply that a dollar received today is more valuable than a dollar to be received in the future. A dollar received in the future is less valuable for three reasons:

☐ *Opportunity cost.* A dollar in hand today can immediately be invested and earn interest. If the dollar is not to be received for one year, the interest which could have been earned must be foregone. The foregone interest represents the opportunity cost associated with the receipt of a dollar in the future rather than today. Consequently, today's value (present value) of the dollar to be received in one year is diminished by the amount of the opportunity cost.

☐ *Inflation.* Inflation represents a reduction in the value of the dollar. When price levels rise, more dollars are required to purchase the same amount of goods and services than previously. When a dollar is to be received in the future, its present value is diminished if inflation occurs prior to its receipt. Conversely, if one borrows money today, dollars used for future repayments will have less value than those originally borrowed if inflation has occurred in the interim.

☐ *Risk.* If a dollar is to be received in the future, there exists some possibility that the dollar will not in fact be repaid. The existence of risk also diminishes the present value of the future dollar.

Note that the three items above are the three components of the discount rate (income approach to value) and the interest rate (the lender's perspective). (Opportunity cost parallels the deferred consumption premium or real return.) Likewise, they will now be the three components of the equity discount rate (the equity required rate of return). However, as discussed in the introductory paragraphs to this chapter, the risk perspectives are different. In the approach to appraisal, NOI was capitalized and the risk premium was based on the overall riskiness of the project. At this stage of the discussion, it is known that the lender has a prior claim and thus a less risky position. Conversely, the equity claim is riskier than the overall project risk precisely because of the prior claim of the lender.

The concept of the time value of money is quite applicable to real estate analysis. Cash inflows and outflows can be analyzed and evaluated by utilizing the theoretical and mathematical concepts of *compounding* and *discounting*. Before going further, the basic mechanics involved will be reviewed as well as the use of the compound interest tables at the end of the book.

Compound Interest and the Discounting Process

Interest is payment for the use of money. Compound interest is no more than interest on interest, and the calculations involved in compounding are very straightforward. Suppose a savings association pays interest at the rate of five percent, with the interest calculated once each year. Then, a dollar invested (deposited) in a savings account yields $1.05 at the end of the year. It therefore may be said that on the day it is deposited the dollar's future value in one year is equal to

- Its present value ($1), plus
- The interest rate times the present value ($0.05).

To this point, simple interest has been described. However, in the second year of the deposit, 5 percent interest would be paid not merely on the $1 original deposit but also on the 5 cents earned as interest during the first year. Thus, the interest earned in the second year would amount to 0.0525 cents ($1.05 × 0.05 = 0.0525), or one-quarter cent more than the first year. This is an example of compound interest.

As a matter of practice, savings institutions have for many years compounded interest semi-annually or quarterly, thus raising the annual interest rate by a small fraction. More recently, banks in areas where competition for funds is very great have been compounding interest daily. The result of this is that an annual interest rate of 7.75 percent will actually pay 8.17 percent at the end of a full year, assuming the funds remain in the account during the entire period.

When interest is to be compounded, the amount of interest to be earned over a period of time can be calculated by painstakingly computing the interest at the end of every interest period (whether daily, monthly, quarterly or otherwise) on the balance outstanding at that time. Another way to calculate the future value is to present the process mathematically:

The future or compound value is equal to the present value times one plus the interest rate raised to a power equal to the number of periods which the money is left in the savings account, or $FV = PV(1 + R)^n$. (See Table 14-2.)

☐ *Discounting.* Discounting is simply the inverse of compounding. In discounting, the future value is known, as is the interest rate and the term.

Table 14-2. COMPOUND INTEREST (FUTURE VALUE) EXAMPLE

How much will $1,000 placed in a 5% annual compounding savings account be worth at the end of the third year?

I. Hand computation $FV = [PV \cdot (1 + r) \cdot (1 + r) \cdot (1 + r)]$

$1,000   Initial principal
   5%   Annual interest rate
$50   First-year interest

$1,000 + $50 = $1,050   Principal during the second year
          5%   Annual interest rate
      $52.50   Second-year interest

$1,050 + $52.50 = $1,102.50   Principal during the third year
          5%   Annual interest rate
    $55.1250   Third-year interest

$1,102.50 + $55.13 = <u>$1,157.63</u>   Future value (end of third year)

II. From the compound interest tables $FV = (1 + r)^n \cdot PV$

  A. Compound interest factor (3 years at 5% — page 502 column 1) = 1.157625
  B. Principal = $1,000
  C. Future value = 1.157625 × $1,000 = <u>$1,157.63</u>

The problem is to find the present value. Suppose a business associate promises to pay you $10,000 in one lump sum at the end of ten years. The question is, what would you pay your associate today (present value) for that promise? The answer is a function of your discount rate and how long you must wait for the payment. Here, too, a formula is available for calculating the present value of a single-payment to be received in the future; it is an algebraic rearrangement of the compounding formula (see Table 14-3):

$$PV = FV \div (1 + r)^n$$

Table 14-3 suggests that if your discount rate were 9% you would pay your business associate $4,224.11 today for that promise. Stated another way with a 9 percent discount rate you would be indifferent to receiving $4,224.11 today or the right to receive $10,000 ten years from today. Also, since discounting is the inverse of compounding, it can be seen that if $4,224.11 were deposited today earning 9 percent interest, the compound value would be $10,000 in ten years.

    □ *Series of payments.* The compounding and discounting formulas can be expanded to handle a series of payments or receipts as easily as a single payment or receipt. The examples in Tables 14-4 and 14-5 present the future value of a series of payments (compound annuity) and the present value of a series of receipts (discounted annuity).

Table 14-3. DISCOUNTING (PRESENT VALUE) EXAMPLE

What is the value today of the right to receive $10,000 at the end of ten years assuming a 9% annual discount rate?

I. Hand computation:

$$PV = \frac{FV}{(1 + r)^n} = \frac{\$10,000}{(1 + .09)^{10}} = \frac{\$10,000}{2.3673637} = \$4,224.11$$

II. From the Compound Interest Tables:
  a. Annual *PV* factor (ten years at 9%, page 516 column 4) = 0.422411
  b. Future value = $10,000
  c. Present value $10,000 × 0.422411 = $4,224.11

Table 14-4. FUTURE VALUE OF AN ANNUITY

How much will $500 set aside each year accumulate to in 7 years if during the interim the funds can be invested at 8 percent compounded annually?

Amount of the annuity	$500
Term	7 years
Interest rate	8%
Annual annuity factor (page 512 column 2)	8.922803
Future value of the annuity ($500 × 8.922803)	$4,461.40

Table 14-5. PRESENT VALUE OF AN ANNUITY

What is the value today of receiving $500 a year for 7 years if the annual discount rate is 8% annual compounding?

Amount of the annuity	$500
Term	7 years
Discount rate	8%
Annual annuity factor (page 512 column 5)	5.206370
Present value of annuity ($500 × 5.206370)	$2,603.19

☐ *Sinking fund accumulation.* When calculating the sinking fund method of the recapture of capital (income approach to value), it is necessary to determine how much must be set aside each period to accumulate to a certain value. This method is demonstrated in Table 14-6. The concept of the sinking fund can be used when an investor needs to determine how much must be set aside to replace certain fixtures. For example, if the floor

Table 14-6. SINKING FUND ACCUMULATION

How much must be set aside each period at 7% compounded monthly so that in 120 *months* $100,000 will accumulate?	
Sinking fund period	120 months
Interest rate	7%
Monthly sinking fund factor (page 507 column 3)	0.005778
Amount to set aside each month ($100,000 × 0.005778)	$577.80

coverings in an apartment have a useful life of five years and are expected to cost $10,000 how much must be set aside each *month* from income to replace the floor coverings. If we assume an 8% annual discount rate it can be seen that each month $136.10 must be set aside to accumulate $10,000 (0.013610 × $10,000).

☐ *Installment to amortize.* A slightly more complex variation in these procedures can be used to arrive at a constant periodic payment necessary to amortize (pay off) a loan. This concept is introduced in Chapter 13 and is illustrated in Table 14-7. This factor is called the annual or monthly constant, depending on the repayment pattern.

Table 14-7. MONTHLY CONSTANT DEBT SERVICE

What are the *monthly* payments on a fully amortizing 30-year $60,000 loan at 9%?	
Term (360 months)	30 years
Interest rate	9%
Initial principal	$60,000.00
Factor (page 515 column 6)	0.008046
Mortgage loan monthly constant payment ($60,000 × 0.008046)	$ 482.76

EFFECT OF FINANCING ON BEFORE-TAX CASH FLOWS

With this background, the equity perspective of debt financing will be considered. Looking back to Table 14-1, two pertinent return measures can be calculated: (1) rate of return on total capital (ROR) and (2) rate of return on equity (ROE).

Rate of Return on Total Capital

The ROR measures the overall productivity of an income-producing property. The major assumption implied by this rate of return measure is that the project has been financed with equity only; and, consequently, there is no debt service. The ROR is calculated as follows:

$$ROR = \frac{NOI}{\text{Total capital invested}}$$

For our example in Table 14-1, the ROR is:

$$ROR = \frac{\$32,189}{\$357,600} = 9\%$$

Rate of Return of Equity

Since most real estate projects involve debt financing, the rate of return on equity measures the performance of a project on an after-financing or equity cash-on-cash basis. The ROE is often referred to as the *cash-on-cash return* and is measured as follows:

$$ROE = \frac{\text{Before-tax equity cash flow}}{\text{Equity investment}}$$

For the example in Table 14-1, the ROE is:

$$ROE = \frac{\$4,369}{\$97,600} = 4.47\%$$

Positive and Negative Leverage

The use of borrowed funds in financing a project is called leverage. The use of leverage requires a division of the project's net operating income between two claims—debt and equity—and has two effects upon the residual (equity) cash flow. First, the use of debt may change the percentage return to equity; and, second, the use of debt will increase the risk to equity.

The impact of leverage upon equity return (ROE) can be analyzed by comparing the ROR with the annual constant (K). The general rule is that if K is greater than ROR, leverage is negative and works against the equity investor by reducing the percentage return to equity. If K is less than ROR, leverage is positive and works for the equity investor by increasing the percentage return to equity.

In Table 14-1, ROR is 9 percent, while K is 10.07 percent (K = annual debt service ÷ original loan amount). Thus leverage is negative. The inequality K > ROR simply indicates that the cost of financing (K) is greater than the overall productivity of the project (ROR). If an investor pays more for borrowed funds than can be earned on those same funds when invested (i.e., K > ROR), ROE will suffer.

If the financing associated with a particular project results in negative leverage, what can the investor do? The investor can either (1) reduce K by negotiating a lower interest rate or longer term or (2) increase ROR by raising rents, reducing operating expenses, or paying less for the project. Generally, the terms of the financing are market-determined, so little can be done to change K. As far as ROR is concerned, both the rents and operating expenses are market determined, leaving the offering price as the only variable generally subject to the investor's control. An example of the impact of positive leverage is presented in Table 14-8.[1]

Table 14-8. POSITIVE LEVERAGE EXAMPLE

Financing of $70,000, with an annual constant of ten percent, is available on a project which costs $100,000 and is expected to generate net operating income of $12,000 per year. What is the expected return to equity?

  I. ROR on total capital (unleveraged return):
     Annual NOI = $12,000
     Total cost invested = $100,000
     Percentage ROR = $12,000 ÷ $100,000 = <u>12%</u>

 II. Leveraged return:
     Annual NOI = $12,000
     Annual debt service = 70,000 × 10% = $7,000
     Before-tax equity cash flow = $12,000 − $7,000 = $5,000
     Equity Investment = $100,000 − $70,000 = $30,000
     Percentage levered return (ROE) = $5,000 ÷ $30,000 = <u>16.66%</u>

III. Since ROR > K, this project demonstrates positive leverage. Note also that if the project were to be financed totally with cash (i.e., no leverage), the ROE would equal the ROR of 12 percent. But since the cost of financing the project (the annual constant) is less than the ROR, the ROE increases to 16.66 percent.

Leverage and Variability of Cash Flow

Whether positive or negative, leverage increases the variability of the equity cash flow. Variability of the equity cash flow is often equated with the riskiness of the equity position. Remember that debt (in the simple debt-equity distinction) has a prior claim on the property's NOI. If a constant amount of the operating cash flows must be paid to the lender, then the impact of any variation in the overall operating cash flows will be felt entirely by the residual (equity) holder. This magnified effect is illus-

---

[1] Traditionally, negative leverage has been viewed as definitionally bad. However, in an inflationary economy where a large part of the total equity return comes from the proceeds from sale and tax shelter, the issue is not quite as clear-cut. In such cases, investors may be content to give a greater amount of the NOI (lower ROE) to the lender knowing the tax shelter and capital gains will not be shared with the lender. This issue will be more easily understood after the investment model is developed in Part VII.

trated in Table 14-9. In sum, debt financing can increase the expected returns to the equity holder but with the penalty of exposing the equity holder to greater risk.

Table 14-9. LEVERAGE-INDUCED VARIABILITY EXAMPLE

An investment alternative is expected (with equal likelihood) to produce a net operating income of $12,000 or $8,000 per year. The total project cost is $100,000, and a 70% loan is available at 9% interest, 10% annual constant. What is the effect of the debt on the equity return?

	Outcome 1	Outcome 2
I. Unleveraged:		
NOI	$ 12,000	$ 8,000
Amount of equity	$100,000	$100,000
Percentage ROE	12%	8%
II. Leveraged:		
NOI	$ 12,000	$ 8,000
Interest ($70,000 at 10% K)	7,000	7,000
Return to equity	$ 5,000	$ 1,000
Amount of equity ($100,000 − $70,000)	$ 30,000	$ 30,000
Percentage ROE	16.66%	3.33%

ADDITIONAL DEBT AND EQUITY DISTINCTIONS

The definition of winning in real estate involves looking at the residual cash flow (the cash flow generated from the project after the prior claims of the lender and the government). This is a useful model, but, at times, it oversimplifies the distinction between debt and equity. There are various ways to divide the claims of the different sources of funds other than the simple debt-equity distinction. There can be several levels (priorities) of debt—first lien, second lien, third lien—and then an equity holder. There can be a group of equity holders and no debt—but with preferred (priority) position within the equity group. A lender may participate in the equity return in ways limited only by the ingenuity of the analyst.

In all of these cases, the logic is the same. Each one of the players—lender, semi-lender, equity investor—wants to win; more precisely, each wants more return for less risk. All want to maximize the NOI from the project and each is in competition with the others when it comes to dividing the NOI among them.

SUMMARY

The mechanics involved in real estate financing are based on the concepts of compounding and discounting. The Compound Interest Tables presented at the end of the book facilitate the use of the basic compounding interest and discounting formulas shown in this chapter.

From the borrower's perspective, debt effects the equity return in two ways. First, leverage may either increase or decrease the expected return to the equity holder. Second and regardless of whether leverage is positive or negative, the existence of the fixed debt obligation increases the variability of the equity cash flow.

In talking about financing, it is appropriate to think in terms of the left- and right-hand sides of the balance sheet. The left-hand side is the asset side, which produces certain operating cash flows. The assets listed in the left-hand side are financed through different sources of funds shown on the right-hand (liability) side. These sources of funds have different claims (in terms of priority and amount) on the NOI. Typically, the sources of funds having a *prior* claim expect a *lower* return because they assume less risk. Similarly, the residual equity return is expected to be higher than the prior return of the lender because the equity holder's claim will be satisfied only if and when the prior claim has been met.

IMPORTANT TERMS

compounding
discounting
opportunity cost
positive leverage
negative leverage

rate of return on equity (ROE)
rate of return on total capital (ROR)
sinking fund
time value of money

REVIEW QUESTIONS

14-1. Why is it important that the sources of financing (debt and equity) understand one another's investment requirements?

14-2. Why is the value of $1 to be received in the future less valuable than $1 to be received today?

14-3. Define and give an example of compound interest.

14-4. What is the difference between the rate of return on total capital and the rate of return on equity?

14-5. If a project has negative leverage how might the equity investor attempt to correct the situation?

14-6. How does the use of leverage affect the variability of equity cash flow?

14-7. Explain the statement, "The net operating income is essentially shared by the sources of financing."

14-8. What is the present value of a series of *monthly* payments of $250 received for 120 months assuming a 12 percent discount rate?

14-9. What would be the annual installment needed to fully amortize (interest and principal) the following loan: $145,000 original balance at 9.5 percent interest for 25 years?

14-10. What variables can be adjusted to correct negative leverage?

VI

Taxation

15

Income and Property Taxation

I N RANKING the priority of claims to operating cash flows from real estate, the first claim is that of the government. The government's claim in the form of property taxes has first priority with respect to the real estate itself; the government's claim in the form of income taxes has first priority on the investor's personal cash flow. Because tax revenues and government expenditures play such a large role in our overall economy and in real estate investing as well, a moment should be taken to amplify some of the macroeconomic numbers that were first presented in the opening chapter.

Governmental spending today represents from 20 to 22 percent of our gross national product (GNP). This total expenditure on goods and services is made up of approximately $150 billion a year in federal government spending and $250 billion a year in state and local government spending. In actuality, the federal government receives considerably more money than state and municipal governments do. However, a large portion of federal funds are transferred to the state and local governments and particularly to individuals.

On the ethical side, who should bear what portion of these common costs? On the purely economic side, which economic activities should be encouraged and which, if any, should be discouraged? Consideration of these policy issues allows the real estate analyst to anticipate and evaluate changes in the tax laws over the investment holding period.

TAXING AUTHORITIES

While considerable overlap in governmental spending exists, some general categorization is possible. The federal government must pay the costs of the following:

- National defense.
- Federal social programs (see Chapter 22 for real-estate-related programs).
- The ongoing operations of the large federal bureaucracy.
- Interest on the national debt.

State governments must handle the costs of their own operations. In addition, they also make transfer payments to various levels of local governments. County and township government is responsible for a variety of service functions, including highway upkeep, parks, recreation areas, etc. Municipal governments must bear the cost of operating city services such as fire and police protection, sanitation, and road maintenance as well as the cost of new construction. At all levels, a court system must be maintained. Finally, school districts bear the important responsibility of operating public schools while special assessment districts, such as water, sewer, and park districts are responsible for a variety of public benefit projects. The analyst is concerned with how these governmental bodies are financed and whether this financing is adequate to provide the services and infrastructure necessary to proper utilization of the particular real estate interest.

TYPES OF TAXES

Taxes: Regressive or Progressive?

A tax may be levied on income, on property, in connection with a transaction (a sales tax), or for benefits received (highway tolls and park fees). A pervasive issue in all tax legislation is whether a particular tax ought to be progressive or regressive. A *progressive tax* is keyed to the ability to pay, with wealthier persons paying relatively more, while a *regressive tax* is one which results in the poor paying a higher percentage of their income in taxes. The latter is exemplified by any straight tax on necessary consumption (sales tax on food) since the poor tend to spend a higher percentage of their income on such items.

In order to raise necessary revenues, the various levels of government are empowered to levy different types of taxes. Taxes can be based on the basis of either the ability to pay (the income tax being the most notable example) or on the benefits received by the taxpayer (e.g., a highway toll or park fee).

☐ *Personal income taxes* (levied by the federal government as well as most state governments) generally are considered to be progressive since rates increase in higher income brackets. However, researchers have found that the middle class pays the highest percentage of income in taxes because high-bracket taxpayers are better able to utilize tax-minimizing and tax-sheltering techniques. Consequently, the income tax system may be progressive up to a certain point but not beyond.

☐ *Corporate income taxes.* It is more difficult to characterize corporate income taxes as progressive or regressive. Following the Revenue Act of 1978, corporate tax rates rise in a series of five steps from 17 percent (for taxable income under $25,000) to 46 percent (for taxable income in excess of $100,000). Thus, at least for small corporations, the corporate income tax may be progressive. For larger corporations, the issue is much more complex and requires an estimate of the corporation's ability to "pass through" the tax to its customers.

☐ *Property tax.* The property tax is the primary revenue tool for funding local governments and school districts. Since the property tax rate is the same for all property, whether of low or high value, the tax can be considered regressive. On the other hand, since owners of higher-priced properties, in fact, pay more taxes, the opposite argument can be made if income and property value are related.[1]

☐ *Sales tax.* The sales tax is used by some state and many municipal governments. It is quite clearly regressive in nature when applied to consumer goods and services since it is a flat percentage of the price and the poor consume a higher percentage of their incomes. When some basic necessities are exempted, the sales tax is less regressive.

☐ *Social security tax.* The social security tax is perhaps the most regressive tax of all since all income up to a specified ceiling is taxed at a flat rate, with income above the ceiling not taxed at all.[2]

FEDERAL GOVERNMENT REVENUES AND EXPENDITURES

By considering how much revenue is raised by the various types of taxes, one can sense who pays for the common costs of government and which economic activities are being encouraged. Some understanding of these policy issues is important in terms of predicting the types of taxes that will be payable over the life of the real property asset.

---

[1] Many states have passed *circuit breaker laws.* These are intended to relieve elderly or low-income homeowners from constantly rising property taxes. When such legislation exists, the property tax becomes progressive to some degree.

[2] Numerous other types of taxes exist, including excise taxes, estate and gift taxes, license taxes, and value-added taxes (VATs), which are primarily found in Western Europe. An analysis of these types of taxes goes beyond the scope of investigation in this book.

Federal government revenues in fiscal 1979 ran around $400 billion. Of this total, 43 percent came from personal income taxes, 15 percent came from corporate income taxes, while 34 percent came from the highly regressive social security tax. Indirect and other taxes accounted for the final 8 percent. In total, then, federal tax collection may be only slightly progressive.

Federal government expenditures in fiscal 1979 ran about $450 billion, indicating an approximate deficit of $50 billion. Of total federal expenditures, defense represents about 23 percent, of which about one-third is for goods and services and two-thirds is for employee compensation. Other federal purchases of goods and services make up another 12 percent of total expenditures.

Transfer payments represent 41 percent of the total, exceeding social security tax collections by a considerable margin. Transfers to state and local government (revenue-sharing) make up another 17 percent. The final 7 percent of federal expenditures are for interest payments on the national debt, which continues to grow and is perhaps an unfortunate legacy for the future.

Federal Deficit

The continuing annual federal deficits have great social importance in terms of who pays and who benefits from federal tax collections. In a more immediate sense, the annual deficit has a pronounced impact on the supply and demand for funds in the economy. This is particularly important for the real estate industry because, as already noted, real estate is tremendously dependent on debt financing, both for new construction and purchases of existing property.

"Crowding Out" and Inflation

A *crowding out* of real estate borrowers can occur when the federal government, considered a risk-free borrower, becomes an important presence in the financial markets. This crowding out will be most pronounced if the deficit is not *monetized*—in other words, if the Federal Reserve System does not increase the money supply in an amount corresponding to the increased deficit. The Federal Reserve often is unwilling to increase the money supply since this tends to increase the rate of inflation.

The usual result in practice is some combination of crowding out plus monetization (and increased inflation). So long as the federal government continues to run a substantial deficit, both can be expected and both have significant implications for the real estate industry, as is noted throughout this book.

STATE AND LOCAL GOVERNMENT REVENUES AND EXPENDITURES

State and local governments collected about $350 billion in fiscal 1979. Of this total, 22 percent came in transfer payments from the federal government. The balance of 78 percent came from direct taxation and was made up of (1) sales taxes (23 percent), (2) property taxes (22 percent), (3) personal income taxes (11 percent), and (4) miscellaneous taxes (22 percent). Since the sales tax is clearly a regressive tax and the property tax is at least partly so, it appears that total state and local taxes generally are less progressive than federal taxes.

About 90 percent of state and local expenditures are for the purchase of goods and services. The balance of 10 percent is for transfer payments. Total expenditures amount to $325 billion in 1979, resulting in surplus of approximately $25 billion. In other words, state and local governments, while running a surplus, were receiving revenue sharing from the federal government, which itself was incurring a substantial deficit. The logic of this can be understood only by recognizing the more progressive nature of federal tax revenues. (See Table 15-1 for a breakdown of tax revenue.)

REAL PROPERTY TAXATION

Following this brief description of the federal, state, and local tax systems, the property tax and then the income tax provisions of the Internal Revenue Code which most directly impact on real property assets are examined. These two taxes—property and income—have a very direct and substantial effect on the cash flow received by the equity investor in real estate.

The property tax varies from locality to locality and may be relatively insignificant in some places, while, in others, it may constitute the single largest operating expense. (See Figure 15-1.) Property taxes are *ad valorem* taxes—that is, they are based on value. Consequently, property taxes are based neither on the ability of the property owner to pay nor on the particular benefits received by the owner.

Real estate taxes are determined by applying *tax rates* to *assessed valuations*. The tax rate is set by the legislature or local governing council. It is often expressed in *mills* (tenths of a cent). For example, a tax rate of 50 mills per $100 is the equivalent of 5 cents per $100 (of assessed valuation). The assessed valuation is the value placed on real (and sometimes personal) property and recorded on the assessment roll of the taxing district. The standard followed in determining assessed valuation, usually specified by law, is the value which would be obtainable for the property in the open market. Assessed valuation may equal 100 percent of such open-market value or a fraction thereof (e.g., 50 percent of full value).

Table 15-1. TAX REVENUE BY SOURCE AND LEVEL: 1950-1976

SOURCE AND YEAR	ALL GOVERNMENT Total (mil. dol.)	Percent of total	FEDERAL Total (mil. dol.)	Percent of all govt.	STATE AND LOCAL State (mil. dol.)	Local (mil. dol.)	ANNUAL PERCENT CHANGE[1] Federal	State	Local	PER CAPITA[2] (dollars) Federal	State and local
Total:											
1950	51,100	100.0	35,186	68.9	7,930	7,984	3.6	8.5	10.0	232	105
1955	81,072	100.0	57,589	71.0	11,597	11,886	10.4	7.9	8.3	348	142
1960	113,120	100.0	77,003	68.1	18,036	18,081	6.0	9.2	8.8	428	201
1965	144,953	100.0	93,710	64.6	26,126	25,116	4.0	7.7	6.8	483	264
1970	232,877	100.0	146,082	62.7	47,962	38,833	9.3	12.9	9.1	719	427
1972	262,534	100.0	153,733	58.6	59,870	48,930	2.6	11.7	12.3	738	522
1973	286,132	100.0	165,030	57.7	68,069	53,032	7.3	13.7	8.4	786	577
1974	314,785	100.0	184,112	58.5	74,207	56,467	11.6	9.0	6.6	871	618
1975	331,435	100.0	189,970	57.3	80,155	61,310	3.2	8.0	8.5	892	664
1976	358,227	100.0	201,414	56.2	89,256	67,557	6.0	11.4	10.2	938	731
Individual income:											
1950	16,533	32.4	15,745	95.2	724	64	9.7	20.5	20.6	104	5
1955	29,984	37.0	28,747	95.9	1,094	143	12.8	8.6	17.4	174	7
1960	43,178	38.2	40,715	94.3	2,209	254[4]	7.2	15.1	12.2	226	14
1965	52,882	36.5	48,792	92.3	3,657	433[4]	3.7	10.6	11.3	252	21
1970	101,224	43.5	90,412	89.3	9,183	1,630[4]	13.1	20.2	30.4	445	53
1972	109,974	41.9	94,737	86.1	12,996	2,241[4]	2.4	19.0	17.3	455	73
1973	121,240	42.3	103,246	85.2	15,587	2,406[4]	9.0	19.9	7.4	492	86
1974	138,443	43.9	118,952	85.9	17,078	2,413[4]	15.2	9.6	.3	563	92
1975	143,840	43.4	122,386	85.1	18,819	2,635[4]	2.9	10.2	9.2	574	101
1976	156,178	43.6	131,603	84.3	21,448	3,127[4]	7.5	14.0	18.7	613	114
Corporation income:											
1950	11,081	21.7	10,488	94.6	586	7	4.1	.1	(NA)	69	4
1955	18,604	22.9	17,861	96.0	737	7	11.2	4.7	–	108	5
1960	22,674	20.0	21,494	94.8	1,180	(4)	3.8	9.9	(4)	119	7
1965	27,390	18.9	25,461	93.0	1,929	(4)	3.4	10.3	(4)	131	10
1970	36,567	15.7	32,829	89.8	3,738	(4)	5.2	14.2	(4)	162	18
1972	36,582	13.9	32,166	87.9	4,416	(4)	−1.0	8.7	(4)	154	21
1973	41,578	14.5	36,153	87.0	5,225	(4)	12.4	22.8	(4)	172	26
1974	44,635	14.1	38,620	86.5	6,015	(4)	6.8	10.9	(4)	183	28
1975	47,263	14.3	40,621	85.9	6,642	(4)	5.2	10.4	(4)	191	31
1976	48,682	13.6	41,409	85.1	7,273	(4)	1.9	9.5	(4)	193	34
Sales, gross receipts:											
1950	12,997	25.4	7,843	60.3	4,670	484	1.3	7.5	10.0	52	34
1955	17,221	21.2	9,578	55.6	6,864	779	4.1	8.0	10.0	58	46
1960	24,452	21.6	12,603	51.5	10,510	1,339	5.6	8.9	11.4	70	66
1965	32,904	22.7	15,786	48.0	15,059	2,059	4.6	7.5	9.0	81	88
1970	48,619	20.9	18,297	37.6	27,254	3,068	3.0	12.6	7.9	90	149
1972	57,589	21.9	20,101	34.9	33,250	4,238	4.8	10.5	18.7	97	180
1973	61,769	21.6	19,722	31.9	37,123	4,924	−1.9	11.6	16.2	94	200
1974	66,632	21.1	20,534	30.8	40,556	5,542	4.1	9.2	12.6	97	218
1975	70,905	21.4	21,090	29.7	43,346	6,468	2.7	6.9	16.7	99	234
1976	76,265	21.3	21,718	28.5	47,391	7,156	3.0	9.3	10.6	101	254
Property:											
1950	7,349	14.4	(X)	(X)	307	7,042	(X)	5.5	9.7	(X)	48
1955	10,735	13.2	(X)	(X)	412	10,323	(X)	6.1	8.0	(X)	65
1960	16,405	14.5	(X)	(X)	607	15,798	(X)	8.1	8.9	(X)	91
1965	22,583	15.6	(X)	(X)	766	21,817	(X)	4.8	6.7	(X)	117
1970	34,054	14.6	(X)	(X)	1,092	32,963	(X)	7.4	8.6	(X)	168
1972	42,133	16.0	(X)	(X)	1,257	40,876	(X)	7.3	11.4	(X)	202
1973	45,283	15.8	(X)	(X)	1,312	43,970	(X)	4.4	7.6	(X)	216
1974	47,705	15.1	(X)	(X)	1,301	46,404	(X)	−.8	5.6	(X)	226
1975	51,491	15.5	(X)	(X)	1,451	50,040	(X)	11.5	7.7	(X)	242
1976	57,001	15.9	(X)	(X)	2,118	54,884	(X)	46.0	9.7	(X)	266
Other taxes:											
1950	3,140	6.1	1,110	35.4	1,643	387	5.5	10.7	(NA)	7	13
1955	4,527	5.6	1,402	31.0	2,490	634	4.8	8.7	10.4	8	19
1960	6,411	5.7	2,191	34.2	3,530	692	9.3	7.2	1.8	12	23
1965	9,191	6.3	3,670	39.9	4,715	807	10.9	6.0	3.1	19	28
1970	12,413	5.3	4,544	36.6	6,695	1,173	4.4	7.3	7.8	22	39
1972	16,256	6.2	6,729	41.4	7,951	1,575	21.7	9.0	15.9	32	46
1973	16,265	5.7	5,909	36.3	8,622	1,731	−12.2	8.4	9.9	28	49
1974	17,370	5.5	6,006	34.6	9,257	2,108	1.6	7.4	21.8	28	54
1975	17,936	5.4	5,873	32.7	9,897	2,166	−2.2	6.9	2.8	28	57
1976	20,101	5.6	6,684	33.3	11,026	2,390	13.8	11.4	10.3	31	63

SOURCE: U.S. Bureau of the Census, Statistical Abstract of the United States: 1978 (99th ed.) (Washington, D.C.: U.S. Government Printing Office, 1978), p. 291.

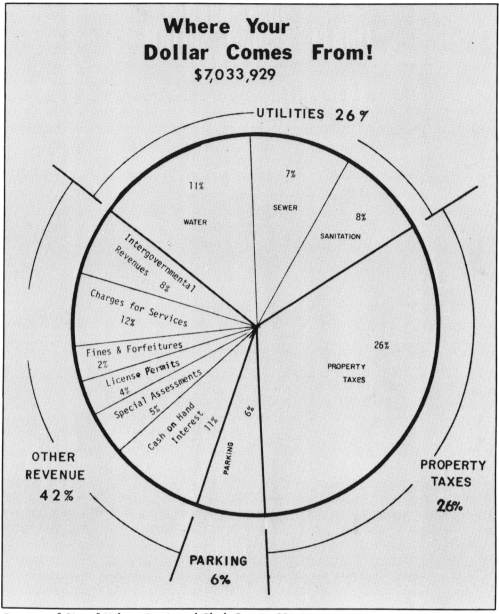

Courtesy of City of Helena, Lewis and Clark County, Montana.

Figure 15-1. SOURCES OF REVENUE—HELENA, MONTANA

The normal procedure when establishing the property tax each year is for the taxing authority to determine the total assessed valuation of property within the taxing district (which will change each year as a result of inflation new construction, property being improved, demolition, etc.).

Then, the total amount of revenues required to be raised from this source by the taxing district will be divided by the assessed valuation and the result will be the tax rate for the current year.

California's Proposition 13

In 1978, California voters approved Proposition 13, a voter-initiated statute that was a harbinger of a significant "tax revolt" in many parts of the country. Under Proposition 13, California real property taxes were reduced by limiting the maximum property tax rate to one percent of "full cash value" of real property and by rolling back assessed property values to 1975-1976 levels, subject only to an annual 2 percent increase. Only when ownership of a property changes may the property be reassessed to reflect its current market value. In addition, the legislature was barred from enacting new property taxes while local governments could impose "special taxes" only if two-thirds of the voters approve.

There were warnings that passage of the proposition would cause catastrophic rollbacks in social and educational programs. Despite all this, the initial impact of the law was relatively mild, primarily because the state government, by virtue of a large surplus in state tax collections, was able to transfer funds to local governments to offset most of the lost revenues. In addition, local communities passed new laws imposing fees on services that previously had been free and increasing other fees. Many of these new and increased charges were directed against builders who, in turn, passed their costs along to tenants and purchasers of space.

A number of other states have since passed Proposition 13-like measures, and indications are that local governments will continue to be required to fit budgets to available property tax revenues rather than the other way around.

Public Education Financing

Another significant trend in real property taxation is that the financing of public education may gradually be transferred to the state from individual school districts. This trend is the result of a number of legal decisions holding that state constitutional provisions are violated when public school financing depends on the assessed valuation of property in the school district. This results in very wide variations in expenditures per student within school districts in a single state. To the extent that the school financing burden is shifted to the state—which normally utilizes taxes other than the property tax to raise revenue—local property taxes may decline.

Property Tax as a Land Planning Tool

Local governments recognize that the property tax is a land planning tool as well as a means of raising revenue. This is particularly true when the property tax is a significant element of a property's operating expenses and so has a great impact on residual equity cash flows. By giving special property tax relief in such cases, local governments can encourage one land use over another or attract a new industry to the community.

For example, farmers near developing urban areas sometimes find their property taxes rising substantially because of sharp increases in assessed valuations reflecting the market value of their land as development acreage rather than as farmland. As a result, the land sometimes must be sold since it can no longer be used profitably for agricultural purposes. In order to prevent this loss of farmland, some communities follow a practice known as *value in use assessment*. This permits farmland to be assessed at a lower value in order to encourage the continuation of agricultural use. (These issues are dealt with in detail in Part IX.)

Tax-Exempt Property

A growing problem in many communities is the percentage of property exempt from tax liability because it is used for public, charitable, or religious purposes. This problem comes into sharp focus in cities which have economic bases dominated by government employment. If a major educational institution is located in a state's capital, a very large percentage—perhaps as much as half—of the property within the city may be tax-exempt. This means that the city either must set high tax rates or develop other sources of revenue.

If property taxes are high, then property owners in the district are being taxed at a higher rate than owners in other districts. This may contribute to increased development outside the city limits to avoid the high city taxes. The result is an eroding city tax base and future city financing difficulties.

Property Tax: Regressive or Progressive?

From the point of view of society in general, a key question about the property tax is: Who bears the major tax burden? Is the tax progressive or regressive? While these questions cannot be answered categorically, a few illustrations offer a clearer perspective on some of the issues involved.

☐ *Property-rich and property-poor districts.* A taxing district with a large number of industrial or business properties, or with many high-priced homes, will have a very large property base for taxation. Consequently, it can utilize relatively low tax rates to raise a great deal of revenue. By contrast, a taxing district with low-priced homes and no industry will have a difficult time, even with relatively high tax rates, in raising sufficient revenue to provide needed services.

As a result, an expensive home in a relatively poor community may be taxed a larger amount than the same home in a more affluent community. What is even more probable is that the home in the wealthier community would pay the same or somewhat higher taxes, but services would be at a much higher level.

☐ *Pass-through to users.* When increases in property taxes can be passed on to tenants of income properties through higher rentals (as may be the case for office buildings and retail stores), the tax tends to be regressive in nature, with final users and consumers shouldering the burden. On the other hand, when competition or rent control statutes prohibit a pass-through of property tax increases, then the consequence is a reduced equity cash flow for the investor.

In such cases, the property tax would be progressive *if* equity holders in the aggregate were wealthier than tenants. On the other hand, if rising taxes forced properties to be abandoned, as has happened in some big, older cities, the more important consequence is that the assessment roll is reduced and less space is available for occupancy. (It should be remembered, too, that property taxes are allowable deductions for federal income tax purposes.)

The progressive-versus-regressive distinction is not totally academic. As cities expand and, through annexation of adjacent areas, place more property on their tax rolls, consideration of who bears which common costs is more acutely focused. Newly annexed areas do not necessarily receive the same level of services as are provided in the central city—at least not immediately.

In many cases, local statutes allow the taxing authority to phase in the provision of complete city services over a two- to five-year period. On the other hand, certain municipal services are available to people living just beyond the boundaries of the taxing district. Such services include park and recreation facilities, museums, and other cultural facilities which are available to those living outside the taxing district and who pay no property taxes to it. Clearly, both policy and ethical questions must be considered in understanding the constantly changing nature of the property tax.

Impact of Property Tax on Cash Flow

From the perspective of a real estate analyst, property taxes are an important element in projecting future cash flows. Such taxes are often an important expense today and give indications of rising in the future. The failure to account for increases in property taxes turned many attractive investments into mistakes during the 1970s. While it is possible that property taxes will increase less rapidly in the future as a result of statutes similar to Proposition 13 in California, this is far from certain.

On the other hand, the real estate analyst is also interested in determining whether the municipality is able to support the level of services required by the populace. Particularly where a project may seek to attract tenants or purchasers from a distance, the quality of public education, fire and police services, sanitation, and the like is an important consideration.

THE FEDERAL INCOME TAX

The federal income tax has a major impact on real estate investment decisions and on the benefits to be derived from property ownership. Real estate has always been a tax-favored investment medium and one of the most important goals of the real estate professional is to *structure* a real estate investment package so as to maximize the tax savings for the equity interests.

The balance of this chapter discusses general provisions of the Internal Revenue Code affecting real estate. Chapter 16 analyzes in some detail the tax law provisions that specifically deal with real estate investment.

Goals of the Real Estate Decision-Maker

In reaching tax decisions, the real estate decision-maker's objective is usually to pay as little as possible as late as possible. This basic objective is accomplished in three ways. The first is *deferring* tax liability as far into the future as possible by accelerating all deductible items and by postponing income recognition where feasible. The second is *converting* ordinary income into capital gain because the latter is taxed at a substantially lower rate than the former. The third is *smoothing* income recognition over several years to avoid peak marginal tax rates that come with unusually high income in any tax year under a progressive tax system.

Ordinary Income Tax versus Capital Gain

Ordinary income includes salary, wages, commissions, and profits earned from carrying on a trade or business. Interest, dividends, royalties, and rents also are ordinary income. The tax rate applied to ordinary income is progressive in nature; rates range from 14 percent to 70 percent on *taxable income* (i.e., after the taxpayer has taken permissible deductions and exemptions).[3]

By comparison, *capital gains* is profit received from the sale or exchange of capital assets.

---

[3] A particular category of ordinary income is termed earned income (wages, salary, and commissions). The maximum tax on earned income is 50 percent which reflects a desire by government to not tax active income as heavily as passive income (rents and dividends).

The logic of the capital gains tax is that capital gains represent the appreciation of property which often has been held for a long period of time. Under our somewhat progressive tax rate structure, it would be unfair to tax the entire gain as if it had entirely occurred in a single year. Congress could have provided that any such gain would be taxed as if it had been realized pro rata over the entire life of the investment. Instead of this more complex way, Congress chose to permit a flat deduction of 60 percent of the total gain, provided the investment was held for a minimum period of one year.

From a public policy perspective, preferential tax treatment of capital gains income provides an inducement to invest (and consequently to save) and also makes capital more mobile so that greater overall economic efficiency is achieved (i.e., investors are not prohibited from moving toward more attractive investments by a heavy tax on the exchange). Such a tax would make the capital markets less efficient in allocating savings to investment.

The definition in the tax law of a capital asset is complex. Basically, the term includes any property not held for sale in the normal course of business. Thus, investment real estate held for income is a capital asset. However, a developer is considered to be in the business of producing real estate for sale and so is not eligible for capital gains treatment. So long as the asset is held longer than one year, it qualifies for the special tax treatment just described.[4]

Avoiding the Two Kinds of Minimum Tax

Since 1969, tax analysts have also been concerned with avoiding the payment of either of the two kinds of *minimum tax* that are now part of the tax law.

□ *The 1969 Tax Reform Act.* The concept of a minimum tax was introduced in the 1969 Tax Reform Act in order to insure that every taxpayer pay at least some income tax no matter what the source of

---

[4] Other rules pertaining to the capital gains tax may be summarized briefly:
- If a capital asset is held for less than one year and is sold at a profit, the gain is short-term and is treated as ordinary income.
- If a capital asset held for more than one year is sold at a loss the loss is deductible (i.e., it may offset ordinary income) but $2 of such long-term capital loss is necessary to offset $1 of ordinary income and in addition, the maximum offset in any one year is $6,000, with any excess carried over to future years.
- In the event of a short-term capital loss (from a capital asset held for less than one year), the loss may be used to offset ordinary income on a dollar-for-dollar basis, but only up to a maximum of $3,000 per year.
- An investor having both capital gains and capital losses must offset one against the other before applying the rules just described.
- In the case of corporations, long-term capital gains are taxed at a flat rate of 30 percent, while short-term gains are taxed as ordinary income.

income. The stimulus for the new tax arose when it became generally known that some very wealthy individuals were paying no taxes whatsoever—in most cases because they were in a position to assume economic risks involved in *tax shelters* and so were able to generate sufficient deductions to offset their full current income.

☐ *The 1978 Revenue Act.* In the 1978 Revenue Act, Congress split the original minimum tax into two separate minimum taxes. The original minimum tax is now known as the *add-on minimum tax* because it is in addition to regular tax liability, while the new minimum tax is called the *alternative minimum tax* (AMT) because it is payable only as an alternative to regular tax liability plus the add-on minimum tax.

The two minimum taxes are quite complex in their application; only a very brief summary of each is given below.

☐ *Add-on minimum tax.* This tax applies to all taxpayers and, as noted, is in addition to regular tax liability. The amount of the minimum tax is 15 percent of certain types of income, called *tax-preference income.* For the real estate investor, the most significant item of tax-preference income is the amount of any accelerated depreciation deduction taken in excess of straight line depreciation.[5] (This "excess depreciation" is discussed in the next chapter.)

☐ *Alternative minimum tax.* The AMT is payable only if it exceeds the regular income tax liability of a taxpayer plus any add-on minimum tax. Basically, the AMT is applied to the 60 percent excluded portion of capital gains plus itemized deductions minus a $20,000 exemption. The AMT is, in effect, a new method of taxing long-term capital gains and will apply only in rare cases to a taxpayer having extremely large capital gains and very little other taxable income. (In Part VII, it is seen that these two minimum taxes can cause considerable problems in developing a workable discounted cash flow model.)

CALCULATING TAXABLE INCOME OR LOSS

The tax consequences of investing in real estate can conveniently be divided into two categories. The first relates to operating the real estate, while the second deals with the proceeds upon sale or other disposition. In both cases, the bottom line figure of concern is taxable income or deduct-

---

[5] From 1969 to 1978, the capital gains exclusion (then 50 percent and now 60 percent) was also a tax preference item.

ible loss. If the bottom line is taxable income, it will be added to any other taxable income of the taxpayer and the whole will be taxed in accordance with the appropriate tax rate schedule. If the result is a deductible tax loss, the loss will offset other taxable income of the taxpayer, with the net taxable income then subject to tax.

Calculating Taxable Income (Loss) From Real Estate Operations

During the period of ownership, the basic tax calculation of the investor each year will be as follows:

☐ *Determine gross income.* First, the investor adds up all rental income, receipts, and other revenues from the property or business operation to determine gross income.

☐ *Deduct operating expenses.* Next, the investor deducts all operating expenses, which include all of the ordinary and necessary expenses in connection with the property, including payroll, real estate taxes, maintenance and repair, insurance premiums, legal and accounting fees, advertising and promotion, supplies, etc.

☐ *Depreciation.* The investor also deducts from gross income an amount representing depreciation of the improvements on the property. Depreciation is a special kind of operating expense, being a bookkeeping entry rather than representing a cash outlay. Because of its crucial importance to real estate investment, it is discussed in detail in the following chapter.

☐ *Interest on mortgages.* Also deducted from gross income are interest payments on any outstanding loans used to finance the property. Note, however, that loan amortization (repayment) is not deductible for tax purposes since the IRS views amortization not as an expense but as a payment or contribution of capital (investment).

☐ *Taxable income (loss).* If gross income exceeds all of the deductions just listed, the balance remaining is taxable income. If, on the other hand, deductions exceed gross income, the property has shown a deductible loss for the year, which may be used to offset (shelter) other income of the investor.

Calculating Taxable Income (Loss) on Sale

When the property is sold or disposed of in certain other ways, such as by a foreclosure of a mortgage, the investor must determine whether any gain or loss has been realized. This involves the following calculation:

☐ *Sales proceeds.* First, the amount of sales proceeds must be determined. This normally will be the sales price stated in the contract of sale less any selling costs such as commissions and legal fees. It will include not only the cash paid to the seller but also the amount of any mortgages of which buyer is relieved. If consideration other than cash is given for the property, then the fair market value of such property is a part of the sales price.

☐ *Adjusted basis (cost).* Next, the seller deducts from the sale proceeds the seller's cost or basis. This figure is developed as follows:

- The seller begins with this original cost (cash or property paid plus the amount of any mortgages to which the property was subject when acquired).
- To this is added any capital expenditures made by the seller during the period of ownership.
- From this is subtracted the cumulative depreciation deductions taken by the seller during ownership.

☐ *Gain or loss.* If the amount of sales proceeds is larger than the adjusted basis of the seller, a gain has been realized; otherwise, a loss has been realized. The gain or loss will be characterized as capital gain (loss) or ordinary income (loss), depending on whether the property was a capital asset in the hands of the seller. If capital gain or loss is realized, it will be long-term gain or loss, provided the seller held the property for at least one year. Only 40 percent of any long-term gain is taxable, giving the investor a 60 percent exclusion.

While this description sets forth the basic outline of the tax calculation for the real estate investor, some of the deductions, most notably that dealing with depreciation, require further elaboration in Chapter 16.

SUMMARY

This chapter has set forth the basics of property and income taxation. Both the property tax and the income tax are methods of providing the financing necessary to support government operations. Since taxation has such a pronounced impact on cash flow, it is a key part of the real estate game. The decision-maker must not only know current tax law, but also have a feel for the historical evolution of tax principles, the social consequences of who bears what part of which common costs, and the implications of the different means of raising the necessary revenue. Only with this broad background will the decision maker be able to anticipate changes in tax law over the expected economic life of the real estate asset.

It is important to remember that the incentives in the tax law are not merely "loopholes." They were placed in the law to produce what are deemed socially desirable activities. So long as these incentives accomplish this goal, the real estate analyst should feel no uneasiness about organizing investment programs to maximize the tax benefits. And because the social purposes sought to be achieved by these incentives are long-lasting ones (adequate housing and employment), the analyst should feel comfortable about anticipating that these tax benefits will be available over the holding period of the asset which may extend for many years.

IMPORTANT TERMS

ad valorem tax
alternative minimum tax
capital gains
corporate income tax
crowding out
equalization procedure
minimum tax
personal income tax
progressive income tax

property tax
regressive income tax
sales tax
taxable income
tax avoidance
tax conversion
tax deferral
value in use assessment

REVIEW QUESTIONS

15-1. Discuss the difference between regressive and progressive taxation. Why might a general sales tax be considered regressive and an income tax progressive?

15-2. How does the federal deficit relate to "crowding out" real estate borrowers in the national financial markets?

15-3. What are some of the difficulties associated with the reliance of local governments on the property tax as their primary source of revenue?

15-4. What services does a municipality normally provide the real estate user?

15-5. Property taxes are often levied on an ad valorem basis. What problems might this cause for property owners?

15-6. How can the property tax be used as an effective land planning tool?

15-7. Why does the federal government, which runs a deficit, transfer funds to state and local governments which run a surplus?

15-8. How is taxable income calculated?

15-9. What is a capital gain and how is it taxed?

15-10. Has the recent growth in government spending, as a percentage of gross national product, occurred at the federal or local level?

16

Income Tax and Real Estate

I N THIS CHAPTER, the specific provisions of the Internal Revenue Code (IRC) affecting real estate investments are examined. These provisions are examined from the point of view of an equity investor in real estate who is seeking to maximize the equity (residual) cash flow. An investor always bears in mind the basic distinction between *tax avoidance* and *tax evasion*. The first involves the individual taxpayer taking an aggressive posture in terms of minimizing tax liability and interpreting tax law liberally (perhaps more liberally than the Internal Revenue Service (IRS) and the courts ultimately will permit). The second, tax evasion, is fraud; it amounts to the willful concealment or misrepresentation of facts in order to avoid the payment of tax. Tax avoidance may be justifiable economic action; tax evasion is criminal activity that can lead to severe penalties. The line between them is not difficult to draw. A taxpayer who *fully and truthfully discloses* all pertinent information on a tax return can draw legal conclusions that differ from those generally accepted, without being guilty of fraud. But when disclosure is either incomplete or untruthful, the line has been overstepped.

RELEVANT TAX PROVISIONS

While the Internal Revenue Code covers many areas, those provisions directly affecting real estate naturally are the focus here. These areas include:

- Depreciation.
- At-risk provisions.
- Depreciation recapture.
- Investment tax credit.
- Energy credit.
- Investment interest deductibility.
- Construction period interest and property taxes.
- Installment sales.
- Tax-free exchanges.

In a simple framework, the important aspects of the above provisions will be introduced. The result will be a tax planning background sufficient to effectively utilize the investment analysis model developed in Part VII.

DEPRECIATION DEDUCTION

A major set of tax provisions affecting real estate investment involves depreciation. Through a combination of depreciation and capital gain, the basic objectives of tax planning can be accomplished.

The logic of depreciation is a simple matching of expenses with revenues as revenue-producing assets wear out. The concept of depreciation allows the investor to deduct a noncash expense (depreciation) from income before calculating taxable income. As such, depreciation provides a significant portion of the tax shelter for which income property has become known. Furthermore, although the general concept of depreciation is to allow investors to write off wasting assets (i.e., those assets which lose value as they are utilized), real estate is not necessarily a wasting asset over most relevant time periods. In fact, in many cases the value of the real estate asset increases rather than declines as time passes.

Determination of depreciation is based on three items: (1) the depreciable basis, (2) the useful life, and (3) the allowable depreciation technique.

Depreciable Basis

The depreciable basis of any item of property is its original cost plus additional capital investments during the period of ownership. The depreciable basis of real estate is the same except that the cost of the land must be subtracted from the total cost since land is not depreciable.

For example, an office building is purchased for $1 million. An appraisal determines that 20 percent of the cost ($200,000) is attributable to the land and 80 percent ($800,000) is attributable to the improvements. The depreciable basis of the property is therefore $800,000. If, two years later, the owner incurs a capital expenditure (say, installing a new elevator system) the cost of that expenditure is added to the depreciable basis.

One further important point must be noted. The depreciable basis for real property is its total cost to the investor, including equity and debt. In the example just given, it makes no difference whether the investor purchasing the $1 million office building utilized all cash or part cash and part debt. It also makes no difference whether the debt was recourse (the borrower assuming personal liability) or nonrecourse (no personal liability). In all cases, the initial depreciable basis remains $800,000.

The justification for allowing an owner to depreciate the entire cost of the improvements undiminished by any debt is that eventually the owner will have to amortize the mortgage obligation and thereby complete his investment in the property. In actual practice, mortgage obligations are usually amortized at a very slow pace during the early years of ownership, whereas depreciation deductions during the same period may represent a much higher percentage of the total cost of the property.

The result often is that the investor can obtain depreciation deductions in the course of a few years that far exceed his cash investment in the real estate.

The "At Risk" Limitation to Non-Real-Estate Investments

It has been noted that a real estate investor is entitled to include as part of his basis (cost) not only the equity investment made but also the amount of any debt used to finance the property. Since the depreciation write-offs in the initial years of ownership may substantially exceed the amount of cash investment, the real estate investor often can quickly recoup the entire equity investment via tax savings.

Until 1976, the right to include debt in an investor's basis applied to any type of investment, real estate or otherwise. But tax reformers believed that this constituted an abuse where the investor was not personally liable on the debt (i.e., the debt was nonrecourse). They felt that only when the investor assumed a personal responsibility to pay the debt should the tax basis be increased by such debt. Put another way, the reformers argued that depreciation should be limited to the amount *at risk* (whether equity or debt involving personal liability).

As a result, the 1976 Tax Reform Act (as later amended by the Revenue Act of 1978) created a new tax provision limiting the amount of any tax write-off by an investor to the amount of capital actually at risk. Any loss not deductible in any one year may be carried forward to be used in a subsequent year, again provided it does not exceed the amount at risk.

This new at-risk provision is applicable to all types of tax shelter investments *except* real estate—that is, it applies to film production, the extraction industries, oil exploration, feed lots, etc. Consequently, real estate is the only remaining major tax-shelter investment where non-recourse debt may be used to increase the basis for depreciation.

Useful Life

The depreciable basis is written off over the *economic life* of the asset. The economic or useful life of an asset is the period of time over which the asset will generate sufficient income to justify the investment. Therefore, if the asset is to last ten years, its depreciation should be accomplished in that ten-year period. The Internal Revenue Service suggests guideline useful lives which are conservative estimates (from the IRS's standpoint) of the useful life of particular types of real property. (See Table 16-1.) However, the individual investor can use a shorter useful life whenever

Table 16-1. USEFUL LIVES

The following useful lives have been approved by the Internal Revenue Service in connection with the calculation of annual depreciation deductions:

	Years
Building services:	
Shelter, space, and related building services for manufacturing and for machinery and equipment repair activities:	
Factories	45
Garages	45
Machine shops	45
Loft buildings	50
Building services for the conduct of wholesale and retail trade,	
includes stores and similar structures:	50
Building services for residential purposes:	
Apartments	40
Dwellings	45
Building services relating to provision of miscellaneous services	
to businesses and consumers:	
Office buildings	45
Storage:	
Warehouses	60
Grain elevators	60
Banks	50
Hotels	40
Theaters	40

SOURCE: *Revenue Procedure 62-21* (Washington, D.C.: U.S. Department of the Treasury, 1962).

the shorter life can be justified. For example, the useful life of a student apartment house might be less than a similarly constructed luxury apartment house for the elderly due to the extra "wear and tear" experienced in the former.

The chronological life or age of a project is only one factor in determining its remaining useful life. That is, if a new apartment building is deemed to have a 45-year useful life, it does not necessarily follow that a 10-year-old apartment building has a 35-year useful life remaining. The remaining useful life of an existing property is affected by its physical condition, which, in turn, is a consequence of its original construction and the manner in which it has been maintained, as well as the market within which the building must compete. Consequently, it is possible to have a 60-year-old (chronological) property with a 20-year remaining useful life.

Composite and Component Depreciation

To this point, a property has been viewed as a single entity in determining its useful life. This approach is known as *composite depreciation.* Another approach is to establish a useful life for each separate component of the asset and depreciate each separately. This is known as *component depreciation.* Components of a building might include the roof and outside walls, plumbing system, heating system, electrical wiring, air conditioning, and elevators. Since many of these components have relatively short lives, the depreciable basis allocated to those components can be recouped much more quickly than under composite depreciation.

As an example of component depreciation, assume that a building costing $1 million and with a 40-year life is depreciated on the straight-line basis under the regular method. Depreciation would amount to $25,000 per year (1/40 × $1,000,000) for the entire 40-year period. Now suppose, instead, the component method were used:

Description	Cost	Life (Years)	Annual Approximate Depreciation
Building	$ 600,000	40	$15,000
Wiring	60,000	15	4,000
Plumbing	45,000	15	3,000
Roofing	50,000	10	5,000
Heating	100,000	10	10,000
Paving	25,000	10	2,500
Ceiling	25,000	10	2,500
Air conditioning	50,000	10	5,000
Elevators	45,000	15	2,000
Total	$1,000,000		$50,000

In this hypothetical example, depreciation under the component method *doubles* the amount of the depreciation deduction in each of the first ten years. Thereafter, assuming that the assets with ten-year lives were not replaced so that the depreciable basis remained unchanged, the depreciation deduction would decline to a lower figure for the next five years. Assuming the assets with fifteen-year lives were not replaced when they were fully depreciated, the depreciation deduction would decline once again after fifteen years of ownership and then would remain level, for the balance of the forty-year building life. (The annual deduction declines because an owner can never recoup more than 100 percent of his cost via depreciation. Thus, the ten-year and fifteen-year life components are fully depreciated at the end of the respective periods and their cost is excluded from any further calculation.)

DEPRECIATION METHODS

☐ *Straight line depreciation.* The simplest way to write off an asset is the *straight line* method of depreciation. In other words, if the asset is to last forty years, the investor takes 2.5 percent of the cost (excluding land) as depreciation each year.

For example, assume an investor acquires real estate for $100,000. Twenty percent, or $20,000, is allocated to nondepreciable land, and 80 percent, or $80,000, is allocable to depreciable improvements. A useful life of forty years is given to the improvements. Using straight line depreciation, the investor is entitled to deduct 2.5 percent of $80,000 each year during his ownership. This deduction of $2,000 is available against ordinary income. Further, the deduction is available regardless of how much or how little equity the investor puts up and whether or not he is personally liable on the mortgage securing the loan.

☐ *Accelerated depreciation.* Since some assets depreciate faster in earlier years than in later years, the straight line method may not reflect a fair depreciation technique. As a result of this, additional allowable depreciation techniques beyond the straight line method were incorporated into the Internal Revenue Code. Essentially, these permit larger depreciation write-offs during the early years of ownership at the expense of smaller write-offs in later years (since total write-offs may never exceed 100 percent of cost). However, such *accelerated methods* are normally preferred since they defer taxes to future years—one of the objectives in tax planning.

Accelerated depreciation actually incorporates three separate methods[1]:

- 200 percent declining balance.
- 150 percent declining balance.
- 125 percent declining balance.

Table 16-2 lists the types of properties eligible for each type of depreciation.

The three methods of accelerated depreciation all are stated as a percentage of the straight line method. The 200 percent method allows a rate of depreciation equal to twice the straight line rate. If the straight line rate is 2.5 percent a year, the 200 percent method permits an annual rate of 5 percent. Similarly, the 150 percent method permits a rate of depreciation equal to 1.5 times the straight line rate, while the 125 percent method allows a rate equal to 1.25 times the straight line rate.

However, one additional element is involved in each of the accelerated methods. Under the straight line method, the rate (whatever it is) is calculated on the *original depreciable basis.* In the example given earlier in

---

[1] A fourth method of accelerated depreciation is known as the *sum-of-the-years'-digits method.* Since the results of this method closely parallel the 200 percent method, its computation is not set out in the book.

Table 16-2. REAL ESTATE DEPRECIATION METHODS

Depreciation Method	Applicable to
1. 200% declining balance	1. New residential housing
2. 150% declining balance	2. New commercial and industrial property
3. 125% declining balance	3. Used residential rental housing with useful life of at least twenty years
4. Straight line	4. Used commercial and industrial property
5. Straight line using sixty-month useful life	5. Low-income rental housing rehabilitation expenditures (subject to dollar limitations)

Items (1) and (5) manifest congressional intent to stimulate participation in new low-income and residential housing development by the private investment sector.

the chapter, the 2.5 percent rate was calculated on the $80,000 basis during each year, giving a constant $2,000 deduction. However, each of the accelerated methods applies the rate to a *declining balance* rather than the original depreciable basis. That is, the rate is applied each year to the original depreciable basis *less* accumulated depreciation for prior taxable years. As a result, the amount of the depreciation deduction is greater in earlier years and declines in each succeeding year of the property's useful life. This is shown in Table 16-3.

At some point in the life of the property—often between the fifth and fifteenth years—the annual deduction from the use of an accelerated method will drop below that available from the straight line method. When that time comes, the investor may shift from the accelerated method to the straight line method of depreciation. However, the reverse is not true. No shift is possible from the straight line method to an accelerated method. And in no event may an investor depreciate more than his depreciable base.[2]

Summing Up the Depreciation Deduction

The owner of improved real estate is entitled to take an annual depreciation deduction in an amount which, in theory at least, is equal to the

---

[2] Another technique which may be used to accelerate depreciation in the early years of ownership is bonus depreciation. Bonus depreciation involves the write-off in the first year of ownership of a particular portion of the depreciable basis, today 20 percent. In other words, it is an even faster way to write off the cost. Bonus depreciation is a tool of federal fiscal policy designed to encourage investment during recessionary periods. Since it applies primarily to *personal property,* it is not covered in this book.

Table 16-3. 200 PERCENT DECLINING BALANCE DEPRECIATION

Assumptions:
- 25-year useful life
- cost $100,000 (including land valued at $20,000)

First-year depreciation:

$$\$80,000 \times \left(\frac{1}{25} \times 200\% = 8\% \right) = \$6,400$$

Second-year depreciation:
$80,000 − 6,400 = 73,600 × 8% = $5,888

Third-year depreciation:
$73,600 − 5,888 = 67,712 × 8% = $5,417

Remaining basis after third-year:
$67,712 − 5,417 + 20,000 (land) = $82,295
Total depreciation taken = $17,705

using up of the improvements during the year. The amount of the deduction is based upon three elements: (1) the depreciable basis, (2) the useful life of the improvements, and (3) the depreciation method chosen.

The investor is permitted to deduct the amount of depreciation even though no cash outlay occurs; the deduction is purely a bookkeeping entry. If the improvements had actually suffered a loss of value equal to the amount of the depreciation deduction, the investor's capital position has not changed since the tax-free cash he has received via the depreciation deduction is exactly matched by the loss of value of the property. However, in practice, well-maintained and well-located property may suffer very little, if any, loss of value during any given year. As a result, the investor is actually receiving portions of the original investment in the form of tax-free or tax-sheltered income from the property.

The income really is not tax-free. The investor has merely deferred the payment of tax to a later date when the property will be sold. Of course, this deferral is a worthwhile goal since the investor has the use of cash that otherwise would have been paid to the government as taxes. In addition, when the time comes to pay the deferred tax, the investor may be able to switch the income from the ordinary income category into the capital gain category which will be taxed at a lower rate.

DEPRECIATION RECAPTURE ON SALE OF REAL ESTATE

The description of the depreciation deduction given to this point is only part of the story. It has been seen that each year during ownership, the investor is entitled to exclude from taxable income an amount deemed to represent the extent to which the asset was used up or investment was returned during the year. As a result, the investor pays less income tax than he would otherwise. Now what happens when the property finally is disposed of, by sale or otherwise, must be determined.

On the sale of any capital asset, any gain that is realized by the seller is subject to tax, either at ordinary income rates or the capital gains rate. The amount of the gain is equal to the difference between the selling price and the seller's *basis* in the property. Basis is equal to original cost plus additional capital investments during the period of ownership and minus *accumulated depreciation deductions*. This is entirely logical since, insofar as the investor's tax returns are concerned, the investor treated a portion of the income from the property each year as a return of capital. As a result, when the property is sold, the seller must report as a gain not only the increase in value over original cost but also any increase in value over the investor's *depreciated basis*.

Table 16-4. RECAPTURE OF DEPRECIATION

Assume that the property in Table 16-3 sells after three years for $120,000 and that straight line depreciation *would have* been $3,200 per year or $9,600 over three years.

Real estate:	
Taxable gain ($120,000 less remaining basis of $82,295)	$37,705
Depreciation taken	17,705
Hypothetical straight line depreciation (4% × $80,000 × 3 years)	9,600
Excess of accelerated over straight line (17,705 − 9,600)	8,105
Taxed as capital gains (37,705 − 8,105)	29,600
Taxed as ordinary income	8,105
Total taxable (29,600 × 40% + 8,105)	$19,945

Deferral of Tax

It can now be seen that the depreciation deduction does not enable the investor to *avoid* tax. It merely *defers* the tax until a later date—that is, when the property is sold. In addition, if the gain realized at sale is taxed at capital gains rates, the investor has *converted* income that otherwise would be taxed at ordinary income rates into income taxed at the much lower capital gains rate.

For example, assume an investor acquires a property with an $80,000 depreciable basis and a 40-year economic life. If the real estate is held for a period of ten years, the investor takes total depreciation deductions of $20,000 (2.5 percent per year × $80,000 × 10 years). Assuming the investor is in the 50 percent bracket, this represents total tax savings of $10,000

(0.5 × $20,000). Assume at the end of ten years, the property sells for $100,000, the same price for which purchased. The investor's basis for tax purposes is $80,000 (cost of $100,000 minus $20,000 of depreciation deductions). Thus a gain of $20,000 is realized. If the property is a capital asset, a capital gain tax of $4,000 is due (40 percent of the $20,000 gain, or $8,000, is subject to a 50 percent tax).

Net result: The investor has *deferred* $4,000 in tax payments which would have been due in equal amounts during the ten-year period of ownership until the ultimate sale and has *switched* ordinary income of $20,000 (which would have been taxable at a 50 percent rate if not for the depreciation deductions) to capital gain of $20,000, thus reducing the tax from $10,000 to $4,000, a saving of $6,000.

Abuses of Depreciation Methods

Until 1964, the ability to convert ordinary income to capital gain could be used no matter what type of depreciation (straight line or accelerated) was used by the investor. However, certain abuses soon developed.

For example, many professional investors bought property, utilized accelerated depreciation for a few years to generate very large tax write-offs, and then sold the property to another investor who could begin the depreciation cycle all over again. This practice is known as *flipping*. Properties could be bought and sold at exactly the same price so no real economic gain or loss was incurred, but, at the same time, tremendous tax savings could be achieved through the switching technique.

Depreciation Recapture

As a result, Congress in 1964 introduced a new concept known as *depreciation recapture* into the tax law. The recapture rule provides that whenever accelerated depreciation is used, any gain on sale attributable to the difference between accelerated and straight line depreciation is to be treated as ordinary income rather than capital gain. Depreciation recapture has no effect whatsoever on gain that is attributable either to the use of straight line depreciation or to the true appreciation in the value of the property over the owner's original cost. (See Table 16.4.)

It would appear that the tax law gives the benefit of accelerated depreciation with one hand (by permitting the method to be used during ownership) and then takes back the benefits with the other hand (by requiring gain attributable to accelerated depreciation to be taxed at ordinary income rates when the property is sold). Would it not be much easier simply to prohibit any accelerated depreciation method at all?

There are two answers to this. The first is an historical or political answer. Accelerated depreciation was first permitted in 1954, at a time when Congress wished to stimulate the flow of capital into real estate and sought to achieve this end by creating a tax "loophole." This is but one of many ways in which the tax law is used as a social policy vehicle as well as a revenue raising one. Then as a result of what it felt to be abuses of accelerated depreciation, Congress sought to restrain the use of accelerated depreciation. But it was not politically possible to simply cancel the method, so instead the concept of recapture was introduced into the tax law.

The second reason why Congress did not simply cancel the use of accelerated depreciation is that the recapture concept still enables investors to realize a tax benefit. This is the benefit of deferring tax on income until property is sold. Recapture merely prevents the conversion of ordinary income into capital gain. Put in other words, the time-value-of-money benefit from accelerated depreciation remains intact.

OTHER SIGNIFICANT TAX PROVISIONS

In addition to depreciation and depreciation recapture, the tax law contains a number of other provisions of particular importance to real estate. These are briefly summarized in the following paragraphs.

Investment Tax Credit

The investment credit is intended to be an incentive for capital expenditures by business persons and investors. It is particularly effective by virtue of being a *credit* rather than a *deduction*. The former reduces the tax liability directly, on a dollar-for-dollar basis, while the latter merely reduces taxable income and so reduces tax liability by a varying percentage, depending on the taxpayer's bracket.[3]

The investment credit is primarily available only for purchases of personal property,[4] but an important provision of the 1976 Tax Reform Act extended it to rehabilitation costs for industrial and commercial (but not apartment) buildings that have been in use for at least twenty years. The extension of the investment credit to used real estate clearly is another use of the tax law to bring about a desired social policy.

The amount of the investment credit is 10 percent of the cost of the qualifying property. However, the property must have a useful life of seven years or more for the taxpayer to obtain the full credit. If the useful life of the property is five to seven years, only two-thirds of the cost qualifies for the credit, while, for a property with the useful life between three and five

---

[3] A $1 credit reduces tax liability by $1 for every taxpayer who can claim it. A deduction of $1 taken by a taxpayer in the 50 percent tax bracket reduces tax liability by 50 cents, with the reduction declining as the tax bracket declines.

[4] Hotel furnishings qualify but the furniture in a furnished apartment houses does not.

years, only one-third of the cost qualifies. No credit may be taken for acquiring property with a useful life of less than three years.

Energy Credits

Two additional investment credits were created by the 1978 Energy Tax Act, and later expanded in 1980: residential energy credit and investment credit for energy property.

☐ *Residential energy credit.* An individual homeowner or residential tenant who spent money on or after April 20, 1977 for energy-saving devices may take a tax credit of 15 percent of the first $2,000 spent (i.e., a maximum credit against tax of $300). Only principal residences substantially built prior to April 20, 1977 (which was the date of President Jimmy Carter's energy message) are eligible. The credit is available for

- Insulation.
- Storm doors and windows.
- Caulking or weatherstripping.
- Heating system efficiency devices.
- Meters to show energy usage.
- Other items (to be determined by the U.S. Department of the Treasury) designed to make homes more energy-efficient.

Homeowners or renters of both new and old homes may obtain a tax credit for the installation of renewable energy source property (primarily solar, wind, or geothermal heating and cooling devices). The credit is equal to 40 percent of $10,000 (a maximum credit of $4,000). Only principal residences located in the United States are eligible. The expenditures had to be made on or after April 20, 1977.

☐ *Investment credit for energy property.* Business firms may claim a 10 percent investment credit (in addition to the regular credit) for certain energy-saving equipment placed in service between October 1, 1978 and December 31, 1982. Qualifying energy property includes:

- Boilers, burners, or the like that utilize fuel other than oil or natural gas.
- Solar and wind energy devices (for which the credit is 15 percent).
- Certain heat-recovery, solid waste recycling, shale oil- and natural gas-producing equipment.

Limits on Deductions for Interest and Property Taxes

Interest paid on debt and real property taxes are deductible on federal income tax returns. Unlike most other types of deductions (including depreciation), which are deductible only if the real property is used for investment or in a trade or business, interest and tax deductions are available for every kind of real estate, including personal residences. The two deductions have been called the "greatest loophole of them all" because, in dollar terms, they far exceed most other kinds of deductions available to special classes of taxpayers. From time to time, attempts have been made to eliminate these deductions from the tax law, but, given the number of homeowners, it is not likely that this will be accomplished.

However, in recent years, Congress has enacted two significant limitations on interest and tax deductions: (1) construction period interest and taxes and (2) limit on investment interest deductions.

☐ *Construction period interest and taxes.* Prior to the 1976 Tax Reform Act, all interest and property taxes paid during the construction period were immediately deductible. This was true even though the property had not yet begun to produce income. The result was that equity investors (often the limited partners in a real estate syndicate) would immediately be entitled to large tax deductions which they could use to offset their outside income.

The rush by highly taxed professionals and business executives to put capital into new construction in order to obtain these "up front" deductions was thought to be one of the causes of the overbuilding of the early 1970s. The 1976 Tax Reform Act, applying the principle of matching deductions to their related income, required that construction period interest and taxes be capitalized and amortized (written off) over a ten-year period.[5]

Clearly, elimination of the immediate deductibility of these construction period items reduces the tax advantages accruing to the equity investor. The results, as is further discussed in the Part VIII, is to increase the required cash return to equity during the construction period.[6]

☐ *Limit on investment interest deductions.* Investors rightly view tax-deductible interest payments on debts connected with real property as one of the key advantages of owning real estate. However, a limitation on such deductions was introduced by the 1969 Tax Reform Act and tightened by the 1976 Act.

The limitation currently applies to all interest in excess of (1) $10,000 plus (2) net investment income, which primarily constitutes income from rents, dividends, and interest. The limitation does not apply to corpora-

---

[5] The ten-year capitalization period is phased in in stages between 1976 and 1982, with the full ten-year amortization period only applicable to 1982 and years thereafter. The purpose is to avoid a too-sudden impact of the new rule that would be unfair to existing investors. For commercial properties, only half of these expenses must be capitalized. Special rules apply to low-income housing.

[6] Put another way, the equity investor cannot recoup as large a portion of his equity via tax deductions during the construction period.

tions but can have a significant impact on the highly leveraged raw land investor.

For example, assume that an investor has paid $50,000 during the year in interest charges on loans to carry a portfolio of stocks and a triple-net leased property. The investor receives $15,000 in dividend income and $15,000 in lease rentals, for a total of $30,000. Adding to this net investment income the initial $10,000 exemption gives a total of $40,000; this amount of interest may be deducted for the current year. Since the investor actually incurred $50,000 in interest charges, the $10,000 excess investment interest of $10,000 must be carried forward to future years. This is the reverse of the tax planning objective of deferring the tax liability.

DEFERRING TAX ON SALE OR DISPOSITION OF REAL ESTATE

Under our tax system, the owner of property—real estate or otherwise—may see its value increase year after year while paying no tax during the entire period of ownership. In other words, *unrealized appreciation* does not constitute taxable income. However, when the property is sold or otherwise disposed of, the owner normally will realize a taxable gain (or loss).

However, under certain circumstances, an owner of property may defer the payment of tax on gain even beyond the time of disposition. This can prove to be a major tax benefit since funds that otherwise would be required for taxes remain available to the investor for varying lengths of time.

Of these various methods for deferring the payment of tax, two are particularly significant: (1) the installment sale and (2) the tax-free exchange.

Installment Sales

The installment sale method was put into the tax law as an exception to the general principle that the full gain on the sale of real estate must be recognized, and the tax paid, in the year of sale. The installment sale method is available only when the seller of real estate receives *30 percent or less* of the total sale price in the year of sale. In that case, the seller can report his gain proportionately over those years during which the purchase price is paid. The purpose of the installment sale method is to enable a seller to avoid a situation where the tax to be paid in any one year is greater than the cash proceeds received by the seller.

For example, property is sold for $50,000, with the seller agreeing to accept $10,000 in cash, with the balance of $40,000 represented by a purchase money mortgage payable in four equal installments during the four years following the year of sale. Assume that the seller's basis in the property was $5,000, so that the total gain is $45,000. If the seller's capital gains tax bracket was 28 percent (40 percent of the maximum bracket of 70 percent), the total tax due is $12,600 (28 percent times $45,000).

If the seller were required to pay the entire tax in the year of sale, he would be out of pocket $2,600, since he received only $10,000 as a cash payment. However, since the amount received in the year of sale is 20 percent ($10,000 of a total price of $50,000), the seller may elect the installment sale method and so report only one-fifth of his gain in the year of sale. This reduces his tax in the first year to $2,520, leaving him with a cash balance of $7,480. In succeeding years, as each payment is received, the seller will pay a similar amount in tax so that at the end of the payment period, the total tax will equal $12,600.

Tax-Free Exchanges

Two special provisions of the tax law confer on real estate investors a special tax benefit: the right to exchange one parcel of real estate for another without paying any tax on the appreciation of value in the original property. Instead, the gain is "carried over" to the new property by assuming the old tax basis in the new property.

This deferral of gain may continue through a whole cycle of exchanges until a property is sold or disposed of in a taxable transaction; at this time, the entire gain, beginning with the original property, is subject to tax.

☐ *Tax-free exchanges of investment and business property.* The first of the two tax-free exchange provisions in the tax law permits *investment or business real estate* to be exchanged directly (swapped) for property of like kind without payment of tax on any appreciation in value in the original property. The obvious advantage of this tax postponement is that the investor can reinvest his full capital into new properties undiminished by tax payments. In effect, the investor has the benefit of an interest-free loan from the government. Other advantages exist, too. (See 16-1.)

By permitting this type of tax-free exchange, Congress sought to minimize the adverse effect of tax payments on the transferability of property. The active movement of property, as already noted, is considered to be beneficial both from a social and economic point of view. Also, it is practically speaking very difficult to increase the gain in such exchanges.

☐ *Tax-free exchange of residential property.* The direct swap of property just described may be utilized only for business or investment property. However, Congress has made separate provision for residential properties in the tax law. Any owner of a personal residence may avoid payment of any tax on the appreciation of value if, following a sale of the

16-1. ADVANTAGES OF A TAX-FREE EXCHANGE

☐ *Deferring capital gains.* As noted in the book, when properties are exchanged, the capital gains tax that would be payable because of any appreciation in the value of the property exchanged is deferred so long as the chain of exchanges is not broken. In theory, the tax may be deferred for many years.

☐ *Making property more salable.* Often, a prospective buyer lacks sufficient cash and may not be able to get a mortgage from a third party to make up the difference. The seller may then have to take back a large purchase money mortgage, which he may not wish to do for a number of reasons. An exchange means he can take other property of the buyer in lieu of taking back a mortgage. Since the buyer himself may not have property that the seller desires, three-party and even four-party exchanges can be set up.

☐ *Changing investment strategy.* A tax-free exchange may appeal to investors who, because of age or changes in personal income, wish to adopt a new investment strategy or change the balance of their real estate portfolio. For example, an investor with a high income may want to exchange real estate producing taxable income for raw land with potential for long-term appreciation. Or, an investor may wish to change the geographical location of his holdings when faced with retirement or transfer.

☐ *Raising cash.* An investor who needs cash but cannot mortgage or refinance his existing investment for one reason or another can exchange for property that is more financeable. For example, property which justifies no more than a 60 percent mortgage might be exchanged for property which will support an 80 percent mortgage. Or property carrying a mortgage which bars prepayment could be exchanged for a property with no mortgage or with one that could be easily refinanced.

residence, the funds received are reinvested in a new personal residence within 18 months or, in the case of new construction, 24 months.

If the purchase price of the new residence is less than the sale price of the old residence, gain is recognized but only to the extent of the difference in price. (See 16-2.)

FORMS OF OWNERSHIP AND INCOME TAXES

In Chapter 4, the most important types of legal entities used for real estate ownership are discussed. These include, in addition to individual ownership (sole proprietorship), the general partnership, limited partnership, regular corporation, and Subchapter S corporation. These are now briefly reviewed in light of the tax considerations that are introduced in this chapter. (See Table 16-5.)

16-2. TAX-FREE SALES OF HOMES

In addition to the tax-free exchange techniques described in the text, the tax law contains a special provision applicable to homeowners who are 55 years of age or over at the time they sell their residence. Such a homeowner may exclude from gross income all of the gain realized, up to a ceiling of $100,000 of gain. The homeowner must have lived in the residence for three out of the previous five years. The tax-free election can be made only once during the owner's lifetime.

This special provision in the tax law reflects the recognition by Congress that value built up in a residence may be the major private source of retirement income for the elderly. By removing the tax on this gain, the elderly are free to move to smaller (possibly rental) quarters and use the proceeds from the sale of their former homes to support themselves.

Individual Ownership

All of the tax planning benefits noted in this chapter are available to an individual owner of real estate. In particular, when real property is owned by one or more individuals (in the latter case, as tenants in common, joint tenants, or tenants by the entirety), any loss shown by real property for tax purposes may be utilized by the individual owners to offset other income that would otherwise be taxable.

The major difficulties with individual ownership (sole proprietorship) are two. First, it is often difficult to raise any substantial amount of capital since any of the forms of individual ownership cannot easily encompass more than a few people. Further, each individual owner will be fully liable for any debts or obligations in connection with the real property. (Nonrecourse financing is possible insofar as a mortgage is concerned, but the individuals will still be liable for all other obligations of the venture.)

Table 16-5. COMPARING INVESTMENT VEHICLES

	Sole Proprietorship	General Partnership	Corporation	Subchapter S Corporation	Limited Partnership
Ability to raise capital	Limited	Yes	Yes	Yes	Yes
Limited liability	No	No	Yes	Yes	Yes
No double taxation	Yes	Yes	No	Yes	Yes
Income retains its character	Yes	Yes	No	Yes	Yes
Deduction of excess losses	Yes	Yes	No	No	Yes

General Partnership

The general partnership is really a further extension of the co-ownership entities described in the preceding paragraph. All of the partners in a general partnership share unlimited liability, just as does an individual owner, and all have an equal say in management—that is, unanimous consent is required unless the partnership agreement specifies otherwise.

Since the general partnership is not a separate entity for tax purposes, gain and loss are "passed through" the partnership form directly to the individual partners. The individual partners thus retain all of the tax benefits that would be available to them as individual or co-owners. Put another way, the general partnership is an *income conduit*.

If the general partnership has no tax or liability advantages over individual or co-ownership, why is it used? Primarily because it is at times a more convenient way for a group of persons to own real estate than co-ownership.

Regular Corporation

The regular business corporation solves the most serious problem of the preceding entities: that of unlimited liability. When a corporate entity owns real estate, it is the entity only and not its individual shareholders which is liable for all obligations. Thus, each individual participant can limit his liability to the amount of capital contributed.

Corporations have three other advantages which normally are not present in other forms involving multiple ownership:

- Interests in the corporation are freely transferable by the endorsement of stock certificates, with no consent by the corporation required.
- The corporation, by its charter, may be given very long or perpetual life.
- Centralized management, through a board of directors, is not only possible but is a requisite of this form of ownership.

The corporation has one major disadvantage. Unlike all other forms of ownership described, it is a separate taxable entity and so cannot pass through losses to the individual shareholders. Alternatively, if the assets of the corporation produce taxable income, a double tax must be paid, once by the corporation at the corporate level and once again to the extent that remaining income is distributed to the shareholders as dividends. Despite this serious limitation, corporations may nevertheless be utilized to own real estate which produces taxable income if

- The corporation's net income may be distributed to its shareholder-employees in the form of compensation (salaries).

Since the compensation is a deductible expense to the corporation, only a single tax is paid at the shareholder-employee level.
- The corporation is to accumulate the net income or use the net income for other investments so that no dividend distributions are projected. However, the accumulation of income above a certain amount will subject the corporation to a substantial penalty tax.

Limited Partnership

Properly designed, the limited partnership combines the best features of both the corporate and general partnership form of ownership. Consequently, the limited partnership is the most frequently used vehicle when more than one investor is participating.

The limited partnership contains at least one general partner and one or more limited partners. The former—often the promoter or developer—assumes unlimited liability for the obligations of the project. The limited partners, on the other hand, may lose only the amount of capital contributed to the venture.

At the same time, the limited partnership retains all the tax advantages of the general partnership. That is, all income and losses are passed through directly to the individual partners and no double taxation results.

Subchapter S Corporation

Just as the limited partnership is a partnership with corporate attributes, the Subchapter S corporation is a corporation with partnership attributes. The name derives from the circumstance that this type of corporation is authorized by Subchapter S of the Internal Revenue Code.

A Subchapter S corporation is limited to fifteen shareholders, who may elect to be taxed as if the corporation was a partnership. In other words, for tax purposes, gains and losses are passed through directly to the shareholders as in the case of a partnership. However, for nontax purposes (limited liability and centralized management), the Subchapter S corporation is treated as if it were a true corporation.

The Subchapter S corporation is not frequently used for real estate because of the rule that such a corporation may not derive more than 20 percent of its gross receipts from passive investment income, which includes, among other things, most residential and commercial rents. Subchapter S corporations are meant for active business endeavors, not passive investments. However, certain types of real estate activities (e.g., operation of a hotel or motel) will qualify for Subchapter S status.

Real Estate Investment Trust

One solution to the tax problems experienced by the corporation was the real estate investment trust (REIT). The REITs were a creation of the tax laws in the early 1960s and became the darlings of Wall Street in the late 1960s. They provided a way for the small investor to participate in the benefits of real estate. The REIT is a corporation in every sense of the word except that it pays no tax at the corporate level so long as it meets certain requirements. These requirements are as follows:

☐ *Income distribution and assets.* Ninety-five percent of a REIT's income must be distributed to the beneficial shareholders annually. Further, at least 95 percent of its gross income must come from passive sources and at least 75 percent must come from real estate (e.g., rents).

☐ *Ownership.* The REIT must be owned by 100 or more persons and not over 50 percent of the ownership can be in the hands of five or fewer persons.

If the REIT meets all of these requirements, there is no tax at the trust level. In addition, capital gains income retains its character. Therefore, if the REIT experiences a capital gain, the dividend resulting from that capital gain is taxed at capital gains rates to the beneficial shareholder. There is, however, no deduction of REIT losses by shareholders.

As already mentioned, the REITs have experienced operating problems due partially to their own errors, partially to the nature of the market and partially to the enabling legislation which created them. This legislation significantly limited their flexibility of operations. The idea of the REIT was to provide a passive vehicle for the small investor. Unfortunately, many small investors investing in REIT shares lost their chips in the real estate game.

SUMMARY

Real estate is the most tax-favored of all investments. In part, this arises from the unique qualities of real estate that makes it particularly appropriate for the utilization of depreciation deductions and other tax provisions which are available to all forms of investment. In addition, however, real estate has been given special treatment by Congress, in its attempt to further certain social and economic objectives.

Nevertheless, the real estate player is ill-advised to choose a real estate investment solely on the basis of tax considerations. The primary stress should always be the before-tax economic viability of the project. Deci-

Table 16-6. THE BASIC TAX PLANNING MODEL

I. Assume no depreciation deduction or favorable capital gains tax

Cost: $100,000	*Year 1*	*Year 2*
Net operating income (taxable income)	$12,000	$ 12,000
Tax at 50%	$ 6,000	$ 6,000
Sales price (end of Year 2)		$120,000
Basis (cost)		100,000
Gain		$ 20,000
Tax at 50%		$ 10,000
Total taxes		$ 22,000

II. Assume depreciation deductions and favorable capital gains tax

Cost: $100,000	*Year 1*	*Year 2*
Net operating income	$12,000	$ 12,000
Depreciation*	4,000	4,000
Taxable income	8,000	8,000
Tax at 50%	$ 4,000	$ 4,000
Sales price (end of Year 2)		$120,000
Basis (cost minus depreciation of $8,000)		92,000
Gain		$ 28,000
Capital gains tax of 20% (50% of 40%)		$ 5,600
Total taxes		$ 13,600

---

* Basis: $100,000 less land of $20,000 = $80,000
  Useful life 20 years; Straight line method (5% rate)

Tax comparison:	I	II
Total taxes	$22,000	$ 13,600
Paid earlier (Year 1)	$ 6,000	$ 4,000
Paid later (Year 2)	$16,000	$ 9,600

sions made solely on the basis of tax elements often result in unfortunate consequences.

Tax planning can be viewed in terms of minimizing and deferring taxable income and of converting ordinary income into capital gain. Put simply, the astute investor wishes to pay as little tax as possible as late as possible. (See Table 16-6.)

IMPORTANT TERMS

accelerated
  depreciation
at-risk provision
bonus depreciation
  method
component
  depreciation
composite
  depreciation
construction period
  interest
declining balance
  depreciation

depreciation
income conduit
investment credit
ordinary income
recapture of depreciation
sole proprietorship
straight line depreciation
subchapter S corporation
tax-free exchange
tax-preference income
tax shelter
useful life

REVIEW QUESTIONS

16-1. What is the difference between tax avoidance and tax evasion?

16-2. List the common sources of ordinary income.

16-3. Briefly discuss how taxable income or loss from real estate operations can be calculated.

16-4. What is the difference between useful life and chronological age?

16-5. How might the use of accelerated depreciation transfer ordinary income to capital gain?

16-6. Since the recapture provisions of the Internal Revenue Code have recently been strengthened how might you justify use of accelerated depreciation over straight-line depreciation?

16-7. How have the current "at risk" provisions affected real estate as an investment vehicle?

16-8. What is the difference between a tax credit and a tax deduction? Which might the average investor prefer?

16-9. How might an installment sale be used to reduce the current tax liability associated with the sale of owner financed real estate?

16-10. Compare and contrast corporate and limited partnership ownership of income producing real estate.

VII
Investment

17

Principles of Investment

$\mathbf{I}$T IS NOW TIME to demonstrate how residual cash flow is determined and, in the process, to pull together the diverse aspects of the real estate industry. This part details the definition of "winning" in the real estate game and leads to dynamic considerations in Part VIII, which follows.

With the game then fully described, in Part IX the rules are checked to see if the "guiding hand" really works. In other words, when the players are playing to win, are they also collectively acting in a manner which is in the best interest of society as a whole?

OBJECTIVES: BENEFITS, RISKS, AND VALUE

The goal here is to develop a methodology whereby the decision-maker can evaluate the benefits associated with real estate investment. These benefits include: (1) cash flow, (2) tax shelter, (3) capital gain, and (4) possibly some nonpecuniary items. The analyst must estimate *expected* benefits associated with a particular investment and then estimate the investment value based on these expectations.

Investment value represents the maximum offering price that an investor can justify for a particular project. The *determination of investment value* is highly dependent on the property's characteristics, the financing and tax situation, and the individual investor's institutional or personal situation. A second approach in investment analysis is to measure the *rate of return* provided by a particular project, given assumptions about expected revenues, operating expenses, financing, taxes, and the holding period. Finally, using either or both of these measures, the objective of investment analysis is to select among *alternative investments*. Since many investment opportunities exist, the investor must be able to evaluate them and choose the investment which best meets the appropriate investment needs. (See **17-1** for a distinction between investment and appraisal.)

359

17-1. INVESTMENT ANALYSIS VERSUS APPRAISAL

Investment analysis should be clearly contrasted with appraisal methodology. Appraisal deals with the estimation of *market value* in terms of a most likely selling price, while investment analysis estimates what maximum offering price an *individual purchaser* can justify.

Appraisal market value is a function of the composite of all investors (weighted by their wealth) operating in the marketplace. Investment analysis is designed to meet the individual investment criteria of the particular investor and assist in making specific investment decisions.

Thus, while appraisal concepts can be useful in investment analysis, the decision-maker, who must reach specific investment decisions, requires more detailed and individualized analysis techniques.

Risk and Expected Return

The expected return to be received from investments constitutes the inducement to invest. The investor will look at the *riskiness* of an investment (the possibility of adverse results) as well as the *expected return* from the investment. In other words, investors must not only estimate expected returns but must also have some idea about how accurate their estimates are. The more confidence the investor has about his estimates, the lower the risk. Based on the aggregate expectations of all investors about investment risk and return, the market allocates savings to investment both directly and through the financial institutions described in Part V.

INVESTMENT GOALS AND CONSTRAINTS

Wealth Maximization

The major objective of most investors is to maximize wealth. However, this wealth maximization idea means different things to different investors. Some investors are concerned with maximizing current cash flow and/or tax shelter, while others wish to maximize future wealth through capital gain. That is why certain types of investments are better suited to one particular group of investors than to another. At this point, it will be assumed that investors have no special requirements. More detailed portfolio considerations are included in Appendix 19A.

Pecuniary and Nonpecuniary Returns

Note that the return on a real estate project can be pecuniary or nonpecuniary. The pecuniary return includes: annual cash flow, tax shelter, and gains from sale.

Since real estate plays many roles in our life-style, nonpecuniary returns also may be realized. What might be termed *psychic income* includes such items as: (1) self-esteem and (2) ego fulfillment. Nonpecuniary items are difficult to incorporate in an accounting framework. However, they must always be in the back of the real estate analyst's mind. All of the investor's objectives must be considered to fully understand the marketplace.

Investment Constraints

In pursuing the goal of wealth maximization, investors face a series of constraints. Among these are: (1) legal constraints, (2) cultural constraints, (3) personal constraints, (4) the investor's initial wealth, (5) the amount of risk the investor is willing to assume, and (6) the availability of investment alternatives.

☐ *Legal constraints* provide the formal rules of the real estate game, and investment decisions are subject to them.

☐ *Cultural constraints* go beyond the immediate pressures of the legal rules. For example, lack of an aggressive maintenance program may lead to an unsavory "slumlord" status. In addition, the investor may pay, in cash flow terms, for negative externalities which a project generates. This is true even if the externalities are technically legal at the inception of the investment. Society will not tolerate certain social and environmental abuses for a long period of time.

☐ *Personal constraints* can be interpreted as the ethical constraints on the investor. As a long-run strategy, the investor may want to avoid specific projects because of personal conviction or moral beliefs. For example, while a local liquor store may prove to be an excellent investment in a financial and legal sense, an investor opposed to liquor consumption may avoid such properties.

☐ *The investor's initial wealth* is an obvious constraint. For most new investors, this is often a critical factor in limiting the range of potential properties. Terminal wealth (at the end of the game) is a function of how much money the investor starts with as well as the results obtained in an investment sense.

☐ *The amount of risk the investor is willing to assume* will influence investment success. This will vary from individual to individual and can have a dramatic impact on terminal wealth. Risk and return are positively related so risk avoidance can have a limiting influence on potential wealth creation.

☐ *Finally, the availability of investment alternatives* represents an investment constraint.

If a project fulfills all of the above constraints, there is no guarantee that it will be available for purchase.

Note that all of these constraints are laid out in the initial analytical framework. Investment analysis focuses on (1) a determination of value based on estimates of the return the project is expected to generate in a particular marketplace over the long run and (2) the certainty of those estimates. Comparing investment value to the cost of the project, the investment decision can be made.

ELEMENTS OF INVESTMENT ANALYSIS

The Accounting Framework

Return is typically analyzed within the following accounting framework:

- Projected revenues to be generated by the project,
- *Less* all anticipated operating expenses,
- *Equals* the net operating income (NOI) expected from the project.

The NOI goes first to satisfy lenders.[1] The residual, or bottom line, is the *cash flow return* to the equity owner.

The investment benefits of long-term appreciation (after tax) are also included within the accounting framework. Consequently, the accounting framework pulls together all of the different elements involved in investment analysis to facilitate decision-making.

The Time Value of Money

The investor is concerned not only with the size of the expected cash flows but also with their timing. Recall from Part V that discounting (present value) is simply the inverse of the compound interest formula and can be used to value future cash flows. Since all of the benefits associated with investment in real estate are received over time (i.e., throughout the holding period), the application of the concept of the time value of money is extremely important in investment analysis.

---

[1] Frequently mentioned here is the prior claim of government, represented by the property tax. In our investment analyses this tax is considered an operating expense and so its payment is reflected in the net operating income figure.

Cash flows translate into lower current investment values if they are to be received further into the future. The worth of future cash flows depends not only on when they will be received but also on the risk that they will not be received at all. This risk is expressed along with the time value of money in the discount rate. Value and the discount rate are inversely related.

In essence, the process of discounting allows the analyst to reduce all anticipated cash flows to a single point in time so that an investment decision can be made. This single-point estimate of the value of the expected cash flows incorporates the *time value of money* and *riskiness* in the investment analysis.

Two Parts of Real Estate Return

It is also important to remember that the expected residual cash flow from real estate comes in two parts. First are the *annual cash flows* to be received throughout the holding period. Second are the *proceeds from sale or other disposition* of the real estate.

For some investments, the periodic cash flows are most important, while for others the proceeds from sale may be most significant. Both of these cash flows must be discounted to the single point in time when the investment is being made.

TYPES OF RISK

Risk is the possibility of suffering adverse consequences resulting from an investment. In this context, there are several types of risk:

- Business risk.
- Financial risk.
- Purchasing power risk.
- Liquidity.

Business Risk

Business risk reflects the possible unsuccessful operation of the particular project. Business risk is determined by (1) the type of project, (2) its management, and (3) the particular market in which it is located. All of these affect the expected operating cash flows from the project.

The possibility that these cash flows will not be sufficient to justify the investment represents the degree of business risk associated with the investment. A regional shopping center fully rented under long-term net leases to triple-A tenants has a lower business risk than a raw land investment which anticipates construction of a motel sometime in the future.

From a practical point of view, business risk is centered in two major areas. The first is *management.* Fixing and collecting rents, maintaining and repairing, and controlling operating expenses are key variables in the management area. *Market changes* represent the other area involving business risk. New competition, changes in local demographic characteristics, new roads bypassing a project, and new employers entering the market all affect the business risk associated with a particular project.

Financial Risk

Financial risk reflects uncertainty about the residual equity return as the result of the use of debt financing. The use of debt increases the variability of the return to equity. This increased variability or uncertainty is the financial risk associated with a particular investment.

Put another way, financial risk is the potential inability of the project's NOI to cover the required debt service. Such an event is more likely to occur when a high proportion of the purchase price is financed with debt. The less debt that is used in the capital structure, the lower the financial risk.

Purchasing Power Risk

Purchasing power risk reflects the fact that inflation may cause the investor to be paid back with less valuable dollars. The expectation of inflation is incorporated in the discount rate, but future rates of inflation may be underestimated. The possibility of higher inflation than was incorporated in the discount rate is the purchasing power risk associated with the investment. In general, purchasing power risk affects all investors equally and does not vary from project to project.

Liquidity Risk

Liquidity risk relates to the conversion of the investment to cash at some future date. An investor wants to be able to sell quickly and without substantially discounting the price below fair market value. The liquidity risk associated with a particular investment is the risk that a quick sale will not be possible or that a significant price reduction will be required to achieve a quick sale.

Real estate is generally considered an *illiquid* asset, not easily convertible to cash without sacrificing price. Consequently, liquidity risk tends to be high for real estate investments.

This liquidity risk leads to a need for balance in the investor's portfolio. For example, the investor should include in the portfolio highly liquid assets, such as government bonds. (Risk in a portfolio context is discussed in Appendix 19A.)

DEFINITIONS OF RISK

Risk as Variance

The four types of risk just mentioned can be collectively measured and quantified by estimating the variance of the expected equity cash flow. The more variance the investor expects in the equity portion of the return generated by the property, the greater the risk associated with receiving that cash flow.

Many times, investors will estimate the cash flow under varying circumstances in order to analyze the sensitivity of the project's rate of return to changes in rental receipts, vacancy, and operating expenses. *Sensitivity analysis* is an appealing method for estimating risk in the real estate field, since changes frequently occur in the elements that affect cash flow.

Risk of Ruin

Although *variance* is the classic finance definition of risk, in many cases an alternative definition more accurately characterizes the perspective of the investor. This alternative definition is the *risk of ruin*. This is the probability that the expected returns will be less than a minimal acceptable level. For some investors, this might be a return of less than 5 percent; for others, the risk of ruin could be the risk of bankruptcy.

The variance and risk of ruin definitions are similar when expected future returns can be characterized by a normal distribution.[2] (See Figure 17-1.)

In investment analysis, risk is incorporated in the discount rate used as an estimate of the required rate of return.[3] Recall that the required rate of return involves: (1) a real return, (2) an inflation premium, and (3) a risk

[2] The normal distribution is a perfectly symmetric distribution. For an example, note the graph below:

[3] An alternative capital market theory (state preference theory) adjusts the expected cash flows to their certainty equivalent and discounts at a risk-free rate. While this is a theoretically appealing idea, it is not often practical to utilize the state preference theory in real world investment analysis.

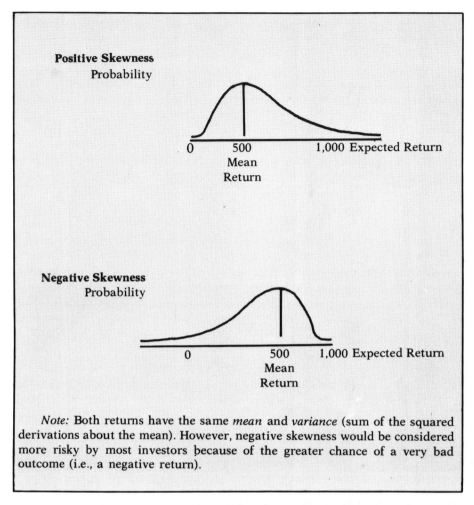

Figure 17-1. POSSIBLE DISTRIBUTIONS OF EXPECTED RETURNS

premium. Unlike the appraisal methodology, no recapture premium is necessary since in investment analysis an indefinitely long or continual return is not assumed, as it was in the appraisal formula $V = NOI/R$.

In investment analysis, a holding period and disposition assumption are made and incorporated into the discounted cash-flow analysis. In effect, what is considered is a two-part return.

Positive Correlation Between Risk and Return

Risk and return are thought to be positively correlated. Harry M. Markowitz, the father of modern portfolio theory, states that the investor seeks to maximize return for given levels of risk or minimize risk for given levels of return. The logic here can be very appealing. The investor expects more compensation if there is a greater chance of adverse financial consequences—that is, the investor wants more return if there is more risk. Investors, in other words, are *risk-averse.*

However, even with no risk, the investor requires a certain minimum return. This minimum return represents the real return and inflation premium portion of the required rate of return. Government bonds are generally considered to be risk-free and are used as an indication of the return required when there is no risk associated with the receipt of expected cash flows. Beyond this risk-free rate, risk and return are positively correlated. (See Figure 17-2.)

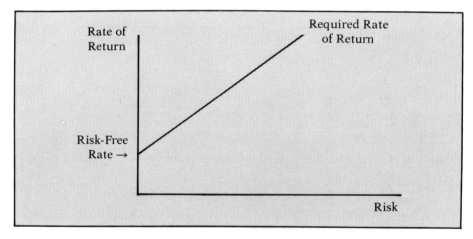

Figure 17-2. THE RISK-RETURN RELATIONSHIP

Risk Aversion

The concept of risk aversion is usually proved by using the theory of the *diminishing marginal utility of money.* (See Figure 17-3.) Given the situation of an investor who has a risky and a riskless alternative, the riskless alternative might be preferred even though a greater return is possible if the risky alternative is chosen. Assume a riskless government bond paying a certain 8 percent and a riskier apartment house with equal likelihood (50-50) of either a 10 or 6 percent return. Both investments have the same expected dollar return, but the expected *utility of the investor*[4] might be less in the case of the risky alternative.

---

[4] The term *utility of the investor* refers to the value of the money to the investor. Simply put, one additional dollar is valued differently by a millionaire and a pauper.

Alternative 1. Government bond paying 8%
Alternative 2. Apartment house, with equal likelihood it will return either 10% or 6%.

Both alternatives have the same mean expected return (8%). However, look at the investor's preference:

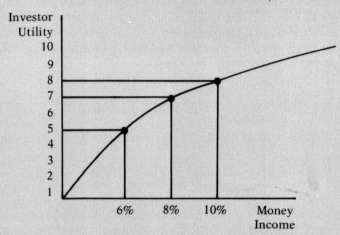

The slope of the curve is based on the diminishing marginal utility of the dollar.

Alternative 1. 8% return = 7 utilities
Alternative 2. 10% = 8 utilities × 50% = 4   utilities
              6% = 5 utilities × 50% = 2.5 utilities
              Total   6.5 utilities

Despite the same mean expected return, the riskier alternative (Alternative 2, with more variance) is less attractive (offers less utility to the investor). Thus if an investor has diminishing marginal utility for money, then the investor will be risk-averse. It should be noted that the assignment of cardinal values—"utilities"—in the above example has been done for presentation purposes only. Utility, of course, is an ordinal concept.

Figure 17-3. DIMINISHING MARGINAL UTILITY

    While most investors are assumed to be risk averse, there are also risk seekers in the world. The developers discussed in Part VIII may belong to this group. In his classic book *Risk Uncertainty and Profits*, Frank Knight describes all entrepreneurs as collective risk seekers. Knight postulates that the true entrepreneur loves action and will take less than a "fair gamble" for the possibility of becoming very wealthy.

DERIVING THE DISCOUNT RATE

Given all of the risk factors discussed, how does the analyst arrive at the required rate of return or the discount rate? There is no perfect methodology, but the following process will allow the analyst to derive a meaningful required rate of return:

□ *Real return.* First, the analyst must estimate the required real return—that is, the premium the investor wants for deferred consumption. This figure can be estimated from historical data by comparing rates of return on government securities with rates of inflation over long periods of time. Various researchers have put this number at between 2 and 3 percent.

□ *Inflation rate.* An estimate of the expected rate of inflation over the holding period is then made by subtracting the real return from the current yield on government bonds. If the investor expects to hold an asset for ten years, he can look at the yield on ten-year government bonds (which are assumed to be free of any risks other than risks associated with inflation) and provide a way to estimate the market's expectations regarding inflation. The current total bond yield less the 2 to 3 percent real return is a composite of investor expectations about inflation over a ten-year period.

□ *Average risk premium.* This can be established by looking at the difference between the returns over long periods of time on common stock and the returns on risk-free government securities over the same period of time. A number of studies have put this difference at 4 to 5 percent.

□ *Adjusted risk premium.* The average risk premium must then be adjusted for the relative riskiness of the particular project. This adjustment is subjective but can be realistically estimated by an analyst who knows the property, the local market, the financial leverage, and the type of investment vehicle to be used as well as the liquidity needs and personal considerations of the investor. It is possible to make meaningful adjustments to the average risk premium and develop a risk premium appropriate for the particular investment.

□ *Before-tax return.* The real return plus the inflation premium plus the adjusted risk premium give the required rate of return before personal income taxes. Normally, however, real estate investment analysis is conducted on an after-tax basis.

□ *After-tax return.* The after-tax required rate of return can be derived from the pre-tax rate of return using the formula: *after-tax required rate of*

17-2. CALCULATION OF AFTER-TAX REQUIRED RATE OF RETURN

An office building investment opportunity is being evaluated. The investor's expected holding period is ten years. The building is well-built, well-located and fully leased. The loan is 60% of the purchase price and offers reasonable terms. The investment is not highly liquid and offers no particular non-pecuniary benefits to the investor. The investor is in the 50% tax bracket and historically about 20 percent of his income is capital gains.

I.   Real return – 2% (from historical data)

II. Inflation premium – 7% (government securities maturing in 10 years are yielding 9%)

III. Risk premium – 3% (average of 4%; less 2% for fully leased property in a good market; plus one percent for illiquidity)

IV. Before-tax rate of return (BTR) = 12%

V.   After-tax rate of return (ATR) = 6.72%

$$ATR = BTR\ (1 - T)$$

T = (marginal tax rate × percentage of ordinary income) + (40% marginal tax rate × percentage capital gains)

T = (50% × 80%) + (40% × 20%)

= 44%

ATR = 12% (1 – 44%)

= 12% (56%)

= 6.72%

return is equal to one minus the tax rate times the before-tax required rate of return.[5] (The tax rate is a weighted average of the ordinary and capital gains rates projected for the investor.) Calculation of a rate of return for a specific real estate investment is illustrated in **17-2.**

SUMMARY

Investment analysis seeks to determine value to the individual investor. Value is a function of the expected returns from a project and the risks associated with those expected returns. A useful methodology in arriving at investment value is the discounted after-tax cash flow technique. In this technique, all the different aspects of risk as well as the time value of money, are incorporated in the discount rate.

Be careful when using the technique. Anyone can be taught to do the mechanics; i.e., to go through the accounting framework, deduct prior

---

[5] Note that this rate is bounded on the lower side by the rate available on tax-free municipal bonds of comparable risk.

Investments can be valued by discounting before tax cash flow at the before-tax discount rate. However, this approach has two disadvantages: (1) It does not incorporate the unique tax situation of the particular investor and (2) it overvalues investments with below-average tax-shelter potential and undervalues assets with above-average tax-shelter potential.

claims, arrive at residual cash flows, and discount these cash flows to a present value. The key in investment analysis is knowledge of the product and the market. Long-run success requires profitable operations and dependable estimates of operations can only be made by an analyst who has a clear understanding of the marketplace.

IMPORTANT TERMS

business risk
cash flow
financial risk
liquidity risk
money risk
psychic income

purchasing power risk
risk
risk aversion
sensitivity analysis
variance

REVIEW QUESTIONS

17-1. Outline the major differences between appraisal and investment analysis.

17-2. How would each of the major investment constraints mentioned in the text affect your personal investment in real estate?

17-3. Why is it justified to think of the real estate return as a two-part return?

17-4. How does the time value of money relate to the concept of a two-part return?

17-5. Compare and contrast the concepts of risk as variance and risk as risk of ruin.

17-6. Distinguish between the average risk premium and an adjusted risk premium.

17-7. Why is it reasonable to suggest that risk and return are positively correlated?

17-8. How can the use of an after-tax rate of return be justified when evaluating real estate investments?

17-9. How should nonpecuniary returns or psychic income be incorporated into real estate investment analysis?

17-10. How might it be possible for two investors analyzing the same investment property to derive different discount rates?

18

The Discounted Cash Flow Model

THE PURPOSE OF the discounted cash flow (DCF) model is to bring together, for purposes of analysis, all the factors which affect the return from a real estate investment. All cash flows are reduced to a single figure, the *present value*. These cash flows include all *cash inflows*, such as rents and proceeds of sale, and all *cash outflows* such as operating expenses, taxes, and debt service. The present value figure represents the value today of the residual equity claim to future cash flows adjusted for both the time value of money and the risk associated with the expected cash flows.

All the cash flows which are used in the DCF model must be estimated from data collected in the marketplace. Estimating the inputs for the model becomes the most difficult portion of investment analysis once the mechanics of the DCF model are mastered. The more accurate the estimated input variables, the more reliable the DCF model becomes as an aid to decision-making. The computer science axiom of "garbage in—garbage out" holds true in the case of DCF real estate investment analysis; the model is only as useful as the accuracy of the input variables allows it to be. Consequently, establishment of operating cash flows is a reflection of the analyst's knowledge of existing market conditions and trends.

Beyond the operating cash flows, the straightforward accounting framework developed in the preceding chapter takes into account the prior claims of the lender (debt service) and the government (income tax liability, if any) in calculating the after-tax residual cash flow. The real estate analyst must also determine the investor's marginal (highest bracket) tax rate, his after-tax required rate of return or discount rate, the expected investment horizon or holding period, and the sales price.

The investor's marginal tax rate will reflect income earned from other sources as well as the taxable income or loss from the property. The methodology for developing the discount rate to be used in turning the expected future cash flows into a present value, discussed in Chapter 17, is a function of the real return, an inflation premium and risk. The investment horizon or anticipated holding period may be affected by tax planning considerations,[1] market trends, and other factors. (See ▮18-1.▮)

---

[1] When the debt is amortized and accelerated depreciation is used, the tax shelter deteriorates over time.

18-1. TIMING OF CASH FLOWS

In 1974, Realty Growth Investors (a Baltimore REIT) made a loan to a group of Houston investors to build the 156-unit Ramblewood Apartments, located north of the city of Houston. The investors had estimated the value of the completed project to be approximately $2 million. Construction went generally according to plan, but lease-up was slow. The investors had estimated the value using the simple $V = \dfrac{NOI}{R}$ formula. In fact, there was no problem with their long-term value estimate, but they had neglected to consider the cash deficit during the lease-up period.

After completion of construction the investors ran out of funds and were unable to pay interest on their debt to Realty Growth Investors due to low occupancy during the lease-up period. The REIT foreclosed on the property, held it for less than twelve months during which time the property achieved its expected occupancy level, and sold the property for a half million dollar profit.

The moral of the story here is that $V = \dfrac{NOI}{R}$ is a good first approach, but a more in-depth investment analysis, considering the exact timing of all cash flows, is warranted in more complex investment situations.

The model presented in this chapter puts all of these items together and allows the analyst to look at a complex problem in a logical way. The purpose of the DCF model, then, is to estimate the present value of a particular real estate investment. The estimated present value will then be compared to project cost to determine the acceptability of the investment for a *particular* individual investor.

THE BASIC DISCOUNTED CASH FLOW MODEL

The preceding chapters have developed the skills necessary to derive appropriate data from the marketplace for use in the DCF model. In this chapter, the accounting mechanics will be examined and the source of information for all the variables incorporated in the model will be reviewed.

The model example integrates all of the material necessary to carry out a real estate investment analysis. Although the specific example is a new apartment property, the DCF framework, both from a practical accounting and a theoretical perspective, can be applied to any income property.

Gross Possible Income

The starting point of the DCF model is gross possible income (GPI). This is the income which is possible if all the space is leased at the projected rent level plus any income from other sources, such as vending income. GPI is estimated by considering the rent received on comparable properties as well as the historic rent received on the subject property. Further, using regional and urban economic techniques discussed in Part I, trends can be established to project potential income over time. The DCF model allows the analyst to project different rent levels at different points in time, thus offering a refinement over the simple $V = NOI/R$ formulation presented in Part III.

Estimates of future rent levels can be presented on an actual (dollar) basis or relative (percentage change) basis. Generally, the analyst assumes an average rate of rent increase over the investment horizon. When the percentage method is used, the analyst must be careful not to overestimate the rate of increase by failing to realize the increase will be compounded over time. As a general rule, most would agree that the estimates of income (and expenses) should represent the "most likely" outlook. In any event, the analyst must not only estimate revenues but must develop a feeling for the accuracy of the estimate for use in calculating the risk premium incorporated in the discount rate.

Vacancy and Collection Loss Expenses

From the gross possible income figure, the vacancy allowance and the collection loss estimate is deducted. The vacancy allowance is, again, a function of the property's history, comparables, and market trends. It represents an average vacancy rate for the project being analyzed and is expressed as a percentage of the GPI. The vacancy rate is directly related to the property's life cycle. A new property often experiences a relatively high vacancy rate during the rent-up period, then may have few vacancies during its prime, followed by increasing vacancies as it ages. Vacancy is also related to rent levels. It is often possible to trade off rent increases with occupancy levels. Collection losses (i.e., rents due but unpaid) vary from insignificant on some properties to a major item on others, particularly apartment buildings in declining areas. Gross possible income reduced by a vacancy allowance and collection loss allowance equals realized revenues or *gross effective income (GEI)*.

Note that the estimate of vacancy and collection losses represents an anticipated average rate for the property being analyzed rather than the current experience. Even if the project is currently 100 percent occupied, a vacancy and collection loss rate should be included. Sooner or later (and probably sooner), the investor will experience some actual vacancy and credit losses.

Operating Expenses

Operating expenses include management fees, payroll, repairs and maintenance, utilities, security, advertising and promotion, property taxes, and insurance premiums. In practice, each of these expenses would be estimated separately. The DCF example, for convenience of presentation, lumps them together as a percentage of gross possible income. Estimates for each of these items will be based on the operating history of the property, comparables and future trends.

Inflation will affect both operating costs and revenues.[2] However, age will also increase operating expenses. As properties get older, they tend to require higher maintenance costs. Conversely, as the property gets older and has higher functional obsolescence, revenues are adversely affected. So while both age and inflation work to increase operating expenses, only inflation increases revenues while the age factor is working in the opposite direction. Consequently, it is generally true that operating expenses tend to rise at a more rapid *rate* than revenues over the holding period.

Property taxes and insurance premiums must also be deducted from gross effective income. In the case of property taxes, current year's taxes are the starting point, but future increases normally can be anticipated, the extent depending on the financial condition of the municipality. Insurance premiums for fire, casualty, and liability coverages should be included.

Major Repairs and Replacements

Also to be deducted from gross effective income is the cost of major repairs and replacements anticipated over the holding period. These might include a new roof, new electrical, heating or plumbing systems, or replacement of appliances in an apartment building. Rather than incorporate an average figure each year for these items, the DCF model charges off each individual expenditure in the year for which it is projected. In this way, the time value of money is more accurately reflected.

Net Operating Income

Realized revenues less operating expenses and major repair items equal *NOI*, as shown in Table 18-1.[3]

---

[2] Property subject to long-term leases may have fixed income (because of flat rentals), fixed expenses (because increases are passed through to tenants), or both. Naturally, the analysis should reflect these provisions.

[3] A standard appraisal would end the income analysis at this point. All that follows would not be of concern to the appraiser using the income method in estimating market value.

Table 18-1. CALCULATION OF NET OPERATING INCOME

	Year 1	Year 2	Year 3	Year 4	Year 5
A. Gross possible income	$24,000	$24,720	$25,462	$26,226	$27,013
B. Less: vacancy and collection allowance	(1,200)	(1,236)	(1,273)	(1,311)	(1,351)
C. Gross effective income	$22,800	$23,484	$24,189	$24,915	$25,662
D. Less: operating expenses (including insurance and property taxes)	(9,600)	(10,080)	(10,584)	(11,113)	(11,669)
E. Major repairs and replacements	-0-	-0-	-0-	-0-	-0-
F. NOI	$13,200	$13,404	$13,605	$13,802	$13,993

A DISCOUNTED CASH FLOW EXAMPLE

The following real estate investment analysis focuses on a new apartment building where the factors of increasing rentals, leverage, accelerated depreciation, investor tax considerations, and price appreciation all have an important bearing on the property's total investment value and rate of return. The property analysis incorporates the following assumptions:

- First-year GPI of $24,000 increases by 3 percent annually (compounded). The building has five units, each with 1,000 square feet and renting for $400 per month.
- The vacancy and collection loss allowance is 5 percent of GPI.
- Total operating expenses are 40 percent of GPI during the first year of operations, or $9,600. (Each component of operating expenses was analyzed separately to obtain the 40 percent collective figure.) Thereafter, expenses increase at a rate of 5 percent per year (compounded). This includes property taxes and insurance premiums. No major repairs are anticipated over the next five years.
- The total cost of the project is $140,000. Land is valued at $10,000 and the improvements at $130,000. Since there are 5,000 square feet in the building (1,000 square feet/unit times 5 units), the square foot cost of the improvements is $26.
- Mortgage debt of $100,000 is available at 9 percent interest, self-liquidating over 26 years. This results in a mortgage constant of approximately 10 percent and annual debt service of $10,000.[4]
- The improvements will be depreciated using the double declining

---

[4] The exact constant, assuming monthly payments in arrears (i.e., paid at the end of each month), is 9.969 percent.

balance method, the economic life of the improvements is thirty years, and composite (rather than component) depreciation will be used.
- The project value is expected to grow at 3 percent per year (based on the original cost of the project).
- The investor's marginal income is taxed at 50 percent.
- An annual after-tax return on equity investment of 12 percent is sought over the entire holding period.
- The investor expects to hold the property five years. No provision is made for a selling commission and other expenses when the property is sold (a simplifying assumption).

Debt Service

NOI is the amount of GEI remaining after deduction of operating expenses and cost of major repairs and replacements. The first claim on this cash is for debt service, which includes payment for interest on the outstanding loan plus an amount for debt reduction (amortization).

As explained in Chapter 14, the debt service constant is the percentage of the original loan amount required to (1) pay periodic interest on the outstanding loan balance and (2) amortize the loan over its term. The constant can be found quickly by the use of loan amortization tables. As shown in Table 18-2, the portion of each year's constant payment allocable to interest and principal payments is easily calculated once the annual debt service constant is known. Table 18-2 shows clearly how the interest portion of the debt service *declines* each period, since current interest is based on the outstanding loan balance (not the original principal). Since the total debt service remains constant, the principal repayment (amortization) rises by the same amount as the interest declines.

Depreciation

The annual depreciation schedule for the example is presented in Table 18-3. Since an accelerated method (200 percent declining balance) is

Table 18-2. CALCULATION OF DEBT SERVICE

	Year 1	Year 2	Year 3	Year 4	Year 5
Mortgage amount	$100,000	$99,000	$97,910	$96,722	$95,427
Interest rate	0.09	0.09	0.09	0.09	0.09
Interest payment	9,000	8,910	8,812	8,705	8,588
Principal payment	1,000	1,090	1,188	1,295	1,412
Debt service (10% constant)	$ 10,000	$10,000	$10,000	$10,000	$10,000

Note: The loan balance at the end of year 5 is ($95,427 − $1,412) = $94,015.

Table 18-3. CALCULATION OF DEPRECIATION

	Year 1	Year 2	Year 3	Year 4	Year 5
Depreciable basis	$130,000	$121,329	$113,236	$105,683	$98,634
Depreciation rate	0.0667	0.0667	0.0667	0.0667	0.0667
Annual depreciation	$ 8,671	$ 8,093	$ 7,553	$ 7,049	$ 6,579

Note the following:
- Initial depreciable basis is $130,000 (cost of improvements). The basis declines each year by the amount of accrued depreciation to that point. Since a constant depreciation rate is applied to a declining balance, the depreciation deduction declines each year, resulting in a gradual loss of tax shelter.

- The accrued depreciation taken after five years is $37,945. If straight-line depreciation had been used, total depreciation after five years would have been $21,667. (Then, 1/30, or 3⅓ percent, of $130,000 depreciable basis written off each year would give an annual deduction of $4,333.30.) The difference of $16,278 ($37,945 minus $21,667) is called *excess depreciation* and is subject to recapture as ordinary income when the property is sold.

- The maximum allowable depreciation rate on residential property is 200 percent if *new* and 125 percent if *used*. Commercial property is 150 percent if *new* and 100 percent if *used*. Whenever the rate is in excess of 100 percent, declining balances must be used in calculating each year's depreciation.

used, the annual depreciation allowance *declines* over the holding period although the percentage rate of 6.67 (1/30 × 200%) percent remains constant. Recall the reason for this. The constant rate is applied each year to a declining figure—the initial depreciable basis *minus* accumulated depreciation to that point. This annual decline in the depreciation deduction will result in gradually declining tax shelter over the holding period.

Taxable Income or Loss

The provision for the claim of government in the form of income taxes follows the determination of interest and depreciation expense. NOI less interest and depreciation equals taxable income or loss. Multiplying the taxable income by the investor's *marginal* tax rate gives the annual tax liability associated with the particular investment. The marginal tax rate should be used, and not the average tax rate, for all investment decisions are made at the margin. A tax loss will arise as in our example if the interest and depreciation expense exceeds the net operating income, as shown in Table 18-4.

In the event that the property shows a tax loss, the investor will receive certain benefits from that loss. By offsetting the loss against his other income, the investor will *shelter income.* Aggregate taxable income

Table 18-4. TAXABLE INCOME (a continuation of Table 18-1)

	Year 1	Year 2	Year 3	Year 4	Year 5
F. NOI	$13,200	$13,404	$13,605	$13,802	$13,993
G. Less: depreciation	(8,671)	(8,093)	(7,553)	(7,049)	(6,579)
H. Less: interest	(9,000)	(8,910)	(8,812)	(8,705)	(8,588)
I. Taxable income (loss)	$(4,471)	$(3,599)	$(2,760)	$(1,952)	$(1,174)

Note: Taxable loss declines each year as a result of three factors: rising NOI, declining depreciation, and declining interest expense.

will be reduced, and, consequently, the overall tax liability will be less. The extent of the tax benefit or savings from any particular loss may be calculated by multiplying the taxable loss times the marginal tax rate as shown on line N of Table 18-5. Therefore, using the taxable loss figure and the marginal tax rate, either the tax due or the tax shelter may be calculated.

Before-Tax Cash Flow

Depreciation deductions (reflected in taxable income or loss) do not represent an actual cash expense; they are merely a bookkeeping entry. Therefore, they must be added back to the taxable income or loss in order to accurately reflect the before-tax cash flow. On the other hand, principal repayment is not a tax-deductible item (so not reflected in the taxable income or loss) but is an actual out-of-pocket cash expense. Therefore, such repayments must be subtracted from taxable income or loss. These calculations are presented in lines J and K of Table 18-5, respectively, with line L showing the before-tax cash flow.

Table 18-5. EQUITY CASH FLOW AFTER TAX (a continuation of Table 18-4)

	Year 1	Year 2	Year 3	Year 4	Year 5
I. Taxable income (loss)	$(4,471)	$(3,599)	$(2,760)	$(1,952)	$(1,174)
J. Plus: depreciation	8,671	8,093	7,553	7,049	6,579
K. Less: principal repaid	(1,000)	(1,090)	(1,188)	(1,295)	(1,412)
L. Before-tax cash flow	3,200	3,404	3,605	3,802	3,993
M. Less: taxes	0	0	0	0	0
N. Plus: tax savings (50% × (I) above)	2,235	1,799	1,380	976	587
O. Equity cash flow after-tax	$5,435	$5,203	$4,985	$4,778	$4,580

After-Tax Equity Cash Flow

The equity cash flow after tax is determined by simply deducting any tax liability or adding any tax savings as in M and N of Table 18-5. In our example, the project is not expected to generate a tax liability during the investment horizon. This means that all of the NOI is sheltered. Tax savings are an important feature in our example. Not only does the investor shelter all of the income generated by the investment, but income earned from other sources is also sheltered. This reduction in aggregate tax liability can be attributed to this investment, because without the investment the investor's taxes would be higher by the amount of the tax savings. As a result, the tax savings are added to the before-tax cash flow to yield the equity cash flow after tax, as shown on lines N and O of Table 18-5.

Present Value of After-Tax Cash Flow

The cash flow to equity calculated above represents the first part of the two-part return to equity: the periodic cash flow from operations. These cash flows can be reduced to their present value using the present value formula $PV = CF_n/(1 + r)^n$. Using the Compound Interest Tables at the end of this book, a present value factor is often easier to work with than the multiplication and division required in the formula. Multiplying the present value factor (associated with the investor's expected after-tax return on equity) by the individual annual equity cash flows and summing the product gives the present value of the after-tax cash flows to equity for the assumed holding period. Table 18-6 indicates that the total present value of the equity cash flow after tax in our example is $18,184.

Table 18-6.   PRESENT VALUE OF THE CASH FLOW AFTER TAX
             (a continuation of Table 18-5)

	Year 1	Year 2	Year 3	Year 4	Year 5
O. Equity cash flow after-tax	$ 5,434	$ 5,203	$ 4,985	$ 4,778	$ 4,580
PV factor @ 12%	0.8929	0.7972	0.7118	0.6355	0.5674
Present value of annual equity cash flow after taxes*	$ 4,853	$ 4,148	$ 3,548	$ 3,036	$ 2,599

* Total present value of equity cash flow after tax for 5 years is $18,184.

Sales Price

The second part of the two-part return on real estate investment requires an assumption about a sale or disposition. Absent any better information, it is often reasonable to assume that a future buyer will be willing to pay the same amount per dollar of income generated by the project as the current investor is willing to pay; in other words, that the capitalization rate or the multiplier (see the discussion of the income approach to value in Part III) will be the same on disposition as on purchase. From the sales price assumption, commissions and closing costs are deducted.

In the example, it was assumed that the market value of the property would increase by 3 percent per year, compounded annually, over the holding period. As shown in Table 18-7, the market value of the project is estimated to be $162,298 at the end of the fifth year. It was further assumed that no selling commission, closing costs, or loan prepayment penalties would be incurred. These are simplifying assumptions and clearly some marketing costs are incurred in most real estate transactions and they would directly reduce the proceeds of the sale.

Table 18-7. SALES PRICE

Market value (3% compound growth)	$144,200	$148,526	$152,982	$157,571	$162,298

Note: No commissions, closing costs or loan prepayment penalties are incurred.

Income Tax on Realized Gain From Sale

Any realized gain upon sale of the property is subject to a government claim for income tax. The gain on sale is the sales price (net of commissions and closing costs) less the seller's tax basis. The tax basis is the original cost plus capital expenditures during ownership (none in our example) less depreciation taken.

As noted in Part VI, the Internal Revenue Code does not permit all of the gain to be taxed at the advantageous capital gains rate if accelerated depreciation had been utilized during ownership. Specifically, the gain on sale that is attributable to the difference between accelerated depreciation and straight line depreciation will be taxed at ordinary rates. Therefore, the gain on sale is divided into two portions: (1) the part which is subject to recapture as ordinary income and (2) the remainder which will be taxed at the advantageous capital gains rate (i.e., only 40 percent of the capital gain portion will be subject to tax).

For our example, the calculation of realized gain is shown in Table 18-8 while the tax due on the sale is shown in Table 18-9. In Table 18-8, the total capital gain is calculated by first determining the tax basis (cost). The tax basis is the difference between the original cost of the project ($140,000) and the depreciation taken during the holding period ($37,945).

Table 18-8. CALCULATION OF GAIN ON SALE

A. Tax basis:	
Cost	$140,000
Depreciation taken (Table 18-3)	(37,945)
Tax basis	$102,055
B. Sales price (Table 18-7)	$162,298
C. Taxable gain:	
Sales price	$162,298
Tax basis	(102,055)
Total taxable gain	$ 60,243

Table 18-9. CALCULATION OF TAX ON SALE

A. Total taxable gain (Table 18-8)		$60,243
B. Portion subject to recapture as ordinary income (Table 18-3, note 2)		16,278
C. Portion subject to capital gain treatment		43,965
D. Tax on portion subject to recapture (50% × $16,278)	$8,139	
E. Tax on capital gain [(40% × 50%) × $43,965]	8,793	
F. Total tax on sale (D + E)		$16,932

The resulting basis ($102,055) is then deducted from the sales price ($162,298) to yield the total gain of $60,243.

Once the total gain has been determined, the tax due on the sale can be as calculated in Table 18-9. Since accelerated depreciation was assumed, the total taxable gain must be divided into two categories: the portion subject to recapture and the portion entitled to capital gains treatment. The portion subject to recapture represents the excess depreciation of $16,278 (see Table 18-2's second bulleted item). This amount is then deducted from the total gain to yield the portion subject to capital gain treatment ($43,965). The total tax on sale is calculated by multiplying the two taxable gain categories by their appropriate tax rates, which results in a total tax on sale liability of $16, 932 for our example.

Cash Proceeds From Sale

The total tax liability and the loan repayment are then subtracted from the net sales price (after commissions and closing costs) to obtain the cash proceeds from the sale. This figure is discounted to its present value by the same method used to discount the annual cash flows. Table 18-10 shows the present value of the proceeds from sale for our example. The total tax liability ($16,932) and the loan repayment ($94,015) are sub-

Table 18-10. PRESENT VALUE OF THE CASH PROCEEDS FROM SALE

Sale price	$162,298
Less: tax on sale (Table 18-9)	(16,932)
Less: loan payoff (Table 18-2)	(94,015)
Net cash to equity from sale	$ 51,351
Present value factor @ 12%	0.5674
Present value of proceeds from sale	$ 29,137

tracted from the sales price ($162,298) to yield the net cash to equity from sale ($51,351). Since this figure will not be received until the end of the holding period, it must be discounted to determine its present value. Therefore, the figure is multiplied by the present value factor at 12 percent to yield the present value of the proceeds from sale ($29,137).

Net Present Value and the Investment Decision

The total present value of the equity is the sum of the total present value of the after-tax equity cash flows and the present value of proceeds from sale. If this total present value exceeds the equity cost of the investment, then the net present value is said to be *positive* and the investment decision is to invest.

In our example, the total present value of equity ($47,321) is greater than the cost of equity ($40,000) resulting in a positive net present value (Table 18-11). Consequently, the decision would be to invest. From a practical point of view, the results of the DCF model indicate that the investment meets all the financial requirements of the investor. It presents

Table 18-11. THE INVESTMENT DECISION

Total present value of equity cash flow after tax (Table 18-6)	$ 18,184
Present value of proceeds from sale (Table 18-10)	29,137
Total present value of equity	$ 47,321
Equity cost ($140,000 − $100,000)	40,000
Net present value	$ 7,321
Decision—Invest	
Justified Investment Price	
Value of debt (face amount)	$100,000
Value of equity (above)	47,321
Price at which investment is expected to yield exactly 12%	$147,321

the investor with a maximum or justified purchase price which could be offered in light of the investor's criteria.

The justified purchase price is the investment value of the project based on the ability of its projected cash flows to satisfy the needs of all the financing parties involved. In other words, the justified price is the value of the debt plus the value of the equity. The value of the equity is the total present value of the equity as shown. The value of the debt is the face amount of the debt (i.e., no discounting is necessary) since the investor will pay the required rate of return to the lender in the form of periodic interest. Therefore, adding the present value of the equity cash flow to the face value of the debt gives the justified purchase price. If the investor can buy for less than this price, then more than the investor's required rate of return will be achieved.

To sum up the possible alternative results from DCF analysis:

☐ *The net present value is zero.* Here, the expected cash flows, when discounted at the required rate (the rate of return sought by the investor), exactly equal the cost of investment. Put another way, the rate of return from the project is exactly equal to the required return. Consequently, the decision will be to invest.

☐ *The net present value is positive.* As in our example, the expected cash flows, when discounted, exceed the cost of investment and so the decision will be to invest.

☐ *The net present value is negative.* The expected cash flows, when discounted, are less than the cost of investment, so that the investor will not receive the desired return and so presumably will not invest at the asking price.

PRESENT VALUE AND THE INTERNAL RATE OF RETURN

Instead of using DCF analysis to determine whether discounted cash flows exceed or fall below a desired return, the analyst may seek to establish the precise return from the property. This return is called the internal rate of return (IRR). IRR is that discount rate which equates all of the project's cash inflows to the outflows. Therefore, IRR measures the yield of the investment. Often, this is very important to the investor, who may feel more comfortable with a *yield* or *return* concept rather than merely with the "invest or not invest" decision.

The actual IRR may be calculated by trial and error methods. Simply increase or decrease the discount rate as needed to move the net present value toward zero. Once the zero net present value has been straddled by two different discount rates, the analyst knows that the internal rate of return is somewhere between the two discount rates. (The reader can experiment with this trial and error method using the Compound Interest Tables provided at the end of the book.)[5] IRR also can be quickly determined with many hand calculators.

In our example, the IRR is greater than 12 percent since the DCF model yielded a positive net present value using a 12 percent discount rate.

Estimating the Internal Rate of Return

The present value tables can be used to choose the appropriate discount factors for our example. As already noted, IRR is greater than 12 percent. Choosing 16 and 18 percent as possible discount rates yields the data in Table 18-12.

Table 18-12. ESTIMATING INTERNAL RATE OF RETURN

Year	18% PV Factor	ECFAT	PV	16% PV Factor	ECFAT	PV
1	0.847458	$ 5,435	$ 4,605	0.862068	$ 5,435	$ 4,685
2	0.718184	5,203	3,736	0.743163	5,203	3,866
3	0.608631	4,985	3,034	0.640658	4,985	3,193
4	0.515789	4,778	2,464	0.552291	4,778	2,638
5	0.437109	4,580	2,001	0.476113	4,580	2,180
5	0.437109	51,351	22,445	0.476113	51,351	24,448
			$38,325			$41,010

The present value of the after-tax equity cash flow is $38,285 at 18 percent and $41,010 at 16 percent. Since the cost of equity, $40,000, falls within this range, the IRR for our example is somewhere between 16 and 18 percent. To get a more accurate estimate of the IRR, the factors must be interpolated. (See Table 18-13.)

The IRR is then compared with the investor's required rate of return. If the IRR exceeds the required rate of return, the decision is to invest. If the IRR is lower than the required rate of return, the decision would be not

---

[5] The internal rate of return and the net present value criteria involve different reinvestment assumptions. On a theoretical basis, they are not interchangeable phrases; yet in the real world, the distinction is seldom made. In a theoretical sense, the two can give different answers in constrained capital budgeting situations at a point known as *Fisher's Intersection.* Both of these concepts involve theoretically incorrect *reinvestment* assumptions. The *financial management rate of return* is a similar idea to the internal rate of return with a theoretically more valid reinvestment assumption which borrows from duration theory. For a further discussion of these items, see the references.

Table 18-13. INTERPOLATING INTERNAL RATE OF RETURN
(a continuation of Table 18-12)

PV @ 16% = $41,010	PV @ 16% = $41,010
PV @ 18% = 38,285	PV @ IRR = 40,000
Difference $ 2,725	Difference $ 1,010

$$IRR = 16\% + \frac{1,010}{2,725}(18\% - 16\%)$$

$$= 16\% + 0.3706\% \,(2\%)$$
$$= 16\% + 0.74\%$$
$$= 16.74\%$$

to invest. In our example the IRR of 16.74 percent exceeds the required rate of return of 12 percent; hence, the invester would be encouraged to make the investment decision. Note that the determination of the required rate of return exactly parallels the determination of the appropriate discount rate.

FURTHER CONSIDERATIONS ABOUT INVESTMENT RETURN

The foregoing model allows the investment analyst to reduce to one figure the numbers associated with the two-part return and compare that figure to the cost. Risk and the time value of money are incorporated in the discount rate. Remember, however, that the model is only as good as the input data—that is, only as good as the analyst's projections of the marketplace. Further, the model may overlook important items in the investment analysis and should always be tested.

One way to test the results of the model is to look at the simple multiplier analysis suggested in the appraisal section. As shown in Table 18-14, the operating expense ratio, the positive or negative leverage, and the tax shelter can all be examined by looking at different multipliers. The critical sales price assumption can also be evaluated by looking at the change in the multiplier between the date of purchase and the projected date of sale.[6]

Whenever unusual situations or inconsistencies are noted in the multiplier/ratio analysis suggested in Table 18-14, the assumptions of the model should be revised and a new net present value computation made.

---

[6] This entire model is easily computerized. Computer models can incorporate subjective probability distributions as well as simple point estimates as suggested above.

Table 18-14. EXAMPLE OF MULTIPLIER ANALYSIS

All of these multipliers neglect the second (sales proceeds) part of the two-part return.

	Original Investor	*Purchaser After Five Years*
Gross income multiplier	$\dfrac{\$140,000}{\$24,000} = 5.8$	$\dfrac{\$162,298}{\$27,013} = 6.0$
Net income multiplier	$\dfrac{\$140,000}{\$13,200} = 10.6$	$\dfrac{\$162,298}{\$13,993} = 11.6$
After-debt service multiplier	$\dfrac{\$40,000}{\$13,200 - \$10,000} = 12.5$	
After-tax multiplier	$\dfrac{\$40,000}{\$5,435} = 7.4$	

Note the following:

- If either the gross or net income multiplier, but not both, are out of line when compared to multipliers for comparable properties, then something is unusual about the operating expense assumptions.

- Again when compared to comparable property multipliers, if the after-debt service multiplier or the net income multiplier, but not both, are out of line; then something is unusual about the subject property's financing.

- As in the first and second notes above, if the after-debt service or the after-tax multiplier, but not both, are out of line, then the investment involves an unusual tax situation.

- The net income multiplier shows that the future purchaser is expected to pay considerably more for a dollar of operating income than the investor is paying. Is this reasonable? Using $V = NOI/R$, first calculate the R involved when the investor buys for $140,000, then use that R and the fifth-year income figure to more accurately estimate a sales price. Based on this projected sales price, what is the investment decision?

- For the new purchaser after 5 years, the after-debt service multiplier and the after-tax multiplier would depend on the purchaser's financing.

SUMMARY

The after-tax DCF model is an organized way to evaluate complex investment alternatives. Essentially, DCF calculates a project value based on the present value of equity and the present value of debt. It is therefore a useful investment decision-making tool. It can also be used on a continuous basis after the initial investment to decide on the appropriate time of disposition. The critical items in using the model are knowledge of the market, an estimation of risk and an estimation of the time value of money. Many people can learn the accounting mechanics. Knowledge of the market is more an art than a science.

APPENDIX 18A

Investment Analysis Case: The Southhills Garden Office

Utilizing the Southhills Garden Office case in Appendix 8A and the additional assumptions listed below, determine the discounted cash flow, net present value, and the internal rate of return for the project. Indicate if the investor should or should not make the investment. Justify your recommendation—that is, based on your analysis why should or why should not the investment be made.

Additional Assumptions

- Financing is available based on $195,000 appraised value with a 75 percent loan to value ratio at 10 percent interest for 27 years.
- The investor considering this project would take the most aggressive tax treatment, in terms of depreciation, as allowed by law.
- The property value can be expected to increase by approximately 4 percent per year.
- The investor's marginal tax bracket is 50 percent and the minimum required rate of return is 12 percent.
- The expected holding period or investment horizon is five years.
- Potential gross income is expected to increase by 3 percent per year.
- The vacancy and bad debt expense will equal 5 percent.
- Building A's value is estimated to be $48,465. It is a new building with an economic life of thirty years.
- Buildings B and C have a combined value of $51,561. They are existing structures with remainng economic lives of twenty years.
- There is a 6 percent sales commission on the sale.
- The purchase price is expected to be $190,000.

IMPORTANT TERMS

amortization	equity cash flow
cash inflow	after tax
cash outflow	internal rate of return (IRR)

net present value   tax basis
proceeds from sale   tax savings
taxable gain   two-part return

REVIEW QUESTIONS

18-1. How does the discounted cash flow model incorporate the concept of present value?

18-2. What data must be collected in order to calculate the estimated gross effective income for an existing income producing property?

18-3. What factors does the discounted cash flow model consider which would be ignored in a typical appraisal?

18-4. In the example presented in the chapter, how can net operating income increase each year when gross possible income is rising by only 3% per year while operating expenses are increasing by 5% per year?

18-5. Again referring to the example in the chapter, why does the tax shelter offered by the project fall in each year of the investment horizon?

18-6. How would an increase in the contract rate of interest affect the taxable income (loss) in Table 18-4?

18-7. In the example in the chapter, would the project be more or less valuable to an investor in the 70 percent marginal tax bracket? Why?

18-8. If an investor reassessed his required rate of return to incorporate a higher inflation premium what impact would this have on the project's internal rate of return?

18-9. If the project in the example in the chapter were a low-income rehabilitated project which could be fully depreciated (straight line method) over five years, what would be the present value of the equity cash flow?

18-10. Since the gain on the sale of the project in the chapter is subject to recapture, and hence a portion of the gain is taxed at ordinary rates, how might an investor justify using accelerated depreciation?

19

Investment Alternatives

I N PARTS I AND III, the general characteristics of the real estate asset which generate benefits for (and hence value to) the owner are developed. Part II examines the rules associated with the use of these assets. In Parts IV, V, and VI, specific aspects associated with the acquisition and ownership of real estate are covered. In this part, all of these elements are combined in a discounted cash flow (DCF) model.

In this model, value is a function of expected return and the riskiness of that return. What follows in this chapter is a discussion of the different types of real estate assets and how the different elements in the DCF model create varying risk-return expectations for those assets. In other words, the model developed in the last chapter is flexible enough to be used in connection with a wide range of property types.

DIFFERENT TYPES OF REAL ESTATE ASSETS

The owner of real estate sells space over time with associated services. When speaking about different types of real estate, the reference is to the (1) type of space being provided (office space, warehouse space, raw land, etc.), (2) particular time horizon (ranging from perpetual in the case of for-sale property, to a single day in the case of a hotel room), and (3) type of services to be provided by the owner, ranging from none in the case of a net lease to intensive personal care in the case of a nursing home or hospital).

In the discussion that follows about specific types of real estate, these differences will be related to the anticipated financial benefits from the property and the degree of risk assumed by the investor. The general scenario is to present the least developed investment alternative first and progress to the more intensively developed properties. In each case, the goal is to understand how the investment's characteristics affect the investor in his effort to reach specific goals.

UNDEVELOPED (RAW) LAND

Of all types of real estate investment, ownership of undeveloped land incorporates the *greatest degree of uncertainty* (with the possible exception of urban redevelopment which involves both raw land considerations and municipal politics). Here, *raw land investment* refers to the purchase of undeveloped acreage on the urban fringe which is anticipated to be ready for development within three to five years. (See 19-1.) Consequently, such acreage must be in the "expected" direction of growth of the urban area. Thus, an understanding of regional and urban dynamics is crucial to successful investment. However, a high level of uncertainty always is associated with raw land investment since the land use decision will not be made until some time in the future.

19-1. AGRICULTURAL LAND

Agricultural land which is in the path of growth of an urban area gradually begins to take on a double aspect, reflecting its present use for food production as well as its potential use for urban development. Since the value of such land for urban purposes will almost always be much higher than its value as agricultural land, several million acres a year in the United States are converted to urban uses. Even when the actual conversion to an urban use does not take place, the potential for such use results in the land being reappraised at much higher values for purposes of determining property taxes. This may place an intolerable burden on the farmer or agricultural user, who may consequently be forced to sell the land to developers. (Potential solutions to this problem are discussed in Part IX.)

The Asset Itself

From a physical standpoint, a number of items must be considered by the investor. They include access to the property from a public road, the slope of the land (since grading can be an expensive process), soil-bearing capacity, configuration of the land, vegetation, and so forth. From a legal standpoint, the current zoning of the property (or possibly the complete absence of zoning) and the likelihood of rezoning in the future are important ingredients in the investment analysis. The availability of public services (fire, police, and sanitation) as well as utilities (gas, electricity, water, and sewer) may make the difference between a successful and unsuccessful land investment.

Financing, Tax Shelter, and Periodic Cash Flow Considerations

As pointed out in Chapter 12, institutional financing for undeveloped land often is unavailable so the buyer probably must look to the seller or his own resources for financing.

Raw land is the least attractive type of investment from the point of view of tax shelter since land cannot be depreciated for tax purposes. Mortgage interest and property taxes are deductible; however, since these are actual cash outlays, they do not create tax shelter. Consequently, an investor seeking tax benefits as a significant objective normally will avoid undeveloped land.

Raw land generates no cash flow in most cases. Indeed, it usually involves a negative cash flow since the investors must pay property taxes, mortgage interest and other carrying charges. Therefore, a distinguishing characteristic of raw land investment is the "carry" problem—that is, does the investor have the financial and psychological resources to absorb several years of carrying costs.

Prospects for Long-Term Appreciation

Rapid appreciation in the value of the property represents the key to successful raw land investment. If the property value does not rise quickly enough, the carrying costs may reduce the aggregate return to the point which does not justify the risks involved. From a rate of return perspective, interest, property taxes, and other payments associated with raw land ownership can be viewed as ongoing equity contributions (on an after-tax basis). Consequently, the investor's equity in the project is continually increasing. (See **19-2.**)

19-2. RECREATIONAL LAND DEVELOPMENT

Recreational land developments present a new set of considerations. These type of developments, usually in the warm climates of the south and southwest, involve the sale of individual building lots to investors who often have the dual purpose of holding the land for appreciation and for building a retirement home in the future. Since both an enjoyment and investment factor is involved, such lots cannot be valued simply by capitalizing a projected income stream. More significantly, the extremely high marketing costs involved with such property mean that price appreciation must be very great in order to bring the purchaser a profit, if indeed a profit can ever be expected.

Because of frequent abuses in this type of investment, Congress passed the Interstate Land Sales Full Disclosure Act (ILSA) in 1968 to regulate the sale and lease of underdeveloped subdivisions in interstate commerce. The law requires developers of subdivisions of 50 lots or more to file a property report and a statement of record with the federal Office of Interstate Land Sales before lots can be offered for sale. These "property reports" are a valuable source of information for the potential recreational land investor.

INDUSTRIAL REAL ESTATE

Industrial property is improved land used for the purpose of manufacturing, processing, or warehousing goods. In its broadest sense, it is improved property used for any purpose other than residential or commercial. Virtually all industrial property is *special purpose* property—that is, not easily convertible to other uses. For this reason, an industrial property is considered somewhat riskier than such general purpose investments as office buildings and apartment houses. The high degree of obsolescence of industrial plants due to constantly changing technology adds a further element of risk. The major profit factor in industrial real estate relates to the relative efficiency of the particular facility in comparison with the competition and is usually evidenced in the bottom line of the industrial firm. (Warehouses are a notable exception to these generalizations.)

A special type of industrial property is the *industrial park*, a large tract of land on which a number of compatible buildings are constructed for a variety of light industrial uses. Individual sites in the park usually are purchased by users, although occasionally sites are leased. The key element of an industrial park is the creation of a controlled environment which includes all required facilities for industrial use, including utilities, streets, railroad sidings, and automobile parking.

WAREHOUSES

Of the various kinds of industrial properties, warehouses are the type most often owned for investment purposes. Warehouses are essentially large boxes for the storage of goods. They are transportation-oriented in order to provide high speed access within and beyond the particular area. They can range in size from several hundred to several hundred thousand square feet. A special type of warehouse is the *miniwarehouse*, which is a one-story building subdivided into numerous cubicles (varying from 50 to 300 square feet or more) intended to be used as storage by families or small businesses.

The Asset Itself

Warehouses typically do not require proximity to operating businesses or amenities; rather, they require access to key transportation arteries. In a physical sense, a warehouse has a long economic life due to minimal functional obsolescence. Relatively little has changed in warehouse design in recent years other than somewhat higher ceilings and somewhat greater floor load capacities designed for mechanized inventory handling equipment.

A warehouse owner must determine at the outset whether to seek out a major tenant under a long-term fixed-rental net lease, which means less risk and a lower return, or lease out space to several small tenants under short-term leases, which means higher risk (since vacancies may occur) but the opportunity to step up the return by increasing rentals as leases expire. In either case, warehouse investments are not management-intensive, because goods require less care than people.

Financing, Tax Shelter, and Periodic Cash Flow Considerations

Because of its particular space, time, and service characteristics, a warehouse provides excellent loan collateral. Consequently, good long-term financing is often available on fully leased warehouse space.

A warehouse will not generate as much tax shelter as an office building or apartment house. The reason is that the major expense is in the structure rather than in short-lived components such as elevators, heating and electrical systems, etc. Consequently, annual depreciation writeoffs will be relatively low. On the other hand, the fact that a warehouse typically is built on inexpensive land means that the bulk of the investment may be attributed to the depreciable structure.

Prospects for Long-Term Appreciation

As with other income properties, cash flow is the key to increases in investment value. The terms in the lease are critical in this regard. Long-term net leases may preclude rentals from rising to keep pace with inflation and so may result in only moderate appreciation. By comparison, a warehouse with short-term leases and with a history of repeated rent increases as space becomes available for re-renting can be an excellent hedge against inflation. (Most of the rent increases are likely to flow directly to the bottom line since operating expenses tend to be a relatively low percentage of GPI.) However, the shorter the lease period, the greater the vacancy risk.

COMMERCIAL REAL ESTATE

Commercial property includes all types of improved real estate held by the owner for the production of income through leases for commercial or business usage, e.g., shopping centers, office buildings, retail stores (see **19-3**), gasoline stations, restaurants, hotels, motels, and parking lots.

19-3. LOCATION CHECKLIST FOR RETAIL BUSINESS

Here is a list of factors affecting retail location:

☐ *Factors indicating a weak location:*
- Numerous vacant stores within a one-block radius.
- Neighbors such as taverns, garages, or pawn shops appealing to nonretail customers.
- Inadequate parking in the immediate area.
- One block, or the equivalent, from the main business area.
- Adjacent businesses needing repair and maintenance.

☐ *Factors indicating a strong location:*
- No vacant stores within one block.
- Middle- to upper-middle income community.
- Adjacent to heavy business traffic.
- Location in main business area and near dominant retail store.
- Diversified economic base.
- Adequate parking facilities.

SHOPPING CENTERS

Shopping centers—integrated and self-contained multistore shopping areas—appeared in their present form following World War II and are both a contributing cause to and a result of the suburban explosion which began at that time and which only recently is showing signs of slowing. There are now close to 20,000 shopping centers of all types in the United States, and they account for close to one-half of total retail sales.

Originally, shopping centers were precisely what the name implies, that is, large open areas which duplicated in large part the local neighborhood shopping districts within a city. However, as suburban families began to rely less and less on the urban centers for their shopping and recreation, shopping centers began to change. The larger ones became fully enclosed malls, offering a controlled climate throughout the year. They also began expanding vertically as well as horizontally, becoming in some cases two or more stories in height. Finally, many began adding a variety of nonshopping facilities, most notably movie theaters, banking services, bowling alleys, medical buildings, and general office buildings. More recently, some centers are offering hospitality and residential facilities as well, thus becoming virtually minicities.

The Asset Itself

Shopping centers are classified into three types:

☐ *Neighborhood centers* (up to perhaps 50,000 square feet). These are more commonly known as "strip centers," because the early ones took the form of a straight line of stores tied together by a canopy over a pedestrian walk running along the storefronts. Variations of the strip include the "L" (a strip pattern with one end turned) and the "U" (a strip pattern with both ends turned in the same direction). Neighborhood centers have remained popular throughout the entire history of shopping center development; however, because of their relatively small size and their exposure to competition from new retail areas which may be developed nearby they are subject to considerable obsolescence (in effect, negative appreciation).

☐ *Community centers* (50,000 to 300,000 square feet). Such a center will feature the "convenience goods" found in the neighborhood centers plus clothing, furniture, banking, professional offices, and possibly recreational facilities. Its principal tenant usually will be a variety or junior department store or large grocery store.

☐ *Regional centers* (300,000 square feet and up). This, the largest of the three types, will have two or more major department stores or other "anchors" to act as traffic generators with up to 100 or more smaller retail outlets. Because of their relative insulation from competition, and the continuing transfer of retail trade to the suburbs from the central business district of the cities, the regional centers are often considered to be among the highest quality real estate investments to be found.

The key to understanding shopping centers is to remember they are merchandising ventures and must serve the merchandise needs of their markets. The success of a particular center will depend on the size of its market area, the quality of the market (i.e., stability and growth of consumer income) and the competitive position of the center.

More specifically, income potential is dependent upon tenant mix, length of leases, and lease terms. Income potential is greatest when

- Nonanchor tenants are carefully selected on the basis of their ability to achieve high sales volume and so pay percentage (overage) rents.
- Lease terms are fairly short (perhaps five years), which permits frequent adjustments of rent.
- Lease terms minimize the landlord's exposure to operating expenses through various types of expense escalation provisions in the leases.

Usually, the minimum (fixed) rentals paid by tenants in the center are sufficient to pay the landlord's basic operating expenses plus debt service on a mortgage loan. The landlord's profit comes primarily from percentage rentals which will become payable as the sales volume of the individual tenants exceeds the "floor" level set in the leases. And when leases also require the tenants to pay any increases in property taxes and other operating expenses over those incurred in a base year, the center becomes an ideal inflation hedge.

Financing, Tax Shelter, and Periodic Cash Flow Considerations

Because of the inclusion of percentage rentals in many shopping center leases, the cash flow position of the landlord improves so long as the sales volume of the center continues to grow. Because percentage rentals are usually tied to gross sales rather than net profits, rentals may increase even though the tenants' profits remain level. In addition, the high degree of debt financing and relatively low operating expenses mean that a large proportion of the cash outlay of the landlord is in the form of a fixed debt service; thus, a large portion of increased rentals flow directly to the landlord.

From a tax standpoint, shopping centers are eligible either for the 150 percent declining balance method (for new centers) or the straight line method (for existing centers). The relatively large investment in nondepreciable land, however, means that depreciation write-offs may be as large as in the case of high-rise structures.

Prospects for Long-Term Appreciation

Well-leased regional centers pass on most of the business risk to the tenants. As noted, they can be ideal inflation hedges. Since inflation is a major factor in long-term appreciation, the well-leased regional mall has excellent long-term prospects for appreciation.

OFFICE BUILDINGS

The Asset Itself

Good location is particularly critical for office buildings because of the elements of prestige and convenience. An office building in the wrong place (for example, at a considerable distance from the central business district) may end up an inefficient warehouse. By comparison, an apartment building often can find tenants at lower rentals no matter where the building is sited.

In the case of suburban buildings, good location generally means good access to major highway arteries (and also to a regional air facility), and location within a high income residential area where property values are stable and growing. Suburban buildings also should be in reasonable proximity to restaurants and shopping facilities, since these often are necessary in order to attract tenants.

The prestige of an office building is directly related to the quality of its tenants. Of the types of real estate considered so far, office buildings are more people-intensive, have higher operating expenses as a percent of revenues and hence require the more management. Capital expenditures may also be required as the building ages, for elevator renovation, new air-conditioning facilities, etc. The construction is much more complex than the "shell space" that constitutes the structure of the shopping center.

Financing, Tax Shelter, and Periodic Cash Flow Considerations

From a financing point of view, office buildings represent excellent collateral and mortgages with high loan-to-value ratios often can be obtained. In recent years, there has been a trend toward involving major tenants in the ownership of the building; for the developer, this is a way to raise equity capital while it gives the major tenant a say in the design and construction of the building as well as a return in the form of cash flow on its investment or a preferred rental for the space it utilizes.

Tax shelter in office building investments generally is quite good since in both downtown and suburban locations, a relatively large proportion of the investment is attributable to the structure and so can be recouped via depreciation deductions. In addition, the use of component depreciation can increase depreciation write-offs during the early years of ownership because of the large investment in short-lived components such as air conditioning, heating and electrical systems, elevators, etc.

Prospects for Long-Term Appreciation

The value of a well-maintained and well-located office building is likely to appreciate at least as fast as the rate of inflation and, during periods of tight demand, considerably faster (since considerable time is needed to create new space). On the other hand, as already noted, the demand by many firms for prestige space means that new facilities often can draw tenants from existing buildings, thus creating a substantial amount of vacant space that must be re-leased. This leads, at least temporarily and sometimes permanently, to lessened cash flow and a possible decline in market value.

HOSPITALITY FACILITIES

The hospitality industry—hotels and motels—with its millions of rooms for sale each day, is a major factor in the real estate market and in the economy in general. Hotel and motel *chains* continue to grow and now account for approximately 50 percent of all rooms. At the same time, many of the public companies (such as Sheraton and Hilton) which formerly owned most of their properties are selling off all or part of their ownership interests and concentrating in both existing and new properties on the franchising and management end. Related fees may run anywhere from 3 to 10 percent of gross revenues.

The Asset Itself

Hotels and motels are relatively speculative investments, being management-intensive and highly subject to such outside influences as competition and energy shortages. In that respect, they are like any retail business. They have one major advantage in an inflationary economy; their rates can be changed every day. But, unlike a shopping center, the investor is not passing on the primary business risk to the tenant.

Hotels and motels fall into two general categories: *transient facilities* and *destination facilities*. Those in the first type usually are located on major highways or at airports and depend primarily on persons in transit from one location to another. Destination facilities, by comparison, seek guests who will remain for at least several days, perhaps to spend a vacation or attend a convention. Consequently, these destination facilities often are located in desirable resort areas or in cities which attract large number of tourists, and they offer complete banquet, meeting room and convention facilities.

Financing, Tax Shelter, and Periodic Cash Flow Considerations

Obtaining financing for hospitality facilities is more difficult than for many other types of real estate because of the risks that cash flow will be substantially reduced at some future date by the existence of new competition, a change in travel patterns, or the sudden unavailability of gasoline for automobile travel.

This reluctance to finance, combined with increasingly heavy costs of construction, means that equity ratios in a new facility often must equal 25 to 50 percent of total capital. Major considerations of lenders are (1) the management capability of the hospitality facility operator (this puts a premium on professional (outside) management or on investors who have had long experience with this type of property) and (2) national reservation systems which are considered vital to high occupancy ratios.

From a tax standpoint, hospitality facilities generate substantial investment tax credits during the construction period and create significant depreciation in the early years of ownership due to the short economic life of many of the components. Note, however, that while such personal property as furniture, drapes, and rugs may be written off over a very few years, they also must be replaced quickly and so adequate replacement reserves must be maintained.

Prospects for Long-Term Appreciation

Since hospitality facilities are more susceptible to changes in the economic cycle than many other types of real estate, the market value of such properties also may vary over a fairly wide range. The physical structures are unique and complex, the number of employees is large, and cash control is a significant problem, all of which increase risk. In general, hotels can be big winners or big losers. Some of the risk of operation can be reduced by obtaining a major chain franchise and hiring a national management firm, but the costs significantly reduce potential residual cash flow.

RESIDENTIAL REAL ESTATE

Residential real estate includes any type of facility that provides permanent (as distinguished from transient) housing for individuals. Types of residential properties include: (1) single-family homes, (2) two-unit (duplex) or four-unit (fourplex) structures, (3) apartment buildings (five units or more), (4) mobile home parks, and (5) nursing homes and rest homes. All of these (except the last) may either be owned outright or may be organized as condominiums, with each unit separately owned.

SMALL RESIDENTIAL RENTAL PROPERTIES

Most investors, from their own experience, are intimately familiar with the operation of a single-family residence. Consequently, investment in a single-family house, duplex or fourplex, is a logical way to enter the investment arena.

Because ownership of a home involves a certain degree of ego satisfaction and social status as well as provision of shelter, prices of small residential properties are frequently higher than can be justified on the basis of projected cash flow. Consequently, an investor may have difficulty finding a reasonably priced property, at least in terms of providing an annual return.

A major difference between single-family homes and the duplex or fourplex property is in the markets in which they are bought and sold. In the case of a single-family house, the investor may end up selling the property either to another investor or to an owner-occupant. By comparison, duplexes and fourplexes are much more difficult to sell as owner-occupied properties and consequently have a much smaller market. It is true that some investors buy a duplex with the intention of living in one unit while leasing the other, but this tends to be a temporary situation.

The Asset Itself

The important physical characteristics of small residential properties include location and property condition. Location is important with respect to transportation for work, schools, shopping, churches, etc. The condition of the improvement is important because it affects rental levels and operating expenses.

The most important economic characteristic of the small residential property is that a single vacancy creates a high vacancy rate (100 percent, in the case of a single-family home). The investor in a small residential property usually cannot afford a property manager or superintendent to handle day-to-day problems. Consequently, the investor himself must perform these functions. Because of the inevitable amount of personal time the investor must spend, it is critically important that the cost of management be incorporated into the investment model. Otherwise, the omission of any return on the investor's own time will mean that the property is not being judged properly vis-à-vis other investment alternatives.

Financing, Tax Shelter, and Periodic Cash Flow Considerations

Good financing generally is available for residential properties since such properties normally maintain their value and so provide good collateral for the loan. However, the loan-to-value ratio may be somewhat smaller for an investor as compared to an owner-occupant. Tax shelter is usually quite good for the properties due to the preferred depreciation rate and relatively high leverage.

Prospects for Long-Term Appreciation

The physical and economic characteristics of small residential properties often produce a low periodic cash flow, with most of the total return anticipated to come from appreciation, to be realized when the property is sold. Relying on potential appreciation is justified only if property values are currently rising and this trend is expected to continue and if the subject property is well located and constructed.

Prices of small residential properties have risen quite rapidly over the past few years, sometimes as much as one percent per month. This substantial appreciation has been one major inducement to investors to come into the residential property market. It is unlikely that appreciation can continue to substantially exceed inflation in the nation generally; however, particular markets may see higher appreciation because of local conditions.

APARTMENT BUILDINGS

Apartment buildings, or apartment complexes, make up a large portion of the nation's housing stock and have always represented a significant area for real estate investors. Since apartment buildings share many features with the small residential property, this type of investment is often the next step up for investors who seek a market in which they have some familiarity.

Apartment buildings fall into two well-defined groups: Conventionally financed buildings are those in which financing is provided by a private or institutional lender and the loan is not government-guaranteed. Subsidized buildings are financed directly by government, either city, state or federal, or by a government-guaranteed loan.

The Asset Itself

As with smaller residential properties, the importance of location is critical. From the physical standpoint, the attractiveness of the property will affect rental levels and the quality of construction will affect operating expenses. In recent years, such amenities as swimming pools and tennis courts have become important features of many buildings. Finally, the mix of apartment units—studio, one bedroom, two bedroom, etc.—is important in relation to the potential demand from single persons, families with children, etc.

Certainly, property management again is a key factor, particularly when the landlord provides utilities and significant amenities.

Financing, Tax Shelter, and Periodic Cash Flow Considerations

Financing is usually good for apartment properties. However, any indication of poor maintenance or a deteriorating neighborhood may discourage lenders. The lender looks primarily to the rental income stream to service the loan; by comparison, the creditworthiness of the borrower is the crucial element for smaller residential properties.

Again, tax shelter generally is excellent because residential rental properties can utilize the most liberal depreciation methods. In addition, the relatively high loan-to-value ratios utilized by lenders creates desirable leverage.

Prospects for Long-Term Appreciation

As a general rule, the value of any income property is a function of the cash flow it generates. For some properties (e.g., shopping centers), investors are willing to pay very high prices (a low capitalization rate) because of expected steady increases in cash flow. This is not true of apartment buildings because of fears that physical and functional obsolescence and possibly even rent control will put a lid on cash flow growth. Consequently, an apartment building's prospects for appreciation will be good only if there is sound reason to believe that cash flow will rise in the future. However, a well-maintained and well-located project represents one of the more stable forms of investment and consequently is a good prospect to appreciate at least in line with the inflation rate.

OTHER TYPES OF REAL PROPERTY INTERESTS

In addition to the major categories of real estate discussed above, investments may be made in recreational properties (resort properties, bowling alleys, indoor tennis courts, etc.) and business operations where location is a critical factor (fast food outlets, automatic laundries, etc.). An investor also may become involved in real estate without taking an equity position. Less risky investments are possible by purchasing participations in mortgage loan packages issued by GNMA or private lenders. (See Appendix 12A.) Indeed, the methods of dividing claims on real estate cash flow is limited only by man's ingenuity (See Table 19-1.)

SUMMARY

In general, real property has certain unique characteristics which must be reflected in real estate investment analysis. Basically, the investor is buying the right to residual cash flows. The residual cash flows will be affected by the property's physical, economic, legal, and social characteristics. Different types of real property can be differentiated along these lines. They involve offering the tenant different types of space over different time periods with different levels of service connected with the space.

By examining both the investment characteristics of real estate as a whole as well as the unique characteristics of the particular types of real estate, an idea of the adjustments to the average risk premium incorporated in the discount rate may be made.

Table 19-1. **COMPARISON OF PROTOTYPE REAL ESTATE INVESTMENTS**

Test	Real Estate Income Properties[1]	Location-oriented Businesses[2]	Raw Land
Income	Relatively secure flow of income which may grow as short-term leases are turned over at higher rentals	Insecure income flow but good growth potential	Nonexistent or very small income flow, but substantial income expected when property is developed
Capital growth	Continuing growth can be anticipated in line with rising income	Can be substantial if income flow grows as expected	May grow in value even before developed as moment of investment realization comes closer
Risk of loss	Greater than for Triple A leased property, but quite small if property is well-selected	Significant risk because of business speculation element	Very high unless the investor is prepared to hold the property as long as necessary to realize growth in value
Ability to finance	Usually very good because of relatively secure and growing income	Poorer financing terms than for "true" (non-business-connected) real estate investment	Financing may be unavailable during tight-money periods; during easy-money periods, terms will be tough
Tax advantages	Usually the same as for other types of developed real estate	Usually the same as for other types of developed real estate	Depreciation deductions unavailable for unimproved real estate; right to capitalize certain carrying charges
Liquidity	Depends on quality of the particular property	Investor may be locked into an unsuccessful business	Very illiquid
Management	Significant burden on investor-owner	Significant burden, both real estate and business	Very little management responsibility

[1] For example, apartment houses, office buildings, and shopping centers.
[2] For example, hospitality facilities, fast-food stores, and recreational facilities.

APPENDIX 19A

Real Property in a Portfolio Context

In both Part V on financing and Part VII on investment, it was noted that in the capital markets saver's funds are matched with investment needs. Since not all prospective investments can be financed, these markets perform an allocation as well as an aggregation function. If a prospective investment is to be financed (through debt, equity or some combination), its expected return must be sufficient to induce savers (or financial inter-mediaries acting for groups of savers) to invest their funds. The saver/ investor is concerned with the expected return and the riskiness of that return. (These ideas are developed in Chapter 17.)

PORTFOLIO RISK

It is important to note that the investor is concerned not only with the riskiness of a particular property, but also how the property will affect the riskiness of the investor's overall portfolio. The discount rate developed in Chapter 17 included a risk premium. That risk premium reflected the risk associated with the expected cash flows to be generated by the project. In this appendix, risk is examined from a portfolio perspective—that is, how the particular project affects the overall risk in the investor's portfolio. In a diversified portfolio, some of the variation in expected cash flows from one property cancels out variation in the opposite direction from another property. However, some aggregate or total variation remains; and it is a particular project's contribution to that remaining variance with which we are concerned.[1]

Investors buy and sell so as to maximize the expected return from their portfolio (for any given level of portfolio risk) or minimize the port-folio risk (for any given level of expected return). As investors buy and sell in the marketplace, the prices of alternative investments adjust to reflect aggregate expectations about the investment's expected return and the degree to which the investments will contribute to the riskiness of a diversified portfolio.[2] (Again, most investors hold more than one invest-ment (i.e., portfolios), and they attempt to reduce portfolio risk by diver-sifying.) Consequently, assets are priced based not on the variance of the asset's expected returns alone (property risk) but the contribution of the asset's expected return to the variance of the diversified portfolio (portfolio risk). It is this risk which must be incorporated into the discount rate used in the discounted cash flow (DCF) model. What follows is an expansion of Chapter 17 to include a more sophisticated approach to derivation of the discount rate, specifically adjustments for portfolio risk.

---

[1] Note that an investor can diversify within a general category of investments (common stocks) and between different general categories of investments (e.g., common stock and real estate). To the extent that real estate returns are countercyclical (i.e., rising when other returns are declining and vice versa), this latter type of diversification can be very attractive to investors.

[2] Theoretically, a fully diversified portfolio includes claims on every asset available in the marketplace in proportion to that asset's relative value in the market. In practice, effective diversification (sufficient diversification to achieve most of the possible canceling out of variance between investments) is achieved by holding claims on each of the major groups of assets available in the marketplace.

ALTERNATE CAPITAL MARKET THEORIES

Two basic financial theories seek to explain how the capital markets allocate investment funds. Both theories work on a general equilibrium concept. Investors are thought to buy and sell assets in the capital markets so as to reach an optimal balance between risk and expected return in all of their portfolios.

State Preference Theory

The state preference theory uses a discounted cash flow framework, and discounts at the risk-free rate. The numerator in the discounting process is not the expected cash flow for the project, but rather, the investor is thought to look at the distribution of possible cash flows in each period and think of a fixed amount which the investor would trade for that expected distribution of cash flows.

For example, an investment might be expected to return either $100 or $200 in the third year, with a probability of 20 percent on the more favorable outcome and 80 percent on the less favorable outcome. Hypothetically, there exists some exact dollar amount (the certainty equivalent) which is exactly equal in terms of investor preference to the distribution of expected returns. In other words, the investor is indifferent between the hypothetical fixed amount and the distribution of expected returns.

In the example above, the expected value is $120 ($100 multiplied by 80 percent plus 200 multiplied by 20 percent), but the theoretically risk-averse investor might be willing to accept a certain $115 in exchange for the uncertain distribution. Using state preference theory, the $115 is discounted at the risk-free rate.

The state preference theory has great intuitive appeal. The discount rate is easily evidenced in the money markets (by looking at government bonds with a similar maturity). Further, the numerator is individually adjustable to the asset, the time period in the future, and the investor's own preferences.

Despite its intuitive appeal, the state preference theory has not been used widely in practice. It is very cumbersome to obtain certainty equivalents and, in fact, to obtain expected distributions of possible returns for each period in the future. Consequently, by far the most popular capital markets theory has been the *capital asset pricing model.*

The Capital Asset Pricing Model

In the capital asset pricing framework, the basic discounted cash flow model is again utilized. Now, the numerator is the expected (most likely) return and the denominator incorporates a risk premium. In addition to the factors considered in the risk premium developed in Chapter 17, the risk premium in this discount rate is also a function of portfolio risk.

Capital asset pricing theory involves a simple mean-variance approach to investment analysis. All assets are priced based on their expected return (the mean of that return) and the riskiness associated with that return (defined as the variance associated with incorporating the given expected return in the portfolio).

The overall variance in any particular asset's expected return can be divided into a *systematic* and an *unsystematic* component. The systematic component is the amount of the asset's variance that can be explained by the variance of the overall market. The unsystematic component is the variance in the individual asset's return which is unique to the particular asset. In other words, the particular security's variance is broken down into two parts: one is a function of the general market and the other part is unique to the particular asset. In a fully diversified portfolio, unique (unsystematic) variance will cancel out in the aggregate. Consequently, it is the only systematic (market-related) risk which is important in pricing assets in the capital markets.

A measure of systematic risk can be determined by regressing the historical return of any particular asset on the historical returns of the market as a whole. The regression coefficient is termed the particular asset's beta. The higher this beta, the greater the systematic risk associated with the security's return. In other words, the higher the beta the more a particular asset will contribute to the variance of the overall portfolio. (Remember, the investor is concerned with the variance of the total portfolio.)

Figure 19A-1 illustrates the typical relationship between return and risk according to the capital asset pricing model. Again, risk and expected return are positively correlated. The higher a particular investment's beta, the greater the investor's required return.

The investor is particularly attracted to any investment whose returns are negatively correlated with the market. Such negative correlation would be indicated by a negative beta. By combining assets which are negatively correlated, the overall return of the portfolio becomes more stable, i.e., the variance is reduced without necessarily sacrificing returns.

Once a particular security's beta is known, the calculation of the appropriate risk premium for use in DCF analysis is very straightforward. The appropriate risk premium (now in a portfolio context) is the market risk premium times beta ($\beta_m \times$ MRP). MRP is simply the average market return less the risk-free return. This product is then added to the risk-free rate appropriate for the anticipated holding period to obtain the appropriate required rate of return (discount rate). (See **19A-1.**)

☐ *Underlying assumptions.* The capital asset pricing model is based on seven key assumptions:

- All investors are single-period expected utility of terminal wealth maximizers who choose among alternative portfolios on the basis of mean and variance (or standard deviation) of return.
- All investors can borrow or lend an unlimited amount at an exogenously given risk-free rate of interest R_F, and there are no restrictions on short sales of any asset.
- All investors have identical subjective estimates of the means, variances, and co-variances of return among all assets.

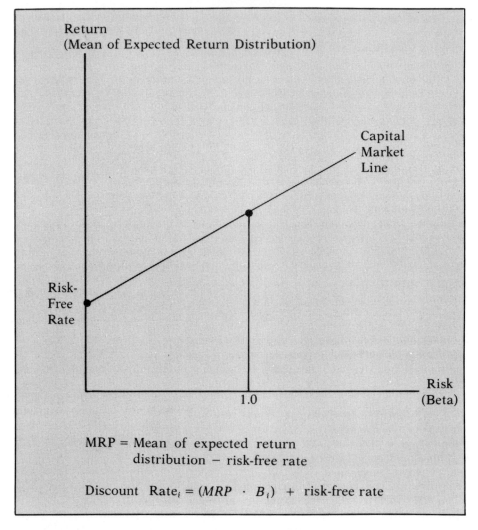

MRP = Mean of expected return
distribution − risk-free rate

Discount Rate$_i$ = $(MRP \cdot B_i)$ + risk-free rate

Figure 19A-1. CAPITAL ASSET PRICE MODEL

19A-1. CALCULATING BETA

The beta is calculated using historical data and estimating the following figures using regression analysis:

$$RR_m = a + b_m(MRP)$$

where:

RR_m = Return on investment m (Both periodic cash flow and appreciation in value)

a = Risk-free rate

b_m = Investment m beta

MRP = Average Market Risk Premium (Historical Average market return less the corresponding historical risk free return)

RR_m and MRP are known for each month over a substantial period, say 20 years. a and b_m are then produced through regression analysis

- All assets are perfectly divisible and perfectly liquid—that is, all assets are marketable and there are no transactions costs.
- There are no taxes.
- All investors are price takers.
- The quantities of all assets are given.

The student should consider at this point whether each of these assumptions holds for real estate investment.

□ *Implications.* Based on these assumptions, the implications of the capital asset pricing model are that all investors hold some combination of the market portfolio and the risk-free asset. The market portfolio is a weighted average of all possible investments. Thus, according to this theory, the price of assets in the capital markets adjusts so that the mean of the expected return and the beta associated with that return correctly price all assets. Investors then fully diversify over all possible claims on assets according to the relationship of the total value embodied in that asset to the total value of all assets.

□ *Implications for real estate investments.* All seven of the basic assumptions are usually violated in the real estate markets. It is equally clear that the implications of the model do not hold to the real world. All investors are not perfectly diversified. Further, there is seldom sufficient historical data to calculate betas for real estate investment. Despite these shortcomings, this theory which developed from Harry M. Markowitz through William F. Sharpe to today's version is useful to the real estate analyst. While the beta measure should not be naively followed, the theory is an excellent learning tool.[3] Even though the very straightforward calculation of a risk premium from the beta is not usually possible, the distinction between systematic and unsystematic risk is very helpful.

Like other investments, real estate is priced in the market place through the interaction of buyers and sellers each attempting to improve his own portfolio position. Consequently, it is the contribution to portfolio risk that should be a measure of the riskiness of an investment—that is, systematic risk is the key to asset pricing. However, to utilize the systematic risk concept to help develop a method of deriving the appropriate discount rate for real estate investment, an alternative definition of risk is useful.

AN ALTERNATIVE DEFINITION OF RISK

Rather than equating risk solely with variance, the *risk of ruin* definition is suggested. Under the risk-of-ruin notion, an investor is not assumed

---

[3] For a more complete description of the capital asset pricing model and related real estate applications, see Mike Miles and Michael Rice, "Toward a More Complete Investigation of the Relation Between Evidenced Money and Capital Market Returns," *The Real Estate Appraiser and Analyst*, November-December 1978.

to be averse to upside fluctuations (as is implicit when risk is defined as variance). What investors seek to minimize is the probability of achieving less than a certain minimum acceptable return.

Adjusting the Risk Premium for Portfolio Considerations

Keeping this new definition in mind, recall the methods for calculating the discount rate suggested in Chapter 17. The average risk premium is calculated on the basis of aggregate returns in the stock market over long periods of time. (Note that this risk premium is prepersonal taxes. It is converted to an after-tax required risk premium according to the formula suggested in Chapter 17—that is, after-tax required rate of return equals one minus the effective marginal tax rate times the before-tax required rate of return.)

The average risk premium is then adjusted for the particular investment. Again, the property type, the property characteristics, the investment vehicle used, the leverage involved, and the *liquidity* of the particular claim are all important. Now, however, the adjustment factors are expanded to incorporate portfolio considerations. Investment diversification is important as are personal factors.

In a relatively inefficient market (most real estate markets), the investor doesn't want to lose control of the timing of the sale. Or, in a more general context, he wants to minimize the risk of ruin. This can be partially accomplished in several ways, such as by including highly liquid assets in the portfolio and by incorporating assets whose returns are *negatively correlated* with existing portfolio returns. The incremental needs of any portfolio are thus a function of the investor's preference and the initial composition of the portfolio.

When determining the risk premium appropriate for use with the DCF model consider both the property and financing characteristics suggested in Chapter 17 and the investor's current portfolio. The more closely the expected returns of the investment alternative under investigation correlate with the expected returns from the assets already in the portfolio, the higher the risk should be. (See ▮19A-2.▮)

COMPARING REAL ESTATE AND COMMON STOCKS

Another way to approach portfolio considerations is to compare investment in real property with investment in common stocks. It is not suggested that one type of investment is always better than the other, but rather that the two are different. Further, most portfolios should include a combination with the weights on each dependent on the needs of the particular investor.

Comparative Advantage

One distinct difference between real property investment and common stock investment involves the possibility for comparative advantage. Common stocks are sold in a fairly efficient central market (e.g., the New York Stock Exchange). Real estate assets are traded in numerous fairly

19A-2. THE BOTTOM LINE

The discount rate to be used in the DCF model includes a risk premium. This risk premium should include consideration of the investor's overall portfolio. In this regard, the investor is concerned with the possibility of a serious adverse consequence, possibly losing control of the timing of the sale. This is most likely to happen when a particular combination of assets in the portfolio all experience adverse conditions at one time. Consequently, the investor should use a lower discount rate (lower risk premium) when evaluating an asset whose return is negatively correlated with return on existing assets in the portfolio and, conversely, use a higher discount rate when evaluating investments whose return is closely correlated with the expected return on assets currently in the portfolio.

inefficient markets (markets defined both by geographic location and product type).

In evaluating the prospects of a particular common stock, the investor typically looks at the prospectus and/or the annual report. Evaluation of product lines, management capability, financial structure, and so forth is termed fundamental analysis. In the 1960s, many investors made a great deal of money using fundamental analysis. Today, however, with the accelerating rate of change, shortened product lives, heightened management mobility, and frequent mergers and acquisitions, it is increasingly difficult to use fundamental analysis.

In the case of real estate investment, it is still possible to "know" the local area, have a feel for not only how the city is growing but why it is growing, and how local politics will affect growth in the future. Since it is possible to "know" the market better in the real estate situation and because the market is inefficient, it is possible to have a comparative advantage in the real estate business.[4] This comparative advantage means that the investor may get more expected return than is justified by the risk assumed, or assume less risk for any particular expected return.

Wealth-Building Potential

The two alternatives are different in terms of wealth-building potential. Two-thirds of the tangible assets of this country are real property assets. Considering financial assets, the value of all real property claims still nearly doubles the value of all corporate stock. If you want to make money, you have to go where the money is.

In terms of making money, *debt capacity* is also important. Certainly, corporations borrow extensively, and the purchase of corporate stock can be 50 percent financed (margin requirement). However, in real property, each asset can often be financed at 75 to 80 percent of the value, and this

---

[4] In an efficient market, the assets are priced so that the expected return is justified by the risk assumed; in other words, it is impossible to make a *good* or *bad* investment in an expectational sense. (Naturally, after the fact, some assets will turn out to be better or worse than others.) Conversely, in an inefficient market, it is possible to make a good or bad investment; in other words, to get less than a fair return for the risk assumed or words, to get less than a fair return for the risk assumed or more than the fair return for the risk assumed.

value does not necessarily equal cost. If value exceeds cost, then the effective debt/equity ratio is even greater. With mortgage insurance, 90 and 95 percent financing is possible. Finally, in terms of debt, it should be noted that nonrecourse financing is more often available in the purchase of real estate assets than in the purchase of common stock. Margin purchases always involve personal liabilities. Conversely, since the real estate asset provides excellent collateral, it is at times possible to use nonrecourse debt in real estate investment.

Wealth building also involves taxes. *Tax shelter* is much more possible in the case of real estate investment. Real estate is a tax-preferred investment alternative. Depreciation and capital gains allow both deferral and switching of income classification. Under the Tax Reform Act of 1976, only real property ventures still provide the complete shelter benefits possible with nonrecourse financing. There need be no double taxation in real estate, and excess losses are deductible. (See Part VI for more detail.)

Finally, from a tax perspective, tax-free equity buildup is the key to wealth building. When a particular asset appreciates in value, the appreciation is not taxed until the asset is sold. Individuals who have become wealthy from securities holdings usually have done so because they were fortunate enough to buy—and hold—stock in a rapidly growing company.

For the past decade, the average corporate stock has not experienced much appreciation. Consequently, tax-free equity buildup of any consequence has been rare. By comparison, real estate assets overall have experienced sharp increases in value and those investors fortunate enough to have well-located portfolios of real estate assets have benefited from rapid appreciation. One reason for this undoubtedly has been the fact that real estate has proven to be a much better hedge against inflation than has common stock.[5]

Related Issues

There are several problems typically associated with real estate investment which should also be mentioned at this time. These include high closing costs, the risk of fraud, high debt costs, government-created uncertainties, the personal time commitment, illiquidity, and difficulty in diversification. Each of these items may be a factor in estimating the riskiness of a real estate investment relative to a common stock investment. (Remember from Chapter 17, the average risk premium came from the stock market and then was adjusted for the particular real estate investment.)

In terms of high closing costs, the 6 percent commission in real estate can represent 30 to 40 percent of the actual equity. However, the client receives considerable services for this commission, and the commission on larger transactions is negotiable. Additionally, the commission is only paid on one end of the transaction. Therefore, to compare a 6 percent real estate commission with a stock market commission, the 6 percent must be reduced to 3 percent. When buying or selling $2,000 or $3,000

---

[5] Finally, it should be remembered that real estate assets may be exchanged tax-free, giving the real estate investor an additional road toward achieving rapid tax-free appreciation.

worth of stock, commissions can well run 1 to 2 percent on each end of the transaction each without similar services being rendered.

Certainly, there have been tremendous *frauds* perpetrated in the real estate industry. Florida swamps and Arizona deserts have been sold many times. However, most states do require that real estate conveyances be in writing and title insurance is possible. Such is not the case in the stock market.

Some people claim that *debt costs more* in the real estate situation. When borrowing to buy common stock, one borrows at only 1 to 2 points over short-term prime. However, over the last few years, 1 to 2 points over short-term prime has often been higher than the long-term mortgage rate. Theory would suggest that short-term rates would be lower than long-term rates. However, this is not always the case.

As noted, *government* has a pronounced role on the different real estate markets. The unwary investor can be hurt by government decisions. However, since real estate is traded in a localized market, it is often possible to know (to a great extent) what government will do. The aware investor should not be hurt too badly by government.

Real property investment very definitely involves a substantial *time commitment*. Therefore, the time factor is important. However, it is possible to have a comparative advantage in real property. The use of one's time and personal expertise can generate higher returns. Further, since one is closer to the real estate investment, it is more possible to evaluate operating management. (As noted in Chapter 11, property management is the key element in determining the cash flow of constructed property.)

Real property is definitely *less liquid* than corporate stock (even considering the fact that corporate stock can change in value rapidly). This necessitates the incorporation of highly liquid assets, such as government bonds, in the investor's portfolio. Still, real estate claims may not be as illiquid as they at first appear. As previously noted, refinancing is often a possibility. As the marketing function in real estate (described in Chapter 10) becomes more efficient, all real estate claims become more liquid. Further, real property values fluctuate less, so that while the sale may take a considerable period, the value is not as volatile as is the case in common stock investment. Finally, choosing the appropriate investment vehicle can enhance the liquidity of real estate claims.

Certainly, it is difficult to *diversify* in real property. The bundle of rights is not perfectly divisible, and real estate assets can be very expensive. It is thus difficult for most investors to diversify either geographically or by product type. In fact, the unfortunate real estate investment trust (REIT) experience suggests that diversification in real estate may not be a good thing. While one can have a comparative advantage in one market, no one is knowledgeable enough to have a comparative advantage in every market. Thus, diversification in real estate may necessitate going into markets where one is at a comparative disadvantage. In an inefficient market, this can be disastrous.

Summary

While many of the negative claims about real estate investment are not justified, the liquidity and diversification arguments are valid. This brings us back to the portfolio concept. The successful real estate investor will pick up the liquidity needed (to offset the illiquidity of individual real estate assets) through the use of highly marketable risk-free securities. Also non-real-estate claims will be included in the portfolio to achieve overall portfolio diversification (reduction in variance of returns). By combining risk-free assets, real estate assets, and common stocks a certain amount of diversification and liquidity can be maintained without sacrificing the potentially attractive returns offered in the real estate marketplace.

Only when the analyst is aware of the overall portfolio can an appropriate estimate of the riskiness of an incremental investment be made. Only then can the justified purchase price derived from the DC7 model be an accurate reflection of both the investment and the investor.

IMPORTANT TERMS

anchor tenant
apartment house
carrying costs
commercial real estate
destination facility
duplex
hospitality facility
industrial park
industrial real estate
Interstate Land Sales
    Disclosure Act (ILSA)

miniwarehouse
negative cash flow
office building
property report
recreational land
    development
shopping center
special purpose
    property
transient facility
warehouse

REVIEW QUESTIONS

19-1. How do you calculate the tax shelter from undeveloped land?
19-2. Why is undeveloped land thought to have a potential "carry" problem?
19-3. Why is a warehouse good collateral for a loan?
19-4. What are the different types of shopping centers?
19-5. How may the inflation risk in shopping centers investment be transferred to the tenants?
19-6. Why are property management concerns more important in office buildings than warehouses?
19-7. What type of property has the most significant cash control problems and why?
19-8. How do franchising agreements with major chains affect the risk-return position of the hotel/motel investor?
19-9. What are the tax advantages in a residential development?
19-10. From a vacancy risk perspective, is location more important in office building or apartment investment?

VIII
Development

20

Development: The Roles of the Participants

T HE DISCUSSION OF real estate development signifies a move from a static world to a dynamic world. It is real property development that creates the jobs and the constructed space which are so important to our general economy. And it is primarily at this stage of the real estate process that crucial issues are raised concerning the impact of the physical environment on society. Finally, in terms of the game, real estate development is one of the few remaining places where entrepreneurial skill can bring a big return.

The developer operates under the same general rules of the game that we have observed throughout the book. The same legal rules set the stage, the same appraisal techniques apply, the same marketing functions are relevant (with an additional focus on marketing research as is detailed in Appendix 21A), and the same financial institutions are involved. Therefore, the same analytical framework is appropriate.

However, now the investor is buying a *pro forma* (hypothetical) bottom line. The improved space does not exist, no historic earnings record can be examined, and the investor must be totally forward-looking in approach. Since there is no history (and in the case of more innovative space, few good comparables), the investor's understanding of the marketplace and the needs of the users of space is even more critical.

The purpose of this part is to introduce the real property development process. Chapter 20 highlights the participants in the development process and their respective roles. The role of the developer as entrepreneur and decision-maker is emphasized, and ten key development decision points are introduced. Also, since a major aspect of the developer's role focuses on managing the risk associated with development, the concept of risk control techniques as decision points is presented. In Chapter 21, the real property development process is presented as a series of seven stages. The role of each of the development participants is integrated into an actual development case. In this manner, the analytical framework developed throughout the book is adapted to the real property development process.

The Creation of Space

It is the architect's role to translate the developer's ideas into working plans and specifications. John Portman is a well-known architect turned developer. As an architect whose ideas could not be fulfilled by existing developers, he became involved in the entrepreneurial effort in order to execute his ideas in bricks and mortar. His work is important in any discussion of the creation of space because he proved that the public would pay (i.e., effective demand exists) for unique and creative space. His idea is that space should be designed for people. An immediate dollars and cents accounting concept must be transcended and a look given at the total needs of the human being in designing the constructed physical environment. (See Figure 20-1.)

IT BEGINS WITH THE LAND

Before moving on to consider how "dreams" are turned into reality, it is appropriate to look first to the land itself. James A. Graaskamp's[1] view of the development perspective encompasses three different possibilities. First "a site looking for a use" is perhaps the most common situation. This involves the investor buying land without first deciding on a particular development plan. Second, there is "a use looking for a site." Here, the developer notes a need in a certain area for a specific kind of constructed space. Then, the most appropriate site must be found. Third, Graaskamp cites the situation of "capital looking for an investment opportunity." An investor has cash and needs to invest.

While all three situations are common in the real world, it is the second alternative which is the most efficient way to turn ideas into reality. The site looking for a use is in some sense putting the cart before the horse. The developer seeks to satisfy needs in society, not pour concrete on every square foot of land. Capital looking for an investment should involve looking at all investment opportunities, not just development. As was seen in the case of the real estate investment trusts (REITs), searching too hard may result in stretching pro formas and finally in bad investments.

THE DEVELOPMENT PROCESS

The *development process* can be defined as the act of bringing an idea or concept to successful fruition in bricks and mortar. It is a complex

---

[1] James A. Graaskamp, *A Guide to Feasibility Analysis* (Chicago: Society of Real Estate Appraisers, 1970), p. 13.

Exterior View

Interior View

Courtesy of Hyatt Regency Atlanta in Peachtree Center, Atlanta, Georgia.

Figure 20-1.   THE HYATT REGENCY ATLANTA HOTEL—ATLANTA, GEORGIA

process requiring the coordinated expertise of many professionals. On the investment side, sources of financing must be attracted by the promise of sharing the cash flow generated by development in a manner which properly allocates risk and return. The physical construction of the project requires coordination among architects, engineers, and contractors. The public sector, especially local government, must approve the legality of the development in terms of zoning, building codes, etc. And ultimately, user needs must be satisfied. This requires the developer to identify a market segment in which sufficient effective market demand will exist for the type of space to be created. In short, successful development requires a team effort or team approach.

The members of the development team can be viewed as co-participants even if they do not have a formal partnership or relationship. At the same time, they have different goals or reasons for becoming involved in development. To understand the development process, it is necessary to know something about these different goals. In addition, some details of the function of each participant can add to the overall picture of what the development process in real estate involves.

The Developer

The developer is the entrepreneur who makes things happen, the quarterback or prime mover of the development process. The developer is first a source of ideas, who translates perceived needs into a concept of space which will satisfy those needs. Next, the developer is the promoter, bringing together the sources of capital, labor, and materials and at the same time, seeing that the project meets the regulations imposed by one or more levels of government. Once the process is under way, the role of the developer changes into that of a manager who must coordinate the efforts of all the participants in the development process and keep them moving toward a common goal. Finally, it is the developer who must supervise the initial operations of the completed project.

It seems true that developers are created, not made. It takes a unique personality combining great ability with a tremendous drive to function successfully in the development environment. As with John Portman, some developers come from the architectural profession. Others come from contracting, lending, marketing, or other specialized aspects of the real estate development business. Rarely, however, does one begin a professional career as a developer. Individuals are hired as participants in the development process, and those with unique talents move on to become the primary decision-makers.

The Developer's Goals   As the project's prime mover, the developer seeks the maximum possible return with a minimum commitment of time and money. This return consists of the following:

- The development fee, the stated direct compensation for "doing the development."
- Profits on the sale to long-term investors (i.e., sales price less cost to construct).
- Possibly a long-term equity position (for which the developer may or may not put in any cash). To the extent that this is done, the developer's goals are similar to those of the passive investor.

The developer's time commitment is a function of the length of the development period. Although the other equity interests also wish to minimize the time of their involvement, they are not "selling their time," as is the developer. They are involved in only a portion of the development process and are less sensitive to the overall length of the development period.

The developer may also profit through ownership of entities which sell services to the development—insurance agencies, mortgage banking firms, leasing companies, management companies, or even general contracting firms. To the extent that these arrangements are on an arm's-length basis and represent ethical agreements, the developer is simply compensated for performing additional functions. If, on the other hand, all parties to the development agree to unusual compensation for one of the outside activities in which the developer has an interest, then any excess above standard compensation should be considered as an addition to the development fee.

The financial exposure of the developer arises in two different ways. First, the developer expends time and money before being assured that the project will be built (i.e., before the commitment point). Naturally, the developer seeks to minimize such expenditures. Second, in addition to the developer's own equity position (both contributed capital and debt on which the developer is personally liable), a certain project cost or a certain initial occupancy level may be guaranteed to the investors and/or lenders. As the *primary risk bearer*, the developer's exposure is a time function of his direct financial commitment as well as the magnitude of any guarantees and the likelihood of their being called upon.

The Joint Venture Partner

Any individual or institution providing the developer with development period equity funding in return for a participation in development profits can be called a joint venture partner. (Remember the term "joint venture" is not a precise legal term.) The partner attempts to achieve the maximum possible portion of returns from development based on the minimum possible financial commitment. The partner's return is based primarily on the difference between project value and project cost and therefore indirectly on the amount and terms of the debt financing. The joint venturer's equity contribution often bridges a portion of the gap between project cost and available construction debt financing (the remainder of the gap must be filled by the developer's equity). The risk to the joint venture partner is a function of the extent of that contribution, assuming no personal liability, or a function of the amount of debt and the extent of the contribution, in the case of personal liability. In either case, the partner is interested in any downside obligations and the financial strength of the developer as these relate to the overall solvency of the project.

The Construction Lender

The construction lender is not concerned with the long-term economic viability of the project so long as a permanent loan (takeout) commitment has been obtained. (See Figure 20-2 for sources of development financing.) With such a commitment in hand, the construction lender is assured of being repaid upon completion of the project. The construction lender (frequently a commercial bank) has the responsibility of seeing that the developer completes the project on time and on budget according to the plans and specifications. (The time frame is important because the permanent loan commitment usually provides that it will expire by a designated date.) This policing role requires that the construction lender monitor the construction process, a process usually done by a *draw* procedure which involves certification of the degree of completion prior to each payment (draw) under the construction loan.

The construction lender faces the risk that construction costs will exceed the final permanent loan amount, forcing recourse to the equity interests or to the developer to cover the difference. If these others are unable or unwilling to do so, the construction lender has the option of foreclosing or taking a long-term loan position as a remedy. The construction lender weighs these undesirable possibilities against the expected

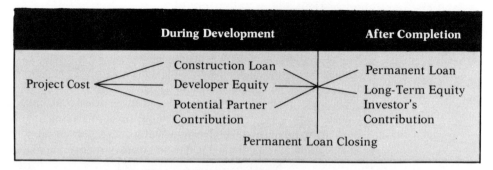

Figure 20-2. SOURCES OF DEVELOPMENT FINANCING

interest return (including compensating origination fees) to be earned by making the loan.

The Permanent Lender

The permanent lender, like the construction lender, seeks a secure loan while achieving the maximum possible return. Because the permanent lender, unlike the construction lender, has no takeout source, the market value of the completed project is critical since it serves as collateral for the loan. The value of the project will be a function of the cash flow generated, market capitalization rates, and the projects' expected economic life. The relationship of the loan to this value is commonly expressed in the *loan-to-value ratio* (LTVR) and the *debt coverage ratio* (DCR).

The LTVR generally is an indication of the safety of the loan; the lower the LTVR, the lower the risk of the lender because the greater is the equity "cushion." The DCR is an indication of the project's ability to meet the debt service requirements from net operating income (NOI). The larger the DCR, the lower the risk to the lender (because the greater is the income "cushion").

The Long-Term Equity Investor

The long-term equity investor may or may not make an appearance during the development period. The investor may contract to purchase the completed property prior to construction (basing the price on preconstruction value estimates) or wait until the project is completed. If the former, the contract usually will be signed before the commitment point—the time immediately preceding the commencement of construction. Whatever the time of sale, the price is usually not payable until completion and so the funds are not available to the developer. (However, a purchase commitment prior to construction may substitute or supplement the permanent loan commitment as a takeout for the construction lender.)

The long-term equity investor plays a passive role during the development period which does not include the sharing of development period risks. On completion of the project, the investor wants the maximum possible operating period returns (sometimes guaranteed by the developer for an initial period of one or more years) for the least possible price. (The situation here directly parallels the investor position described in Part VII.) These returns will normally be lower than those accruing to development period investors because the latter assume more risk due to the uncertainties surrounding the construction process.

In the past, construction period tax deductions (primarily for interest and real estate taxes) encouraged early investment by long-term equity interests. However, the Tax Reform Act of 1976 substantially reduced the tax incentive for early investment by requiring all or most of these costs to be capitalized. Consequently, early equity commitments have become more difficult to obtain. However, the developer's incentive remains for preselling the long-term equity interest. The sale enables the developer to avoid or minimize the market risks associated with changing value estimates over the development period. Presale of the equity may also facilitate the procurement of permanent financing.

The Architect

As previously mentioned, the architect's function is to translate the developer's ideas into working drawings and specifications which guide the construction workers in building the project. The architect typically begins with renderings which are rough sketches of what the project will look like when completed on the chosen site. If these prove to be an accurate reflection of the developer's ideas, the architect moves on to preliminary drawings which are more technical descriptions of the earlier sketches. From preliminary drawings, building cost estimates will be made (in more sophisticated development situations, operating cost estimates will also be adjusted to reflect specific project construction specifications).

These building cost estimates are part of the feasibility study, which has a primary role in the decision-making process. (See Appendix 21A.) If the overall feasibility indicates the project should be developed (i.e., projected value exceeds estimated construction cost), the architect will turn the preliminary drawings into final drawings. The architect may also be involved during the actual construction process. In such cases, the architect observes the construction process and verifies to the developer and/or the lender that the work is being done according to the plans and specifications established in the final drawings.

The Engineer

The engineer most often works with the architect. The architect uses the engineer to insure that the plans are structurally sound. It is the engineer who is responsible for determining soil-bearing capacity, the depth of footings, stress, and related items. In more complex development situations, an engineer may also be used as a construction manager. In such cases, the engineer replaces the architect in supervising the construction process. The construction manager, unlike the architect, is on the construction site continually and serves as the developer's representative or interface with the general contractor.

The General Contractor

The general contractor (GC) executes a contract with the developer to build the project according to the plans and specifications of the architect and engineer. The GC then retains whatever outside assistance he will need to actually build the project. The general contracting function is basically to subdivide the contract with the developer among different construction firms which then perform the actual construction work. In other words, the GC will hire excavation crews, concrete crews, a rough carpentry group, mechanical systems firms, a finish carpentry group, and all the other related worker groups involved in the particular job. The GC schedules their work and monitors the quality of that work to assure that their performance will, in the aggregate, satisfy his contractual obligations to the developer. *The subcontractors* are the individual workers or construction firms who are retained by the general contractor to do specific portions of the work. Their contract is with the GC and they look to the general contractor for payment as the work is completed.

Final Users

The description of all the participants in the development process would not be complete without mention of the final users of the space being created. It is anticipation of the needs of these users that leads to the idea which the developer asks the architect to translate into plans and specifications. As is seen in the next chapter, users often contract for space before it is actually completed. In this manner, they can assure that their needs will be met by the finished product. And as a result, they may become more than passive participants in the development process. Working through the marketing representative of the developer, the final users may interact with the financial and construction representatives of the developer during the actual building of a project.

Regulators

There are numerous regulators of the development process. On the local level, zoning officials assure compliance with local zoning ordinances. Local building inspectors enforce local building codes. On a regional, state, and national basis, there are a host of additional regulators. Their functions range from environmental and consumer protection to enforcement of antitrust statutes. The regulators enforce the rules of the game. If society's needs are to be met through the private sector development process, the rules must adjust to changing times. In fact, the development process has become so complex that regulators must often be active participants in that process, not merely passive critics, if social goals are to be achieved.

To conclude the discussion of participants in the asset creation process, note that quite often one individual or institution will fulfill more than one development function. However, the decision-maker can better evaluate the development environment by a consideration of each function individually, even when the goals and risk perspectives inherent in different functions are combined in a single entity.

Different Risk-Return Perspectives of Participants

The various measures of return used by the different participants in the development process are derived primarily from anticipated *project cost* and *project value*. These are the two key accounting statements in the feasibility report. The participants need to evaluate different possible combinations of these factors in light of their particular goals in the development process. As is seen in the next chapter, the feasibility study thus provides sufficient information for many different participants to make development decisions. (See Figure 20-3.)

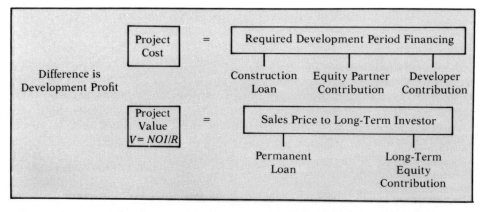

Figure 20-3.   RELATIONSHIP OF PROJECT COST TO PROJECT VALUE

PRIMARY DECISIONS

Since the development decision is in essence an investment decision, development analysis encompasses all aspects of the real estate process just as does investment analysis. However, in the development situation, greater uncertainties result from the fact that the space being considered has not yet been created. The developer, the key decision-maker on the development team, must make certain primary decisions during the development process.

How Should the Site Be Acquired?

An option or low down payment time purchase can significantly reduce early capital requirements, though usually with an adverse effect on total land cost. Note that this is not the decision to commit to the development of the proposed project, but only the decision how best to "tie up" the land so that it will be available if, upon completion of the feasibility study, the developer decides to proceed.

How Extensive Should the Feasibility Study Be?

Estimates of most variables in the development process can be made more accurate by expanding the feasibility study (and related studies, as described in Appendix 21A). However, the cost of these studies and the time required to complete them place limits on the extent to which they can be utilized. It is the feasibility study that contains project cost and value estimates which frequently are the basis for decisions of several participants in the development process.

What Types of Financing Should Be Obtained?

Should a permanent loan commitment be obtained before initiating construction? Possibly better permanent loan terms could be obtained after construction and lease up. The commitment fee is an additional expense. However, construction loan terms may suffer if no permanent loan commitment is obtained. There also is the risk that only less advantageous permanent loan terms will be available at the end of the development period. Also, obtaining a construction loan without first obtaining a permanent commitment may be impossible. (Less advantageous terms would include some combination of a lower loan amount, a shorter loan maturity, a higher interest rate, and more restrictive loan covenants.)

Who Should the General Contractor Be?

How should the construction contract price be established? Who should supervise the construction process? Should the general contractor be bonded? All of these questions directly affect the largest single component of development costs: basic construction cost per square foot.

Should a Major Tenant or Tenants Be Presigned?

Often rental concessions will be necessary to pre-sign quality tenants. However such pre-signings improve the prospects for high initial occupancy and may result in more attractive long-term financing.

Should the Developer Take in a Joint Venture Partner?

Such a partner would provide needed construction period financing and possibly ease borrowing problems, but the developer might otherwise keep all development profits for himself.

Should the Developer Presell the Equity to Passive Investors?

In the case of a presale, the escrowed proceeds might advantageously affect negotiations for a permanent loan commitment, and certainly such a sale lessens the risk of a decline in expected operating profits during the development period. However, if the developer waits to sell to the eventual investors, rental levels may increase and the completed project sell at a higher price. Certainly the capitalization rate applied to a completed project would normally be lower because the project would then be real.

Should an Outside Leasing Agent or Sales Firm Be Used?

Outside agents reduce the extent of leasing or sales activity required by the development team, but at a monetary cost and with a reduction in developer control of the marketing function.

Should an Outside Management Firm Be Employed?

Considerations here parallel those the use of outside leasing agents.

What Government Approvals Will Be Required?

A major element of the construction process today is compliance with municipal, state and federal regulations. If any federal agency will be involved in the development, an environmental impact statement (EIS) may have to be prepared to document the environmental impact of the proposed development. Some states also have their own EIS requirements. On the local level, the project must comply with zoning regulations and may require approvals pursuant to a master plan. Permits will be required during the construction process and a *certificate of occupancy* (CO) may be required when the building is completed.

ADDITIONAL DECISION POINTS

While the above issues represent key development decision points, they are by no means the only decision points in the real property development process. As the manager of the development process, the developer is keenly aware of minimizing development risks. Consequently, there are several risk control techniques that can be utilized in the management of the development process. Whenever the developer (or another participant in the development process) considers the use of any of the risk control techniques described in **20-1**, a decision point has been reached. The use

20-1. RISK CONTROL TECHNIQUES

A. *Initiation and Overview*
1. Evaluate the developer's capabilities and resources.
2. Determine the qualifications of the possible participants in the development—that is, examine their track record, financial strength and performance capabilities.
3. Coordinate the individuals performing the different activities involved in the real property development process.

B. *Government Regulation*
1. Coordinate with the city master plan.
2. Increase the frequency of building inspections by city officials.
3. Increase the extent and quality of environmental impact study.

C. *Feasibility Analysis*
1. The feasibility study is in itself a risk control technique. Increased effort in any area of the feasibility analysis can be looked on as a risk control technique having the purpose of improving the quality of the estimates of the variables used in development analysis.

D. *Site Selection and Land Acquisition*
1. The acquisition method can limit exposure prior to the commitment point.
2. Obtain protective warranties in deeds.
3. Include release clauses and subordination agreements in contracts if possible.

E. *Site Planning and Design*
1. Provide for a review of design plans by operations, marketing, and financial personnel.
2. Check for utility availability and possible city concessions such as property tax relief.
3. Provide for structural warranties in the architect's contract.

4. Check for the possibility of cost sharing through joint venture efforts on site utilities.

F. *Financing the Development*
1. The construction lender wants a floating rate loan, strict draw procedures, early equity contributions, personal liability of the investors and the developer, and a permanent loan commitment.
2. The permanent lender wants either the interest rate or the principal balance to be adjusted periodically for inflation, a lower loan-to-value ratio, a higher debt-service coverage ratio, and the personal liability of the investors.
3. The investors want to make their cash contributions late, avoid cash calls and personal liability, and reduce the equity amount.
4. The developer wants a fixed rate construction loan, relaxed draw procedures, substantial equity, large contingency provisions, and no personal liability.

G. *Construction*
1. The level of construction risk may be affected by performance and payment bonds, retainage, union relations, general contractor participations, architectural supervision and/or construction management.
2. When construction management is used, PERT and CPM may be useful control devices.

H. *Leasing*
1. Tenant equity participations may help attract quality lead tenants. Tenant mix will be based on the market study. Net leases and expense stops may be used to limit exposure to increases in operating costs. Outside leasing agents may be used to reduce certain leasing risks.

of these risk control techniques are more fully developed in the next chapter.

The Termination Option

Since development is a dynamic process, decisions are made in a time sequence. When any variable changes, the developer can reconsider the "go—no-go" decision and is therefore at a decision point. As time passes in the process, certain variables which could previously only be estimated become historical facts, while the estimates of other variables change. The project can then be reevaluated on the basis of the new data and estimates revised. Resulting changes in anticipated results could cause the developer to reexamine his participation in the development. Thus, any time movement through the process can represent a decision point in the process.

The complexity of the real property development process indicates the need for a decision model—in other words, a specialized analytical framework unique to the development process. In the following chapter, such a model, or specialized analytical framework, is developed as a variation on the basic analytical framework used throughout the book. The variation will encompass the dynamic element which is the key to the development process.

SUMMARY

Development is a focal point of the real estate industry and the developer is the focal point of the development process. He is an entrepreneur, promoter, manager, and, in fact, the individual most responsible for the constructed physical environment in which we all live.

IMPORTANT TERMS

architect
certificate of occupancy (CO)
construction loan draw
development
general contractor (GC)

joint venture
passive investor
pro forma
risk control techniques
subcontractor

REVIEW QUESTIONS

20-1. What is the role of the developer in the real estate development process?

20-2. How might a landowner become involved in real estate development as a joint venture partner?

20-3. What are the major risks that a construction lender faces as a participant in the real estate development process?

20-4. Why can it be said that the equity-investor in the real estate development process is buying a *pro forma* operating statement?

20-5. How might a site for development be obtained in order to reduce the capital necessary to get the development under way.

20-6. What factors might a developer consider when deciding to presell the equity interest to passive investors?

20-7. Why might investment in a development situation have more risk than investing in an existing project?

20-8. Should a developer maintain a continual termination option as a realistic decision point after development has begun?

20-9. What are the advantages and disadvantages of pre-signing major tenants in an income producing property?

20-10. How is the lending position of the permanent lender different from that of the construction lender?

21

The Development Process

THE REAL PROPERTY DEVELOPMENT PROCESS may be viewed in seven stages
(as shown in Figure 21-1). The flow of activities through the stages represents a typical sequence in real property development. Although this
particular sequence is not necessarily followed in all cases, it does provide
a good framework for analyzing the process and it creates a structured
environment within which projects can be accurately evaluated. Viewing
development as a series of stages allows a needed flexibility not present in
traditional appraisal models. The developer is thus able to review the
project at each stage of completion and to consider the implications of
proceeding or not.

The seven-stage framework also contributes to an understanding of
how the various development activities interact. The stages interact in two
ways. First, some development activities span several different stages, and
several different activities will be ongoing during any one stage. Second,
the process is interactive in the sense that the values of certain variables in
the process are conditioned by the values of other variables. The variables
which quantify a particular action initiated in one stage may be a function
of a variable resulting from a separate action completed in a different
stage. For instance, the availability of a permanent loan which will be
closed at the end of the development period will probably improve the
terms of the construction loan initially funded at the beginning of the
construction stage. (See 21-1.)

As the seven-stage development model is presented, the development
of a hypothetical regional shopping center (Military Mall) is used as an
example to illustrate the different stages. The hypothetical example is
patterned after Military Circle, located in Norfolk, Virginia, one of the
most successful shopping centers on the East Coast. (See Figure 21-2.)

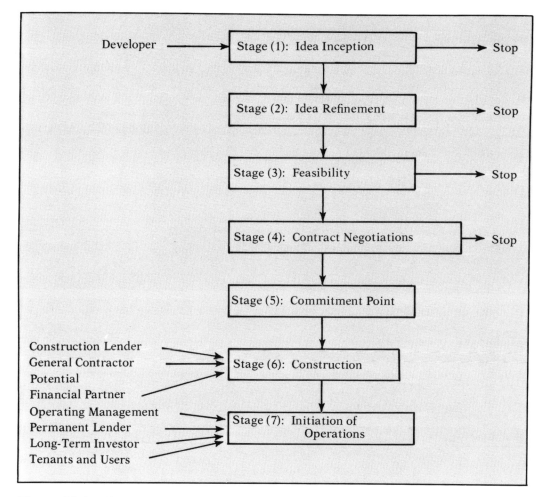

Figure 21-1. THE REAL PROPERTY DEVELOPMENT MODEL

STAGE 1: IDEA INCEPTION

The development process begins with the idea inception stage. In this stage, the developer generates an idea for a particular type of project (motel, office building, warehouse, etc.) and considers what project size might be appropriate for a particular urban area. The developer then reflects on the type of tenants who might be interested in the projected space and the possible sources of financing.

21-1. THE VOLITIONAL FALLACY

There is something about many projects that make those involved fall in love with them. As a result, the "volitional fallacy" becomes a common problem. The developer's and analyst's beliefs become "because it ought to be true, it will be true." Such a volitional fallacy appears to have affected market studies done for projects like the many "new towns" that were started before the recession. Analysts accepted the idea that the unique character of a new town environment or some design features would help a project achieve capture rates far in excess of the norm.

The idea that an attractive supply creates its own demand contains elements of truth, but an attractive product rarely causes radical changes in traditional patterns. Many of the "new towns" studies estimated capture rates of more than 10 percent of the metropolitan market, although normally 3 percent would have been considered ambitious. Gananda, an ill-conceived and poorly located "new town" outside of Rochester, was projected to capture 500 to 600 units per year in an SMSA that had peaked at 6,000. In reality, only two houses were built and one of these burned down. What was overlooked in the enthusiasm for the concept was the obvious fact that for years "new towns" would just be small new land developments in the middle of cornfields. The reported advantages of a comprehensively planned environment would not become evident until many of the initial buyers had moved on to other communities.

The "Pro Forma"

Next, the developer will put together a "back-of-the-envelope pro forma." The pro forma will include a very rough "guesstimate" of a cost and value statement. (See Table 21-1.) The type of tenant needs to be satisfied and the construction requirements will be combined on a rough basis to come up with a cost figure. Looking at what rental rate the projected space presently commands in the marketplace, the developer will devise an equally rough estimate of the income stream to be generated by the property.

From that income stream, a project value can be established based upon current capitalization rates. Based on the project value, an approximation can be made of the amount and cost of financing. Finally, the developer can make a stab at the bottom-line cash flow for the residual (equity) interest.

The developer may go through this process many times, usually discarding the results. When a rough idea does look good at this early stage, the developer moves on to the second stage in the process.

The Military Mall Example

In the Military Mall hypothetical example, the developer felt that Norfolk, Virginia needed a regional shopping center. His plan was to

Courtesy of Military Circle—Equitable Life, owned by the Equitable Life Assurance Society of the United States and managed by Alpert Corporation—Virginia Division.

Figure 21-2.   NORFOLK, VIRGINIA MILITARY CIRCLE AND RING ROAD CONCEPT

Table 21-1. BACK-OF-THE-ENVELOPE PRO FORMA

Cost:	
Land	$1,500,000
Site work	2,000,000
Construction (200,000 sq. ft. @ $20/sq. ft.) =	4,000,000
	$7,500,000
Value:	
Rent (200,000 sq. ft. @ $7/sq. ft.)	$1,400,000 (mall only)
Operating expenses (40%)	560,000
Cash flow	$ 840,000
Capitalization rate (10%)	$8,400,000
Conclusion: Move to Stage 2	

induce three major department stores (the projected anchor tenants) to locate on the site by offering free land for store construction and free use of the center's infrastructure (roads, common areas, etc.). The developer would build a mall connecting the three anchors and make his profit by leasing space to smaller tenants attracted to the site by the large department stores which would act as traffic generators.

STAGE 2: IDEA REFINEMENT

The second stage of the process involves refining the rough idea conceptualized in stage (1). First, the developer must find a specific location within the given area. The site must be checked to see that zoning is appropriate or that rezoning is possible. Further, there must be access to major transportation arteries, and municipal services must be available.

Next, the developer will seek to "tie up" the site. At this early stage in the development process, the developer is leary of committing large sums of money to a tract of land which may not end up being developed. However, doing extensive planning work prior to gaining control of the site can leave the developer in a disadvantageous negotiating position with the land owner. Consequently, the objective at this time is to arrange for an option on the land or possibly a low down payment purchase with no personal liability (in effect, also an option). In this manner, the site will be available when needed while present investment is minimized.

The next step is to determine physical feasibility and prepare an architectural layout. The developer will arrange for soil tests to determine the load-bearing capacity of the ground, examine the grade and configuration of the site, and consider any other unique physical characteristics. The developer's architect determines whether the general type and size of the envisioned project can be placed on the site. For example, the architect will judge if the number of square feet to be developed will leave sufficient space to meet municipal parking requirements.

Also during the idea refinement stage, the developer will begin to look for general contractors (GCs) who are available to do work in the area. Some very tentative discussion may be initiated with possible tenants, with a view to obtaining the right mix for the project. Potential permanent and construction lenders will be approached to ascertain their general interest in providing loans. Finally, a check of possible sources of equity capital will be made and tax ramifications of alternative financing structures will be considered.

The Military Mall Example

In the Norfolk, Virginia Military Mall example, the developer had an eye on a location on the corner of Military Drive and Virginia Beach Boulevard. The site seemed ideal for a regional center. It was at the intersection of two major arteries and within a reasonable driving distance of a considerable residential population.

The proposed use was permitted under the zoning ordinance while access to the major arteries as well as necessary municipal services could be obtained. The developer then acquired options to purchase 100 contiguous acres from several landowners working through a local broker. Even though forty acres would be sufficient for the proposed center, the developer knew that the center would generate a demand for adjacent uses. As a result, the land peripheral to the shopping center could be expected to increase sharply in value. The developer wished to capture this value increase for the development group.

With the land "tied up," the developer considered the best layout for the shopping center and determined that a ring road would be the most advantageous design. The developer would put the shopping center in the middle of a circular road which would connect with the arterial highways. In this way, each tenant could be given frontage—always considered a choice spot. Using the ring road also allowed access to the additional sixty acres which the developer hoped to market after the shopping center opened for business.

The developer then made sure that a competent general contractor was available. Next, the GC obtained "expressions of interest" from certain major department stores and ascertained which permanent and construction lenders were currently in the market for shopping center loans. Finally, consideration was given to possible sources of long-term equity funds.

STAGE 3: FEASIBILITY

The third stage in the development process is the precommitment stage. At the beginning of this stage, the formal feasibility study is begun. As indicated in Appendix 21A, varying degrees of market research are possible. In essence, the developer will use regional and urban economic data to look at the market possibilities for the chosen product (constructed space). Preliminary drawings will be made trading off an aesthetic market appeal against the cost of the particular project. (Operating costs ramifications of any particular design concept also will be considered.) From the preliminary drawings, initial construction cost estimates will be made using such sources as the Dodge Building Cost Calculator.

At this point, discussions with both permanent and construction lenders will become more specific. A developer lacking the necessary contacts may retain a mortgage banker to facilitate these discussions. Based on the costs projected in the preliminary drawings as well as the estimate of market demand for the space, the feasibility study is completed, permitting a more refined cost and value statement to be developed which will determine the economic viability of the proposed project.

The feasibility study is a resource document and should include sufficient data to allow each participant in the process to evaluate objectives in a risk-return perspective. Finally, any building permits or other local government requirements are obtained or met.

The Military Mall Example

In the Military Mall example, the architect located the regional center inside the planned ring road. The cost estimates for the center were checked for reasonableness with GCs doing business in the area. The most likely permanent lender was given a rough idea of the design to be sure that nothing in the proposed development created unusual financing problems. Based on the construction cost estimates as well as the market feasibility, the developer produced cost and value statements similar to those shown in Tables 21-2 and 21-3.

STAGE 4: CONTRACT NEGOTIATIONS

The fourth stage is the contract stage, at which point written agreements are entered into with all the key participants in the project. On the financial side, a permanent loan commitment will be obtained. The permanent lender, relying on the feasibility study of the developer as well as on its own analysis and appraisal of the site and project, agrees by this

Table 21-2. COST STATEMENT

Land (including closing costs)	$1,400,000
Site work (including utilities)	650,000
Building (mall only)	3,750,000
Tenant allowances	460,000
Architectural and engineering fees	230,000
Construction interest	360,000
Permanent loan commitment fee (1%)	80,000
Marketing (leasing, advertising, and promotion)	100,000
Operating personnel before opening	50,000
Development fee	200,000
Permits, miscellaneous, and contingencies	100,000
	$7,380,000

commitment to make a loan if the project is built according to plans and specifications. The developer will then take the permanent loan commitment to a potential construction lender. After convincing the construction lender that the shopping center is likely to be completed on time according to plans and specifications, the developer obtains a construction loan, to be funded in stages as the center is built.

Also at this point, the developer must decide on how to retain the GC. Should a construction contract be negotiated on a one-to-one basis, or should construction bids be solicited from all interested GCs? Should the architect supervise the construction process, or should a construction

Table 21-3. VALUE STATEMENT

Revenues*			
120,000 sq. ft. prime space @ 7.50/sq. ft.		$840,000	
85,000 sq. ft. back space @ 5.00/sq. ft.		425,000	$1,265,000
Operating Expenses**			
Building maintenance	8%		
Utility systems	14%		
Property taxes	12%		
Insurance	2%		
Management	5%		
	41%		$ 519,000
Cash flow before income taxes and debt service			$ 746,000
Project value (9.8% capitalization rate)			$7,612,000

* Per proposed rental roll using desired tenant mix. No percentage rents included.
** Based on industry averages adjusted for local economic conditions. Expense escalation clauses in leases are not needed in first-year example.

manager be hired? Should the general contractor be required to post payment or performance bonds, i.e., should insurance be taken out to assure satisfaction of the GC's contractual obligations?

In most private (as distinguished from government) construction situations, contracts are negotiated. This is primarily due to the fact that not all of the plans are complete when the GC is hired. On the other hand, most government jobs involve bidding. In government projects, plans and specifications are usually fully complete, and, therefore, the bidding process makes sense.

At this stage, the developer must also decide whether to seek to pre-lease to major tenants. If major tenants are pre-signed, financing will be easier to obtain and smaller tenants will be drawn to the area. On the other hand, major tenants know their value to the developer and will be able to bargain for a better deal if they are drawn into the process early. In either case, overall leasing parameters, including tenant allowances (for store construction and fixturing) common area charges, heating, ventilating and air conditioning (HVAC) charges, minimum and percentage rent, length of lease, renewal options, and so forth must be established. This is necessary so that the marketing function may go on during the construction process.

Finally, a decision on financing the equity must be made. Should a money partner be brought in to share development risks? Should the project be presold to long-term equity investors? What particular investment vehicle would be most advantageous considering the tax shelter possibilities as well as the risks involved in the particular development?

The Military Mall Example

In the Military Mall example, a permanent financing commitment was obtained from a life insurance company. Based on the commitment, a local commercial bank agreed to make the construction loan. Since the project was quite large, even for the Norfolk area, one of the large general contractors in the area was chosen and a construction contract negotiated.

Three major department stores were selected as anchor tenants and leases were executed, such preleasing being a requirement of the permanent loan agreement. Leasing parameters for the remaining tenants were established so that revenues from the project would be sufficient to support the value estimate shown in the feasibility study. (The market research portion of the feasibility study indicated that the leasing guidelines were reasonable.)

The developer decided to use his own capital during the development period and then sell after completion to a long-term equity investor. By waiting until completion, the developer believed a higher price would be obtainable since the purchaser would view the project as less risky.

STAGE 5: COMMITMENT POINT

The fifth stage of the development process is termed the commitment point. Here, the contracts negotiated in stage (4) are signed, or conditions required to make them effective are satisfied. Frequently, contracts negotiated in stage four are contingent on other contracts, for example, the permanent loan commitment may be contingent on signing a certain major tenant. Since the developer does not want to be bound under one contract unless all the contracts are in force and because the contracts may in fact be contingent on one another, it is frequently necessary to arrange a simultaneous execution of several contracts.

In the fifth stage, the partnership or joint venture agreement is closed (if the developer needs a money partner). Any presale to passive investors is closed. The construction loan is closed and the permanent commitment fee is paid, binding the permanent lender. The construction contract is signed with the general contractor. Any presigned major tenants execute their leases. Land optioned in stage (2) is acquired by exercising the option. Finally, the informal accounting system, in use since successful completion of the "back-of-the-envelope pro forma" in stage 1, is replaced by a more formal accounting system.

A budget is drawn, based on the agreements negotiated above. Cash control is maintained through construction loan draw procedures which are explained below. Time control is established by relating the different contracts in a PERT or CPM chart.

The Military Mall Example

In the Military Mall example, the construction loan was contingent on the permanent loan commitment. This, in turn, was contingent on the major tenant leases. Therefore, all of the contracts were executed at approximately the same time, so that the major tenants, the construction and permanent lenders, and the general contractor, all became bound simultaneously. A budget was developed, adhering to the cost statement shown in the feasibility study and tied to the contracts just executed. The construction lender was then ready to begin advancing funds based on this budget. The first draw (i.e., the first request for funds from the bank) was to pay off the land purchase. (The construction lender took a first lien position in the land through a mortgage executed by the developer.)

STAGE 6: CONSTRUCTION

Stage 6 is the construction period. At this point, the developer's emphasis switches from that of stressing minimal financing exposure in the event the project does not go forward, to that of seeking to reduce the construction time during which the developer experiences maximum financial exposure. The commitment point is past, and now the developer will be called upon to function more as a manager and less as a promoter.

During this period, the physical structure is built. Periodically, the subcontractors submit bills or vouchers for their costs to the general contractor. The developer adds his soft-dollar costs (insurance, interest, marketing, etc.) to the hard-dollar costs and sends a draw request to the commercial bank. The commercial bank funds the loan according to the loan agreement executed in the previous stage, by placing funds in the developer's bank account. The developer writes a check to the GC, and the GC pays the subcontractors.

To protect the construction lender, the GC's work must be approved either by the architect or the construction manager in order to assure that it has been done according to plans and specifications. Further, a portion of the payments due the GC and the subcontractors (perhaps 10 percent) will be withheld. This practice, known as *retainage*, is also intended to protect the lender (and developer) against incomplete or defective work. The retained sums are paid after the architect or construction manager certifies that the project has been completed in accordance with the plans and specifications.

The construction manager, marketing representative and financial officer, all members of the development team, work closely together during this stage. The construction manager must be sure that the project is being built according to plans and specifications and on time. The marketing representative must see to it that presigned major tenants are receiving what they expected and any remaining space is being leased or sold. The financial officer is the coordinator between the construction process and the marketing function on one side and sources of financing on the other. That officer transmits the draw request from the construction manager and supervises banking relations. At the same time, he approves adjustments that must be made to reflect the realities of the marketplace as described by the marketing representative. (See Figure 21-3.)

The Military Mall Example

In the Military Mall example, a construction manager (CM) was selected to represent the developer. The CM monitored the progress of the general contractor and approved draw requests which were forwarded to the controller of the development company. The controller added soft-dollar costs and made a draw request, net of the retainage to be withheld, to the construction lender. The developer's leasing agent handled construction problems of the major tenants and negotiated the leasing of the smaller shops on the mall.

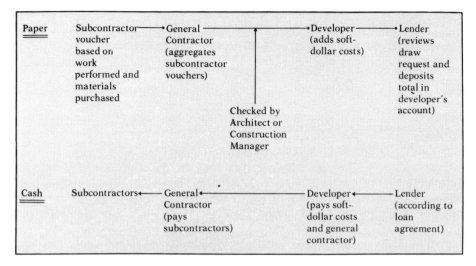

Figure 21-3. CASH AND PAPER IN THE CONSTRUCTION STAGE

STAGE 7: INITIATION OF OPERATIONS

In the final stage of the development process, construction is completed and operating personnel are brought on the scene. Preopening advertising and promotion take place; utilities are connected; municipal requirements such as inspections and certificates of occupancy are satisfied; and the tenants move in.

On the financial side, the permanent loan is closed and the construction loan paid off. Unless the developer is keeping the property as an investment, long-term equity interests take over from the developer (based on a presale contract or a sale after completion), and the formal opening is held.

The Military Mall Example

In Military Mall, the developer hired a shopping center manager and promotions manager. Both were brought on site approximately six weeks before the planned opening. The operating manager designed the operating system, including maintenance and security schedules, and began to work with the tenants. The advertising manager arranged the formal opening as well as the media campaign intended to bring large numbers of shoppers to the center during the first few weeks. As the project was completed, utilities were connected and a city occupancy permit obtained. The anchor tenants (major department stores) moved in as soon as their space was finished. The smaller tenants occupied their premises when the mall area was completed. The permanent loan was closed, permitting the construction loan to be satisfied. The developer then began to look for a long-term equity investor who would be interested in buying the center.

SUMMARY

Development is the most exciting part of the real estate game. An understanding of all facets of the industry is required to fully understand the dynamics of the creation of space. Before changes in the rules of the game (public policy) are considered, a firm analytical foundation is essential, so a review of previous chapters may be in order at this point.

APPENDIX 21A

Land Use Feasibility Analysis

Feasibility analysis can be as simple as evaluating a one-year cash-flow pro forma or as complex as a multiyear market and economic study. While the depth of analysis, which can be economically justified, varies depending on the importance of the decision; the feasibility study should always be developed according to an analytical framework similar to the one described in this appendix. This framework is flexible enough to cover a wide variety of real estate projects, with the level of detail depending on the importance of the decision.

A complete real estate feasibility analysis requires a market and economic study undertaken with a clear understanding of the decision environment. The *decision environment* consists of the motivations and capacities of a myriad of individuals and institutions as well as the concept of *the general public*. The specific group of individuals involved varies from project to project, but the basic theme remains: Land-use decisions cannot be made in a vacuum. They are, in fact, public issues. Examined here will be this environment, site and participant relationships, exogenous shocks to the relationship, and related implications for the participants. On this basis, the mechanics of feasibility analysis are examined, and a practical framework for analysis is developed.

THE LAND-USE DECISION ENVIRONMENT

Analysis of the land-use decision environment requires first a realistic view of the key participants involved.[1] These participants include, in general terms, the public sector, developers/investors or producers, and consumers or users. Any land-use decisions affecting a parcel of land will involve interaction between these three parties. This necessary interaction suggests a need for cooperation rather than confrontation; ultimately, the three groups must view themselves not as adversaries but as partners.

The participants must recognize the others' needs and be willing to work within a partnership atmosphere, even though specific goals may differ. Each must survive the short run and prosper through the long run if societal equilibrium in the development field is to be achieved.

Short-Run Considerations

The short-run considerations for each participant revolve around their cash management cycle. Developers must be able to meet their short-run cash needs and remain financially solvent in order to successfully complete the development process. This requires them to accurately estimate and control development expenditures, finance the expenditures, and complete the project on time.

The public sector participants are faced with a similar cash management problem. They also must be able to finance or fund public expenditures associated with development. For example, public services to a site usually must be provided. The initial costs of providing such services may exceed the revenue generated by property taxes from the locality. As a result, the municipality's master plan may seek to coordinate growth with the public sector's ability to provide and pay for public services.

Users or consumers of real estate must also operate within a cash management cycle. Owner-occupants and tenants must be able to pay the market price for the real estate they use. In the case of commercial real estate, users must be able to meet monthly rental payments and still earn a market profit on their own goods or services. Residential real estate users must be able to pay market prices for real estate services and still meet all other consumption and saving demands.

In the short run, then, land-use decisions affecting any site must recognize each participant's cash management needs. This does not suggest that one or two of the participants must cater to the specific needs or demands of the third, but rather that each must be aware of the role and responsibility of each of the others and be prepared to work within a partnership atmosphere.

---

[1] Much of the material in the following section was adapted and expanded on from a two-day workshop, "Real Estate Feasibility for the Appraiser," prepared by James A. Graaskamp and sponsored by the American Institute of Real Estate Appraisers.

Long-Run Considerations

Long-run constraints affecting the development participants revolve around the economic and cultural stability of the community within which development occurs. This long-run stability, or societal equilibrium, requires continued communication between the participants. Developers must make a lasting commitment to the community itself. That is, developers have a responsibility to the community to create or produce real estate services which will provide an acceptable environment in the long run. Community involvement and leadership in the political arena may be an example of such a commitment.

The public sector needs to plan for future growth taking into consideration expected demographic and economic changes. By determining where growth is likely to occur, the public sector is in a better position to encourage development and planning and provide the necessary "infrastructure" to support future real estate needs.

Users or consumers of real estate also participate in and contribute to societal equilibrium. This requires an active contribution to the development of local land use policy. Users can also support less specific policy decisions made in the public sector which affect the overall attractiveness and/or economic health of the community. Examples might include support of a public transportation system or of the construction of housing geared to the needs of "senior citizens."

Clearly, there are trade-offs between short- and long-run considerations. The developer has limited resources, and certain public officials face periodic reelection challenges. Short-run pressures cannot be ignored, but neither can they be allowed to totally dominate longer-term considerations. (In the Part IX, possible "changes in the rules" will be considered to assure that this is the case.)

SITE AND PARTICIPANT RELATIONSHIPS

Each participant in the land-use decision process must interact with each of the other participants and, of course, with the site itself. These relationships reflect the fact that the participants rely upon one another in many ways in an effort to successfully develop a particular site. Responsibilities, decisions, and services contributed and/or received by each participant must be recognized as the culmination of extensive cooperation between the participants. Figure 21A-1 represents a simplified representation of the participants' relationship to each other and to the site.

Public Sector/Site Relationship

The fundamental relationship between the public sector and the site is dominated by the provision of services to the site and the implementation of policy decisions affecting the site, as indicated by ① in Figure 21A-1. In return, the site represents the basis for levying real estate taxes which

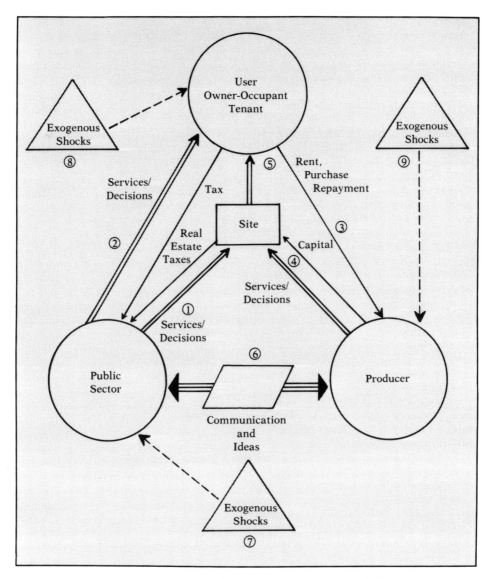

**Figure 21A-1. SIMPLIFIED SITE AND PARTICIPANTS'
RELATIONSHIP**

finance the many services provided to the site. Services provided by the public sector to the site would normally include police and fire protection, utilities, schools, libraries, roadway maintenance, etc. Policy decisions affecting the site would include master planning, zoning, building codes, environmental controls, and capital improvement programs, to name a few. The combination of the availability of public services and the implementation of policy decisions may encourage, discourage, or even preclude development.

Public Sector/User Relationships

The relationship between the public sector and the user, as indicated by ② in Figure 21A-1, concentrates on policy decisions affecting and services offered to the user and tax payments and political input directed to the public sector. Services provided directly to the user include health facilities, schools, transportation, recreational facilities, etc. Policy decisions which affect the user might include utility charges, neighborhood zoning decisions, and tax rate decisions. The user pays real estate, personal property, sales, and income taxes. These funds are used to finance public sector operations.

Users also provide, or should provide, a great deal of input to the public sector. Such input is directed to the public sector through the elective process and through direct participation in government. This government participation may be achieved through service on appointed boards and commissions or lobbying for specific legislation.

User/Producer Relationships

User and producer relationships are developed through the market system. Rental levels and purchase prices are the result of the interaction of supply and demand for real estate service within the marketplace, as indicated by ③ in Figure 21A-1. Relative increases in profits may stimulate new development while relative declines would discourage new development. The microlevel essentials of this important interface were discussed in Chapters 9, 10, and 11.

Producer/Site Relationships

The relationship between the producer and the site is presented by ④ in the figure. This relationship is dominated by services and policy decisions of the producer which affect the site and the capital applied to the site by the producer. The services and decisions affecting the site include development concept, design, and actual construction. Capital applied to the site includes materials, labor, and management skill.

User/Site Relationships

As indicated by ⑤ in Figure 21A-1, the primary relationship between the user and the site is represented by the net benefits which accrue to the user. These benefits may be either pecuniary or nonpecuniary and represent the utility derived from the site by the user. Pecuniary benefits could include increased sales due to location or design while nonpecuniary benefits might include prestige associated with the site.

Public Sector/Producer Relationships

The relationship between the public sector and the producer is represented by ⑥ in the figure. This relationship is perhaps the least understood and recognized of all of the relationships. With the recent increase of public sector influence in the development process, difficulties emerged which have tended to put the two participants in an adversary position. The primary relationship between the public sector and the producer includes communication and an exchange of ideas. In general, however, this necessary two-way communication is informal at best and nonexistent at its worst. The idea exchange portion is many times even less developed than the communication process.

Producers may perceive the public sector as merely representing a series of obstacles to development. The public sector may perceive the producers as being insensitive to macro-socioeconomic issues as they pursue profit at all costs. Naturally, neither of these perceptions represents the typical attitude of the participants. In fact, in most cases, the participants are making what at least they consider to be an honest effort to be fair and responsive to the other's needs.

A major problem area in the relationship between the public sector and producers lies in the nature of their day-to-day interaction. In many instances the parties only communicate with one another when a problem arises. For example, a request for a zoning change may require interaction. This site or problem specific interaction is usually carried out through a fairly well-defined series of official steps. Application is made requesting the zoning change which is followed by review and recommendation by the public sector. During the process, both parties are aware of the fact that something is at stake. Many times, the applicant is requesting something that the public sector does not wish to grant. As a result, the parties are often placed in a direct adversary position. To remedy this situation there is a need to develop a parallel communication network or medium devoid of specific confrontation. This might include workshops sponsored by the public sector or by producers. Explanations of city growth management policy and producer involvement in the development of the growth policy can help provide understanding between the two parties.

EXOGENOUS SHOCKS TO THE PARTNERSHIP

In addition to the relationships among the public sector, producers and users, there exist potential exogenous shocks which affect how each of the participants is able to affect the site. These shocks are represented as triangles in Figure 21A-1. The shocks are external to the participants—that is the participants can respond or react to the shocks but do not initiate the shocks.

Exogenous Shocks to the Public Sector

Exogenous shocks affecting the public sector's impact upon land use decisions can be the result of several factors. Changes in elected officials may cause a change in policy regarding land-use decisions. This may come about via appointments to boards and commissions or through a change in support for certain policy decisions. As elected officials come and go over the years, local government's attitude toward land-use policy may change. These changes are usually not controlled by public sector administrators and therefore while the employees remain, the policies they must implement may vary.

Changes in key (nonelected) personnel may also cause changes in public sector land use decisions. For example, a new planning department head may recommend new policy guidelines for growth management. Other lower-level personnel changes may also cause changes, although probably to a lesser extent.

Citizen support of public sector land use policy could also affect specific programs. This type of exogenous shock does not necessarily result in personnel change but rather in attitudinal changes. For example, a desire for less government may result in a demand by citizens for tax cuts. Existing public sector land-use policy may require substantial expenditures of public funds generated by either taxes or bond proceeds. Unwillingness to approve tax increases or bond referendums could result in reduced public sector activity in land use policy areas.

These exogenous shocks are basically outside of the control of the individuals who make up the public sector. Still, public sector land use decisions must respond to such shocks on almost a continuous basis. Policy changes cause difficulties not only for the public sector but also for producers and users. Producers and users discover that the "rules of the game" have changed as reflected in land-use policies and guidelines.

Exogenous Shocks to Users

Owner-occupants and tenants are affected by a number of exogenous shocks. The majority of these shocks affect users' ability or willingness to pay for real estate services. Macro-economic changes which affect general economic activity, employment, and inflation can significantly affect user decisions. Corporate users will plan plant and office expansions based upon expectations of future economic growth. If their expectations are jolted by major economic changes, the response to the shock may greatly affect utilization of particular sites. Adverse economic news may cause a reduction in demand while optimistic news may increase demand.

An additional source of exogenous shocks may more directly affect individual users. These microshocks might include job transfers, promotions, loss of job, death, illness, or divorce. Each of these shocks, and many more not listed, can significantly alter personal land use decisions. Again, these shocks cannot normally be controlled, but they elicit a response.

Exogenous Shocks to Producers

Exogenous shocks which adversely affect producers could develop in the market place in general and thus affect all producers, or develops so as to affect an individual producer. Market shocks generally would have relatively the same impact upon all producers. These shocks would include the same macro-economic changes which affect users. Increases in unemployment and inflation can directly affect producers on both the supply and the demand side. In the supply area, inflation increases cost which must be passed onto the ultimate consumer. On the demand side, unemployment can reduce demand for real estate services.

Micro-exogenous shocks which might affect individual producers would include such factors as increased competition, major local employer relocations, and producer-employee labor problems. Policy decisions instituted by the public sector may also materially affect a producer's ability to develop a site in a certain manner. These factors would include growth policy, zoning decisions, and local ordinances affecting development. Finally, changes in a producer's financial strength may limit his ability to attract adequate financing for future projects. This could occur if several projects failed and, as a result, the track record of the developer was damaged.

IMPLICATIONS FOR THE PARTICIPANTS

The issues just outlined demonstrates the need to develop relationships among the participants which have not traditionally been in evidence. The public sector, producers, and users must realize that they are partners in the growth and development of a community and therefore need to establish a framework for the partnership to develop. Because of the nature of decisions made by the public sector affecting a particular site (and the organizational form of the public sector), the public sector has the greatest responsibility in developing this partnership.

Of course, users contribute to the partnership through the market system and through public forums and involvement in government activities. However, users are generally not organized structurally as well as the public sector or producers. As a consequence users generally cannot provide the physical framework for partnership development.

Public sector and producer responsibility in the development of the partnership lie in the area of communication and idea exchange. Many past attempts have been unsuccessful because the producer was ill prepared. The concept of a public-private partnership requires a forum to be created to enable the producer to understand public sector requirements for development. This could be facilitated through workshops, seminars, and informal presentations where the public sector and interested producers discuss development policy.

The development of such a framework of cooperation may require the creation of a new professional role in the land use decision environment.

This new role might be filled by government relations specialists who act as consultants to both the public sector and producers. Such specialists could concentrate on providing the linkage necessary to advance communication and idea exchange between the participants. The specialist would need to be versatile enough to effectively empathize with both the public sector and the producer. The development of this kind of expertise would be a natural and useful extension of the role of a market and economic feasibility analyst. In fact, the input of a land use government relations specialist should become an integral part of the total real estate feasibility analysis.

Given the emerging relationship between the public and private sector, it is necessary to develop a feasibility study format which addresses all of the complex issues affecting modern real estate investment and development. The real estate analyst must incorporate the short- and long-term needs of the three participants cited above in terms of their interaction with each other and the site. This becomes a prerequisite of feasibility analysis since it is becoming more and more difficult to successfully develop a site without taking all of the participant's constraints into consideration.

In the sections which follow, a framework for detailed real estate feasibility analysis is presented. The framework relies on two interdependent studies: (1) market and (2) economic. It is within the market study segment of the feasibility report that the relationship between the public sector, user, developer, and site are analyzed. The economic study combines this information in a discounted cash flow framework. Figure 21A-2 presents an outline of a complete feasibility analysis along with suggested sources of data.

ROLE OF THE MARKET STUDY

The role of the market study in the land-use decision environment is to provide all the data necessary to allow the real estate analyst to make an informed investment decision about a specific project. The economic study then uses these data to determine if the proposed project appears to be a viable investment. The resulting investment decision can be to reject the project, accept it, or modify it. The market study itself must disaggregate the data sources in Figure 21A-2 in such a way that they relate to a specific situation since in most instances, land-use feasibility analysis deals with a specific site, user, and investor/developer. In other words, macrodata must be related to a microsituation.

The perspective of the market study will depend on the purpose of the analysis. In general, the analyst is faced with one of four scenarios:

- A site in search of a use.
- A use in search of a site.

Feasibility Outline	Data Sources	
I. Market study		
A. Regional and urban analysis		
1. Regional economic activity	Federal Reserve district banks	(1, 2)
2. Economic base analysis	Major financial institutions	(1, 2)
3. Population analysis	State economic agencies	(1, 2, 6)
4. Income analysis	U.S. Bureau of the Census	(3, 4)
5. Transportation networks		
6. Growth and development patterns	State and local chambers of commerce	(1, 2, 3, 4, 5, 6)
	University bureaus of business research	(1, 2, 3, 4, 5)
	State real estate research centers	(1, 2, 3, 4, 6)
	Major city planning departments	(6)
	State department of highways	(5)
B. Site analysis		
1. Zoning and building codes	Local planning departments and commissions	
2. Utility	Local utility companies	
3. Access	Local highway department and transportation offices	
4. Size and shape	Plat records	
5. Topography	Survey, soil samples	
C. Demand analysis		
1. Competition	Survey, market knowledge	
2. Demographic	U.S. Bureau of the Census	
3. Trend analysis	Building permits, starts, and zoning change requests	
D. Supply analysis		
1. Vacancy rates and rental levels	Survey, local appraisers	
2. Starts and building permits	Building permits, starts and zoning change requests	
3. City services	Survey, planning departments	
4. Community planning	Planning department	
5. Construction cost/financing	Local builders, financial institutions	
II. Economic study		
A. Before-tax cash flow	Complete discussion of economic analysis can be found in Chapter 18	
1. Gross possible rents	} Market survey, appraiser, property managers	
2. Vacancy and bad debt		
3. Operating expenses		
4. Net operating income		
5. Debt service	Survey of Financial institutions	
B. After-tax discounted cash flow		
1. Depreciation		
2. Tax liability		
a. Ordinary income	Investors criteria and tax law	
b. Capital gain	(see Chapter 16)	
C. Present value and justified investment price	See Chapter 18	
D. Yield or internal rate of return	See Chapter 18	
E. Invest—do not invest decision	See Chapter 18	

Figure 21A-2. FEASIBILITY OUTLINE AND DATA SOURCES

- Capital in search of an investment.
- An existing development.

While these four scenarios will affect the nature of the market study, the basic objective of the study always is to provide the data necessary for making an informed decision. The data collection process will focus upon four areas: (1) regional (area) analysis, (2) site analysis, (3) demand analysis, and (4) supply analysis.

Regional Analysis

The purpose of the regional analysis is to provide information which will highlight the activity—past, present, and future—in the *region* which the study encompasses. The region might be a state, SMSA, county, or city. The key elements of the regional analysis will include:

☐ *Impact of the national economy upon the region.* For example, how would a nationwide recession affect the region? What is the role of the region in the national economy?

☐ *Economic base analysis.* The region is analyzed as a separate economy. What industries dominate the economy? What is their impact upon demand for service and eventually the demand for space? What does the future of the economic base look like?

☐ *Population analysis.* Population changes and trends can indicate market strengths and weaknesses. Migration patterns, age, education, mobility, etc., should be evaluated.

☐ *Income levels.* Average income of the area, sources of income, unemployment patterns, and new employment opportunities will affect the needs of the area.

☐ *Transportation.* Does the region act as a transportation hub or is it isolated? Check highway routes to various markets as well as train, air, and possible water service.

☐ *Growth or development patterns.* Is the region a growth-oriented area or has the growth leveled off? Where will future development occur and why?

Site Analysis

As the name implies, the site analysis deals with legal and physical characteristics of the site being evaluated. The following items must be considered before a site can be judged appropriate for development. (In the case of an existing development, these characteristics remain important and should not be overlooked.)

☐ *Zoning.* In almost all cities, zoning can be the key to site analysis. If demand exists for a particular use but the proper zoning cannot be obtained, the site cannot be utilized. A site requiring a zoning change is less attractive than a site which is properly zoned. The number of sites zoned for competitive space is also important.

☐ *Utilities.* All developed property requires certain minimum utility connections. Electric, gas, water, and waste water availability can be critical.

☐ *Access.* Lack of access to the site can severely limit its potential. The evaluation of accessibility usually focuses on immediate ingress and egress, but often also includes the position of the site relative to the local transportation arteries.

☐ *Size and shape.* In many instances, the size and shape of a parcel can limit its attractiveness as a developable site. Parking and site planning requirements can have a significant impact upon the success of any project.

☐ *Topographical considerations.* The vegetation, slope, load-bearing capacity, etc., of a site can greatly affect developmental potential. Severe slope may result in run-off problems which could result in flooding and damage the project.

Demand Analysis

Demand analysis involves evaluation of the market in an effort to estimate the *effective* demand for a particular real estate project. The first step is to define the market itself. This can be done on the basis of geographic limits and property type. After the market has been defined, the next step is to evaluate the forces which influence demand. These would include the following matters:

☐ *Competition.* A survey of the market area must be made to determine existing and planned competition. Such a survey would include the location, rental level or sales price, vacancy, etc., of each comparable project.

☐ *Demographic analysis.* The characteristics of the population surrounding the site can indicate consumer preferences in the area. Income, age, etc., are important factors when analyzing residential and retail real estate developments. Although less important for office and industrial uses, demographic analysis can indicate available labor pools.

☐ *Trend analysis.* After evaluating the site's market, the analyst will find it necessary to forecast future demand. This is very important since feasibility analysis is a forward looking process which should help the decision maker evaluate a long-term investment.

In total, the demand analysis must provide the data necessary for the decision-maker to make the market segmentation and market share calculations described in Part IV.

Supply Analysis

Analysis of the supply side of the market requires that the analyst examine existing supply and expected future supply. Existing supply can be evaluated by an inventory of the market. The inventory should include current rents, vacancy rates, location, and amenities of each project. *Future* supply, expected additions to the market, can be estimated by examining the following areas:

☐ *Vacancy rates and rental trends.* Current vacancy rates can indicate future needs; e.g., high vacancy indicates current demand does not equal supply and vice versa. Rising rental rates can make future development at higher prices feasible.

☐ *Starts and building permits.* Construction starts indicate additions to supply in the near future while recorded building permits indicate projects soon to be built.

☐ *Availability of government services.* Utilities may again be the key here; i.e., the absence of utilities can severely restrict supply. Transportation and other government services may also affect supply.

☐ *Comprehensive community planning.* The attitude and policy of the local planning department may be designed to encourage or discourage certain types of development in specific areas. For example, industrial development may be concentrated in one area and forbidden in another.

☐ *Construction cost trends and available financing.* Rapidly rising construction costs can limit future supply if rental rates are not expected to rise. Available financing can be a factor in encouraging or discouraging additions to supply. If interest rates are high, residual cash flow will be adversely affected—thus discouraging construction.

ROLE OF THE ECONOMIC STUDY

After having completed the market study, the analyst's next step in a total feasibility analysis is to carry out an economic study. The economic study utilizes the data collected in the market study to evaluate the potential profitability of the investment development. The discounted cash-flow model presented in Chapter 18 presents the detailed framework of the mechanics of an economic study. Just as the market study was designed to evaluate the acceptability of the project in a market sense, the economic study will be designed to evaluate the attractiveness of the project in an economic sense. This is a key part of feasibility analysis. Although there may be significant demand for a particular project as revealed in the market study, the economic study may reveal that market rents may not be sufficient enough to justify the investment.

The economic study can be broken down into four major areas. First, a cost analysis will indicate the estimated total capital required for the project and the breakdown between land and improvements. Next, a simple single-period before-tax cash-flow pro forma will be developed. This statement presents the analyst's estimates of what the first year's cash-flow statement is likely to be. Next, this pro forma is expanded to an after-tax discounted cash-flow present value analysis. This process, as described in Chapter 18, provides the investor with a feeling for the project's expected performance over time and an estimated maximum offering price or investment value. Finally, a yield or rate of return analysis and ratio analysis is prepared. These last two steps collectively allow the analyst to recommend decision options to the developer and eventually to the investor.

Cost or Purchase Price

An important part of the economic study deals with the cost or purchase price of the proposed investment. Since investment value (for an income property) is a function of income, a justified cost or purchase price cannot exceed the investment value—that is, if sufficient rent is *not* generated, the cost of the project is not justifiable. In the case of a project to be developed, the cost estimate of the improvements plus the purchase price of the land represent the project cost. It should be stressed that actual costs should be used whenever possible. However, since all costs cannot be known before a project is built, estimates must be made by the developer or architect.

In the case of an existing project, the asking price is generally used as a surrogate for the purchase price. The economic study then proceeds to evaluate the reasonableness of the asking price—that is, is the project overpriced or underpriced?

SUMMARY

A market and economic study can be combined to provide the real estate decision-maker with a complete feasibility analysis. The relationship between the public sector and the developer, too often ignored, is a critical portion of the analysis. This relationship should be carried out as a partnership rather than an adversary relationship if the project is to have the maximum chance of success.

IMPORTANT TERMS

anchor tenant
construction
  manager
hard-dollar costs

pro forma
retainage
soft-dollar costs
tenant allowances

REVIEW QUESTIONS

21-1. It has been suggested that the development process can be viewed as seven interactive stages. How do the various development activities interact?

21-2. List and discuss the seven stages of the development model suggested in Chapter 21.

21-3. What is retainage? How does this practice protect construction lenders?

21-4. What sources of data may be relied upon in developing a pro forma operating statement for a new income producing property? In which of the development stages should this data be collected.

21-5. Why might a developer utilize a land option to gain control of property in the idea refinement stage?

21-6. Why does the developers role change from one of a promoter to a manager in the construction stage?

21-7. Why might it be advisable to execute the permanent loan commitment and major tenant leases at the same time.

21-8. Would it be advisable to have a promotion or advertising manager on site prior to opening a new development? Why?

21-9. Why might a developer be willing to offer very attractive lease concessions to an anchor tenant in a new shopping center.

21-10. What might be the impact on the value of land adjacent to a new shopping center development? What might a developer do to take advantage of the situation?

IX
Public Policy

22

Government Involvement

P ROBABLY THE MOST logical reason for a government role in the real estate industry is the macroeconomic importance of the industry. As noted in Chapter 1, over half of all private domestic investment is involved in real property development. Over two-thirds of the tangible assets of the country are real property assets. Ten to fifteen percent of gross national product (GNP) and a significant portion of national employment are directly related to the real estate industry. Since the government itself represents over 20 percent of GNP and is a major employer, it makes sense that each would play a role in the other's activities.

Additionally, real estate services represent one of modern man's basic needs, in terms of both shelter and commerce. Individuals interact continuously with the concept of real property. The exact nature of this interaction varies (e.g., an igloo versus a high-rise apartment), but the concept of real property and the basic need it satisfies remains the same.

PUBLIC POLICY OBJECTIVES

In an economic sense, government policy can generally be said to seek balanced growth, acceptable inflation, low unemployment, and a better quality of life for all. In the pursuit of these general goals, the real estate industry has an important role. Since the industry is so large, its performance has an effect on the overall performance of the economy. In fact, over the past few decades, the real estate industry has been a target of government monetary and fiscal policy aimed at achieving balanced growth and lower inflation. Many times, this effort has caused a reduction in the level of activity within the real estate industry or has been at the expense of growth within the industry. For example, during 1974-75 relatively high interest rates in the money markets caused funds to flow out of lending institutions (disintermediation) and was a major cause of the large downswing in the housing sector of the real estate industry. This contributed to the general slowdown in the economy and eventually helped reduce the rate of inflation.

Today, there is a greater awareness that this is a world of limited resources, and consequently, government has gone from a pure growth goal to an effort to preserve resources. A significant question for the real estate decision-maker is whether planning is compatible with the free enterprise system. Certainly, no market is completely free, but how many and what types of controls can be placed on a market before the marketplace ceases to function efficiently? Put another way, does planning result in a more efficient allocation of resources than market allocation, and is planning fairer to all the people than market allocation? These ideas should be kept in mind as the different government influences on land use decisions are examined. Answers to these questions will help us anticipate government action which can cause changes in the "rules of the game."

AREAS OF GOVERNMENT INVOLVEMENT AND RESPONSIBILITY

The Courts

The oldest form of control in the real estate industry is through litigation in the courts. Development in the past often proceeded without prior approval or permission. When a project was started which others felt might be damaging to them as individuals or to the whole community, little could be done except by a lawsuit "after the fact." Any legal remedy came from the *nuisance concept* under common law—the idea that one property owner could not unduly burden a neighbor's property. As our economy became increasingly interrelated and as real estate development became more complex, litigation after the fact became an unsatisfactory method of control. It was more rational and efficient to require advance permission to avoid conflicting uses.

Advance permission was first evidenced through districting (an early form of zoning) in New York City in 1916. Today, advance permitting has gone beyond zoning and is also used to protect the environment and achieve more efficient overall land use. The courts have generally supported most of these permit systems. Further, the courts, both of their own initiative and through the enforcement of statutory laws, became actively involved in the real estate industry in efforts to prevent discrimination on the basis of both income and race. Remember that the enthusiasm of the courts for different government policy tools goes a long way in determining how effective they will be. Therefore, the decision-maker must be aware of both "new rules" and the courts' "interpretation" of these rules.

Public Goods

Government has a hand in the real estate industry simply because some goods are more efficiently owned or produced on a common basis. Even the most adamant free enterprise advocate would probably not suggest that highways be individually owned. It has been found to be most efficient to have the government be responsible for certain forms of transportation—specifically roads, waterways, airports, and, in some cases, railroads—and other elements of the infrastructure which are essential before significant real estate development can occur.

Energy production, while never a nationalized industry, has always been closely regulated and in some sense subsidized by government. Many utilities are municipally owned. Recreation areas are provided by all levels of government. Reservation of land for native Americans is considered a government function. Public education, public hospitals, and prisons are other areas where it has seemed most efficient to produce goods jointly. In other words, provision of common goods is a very significant government role which is generally accepted by society, even though there are questions as to the extent of this government role.

Environmental Protection

During the 1960s, the nation became more aware of the need to protect the environment. In the 1970s, this need became more acute as the nation recognized it was moving into an era of limited resources. Previously, certain natural resources were viewed by many to be free goods. That is, in an economic sense, their supply was considered to be unlimited and the assets as renewable. Water and air were the first of such "free" resources to be recognized as limited or scarce. Additionally, water and air were easily identifiable as public goods. It became the responsibility of government to limit or prohibit activities which infringed the general public's right to clean air and clean water. This is a very sensitive area since much of the nation's industrial activity involves air and water pollution. So while it is generally accepted that the government should have a role in protecting the environment, just how clean the air and water should be is a hotly debated topic.

As in many areas of government impact in the real estate industry, two major trade-offs must be recognized and dealt with. First, individual rights versus public rights are often the centerpiece of environmental questions affecting real estate decision-making. The questionable areas usually revolve around limiting or restricting individual rights in order to protect the rights of the public. For example, if a river flows through a property, can the owner expel pollutants into the water which will adversely affect the owners downstream? Do public rights supersede individual rights? Recent trends have generally favored public over individual rights.

Second, a significant trade-off relationship can be identified in the area of economic activity and environmental protection. The cost and implementation of environmental protection measures can be expensive and time-consuming. During periods of slow economic growth, certain environmental protection measures might unduly restrict economic development. At such times, decisions must be made as to what is most important—economic growth or environmental protection.

The Tax System

Both the production of public goods and the provision of public services require funding. In order for the government to function, certain resources must be committed to the public sector. In Part VI, the different types of taxes collected by different levels of government were described. If government has a clear role or responsibility to provide certain public goods as well as to enforce certain regulations, then it just as clearly has a right to raise the necessary capital to do so. The question becomes who should pay for the common goods?

Since taxes perform not only a revenue raising function, but also an economic planning function, the question also involves what economic activities should be encouraged or discouraged through the tax laws. The question is broadened when one considers whether the goal should be fairer taxation[1] or taxation designed to help the general economy.

Consumer Protection

As the world has become ever more complex, government has come to provide certain consumer protection as part of its general role of overseeing the public's health and well-being. In the real estate industry, this takes many forms including licensing salespersons and requiring lenders to disclose fully all the costs associated with financing. In the real estate development and investment areas, government responsiveness to neighborhood associations and tenant groups has often resulted in limits on the right to use property (e.g., to convert from rental to condominium operation) and to earn a market return from property (e.g., rent control).

Data Collection

Data collection has also come to be accepted as a legitimate role of government. In order to assess taxes, the government must have tax rolls (i.e., lists of property owners). In order to design programs which serve the needs of the people, the government must collect pertinent information about housing patterns, family income, etc. In the development area, a significant amount of market resource data is available from the federal government, which maintains not only results of the national census, but also large amounts of regional and national economic information.

---

[1] And does this mean a progressive tax where those more able to pay carry a greater share of the load or a regressive tax which might encourage savings and hence investment?

Housing

As indicated earlier, one of the basic human needs is shelter. Some have suggested that a deteriorating physical environment can aggravate social and economic problems and contribute to an increasing incidence of crime and violence. For these reasons, many—but by no means all—citizens see a government role in dealing with shelter needs not adequately satisfied in the private market. In the United States, this concern has led to the development of housing programs that meet the needs of specific groups. Performance in this area is difficult to measure, most would agree that such programs have met with some success.

Coordination

Finally, the government, of necessity, has assumed a coordination function. In the private sector, this evolved naturally as the nuisance law concept gave way to advance planning and permitting. In addition to coordinating private sector activities, the government has begun to try to coordinate its own activities. This is possibly an even more difficult problem. Between levels of government and within levels of government, significant conflicts arise both of a political and a practical nature. Coordinating government activity in our political system is a far from simple task.

LOCAL PLANNING TOOLS

Most land use regulation under the police powers has come at the local level as authorized by state enabling statutes. Essentially, there are three primary regulatory tools: (1) the zoning ordinance, (2) the subdivision ordinance, and (3) the building code. Other important tools are: (4) growth planning programs, (5) the provision of public goods, and (6) taxation.

Zoning

Zoning involves the use of both a *map* and a *text*. The subject area is mapped into a series of zones or districts which are classified as residential, commercial, industrial, and in some cases as combinations of the three. In most cities these classifications are subdivided; for example, several types of residential development may be allowed in different zones of the city. The text then describes the specific use allowed in each of these classifications. The allowed intensity of use in each of these classifications is also described in the text as are associated parking provisions, etc.[2] (See Figure 22-1.)

---

[2] Note that counties and even states may also have zoning ordinances.

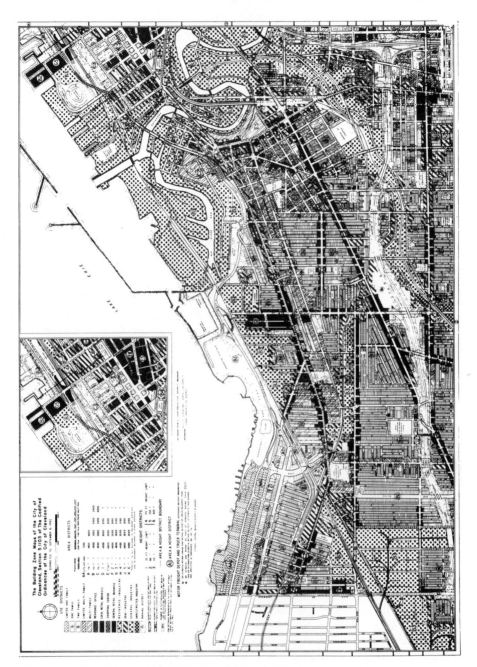

Figure 22-1.   ZONING ORDINANCE—CLEVELAND, OHIO

The first court test of zoning, in 1926, concerned an ordinance in Euclid, Ohio. An application to have property rezoned to multifamily residential from single-family residential was denied. The owner sued, claiming an unfair government taking against which citizens are protected by the Fifth and Fourteenth Amendments to the U.S. Constitution. The case eventually reached the U.S. Supreme Court, which ruled that refusal of a municipal government to rezone, so long as the refusal was logically based, did not constitute a taking requiring compensation. Following this decision, the Supreme Court was silent on zoning matters until the 1970s when a number of important court decisions were rendered. These decisions created standards which restricted the ways municipalities could use zoning ordinances, as is described in subsequent sections. (See 22-1.)

Subdivision Regulation

Subdivision regulation works in conjunction with zoning regulation to accomplish municipal land-use objectives. Subdivision ordinances set out minimum standards for the subdivision of land which is to be developed. In most areas, the subdivision cannot be platted (recorded in the title records as a subdivision) unless it meets certain standards.

The logic behind subdivision regulation is that eventually the municipal government expects to assume responsibility for operation and maintenance of streets, sewers and sometimes utilities. Therefore, it is in the best interest of the public if these facilities meet certain minimum standards so as to be easily integrated at a future date with existing municipal systems.

22-1. POLICE POWERS VERSUS CONDEMNATION

Note the distinction between accomplishing government goals through zoning and by use of the power of eminent domain. Eminent domain requires compensation while zoning does not. Governments thus find it financially more feasible to use zoning wherever possible. However, from the perspective of private property rights, zoning may involve the loss of rights without compensation.

How much can the government take through zoning before it is, in law, condemning property? In other words, how much can a city accomplish through zoning without paying? The general rule is that government can *downzone* (zone to a less intensive and hence less profitable use) without paying compensation so long as the downzoning is consistent with an overall master plan. However, when the zoning becomes so extensive as to involve the actual taking of an easement (such as air rights around an airport) or to completely eliminate the potential for development, then zoning is not allowed. In such cases, eminent domain must be used, and the private owner must be compensated.

In many areas, the law allows municipalities to control development which is occurring beyond the city limits—in effect, providing the municipality with extraterritorial jurisdiction (ETJ). The ETJ frequently ranges from two to five miles beyond the corporate city limits. Since zoning requirements apply only within the city limits, subdivision requirements may represent the only type of municipal control which can affect development within the ETJ.

Building Codes

Building codes are another way to protect the public health and safety, most particularly to avoid structural defects and fire hazards that can cause injury and loss of life. Building codes in most areas require that inspections be made during the development process to assure that minimum safety standards are being incorporated in the construction of the project.[3]

Growth Planning

As noted in Chapter 1, there is a growing awareness in the country that a period of limited resources has begun. In light of this, government at various levels is expanding its advance planning, while the courts are cooperating by showing an increasing willingness to uphold municipal regulation that limits private property rights. Remember that the permitting system overlaps, to some extent, the zoning ordinance. That is, in addition to satisfying the zoning ordinance, the developer must obtain specified permits. Through the zoning ordinance and the permitting system, growth policy consistent with the master plan may be achieved.[4] The assorted permitting systems have become so complex and intertwined that many developers complain that a disproportionate amount of time and effort goes into meeting sometimes conflicting government standards.

---

[3] It should be noted that in addition to the laudable goal of protecting public health and safety, building codes have in the past often protected existing monopolies. This has resulted because certain building codes were written not to require minimum standards, but rather to require certain specific materials and construction techniques. In other words, rather than saying a certain type of multifamily unit must have a thirty-minute fire wall between each unit, some building codes stated that a particular material installed in a particular way must be used. In the latter case, those involved in the supply and installation of that material were, in some sense, granted a monopoly. Further, the incorporation of cost saving innovations in the construction process has been slowed by such restrictive building codes.

[4] One of the most far-reaching and imaginative regional master plans is the Year 2000 Plan in Washington, D.C.

Provision of Public Goods

In addition to direct regulation, it is clear that government, especially local government, influences land use decisions through provision of public goods. All three levels of government are involved in transportation and in the location of their own operating facilities. In providing for these public goods, the various levels of government often use the power of *eminent domain*. As noted in Chapter 5, the power of eminent domain permits government to take private property for a public purpose provided fair value is paid. It would be impossible, for example, to have an efficient national highway system without allowing the government such power.

The key question in eminent domain cases is the exact amount of fair compensation for property condemned. The three basic approaches to value are utilized; but, in addition to judgmental questions involving the determination of value, timing questions are also important. If the government announces the construction of a major transportation artery, land around that particular location normally will increase in value. The owner of the condemned land is entitled to its value before, not after, the announcement. Similarly, if a government condemns a site as a nuclear power waste dump, surrounding land values are likely to decrease in value, but the land owner is entitled to receive the value of his property before the announcement of the proposed use.

The provision of public utilities and services often is used by local governments to control the direction of growth. This is based on the assumption that new growth is discouraged in areas where municipal services do not meet the needs of new development. Capacity limitation can be the result of existing heavy use (e.g., a sewer main has reached its capacity) or of lack of services (e.g., no sewer system serves a particular area). In either case, the decision to expand or extend service involves high fixed costs. The municipality must examine the trade-off between the cost involved and the desire to accommodate or encourage growth. This decision often can be very difficult for government to make but very profitable for the private sector if correctly anticipated.

Taxation

The federal, state and local governments are able to provide public service in part because of the power to levy property taxes. In a real estate context, the property tax is not only a revenue tool but also a land planning tool.[5] Recall that local government has a first lien on the property for

---

[5] As noted in Part VI, the income tax is also an economic planning tool. Specific provisions of the Internal Revenue Code definitely encourage certain types of real estate investment and development.

unpaid taxes. Government can (when combining high property taxes with rent controls) in effect eliminate residual equity cash flow. This has been the case in many parts of New York City. Taxing away the equity value is generally not thought to be wise from either an individual equity standpoint (fairness) or a public benefit perspective. However, the property tax can be used as an effective land planning tool in relatively free markets. In other words, property taxes can be used to encourage certain types of socially beneficial development.

Certain variances on the basic property tax framework described in Part VI can be used to accomplish public goals. In the basic property tax scheme, both land and buildings in the taxing district are valued. The total value constitutes the property tax base of the particular taxing authority. A tax rate then is set based on the revenue sought to be raised. One problem with most property tax systems is that vacant land may not be taxed as heavily as improved property. Thus, development is penalized and speculative holding of raw land is encouraged. As municipal governments experience increasing costs for municipal services, they must seek ways to provide such services more efficiently.

☐ *In-fill incentives.* One serious problem in rapidly developing areas has been "leap-frogging." This occurs when developers skip close-in land to develop property in outlying areas of the municipality. Developers usually leap-frog because land closer to the urban center is often much more expensive. (One reason is that public services are available.) From a public policy standpoint, it is much more desirable for land already serviced by municipal facilities to be developed than outlying areas which require the extension of municipal services. Thus, local governments are concerned with ways to create *in-fill incentives*—that is, inducements to developers to use land in the central city, thus avoiding urban sprawl and reducing the cost of providing municipal services.

☐ *Site value taxation.* One possible way is *site value taxation.* In site value taxation, the property tax base includes land only and ignores any improvements. As a result, the overall tax base is lower, requiring a higher tax rate to achieve the same total revenues. This means that vacant land will be taxed at higher rates than under the standard system while developed land has a lower tax. Consequently, holders of raw land will see their carrying burden increase—cash outlays will rise even though the land generates little if any revenue. Site value taxation is supposed to encourage, if not force, landowners in the central city to develop their land. Site value taxation would presumably lessen the attractiveness of land on the fringe of the city and, consequently, help achieve the objective of reducing the cost of providing municipal services.[6]

---

[6] Few major urban areas are currently using site value taxation, although the idea is part of the literature that is being studied in many cities.

☐ *Value in use taxation.* Another approach to property taxation is *value in use taxation.* Under this approach, land is taxed based on its current use rather than its highest and best use. In this way, naturally productive lands in agriculture or forestry are kept free from development. For example, farmland on the boundary of a major urban area may have significant development potential. Its highest and best use (the use which produces the highest residual value to the land) is most often a development use, not an agricultural use. Under standard property tax system, the farmer pays taxes based on the value of the land for development purposes. This may force a sell-out even though this is not in the public interest. Consequently, many local governments have passed provisions allowing for value in use taxation for agriculture and, in some cases, for forestry. These provide that so long as the land is used for the particular productive purpose, it will be taxed according to its value in use and not according to its highest and best use.

Consider what might happen from a combination of more restrictive zoning, site value taxation, and value in use taxation. Assume that a city zones a small amount of land for development. Then through site value taxation, the city seriously encourages the owners of that land to develop it. (In fact, in such situations, the cost of not developing could be prohibitive.) Then, through value in use assessment, the government makes it easier for surrounding landowners (farmers) to keep their land in agricultural production. If they allow their land to be rezoned, the property taxes increase very significantly. The combination of these three items would allow the government to determine to a great extent exactly where development would occur. This would certainly help accomplish the purpose of reducing the cost of providing municipal services; however, it would also remove land use decisions from the marketplace. A government official or agency would make the decisions which the market previously made. The question becomes "are the benefits from reduced municipal service costs sufficient to offset the less efficient allocation which would result from removing marketplace controls?"[7]

FEDERAL CONTROLS

In addition to the foregoing controls, which are usually enacted by local government (jointly in some cases with state government), other controls are imposed by the federal government. These controls are at times enforced by the federal government directly and at other times are combined with local and state planning tools and enforced at those levels.

---

[7] Removing the development decision from the marketplace and placing it in the hands of a government agency seems very foreign to most Americans; this has, in fact, been done in many if not most Western European countries.

Environmental Protection

In the 1960s, the general public became more concerned with environmental issues. Reacting to this concern, various levels of government passed statutes requiring certain forms of environmental protection and/or conservation. Most of these statutes involve some type of local land use planning, coupled with a permitting system to assure the minimization of environmental damage from development. At the national level, the U.S. Environmental Protection Agency (EPA) was created by the National Environmental Policy Act (NEPA). After this, in rapid succession, air, water, and noise amendments to the basic statute were enacted. The specific inclusion of land use plans in these amendments illustrates once again how important land is in the general economic and social framework of the nation.

While environmental legislation may not seem to be directly related to land use, implementation of environmental protection usually requires specific land use controls. In the case of the clean air amendments to NEPA, automobile usage was cited as an indirect but troublesome source of pollution. Based on this, local governments were directed to develop land use plans which would minimize automobile trips and so reduce air pollution.

The water amendments were aimed at both direct and nonpoint sources of water pollution. In addition to requiring all dumping into public waterways to meet certain standards, these amendments cited numerous types of land use (even agricultural) as nonpoint sources of pollution. In cases where waterways did not meet certain minimum standards, no additional development was permitted which would in any way affect the quality of water. In other words, development was prohibited if the water did not meet a certain standard, even if the new development did less environmental damage than existing development.

Last in the EPA trilogy are the noise amendments. These have not received the vigorous federal support given the air and water rules. It is interesting to note that conflicts can arise among these amendments. For example, a municipality considering a new airport must be concerned with meeting environmental standards. The clean air rules, in light of the automobile as an indirect source of pollution, would support an airport site close to the most populous areas of the city, thus limiting the length of automobile trips. On the other hand, the rules pertaining to noise would point to a site far from the city so that the fewest number of people would be burdened with the earthshaking sounds associated with jet aircraft. This is merely one illustration of numerous possible conflicts at various levels of government.

Note also that environmental legislation begins at the federal level but requires local enforcement through local land use planning. The courts have been particularly active in this area as well. Courts have supported and, in some cases, gone beyond specific enabling legislation to assure that underlying objectives of the environmental legislation are promoted through local planning and permitting systems.[8]

Urban Renewal

The Urban Renewal Program was designed to alleviate slum conditions. Essentially, it provided that the federal government would provide the bulk of the funds needed to enable local governments to (1) buy up slum properties (under eminent domain if necessary), (2) demolish the slums, and (3) sell the land at below-market prices to private developers. The underlying justification for the program was that the private marketplace could not achieve the rehabilitation of large slum areas without some form of subsidy. Private developers would probably be unable to obtain the necessary financing. And without the power of eminent domain, the possibility was very real that one or more landowners would refuse to sell, thus preventing comprehensive redevelopment. Most important, there could be no assurance that the redeveloped properties would generate sufficient cash flow to permit a satisfactory return on the large investment required.

The program looked good on paper but was, in practice, a relative failure. The unfortunate result was that many poor families were removed from neighborhoods where they had lived for many years without provision for new housing. Consequently, they crowded even more densely into the remaining slums. In later years of the urban renewal program, local government agencies were required to provide adequate housing for evicted persons. Further, regulations required that redevelopment of the area provide for at least as much low-income housing as was there originally. These two provisions eliminated some of the abuses of the earlier urban renewal program but greatly increased the cost. Land in the central city which was cleared and free of restrictive government regulations was very valuable to the private developer. However, the private developer would not pay as much for land when development required a certain amount of relatively unprofitable low-income housing. When local governments were forced to resell the land to the private sector at a lower cost and at the same time provide for housing the poor during the intervening period, the cost of urban renewal greatly escalated.

---

[8] The various amendments to the Environmental Policy Act are certainly not the only pieces of federal legislation involving environmental protection. The U.S. Department of Commerce's floodplain insurance is an attempt to force local areas to move development out of flood-prone areas. It is particularly interesting in that it is implemented partially by financial institutions.

The U.S. Department of the Interior manages the Coastal Zone Management Program, which affects the coastal areas of some thirty states and involves significant federal funding if the state is willing to plan and closely regulate development in hazardous and fragile areas along coastlines.

Low-Income Housing

Using even more direct methods, the U.S. Department of Housing and Urban Development (HUD) provides loans at below-market interest rates and direct rent subsidies to encourage provision of low-income housing. Changes in the myriad HUD programs occur rapidly, making documentation in textbook form very difficult. Our purpose will not be to look at any particular program, but to look at the general approaches that HUD has taken.

Under the old 236 program, HUD provided interest subsidies to developers of low-income, multifamily housing. This was done by HUD paying most of the interest on the mortgage, which was made by an institutional lender such as a savings and loan (S & L) association. Imagining the problems involved is not difficult. For example, what standards should apply to the housing? The developer-investor is likely to prefer to build more luxurious units (which are easier to rent) than many people might deem appropriate for subsidized housing. Further, what income limits should be set in determining who are low income families? It is not easy to audit the income of a tenant, particularly when family situations are in a state of flux.

Some of these problems were dealt with in later programs designed to provide interest rate subsidies in connection with financing for qualified low-income families to *purchase* single-family homes (235 program). This program was more expensive because the housing cost more. Problems arose because of the difficulty in determining who should be chosen to receive subsidy benefits since the government could not afford to provide subsidies to all low-income families.

Other HUD programs have provided for direct subsidies to tenants and, at the other extreme, for public housing—ownership by government agencies of units to be rented to low-income families. In total, the various HUD programs have provided jobs and stimulated investment. There are some questions, however, as to their long-run cost effectiveness.[9] (See 22-2.)

SUMMARY

Numerous tools are available to governments for use in accomplishing their diverse real-estate-related goals. Most of these tools imply some reduction in private property rights. They involve the federal, state, or local governments providing for the public benefit at a distinct cost to

---

[9] Today, most of the action in subsidized housing comes under the HUD Section 8 Program. The interested student should begin there in his search for which programs currently have funding.

22-2.   THE COURTS AND LOW-INCOME HOUSING

In the late 1960s and early 1970s, the courts became concerned about provisions for low-income housing. The U.S. Supreme Court, which chooses which cases it will hear based on the importance of the issues involved, had avoided zoning-related issues for nearly fifty years before the questions of low-income housing and racial discrimination brought zoning back to its attention. In general, the courts have recently taken a very active role, sometimes striking down municipal zoning ordinances on the basis that they restricted the amount of low-income housing which could be constructed.

In some cases, the federal courts moved in a different direction from state courts. This can occur because, unless some federal issue is involved, a state court ruling is not subject to review by the U.S. Supreme Court. The two most publicized and precedent-setting cases in past years have been the *Mount Laurel* and the *Arlington Heights* decisions. In the *Mount Laurel* case, the New Jersey Supreme Court stated that every municipality must make provision in its zoning ordi-nance for a fair share of the low-income housing which is needed in the region as a whole. Put another way, a municipality could not take a narrow view of its own housing requirements and ignore the needs of the region.

Contrasting with this decision is that of the U.S. Supreme Court in the *Arlington Heights* case. The Court said that mere evidence of segregation (note the implied correlation between low-income housing and racial dis-crimination) does not, in and of itself, mean that any particular zoning ordi-nance is discriminatory. The evidence must show that a zoning ordinance was intended to discriminate against particular income or racial groups, be-fore the ordinance is invalid. The two cases thus can be clearly distin-guished. On the one hand, the absence of zoning for low-income housing is sufficient to strike down restrictive zoning; on the other, intent must be proved. Contrasting decisions within the court system are quite obviously a problem to the real estate industry. However, they seem inevitable under the dual court system in the United States.

particular private interests. The basic rules of the real estate game must incorporate the government role in order to remit a complete understand-ing of the marketplace. Remembering that real property has a long eco-nomic life in a fixed location, one cannot ignore the possibility that the basic rules, and more likely the government role, will change over the holding period of the asset. Anticipating changes in the government role is difficult, but not impossible. It revolves around two considerations: what is fair and what makes the game more efficient. Politics distort these items over the short run, but over the long run those two considerations are the keys to successful decision-making.

IMPORTANT TERMS

building code
density
downzoning
eminent domain
in-fill incentive
infrastructure
land use regulation

"leap-frogging"
map
nuisance
plat
subdivision ordinance
upzoning
zoning ordinance

REVIEW QUESTIONS

22-1. Suggest a logical reason why the real estate industry might be a target for government programs and policies.

22-2. In an economic sense, what are the goals of government public policy?

22-3. What is the role of the court system in the area of real estate development?

22-4. Why might the production of "public goods" be handled more efficiently by the public sector as opposed to the private sector?

22-5. How might there develop a conflict between economic activity and environmental protection?

22-6. Under what circumstances might the rights of an individual landowner conflict with the rights of the public?

22-7. Discuss the dual dilemma of what public goods should be produced and who should pay for those public goods.

22-8. In general, what types of programs has the U.S. Department of Housing and Urban Development relied upon to encourage provision of low-income housing.

22-9. What is the likely impact of the development phenomenon called "leap-frogging"?

22-10. The National Housing Act established as a national goal the provision of "a decent home and suitable living environment for every American." Do you believe this is an achievable goal? If yes, how? If no, why not?

23
Ethics

CONSIDERATION AND ANALYSIS of the real estate industry and the various real estate markets would not be complete without a discussion of individual business ethics. As noted earlier, certain of the rules of the game are enforced in the courts. Others, however, can be enforced only by social and personal pressures. The real estate industry could not provide as great a package of benefits for society, with as much overall efficiency, if the players relied solely on the formal rules. Thus, personal ethics are important in making the game work.

PHILOSOPHICAL BACKGROUND

Philosophically, *ethics* can be defined, at least in part, as the individual's duty to society. In this sense, what is ethical depends on the particular society and precedents in that society. More simply, ethics can be called the "right way of living." Ethics involves a striving by the individual for the greatest good for the greatest number. As such, business ethics may conflict with pure profit motivation. An understanding of the implications and resolution of such conflicts is important to the real estate decision-maker.

American business practices are highly influenced by the Judeo-Christian ethic. Ethical behavior is defined by past precedent and a view toward what is good for society. In this regard, a trade-off exists between individual freedom (which our society encourages and defends) and what, in the last chapter, is defined as public rights. Our social ethic supports and protects individual freedom while striving to maintain the general public good. The public good, conversely, seeks to balance what is good business for the individual with efficient use of resources in a macroeconomic sense. In the final analysis, the social ethic is implemented at the individual level, and this is where attention is now focused.

ETHICAL CONFLICTS AND REAL ESTATE POLICIES

Ethical issues can have a significant impact on real estate patterns and on property values. Redlining is an example of such an issue. *Redlining* is defined as the supposed policy of a lending institution against making mortgage loans on any property within a specific geographic area (often, say critics of the practice, designated by a red line on a map). Usually, such neighborhoods are blighted slum areas where property values are low and are likely to remain so.

While few if any lenders admit to the arbitrary approach just described, most lenders argue that the application of sound lending and appraisal guidelines inevitably means that property owners in slum and near-slum neighborhoods have difficulty obtaining mortgages. The lenders say their primary responsibility is to protect the assets of the institution— that is, the funds deposited by persons seeking security for their savings.

If redlining lending policies are followed, many good properties located in otherwise unpromising neighborhoods are ignored. A flat refusal to make *any* loans eliminates any chance that the area will improve. Critics of lenders assume that (1) lending institutions have an ethical responsibility to help the cities in which they are located and to invest in areas from which they draw their deposits and (2) selective lending in blighted areas will produce sound assets and perhaps change the area.

What is the proper view of a lender's role? Can it be argued that, in the long run, if something is good for the city, it is good for its institutions—including those called on to finance and so risk loss of assets? Or should a lender think first of its depositors, many of whom are likely to favor a policy of avoiding loans carrying high risk? Suppose a lender does invest in a blighted area to the point that the area becomes prosperous and stable. Then, is the institution to be confronted with the ethical issue of having driven out the poor?

PRIVATE VERSUS PUBLIC RIGHTS

This issue is one of the role of business in society. Remember that the guiding hand works only when externalities are incorporated in the decision-making process. The physical environment and the social and cultural environment provide numerous examples which support this claim. However, will the allocation of resources in society be more efficient if there is greater emphasis on private rights or greater emphasis on public rights?

There *are* public rights, and it is the function of government to define and protect these public rights. However, it seems that the most efficient way to allocate resources in this society is to rely, wherever possible, on the free market. Profits serve to allocate capital by first serving as a reward for risk taking and second as a reward for efficient management. Profit therefore is not the goal, but the yardstick by which performance is measured. In terms of the real estate game, the player who ends up with the chips is the player who has taken risks and managed resources so as to enhance the wealth of society as a whole. Perhaps it is even fair to say that the individual or firm that is not making a profit (in the long run) is unethical—that is, not supplying goods and services for society as efficiently as possible.

The emphasis on private versus public rights is likely to shift back and forth as society responds to specific problems. Nevertheless, the marketplace is likely to remain the primary allocator of resources. In the short run, it may be possible to generate a profit through unethical behavior. However, particularly in real estate, a long-run approach is the better one. A long-run discounted present value definition of winning is used in this book, and, in the long run, the implied adherence to general social ethics is critical to winning.

INDIVIDUAL ETHICAL CONSIDERATIONS

A code of ethics, viewed in its most pragmatic light, is an effort to restrain individual conduct in the interests of a larger group. An ethical question arises only when there is a conflict between what an individual wants (or is directed) to do and what the ethical code directs. (See Appendix 10C for the code of ethics the National Association of Realtors® has set out for its membership.)

There is a certain logic in considering ethical questions in the abstract, as is done in the pages that follow. When faced with the daily pressures of business, many persons reach decisions on the basis of short-term consequences, whereas reflection at a calmer time might well yield different results. Lack of forethought about ethical questions makes rationalization easy—that is, finding reasons which justify a short-run profit decision and which "glosses over" the moral issue.

Certainly, there is no intention here to discuss a particular ethical code. It is possible, however, to suggest approaches that can help an individual test or evaluate a decision in a particular situation. Here are six tests which might prove useful when evaluating the ethics of a situation.

The first is the test of *common sense*. In this very simple approach, the question is asked whether the decision or action makes sense. What are the practical consequences? This requires that the decision be thought through to the ultimate conclusion. Thus, the long-run perspective is emphasized over the short-run consequences.

Another test is to determine if the action or decision will *hurt someone else*. For example, will the decision damage someone's reputation unjustifiably? Or, will the decision hurt someone in a financial sense? It is important to evaluate how your action will directly affect those involved.

A third possible test is an evaluation of how the decision affects the concept of one's *best self*. Psychologists say that a sense of self-esteem is vital to a person's mental health. Does the action fit in with the person's concept of himself at his best? If he has lowered his standards in order to come to a decision, it may be the wrong one.

Many times, a decision can be evaluated in terms of how the action would stand up to *public scrutiny*. If the action were made public through the media, could it stand up to the light of public knowledge? This test may be particularly applicable to the real estate industry since real estate decisions often directly involve the public good.

Another relatively simple test is that of *one's most admired personality*. Most people have someone whom they trust and look up to more than any other. How would that person evaluate the decision or action? If he would disapprove, perhaps reconsideration is in order.

The final test for evaluating ethical decisions is that of *foresight*. Before reaching a decision which involves an ethical question, one should evaluate all of its possible consequences. How will the contemplated action affect loved ones, co-workers, peers, and the public?

In the day-to-day world of the real estate industry, there exist conflicts of interest, ignorance and confusion, a lack of empathy, inconsistencies, human weaknesses, and inadequate formal standards. In light of these, it is useful to consider some possible real world situations. The examples which follow offer the opportunity for deciding on what is ethical behavior. There are no solutions to these issues presented in the book. Evaluate your decisions in terms of your own ethical standards.

Situation 1

Through hard work, you have risen to the position of controller of a real estate development firm. Your next goal is to become the financial vice-president. The company president indicates that he is looking for permanent financing on a new development project. Normally finding this financing is the job of the financial vice-president, but this time, the president wants to see if you can handle this task. He says that a representative of Mutual Mutual Mutual Insurance will be in the office the next day to discuss the project.

You are familiar with the project, having done the feasibility analysis. The lender's representative arrives, and three days are spent showing him the project and convincing him of the validity of the feasibility study. You know that the market rate of interest for this type of loan is 10.5 percent.

However, you are asking for 10 percent with the idea that you will negotiate up.

On the evening of the final day of the lender's representative's visit, you are having drinks and a final discussion. It appears that the representative is going to recommend to his company that they make the commitments you seek and at 10 percent. Your career is about to take off. You enjoy a second drink.

The lender's representative begins to talk about a problem he is having with one of his children. His daughter has been in college and has drug problems. The father feels that the only way to really pull her out is to get her closer to her family—in fact, to find a place up in the mountains where the family can go on weekends, be away from it all, and be together as they were in earlier years. He indicates that he has a particular cabin in mind but that he needs $10,000 for the down payment.

In the glow of the second drink, it finally comes through to you that he is asking you for $10,000. Suddenly, the meteoric rise in your career is in jeopardy. As controller, you know that you can pay the $10,000 without discovery by the auditors. You know your boss will not want to know about this situation, but he would be very happy to pay $10,000 on the side for this loan. The value to the company of the half-point lower interest rate far exceeds $10,000.

Do you say, "Well, I personally want to see you have that place in the country and I'll find a way to find you that $10,000," shake hands, put the man on the plane, and become the financial vice-president. Or do you stand up and say "You're asking for a bribe—get out!"

Obviously, there are some intermediate positions, but as you consider them, be careful that you are not rationalizing. You must make an immediate decision; what do you do? The lender's representative was quite clear. Between the lines he has said, "I will recommend this loan, and in all probability, it will be approved, if you find a way to get me that $10,000." You can do it and not get caught. In fact, you might even pay it out of your own pocket considering the benefits to you. What are the ethical issues? What are you going to do?

Situation 2

You are running your own real estate marketing firm and have just been engaged to handle the marketing (on an exclusive basis) of a major second home development. This is the biggest contract your firm has ever had. It promises commissions which will put you and most of your agents into the country club set.

You are seated at a meeting with the top officials of the development company. They are discussing a problem they are having with one section of the development. It appears the development company is installing its own water and sewer system and doing this through the creation of a municipal utility district. (The advantage of this is that the district can issue tax-free bonds to finance the system.) The problem is that one parcel of land in the development already is part of an existing water district. The developer cannot find a way to install the water and sewer system needed for the proposed development unless the existing water district releases the parcel in question and permits it to be incorporated into the new district.

The situation is somewhat complex and is shown in Figure 23-1. The existing water district has issued bonds to provide water service only. The envisioned development (which you will market) involves a much more extensive system with sewer services.

How is the land removed from one district and put in another? It is necessary that all the holders of the existing district's bonds release their claim on the land. They have no incentive to do this and the developer is not sure how to convince them.

A representative of the developer points out that the existing water district has one operating officer who wants to buy a lot in the new subdivision. The lot has not yet been platted, but it will probably be priced at about $20,000. The existing water district's operating officer has offered $4,000 for it while suggesting that he would use his influence to gain the release necessary from the bondholders. It appears to be an easy thing to cover, no one will ever see what has happened, but, in the back of your mind, you figure it out.

A bribe is being suggested by the officer of the water district to use his influence to induce bondholders to release certain land. While there is some logic in the land being part of the planned district, the release definitely reduces the collateral for the existing bonds. What can you do? You can keep quiet, let it happen, and make your money selling the lots. At the other extreme, you can go to the district attorney and report what you feel to be a bribe.

In deciding where you come down, you might consider what jobs are now held by the people who blew the whistle on other shady deals. You have done nothing wrong yourself, but you are aware of unethical behavior. What do you do?

SUMMARY

The last two chapters discuss protection of the overall social ethic as evidenced in concerns about the physical and cultural environment. These are all evolving concepts which respond to the technological and social changes in society. The real estate analyst needs an understanding of these issues to project future government policies which can change the rules of the game and consequently have a significant influence on future proj-

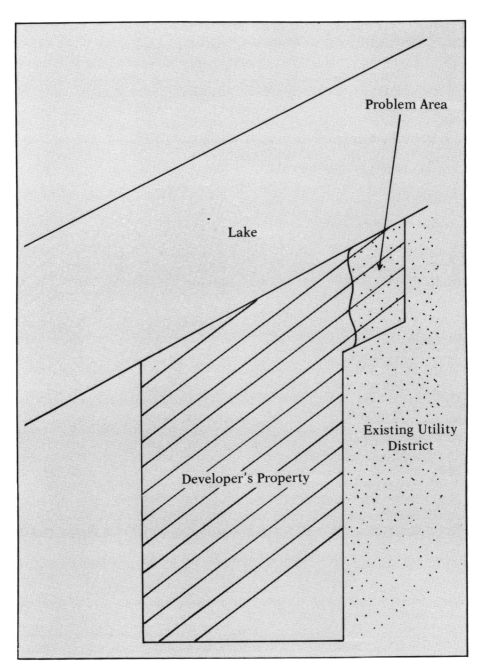

Figure 23-1. GRAPHIC ILLUSTRATION OF SITUATION 2

ect's net operating income. Individual business ethics also change over time. The analyst must be aware of such changes in this important, if informal, part of the rules of the game to fully understand the workings of the real estate markets.

Ethical behavior is important in its own right; it should be viewed as good business. Unethical behavior will be costly in the long run. But ethics can certainly cost money in the short run and where does one draw the line? That decision must be made over and over again in the course of a business career. The decision is more likely to be right if ethical issues are considered in advance.

IMPORTANT TERMS

bribery   externalities
discounted present value   neighborhood
ethics   redlining

REVIEW QUESTIONS

23-1. Define ethics in a broad sense which would be applicable to activity in the real estate industry.

23-2. How might rationalization affect an individual's ability to deal with ethical problems.

23-3. Can individuals in business rely solely upon formal laws as guidance in their day-to-day activities or must they also implement informal rules? Why?

23-4. Fully discuss the ramifications of facing the business decision-making environment as presented in Situation 1 in the text.

23-5. Fully discuss the ramifications of facing the business decision-making environment as presented in Situation 2 in the text.

23-6. How might the public right of eminent domain conflict with private property rights?

23-7. How might the evaluation of an action in terms of how the action would stand up to public scrutiny be used to test ethical considerations involved in the decision making process.

23-8. Discuss the possible impact of redlining upon real estate patterns and property values.

23-9. How might the concept of one's best self be used to evaluate a situation which has ethical considerations.

23-10. Discuss how, in the long run, adherence to general social ethics is critical to the definition of winning developed in this book.

24
Significant Trends

T HE EMPHASIS THROUGHOUT this book has been on the role of the decision-maker in real estate investing. The point has been made several times that the viewpoint of the decision-maker is a forward-looking one. Historical patterns and past trends are very important in establishing a background for decision-making, but no historical pattern is permanent and no trend continues forever. The ultimate success of an investor, analyst, or other real estate professional depends on the ability to anticipate changes and, what may be just as important, the ability to recognize the significance and importance of a change after it has become apparent.

This final chapter attempts to identify what will be the most significant trends in real estate in the last two decades of the twentieth century. All of these trends already have had an impact on the environment in which real estate is developed, used, bought, and sold. Some, such as the higher cost of energy, continuing inflation, and foreign investment, impact primarily on investment objectives and financing patterns. Others, such as the increase in legislation to protect consumers and the environment, increase and modify the role of government in the real estate investing and development process. Yet others, such as the rise of brokerage franchise firms and large development organizations, reflect the growing institutionalization of the professionals who serve the industry.

ECONOMIC AND POLITICAL CLIMATE

The most important impact on the real estate industry will come from the overall economy—its health and growth (or lack of growth). The successful analyst will need to continually review both short- and long-term economic projections.

Further, the analyst must anticipate how this economy will be managed and how the rewards of its success will be distributed. There appear to be real differences among competing political philosophies as expressed by the ideologically opposed Republican and Democratic Parties. The political road the nation chooses to follow has a very significant influence on the real estate industry.

For example, in the 1970s, the real estate industry did not experience the boom and bust traditionally accompanying (in a somewhat counter-cyclical manner) the national business cycle. Debt financing continued to be available during periods of high interest rates (periods which tradition-ally were difficult for the real estate industry due to disintermediation). Stopping the credit squeeze on real estate removed one of the major "stops" on inflation. Given today's concern about high inflation, will the country continue to be willing to accommodate the flow of funds into the real estate sector?

DEMOGRAPHIC CHANGES

Another important macroconsideration involves demographic changes. Demand is a function of the number of persons in the area as well as the incomes and preferences of these consumers. Is the baby boom generation going to have more than 3.2 children? Will jobs and climate continue to attract people to the Sun Belt?

INFLATION

Inflation has become a pervasive part of the American economy. As a result, more and more Americans are "fleeing from cash" and seeking ownership of tangible property (real estate, gold and silver, diamonds, and fine art). From time to time, one or another kind of these investments is proclaimed to be the best type of inflation hedge. It seems fair to say that real estate, in general, has met the key requirement of any inflation hedge—that its value rise at least enough to offset the declining purchas-ing power of the dollar.

In the case of single-family houses, a major reason for rising values has been the desire of individuals to obtain the tax benefits available to homeowners and not to renters—particularly the right to deduct mortgage interest and real estate taxes for federal income tax purposes. Another factor favoring rising prices for private homes is the growth of land use controls and a "no growth" philosophy in many areas that makes it much harder than ever before to obtain approval for new residential construc-tion. And where such construction does take place, the longer construction time and the sharp increases in local fees has meant fairly substantial price increases. As a result, prices of existing homes rise as well.

In the case of income real estate, a number of factors contribute to the ease with which rents can be raised to keep pace with inflation—which, in turn, causes the value of the property to rise.

☐ *The real estate commodity–space–is a basic requirement for every person and every business.* Furthermore, in the case of most businesses, rent represents a quite small percentage of total operating costs. As a result, many tenants are willing to pay high rentals provided the location is desirable.

☐ *Increasingly, rents will be raised through the application of cost-of-living, net, or percentage clauses in lease agreements.* As a result, the increases are more or less automatic, rather than being subject to day-to-day or week-to-week movement. By comparison, goods and services provided by large companies must compete in the marketplace each day, and this often prevents their price from rising as fast as the inflation rate.

☐ *Finally, increased construction and financing costs are making it less likely that a large amount of new space will come to the market and create a condition of oversupply.* Consequently, the demand-supply ratio seems likely to remain quite favorable for improved real estate.

Another reason why all forms of mortgaged real estate is a good inflation hedge relates to the fact that interest rates rise during inflation to cover the declining value of money. However, the interest rate on an *existing* mortgage remains fixed. Consequently, the major cash outflow of the real estate investor (debt service on the mortgage) remains unchanged even though the value of the property and the amount of rent income is likely to rise with inflation.

An offset to real estate adjustments to inflation is the spread of rent controls. Such controls retard new investment in rental property and increase market pressures on the values and prices of owner-occupied units. While rent controls may hold down increases in rental stock, they exacerbate upward spiraling prices in ownership markets.

ENERGY

Building structures in the United States, for heating, cooling, and lighting purposes, account for about one-third of total U.S. energy consumption. This means that any important changes in the availability and cost of energy have significant consequences for real estate development and ownership. In particular, builders and developers should not underestimate the importance of utilizing energy-saving techniques in new buildings which are likely to be still standing in the year 2050 and beyond. Decisions made today concerning energy efficiency and energy use are likely to affect the value of improved real estate—in terms of resale or refinancing—for many years to come. (See **24-1.**)

24-1. ENERGY AFTER THE YEAR 2000

No reliable energy forecasts have been made for the first part of the twenty-first century, even though it begins in less than 21 years. Most experts, however, generally agree in principle about the following:

- Possibly as early as 2025, oil and natural gas will have become too expensive and scarce to use as ordinary fuel.
- Either nuclear power will be utilized as a common source of electricity or the energy growth rate on a per-capita basis will approach zero.
- Solar heating and cooling for both residential and commercial buildings will be commonplace.
- Many buildings will require no energy for space conditioning beyond that available from their own solar-energy systems.
- At the same time, most buildings will still purchase electricity from conventional utility systems.

According to a report prepared by the U.S. Department of Commerce,[1] it seems likely that the period between now and the year 2000 will see decreasing availability of oil and gas (whether because of absolute unavailability or rising costs). Consequently, two important conclusions can be drawn:

□ *To keep energy demand within the realistic bounds of energy supply expected to be available by the end of the century,* our national energy growth rate will have to be reduced to 2 percent or less—or to the point where it parallels the population growth rate.

□ *A significant and effective national effort in energy conservation* will be necessary if this energy goal is to be attained.

Prospects for an improved energy situation beyond 2000 appear no better at this point. It seems likely that oil and natural gas will become too expensive and scarce to use as an ordinary fuel; therefore, increasing reliance will have to be placed on coal and nuclear-based electrical generation, development of synthetic fuels, and renewable energy sources (e.g., solar, goethermal, etc.).

Because of the long life of buildings, the energy challenge to the construction industry is unique. Industry goals must be threefold:

---

[1] J. F. Gustaferro, *Implication for Construction of Future Energy Availability* (Washington, D.C.: U.S. Government Printing Office, 1979).

- To use building products that are energy-efficient (rather than energy-intensive) in their manufacture.
- To use siting techniques, insulation, and building technology that are energy-efficient.
- To reduce the use of short-supply energy sources in construction operations themselves.

Conserving Fuel in Existing Buildings

When it comes to buildings already constructed, some significant changes are expected in the types of energy used. The most important change will be the substitution of electricity, coal, and solar energy for oil and gas. Just as important will be a trend to less energy usage either by being more efficient or by doing without.

Continuing emphasis will be placed on conservation measures and good insulation, including such measures as judicious use of trees for shading, proper siting of structures, thermal window panels, and insulated foundations. In addition, much greater use must be made of such energy-efficient devices as high-efficiency furnaces, hot water heaters, and heat pumps.

Trade-Off Between Capital Cost and Energy Saving

One significant issue that will face lenders, appraisers, and investors is whether, from an investment point of view, the extra costs for energy-saving features will be justified by the savings in energy costs over the life of the building. This is an illustration of the concept of contribution, one of the appraisal concepts discussed in Chapter 7. The issue is most important in connection with the installation of solar energy systems to single-family homes, since these may add a significant cost (e.g., $5,000 or more) to the total. A lender will be interested not only in the lessened cost of operation but also the extent to which the resale value of the house will be increased because of the energy-saving features.

Gasoline Shortages

A special aspect of the energy shortage concerns the availability and price of gasoline and its effect on real estate location. Perhaps the most significant socioeconomic phenomenon since the end of World War II has been the dispersal of population from the cities to the suburbs. This dispersal has been made possible by the automobile, which permits living some distance from employment, schools, shopping, and recreation.

The effect of gasoline unavailability or high price will be just opposite to that of the automobile. In brief, increased values can be anticipated for

- Areas that concentrate related services.
- Sites that minimize auto travel.
- Buildings with assured access to necessary fuel and power.

Over the long run, the shortage should stimulate the revival of downtowns and central cities. Well-located existing properties should almost certainly increase in value. With respect to new development, a change may occur in the trend of the past thirty years, which has been to develop land along existing highways and access routes, creating the typical "spoke" or "strip" pattern of land development. During these years, land lacking easy access to highways (so-called *dead land*) has been passed over. But now, such land will be in demand as density levels increase in both residential and commercial neighborhoods.

PROTECTION OF THE ENVIRONMENT

The number of controls on land use and development has risen to a level which now significantly effects the cost of new constructed space. As the economy becomes more complex, increasing the number and significance of development externalities, the demand for even more controls will be strong. However, there is a potentially counterbalancing desire for deregulation in the economy overall. Future resolution of these conflicting trends will have a pronounced influence on the "rules of the real estate game." Remember that growth is measured by GNP, but the GNP figure takes no direct account of improvements in air or water quality.

CONSUMERISM

There has been a sharp upsurge in legislation by government at all levels in the realm of consumer protection. The rationale of such legislation is that government has a responsibility, in its upholding of the general welfare, to assure that members of the general public can protect their interests when they become involved in certain types of transactions. Three significant federal statutes in this area are:

☐ *The Truth in Lending Act,* which requires real estate and other lenders to clearly set forth the annual percentage rate (APR) and finance charges on borrowed funds.

☐ *The Real Estate Settlement Procedures Act* (RESPA), which requires lenders to make full disclosure of all matters affecting real estate mortgages.

☐ *The Interstate Land Sales Disclosure Act* (ILSA), which requires developers of land subdivisions to provide purchases with an offering statement setting forth all of the pertinent facts affecting the development.

In general, government regulation in aid of consumers emphasizes full disclosure of all pertinent information rather than flat prohibition of certain types of sales or transactions. Thus, in connection with the offering of interests in real estate syndicates and partnerships, federal and state regulations do not ban such offerings but require a detailed offering statement describing all aspects of the transaction as well as the experience of the promoters. The federal government also has sought to apply the antitrust laws to such services as real estate brokerage and title insurance in an effort to increase competition.

FOREIGN INVESTMENT

Since the late 1960s, foreign investment in United States real estate has been increasing at a significant rate. U.S. real estate is attractive for a number of reasons.

☐ The United States has had an open door policy toward foreign investments generally.

☐ Trends toward socialism in many foreign countries encourage the movement of capital to the United States.

☐ The United States has a political environment in which private property rights are more protected than in most other countries.

☐ The overall size of the U.S. economy and the percentage of the wealth of the economy invested in real estate dictate some U.S. real estate investment for large internationally diversified investors.

☐ Although the annual cash flow return on real estate investments in many U.S. markets appears low today relative to other U.S. investment alternatives, demand-supply conditions in many growing regional markets still appear attractive.

☐ U.S. real estate prices are still low relative to other developed economies. Income properties in the United States can be purchased at square footage costs considerably below comparable property in the more developed foreign countries, especially in Western Europe.

☐ Over the last decade, real estate has been an excellent inflation hedge compared to many other types of available investments.

☐ Recent U.S. currency devaluations have made U.S. investments more attractive to foreign investors.

☐ It is relatively easy to finance real estate purchases in the United States (although there are potential pitfalls in this area for foreign investors).

☐ Tax avoidance is possible both in the United States and the country of origin. There are several ways for foreign investors to avoid capital gains taxation in the United States. In an inflationary period, a large portion of the total return on real estate comes in the form of capital gains and thus the foreign investor has a considerable advantage over the domestic investor.

Despite intense speculation, there is little precise information as to how much American real estate is in foreign hands. It is not likely that the figure can be much over one percent, although in certain areas of the country and for certain types of property, the percentage may be higher. In 1979, Congress passed the Agricultural Foreign Investment Disclosure Act (AFIDA), which requires all foreign persons owning U.S. agricultural land to file a disclosure statement with the Secretary of Agriculture. This law was in response to fears that foreign interests might come to control significant portions of American farmland and hence farm production.

It should be noted that foreign investment in the United States is far below U.S. investment in other countries.

The Foreign Investor's Viewpoint

Although the absolute amount of land under foreign control is minimal, the fact that many foreign investors focus on particular types of real estate has made their purchases a significant factor in the some markets. In general, foreign investors seek out prime properties in good locations which are likely to resist obsolescence and so maintain their ability to generate rental income in a competitive market. They are often willing to sacrifice current cash flow for future appreciation since one of their main objectives is to obtain a hedge against inflation. (See 24-2.)

24-2. WHY FOREIGNERS INVEST HERE

While certain other countries may be first on particular items in this list, the overall balance is strongly favorable to the United States:

- Political stability.
- Large quantities of relatively low-cost land and improved real estate.
- Inexpensive and productive labor force.
- Favorable tax system for real estate.
- Free currency remittance.
- Lack of legal restriction on foreign ownership.
- Ease of transferability of ownership interests.
- Small risk of expropriation.
- Availability of experienced property managers.
- Ease of communication (both technological and linguistic).
- Likelihood of national survival (i.e., military strength).
- Established and predictable legal system.
- Opportunity for, and likelihood of, property appreciation.
- Capable accountants, developed auditing standards and techniques.
- Lack of restrictions as to property usage.
- Receptivity of the host country and its citizens to foreign investment.
- Opportunities for both small and large-scale investments.
- Availability of financing.

DEBT FINANCING

One of the major advantages of real estate investment, a point made several times in this book, is that a very large portion of the purchase price may be financed by loans. The most obvious benefit of this is that an investor with a relatively small amount of capital can obtain control of a very substantial parcel of real estate and thus gain the leverage and tax benefits described in Parts V and VI. (See 24-3.)

24-3. FUTURE DEBT FINANCING ISSUES

In the future, will liquidity and profit squeezes at financial intermediaries (resulting from inflation) and usury ceilings restrict credit availability? Will changes in regulation change the structure of the institutions which provide mortgage credit and consequently alter the best source for particular types of real estate financing? (What will be the impact of NOW accounts for example?)

Taking a broader view of financing, will municipal governments be able to finance the provision of the infrastructure needed to support anticipated private development? (How long can New York run a deficit?) Will some state and local governments continue to issue tax exempt bonds to raise money for mortgage finance?

INSTITUTIONALIZATION OF THE INDUSTRY

Until quite recently, both real estate development and real estate investment were carried on primarily in local markets by local firms and individuals. There were several reasons for this. Real estate is immobile and its location is often the most important factor to be considered; this puts great importance on knowing the particular property. The laws and practices affecting real estate differ from state to state, which impedes transactions across state lines. Perhaps most important, real estate projects until fairly recently were generally small enough to be handled by local groups who did not have to seek the participation of large and distant institutions.

Development Financing

This situation, however, is changing rapidly. Because of inflation and the reduced availability of traditional financing, developers are finding it more and more difficult to raise the necessary capital for large projects. As a result, they are seeking out large lending institutions, insurance companies, real estate investment trusts and public limited partnerships are utilized.

Investment

Particularly significant has been the increasing interest shown by major brokerage and investment banking organizations in real estate financing and investment. One reason is the desire of Wall Street firms to expand their base of operations as income from stock trading and stock brokerage has declined. Another reason is the demand by investors for ways to participate in the real estate market, which many perceive as offering more substantial long term profit opportunities than common stock. In addition, Wall Street firms have played an important role in expanding the secondary mortgage market, particularly the market for Ginnie Mae mortgage-backed securities (of which more than $70 billion dollars had been issued by the end of 1979).

Brokerage

Even in the field of real estate brokerage, a trend toward national and institutional ownership is strong. This trend began with the development of franchise organizations which have sought by national advertising and promotion to create a form of "brand name" identification for affiliated local firms. The market at which such advertising is aimed is that of the millions of American families and businesses which move from one part of the country to another each year.

In development financing, investment, and brokerage, the days of the completely independent entrepreneur may be numbered. On the other hand, it is this entrepreneur who has made the industry what it is today.

COMPUTERS

Closely related to the institutionalization of real estate brokerage has been the development of computerized information systems. These systems are gradually replacing the traditional practice of a real estate broker or salesperson personally escorting prospects from house to house, a practice that is time-wasting in the extreme. Computerized systems not only sharply reduce the time required of the prospective purchaser but also make the broker's operation far more efficient.

In its most common form, a computerized information system lists all properties available for sale according to a variety of criteria. A buyer seeking a property fills out a form listing the most important considerations, such as location, price, number of bedrooms, accessibility to transportation, etc. The computer identifies properties meeting several or all of the criteria and displays on a screen a series of pictures of each property. The purchaser then visits selected properties accompanied possibly only by a driver who brings the purchaser back to the brokerage office after the inspection.

The benefits of such a system are even more obvious for persons moving from one part of the country to the other. Such a prospect can visit the local branch office of a national chain, or the local firm affiliated with a national franchise, and view pictures of properties in the desired location.

Similar systems can be anticipated for income properties as well. Institutional investors or large syndicates interested in assembling a portfolio of properties in different parts of the country would clearly benefit from a system giving access, via a computer system, to a national set of listings. Eventually, computer systems might be developed to show land availability throughout the country, as well as sources of financing at different rates of interest and loan terms.

Property tax records have also been computerized in many areas. Investment analysis is aided by computer models. (Most of these computer models are high-speed adaptations of the investment model developed in Part VII.) Additionally, large-scale land planning is now often a computer-assisted function. The real estate industry is a fertile field for advancing technology and the decision maker of the future will need to be comfortable with this technology.

SUMMARY

In the past thirty years, the real estate industry has gradually changed from a series of small locally oriented markets dominated by individual investors into a national (and even international) market significantly influenced by large developers and financial institutions, and organizations representing giant pools of capital. This is not to deny that the majority of real estate transactions still take place between individuals who negotiate face to face about a property familiar to both of them. However, any major transaction today usually requires the financing, skills and know-how of large organizations and it is they who are setting many of the future patterns for real estate development and ownership. Also playing a more significant role than ever before are federal, state, and local governments, as real estate development becomes closely involved with questions of public policy such as environmental protection, energy shortgages, the rising costs of municipal services, and tax favoritism.

Closely related to these considerations is the importance of the real estate industry to the general economy, with real estate development constituting a major source of employment and making up the single largest portion of the gross national product (GNP). Finally, as inflation continues, more and more investors seek in real estate a means of protecting capital from continuing erosion.

The increased interest in real estate as an investment, and its growing impact on society in general, means that the real estate decision-maker's role becomes increasingly difficult, significant, and challenging. The simple rule of maximum return to the equity investor is giving way to a formula that seeks to provide fair shares to all participants in the development and ownership process. Investment policies that further the welfare of all and recognize the rights of the public relative to real estate developments are significant and prominent "business in society" issues.

Notice that this chapter has only *suggested possible* trends. Parts I to VIII developed a framework for real estate decision making. The framework is both logical and decision-oriented. However, to use it effectively, the analyst must incorporate subjective estimates of future trends affecting the industry. While the framework of the analysis can be taught as well as a rational approach for gathering projections, there is little about the future which is certain. Hence, the all important concrete decision-making must be left to the judgment of the reader. The authors believe that real estate decision-making will become significantly more complex and that the decision tools will become much more sophisticated over the next two decades. The future winners in this great game of real estate will be those who are ready to handle the complexity and sophistication.

IMPORTANT TERMS

consumerism
dead land
debt financing

deflation
inflation

REVIEW QUESTIONS

24-1. Give reasons why income real estate values have been able to keep pace with inflation.

24-2. Why are fixed mortgage costs desirable in an inflationary economy and undesirable in a deflationary one?

24-3. Name ways in which buildings can be made more energy-efficient.

24-4. What has the concept of contribution to do with solar energy systems?

24-5. What types of properties should best be able to maintain their value in an era of rising gasoline costs and possible shortages?

24-6. What is the basic goals of the major consumer protection statutes?

24-7. Give four reasons why foreign capital is attracted to U.S. real estate.

24-8. What is one reason for the trend to less debt financing for real estate investments?

24-9. Why is Wall Street becoming interested in real estate?

24-10. How does a computerized information system make the real estate marketing system more efficient?

Compound Interest Tables

	1 AMOUNT OF $1 AT COMPOUND INTEREST	2 ACCUMULATION OF $1 PER PERIOD	3 SINKING FUND FACTOR	4 PRESENT VALUE REVERSION OF $1	5 PRESENT VALUE ORD. ANNUITY $1 PER PERIOD	6 INSTALMENT TO AMORTIZE $1	
MONTHS							
1	1.002500	1.000000	1.000000	0.997506	0.997506	1.002500	
2	1.005006	2.002500	0.499376	0.995019	1.992525	0.501876	
3	1.007519	3.007506	0.332501	0.992537	2.985062	0.335001	
4	1.010038	4.015025	0.249064	0.990062	3.975124	0.251564	
5	1.012563	5.025063	0.199002	0.987593	4.962718	0.201502	
6	1.015094	6.037625	0.165628	0.985130	5.947848	0.168128	
7	1.017632	7.052719	0.141789	0.982674	6.930522	0.144289	
8	1.020176	8.070351	0.123910	0.980223	7.910745	0.126410	
9	1.022726	9.090527	0.110005	0.977779	8.888524	0.112505	
10	1.025283	10.113253	0.098880	0.975340	9.863864	0.101380	
11	1.027846	11.138536	0.089778	0.972908	10.836772	0.092278	
12	1.030416	12.166383	0.082194	0.970482	11.807254	0.084694	
YEARS							**MONTHS**
1	1.030416	12.166383	0.082194	0.970482	11.807254	0.084694	12
2	1.061757	24.702818	0.040481	0.941835	23.265980	0.042981	24
3	1.094051	37.620560	0.026581	0.914034	34.386465	0.029081	36
4	1.127328	50.931208	0.019634	0.887053	45.178695	0.022134	48
5	1.161617	64.646713	0.015469	0.860869	55.652358	0.017969	60
6	1.196946	78.779387	0.012694	0.835458	65.816858	0.015194	72
7	1.233355	93.341920	0.010713	0.810797	75.681321	0.013213	84
8	1.270868	108.347387	0.009230	0.786863	85.254603	0.011730	96
9	1.309523	123.809259	0.008077	0.763637	94.545300	0.010577	108
10	1.349354	139.741419	0.007156	0.741096	103.561753	0.009656	120
11	1.390395	156.158171	0.006404	0.719220	112.312057	0.008904	132
12	1.432686	173.074254	0.005778	0.697990	120.804069	0.008278	144
13	1.476262	190.504855	0.005249	0.677386	129.045412	0.007749	156
14	1.521164	208.465626	0.004797	0.657391	137.043486	0.007297	168
15	1.567432	226.972690	0.004406	0.637986	144.805471	0.006906	180
16	1.615107	246.042664	0.004064	0.619154	152.338338	0.006564	192
17	1.664232	265.692670	0.003764	0.600878	159.648848	0.006264	204
18	1.714851	285.940350	0.003497	0.583141	166.743566	0.005997	216
19	1.767010	306.803882	0.003259	0.565928	173.628861	0.005759	228
20	1.820755	328.301998	0.003046	0.549223	180.310914	0.005546	240
21	1.876135	350.454000	0.002853	0.533011	186.795726	0.005353	252
22	1.933199	373.279777	0.002679	0.517277	193.089119	0.005179	264
23	1.992000	396.799821	0.002520	0.502008	199.196742	0.005020	276
24	2.052588	421.035250	0.002375	0.487190	205.124080	0.004875	288
25	2.115020	446.007823	0.002242	0.472809	210.876453	0.004742	300
26	2.179350	471.739961	0.002120	0.458852	216.459028	0.004620	312
27	2.245637	498.254766	0.002007	0.445308	221.876815	0.004507	324
28	2.313940	525.576044	0.001903	0.432163	227.134679	0.004403	336
29	2.384321	553.728325	0.001806	0.419407	232.237341	0.004306	348
30	2.456842	582.736885	0.001716	0.407027	237.189382	0.004216	360
31	2.531569	612.627767	0.001632	0.395012	241.995247	0.004132	372
32	2.608570	643.427810	0.001554	0.383352	246.659253	0.004054	384
33	2.687912	675.164665	0.001481	0.372036	251.185586	0.003981	396
34	2.769667	707.866827	0.001413	0.361054	255.578310	0.003913	408
35	2.853909	741.563657	0.001349	0.350397	259.841368	0.003849	420
36	2.940714	776.285408	0.001288	0.340054	263.978590	0.003788	432
37	3.030158	812.063254	0.001231	0.330016	267.993688	0.003731	444
38	3.122323	848.929318	0.001178	0.320274	271.890268	0.003678	456
39	3.217292	886.916698	0.001128	0.310820	275.671828	0.003628	468
40	3.315149	926.059501	0.001080	0.301646	279.341764	0.003580	480

SOURCE: Paul Wendt and Alan R. Cerf, *Tables for Investment Analysis* (Center for Real Estate and Urban Economics, 1966; reprinted by the Institute of Business and Economic Research, 1977 and 1979, University of California, Berkeley.

3.00%   ANNUAL COMPOUND INTEREST TABLES   3.00%
                              EFFECTIVE RATE 3.00

	1 AMOUNT OF $1 AT COMPOUND INTEREST	2 ACCUMULATION OF $1 PER PERIOD	3 SINKING FUND FACTOR	4 PRESENT VALUE REVERSION OF $1	5 PRESENT VALUE ORD. ANNUITY $1 PER PERIOD	6 INSTALMENT TO AMORTIZE $1
YEARS						
1	1.030000	1.000000	1.000000	0.970874	0.970874	1.030000
2	1.060900	2.030000	0.492611	0.942596	1.913470	0.522611
3	1.092727	3.090900	0.323530	0.915142	2.828611	0.353530
4	1.125509	4.183627	0.239027	0.888487	3.717098	0.269027
5	1.159274	5.309136	0.188355	0.862609	4.579707	0.218355
6	1.194052	6.468410	0.154598	0.837484	5.417191	0.184598
7	1.229874	7.662462	0.130506	0.813092	6.230283	0.160506
8	1.266770	8.892336	0.112456	0.789409	7.019692	0.142456
9	1.304773	10.159106	0.098434	0.766417	7.786109	0.128434
10	1.343916	11.463879	0.087231	0.744094	8.530203	0.117231
11	1.384234	12.807796	0.078077	0.722421	9.252624	0.108077
12	1.425761	14.192030	0.070462	0.701380	9.954004	0.100462
13	1.468534	15.617790	0.064030	0.680951	10.634955	0.094030
14	1.512590	17.086324	0.058526	0.661118	11.296073	0.088526
15	1.557967	18.598914	0.053767	0.641862	11.937935	0.083767
16	1.604706	20.156881	0.049611	0.623167	12.561102	0.079611
17	1.652848	21.761588	0.045953	0.605016	13.166118	0.075953
18	1.702433	23.414435	0.042709	0.587395	13.753513	0.072709
19	1.753506	25.116868	0.039814	0.570286	14.323799	0.069814
20	1.806111	26.870374	0.037216	0.553676	14.877475	0.067216
21	1.860295	28.676486	0.034872	0.537549	15.415024	0.064872
22	1.916103	30.536780	0.032747	0.521893	15.936917	0.062747
23	1.973587	32.452884	0.030814	0.506692	16.443608	0.060814
24	2.032794	34.426470	0.029047	0.491934	16.935542	0.059047
25	2.093778	36.459264	0.027428	0.477606	17.413148	0.057428
26	2.156591	38.553042	0.025938	0.463695	17.876842	0.055938
27	2.221289	40.709634	0.024564	0.450189	18.327031	0.054564
28	2.287928	42.930923	0.023293	0.437077	18.764108	0.053293
29	2.356566	45.218850	0.022115	0.424346	19.188455	0.052115
30	2.427262	47.575416	0.021019	0.411987	19.600441	0.051019
31	2.500080	50.002678	0.019999	0.399987	20.000428	0.049999
32	2.575083	52.502759	0.019047	0.388337	20.388766	0.049047
33	2.652335	55.077841	0.018156	0.377026	20.765792	0.048156
34	2.731905	57.730177	0.017322	0.366045	21.131837	0.047322
35	2.813862	60.462082	0.016539	0.355383	21.487220	0.046539
36	2.898278	63.275944	0.015804	0.345032	21.832252	0.045804
37	2.985227	66.174223	0.015112	0.334983	22.167235	0.045112
38	3.074783	69.159449	0.014459	0.325226	22.492462	0.044459
39	3.167027	72.234233	0.013844	0.315754	22.808215	0.043844
40	3.262038	75.401260	0.013262	0.306557	23.114772	0.043262
41	3.359899	78.663298	0.012712	0.297628	23.412400	0.042712
42	3.460696	82.023196	0.012192	0.288959	23.701359	0.042192
43	3.564517	85.483892	0.011698	0.280543	23.981902	0.041698
44	3.671452	89.048409	0.011230	0.272372	24.254274	0.041230
45	3.781596	92.719861	0.010785	0.264439	24.518713	0.040785
46	3.895044	96.501457	0.010363	0.256737	24.775449	0.040363
47	4.011895	100.396501	0.009961	0.249259	25.024708	0.039961
48	4.132252	104.408396	0.009578	0.241999	25.266707	0.039578
49	4.256219	108.540648	0.009213	0.234950	25.501657	0.039213
50	4.383906	112.796867	0.008865	0.228107	25.729764	0.038865

	1 AMOUNT OF $1 AT COMPOUND INTEREST	2 ACCUMULATION OF $1 PER PERIOD	3 SINKING FUND FACTOR	4 PRESENT VALUE REVERSION OF $1	5 PRESENT VALUE ORD. ANNUITY $1 PER PERIOD	6 INSTALMENT TO AMORTIZE $1	
MONTHS							
1	1.004167	1.000000	1.000000	0.995851	0.995851	1.004167	
2	1.008351	2.004167	0.498960	0.991718	1.987569	0.503127	
3	1.012552	3.012517	0.331948	0.987603	2.975173	0.336115	
4	1.016771	4.025070	0.248443	0.983506	3.958678	0.252610	
5	1.021008	5.041841	0.198340	0.979425	4.938103	0.202507	
6	1.025262	6.062848	0.164939	0.975361	5.913463	0.169106	
7	1.029534	7.088110	0.141081	0.971313	6.884777	0.145248	
8	1.033824	8.117644	0.123188	0.967283	7.852060	0.127355	
9	1.038131	9.151467	0.109272	0.963269	8.815329	0.113439	
10	1.042457	10.189599	0.098139	0.959272	9.774602	0.102306	
11	1.046800	11.232055	0.089031	0.955292	10.729894	0.093198	
12	1.051162	12.278855	0.081441	0.951328	11.681222	0.085607	

YEARS							MONTHS
1	1.051162	12.278855	0.081441	0.951328	11.681222	0.085607	12
2	1.104941	25.185921	0.039705	0.905025	22.793898	0.043871	24
3	1.161472	38.753336	0.025804	0.860976	33.365701	0.029971	36
4	1.220895	53.014885	0.018863	0.819071	43.422956	0.023029	48
5	1.283359	68.006083	0.014705	0.779205	52.990706	0.018871	60
6	1.349018	83.764259	0.011938	0.741280	62.092777	0.016105	72
7	1.418036	100.328653	0.009967	0.705201	70.751835	0.014134	84
8	1.490585	117.740512	0.008493	0.670877	78.989441	0.012660	96
9	1.566847	136.043196	0.007351	0.638225	86.826108	0.011517	108
10	1.647009	155.282279	0.006440	0.607161	94.281350	0.010607	120
11	1.731274	175.505671	0.005698	0.577609	101.373733	0.009864	132
12	1.819849	196.763730	0.005082	0.549496	108.120917	0.009249	144
13	1.912956	219.109391	0.004564	0.522751	114.539704	0.008731	156
14	2.010826	242.598299	0.004122	0.497308	120.646077	0.008289	168
15	2.113704	267.288944	0.003741	0.473103	126.455243	0.007908	180
16	2.221845	293.242809	0.003410	0.450076	131.981666	0.007577	192
17	2.335519	320.524523	0.003120	0.428170	137.239108	0.007287	204
18	2.455008	349.202022	0.002864	0.407331	142.240661	0.007030	216
19	2.580611	379.346715	0.002636	0.387505	146.998780	0.006803	228
20	2.712640	411.033669	0.002433	0.368645	151.525313	0.006600	240
21	2.851424	444.341787	0.002251	0.350702	155.831532	0.006417	252
22	2.997306	473.354011	0.002086	0.333633	159.928159	0.006253	264
23	3.150656	516.157528	0.001937	0.317394	163.825396	0.006104	276
24	3.311850	554.843982	0.001802	0.301946	167.532948	0.005969	288
25	3.481290	595.509709	0.001679	0.287250	171.060047	0.005846	300
26	3.659400	638.255971	0.001567	0.273269	174.415476	0.005733	312
27	3.846622	683.189213	0.001464	0.259968	177.607590	0.005630	324
28	4.043422	730.421325	0.001369	0.247315	180.644338	0.005536	336
29	4.250291	780.069922	0.001282	0.235278	183.533283	0.005449	348
30	4.467744	832.258635	0.001202	0.223827	186.281617	0.005368	360
31	4.696323	887.117422	0.001127	0.212933	188.896185	0.005294	372
32	4.936595	944.782889	0.001058	0.202569	191.383498	0.005225	384
33	5.189161	1005.398630	0.000995	0.192709	193.749748	0.005161	396
34	5.454648	1069.115587	0.000935	0.183330	196.000829	0.005102	408
35	5.733716	1136.092425	0.000880	0.174407	198.142346	0.005047	420
36	6.027066	1206.495925	0.000829	0.165918	200.179632	0.004996	432
37	6.335423	1280.501402	0.000781	0.157843	202.117759	0.004948	444
38	6.659555	1358.293140	0.000736	0.150160	203.961555	0.004903	456
39	7.000270	1440.064850	0.000694	0.142852	205.715609	0.004861	468
40	7.358417	1526.020157	0.000655	0.135899	207.384291	0.004822	480

	1	2	3	4	5	6
	AMOUNT OF $1 AT COMPOUND INTEREST	ACCUMULATION OF $1 PER PERIOD	SINKING FUND FACTOR	PRESENT VALUE REVERSION OF $1	PRESENT VALUE ORD. ANNUITY $1 PER PERIOD	INSTALMENT TO AMORTIZE $1
YEARS						
1	1.050000	1.000000	1.000000	0.952381	0.952381	1.050000
2	1.102500	2.050000	0.487805	0.907029	1.859410	0.537805
3	1.157625	3.152500	0.317209	0.863838	2.723248	0.367209
4	1.215506	4.310125	0.232012	0.822702	3.545951	0.282012
5	1.276282	5.525631	0.180975	0.783526	4.329477	0.230975
6	1.340096	6.801913	0.147017	0.746215	5.075692	0.197017
7	1.407100	8.142008	0.122820	0.710681	5.786373	0.172820
8	1.477455	9.549109	0.104722	0.676839	6.463213	0.154722
9	1.551328	11.026564	0.090690	0.644609	7.107822	0.140690
10	1.628895	12.577863	0.079505	0.613913	7.721735	0.129505
11	1.710339	14.206787	0.070389	0.584679	8.306414	0.120389
12	1.795856	15.917127	0.062825	0.556837	8.863252	0.112825
13	1.885649	17.712983	0.056456	0.530321	9.393573	0.106456
14	1.979932	19.598632	0.051024	0.505068	9.898641	0.101024
15	2.078928	21.578564	0.046342	0.481017	10.379658	0.096342
16	2.182875	23.657492	0.042270	0.458112	10.837770	0.092270
17	2.292018	25.840366	0.038699	0.436297	11.274066	0.088699
18	2.406619	28.132385	0.035546	0.415521	11.689587	0.085546
19	2.526950	30.539004	0.032745	0.395734	12.085321	0.082745
20	2.653298	33.065954	0.030243	0.376889	12.462210	0.080243
21	2.785963	35.719252	0.027996	0.358942	12.821153	0.077996
22	2.925261	38.505214	0.025971	0.341850	13.163003	0.075971
23	3.071524	41.430475	0.024137	0.325571	13.488574	0.074137
24	3.225100	44.501999	0.022471	0.310068	13.798642	0.072471
25	3.386355	47.727099	0.020952	0.295303	14.093945	0.070952
26	3.555673	51.113454	0.019564	0.281241	14.375185	0.069564
27	3.733456	54.669126	0.018292	0.267848	14.643034	0.068292
28	3.920129	58.402583	0.017123	0.255094	14.898127	0.067123
29	4.116136	62.322712	0.016046	0.242946	15.141074	0.066046
30	4.321942	66.438848	0.015051	0.231377	15.372451	0.065051
31	4.538039	70.760790	0.014132	0.220359	15.592811	0.064132
32	4.764941	75.298829	0.013280	0.209866	15.802677	0.063280
33	5.003189	80.063771	0.012490	0.199873	16.002549	0.062490
34	5.253348	85.066959	0.011755	0.190355	16.192904	0.061755
35	5.516015	90.320307	0.011072	0.181290	16.374194	0.061072
36	5.791816	95.836323	0.010434	0.172657	16.546852	0.060434
37	6.081407	101.628139	0.009840	0.164436	16.711287	0.059840
38	6.385477	107.709546	0.009284	0.156605	16.867893	0.059284
39	6.704751	114.095023	0.008765	0.149148	17.017041	0.058765
40	7.039989	120.799774	0.008278	0.142046	17.159086	0.058278
41	7.391988	127.839763	0.007822	0.135282	17.294368	0.057822
42	7.761588	135.231751	0.007395	0.128840	17.423208	0.057395
43	8.149667	142.993339	0.006993	0.122704	17.545912	0.056993
44	8.557150	151.143006	0.006616	0.116861	17.662773	0.056616
45	8.985008	159.700156	0.006262	0.111297	17.774070	0.056262
46	9.434258	168.685164	0.005928	0.105997	17.880066	0.055928
47	9.905971	178.119422	0.005614	0.100949	17.981016	0.055614
48	10.401270	188.025393	0.005318	0.096142	18.077158	0.055318
49	10.921333	198.426663	0.005040	0.091564	18.168722	0.055040
50	11.467400	209.347996	0.004777	0.087204	18.255925	0.054777

6.00%   MONTHLY COMPOUND INTEREST TABLES   6.00%
                             EFFECTIVE RATE 0.500

	1 AMOUNT OF $1 AT COMPOUND INTEREST	2 ACCUMULATION OF $1 PER PERIOD	3 SINKING FUND FACTOR	4 PRESENT VALUE REVERSION OF $1	5 PRESENT VALUE ORD. ANNUITY $1 PER PERIOD	6 INSTALMENT TO AMORTIZE $1	
MONTHS							
1	1.005000	1.000000	1.000000	0.995025	0.995025	1.005000	
2	1.010025	2.005000	0.498753	0.990075	1.985099	0.503753	
3	1.015075	3.015025	0.331672	0.985149	2.970248	0.336672	
4	1.020151	4.030100	0.248133	0.980248	3.950496	0.253133	
5	1.025251	5.050251	0.198010	0.975371	4.925866	0.203010	
6	1.030378	6.075502	0.164595	0.970518	5.896384	0.169595	
7	1.035529	7.105879	0.140729	0.965690	6.862074	0.145729	
8	1.040707	8.141409	0.122829	0.960885	7.822959	0.127829	
9	1.045911	9.182116	0.108907	0.956105	8.779064	0.113907	
10	1.051140	10.228026	0.097771	0.951348	9.730412	0.102771	
11	1.056396	11.279167	0.088659	0.946615	10.677027	0.093659	
12	1.061678	12.335562	0.081066	0.941905	11.618932	0.086066	
YEARS							MONTHS
1	1.061678	12.335562	0.081066	0.941905	11.618932	0.086066	12
2	1.127160	25.431955	0.039321	0.887186	22.562866	0.044321	24
3	1.196681	39.336105	0.025422	0.835645	32.871016	0.030422	36
4	1.270489	54.097832	0.018485	0.787098	42.580318	0.023485	48
5	1.348850	69.770031	0.014333	0.741372	51.725561	0.019333	60
6	1.432044	86.408856	0.011573	0.698302	60.339514	0.016573	72
7	1.520370	104.073927	0.009609	0.657735	68.453042	0.014609	84
8	1.614143	122.828542	0.008141	0.619524	76.095218	0.013141	96
9	1.713699	142.739900	0.007006	0.583533	83.293424	0.012006	108
10	1.819397	163.879347	0.006102	0.549633	90.073453	0.011102	120
11	1.931613	186.322629	0.005367	0.517702	96.459599	0.010367	132
12	2.050751	210.150163	0.004759	0.487626	102.474743	0.009759	144
13	2.177237	235.447328	0.004247	0.459298	108.140440	0.009247	156
14	2.311524	262.304766	0.003812	0.432615	113.476990	0.008812	168
15	2.454094	290.818712	0.003439	0.407482	118.503515	0.008439	180
16	2.605457	321.091337	0.003114	0.383810	123.238025	0.008114	192
17	2.766156	353.231110	0.002831	0.361513	127.697486	0.007831	204
18	2.936766	387.353194	0.002582	0.340511	131.897876	0.007582	216
19	3.117899	423.579854	0.002361	0.320729	135.854246	0.007361	228
20	3.310204	462.040895	0.002164	0.302096	139.580772	0.007164	240
21	3.514371	502.874129	0.001989	0.284546	143.090806	0.006989	252
22	3.731129	546.225867	0.001831	0.268015	146.396927	0.006831	264
23	3.961257	592.251446	0.001688	0.252445	149.510979	0.006688	276
24	4.205579	641.115782	0.001560	0.237779	152.444121	0.006560	288
25	4.464970	692.993962	0.001443	0.223966	155.206864	0.006443	300
26	4.740359	748.071876	0.001337	0.210954	157.809106	0.006337	312
27	5.032734	806.546875	0.001240	0.198699	160.260172	0.006240	324
28	5.343142	868.628484	0.001151	0.187156	162.568844	0.006151	336
29	5.672696	934.539150	0.001070	0.176283	164.743394	0.006070	348
30	6.022575	1004.515043	0.000996	0.166042	166.791614	0.005996	360
31	6.394034	1078.806895	0.000927	0.156396	168.720644	0.005927	372
32	6.788405	1157.680906	0.000864	0.147310	170.537996	0.005864	384
33	7.207098	1241.419693	0.000806	0.138752	172.249581	0.005806	396
34	7.651617	1330.323306	0.000752	0.130691	173.861732	0.005752	408
35	8.123551	1424.710299	0.000702	0.123099	175.380226	0.005702	420
36	8.624594	1524.918875	0.000656	0.115947	176.810504	0.005656	432
37	9.156540	1631.308097	0.000613	0.109212	178.157690	0.005613	444
38	9.721296	1744.259173	0.000573	0.102867	179.426611	0.005573	456
39	10.320884	1864.176825	0.000536	0.096891	180.621815	0.005536	468
40	10.957454	1991.490734	0.000502	0.091262	181.747584	0.005502	480

6.00%   ANNUAL COMPOUND INTEREST TABLES   6.00%
EFFECTIVE RATE 6.00

	1	2	3	4	5	6
	AMOUNT OF $1 AT COMPOUND INTEREST	ACCUMULATION OF $1 PER PERIOD	SINKING FUND FACTOR	PRESENT VALUE REVERSION OF $1	PRESENT VALUE ORD. ANNUITY $1 PER PERIOD	INSTALMENT TO AMORTIZE $1
YEARS						
1	1.060000	1.000000	1.000000	0.943396	0.943396	1.060000
2	1.123600	2.060000	0.485437	0.889996	1.833393	0.545437
3	1.191016	3.183600	0.314110	0.839619	2.673012	0.374110
4	1.262477	4.374616	0.228591	0.792094	3.465106	0.288591
5	1.338226	5.637093	0.177396	0.747258	4.212364	0.237396
6	1.418519	6.975319	0.143363	0.704961	4.917324	0.203363
7	1.503630	8.393838	0.119135	0.665057	5.582381	0.179135
8	1.593848	9.897468	0.101036	0.627412	6.209794	0.161036
9	1.689479	11.491316	0.087022	0.591898	6.801692	0.147022
10	1.790848	13.180795	0.075868	0.558395	7.360087	0.135868
11	1.898299	14.971643	0.066793	0.526788	7.886875	0.126793
12	2.012196	16.869941	0.059277	0.496969	8.383844	0.119277
13	2.132928	18.882138	0.052960	0.468839	8.852683	0.112960
14	2.260904	21.015066	0.047585	0.442301	9.294984	0.107585
15	2.396558	23.275970	0.042963	0.417265	9.712249	0.102963
16	2.540352	25.672528	0.038952	0.393646	10.105895	0.098952
17	2.692773	28.212880	0.035445	0.371364	10.477260	0.095445
18	2.854339	30.905653	0.032357	0.350344	10.827603	0.092357
19	3.025600	33.759992	0.029621	0.330513	11.158116	0.089621
20	3.207135	36.785591	0.027185	0.311805	11.469921	0.087185
21	3.399564	39.992727	0.025005	0.294155	11.764077	0.085005
22	3.603537	43.392290	0.023046	0.277505	12.041582	0.083046
23	3.819750	46.995828	0.021278	0.261797	12.303379	0.081278
24	4.048935	50.815577	0.019679	0.246979	12.550358	0.079679
25	4.291871	54.864512	0.018227	0.232999	12.783356	0.078227
26	4.549383	59.156383	0.016904	0.219810	13.003166	0.076904
27	4.822346	63.705766	0.015697	0.207368	13.210534	0.075697
28	5.111687	68.528112	0.014593	0.195630	13.406164	0.074593
29	5.418388	73.639798	0.013580	0.184557	13.590721	0.073580
30	5.743491	79.058186	0.012649	0.174110	13.764831	0.072649
31	6.088101	84.801677	0.011792	0.164255	13.929086	0.071792
32	6.453387	90.889778	0.011002	0.154957	14.084043	0.071002
33	6.840590	97.343165	0.010273	0.146186	14.230230	0.070273
34	7.251025	104.183755	0.009598	0.137912	14.368141	0.069598
35	7.686087	111.434780	0.008974	0.130105	14.498246	0.068974
36	8.147252	119.120867	0.008395	0.122741	14.620987	0.068395
37	8.636087	127.268119	0.007857	0.115793	14.736780	0.067857
38	9.154252	135.904206	0.007358	0.109239	14.846019	0.067358
39	9.703507	145.058458	0.006894	0.103056	14.949075	0.066894
40	10.285718	154.761966	0.006462	0.097222	15.046297	0.066462
41	10.902861	165.047684	0.006059	0.091719	15.138016	0.066059
42	11.557033	175.950545	0.005683	0.086527	15.224543	0.065683
43	12.250455	187.507577	0.005333	0.081630	15.306173	0.065333
44	12.985482	199.758032	0.005006	0.077009	15.383182	0.065006
45	13.764611	212.743514	0.004700	0.072650	15.455832	0.064700
46	14.590487	226.508125	0.004415	0.068538	15.524370	0.064415
47	15.465917	241.098612	0.004148	0.064658	15.589028	0.064148
48	16.393872	256.564529	0.003898	0.060998	15.650027	0.063898
49	17.377504	272.958401	0.003664	0.057546	15.707572	0.063664
50	18.420154	290.335905	0.003444	0.054288	15.761861	0.063444

6.50%
MONTHLY COMPOUND INTEREST TABLES
EFFECTIVE RATE 0.542
6.50%

	1 AMOUNT OF $1 AT COMPOUND INTEREST	2 ACCUMULATION OF $1 PER PERIOD	3 SINKING FUND FACTOR	4 PRESENT VALUE REVERSION OF $1	5 PRESENT VALUE ORD. ANNUITY $1 PER PERIOD	6 INSTALMENT TO AMORTIZE $1	
MONTHS							
1	1.005417	1.000000	1.000000	0.994613	0.994613	1.005417	
2	1.010863	2.005417	0.498649	0.989254	1.983867	0.504066	
3	1.016338	3.016279	0.331534	0.983924	2.967791	0.336951	
4	1.021843	4.032618	0.247978	0.978624	3.946415	0.253395	
5	1.027378	5.054461	0.197845	0.973351	4.919766	0.203262	
6	1.032943	6.081839	0.164424	0.968107	5.887873	0.169841	
7	1.038538	7.114782	0.140552	0.962892	6.850765	0.145969	
8	1.044164	8.153321	0.122649	0.957704	7.808469	0.128066	
9	1.049820	9.197485	0.108725	0.952545	8.761014	0.114142	
10	1.055506	10.247304	0.097587	0.947413	9.708426	0.103003	
11	1.061224	11.302811	0.088474	0.942309	10.650735	0.093890	
12	1.066972	12.364034	0.080880	0.937232	11.587967	0.086296	
YEARS							MONTHS
1	1.066972	12.364034	0.080880	0.937232	11.587967	0.086296	12
2	1.138429	25.556111	0.039130	0.878404	22.448578	0.044546	24
3	1.214672	39.631685	0.025232	0.823268	32.627489	0.030649	36
4	1.296020	54.649927	0.018298	0.771593	42.167488	0.023715	48
5	1.382817	70.673968	0.014149	0.723161	51.108680	0.019566	60
6	1.475427	87.771168	0.011393	0.677770	59.488649	0.016810	72
7	1.574239	106.013400	0.009433	0.635227	67.342623	0.014849	84
8	1.679669	125.477348	0.007970	0.595355	74.703617	0.013386	96
9	1.792160	146.244833	0.006838	0.557986	81.602576	0.012255	108
10	1.912184	168.403154	0.005938	0.522962	88.068500	0.011355	120
11	2.040246	192.045460	0.005207	0.490137	94.128569	0.010624	132
12	2.176885	217.271134	0.004603	0.459372	99.808260	0.010019	144
13	2.322675	244.186218	0.004095	0.430538	105.131446	0.009512	156
14	2.478229	272.903856	0.003664	0.403514	110.120506	0.009081	168
15	2.644201	303.544767	0.003294	0.378186	114.796412	0.008711	180
16	2.821288	336.237756	0.002974	0.354448	119.178820	0.008391	192
17	3.010235	371.120256	0.002695	0.332200	123.286152	0.008111	204
18	3.211836	408.338901	0.002449	0.311348	127.135675	0.007866	216
19	3.426938	448.050147	0.002232	0.291806	130.743570	0.007649	228
20	3.656447	490.420930	0.002039	0.273490	134.125004	0.007456	240
21	3.901326	535.629362	0.001867	0.256323	137.294192	0.007284	252
22	4.162605	583.865486	0.001713	0.240234	140.264456	0.007129	264
23	4.441382	635.332073	0.001574	0.225155	143.048282	0.006991	276
24	4.738830	690.245473	0.001449	0.211023	145.657372	0.006865	288
25	5.056198	748.836525	0.001335	0.197777	148.102695	0.006752	300
26	5.394821	811.351528	0.001233	0.185363	150.394529	0.006649	312
27	5.756122	878.053277	0.001139	0.173728	152.542509	0.006556	324
28	6.141620	949.222165	0.001053	0.162823	154.555664	0.006470	336
29	6.552936	1025.157366	0.000975	0.152603	156.442457	0.006392	348
30	6.991798	1106.178087	0.000904	0.143025	158.210820	0.006321	360
31	7.460052	1192.624917	0.000838	0.134047	159.868185	0.006255	372
32	7.959665	1284.861250	0.000778	0.125633	161.421521	0.006195	384
33	8.492739	1383.274822	0.000723	0.117748	162.877357	0.006140	396
34	9.061513	1488.279333	0.000672	0.110357	164.241813	0.006089	408
35	9.668379	1600.316190	0.000625	0.103430	165.520625	0.006042	420
36	10.315889	1719.856364	0.000581	0.096938	166.719167	0.005998	432
37	11.006763	1847.402364	0.000541	0.090853	167.842480	0.005958	444
38	11.743906	1983.040356	0.000504	0.085151	168.895284	0.005921	456
39	12.530417	2128.692413	0.000470	0.079806	169.882006	0.005886	468
40	13.369602	2283.618920	0.000438	0.074797	170.806793	0.005855	480

6.50%   ANNUAL COMPOUND INTEREST TABLES   6.50%
EFFECTIVE RATE 6.50

	1 AMOUNT OF $1 AT COMPOUND INTEREST	2 ACCUMULATION OF $1 PER PERIOD	3 SINKING FUND FACTOR	4 PRESENT VALUE REVERSION OF $1	5 PRESENT VALUE ORD. ANNUITY $1 PER PERIOD	6 INSTALMENT TO AMORTIZE $1
YEARS						
1	1.065000	1.000000	1.000000	0.938967	0.938967	1.065000
2	1.134225	2.065000	0.484262	0.881659	1.820626	0.549262
3	1.207950	3.199225	0.312576	0.827849	2.648476	0.377576
4	1.286466	4.407175	0.226903	0.777323	3.425799	0.291903
5	1.370087	5.693641	0.175635	0.729881	4.155679	0.240635
6	1.459142	7.063728	0.141568	0.685334	4.841014	0.206568
7	1.553987	8.522870	0.117331	0.643506	5.484520	0.182331
8	1.654996	10.076856	0.099237	0.604231	6.088751	0.164237
9	1.762570	11.731852	0.085238	0.567353	6.656104	0.150238
10	1.877137	13.494423	0.074105	0.532726	7.188830	0.139105
11	1.999151	15.371560	0.065055	0.500212	7.689042	0.130055
12	2.129096	17.370711	0.057568	0.469683	8.158725	0.122568
13	2.267487	19.499808	0.051283	0.441017	8.599742	0.116283
14	2.414874	21.767295	0.045940	0.414100	9.013842	0.110940
15	2.571841	24.182169	0.041353	0.388827	9.402669	0.106353
16	2.739011	26.754010	0.037378	0.365095	9.767764	0.102378
17	2.917046	29.493021	0.033906	0.342813	10.110577	0.098906
18	3.106654	32.410067	0.030855	0.321890	10.432466	0.095855
19	3.308587	35.516722	0.028156	0.302244	10.734710	0.093156
20	3.523645	38.825309	0.025756	0.283797	11.018507	0.090756
21	3.752682	42.348954	0.023613	0.266476	11.284983	0.088613
22	3.996606	46.101636	0.021691	0.250212	11.535196	0.086691
23	4.256386	50.098242	0.019961	0.234941	11.770137	0.084961
24	4.533051	54.354628	0.018398	0.220602	11.990739	0.083398
25	4.827699	58.887679	0.016981	0.207138	12.197877	0.081981
26	5.141500	63.715378	0.015695	0.194496	12.392373	0.080695
27	5.475697	68.856877	0.014523	0.182625	12.574998	0.079523
28	5.831617	74.332574	0.013453	0.171479	12.746477	0.078453
29	6.210672	80.164192	0.012474	0.161013	12.907490	0.077474
30	6.614366	86.374864	0.011577	0.151186	13.058676	0.076577
31	7.044300	92.989230	0.010754	0.141959	13.200635	0.075754
32	7.502179	100.033530	0.009997	0.133295	13.333929	0.074997
33	7.989821	107.535710	0.009299	0.125159	13.459088	0.074299
34	8.509159	115.525531	0.008656	0.117520	13.576609	0.073656
35	9.062255	124.034690	0.008062	0.110348	13.686957	0.073062
36	9.651301	133.096945	0.007513	0.103613	13.790570	0.072513
37	10.278636	142.748247	0.007005	0.097289	13.887859	0.072005
38	10.946747	153.026883	0.006535	0.091351	13.979210	0.071535
39	11.658286	163.973630	0.006099	0.085776	14.064986	0.071099
40	12.416075	175.631916	0.005694	0.080541	14.145527	0.070694
41	13.223119	188.047990	0.005318	0.075625	14.221152	0.070318
42	14.082622	201.271110	0.004968	0.071010	14.292161	0.069968
43	14.997993	215.353732	0.004644	0.066676	14.358837	0.069644
44	15.972862	230.351725	0.004341	0.062606	14.421443	0.069341
45	17.011098	246.324587	0.004060	0.058785	14.480228	0.069060
46	18.116820	263.335685	0.003797	0.055197	14.535426	0.068797
47	19.294413	281.452504	0.003553	0.051828	14.587254	0.068553
48	20.548550	300.746917	0.003325	0.048665	14.635919	0.068325
49	21.884205	321.295467	0.003112	0.045695	14.681615	0.068112
50	23.306679	343.179672	0.002914	0.042906	14.724521	0.067914

7.00%   MONTHLY COMPOUND INTEREST TABLES   7.00%
EFFECTIVE RATE 0.583

	1	2	3	4	5	6	
	AMOUNT OF $1 AT COMPOUND INTEREST	ACCUMULATION OF $1 PER PERIOD	SINKING FUND FACTOR	PRESENT VALUE REVERSION OF $1	PRESENT VALUE ORD. ANNUITY $1 PER PERIOD	INSTALMENT TO AMORTIZE $1	
MONTHS							
1	1.005833	1.000000	1.000000	0.994200	0.994200	1.005833	
2	1.011701	2.005833	0.498546	0.988435	1.982635	0.504379	
3	1.017602	3.017534	0.331396	0.982702	2.965337	0.337230	
4	1.023538	4.035136	0.247823	0.977003	3.942340	0.253656	
5	1.029509	5.058675	0.197680	0.971337	4.913677	0.203514	
6	1.035514	6.088184	0.164253	0.965704	5.879381	0.170086	
7	1.041555	7.123698	0.140377	0.960103	6.839484	0.146210	
8	1.047631	8.165253	0.122470	0.954535	7.794019	0.128304	
9	1.053742	9.212883	0.108544	0.948999	8.743018	0.114377	
10	1.059889	10.266625	0.097403	0.943495	9.686513	0.103236	
11	1.066071	11.326514	0.088288	0.938024	10.624537	0.094122	
12	1.072290	12.392585	0.080693	0.932583	11.557120	0.086527	
YEARS							MONTHS
1	1.072290	12.392585	0.080693	0.932583	11.557120	0.086527	12
2	1.149806	25.681032	0.038939	0.869712	22.335099	0.044773	24
3	1.232926	39.930101	0.025044	0.811079	32.386464	0.030877	36
4	1.322054	55.209236	0.018113	0.756399	41.760201	0.023946	48
5	1.417625	71.592902	0.013968	0.705405	50.501993	0.019801	60
6	1.520106	89.160944	0.011216	0.657849	58.654444	0.017049	72
7	1.629994	107.998981	0.009259	0.613499	66.257285	0.015093	84
8	1.747826	128.198821	0.007800	0.572139	73.347569	0.013634	96
9	1.874177	149.858909	0.006673	0.533568	79.959850	0.012506	108
10	2.009661	173.084807	0.005778	0.497596	86.126354	0.011611	120
11	2.154940	197.989707	0.005051	0.464050	91.877134	0.010884	132
12	2.310721	224.694985	0.004450	0.432765	97.240216	0.010284	144
13	2.477763	253.330789	0.003947	0.403590	102.241738	0.009781	156
14	2.656881	284.036677	0.003521	0.376381	106.906074	0.009354	168
15	2.848947	316.962297	0.003155	0.351007	111.255958	0.008988	180
16	3.054897	352.268112	0.002839	0.327343	115.312587	0.008672	192
17	3.275736	390.126188	0.002563	0.305275	119.095732	0.008397	204
18	3.512539	430.721027	0.002322	0.284694	122.623831	0.008155	216
19	3.766461	474.250470	0.002109	0.265501	125.914077	0.007942	228
20	4.038739	520.926660	0.001920	0.247602	128.982506	0.007753	240
21	4.330700	570.977075	0.001751	0.230910	131.844073	0.007585	252
22	4.643766	624.645640	0.001601	0.215342	134.512723	0.007434	264
23	4.979464	682.193909	0.001466	0.200825	137.001461	0.007299	276
24	5.339430	743.902347	0.001344	0.187286	139.322418	0.007178	288
25	5.725418	810.071693	0.001234	0.174660	141.486903	0.007068	300
26	6.139309	881.024426	0.001135	0.162885	143.505467	0.006968	312
27	6.583120	957.106339	0.001045	0.151904	145.387946	0.006878	324
28	7.059015	1038.688219	0.000963	0.141663	147.143515	0.006796	336
29	7.569311	1126.167659	0.000888	0.132112	148.780729	0.006721	348
30	8.116497	1219.970996	0.000820	0.123206	150.307568	0.006653	360
31	8.703240	1320.555383	0.000757	0.114900	151.731473	0.006591	372
32	9.332398	1428.411024	0.000700	0.107154	153.059383	0.006533	384
33	10.007037	1544.063557	0.000648	0.099930	154.297770	0.006481	396
34	10.730447	1668.076622	0.000599	0.093193	155.452669	0.006433	408
35	11.506152	1801.054601	0.000555	0.086910	156.529709	0.006389	420
36	12.337932	1943.645569	0.000514	0.081051	157.534139	0.006348	432
37	13.229843	2096.544450	0.000477	0.075587	158.470853	0.006310	444
38	14.186229	2260.496403	0.000442	0.070491	159.344418	0.006276	456
39	15.211753	2436.300456	0.000410	0.065739	160.159090	0.006244	468
40	16.311411	2624.813398	0.000381	0.061307	160.918839	0.006214	480

7.00%   ANNUAL COMPOUND INTEREST TABLES   7.00%
                       EFFECTIVE RATE 7.00

	1	2	3	4	5	6
	AMOUNT OF $1 AT COMPOUND INTEREST	ACCUMULATION OF $1 PER PERIOD	SINKING FUND FACTOR	PRESENT VALUE REVERSION OF $1	PRESENT VALUE ORD. ANNUITY $1 PER PERIOD	INSTALMENT TO AMORTIZE $1
YEARS						
1	1.070000	1.000000	1.000000	0.934579	0.934579	1.070000
2	1.144900	2.070000	0.483092	0.873439	1.808018	0.553092
3	1.225043	3.214900	0.311052	0.816298	2.624316	0.381052
4	1.310796	4.439943	0.225228	0.762895	3.387211	0.295228
5	1.402552	5.750739	0.173891	0.712986	4.100197	0.243891
6	1.500730	7.153291	0.139796	0.666342	4.766540	0.209796
7	1.605781	8.654021	0.115553	0.622750	5.389289	0.185553
8	1.718186	10.259803	0.097468	0.582009	5.971299	0.167468
9	1.838459	11.977989	0.083486	0.543934	6.515232	0.153486
10	1.967151	13.816448	0.072378	0.508349	7.023582	0.142378
11	2.104852	15.783599	0.063357	0.475093	7.498674	0.133357
12	2.252192	17.888451	0.055902	0.444012	7.942686	0.125902
13	2.409845	20.140643	0.049651	0.414964	8.357651	0.119651
14	2.578534	22.550488	0.044345	0.387817	8.745468	0.114345
15	2.759032	25.129022	0.039795	0.362446	9.107914	0.109795
16	2.952164	27.888054	0.035858	0.338735	9.446649	0.105858
17	3.158815	30.840217	0.032425	0.316574	9.763223	0.102425
18	3.379932	33.999033	0.029413	0.295864	10.059087	0.099413
19	3.616528	37.378965	0.026753	0.276508	10.335595	0.096753
20	3.869684	40.995492	0.024393	0.258419	10.594014	0.094393
21	4.140562	44.865177	0.022289	0.241513	10.835527	0.092289
22	4.430402	49.005739	0.020406	0.225713	11.061240	0.090405
23	4.740530	53.436141	0.018714	0.210947	11.272187	0.088714
24	5.072367	58.176671	0.017189	0.197147	11.469334	0.087189
25	5.427433	63.249038	0.015811	0.184249	11.653583	0.085811
26	5.807353	68.676470	0.014561	0.172195	11.825779	0.084561
27	6.213868	74.483823	0.013426	0.160930	11.986709	0.083426
28	6.648838	80.697691	0.012392	0.150402	12.137111	0.082392
29	7.114257	87.346529	0.011449	0.140563	12.277674	0.081449
30	7.612255	94.460786	0.010586	0.131367	12.409041	0.080586
31	8.145113	102.073041	0.009797	0.122773	12.531814	0.079797
32	8.715271	110.218154	0.009073	0.114741	12.646555	0.079073
33	9.325340	118.933425	0.008408	0.107235	12.753790	0.078408
34	9.978114	128.258765	0.007797	0.100219	12.854009	0.077797
35	10.676581	138.236878	0.007234	0.093663	12.947672	0.077234
36	11.423942	148.913460	0.006715	0.087535	13.035208	0.076715
37	12.223618	160.337402	0.006237	0.081809	13.117017	0.076237
38	13.079271	172.561020	0.005795	0.076457	13.193473	0.075795
39	13.994820	185.640292	0.005387	0.071455	13.264928	0.075387
40	14.974458	199.635112	0.005009	0.066780	13.331709	0.075009
41	16.022670	214.609570	0.004660	0.062412	13.394120	0.074660
42	17.144257	230.632240	0.004336	0.058329	13.452449	0.074336
43	18.344355	247.776496	0.004036	0.054513	13.506962	0.074036
44	19.628460	266.120851	0.003758	0.050946	13.557908	0.073758
45	21.002452	285.749311	0.003500	0.047613	13.605522	0.073500
46	22.472623	306.751763	0.003260	0.044499	13.650020	0.073260
47	24.045707	329.224386	0.003037	0.041587	13.691608	0.073037
48	25.728947	353.270093	0.002831	0.038867	13.730474	0.072831
49	27.529930	378.999000	0.002639	0.036324	13.766799	0.072639
50	29.457025	406.528929	0.002460	0.033948	13.800746	0.072460

7.50%   MONTHLY COMPOUND INTEREST TABLES   7.50%
                              EFFECTIVE RATE 0.625

	1 AMOUNT OF $1 AT COMPOUND INTEREST	2 ACCUMULATION OF $1 PER PERIOD	3 SINKING FUND FACTOR	4 PRESENT VALUE REVERSION OF $1	5 PRESENT VALUE ORD. ANNUITY $1 PER PERIOD	6 INSTALMENT TO AMORTIZE $1	
MONTHS							
1	1.006250	1.000000	1.000000	0.993789	0.993789	1.006250	
2	1.012539	2.006250	0.498442	0.987616	1.981405	0.504692	
3	1.018867	3.018789	0.331259	0.981482	2.962887	0.337509	
4	1.025235	4.037656	0.247668	0.975386	3.938273	0.253918	
5	1.031643	5.062892	0.197516	0.969327	4.907600	0.203766	
6	1.038091	6.094535	0.164081	0.963307	5.870907	0.170331	
7	1.044579	7.132626	0.140201	0.957324	6.828231	0.146451	
8	1.051108	8.177205	0.122291	0.951377	7.779608	0.128541	
9	1.057677	9.228312	0.108362	0.945468	8.725076	0.114612	
10	1.064287	10.285989	0.097220	0.939596	9.664672	0.103470	
11	1.070939	11.350277	0.088104	0.933760	10.598432	0.094354	
12	1.077633	12.421216	0.080507	0.927960	11.526392	0.086757	
YEARS							**MONTHS**
1	1.077633	12.421216	0.080507	0.927960	11.526392	0.086757	12
2	1.161292	25.806723	0.038750	0.861110	22.222423	0.045000	24
3	1.251446	40.231382	0.024856	0.799076	32.147913	0.031106	36
4	1.348599	55.775864	0.017929	0.741510	41.358371	0.024179	48
5	1.453294	72.527105	0.013788	0.688092	49.905308	0.020038	60
6	1.566117	90.578789	0.011040	0.638522	57.836524	0.017290	72
7	1.687699	110.031871	0.009088	0.592523	65.196376	0.015338	84
8	1.818720	130.995147	0.007634	0.549837	72.026024	0.013884	96
9	1.959912	153.585857	0.006511	0.510227	78.363665	0.012761	108
10	2.112065	177.930342	0.005620	0.473470	84.244743	0.011870	120
11	2.276030	204.164753	0.004898	0.439362	89.702148	0.011148	132
12	2.452724	232.435809	0.004302	0.407710	94.766401	0.010552	144
13	2.643135	262.901620	0.003804	0.378339	99.465827	0.010054	156
14	2.848329	295.732572	0.003381	0.351083	103.826705	0.009631	168
15	3.069452	331.112276	0.003020	0.325791	107.873427	0.009270	180
16	3.307741	369.238599	0.002708	0.302321	111.628623	0.008958	192
17	3.564530	410.324766	0.002437	0.280542	115.113294	0.008687	204
18	3.841254	454.600560	0.002200	0.260332	118.346930	0.008450	216
19	4.139460	502.313599	0.001991	0.241577	121.347615	0.008241	228
20	4.460817	553.730725	0.001806	0.224174	124.132131	0.008056	240
21	4.807122	609.139496	0.001642	0.208025	126.716051	0.007892	252
22	5.180311	668.849794	0.001495	0.193039	129.113825	0.007745	264
23	5.582472	733.195558	0.001364	0.179132	131.338863	0.007614	276
24	6.015854	802.536650	0.001246	0.166227	133.403610	0.007496	288
25	6.482880	877.260872	0.001140	0.154252	135.319613	0.007390	.300
26	6.986163	957.786129	0.001044	0.143140	137.097587	0.007294	312
27	7.528517	1044.562771	0.000957	0.132828	138.747475	0.007207	324
28	8.112976	1138.076109	0.000879	0.123259	140.278506	0.007129	336
29	8.742807	1238.849131	0.000807	0.114380	141.699242	0.007057	348
30	9.421534	1347.445425	0.000742	0.106140	143.017627	0.006992	360
31	10.152952	1464.472331	0.000683	0.098494	144.241037	0.006933	372
32	10.941152	1590.584339	0.000629	0.091398	145.376312	0.006879	384
33	11.790542	1726.486751	0.000579	0.084814	146.429801	0.006829	396
34	12.705873	1872.939621	0.000534	0.078704	147.407398	0.006784	408
35	13.692263	2030.762007	0.000492	0.073034	148.314568	0.006742	420
36	14.755228	2200.836555	0.000454	0.067773	149.156386	0.006704	432
37	15.900715	2384.114432	0.000419	0.062890	149.937560	0.006669	444
38	17.135129	2581.620647	0.000387	0.058360	150.662457	0.006637	456
39	18.465374	2794.459783	0.000358	0.054155	151.335133	0.006608	468
40	19.898889	3023.822174	0.000331	0.050254	151.959350	0.006581	480

	1	2	3	4	5	6
	AMOUNT OF $1 AT COMPOUND INTEREST	ACCUMULATION OF $1 PER PERIOD	SINKING FUND FACTOR	PRESENT VALUE REVERSION OF $1	PRESENT VALUE ORD. ANNUITY $1 PER PERIOD	INSTALMENT TO AMORTIZE $1

YEARS

1	1.075000	1.000000	1.000000	0.930233	0.930233	1.075000
2	1.155562	2.075000	0.481928	0.865333	1.795565	0.556928
3	1.242297	3.230625	0.309538	0.804961	2.600526	0.384538
4	1.335469	4.472922	0.223568	0.748801	3.349326	0.298568
5	1.435629	5.808391	0.172165	0.696559	4.045885	0.247165
6	1.543302	7.244020	0.138045	0.647962	4.693846	0.213045
7	1.659049	8.787322	0.113800	0.602755	5.296601	0.188800
8	1.783478	10.446371	0.095727	0.560702	5.857304	0.170727
9	1.917239	12.229849	0.081767	0.521583	6.378887	0.156767
10	2.061032	14.147087	0.070686	0.485194	6.864081	0.145686
11	2.215609	16.208119	0.061697	0.451343	7.315424	0.136697
12	2.381780	18.423728	0.054278	0.419854	7.735278	0.129278
13	2.560413	20.805508	0.048064	0.390562	8.125840	0.123064
14	2.752444	23.365921	0.042797	0.363313	8.489154	0.117797
15	2.958877	26.118365	0.038287	0.337966	8.827120	0.113287
16	3.180793	29.077242	0.034391	0.314387	9.141507	0.109391
17	3.419353	32.258035	0.031000	0.292453	9.433960	0.106000
18	3.675804	35.677388	0.028029	0.272049	9.706009	0.103029
19	3.951489	39.353192	0.025411	0.253069	9.959078	0.100411
20	4.247851	43.304681	0.023092	0.235413	10.194491	0.098092
21	4.566440	47.552532	0.021029	0.218989	10.413480	0.096029
22	4.908923	52.118972	0.019187	0.203711	10.617191	0.094187
23	5.277092	57.027895	0.017535	0.189498	10.806689	0.092535
24	5.672874	62.304987	0.016050	0.176277	10.982967	0.091050
25	6.098340	67.977862	0.014711	0.163979	11.146946	0.089711
26	6.555715	74.076201	0.013500	0.152539	11.299485	0.088500
27	7.047394	80.631916	0.012402	0.141896	11.441381	0.087402
28	7.575948	87.679310	0.011405	0.131997	11.573378	0.086405
29	8.144144	95.255258	0.010498	0.122788	11.696165	0.085498
30	8.754955	103.399403	0.009671	0.114221	11.810386	0.084671
31	9.411577	112.154358	0.008916	0.106252	11.916638	0.083916
32	10.117445	121.565935	0.008226	0.098839	12.015478	0.083226
33	10.876253	131.683380	0.007594	0.091943	12.107421	0.082594
34	11.691972	142.559633	0.007015	0.085529	12.192950	0.082015
35	12.568870	154.251606	0.006483	0.079562	12.272511	0.081483
36	13.511536	166.820476	0.005994	0.074011	12.346522	0.080994
37	14.524901	180.332012	0.005545	0.068847	12.415370	0.080545
38	15.614268	194.856913	0.005132	0.064044	12.479414	0.080132
39	16.785339	210.471181	0.004751	0.059576	12.538989	0.079751
40	18.044239	227.256520	0.004400	0.055419	12.594409	0.079400
41	19.397557	245.300759	0.004077	0.051553	12.645962	0.079077
42	20.852374	264.698315	0.003778	0.047956	12.693918	0.078778
43	22.416302	285.550689	0.003502	0.044610	12.738528	0.078502
44	24.097524	307.966991	0.003247	0.041498	12.780026	0.078247
45	25.904839	332.064515	0.003011	0.038603	12.818629	0.078011
46	27.847702	357.969354	0.002794	0.035910	12.854539	0.077794
47	29.936279	385.817055	0.002592	0.033404	12.887943	0.077592
48	32.181500	415.753334	0.002405	0.031074	12.919017	0.077405
49	34.595113	447.934835	0.002232	0.028906	12.947922	0.077232
50	37.189746	482.529947	0.002072	0.026889	12.974812	0.077072

8.00% MONTHLY COMPOUND INTEREST TABLES 8.00%
EFFECTIVE RATE 0.667

	1 AMOUNT OF $1 AT COMPOUND INTEREST	2 ACCUMULATION OF $1 PER PERIOD	3 SINKING FUND FACTOR	4 PRESENT VALUE REVERSION OF $1	5 PRESENT VALUE ORD. ANNUITY $1 PER PERIOD	6 INSTALMENT TO AMORTIZE $1	
MONTHS							
1	1.006667	1.000000	1.000000	0.993377	0.993377	1.006667	
2	1.013378	2.006667	0.498339	0.986799	1.980176	0.505006	
3	1.020134	3.020044	0.331121	0.980264	2.960440	0.337788	
4	1.026935	4.040178	0.247514	0.973772	3.934212	0.254181	
5	1.033781	5.067113	0.197351	0.967323	4.901535	0.204018	
6	1.040673	6.100893	0.163910	0.960917	5.862452	0.170577	
7	1.047610	7.141566	0.140025	0.954553	6.817005	0.146692	
8	1.054595	8.189176	0.122112	0.948232	7.765237	0.128779	
9	1.061625	9.243771	0.108181	0.941952	8.707189	0.114848	
10	1.068703	10.305396	0.097037	0.935714	9.642903	0.103703	
11	1.075827	11.374099	0.087919	0.929517	10.572420	0.094586	
12	1.083000	12.449926	0.080322	0.923361	11.495782	0.086988	

YEARS							**MONTHS**
1	1.083000	12.449926	0.080322	0.923361	11.495782	0.086988	12
2	1.172888	25.933190	0.038561	0.852596	22.110544	0.045227	24
3	1.270237	40.535558	0.024670	0.787255	31.911806	0.031336	36
4	1.375666	56.349915	0.017746	0.726921	40.961913	0.024413	48
5	1.489846	73.476856	0.013610	0.671210	49.318433	0.020276	60
6	1.613502	92.025325	0.010867	0.619770	57.034522	0.017533	72
7	1.747422	112.113308	0.008920	0.572272	64.159261	0.015586	84
8	1.892457	133.868583	0.007470	0.528414	70.737970	0.014137	96
9	2.049530	157.429535	0.006352	0.487917	76.812497	0.013019	108
10	2.219640	182.946035	0.005466	0.450523	82.421481	0.012133	120
11	2.403869	210.580392	0.004749	0.415996	87.600600	0.011415	132
12	2.603389	240.508387	0.004158	0.384115	92.382800	0.010825	144
13	2.819469	272.920390	0.003664	0.354677	96.798498	0.010331	156
14	3.053484	308.022574	0.003247	0.327495	100.875784	0.009913	168
15	3.306921	346.038222	0.002890	0.302396	104.640592	0.009557	180
16	3.581394	387.209149	0.002583	0.279221	108.116871	0.009249	192
17	3.878648	431.797244	0.002316	0.257822	111.326733	0.008983	204
18	4.200574	480.086128	0.002083	0.238063	114.290596	0.008750	216
19	4.549220	532.382966	0.001878	0.219818	117.027313	0.008545	228
20	4.926803	589.020416	0.001698	0.202971	119.554292	0.008364	240
21	5.335725	650.358746	0.001538	0.187416	121.887606	0.008204	252
22	5.778588	716.788127	0.001395	0.173053	124.042099	0.008062	264
23	6.258207	788.731114	0.001268	0.159790	126.031475	0.007935	276
24	6.777636	866.645333	0.001154	0.147544	127.868388	0.007821	288
25	7.340176	951.026395	0.001051	0.136237	129.564523	0.007718	300
26	7.949407	1042.411042	0.000959	0.125796	131.130668	0.007626	312
27	8.609204	1141.380571	0.000876	0.116155	132.576786	0.007543	324
28	9.323763	1248.564521	0.000801	0.107253	133.912076	0.007468	336
29	10.097631	1364.644687	0.000733	0.099033	135.145031	0.007399	348
30	10.935730	1490.359449	0.000671	0.091443	136.283494	0.007338	360
31	11.843390	1626.508474	0.000615	0.084435	137.334707	0.007281	372
32	12.826385	1773.957801	0.000564	0.077964	138.305357	0.007230	384
33	13.890969	1933.645350	0.000517	0.071989	139.201617	0.007184	396
34	15.043913	2106.586886	0.000475	0.066472	140.029190	0.007141	408
35	16.292550	2293.882485	0.000436	0.061378	140.793338	0.007103	420
36	17.644824	2496.723526	0.000401	0.056674	141.498923	0.007067	432
37	19.109335	2716.400273	0.000368	0.052330	142.150433	0.007035	444
38	20.695401	2954.310082	0.000338	0.048320	142.752013	0.007005	456
39	22.413109	3211.966288	0.000311	0.044617	143.307488	0.006978	468
40	24.273386	3491.007831	0.000286	0.041197	143.820392	0.006953	480

8.00%   ANNUAL COMPOUND INTEREST TABLES   8.00%
                              EFFECTIVE RATE 8.00

	1	2	3	4	5	6
	AMOUNT OF $1 AT COMPOUND INTEREST	ACCUMULATION OF $1 PER PERIOD	SINKING FUND FACTOR	PRESENT VALUE REVERSION OF $1	PRESENT VALUE ORD. ANNUITY $1 PER PERIOD	INSTALMENT TO AMORTIZE $1
YEARS						
1	1.080000	1.000000	1.000000	0.925926	0.925926	1.080000
2	1.166400	2.080000	0.480769	0.857339	1.783265	0.560769
3	1.259712	3.246400	0.308034	0.793832	2.577097	0.388034
4	1.360489	4.506112	0.221921	0.735030	3.312127	0.301921
5	1.469328	5.866601	0.170456	0.680583	3.992710	0.250456
6	1.586874	7.335929	0.136315	0.630170	4.622880	0.216315
7	1.713824	8.922803	0.112072	0.583490	5.206370	0.192072
8	1.850930	10.636628	0.094015	0.540269	5.746639	0.174015
9	1.999005	12.487558	0.080080	0.500249	6.246888	0.160080
10	2.158925	14.486562	0.069029	0.463193	6.710081	0.149029
11	2.331639	16.645487	0.060076	0.428883	7.138964	0.140076
12	2.518170	18.977126	0.052695	0.397114	7.536078	0.132695
13	2.719624	21.495297	0.046522	0.367698	7.903776	0.126522
14	2.937194	24.214920	0.041297	0.340461	8.244237	0.121297
15	3.172169	27.152114	0.036830	0.315242	8.559479	0.116830
16	3.425943	30.324283	0.032977	0.291890	8.851369	0.112977
17	3.700018	33.750226	0.029629	0.270269	9.121638	0.109629
18	3.996019	37.450244	0.026702	0.250249	9.371887	0.106702
19	4.315701	41.446263	0.024128	0.231712	9.603599	0.104128
20	4.660957	45.761964	0.021852	0.214548	9.818147	0.101852
21	5.033834	50.422921	0.019832	0.198656	10.016803	0.099832
22	5.436540	55.456755	0.018032	0.183941	10.200744	0.098032
23	5.871464	60.893296	0.016422	0.170315	10.371059	0.096422
24	6.341181	66.764759	0.014978	0.157699	10.528758	0.094978
25	6.848475	73.105940	0.013679	0.146018	10.674776	0.093679
26	7.396353	79.954415	0.012507	0.135202	10.809978	0.092507
27	7.988061	87.350768	0.011448	0.125187	10.935165	0.091448
28	8.627106	95.338830	0.010489	0.115914	11.051078	0.090489
29	9.317275	103.965936	0.009619	0.107328	11.158406	0.089619
30	10.062657	113.283211	0.008827	0.099377	11.257783	0.088827
31	10.867669	123.345868	0.008107	0.092016	11.349799	0.088107
32	11.737083	134.213537	0.007451	0.085200	11.434999	0.087451
33	12.676050	145.950620	0.006852	0.078889	11.513888	0.086852
34	13.690134	158.526670	0.006304	0.073045	11.586934	0.086304
35	14.785344	172.316804	0.005803	0.067635	11.654568	0.085803
36	15.968172	187.102148	0.005345	0.062625	11.717193	0.085345
37	17.245626	203.070320	0.004924	0.057986	11.775179	0.084924
38	18.625276	220.315945	0.004539	0.053690	11.828869	0.084539
39	20.115298	238.941221	0.004185	0.049713	11.878582	0.084185
40	21.724521	259.056519	0.003860	0.046031	11.924613	0.083860
41	23.462483	280.781040	0.003561	0.042621	11.967235	0.083561
42	25.339482	304.243523	0.003287	0.039464	12.006699	0.083287
43	27.366640	329.583005	0.003034	0.036541	12.043240	0.083034
44	29.555972	356.949646	0.002802	0.033834	12.077074	0.082802
45	31.920449	386.505617	0.002587	0.031328	12.108402	0.082587
46	34.474085	418.426067	0.002390	0.029007	12.137409	0.082390
47	37.232012	452.900152	0.002208	0.026859	12.164267	0.082208
48	40.210573	490.132164	0.002040	0.024869	12.189136	0.082040
49	43.427419	530.342737	0.001886	0.023027	12.212163	0.081886
50	46.901613	573.770156	0.001743	0.021321	12.233485	0.081743

8.50%   MONTHLY COMPOUND INTEREST TABLES   8.50%
                        EFFECTIVE RATE 0.708

	1 AMOUNT OF $1 AT COMPOUND INTEREST	2 ACCUMULATION OF $1 PER PERIOD	3 SINKING FUND FACTOR	4 PRESENT VALUE REVERSION OF $1	5 PRESENT VALUE ORD. ANNUITY $1 PER PERIOD	6 INSTALMENT TO AMORTIZE $1	
MONTHS							
1	1.007083	1.000000	1.000000	0.992966	0.992966	1.007083	
2	1.014217	2.007083	0.498235	0.985982	1.978949	0.505319	
3	1.021401	3.021300	0.330983	0.979048	2.957996	0.338067	
4	1.028636	4.042701	0.247359	0.972161	3.930158	0.254443	
5	1.035922	5.071337	0.197187	0.965324	4.895482	0.204270	
6	1.043260	6.107259	0.163740	0.958534	5.854016	0.170823	
7	1.050650	7.150519	0.139850	0.951792	6.805808	0.146933	
8	1.058092	8.201168	0.121934	0.945098	7.750906	0.129017	
9	1.065586	9.259260	0.108000	0.938450	8.689356	0.115083	
10	1.073134	10.324846	0.096854	0.931850	9.621206	0.103937	
11	1.080736	11.397980	0.087735	0.925296	10.546501	0.094818	
12	1.088391	12.478716	0.080136	0.918788	11.465289	0.087220	
YEARS							MONTHS
1	1.088391	12.478716	0.080136	0.918788	11.465289	0.087220	12
2	1.184595	26.060437	0.038372	0.844171	21.999453	0.045456	24
3	1.289302	40.842659	0.024484	0.775613	31.678112	0.031568	36
4	1.403265	56.931495	0.017565	0.712624	40.570744	0.024648	48
5	1.527301	74.442437	0.013433	0.654750	48.741183	0.020517	60
6	1.662300	93.501188	0.010695	0.601576	56.248080	0.017778	72
7	1.809232	114.244559	0.008753	0.552721	63.145324	0.015836	84
8	1.969152	136.821455	0.007309	0.507833	69.482425	0.014392	96
9	2.143207	161.393943	0.006196	0.466590	75.304875	0.013279	108
10	2.332647	188.138416	0.005315	0.428698	80.654470	0.012399	120
11	2.538832	217.246858	0.004603	0.393882	85.569611	0.011686	132
12	2.763242	248.928220	0.004017	0.361894	90.085581	0.011101	144
13	3.007487	283.409927	0.003528	0.332504	94.234798	0.010612	156
14	3.273321	320.939504	0.003116	0.305500	98.047046	0.010199	168
15	3.562653	361.786353	0.002764	0.280690	101.549693	0.009847	180
16	3.877559	406.243693	0.002462	0.257894	104.767881	0.009545	192
17	4.220300	454.630657	0.002200	0.236950	107.724713	0.009283	204
18	4.593337	507.294589	0.001971	0.217707	110.441412	0.009055	216
19	4.999346	564.613533	0.001771	0.200026	112.937482	0.008854	228
20	5.441243	626.998951	0.001595	0.183782	115.230840	0.008678	240
21	5.922199	694.898672	0.001439	0.168856	117.337948	0.008522	252
22	6.445667	768.800112	0.001301	0.155143	119.273933	0.008384	264
23	7.015406	849.233766	0.001178	0.142543	121.052692	0.008261	276
24	7.635504	936.777024	0.001067	0.130967	122.686994	0.008151	288
25	8.310413	1032.058310	0.000969	0.120331	124.188570	0.008052	300
26	9.044978	1135.761595	0.000880	0.110559	125.568199	0.007964	312
27	9.844472	1248.631307	0.000801	0.101580	126.835785	0.007884	324
28	10.714634	1371.477676	0.000729	0.093330	128.000428	0.007812	336
29	11.661710	1505.182546	0.000664	0.085751	129.070487	0.007748	348
30	12.692499	1650.705711	0.000606	0.078787	130.053643	0.007689	360
31	13.814400	1809.091800	0.000553	0.072388	130.956956	0.007636	372
32	15.035468	1981.477780	0.000505	0.066509	131.786908	0.007588	384
33	16.364466	2169.101112	0.000461	0.061108	132.549457	0.007544	396
34	17.810936	2373.308640	0.000421	0.056145	133.250078	0.007505	408
35	19.385261	2595.566257	0.000385	0.051586	133.893800	0.007469	420
36	21.098742	2837.469426	0.000352	0.047396	134.485244	0.007436	432
37	22.963679	3100.754635	0.000323	0.043547	135.028655	0.007406	444
38	24.993459	3387.311862	0.000295	0.040010	135.527934	0.007379	456
39	27.202654	3699.198142	0.000270	0.036761	135.986665	0.007354	468
40	29.607121	4038.652333	0.000248	0.033776	136.408142	0.007331	480

COMPOUND INTEREST TABLES

	1	2	3	4	5	6
	AMOUNT OF $1 AT COMPOUND INTEREST	ACCUMULATION OF $1 PER PERIOD	SINKING FUND FACTOR	PRESENT VALUE REVERSION OF $1	PRESENT VALUE ORD. ANNUITY $1 PER PERIOD	INSTALMENT TO AMORTIZE $1
YEARS						
1	1.085000	1.000000	1.000000	0.921659	0.921659	1.085000
2	1.177225	2.085000	0.479616	0.849455	1.771114	0.564616
3	1.277289	3.262225	0.306539	0.782908	2.554022	0.391539
4	1.385859	4.539514	0.220288	0.721574	3.275597	0.305288
5	1.503657	5.925373	0.168766	0.665045	3.940642	0.253766
6	1.631468	7.429030	0.134607	0.612945	4.553587	0.219607
7	1.770142	9.060497	0.110369	0.564926	5.118514	0.195369
8	1.920604	10.830639	0.092331	0.520669	5.639183	0.177331
9	2.083856	12.751244	0.078424	0.479880	6.119063	0.163424
10	2.260983	14.835099	0.067408	0.442285	6.561348	0.152408
11	2.453167	17.096083	0.058493	0.407636	6.968984	0.143493
12	2.661686	19.549250	0.051153	0.375702	7.344686	0.136153
13	2.887930	22.210936	0.045023	0.346269	7.690955	0.130023
14	3.133404	25.098866	0.039842	0.319142	8.010097	0.124842
15	3.399743	28.232269	0.035420	0.294140	8.304237	0.120420
16	3.688721	31.632012	0.031614	0.271097	8.575333	0.116614
17	4.002262	35.320733	0.028312	0.249859	8.825192	0.113312
18	4.342455	39.322995	0.025430	0.230285	9.055476	0.110430
19	4.711563	43.665450	0.022901	0.212244	9.267720	0.107901
20	5.112046	48.377013	0.020671	0.195616	9.463337	0.105671
21	5.546570	53.489059	0.018695	0.180292	9.643628	0.103695
22	6.018028	59.035629	0.016939	0.166167	9.809796	0.101939
23	6.529561	65.053658	0.015372	0.153150	9.962945	0.100372
24	7.084574	71.583219	0.013970	0.141152	10.104097	0.098970
25	7.686762	78.667792	0.012712	0.130094	10.234191	0.097712
26	8.340137	86.354555	0.011580	0.119902	10.354093	0.096580
27	9.049049	94.694692	0.010560	0.110509	10.464602	0.095560
28	9.818218	103.743741	0.009639	0.101851	10.566453	0.094639
29	10.652766	113.561959	0.008806	0.093872	10.660326	0.093806
30	11.558252	124.214725	0.008051	0.086518	10.746844	0.093051
31	12.540703	135.772977	0.007365	0.079740	10.826584	0.092365
32	13.606663	148.313680	0.006742	0.073493	10.900078	0.091742
33	14.763229	161.920343	0.006176	0.067736	10.967813	0.091176
34	16.018104	176.683572	0.005660	0.062429	11.030243	0.090660
35	17.379642	192.701675	0.005189	0.057539	11.087781	0.090189
36	18.856912	210.081318	0.004760	0.053031	11.140812	0.089760
37	20.459750	228.938230	0.004368	0.048876	11.189689	0.089368
38	22.198828	249.397979	0.004010	0.045047	11.234736	0.089010
39	24.085729	271.596808	0.003682	0.041518	11.276255	0.088682
40	26.133016	295.682536	0.003382	0.038266	11.314520	0.088382
41	28.354322	321.815552	0.003107	0.035268	11.349788	0.088107
42	30.764439	350.169874	0.002856	0.032505	11.382293	0.087856
43	33.379417	380.934313	0.002625	0.029959	11.412252	0.087625
44	36.216667	414.313730	0.002414	0.027612	11.439864	0.087414
45	39.295084	450.530397	0.002220	0.025448	11.465312	0.087220
46	42.635166	489.825480	0.002042	0.023455	11.488767	0.087042
47	46.259155	532.460646	0.001878	0.021617	11.510384	0.086878
48	50.191183	578.719801	0.001728	0.019924	11.530308	0.086728
49	54.457434	628.910984	0.001590	0.018363	11.548671	0.086590
50	59.086316	683.368418	0.001463	0.016924	11.565595	0.086463

9.00% MONTHLY COMPOUND INTEREST TABLES 9.00%
EFFECTIVE RATE 0.750

	1 AMOUNT OF $1 AT COMPOUND INTEREST	2 ACCUMULATION OF $1 PER PERIOD	3 SINKING FUND FACTOR	4 PRESENT VALUE REVERSION OF $1	5 PRESENT VALUE ORD. ANNUITY $1 PER PERIOD	6 INSTALMENT TO AMORTIZE $1	
MONTHS							
1	1.007500	1.000000	1.000000	0.992556	0.992556	1.007500	
2	1.015056	2.007500	0.498132	0.985167	1.977723	0.505632	
3	1.022669	3.022556	0.330846	0.977833	2.955556	0.338346	
4	1.030339	4.045225	0.247205	0.970554	3.926110	0.254705	
5	1.038067	5.075565	0.197022	0.963329	4.889440	0.204522	
6	1.045852	6.113631	0.163569	0.956158	5.845598	0.171069	
7	1.053696	7.159484	0.139675	0.949040	6.794638	0.147175	
8	1.061599	8.213180	0.121756	0.941975	7.736613	0.129256	
9	1.069561	9.274779	0.107819	0.934963	8.671576	0.115319	
10	1.077583	10.344339	0.096671	0.928003	9.599580	0.104171	
11	1.085664	11.421922	0.087551	0.921095	10.520675	0.095051	
12	1.093807	12.507586	0.079951	0.914238	11.434913	0.087451	
YEARS							MONTHS
1	1.093807	12.507586	0.079951	0.914238	11.434913	0.087451	12
2	1.196414	26.188471	0.038185	0.835831	21.889146	0.045685	24
3	1.308645	41.152716	0.024300	0.764149	31.446805	0.031800	36
4	1.431405	57.520711	0.017385	0.698614	40.184782	0.024885	48
5	1.565681	75.424137	0.013258	0.638700	48.173374	0.020758	60
6	1.712553	95.007028	0.010526	0.583924	55.476849	0.018026	72
7	1.873202	116.426928	0.008589	0.533845	62.153965	0.016089	84
8	2.048921	139.856164	0.007150	0.488062	68.258439	0.014650	96
9	2.241124	165.483223	0.006043	0.446205	73.839382	0.013543	108
10	2.451357	193.514277	0.005168	0.407937	78.941693	0.012668	120
11	2.681311	224.174837	0.004461	0.372952	83.606420	0.011961	132
12	2.932837	257.711570	0.003880	0.340967	87.871092	0.011380	144
13	3.207957	294.394279	0.003397	0.311725	91.770018	0.010897	156
14	3.508886	334.518079	0.002989	0.284991	95.334564	0.010489	168
15	3.838043	378.405769	0.002643	0.260549	98.593409	0.010143	180
16	4.198078	426.410427	0.002345	0.238204	101.572769	0.009845	192
17	4.591887	478.918252	0.002088	0.217775	104.296613	0.009588	204
18	5.022638	536.351674	0.001864	0.199099	106.786856	0.009364	216
19	5.493796	599.172747	0.001669	0.182024	109.063531	0.009169	228
20	6.009152	667.886870	0.001497	0.166413	111.144954	0.008997	240
21	6.572851	743.046852	0.001346	0.152141	113.047870	0.008846	252
22	7.189430	825.257358	0.001212	0.139093	114.787589	0.008712	264
23	7.863848	915.179777	0.001093	0.127164	116.378106	0.008593	276
24	8.601532	1013.537539	0.000987	0.116258	117.832218	0.008487	288
25	9.408415	1121.121937	0.000892	0.106288	119.161622	0.008392	300
26	10.290989	1238.798494	0.000807	0.097172	120.377014	0.008307	312
27	11.256354	1367.513924	0.000731	0.088839	121.488172	0.008231	324
28	12.312278	1508.303750	0.000663	0.081220	122.504035	0.008163	336
29	13.467255	1662.300631	0.000602	0.074254	123.432776	0.008102	348
30	14.730576	1830.743483	0.000546	0.067886	124.281866	0.008046	360
31	16.112406	2014.987436	0.000496	0.062064	125.058136	0.007996	372
32	17.623861	2216.514743	0.000451	0.056741	125.767832	0.007951	384
33	19.277100	2436.946701	0.000410	0.051875	126.416664	0.007910	396
34	21.085425	2678.056697	0.000373	0.047426	127.009850	0.007873	408
35	23.063384	2941.784473	0.000340	0.043359	127.552164	0.007840	420
36	25.226888	3230.251735	0.000310	0.039640	128.047967	0.007810	432
37	27.593344	3545.779215	0.000282	0.036241	128.501250	0.007782	444
38	30.181790	3890.905350	0.000257	0.033133	128.915659	0.007757	456
39	33.013050	4268.406696	0.000234	0.030291	129.294526	0.007734	468
40	36.109902	4681.320272	0.000214	0.027693	129.640902	0.007714	480

9.00%   ANNUAL COMPOUND INTEREST TABLES   9.00%
                              EFFECTIVE RATE 9.00

	1 AMOUNT OF $1 AT COMPOUND INTEREST	2 ACCUMULATION OF $1 PER PERIOD	3 SINKING FUND FACTOR	4 PRESENT VALUE REVERSION OF $1	5 PRESENT VALUE ORD. ANNUITY $1 PER PERIOD	6 INSTALMENT TO AMORTIZE $1
YEARS						
1	1.090000	1.000000	1.000000	0.917431	0.917431	1.090000
2	1.188100	2.090000	0.478469	0.841680	1.759111	0.568469
3	1.295029	3.278100	0.305055	0.772183	2.531295	0.395055
4	1.411582	4.573129	0.218669	0.708425	3.239720	0.308669
5	1.538624	5.984711	0.167092	0.649931	3.889651	0.257092
6	1.677100	7.523335	0.132920	0.596267	4.485919	0.222920
7	1.828039	9.200435	0.108691	0.547034	5.032953	0.198691
8	1.992563	11.028474	0.090674	0.501866	5.534819	0.180674
9	2.171893	13.021036	0.076799	0.460428	5.995247	0.166799
10	2.367364	15.192930	0.065820	0.422411	6.417658	0.155820
11	2.580426	17.560293	0.056947	0.387533	6.805191	0.146947
12	2.812665	20.140720	0.049651	0.355535	7.160725	0.139651
13	3.065805	22.953385	0.043567	0.326179	7.486904	0.133567
14	3.341727	26.019189	0.038433	0.299246	7.786150	0.128433
15	3.642482	29.360916	0.034059	0.274538	8.060688	0.124059
16	3.970306	33.003399	0.030300	0.251870	8.312558	0.120300
17	4.327633	36.973705	0.027046	0.231073	8.543631	0.117046
18	4.717120	41.301338	0.024212	0.211994	8.755625	0.114212
19	5.141661	46.018458	0.021730	0.194490	8.950115	0.111730
20	5.604411	51.160120	0.019546	0.178431	9.128546	0.109546
21	6.108808	56.764530	0.017617	0.163698	9.292244	0.107617
22	6.658600	62.873338	0.015905	0.150182	9.442425	0.105905
23	7.257874	69.531939	0.014382	0.137781	9.580207	0.104382
24	7.911083	76.789813	0.013023	0.126405	9.706612	0.103023
25	8.623081	84.700896	0.011806	0.115968	9.822580	0.101806
26	9.399158	93.323977	0.010715	0.106393	9.928972	0.100715
27	10.245082	102.723135	0.009735	0.097608	10.026580	0.099735
28	11.167140	112.968217	0.008852	0.089548	10.116128	0.098852
29	12.172182	124.135356	0.008056	0.082155	10.198283	0.098056
30	13.267678	136.307539	0.007336	0.075371	10.273654	0.097336
31	14.461770	149.575217	0.006686	0.069148	10.342802	0.096686
32	15.763329	164.036987	0.006096	0.063438	10.406240	0.096096
33	17.182028	179.800315	0.005562	0.058200	10.464441	0.095562
34	18.728411	196.982344	0.005077	0.053395	10.517835	0.095077
35	20.413968	215.710755	0.004636	0.048986	10.566821	0.094636
36	22.251225	236.124723	0.004235	0.044941	10.611763	0.094235
37	24.253835	258.375948	0.003870	0.041231	10.652993	0.093870
38	26.436680	282.629783	0.003538	0.037826	10.690820	0.093538
39	28.815982	309.066463	0.003236	0.034703	10.725523	0.093236
40	31.409420	337.882445	0.002960	0.031838	10.757360	0.092960
41	34.236268	369.291865	0.002708	0.029209	10.786569	0.092708
42	37.317532	403.528133	0.002478	0.026797	10.813366	0.092478
43	40.676110	440.845665	0.002268	0.024584	10.837950	0.092268
44	44.336960	481.521775	0.002077	0.022555	10.860505	0.092077
45	48.327286	525.858734	0.001902	0.020692	10.881197	0.091902
46	52.676742	574.186021	0.001742	0.018984	10.900181	0.091742
47	57.417649	626.862762	0.001595	0.017416	10.917597	0.091595
48	62.585237	684.280411	0.001461	0.015978	10.933575	0.091461
49	68.217908	746.865648	0.001339	0.014659	10.948234	0.091339
50	74.357520	815.083556	0.001227	0.013449	10.961683	0.091227

9.50%   MONTHLY COMPOUND INTEREST TABLES   9.50%
EFFECTIVE RATE 0.792

	1 AMOUNT OF $1 AT COMPOUND INTEREST	2 ACCUMULATION OF $1 PER PERIOD	3 SINKING FUND FACTOR	4 PRESENT VALUE REVERSION OF $1	5 PRESENT VALUE ORD. ANNUITY $1 PER PERIOD	6 INSTALMENT TO AMORTIZE $1	
MONTHS							
1	1.007917	1.000000	1.000000	0.992146	0.992146	1.007917	
2	1.015896	2.007917	0.498029	0.984353	1.976498	0.505945	
3	1.023939	3.023813	0.330708	0.976621	2.953119	0.338625	
4	1.032045	4.047751	0.247051	0.968950	3.922070	0.254967	
5	1.040215	5.079796	0.196858	0.961340	4.883409	0.204775	
6	1.048450	6.120011	0.163398	0.953789	5.837198	0.171315	
7	1.056750	7.168461	0.139500	0.946297	6.783496	0.147417	
8	1.065116	8.225211	0.121577	0.938865	7.722360	0.129494	
9	1.073548	9.290328	0.107639	0.931490	8.653851	0.115555	
10	1.082047	10.363876	0.096489	0.924174	9.578024	0.104406	
11	1.090614	11.445923	0.087367	0.916915	10.494940	0.095284	
12	1.099248	12.536537	0.079767	0.909713	11.404653	0.087684	
YEARS							MONTHS
1	1.099248	12.536537	0.079767	0.909713	11.404653	0.087684	12
2	1.208345	26.317295	0.037998	0.827578	21.779615	0.045914	24
3	1.328271	41.465760	0.024116	0.752859	31.217856	0.032033	36
4	1.460098	58.117673	0.017206	0.684885	39.803947	0.025123	48
5	1.605009	76.422249	0.013085	0.623049	47.614827	0.021002	60
6	1.764303	96.543509	0.010358	0.566796	54.720488	0.018275	72
7	1.939406	118.661756	0.008427	0.515622	61.184601	0.016344	84
8	2.131887	142.975186	0.006994	0.469068	67.065090	0.014911	96
9	2.343472	169.701665	0.005893	0.426717	72.414648	0.013809	108
10	2.576055	199.080682	0.005023	0.388190	77.281211	0.012940	120
11	2.831723	231.375495	0.004322	0.353142	81.708388	0.012239	132
12	3.112764	266.875491	0.003747	0.321258	85.735849	0.011664	144
13	3.421699	305.898776	0.003269	0.292253	89.399684	0.011186	156
14	3.761294	348.795027	0.002867	0.265866	92.732722	0.010784	168
15	4.134593	395.948628	0.002526	0.241862	95.764831	0.010442	180
16	4.544942	447.782110	0.002233	0.220025	98.523180	0.010150	192
17	4.996016	504.759939	0.001981	0.200159	101.032487	0.009898	204
18	5.491859	567.392681	0.001762	0.182088	103.315236	0.009679	216
19	6.036912	636.241570	0.001572	0.165648	105.391883	0.009488	228
20	6.636061	711.923546	0.001405	0.150692	107.281037	0.009321	240
21	7.294674	795.116775	0.001258	0.137086	108.999624	0.009174	252
22	8.018653	886.566731	0.001128	0.124709	110.563046	0.009045	264
23	8.814485	987.092874	0.001013	0.113450	111.985311	0.008930	276
24	9.689302	1097.595994	0.000911	0.103207	113.279165	0.008828	288
25	10.650941	1219.066282	0.000820	0.093888	114.456200	0.008737	300
26	11.708022	1352.592202	0.000739	0.085412	115.526965	0.008656	312
27	12.870014	1499.370247	0.000667	0.077700	116.501054	0.008584	324
28	14.147332	1660.715658	0.000602	0.070685	117.387195	0.008519	336
29	15.551421	1838.074212	0.000544	0.064303	118.193330	0.008461	348
30	17.094862	2033.035174	0.000492	0.058497	118.926681	0.008409	360
31	18.791486	2247.345541	0.000445	0.053216	119.593820	0.008362	372
32	20.656495	2482.925693	0.000403	0.048411	120.200725	0.008319	384
33	22.706602	2741.886606	0.000365	0.044040	120.752835	0.008281	396
34	24.960178	3026.548765	0.000330	0.040064	121.255097	0.008247	408
35	27.437415	3339.462955	0.000299	0.036447	121.712011	0.008216	420
36	30.160512	3683.433122	0.000271	0.033156	122.127671	0.008188	432
37	33.153870	4061.541498	0.000246	0.030162	122.505803	0.008163	444
38	36.444312	4477.176216	0.000223	0.027439	122.849795	0.008140	456
39	40.061322	4934.061676	0.000203	0.024962	123.162729	0.008119	468
40	44.037311	5436.291914	0.000184	0.022708	123.447408	0.008101	480

	1	2	3	4	5	6
	AMOUNT OF $1 AT COMPOUND INTEREST	ACCUMULATION OF $1 PER PERIOD	SINKING FUND FACTOR	PRESENT VALUE REVERSION OF $1	PRESENT VALUE ORD. ANNUITY $1 PER PERIOD	INSTALMENT TO AMORTIZE $1
YEARS						
1	1.095000	1.000000	1.000000	0.913242	0.913242	1.095000
2	1.199025	2.095000	0.477327	0.834011	1.747253	0.572327
3	1.312932	3.294025	0.303580	0.761654	2.508907	0.398580
4	1.437661	4.606957	0.217063	0.695574	3.204481	0.312063
5	1.574239	6.044618	0.165436	0.635228	3.839709	0.260436
6	1.723791	7.618857	0.131253	0.580117	4.419825	0.226253
7	1.887552	9.342648	0.107036	0.529787	4.949612	0.202036
8	2.066869	11.230200	0.089046	0.483824	5.433436	0.184046
9	2.263222	13.297069	0.075205	0.441848	5.875284	0.170205
10	2.478228	15.560291	0.064266	0.403514	6.278798	0.159266
11	2.713659	18.038518	0.055437	0.368506	6.647304	0.150437
12	2.971457	20.752178	0.048188	0.336535	6.983839	0.143188
13	3.253745	23.723634	0.042152	0.307338	7.291178	0.137152
14	3.562851	26.977380	0.037068	0.280674	7.571852	0.132068
15	3.901322	30.540231	0.032744	0.256323	7.828175	0.127744
16	4.271948	34.441553	0.029035	0.234085	8.062260	0.124035
17	4.677783	38.713500	0.025831	0.213777	8.276037	0.120831
18	5.122172	43.391283	0.023046	0.195230	8.471266	0.118046
19	5.608778	48.513454	0.020613	0.178292	8.649558	0.115613
20	6.141612	54.122233	0.018477	0.162824	8.812382	0.113477
21	6.725065	60.263845	0.016594	0.148697	8.961080	0.111594
22	7.363946	66.988910	0.014928	0.135797	9.096876	0.109928
23	8.063521	74.352856	0.013449	0.124015	9.220892	0.108449
24	8.829556	82.416378	0.012134	0.113256	9.334148	0.107134
25	9.668364	91.245934	0.010959	0.103430	9.437578	0.105959
26	10.586858	100.914297	0.009909	0.094457	9.532034	0.104909
27	11.592610	111.501156	0.008969	0.086262	9.618296	0.103969
28	12.693908	123.093766	0.008124	0.078778	9.697074	0.103124
29	13.899829	135.787673	0.007364	0.071943	9.769018	0.102364
30	15.220313	149.687502	0.006681	0.065702	9.834719	0.101681
31	16.666242	164.907815	0.006064	0.060002	9.894721	0.101064
32	18.249535	181.574057	0.005507	0.054796	9.949517	0.100507
33	19.983241	199.823593	0.005004	0.050042	9.999559	0.100004
34	21.881649	219.806834	0.004549	0.045700	10.045259	0.099549
35	23.960406	241.688483	0.004138	0.041736	10.086995	0.099138
36	26.236644	265.648889	0.003764	0.038115	10.125109	0.098764
37	28.729126	291.885534	0.003426	0.034808	10.159917	0.098426
38	31.458393	320.614659	0.003119	0.031788	10.191705	0.098119
39	34.446940	352.073052	0.002840	0.029030	10.220735	0.097840
40	37.719399	386.519992	0.002587	0.026512	10.247247	0.097587
41	41.302742	424.239391	0.002357	0.024211	10.271458	0.097357
42	45.226503	465.542133	0.002148	0.022111	10.293569	0.097148
43	49.523020	510.768636	0.001958	0.020193	10.313762	0.096958
44	54.227707	560.291656	0.001785	0.018441	10.332203	0.096785
45	59.379340	614.519364	0.001627	0.016841	10.349043	0.096627
46	65.020377	673.898703	0.001484	0.015380	10.364423	0.096484
47	71.197313	738.919080	0.001353	0.014045	10.378469	0.096353
48	77.961057	810.116393	0.001234	0.012827	10.391296	0.096234
49	85.367358	888.077450	0.001126	0.011714	10.403010	0.096126
50	93.477257	973.444808	0.001027	0.010698	10.413707	0.096027

10.00%   MONTHLY COMPOUND INTEREST TABLES   10.00%
                                     EFFECTIVE RATE 0.833

	1 AMOUNT OF $1 AT COMPOUND INTEREST	2 ACCUMULATION OF $1 PER PERIOD	3 SINKING FUND FACTOR	4 PRESENT VALUE REVERSION OF $1	5 PRESENT VALUE ORD. ANNUITY $1 PER PERIOD	6 INSTALMENT TO AMORTIZE $1	
MONTHS							
1	1.008333	1.000000	1.000000	0.991736	0.991736	1.008333	
2	1.016736	2.008333	0.497925	0.983539	1.975275	0.506259	
3	1.025209	3.025069	0.330571	0.975411	2.950686	0.338904	
4	1.033752	4.050278	0.246897	0.967350	3.918036	0.255230	
5	1.042367	5.084031	0.196694	0.959355	4.877391	0.205028	
6	1.051053	6.126398	0.163228	0.951427	5.828817	0.171561	
7	1.059812	7.177451	0.139325	0.943563	6.772381	0.147659	
8	1.068644	8.237263	0.121400	0.935765	7.708146	0.129733	
9	1.077549	9.305907	0.107459	0.928032	8.636178	0.115792	
10	1.086529	10.383456	0.096307	0.920362	9.556540	0.104640	
11	1.095583	11.469985	0.087184	0.912756	10.469296	0.095517	
12	1.104713	12.565568	0.079583	0.905212	11.374508	0.087916	
YEARS							**MONTHS**
1	1.104713	12.565568	0.079583	0.905212	11.374508	0.087916	12
2	1.220391	26.446915	0.037812	0.819410	21.670855	0.046145	24
3	1.348182	41.781821	0.023934	0.741740	30.991236	0.032267	36
4	1.489354	58.722492	0.017029	0.671432	39.428160	0.025363	48
5	1.645309	77.437072	0.012914	0.607789	47.065369	0.021247	60
6	1.817594	98.111314	0.010193	0.550178	53.978665	0.018526	72
7	2.007920	120.950418	0.008268	0.498028	60.236667	0.016601	84
8	2.218176	146.181076	0.006841	0.450821	65.901488	0.015174	96
9	2.450448	174.053713	0.005745	0.408089	71.029355	0.014079	108
10	2.707041	204.844979	0.004882	0.369407	75.671163	0.013215	120
11	2.990504	238.860493	0.004187	0.334392	79.872986	0.012520	132
12	3.303649	276.437876	0.003617	0.302696	83.676528	0.011951	144
13	3.649584	317.950102	0.003145	0.274004	87.119542	0.011478	156
14	4.031743	363.809201	0.002749	0.248032	90.236201	0.011082	168
15	4.453920	414.470346	0.002413	0.224521	93.057439	0.010746	180
16	4.920303	470.436376	0.002126	0.203240	95.611259	0.010459	192
17	5.435523	532.262780	0.001879	0.183975	97.923008	0.010212	204
18	6.004693	600.563216	0.001665	0.166536	100.015633	0.009998	216
19	6.633463	676.015601	0.001479	0.150751	101.909902	0.009813	228
20	7.328074	759.368836	0.001317	0.136462	103.624619	0.009650	240
21	8.095419	851.450244	0.001174	0.123527	105.176801	0.009508	252
22	8.943115	953.173779	0.001049	0.111818	106.581856	0.009382	264
23	9.879576	1065.549097	0.000938	0.101219	107.853730	0.009272	276
24	10.914097	1189.691580	0.000841	0.091625	109.005045	0.009174	288
25	12.056945	1326.833403	0.000754	0.082940	110.047230	0.009087	300
26	13.319465	1478.335767	0.000676	0.075078	110.990629	0.009010	312
27	14.714187	1645.702407	0.000608	0.067962	111.844605	0.008941	324
28	16.254954	1830.594523	0.000546	0.061520	112.617635	0.008880	336
29	17.957060	2034.847259	0.000491	0.055688	113.317392	0.008825	348
30	19.837399	2260.487925	0.000442	0.050410	113.950820	0.008776	360
31	21.914634	2509.756117	0.000398	0.045632	114.524207	0.008732	372
32	24.209383	2785.125947	0.000359	0.041306	115.043244	0.008692	384
33	26.744422	3089.330596	0.000324	0.037391	115.513083	0.008657	396
34	29.544912	3425.389448	0.000292	0.033847	115.938387	0.008625	408
35	32.638650	3796.638052	0.000263	0.030639	116.323377	0.008597	420
36	36.056344	4206.761236	0.000238	0.027734	116.671876	0.008571	432
37	39.831914	4659.829677	0.000215	0.025105	116.987340	0.008548	444
38	44.002836	5160.340305	0.000194	0.022726	117.272903	0.008527	456
39	48.610508	5713.260935	0.000175	0.020572	117.531398	0.008508	468
40	53.700663	6324.079581	0.000158	0.018622	117.765391	0.008491	480

	1 AMOUNT OF $1 AT COMPOUND INTEREST	2 ACCUMULATION OF $1 PER PERIOD	3 SINKING FUND FACTOR	4 PRESENT VALUE REVERSION OF $1	5 PRESENT VALUE ORD. ANNUITY $1 PER PERIOD	6 INSTALMENT TO AMORTIZE $1
YEARS						
1	1.100000	1.000000	1.000000	0.909091	0.909091	1.100000
2	1.210000	2.100000	0.476190	0.826446	1.735537	0.576190
3	1.331000	3.310000	0.302115	0.751315	2.486852	0.402115
4	1.464100	4.641000	0.215471	0.683013	3.169865	0.315471
5	1.610510	6.105100	0.163797	0.620921	3.790787	0.263797
6	1.771561	7.715610	0.129607	0.564474	4.355261	0.229607
7	1.948717	9.487171	0.105405	0.513158	4.868419	0.205405
8	2.143589	11.435888	0.087444	0.466507	5.334926	0.187444
9	2.357948	13.579477	0.073641	0.424098	5.759024	0.173641
10	2.593742	15.937425	0.062745	0.385543	6.144567	0.162745
11	2.853117	18.531167	0.053963	0.350494	6.495061	0.153963
12	3.138428	21.384284	0.046763	0.318631	6.813692	0.146763
13	3.452271	24.522712	0.040779	0.289664	7.103356	0.140779
14	3.797498	27.974983	0.035746	0.263331	7.366687	0.135746
15	4.177248	31.772482	0.031474	0.239392	7.606080	0.131474
16	4.594973	35.949730	0.027817	0.217629	7.823709	0.127817
17	5.054470	40.544703	0.024664	0.197845	8.021553	0.124664
18	5.559917	45.599173	0.021930	0.179859	8.201412	0.121930
19	6.115909	51.159090	0.019547	0.163508	8.364920	0.119547
20	6.727500	57.274999	0.017460	0.148644	8.513564	0.117460
21	7.400250	64.002499	0.015624	0.135131	8.648694	0.115624
22	8.140275	71.402749	0.014005	0.122846	8.771540	0.114005
23	8.954302	79.543024	0.012572	0.111678	8.883218	0.112572
24	9.849733	88.497327	0.011300	0.101526	8.984744	0.111300
25	10.834706	98.347059	0.010168	0.092296	9.077040	0.110168
26	11.918177	109.181765	0.009159	0.083905	9.160945	0.109159
27	13.109994	121.099942	0.008258	0.076278	9.237223	0.108258
28	14.420994	134.209936	0.007451	0.069343	9.306567	0.107451
29	15.863093	148.630930	0.006728	0.063039	9.369606	0.106728
30	17.449402	164.494023	0.006079	0.057309	9.426914	0.106079
31	19.194342	181.943425	0.005496	0.052099	9.479013	0.105496
32	21.113777	201.137767	0.004972	0.047362	9.526376	0.104972
33	23.225154	222.251544	0.004499	0.043057	9.569432	0.104499
34	25.547670	245.476699	0.004074	0.039143	9.608575	0.104074
35	28.102437	271.024368	0.003690	0.035584	9.644159	0.103690
36	30.912681	299.126805	0.003343	0.032349	9.676508	0.103343
37	34.003949	330.039486	0.003030	0.029408	9.705917	0.103030
38	37.404343	364.043434	0.002747	0.026735	9.732651	0.102747
39	41.144778	401.447778	0.002491	0.024304	9.756956	0.102491
40	45.259256	442.592556	0.002259	0.022095	9.779051	0.102259
41	49.785181	487.851811	0.002050	0.020086	9.799137	0.102050
42	54.763699	537.636992	0.001860	0.018260	9.817397	0.101860
43	60.240069	592.400692	0.001688	0.016600	9.833998	0.101688
44	66.264076	652.640761	0.001532	0.015091	9.849089	0.101532
45	72.890484	718.904837	0.001391	0.013719	9.862808	0.101391
46	80.179532	791.795321	0.001263	0.012472	9.875280	0.101263
47	88.197485	871.974853	0.001147	0.011338	9.886618	0.101147
48	97.017234	960.172338	0.001041	0.010307	9.896926	0.101041
49	106.718957	1057.189572	0.000946	0.009370	9.906296	0.100946
50	117.390853	1163.908529	0.000859	0.008519	9.914814	0.100859

12.00% MONTHLY COMPOUND INTEREST TABLES 12.00%
EFFECTIVE RATE 1.000

	1 AMOUNT OF $1 AT COMPOUND INTEREST	2 ACCUMULATION OF $1 PER PERIOD	3 SINKING FUND FACTOR	4 PRESENT VALUE REVERSION OF $1	5 PRESENT VALUE ORD. ANNUITY $1 PER PERIOD	6 INSTALMENT TO AMORTIZE $1	
MONTHS							
1	1.010000	1.000000	1.000000	0.990099	0.990099	1.010000	
2	1.020100	2.010000	0.497512	0.980296	1.970395	0.507512	
3	1.030301	3.030100	0.330022	0.970590	2.940985	0.340022	
4	1.040604	4.060401	0.246281	0.960980	3.901966	0.256281	
5	1.051010	5.101005	0.196040	0.951466	4.853431	0.206040	
6	1.061520	6.152015	0.162548	0.942045	5.795476	0.172548	
7	1.072135	7.213535	0.138628	0.932718	6.728195	0.148628	
8	1.082857	8.285671	0.120690	0.923483	7.651678	0.130690	
9	1.093685	9.368527	0.106740	0.914340	8.566018	0.116740	
10	1.104622	10.462213	0.095582	0.905287	9.471305	0.105582	
11	1.115668	11.566835	0.086454	0.896324	10.367628	0.096454	
12	1.126825	12.682503	0.078849	0.887449	11.255077	0.088849	
YEARS							**MONTHS**
1	1.126825	12.682503	0.078849	0.887449	11.255077	0.088849	12
2	1.269735	26.973465	0.037073	0.787566	21.243387	0.047073	24
3	1.430769	43.076878	0.023214	0.698925	30.107505	0.033214	36
4	1.612226	61.222608	0.016334	0.620260	37.973959	0.026334	48
5	1.816697	81.669670	0.012244	0.550450	44.955038	0.022244	60
6	2.047099	104.709931	0.009550	0.488496	51.150391	0.019550	72
7	2.306723	130.672274	0.007653	0.433515	56.648453	0.017653	84
8	2.599273	159.927293	0.006253	0.384723	61.527703	0.016253	96
9	2.928926	192.892579	0.005184	0.341422	65.857790	0.015184	108
10	3.300387	230.038689	0.004347	0.302995	69.700522	0.014347	120
11	3.718959	271.895856	0.003678	0.268892	73.110752	0.013678	132
12	4.190616	319.061559	0.003134	0.238628	76.137157	0.013134	144
13	4.722091	372.209054	0.002687	0.211771	78.822939	0.012687	156
14	5.320970	432.096982	0.002314	0.187936	81.206434	0.012314	168
15	5.995802	499.580198	0.002002	0.166783	83.321664	0.012002	180
16	6.756220	575.621974	0.001737	0.148012	85.198824	0.011737	192
17	7.613078	661.307751	0.001512	0.131353	86.864707	0.011512	204
18	8.578606	757.860630	0.001320	0.116569	88.343095	0.011320	216
19	9.666588	866.658830	0.001154	0.103449	89.655089	0.011154	228
20	10.892554	989.255365	0.001011	0.091806	90.819416	0.011011	240
21	12.274002	1127.400210	0.000887	0.081473	91.852698	0.010887	252
22	13.830653	1283.065278	0.000779	0.072303	92.769683	0.010779	264
23	15.584726	1458.472574	0.000686	0.064165	93.583461	0.010686	276
24	17.561259	1656.125905	0.000604	0.056944	94.305647	0.010604	288
25	19.788466	1878.846626	0.000532	0.050534	94.946551	0.010532	300
26	22.298139	2129.813909	0.000470	0.044847	95.515321	0.010470	312
27	25.126101	2412.610125	0.000414	0.039799	96.020075	0.010414	324
28	28.312720	2731.271980	0.000366	0.035320	96.468019	0.010366	336
29	31.903481	3090.348134	0.000324	0.031345	96.865546	0.010324	348
30	35.949641	3494.964133	0.000286	0.027817	97.218331	0.010286	360
31	40.508956	3950.895567	0.000253	0.024686	97.531410	0.010253	372
32	45.646505	4464.650519	0.000224	0.021907	97.809252	0.010224	384
33	51.435625	5043.562459	0.000198	0.019442	98.055822	0.010198	396
34	57.958949	5695.894923	0.000176	0.017254	98.274641	0.010176	408
35	65.309595	6430.959471	0.000155	0.015312	98.468831	0.010155	420
36	73.592486	7259.248603	0.000138	0.013588	98.641166	0.010138	432
37	82.925855	8192.585529	0.000122	0.012059	98.794103	0.010122	444
38	93.442929	9244.292938	0.000108	0.010702	98.929828	0.010108	456
39	105.293832	10429.383172	0.000096	0.009497	99.050277	0.010096	468
40	118.647725	11764.772510	0.000085	0.008428	99.157169	0.010085	480

	1	2	3	4	5	6
	AMOUNT OF $1 AT COMPOUND INTEREST	ACCUMULATION OF $1 PER PERIOD	SINKING FUND FACTOR	PRESENT VALUE REVERSION OF $1	PRESENT VALUE ORD. ANNUITY $1 PER PERIOD	INSTALMENT TO AMORTIZE $1
YEARS						
1	1.120000	1.000000	1.000000	0.892857	0.892857	1.120000
2	1.254400	2.120000	0.471698	0.797194	1.690051	0.591698
3	1.404928	3.374400	0.296349	0.711780	2.401831	0.416349
4	1.573519	4.779328	0.209234	0.635518	3.037349	0.329234
5	1.762342	6.352847	0.157410	0.567427	3.604776	0.277410
6	1.973823	8.115189	0.123226	0.506631	4.111407	0.243226
7	2.210681	10.089012	0.099118	0.452349	4.563757	0.219118
8	2.475963	12.299693	0.081303	0.403883	4.967640	0.201303
9	2.773079	14.775656	0.067679	0.360610	5.328250	0.187679
10	3.105848	17.548735	0.056984	0.321973	5.650223	0.176984
11	3.478550	20.654583	0.048415	0.287476	5.937699	0.168415
12	3.895976	24.133133	0.041437	0.256675	6.194374	0.161437
13	4.363493	28.029109	0.035677	0.229174	6.423548	0.155677
14	4.887112	32.392602	0.030871	0.204620	6.628168	0.150871
15	5.473566	37.279715	0.026824	0.182696	6.810864	0.146824
16	6.130394	42.753280	0.023390	0.163122	6.973986	0.143390
17	6.866041	48.883674	0.020457	0.145644	7.119630	0.140457
18	7.689966	55.749715	0.017937	0.130040	7.249670	0.137937
19	8.612762	63.439681	0.015763	0.116107	7.365777	0.135763
20	9.646293	72.052442	0.013879	0.103667	7.469444	0.133879
21	10.803848	81.698736	0.012240	0.092560	7.562003	0.132240
22	12.100310	92.502584	0.010811	0.082643	7.644646	0.130811
23	13.552347	104.602894	0.009560	0.073788	7.718434	0.129560
24	15.178629	118.155241	0.008463	0.065882	7.784316	0.128463
25	17.000064	133.333870	0.007500	0.058823	7.843139	0.127500
26	19.040072	150.333934	0.006652	0.052521	7.895660	0.126652
27	21.324881	169.374007	0.005904	0.046894	7.942554	0.125904
28	23.883866	190.698887	0.005244	0.041869	7.984423	0.125244
29	26.749930	214.582754	0.004660	0.037383	8.021806	0.124660
30	29.959922	241.332684	0.004144	0.033378	8.055184	0.124144
31	33.555113	271.292606	0.003686	0.029802	8.084986	0.123686
32	37.581726	304.847719	0.003280	0.026609	8.111594	0.123280
33	42.091533	342.429446	0.002920	0.023758	8.135352	0.122920
34	47.142517	384.520979	0.002601	0.021212	8.156564	0.122601
35	52.799620	431.663496	0.002317	0.018940	8.175504	0.122317
36	59.135574	484.463116	0.002064	0.016910	8.192414	0.122064
37	66.231843	543.598690	0.001840	0.015098	8.207513	0.121840
38	74.179664	609.830533	0.001640	0.013481	8.220993	0.121640
39	83.081224	684.010197	0.001462	0.012036	8.233030	0.121462
40	93.050970	767.091420	0.001304	0.010747	8.243777	0.121304
41	104.217087	860.142391	0.001163	0.009595	8.253372	0.121163
42	116.723137	964.359478	0.001037	0.008567	8.261939	0.121037
43	130.729914	1081.082615	0.000925	0.007649	8.269589	0.120925
44	146.417503	1211.812529	0.000825	0.006830	8.276418	0.120825
45	163.987604	1358.230032	0.000736	0.006098	8.282516	0.120736
46	183.666116	1522.217636	0.000657	0.005445	8.287961	0.120657
47	205.706050	1705.883752	0.000586	0.004861	8.292822	0.120586
48	230.390776	1911.589803	0.000523	0.004340	8.297163	0.120523
49	258.037669	2141.980579	0.000467	0.003875	8.301038	0.120467
50	289.002190	2400.018249	0.000417	0.003460	8.304498	0.120417

	1 AMOUNT OF $1 AT COMPOUND INTEREST	2 ACCUMULATION OF $1 PER PERIOD	3 SINKING FUND FACTOR	4 PRESENT VALUE REVERSION OF $1	5 PRESENT VALUE ORD. ANNUITY $1 PER PERIOD	6 INSTALMENT TO AMORTIZE $1	
MONTHS							
1	1.012500	1.000000	1.000000	0.987654	0.987654	1.012500	
2	1.025156	2.012500	0.496894	0.975461	1.963115	0.509394	
3	1.037971	3.037656	0.329201	0.963418	2.926534	0.341701	
4	1.050945	4.075627	0.245361	0.951524	3.878058	0.257861	
5	1.064082	5.126572	0.195062	0.939777	4.817835	0.207562	
6	1.077383	6.190654	0.161534	0.928175	5.746010	0.174034	
7	1.090850	7.268038	0.137589	0.916716	6.662726	0.150089	
8	1.104486	8.358888	0.119633	0.905398	7.568124	0.132133	
9	1.118292	9.463374	0.105671	0.894221	8.462345	0.118171	
10	1.132271	10.581666	0.094503	0.883181	9.345526	0.107003	
11	1.146424	11.713937	0.085368	0.872277	10.217803	0.097868	
12	1.160755	12.860361	0.077758	0.861509	11.079312	0.090258	
YEARS							**MONTHS**
1	1.160755	12.860361	0.077758	0.861509	11.079312	0.090258	12
2	1.347351	27.788084	0.035987	0.742197	20.624235	0.048487	24
3	1.563944	45.115506	0.022165	0.639409	28.847267	0.034665	36
4	1.815355	65.228388	0.015331	0.550856	35.931481	0.027831	48
5	2.107181	88.574508	0.011290	0.474568	42.034592	0.023790	60
6	2.445920	115.673621	0.008645	0.408844	47.292474	0.021145	72
7	2.839113	147.129040	0.006797	0.352223	51.822185	0.019297	84
8	3.295513	183.641059	0.005445	0.303443	55.724570	0.017945	96
9	3.825282	226.022551	0.004424	0.261419	59.086509	0.016924	108
10	4.440213	275.217058	0.003633	0.225214	61.982847	0.016133	120
11	5.153998	332.319805	0.003009	0.194024	64.478068	0.015509	132
12	5.982526	398.602077	0.002509	0.167153	66.627722	0.015009	144
13	6.944244	475.539523	0.002103	0.144004	68.479668	0.014603	156
14	8.060563	564.845011	0.001770	0.124061	70.075134	0.014270	168
15	9.356334	668.506759	0.001496	0.106879	71.449643	0.013996	180
16	10.860408	788.832603	0.001268	0.092078	72.633794	0.013768	192
17	12.606267	928.501369	0.001077	0.079326	73.653950	0.013577	204
18	14.632781	1090.622520	0.000917	0.068340	74.532823	0.013417	216
19	16.985067	1278.805378	0.000782	0.058875	75.289980	0.013282	228
20	19.715494	1497.239481	0.000668	0.050722	75.942278	0.013168	240
21	22.884848	1750.787854	0.000571	0.043697	76.504237	0.013071	252
22	26.563691	2045.095272	0.000489	0.037645	76.988370	0.012989	264
23	30.833924	2386.713938	0.000419	0.032432	77.405455	0.012919	276
24	35.790617	2783.249347	0.000359	0.027940	77.764777	0.012859	288
25	41.544120	3243.529615	0.000308	0.024071	78.074336	0.012808	300
26	48.222525	3777.802015	0.000265	0.020737	78.341024	0.012765	312
27	55.974514	4397.961118	0.000227	0.017865	78.570778	0.012727	324
28	64.972670	5117.813598	0.000195	0.015391	78.768713	0.012695	336
29	75.417320	5953.385616	0.000168	0.013260	78.939236	0.012668	348
30	87.540995	6923.279611	0.000144	0.011423	79.086142	0.012644	360
31	101.613606	8049.088447	0.000124	0.009841	79.212704	0.012624	372
32	117.948452	9355.876140	0.000107	0.008478	79.321738	0.012607	384
33	136.909198	10872.735858	0.000092	0.007304	79.415671	0.012592	396
34	158.917970	12633.437629	0.000079	0.006293	79.496596	0.012579	408
35	184.464752	14677.180163	0.000068	0.005421	79.566313	0.012568	420
36	214.118294	17049.463544	0.000059	0.004670	79.626375	0.012559	432
37	248.538777	19803.102194	0.000050	0.004024	79.678119	0.012550	444
38	288.492509	22999.400698	0.000043	0.003466	79.722696	0.012543	456
39	334.868983	26709.518627	0.000037	0.002986	79.761101	0.012537	468
40	388.700685	31016.054774	0.000032	0.002573	79.794186	0.012532	480

COMPOUND INTEREST TABLES

ANNUAL COMPOUND INTEREST TABLES
EFFECTIVE RATE 15.00

	1	2	3	4	5	6
	AMOUNT OF $1 AT COMPOUND INTEREST	ACCUMULATION OF $1 PER PERIOD	SINKING FUND FACTOR	PRESENT VALUE REVERSION OF $1	PRESENT VALUE ORD. ANNUITY $1 PER PERIOD	INSTALMENT TO AMORTIZE $1
YEARS						
1	1.150000	1.000000	1.000000	0.869565	0.869565	1.150000
2	1.322500	2.150000	0.465116	0.756144	1.625709	0.615116
3	1.520875	3.472500	0.287977	0.657516	2.283225	0.437977
4	1.749006	4.993375	0.200265	0.571753	2.854978	0.350265
5	2.011357	6.742381	0.148316	0.497177	3.352155	0.298316
6	2.313061	8.753738	0.114237	0.432328	3.784483	0.264237
7	2.660020	11.066799	0.090360	0.375937	4.160420	0.240360
8	3.059023	13.726819	0.072850	0.326902	4.487322	0.222850
9	3.517876	16.785842	0.059574	0.284262	4.771584	0.209574
10	4.045558	20.303718	0.049252	0.247185	5.018769	0.199252
11	4.652391	24.349276	0.041069	0.214943	5.233712	0.191069
12	5.350250	29.001667	0.034481	0.186907	5.420619	0.184481
13	6.152788	34.351917	0.029110	0.162528	5.583147	0.179110
14	7.075706	40.504705	0.024688	0.141329	5.724476	0.174688
15	8.137062	47.580411	0.021017	0.122894	5.847370	0.171017
16	9.357621	55.717472	0.017948	0.106865	5.954235	0.167948
17	10.761264	65.075093	0.015367	0.092926	6.047161	0.165367
18	12.375454	75.836357	0.013186	0.080805	6.127966	0.163186
19	14.231772	88.211811	0.011336	0.070265	6.198231	0.161336
20	16.366537	102.443583	0.009761	0.061100	6.259331	0.159761
21	18.821518	118.810120	0.008417	0.053131	6.312462	0.158417
22	21.644746	137.631638	0.007266	0.046201	6.358663	0.157266
23	24.891458	159.276384	0.006278	0.040174	6.398837	0.156278
24	28.625176	184.167841	0.005430	0.034934	6.433771	0.155430
25	32.918953	212.793017	0.004699	0.030378	6.464149	0.154699
26	37.856796	245.711970	0.004070	0.026415	6.490564	0.154070
27	43.535315	283.568766	0.003526	0.022970	6.513534	0.153526
28	50.065612	327.104080	0.003057	0.019974	6.533508	0.153057
29	57.575454	377.169693	0.002651	0.017369	6.550877	0.152651
30	66.211772	434.745146	0.002300	0.015103	6.565980	0.152300
31	76.143538	500.956918	0.001996	0.013133	6.579113	0.151996
32	87.565068	577.100456	0.001733	0.011420	6.590533	0.151733
33	100.699829	664.665525	0.001505	0.009931	6.600463	0.151505
34	115.804803	765.365353	0.001307	0.008635	6.609099	0.151307
35	133.175523	881.170156	0.001135	0.007509	6.616607	0.151135
36	153.151852	1014.345680	0.000986	0.006529	6.623137	0.150986
37	176.124630	1167.497532	0.000857	0.005678	6.628815	0.150857
38	202.543324	1343.622161	0.000744	0.004937	6.633752	0.150744
39	232.924823	1546.165485	0.000647	0.004293	6.638045	0.150647
40	267.863546	1779.090308	0.000562	0.003733	6.641778	0.150562
41	308.043078	2046.953854	0.000489	0.003246	6.645025	0.150489
42	354.249540	2354.996933	0.000425	0.002823	6.647848	0.150425
43	407.386971	2709.246473	0.000369	0.002455	6.650302	0.150369
44	468.495017	3116.633443	0.000321	0.002134	6.652437	0.150321
45	538.769269	3585.128460	0.000279	0.001856	6.654293	0.150279
46	619.584659	4123.897729	0.000242	0.001614	6.655907	0.150242
47	712.522358	4743.482388	0.000211	0.001403	6.657310	0.150211
48	819.400712	5456.004746	0.000183	0.001220	6.658531	0.150183
49	942.310819	6275.405458	0.000159	0.001061	6.659592	0.150159
50	1083.657442	7217.716277	0.000139	0.000923	6.660515	0.150139

20.00%   MONTHLY COMPOUND INTEREST TABLES   20.00%
                                          EFFECTIVE RATE 1.667

	1 AMOUNT OF $1 AT COMPOUND INTEREST	2 ACCUMULATION OF $1 PER PERIOD	3 SINKING FUND FACTOR	4 PRESENT VALUE REVERSION OF $1	5 PRESENT VALUE ORD. ANNUITY $1 PER PERIOD	6 INSTALMENT TO AMORTIZE $1	
MONTHS							
1	1.016667	1.000000	1.000000	0.983607	0.983607	1.016667	
2	1.033611	2.016667	0.495868	0.967482	1.951088	0.512534	
3	1.050838	3.050278	0.327839	0.951622	2.902710	0.344506	
4	1.068352	4.101116	0.243836	0.936021	3.838731	0.260503	
5	1.086158	5.169468	0.193444	0.920677	4.759408	0.210110	
6	1.104260	6.255625	0.159856	0.905583	5.664991	0.176523	
7	1.122665	7.359886	0.135872	0.890738	6.555729	0.152538	
8	1.141376	8.482551	0.117889	0.876136	7.431865	0.134556	
9	1.160399	9.623926	0.103908	0.861773	8.293637	0.120574	
10	1.179739	10.784325	0.092727	0.847645	9.141283	0.109394	
11	1.199401	11.964064	0.083584	0.833749	9.975032	0.100250	
12	1.219391	13.163465	0.075968	0.820081	10.795113	0.092635	
YEARS							MONTHS
1	1.219391	13.163465	0.075968	0.820081	10.795113	0.092635	12
2	1.486915	29.214877	0.034229	0.672534	19.647986	0.050896	24
3	1.813130	48.787826	0.020497	0.551532	26.908062	0.037164	36
4	2.210915	72.654905	0.013764	0.452301	32.861916	0.030430	48
5	2.695970	101.758208	0.009827	0.370924	37.744561	0.026494	60
6	3.287442	137.246517	0.007286	0.304188	41.748727	0.023953	72
7	4.008677	180.520645	0.005540	0.249459	45.032470	0.022206	84
8	4.888145	233.288730	0.004287	0.204577	47.725406	0.020953	96
9	5.960561	297.633662	0.003360	0.167769	49.933833	0.020027	108
10	7.268255	376.095300	0.002659	0.137585	51.744924	0.019326	120
11	8.862845	471.770720	0.002120	0.112831	53.230165	0.018786	132
12	10.807275	588.436476	0.001699	0.092530	54.448184	0.018366	144
13	13.178294	730.697658	0.001369	0.075882	55.447059	0.018035	156
14	16.069495	904.169675	0.001106	0.062230	56.266217	0.017773	168
15	19.594998	1115.699905	0.000896	0.051033	56.937994	0.017563	180
16	23.893966	1373.637983	0.000728	0.041852	57.488906	0.017395	192
17	29.136090	1688.165376	0.000592	0.034322	57.940698	0.017259	204
18	35.528288	2071.697274	0.000483	0.028147	58.311205	0.017149	216
19	43.322878	2539.372652	0.000394	0.023082	58.615050	0.017060	228
20	52.827531	3109.651838	0.000322	0.018930	58.864229	0.016988	240
21	64.417420	3805.045193	0.000263	0.015524	59.068575	0.016929	252
22	78.550028	4653.001652	0.000215	0.012731	59.236156	0.016882	264
23	95.783203	5686.992197	0.000176	0.010440	59.373585	0.016843	276
24	116.797184	6947.831050	0.000144	0.008562	59.486289	0.016811	288
25	142.421445	8485.286707	0.000118	0.007021	59.578715	0.016785	300
26	173.667440	10360.046428	0.000097	0.005758	59.654512	0.016763	312
27	211.768529	12646.111719	0.000079	0.004722	59.716672	0.016746	324
28	258.228656	15433.719354	0.000065	0.003873	59.767648	0.016731	336
29	314.881721	18832.903252	0.000053	0.003176	59.809452	0.016720	348
30	383.963963	22977.837794	0.000044	0.002604	59.843735	0.016710	360
31	468.202234	28032.134021	0.000036	0.002136	59.871850	0.016702	372
32	570.921630	34195.297781	0.000029	0.001752	59.894907	0.016696	384
33	696.176745	41710.604725	0.000024	0.001436	59.913815	0.016691	396
34	848.911717	50874.703013	0.000020	0.001178	59.929321	0.016686	408
35	1035.155379	62049.322767	0.000016	0.000966	59.942038	0.016683	420
36	1262.259241	75675.554472	0.000013	0.000792	59.952466	0.016680	432
37	1539.187666	92291.259934	0.000011	0.000650	59.961018	0.016678	444
38	1876.871717	112552.303044	0.000009	0.000533	59.968032	0.016676	456
39	2288.640640	137258.438382	0.000007	0.000437	59.973784	0.016674	468
40	2790.747993	167384.879554	0.000006	0.000358	59.978500	0.016673	480

20.00%   ANNUAL COMPOUND INTEREST TABLES   20.00%
EFFECTIVE RATE 20.00

	1 AMOUNT OF $1 AT COMPOUND INTEREST	2 ACCUMULATION OF $1 PER PERIOD	3 SINKING FUND FACTOR	4 PRESENT VALUE REVERSION OF $1	5 PRESENT VALUE ORD. ANNUITY $1 PER PERIOD	6 INSTALMENT TO AMORTIZE $1
YEARS						
1	1.200000	1.000000	1.000000	0.833333	0.833333	1.200000
2	1.440000	2.200000	0.454545	0.694444	1.527778	0.654545
3	1.728000	3.640000	0.274725	0.578704	2.106481	0.474725
4	2.073600	5.368000	0.186289	0.482253	2.588735	0.386289
5	2.488320	7.441600	0.134380	0.401878	2.990612	0.334380
6	2.985984	9.929920	0.100706	0.334898	3.325510	0.300706
7	3.583181	12.915904	0.077424	0.279082	3.604592	0.277424
8	4.299817	16.499085	0.060609	0.232568	3.837160	0.260609
9	5.159780	20.798902	0.048079	0.193807	4.030967	0.248079
10	6.191736	25.958682	0.038523	0.161506	4.192472	0.238523
11	7.430084	32.150419	0.031104	0.134588	4.327060	0.231104
12	8.916100	39.580502	0.025265	0.112157	4.439217	0.225265
13	10.699321	48.496603	0.020620	0.093464	4.532681	0.220620
14	12.839185	59.195923	0.016893	0.077887	4.610567	0.216893
15	15.407022	72.035108	0.013882	0.064905	4.675473	0.213882
16	18.488426	87.442129	0.011436	0.054088	4.729561	0.211436
17	22.186111	105.930555	0.009440	0.045073	4.774634	0.209440
18	26.623333	128.116666	0.007805	0.037561	4.812195	0.207805
19	31.948000	154.740000	0.006462	0.031301	4.843496	0.206462
20	38.337600	186.688000	0.005357	0.026084	4.869580	0.205357
21	46.005120	225.025600	0.004444	0.021737	4.891316	0.204444
22	55.206144	271.030719	0.003690	0.018114	4.909430	0.203690
23	66.247373	326.236863	0.003065	0.015095	4.924525	0.203065
24	79.496847	392.484236	0.002548	0.012579	4.937104	0.202548
25	95.396217	471.981083	0.002119	0.010483	4.947587	0.202119
26	114.475460	567.377300	0.001762	0.008735	4.956323	0.201762
27	137.370552	681.852760	0.001467	0.007280	4.963602	0.201467
28	164.844662	819.223312	0.001221	0.006066	4.969668	0.201221
29	197.813595	984.067974	0.001016	0.005055	4.974724	0.201016
30	237.376314	1181.881569	0.000846	0.004213	4.978936	0.200846
31	284.851577	1419.257883	0.000705	0.003511	4.982447	0.200705
32	341.821892	1704.109459	0.000587	0.002926	4.985372	0.200587
33	410.186270	2045.931351	0.000489	0.002438	4.987810	0.200489
34	492.223524	2456.117621	0.000407	0.002032	4.989842	0.200407
35	590.668229	2948.341146	0.000339	0.001693	4.991535	0.200339
36	708.801875	3539.009375	0.000283	0.001411	4.992946	0.200283
37	850.562250	4247.811250	0.000235	0.001176	4.994122	0.200235
38	1020.674700	5098.373500	0.000196	0.000980	4.995101	0.200196
39	1224.809640	6119.048200	0.000163	0.000816	4.995918	0.200163
40	1469.771568	7343.857840	0.000136	0.000680	4.996598	0.200136
41	1763.725882	8813.629408	0.000113	0.000567	4.997165	0.200113
42	2116.471058	10577.355290	0.000095	0.000472	4.997638	0.200095
43	2539.765269	12693.826348	0.000079	0.000394	4.998031	0.200079
44	3047.718323	15233.591617	0.000066	0.000328	4.998359	0.200066
45	3657.261988	18281.309940	0.000055	0.000273	4.998633	0.200055
46	4388.714386	21938.571928	0.000046	0.000228	4.998861	0.200046
47	5266.457263	26327.286314	0.000038	0.000190	4.999051	0.200038
48	6319.748715	31593.743577	0.000032	0.000158	4.999209	0.200032
49	7583.698458	37913.492292	0.000026	0.000132	4.999341	0.200026
50	9100.438150	45497.190751	0.000022	0.000110	4.999451	0.200022

25.00% MONTHLY COMPOUND INTEREST TABLES 25.00%
EFFECTIVE RATE 2.083

	1 AMOUNT OF $1 AT COMPOUND INTEREST	2 ACCUMULATION OF $1 PER PERIOD	3 SINKING FUND FACTOR	4 PRESENT VALUE REVERSION OF $1	5 PRESENT VALUE ORD. ANNUITY $1 PER PERIOD	6 INSTALMENT TO AMORTIZE $1	
MONTHS							
1	1.020833	1.000000	1.000000	0.979592	0.979592	1.020833	
2	1.042101	2.020833	0.494845	0.959600	1.939192	0.515679	
3	1.063811	3.062934	0.326484	0.940016	2.879208	0.347318	
4	1.085974	4.126745	0.242322	0.920832	3.800041	0.263155	
5	1.108598	5.212719	0.191838	0.902040	4.702081	0.212672	
6	1.131694	6.321317	0.158195	0.883631	5.585712	0.179028	
7	1.155271	7.453011	0.134174	0.865598	6.451310	0.155007	
8	1.179339	8.608283	0.116167	0.847932	7.299242	0.137001	
9	1.203909	9.787622	0.102170	0.830628	8.129870	0.123003	
10	1.228990	10.991531	0.090979	0.813676	8.943546	0.111812	
11	1.254594	12.220521	0.081830	0.797070	9.740616	0.102663	
12	1.280732	13.475115	0.074211	0.780804	10.521420	0.095044	
YEARS							MONTHS
1	1.280732	13.475115	0.074211	0.780804	10.521420	0.095044	12
2	1.640273	30.733120	0.032538	0.609654	18.736585	0.053372	24
3	2.100750	52.835991	0.018926	0.476021	25.151016	0.039760	36
4	2.690497	81.143837	0.012324	0.371679	30.159427	0.033157	48
5	3.445804	117.398588	0.008518	0.290208	34.070014	0.029351	60
6	4.413150	163.831191	0.006104	0.226596	37.123415	0.026937	72
7	5.652060	223.298892	0.004478	0.176927	39.507522	0.025312	84
8	7.238772	299.461053	0.003339	0.138145	41.369041	0.024173	96
9	9.270924	397.004337	0.002519	0.107864	42.822522	0.023352	108
10	11.873565	521.931099	0.001916	0.084221	43.957406	0.022749	120
11	15.206849	681.928746	0.001466	0.065760	44.843528	0.022300	132
12	19.475891	886.842782	0.001128	0.051346	45.535414	0.021961	144
13	24.943389	1149.282656	0.000870	0.040091	46.075642	0.021703	156
14	31.945785	1485.397684	0.000673	0.031303	46.497454	0.021507	168
15	40.913975	1915.870809	0.000522	0.024442	46.826807	0.021355	180
16	52.379817	2467.191326	0.000405	0.019084	47.083966	0.021239	192
17	67.110102	3173.284913	0.000315	0.014901	47.284757	0.021148	204
18	85.950026	4077.601254	0.000245	0.011635	47.441536	0.021079	216
19	110.078911	5235.787733	0.000191	0.009084	47.563949	0.021024	228
20	140.981536	6719.113709	0.000149	0.007093	47.659530	0.020982	240
21	180.559502	8618.856102	0.000116	0.005538	47.734160	0.020949	252
22	231.248255	11051.916141	0.000090	0.004324	47.792431	0.020924	264
23	296.166936	14168.012922	0.000071	0.003376	47.837929	0.020904	276
24	379.310342	18158.896417	0.000055	0.002636	47.873455	0.020888	288
25	485.794726	23270.146862	0.000043	0.002058	47.901193	0.020876	300
26	622.172638	29816.286623	0.000034	0.001607	47.922851	0.020867	312
27	796.836134	38200.134414	0.000026	0.001255	47.939762	0.020860	324
28	1020.533185	48937.592880	0.000020	0.000980	47.952966	0.020854	336
29	1307.029059	62689.394819	0.000016	0.000765	47.963275	0.020849	348
30	1673.953366	80301.761578	0.000012	0.000597	47.971325	0.020846	360
31	2143.884907	102858.475544	0.000010	0.000466	47.977611	0.020843	372
32	2745.741063	131747.571026	0.000008	0.000364	47.982518	0.020841	384
33	3516.557237	168746.747367	0.000006	0.000284	47.986350	0.020839	396
34	4503.765838	216132.760226	0.000005	0.000222	47.989342	0.020838	408
35	5768.115051	276821.522428	0.000004	0.000173	47.991678	0.020837	420
36	7387.406991	354547.535558	0.000003	0.000135	47.993502	0.020836	432
37	9461.285285	454093.693657	0.000002	0.000106	47.994927	0.020836	444
38	12117.366668	581585.600079	0.000002	0.000083	47.996039	0.020835	456
39	15519.093924	744868.508353	0.000001	0.000064	47.996907	0.020835	468
40	19875.793381	953990.082294	0.000000	0.000050	47.997585	0.020834	480

25.00 %   ANNUAL COMPOUND INTEREST TABLES   25.00 %
                                    EFFECTIVE RATE 25.00

	1 AMOUNT OF $1 AT COMPOUND INTEREST	2 ACCUMULATION OF $1 PER PERIOD	3 SINKING FUND FACTOR	4 PRESENT VALUE REVERSION OF $1	5 PRESENT VALUE ORD. ANNUITY $1 PER PERIOD	6 INSTALMENT TO AMORTIZE $1
YEARS						
1	1.250000	1.000000	1.000000	0.800000	0.800000	1.250000
2	1.562500	2.250000	0.444444	0.640000	1.440000	0.694444
3	1.953125	3.812500	0.262295	0.512000	1.952000	0.512295
4	2.441406	5.765625	0.173442	0.409600	2.361600	0.423442
5	3.051758	8.207031	0.121847	0.327680	2.689280	0.371847
6	3.814697	11.258789	0.088819	0.262144	2.951424	0.338819
7	4.768372	15.073486	0.066342	0.209715	3.161139	0.316342
8	5.960464	19.841858	0.050399	0.167772	3.328911	0.300399
9	7.450581	25.802322	0.038756	0.134218	3.463129	0.288756
10	9.313226	33.252903	0.030073	0.107374	3.570503	0.280073
11	11.641532	42.566129	0.023493	0.085899	3.656403	0.273493
12	14.551915	54.207661	0.018448	0.068719	3.725122	0.268448
13	18.189894	68.759576	0.014543	0.054976	3.780098	0.264543
14	22.737368	86.949470	0.011501	0.043980	3.824078	0.261501
15	28.421709	109.686838	0.009117	0.035184	3.859263	0.259117
16	35.527137	138.108547	0.007241	0.028147	3.887410	0.257241
17	44.408921	173.635684	0.005759	0.022518	3.909928	0.255759
18	55.511151	218.044605	0.004586	0.018014	3.927942	0.254586
19	69.388939	273.555756	0.003656	0.014412	3.942354	0.253656
20	86.736174	342.944695	0.002916	0.011529	3.953883	0.252916
21	108.420217	429.680869	0.002327	0.009223	3.963107	0.252327
22	135.525272	538.101086	0.001858	0.007379	3.970485	0.251858
23	169.406589	673.626358	0.001485	0.005903	3.976388	0.251485
24	211.758237	843.032947	0.001186	0.004722	3.981111	0.251186
25	264.697796	1054.791184	0.000948	0.003778	3.984888	0.250948
26	330.872245	1319.488980	0.000758	0.003022	3.987911	0.250758
27	413.590306	1650.361225	0.000606	0.002418	3.990329	0.250606
28	516.987883	2063.951531	0.000485	0.001934	3.992263	0.250485
29	646.234854	2580.939414	0.000387	0.001547	3.993810	0.250387
30	807.793567	3227.174268	0.000310	0.001238	3.995048	0.250310
31	1009.741959	4034.967835	0.000248	0.000990	3.996039	0.250248
32	1262.177448	5044.709793	0.000198	0.000792	3.996831	0.250198
33	1577.721810	6306.887242	0.000159	0.000634	3.997465	0.250159
34	1972.152263	7884.609052	0.000127	0.000507	3.997972	0.250127
35	2465.190329	9856.761315	0.000101	0.000406	3.998377	0.250101
36	3081.487911	12321.951644	0.000081	0.000325	3.998702	0.250081
37	3851.859889	15403.439555	0.000065	0.000260	3.998962	0.250065
38	4814.824861	19255.299444	0.000052	0.000208	3.999169	0.250052
39	6018.531076	24070.124305	0.000042	0.000166	3.999335	0.250042
40	7523.163845	30088.655381	0.000033	0.000133	3.999468	0.250033

Suggested Readings

I The Analytical Framework

Arnold, Alvin L., and Kusnet, Jack, *The Arnold Encyclopedia of Real Estate* (Boston and New York: Warren, Gorham & Lamont, Inc., 1978).

Creedy, Judith, and Wall, Norbert F., *Real Estate Investment by Objective* (New York: McGraw-Hill Book Company, 1979).

Edel, Matthew, and Ruthenberg, Jerome, *Readings in Urban Economics* (New York: Macmillan, Inc. 1972).

Hoover, Edgar, *Introduction to Regional Economics*, 2nd ed. (New York: Alfred A. Knopf, Inc., 1975).

Lifton, Robert K., *Practical Real Estate: Legal, Tax and Business Strategies* (New York: Harcourt Brace Jovanovich, 1979).

McMahan, John, "The Future of the Real Estate Industry: Changing Supply Patterns," *Real Estate Review*, Spring 1977, p. 68.

Redman, Arnold L., and Sirmans, C.F., "Regional/Local Economic Analysis: A Discussion of Data Sources," *The Appraisal Journal*, April 1977, p. 261.

Schreiber, Arthur C., Gatons, Paul K., and Clemmer, Richard B., *Economics of Urban Problems*, 2nd ed. (Boston: Houghton Mifflin Co., 1976).

Wendt, Paul F., "Inflation and the Real Estate Investor," *The Appraisal Journal*, July 1977, p. 343.

II The Legal Environment

Arnold, Alvin L., and Smith, Owen, *Real Estate Review Portfolio No. 1, Negotiating the Commercial Lease* (Boston and New York: Warren, Gorham & Lamont, Inc., 1973).

Casey, William J., *Real Estate Desk Book*, 4th ed. (New York: Institute for Business Planning, Inc., 1973).

Goldstein, Charles A., "Real Estate Transactions and the Lawyer," *Real Estate Review*, Summer 1974, p. 34.

Henszey, Benjamin N., and Friedman, Ronald M., *Real Estate Law* (Boston and New York: Warren, Gorham and Lamont, Inc., 1979).

Kratovil, Robert, *Modern Mortgage Law and Practice* (Englewood Cliffs: Prentice-Hall, Inc., 1972).

Kratovil, Robert, and Werner, Raymond J., *Real Estate Law*, 7th ed. (Englewood Cliffs: Prentice-Hall, Inc., 1979).

Kusnet, Jack, and Holzman, Lee J., *Real Estate Review Portfolio No. 14, How to Choose a Form of Ownership for Real Estate* (Boston and New York: Warren, Gorham & Lamont, Inc., 1977).

Kusnet, Jack, and Kucker, Marvin H., *Real Estate Review Portfolio No. 6, Negotiating the Ground Lease* (Boston and New York: Warren, Gorham & Lamont, Inc., 1974).

French, William B., and Lusk, Harold F., 4th ed. (Homewood: Richard D. Irwin, Inc., 1979).

Morris, Jackson L., *Real Estate Review Portfolio No. 12, How Securities Laws Affect Real Estate Offerings* (Boston and New York: Warren, Gorham & Lamont, Inc., 1977).

Thau, William A., *Real Estate Review Portfolio No. 8, Negotiating the Purchase and Sale of Real Estate* (Boston and New York: Warren, Gorham & Lamont, Inc., 1975).

III Valuation and the Appraisal Process

American Institute of Real Estate Appraisers, *Readings in Real Estate Investment Analysis* (Chicago: American Institute of Real Appraisers, 1977).

American Institute of Real Estate Appraisers, *Readings in Real Property Valuation Principles* (Chicago: American Institute of Real Estate Appraisers, 1977).

American Institute of Real Estate Appraisers, *Real Estate Appraisal Terminology* (Chicago: American Institute of Real Estate Appraisers and Society of Real Estate Appraisers, 1975).

American Institute of Real Estate Appraisers, *The Appraisal of Real Estate*, 7th ed. (Chicago: American Institute of Real Estate Appraisers, 1978).

Bloom, George F., and Harrison, Henry S., *Appraising the Single Family Residence* (Chicago: American Institute of Real Estate Appraisers, 1978).

Shenkel, William M., *Modern Real Estate Appraisal* (New York: McGraw-Hill Book Company, 1978).

Kinnard, William N., Jr., *Income Property Valuation* (Lexington: D.C. Heath & Company 1971).

Friedman, Edith J. (Ed.), *Encyclopedia of Real Estate Appraising* (Englewood Cliffs: Prentice-Hall, Inc., 1978).

Kahn, Sanders A., and Case, Frederick E., *Real Estate Appraisal and Investment*, 2nd ed. (New York: The Ronald Press Company, 1977).

Murray, William G., *Farm Appraisal and Valuation* 5th ed. (Ames: Iowa State University Press, 1969).

Ring, Alfred A., *The Valuation of Real Estate*, 2nd ed. (Englewood Cliffs: Prentice-Hall, Inc., 1970).

Rushmore, Stephen, *The Valuation of Hotels and Motels* (Chicago: American Institute of Real Estate Appraisers, 1978).

IV Marketing, Brokerage, and Management

Allen, John B., *Selling Income Property Successfully*, rev. ed. (Los Angeles: California Association of Realtors®, 1976).

Cronkhite, Gary, *Communication and Awareness* (Menlo Park: Cummings Publishing Co., 1976).

Cyr, John E., *Training and Supervising Real Estate Salesmen* (Englewood Cliffs: Prentice-Hall, Inc., 1973).

Downs, James C., Jr., *Principles of Real Estate Management*, 11th ed. (Chicago: Institute of Real Estate Management, 1975).

French, William B., Martin, Stephen J., and Battle, Thomas E., III, *Guide to Real Estate Licensing Examinations* (Boston and New York: Warren, Gorham & Lamont, Inc., 1978).

Glassman, Sidney, *A Guide to Residential Management*, 3rd ed. (Washington, D.C.: National Association of Home Builders, 1978).

Gordon, Edward S., *Real Estate Review Portfolio No. 10, How to Market Space in an Office Building* (Boston and New York: Warren, Gorham & Lamont, Inc., 1976).

Kelly, Edward N., *Practical Apartment Management* (Chicago: Institute of Real Estate Management, 1976).

Kirkpatrick, C.A., and Russ, F.A., *Salesmanship*, 6th ed. (Cincinnati: South-Western Publishing Company, 1976).

Kotler, Philip, *Marketing Management: Analysis, Planning, and Control*, 3rd ed. (Englewood Cliffs: Prentice-Hall, Inc., 1976).

Leathers, Dale G., *Nonverbal Communication Systems* (Boston: Allyn and Bacon, 1976).

National Association of Realtors®, *An Accounting System for Real Estate Brokers* (Chicago: National Association of Realtors®, 1972).

National Association of Realtors®, *Real Estate Office Management: People, Functions, Systems* (Chicago: National Association of Realtors® National Marketing Institute, 1975).

National Association of Realtors®, *Real Estate Sales Handbook*, 7th ed. (Chicago: National Association of Realtors® National Marketing Institute, 1975).

Walters, William, Jr., *The Practice of Real Estate Management* (Chicago: Institute of Real Estate Management, 1979).

V Financing

Arnold, Alvin L., *Real Estate Review Portfolio No. 5, Real Estate Financing Techniques* (Boston and New York: Warren, Gorham & Lamont, Inc., 1974).

Arnold, Alvin L., and Furner, Joanne F., *Real Estate Review Portfolio No. 2, The Sale-Leaseback* (Boston and New York: Warren, Gorham & Lamont, Inc., 1973).

Bagby, Joseph R., *Real Estate Financing Desk Book* (Englewood Cliffs: Institute for Business Planning, Inc., 1975).

Boykin, James H., *Financing Real Estate* (Lexington: D.C. Heath & Company, 1979).

Britton, James A., Jr., and Kerwood, Lewis O., *Financing Income-Producing Real Estate* (New York: McGraw-Hill Book Company, 1977).

California Association of Realtors®, *Creative Real Estate Financing* (Los Angeles: California Association of Realtors®, 1975).

Case, Frederick E., and Clapp, John M., *Real Estate Financing* (New York: John Wiley & Sons, 1978).

Hoagland, Henry E., Stone, Leo D., Brueggeman, William, *Real Estate Finance*, 6th ed. (Homewood: Richard D. Irwin, Inc., 1977).

Knight, Frank H., *Risk Uncertainty and Profit* (Chicago: University of Chicago Press, 1971).

Shapiro, Ivan, *Real Estate Review Portfolio No. 5A, Case Studies in Creative Real Estate Financing* (Boston and New York: Warren, Gorham & Lamont, Inc., 1979).

Starr, Roger, *Housing and the Money Market* (New York: Basic Books, 1975).

VI Income and Property Taxation

Arnold, Alvin L., *Tax Shelter in Real Estate Today* (Boston and New York: Warren, Gorham & Lamont, Inc., 1979).

Blew, Joseph Miller, and Stevenson, Howard H., "How to Understand a Subsidized-Housing Syndication," *Real Estate Review*, Summer 1978, p. 42.

Corgel, John B., and Goebel, Paul R., "Choosing Depreciable Lives: Weighing Gains vs. Risks," *Real Estate Review*, Summer 1979, p. 80.

Gettel, Ronald E., *How to Get Real Estate Taxes Reduced* (New York: McGraw-Hill Book Company, 1977).

Halperin, Jerome Y., Grey, Francis J., Moser, Carl M., and Huene, Herbert A., *Tax Planning for Real Estate Transactions* (Detroit: Coopers & Lybrand, 1978).

Katz, Neil J., and Priore, Robert A., *Real Estate Review Portfolio No. 15, Real Estate Exchanges and How to Make Them* (Boston and New York: Warren, Gorham & Lamont, Inc., 1977).

Kusnet, Jack, and Sacks, Mason J., *Real Estate Review Portfolio No. 16, Tax Planning for Landlords and Tenants* (Boston and New York: Warren, Gorham & Lamont, Inc., 1978).

Lynn, Theodore S., *et al.*, *Real Estate Limited Partnerships* (New York: Wiley-Interscience, 1977).

Maisel, Sherman J., and Roulac, Stephen E., *Real Estate Investment and Finance* (New York: McGraw-Hill Book Company, 1976).

Robinson, Gerald J., *Federal Income Taxation of Real Estate*, rev. ed. (Boston and New York: Warren, Gorham & Lamont, Inc., 1979).

Rosen, Lawrence R., *Calculator Mathematics for the Real Estate Professional* (Homewood: Dow Jones-Irwin, Inc., 1978).

Sacks, Mason J., and Kusnet, Jack, *Real Estate Review Portfolio No. 13, Real Estate Tax-Shelter Techniques* rev. ed. (Boston and New York: Warren, Gorham & Lamont, Inc., 1973).

Treadwell, Donald H., "Value in Use in Perspective," *The Appraisal Journal*, April 1978, p. 223.

Valachi, Donald J., "The Tax-Deferred Exchange: Some Planning Considerations," *The Appraisal Journal*, January 1979, p. 76.

VII   Investment

Arnold, Alvin L., *Real Estate Review Portfolio No. 4, Analyzing a Real Estate Investment* (Boston and New York: Warren, Gorham & Lamont, Inc., 1974).

Arnold, Alvin L., *Real Estate Review Portfolio No. 18, How to Evaluate Apartment Building Investments* (Boston and New York: Warren, Gorham & Lamont, Inc., 1978).

Case, Frederick E., *Investing in Real Estate* (Englewood Cliffs: Prentice-Hall, Inc., 1978).

Farm Land Institute, *Farm and Land Real Estate Manual* (Chicago: Farm and Land Institute, 1975).

Gettel, Ronald E., *Real Estate Guidelines and Rules of Thumb* (New York: McGraw-Hill Book Company, 1976).

Kinnard, William N., Jr., and Messner, Stephen D., *Industrial Real Estate*, 2nd ed. (Washington, D.C.: Society of Industrial Realtors, 1973).

Kusnet, Jack, and Parisse, Alan, *Real Estate Review Portfolio No. 7, Financial Analysis of a Real Estate Investment* (Boston and New York: Warren, Gorham & Lamont, Inc., 1975).

Lion, Edgar, *Shopping Centers* (New York: John Wiley & Sons, 1976).

Miller, Daniel A., *How to Invest in Real Estate Syndicates* (Homewood: Dow Jones-Irwin, Inc., 1978).

Roulac, Stephen E., *Modern Real Estate Investment* (San Francisco: Property Press, 1976).

Seldin, Maury, and Swesnik, Richard H., *Real Estate Investment Strategy*, 2nd ed. (New York: John Wiley & Sons, 1979).

Sharpe, William F., *Investments* (Englewood Cliffs: Prentice-Hall, Inc. 1978).

Wendt, Paul F., and Cerf, Alan R., *Real Estate Investment Analysis and Taxation*, 2nd ed. (New York: McGraw-Hill Book Co., 1979).

Wiley, Robert J., *Real Estate Investment* (New York: The Ronald Press Company, 1977).

VIII   Development

Cheezem, Mike, and Miles, Mike E., "The Care and Feeding of Giants," *Real Estate Review*, Winter 1979, p. 57.

Dumouchel, J. Robert, *Dictionary of Development Terminology* (New York: McGraw-Hill Book Company, 1975).

Graaskamp, James A., *A Guide to Feasibility Analysis* (Chicago: Society of Real Estate Appraisers, 1970).

Hanford, Lloyd D., Sr., *Feasibility Study Guidelines* (Chicago: Institute of Real Estate Management, 1972).

Harris, Cyril M., *Dictionary of Architecture and Construction* (New York: McGraw-Hill Book Company, 1975).

Martin, Thomas J., *et al.*, *Adaptive Use* (Washington, D.C.: Urban Land Institute, 1978).

McKeever, J. Ross (Ed.), *The Community Builders Handbook* (Washington, D.C.: Urban Land Institute, 1968).

McMahan, John, *Property Development* (New York: McGraw-Hill Book Company, 1976).

Phillippo, Gene, *The Professional Guide to Real Estate Development* (Homewood: Dow Jones-Irwin, Inc., 1976).

Romney, Keith B., *Condominium Development Guide* (Boston and New York: Warren, Gorham & Lamont, Inc., 1974).

Urban Land Institute, *Industrial Development Handbook* (Washington, D.C.: Urban Land Institute, 1975).

Urban Land Institute, *Land Development Manual*, 2nd ed. (Washington, D.C.: National Association of Home Builders, 1974).

Urban Land Institute, *Shopping Center Development Handbook* (Washington, D.C.: Urban Land Institute, 1977).

Watson, Don A., *Construction Materials and Processes* (New York: McGraw-Hill Book Company, 1972).

IX   Public Policy

Clawson, Marion, *America's Land and Its Uses* (Baltimore: Johns Hopkins University Press, 1972).

Downs, Anthony, *Federal Housing Subsidies: How Are They Working?* (Lexington: D.C. Heath and Company, 1973).

Downs, Anthony, "Public Policy and the Rising Cost of Housing," *Real Estate Review*, Spring 1978, p. 27.

Haar, Charles M., *Land Use Planning* (Boston: Little, Brown and Company, 1976).

Hagman, Donald G., *Public Planning and Control of Urban Land Development* (Chicago: West Publishing Company, 1973).

Hansen, Niles M., *The Challenge of Urban Growth* (Lexington: D.C. Heath and Company, 1975).

Klepper, Martin, "The National Energy Act: Its Impact on Real Estate and Real Estate Financing," *Real Estate Review*, Spring 1979, p. 40.

McMahan, John, "The Future of the Real Estate Industry: New Directions and New Roles," *Real Estate Review*, Summer 1977, p. 91.

Proctor, Mary, and Maturzeski, Bill, *Gritty Cities* (Philadelphia: Temple University Press, 1978).

Rose, Jerome G., and Rothman, Robert E., (Eds.), *After* Mount Laurel: *The New Suburban Zoning* (New Brunswick: The Center for Urban Policy Research, 1977).

Silverman, Jane A., *Real Estate Review Portfolio No. 17, Environmental Factors of Real Estate Development: An Approach for Achieving Acceptable Solutions* (Boston and New York: Warren, Gorham & Lamont, Inc., 1978).

White, John R., "How Foreign Money Buys U.S. Real Estate," *The Appraisal Journal*, January 1979, p. 59.

Glossary*

A

absorption schedule the estimated schedule or rate at which properties for sale or lease can be marketed in a given locality; usually used when preparing a forecast of the sales or leasing rate to substantiate a development plan and to obtain financing.

abstract of title a summary of the essential facts contained in consecutive deeds to a parcel of real estate and in other public records affecting the property such as mortgages, judgments, etc. The purpose is to determine if the present owner has a marketable title.

accelerated deprecation a method of depreciation for tax purposes under which a greater amount is written off as an annual deduction each year during the early years of ownership than would be deductible under a straight line method.

acceleration clause a clause in a mortgage that permits the lender to accelerate (i.e., make payable at once) the entire unpaid debt in the event the borrower breaches the mortgage (e.g., by not making an installment payment when due).

add-on minimum tax a tax, in addition to regular income tax, on certain tax-preference items, the most important of which is the excess of accelerated depreciation over straight line depreciation.

ad valorem tax a tax or duty based on value and levied as a percentage of that value (e.g., 30 mills (3 percent) per dollar of property value).

adverse possession a method of acquiring title to property by occupying it under a claim of ownership for the period of years specified by the laws of the particular state.

after-tax equity cash flow the amount of the actual cash returned to the equity interest after deducting from net operating income the amount of any debt service and any tax liability (or adding any tax savings).

agent one who is authorized to represent or act for another person (the *principal*) in dealing with third parties. A real estate broker is the agent of a person who retains the broker to buy, sell, or lease real estate.

agreement of sale a contrast between a purchaser and seller of real estate which, to be binding, must identify the property and specify the purchase price.

air space the space above the surface of land which is owned by the landowner and which may be sold or leased to others independent of the land itself.

allodial system a system of individual land ownership in fee simple which is the

* For more detail, see Alvin L. Arnold, and Jack Kusnet, *The Arnold Encyclopedia of Real Estate* (Boston and New York: Warren, Gorham & Lamont, Inc., 1978).

basis of real property law in the United States. It contrasts with the feudal system under which land was owned in Europe in the Middle Ages.

alternative minimum tax a tax paid instead of regular income tax, payable in relatively rare situations when a taxpayer's long-term capital gains are substantially greater than ordinary income.

amortization the gradual reduction of a debt by means of periodic payments. *Full amortization* exists when the payments are sufficient to liquidate the loan within the term of the mortgage. *Partial amortization* occurs when the payments liquidate a portion, but not all, of the loan principal during the mortgage term (the mortgage then being known as a *balloon mortgage*).

anchor tenant a major department store, supermarket, or other retail operation which is the major generator of customer traffic in a shopping center.

annual percentage rate (APR) a term used in the Truth in Lending Act to describe simple annual interest charged to the borrower.

anticipation an appraisal concept that real estate value is created by the expectation of benefits to be received in the future.

apartment house a building containing independent living units which share certain common facilities, such as utilities, a lobby, etc.

appraisal an estimate and opinion of value, usually set forth in a written statement and as of a specified date.

appraiser one who is qualified in estimating the value of real estate. Most appraisers belong to one or more appraisal organizations which establish standards for membership.

APR the acronym for annual percentage rate.

architect one who practices the profession of architecture; a designer of buildings and supervisor of construction. All states require architects to be licensed.

at-risk provision a provision in the tax law that restricts a taxpayer's loss deductions to the amount of his capital at risk in an investment.

axial theory a theory that urban areas grow by developing outward around the major transportation arteries to the central business district (the arteries constituting the axes of circles around the urban center).

B

balloon mortgage a mortgage which is only partially amortized and so requires a lump sum (balloon) payment at maturity.

band of investment approach a method of finding an appropriate capitalization rate for appraisal purposes by developing a weighted average of the mortgage and equity positions in the particular property. These positions constitute the band of investment in the sense that they require different returns in light of the different risks assumed.

bilateral contract a contract which involves the exchange of one promise for another promise. By comparison, a *unilateral contract* involves the exchange of a promise for the performance of an act.

blanket mortgage a mortgage covering more than one property.

BOMAI The acronym for Building Owners and Managers Association International.

bonus depreciation an additional depreciation deduction for tangible personal property during its first year of use.

bribery the criminal act of giving or receiving something of value with the corrupt intent to influence or be influenced with respect to an action. The specific acts subject to bribery are set forth in the penal law.

broker one who acts as an intermediary between other parties and assists in negotiating agreements between them. Under the law of agency, a broker is a "special agent" who acts on behalf of a principal.

brokerage license the privilege to carry on the business of a real estate broker, granted by a state usually on passage of a written examination and satisfaction of other requirements.

builder's method a method of estimating reproduction cost in which direct cost for labor and materials are added to indirect costs for financing, selling, insurance, etc., to arrive at the estimated reproduction cost new of the improvement on the site.

building code an ordinance promulgated by a municipality that regulates building and construction standards and is designed to preserve and protect the public's health, safety, and welfare.

Building Owners and Managers Association International (BOMAI) a trade association of owners and managers of apartment and office buildings.

building residual approach a method of valuing improved real estate where the value of the land is known or assumed and the object is to find the value of the building.

built-up method a method of developing a capitalization rate which involves estimated a safe or riskless return and then adding to it (building it up) by increments in light of additional risks and burdens assumed by the investor.

bundle of rights the total group of rights associated with the ownership of land and consisting primarily of the rights to possession, enjoyment without interference by others, disposition, and control of the land.

business risk in loan underwriting, the ability of the managers of an enterprise to operate the business successfully and produce profits over a period of time.

C

capital in accounting, the excess of the assets of a business or investment over the liabilities (i.e., net worth). In a partnership, for example, capital is the sum of the individual partners' capital accounts.

capital gain gain from the sale of a capital asset (e.g., investment real estate) which is taxable at a favorable rate if the assets was held for more than one year.

capital improvement the expenditures which cure or arrest deterioration of property and appreciably prolong its life. By comparison, repairs merely maintain property in an efficient operating condition.

capitalization the process of estimating the value of income-producing real estate by applying an appropriate capitalization rate to the projected flow of annual net income.

carrying costs cash outlays required to continue an investment position. For example, owning raw land which produces no income involves carrying costs for real estate taxes (and interest charges if financing is used).

cash flow   the actual spendable income from a real estate investment. To convert taxable income to cash flow, it is necessary to add back the depreciation deduction and then subtract mortgage amortization payments.

cash inflow   in investment analysis, all of the cash payments made in connection with the investment (i.e., the amount of equity).

cash outflow   in investment analysis, all of the cash receipts received by the investor (i.e., annual cash flows plus proceeds of sale).

CBD   the acronym for central business district.

central business district (CBD)   generally, the main shopping or business area of a town or city and consequently the place where real estate values are the highest.

certificate of occupancy (CO)   a certificate issued by a zoning board or building department to indicate that a structure complies with the building code and may legally be occupied.

city   in a legal sense, a municipal corporation; in a broader sense, an organized settlement of people subject to a local government that provides services for those who reside there and which raises money by taxation.

close corporation   a corporation organized and controlled by a single individual or a small group, such as a family.

CO   the acronym for certificate of occupancy.

commercial bank   bank whose primary function is to finance the production, distribution, and sale of goods (i.e., the lending of funds short-term, as distinguished from lending long-term or capital, funds).

commercial real estate   improved real estate held for the production of income through leases for commercial or business usage (e.g., office buildings, retail shops, and shopping centers).

community property   a type of concurrent ownership which exists between spouses residing in certain states and under which each spouse is an equal co-owner of all the property acquired during the marriage, except for certain specified exceptions.

comparables   in the market data approach, other properties to which the subject property can be compared in order to reach a judgment about market value.

comparative unit method   a method used to estimate reproduction or replacement cost of an improvement, whereby the actual costs of similar buildings are divided by the number of cubic or square feet in order to yield a unit cost per cubic foot or per square foot.

component depreciation   a method of depreciation whereby the separate components of a building (e.g., shell and heating equipment) are depreciated on separate schedules.

composite depreciation   a method of depreciation in which the entire structure is depreciated at the same rate; the opposite of component depreciation.

compounding   paying interest on interest (i.e., adding earned interest to the principal so that interest is figured on a progressively larger amount). Compounding translates present value into future value.

concentric circle theory   a theory that urban growth develops in circles around the central business district.

concurrent ownership   ownership interests in property by more than one person at the same time.

condemnation   the taking of real property from an owner for a public purpose under the right of eminent domain, on payment of fair compensation.

condominium a form of joint ownership and control of property by which specified volumes of air space (e.g., apartments) are owned individually while the common elements of the building (e.g., outside walls) are jointly owned.

conformity an appraisal concept that property achieves its maximum value when it is in a neighborhood of compatible land uses and architectural homogeneity.

consideration the promise or performance given by each party to a contract in exchange for the promise or performance of the other. Consideration is a necessary element for a valid contract.

construction cost services published services that provide estimates of construction costs for different types of properties in different parts of the United States.

construction loan a loan made usually by a commercial bank to a builder to be used for the construction of improvements on real estate and usually running six months to two years.

construction loan draw one of a series of payments (advances) made by a lender under a construction loan. The lender seeks to advance only the amount of money already reflected in construction so that in the event of a default, the value of the partially completed property will at least equal the outstanding loan amount.

construction period interest loan interest payable during construction. It cannot be deducted at once but must be amortized over a period of years.

consultant one who provides guidance or advice for a client, usually in consideration of a fixed fee. By comparison, a broker usually receives a percentage fee only if a transaction is consummated.

consumerism the name given to the movement for legislation to protect the interests of the general public in the purchases of goods and services. The legislation usually requires the seller to disclose fully all pertinent facts about the transaction.

contract an agreement between two or more persons which is enforceable by the courts and under which each party acquires certain rights as against the others.

contract rent the rents specified in a lease agreement; the actual rent.

contribution an appraisal concept that the value of an item in production is measured by its contribution to the net return of the enterprise or investment.

cooperative a form of ownership under which a building is owned by a corporation whose stockholders are each entitled to lease a specific unit in the building.

co-ownership ownership interests in property by more than one person at the same time.

corporate income tax an income tax levied on corporations and certain associations treated as corporations. A partnership is not subjected to this tax.

cost approach one of the three methods of appraising real property. In this approach, the value of the improvements is considered to be "reproduction cost new" minus accrued depreciation. The value of the land, derived by another method, is then added to the value of the improvement.

"crowding out" The name of the process, during periods of prosperity, when interest rates rise and the demand for business loans increases, in which lenders shift more and more funds from relatively low-yielding real estate loans to business loans.

D

DCR the acronym for debt coverage ratio.

dead land real estate which, by virtue of its location, lack of access, or topography, is not capable of being developed.

dealer one who operates on his own behalf (e.g., one who buys and sells real estate which he owns). By comparison, a broker has no personal interest in a transaction in which he is involved.

debt coverage ratio (DCR) the ratio between net operating income and the debt service on outstanding loans. The higher the ratio, the lower the risk to the lender.

debt service periodic payments on a loan, with a portion of the payment for interest and the balance for repayment (amortization) of principal. The payments usually, but not always, are equal (level).

declining balance depreciation a form of accelerated depreciation in which the depreciation rate is applied against a declining balance cost rather than original cost. The three types are 125 percent, 150 percent, and 200 percent declining balance.

deed a formal written instrument by which title to real property is conveyed from one person to another.

deed of trust the instrument used in some states (rather than a mortgage) to make real estate security for a debt. It is a three-party instrument, among a trustor (borrower), trustee, and beneficiary (lender).

default the failure of a party to fulfill a contractual obligation. This permits the other party to exercise remedies specified in the contract or by law.

defeasible fee fee simple interest in land that is capable of being terminated on the happening of a specified event; also called a base or qualified fee.

deferred maintenance inadequacies in maintaining and repairing property; also known as curable physical depreciation.

deficiency judgment a personal judgment entered against the mortgagor (borrower) when the amount realized at a foreclosure sale is less than the sum due on the foreclosed mortgage or deed of trust.

density the number of persons or the amount of improved space within a specified unit of land (e.g., an acre). Control of density is one of the primary functions of a zoning ordinance.

Department of Housing and Urban Development (HUD) a cabinet-level federal department responsible for the carrying out of national housing programs, including Federal Housing Administration subsidy programs, home mortgage insurance, urban renewal, and urban planning assistance.

depreciation (economic) as an economic or accounting term, the gradual loss or shrinkage of value of property (except land), the three types being physical, functional, and locational (or economic) depreciation.

depreciation (tax) as a tax term, a deductible expense for investment or business property which reflects the presumed "using up" of the asset. Land may not be depreciated.

destination facility hospitality facility (motel or hotel) located in a resort, city, or other area which attracts tourists and others for vacations or other purposes.

developer one who prepares raw land for improvement by installing roads and utilities, etc.; also used to describe a builder (i.e., one who actually constructs improvements on real estate).

development the process of preparing raw land so that its becomes suitable for the erection of buildings; generally involves clearing and grading land and installing roads and utility services.

devise a transfer of real property under a will. The *devisor* is the decedent, and the *devisee* is the recipient.

diminishing marginal utility the concept that, beyond some point, any further increase in the input of factors of production will decrease the margin between cost and gross income, thus resulting in decreased net income returns.

discounted present value the current value of an income-producing asset which is arrived at by working backward from a known future value through the process of discounting.

discounting the process of translating future value into present value (i.e., seeking to determine the present value of a dollar to be received at some date in the future); the opposite of compounding. The present value will depend on the discount rate (i.e., the rate at which current funds are expected to earn interest).

disintermediation the process whereby persons with excess cash invest directly in short-term instruments such as government paper, instead of depositing the funds in intermediary financial institutions such as savings and loan associations.

downside leverage the reduction of cash flow from property which occurs when the debt service on the mortgage is greater than the free and clear return from the property. In other words, the borrowed funds are earning less than the cost of those funds to the property owner.

downzoning a change in the zoning classification of property from a higher use to a lower use (e.g., from one-acre residential lots to one-half acre lots).

duplex a residential unit containing two living units. A fourplex and a sixplex are four- and six-unit buildings, respectively.

E

easement a nonpossessory interest in land owned by another which gives the holder of the easement the right to use the land for a specific purpose (e.g., a right of way).

economic (or locational) depreciation a loss of value of improved real estate resulting from changes other than those directly occurring to the property itself (e.g., a decline in neighborhood).

effective demand demand which is backed up by purchasing power and so which operates as a force in the marketplace.

Ellwood technique an advanced method of developing a capitalization rate based on the proportion of investment represented by debt and by equity.

eminent domain the power of a public authority to acquire interests in land by condemnation, when necessary to carry on the necessary functions of government. The property owner must receive "just compensation."

equalization procedure the adjustment of real property assessments (valuations) within a taxing district in order to achieve a uniform proportion between assessed values and actual cash values of real estate so that all property owners are taxed at an equal rate.

escalation clause   a provision in a lease that permits the landlord to pass through increases in real estate taxes and operating expenses to the tenants, with each tenant paying its pro rata share.

escheat   the reversion of property to the state when a person dies intestate without known heirs.

estate at will   an interest in property which arises when the owner leases the property to another and the duration of the lease is at the will of the owner or the tenant.

estate from year to year   the leasehold interest of a tenant in property which automatically renews itself for the period specified in the original lease, until terminated by either tenant or owner.

ethics   a code or body of moral rules, particularly a code for persons living together in a community or working in a common profession or business, such as real estate.

excess profit   in appraisal theory, profit which is in excess of that necessary to satisfy the four agents of production. The existence of excess profit will encourage new competition.

exclusive agency   an agreement between a real estate broker and a property owner designating the broker as the exclusive agent to sell or lease the subject property. The owner, however, may sell or lease directly without being liable for a commission.

exclusive right of sale   an agreement between a real estate broker and a property owner in which the broker is designated as the sole party authorized to sell or lease the subject property. Consequently, if the owner sells or leases directly, a commission is still due to the broker.

exogenous   the state of being outside or not a part of a particular thing. For example, the quality of a neighborhood is an exogenous factor that affects the value of a particular parcel of property.

export base multiplier   a mathematical technique used to project employment that will be created by new industry locating within a particular region.

external diseconomies   detriments to the value of property because of nearby activities which are not compatible with the use of the property in question.

external economies   benefits to property that arise from the existence of supporting and like-kind facilities nearby.

externalities   factors external to a parcel of property that affect its value. For example, a noisy or polluted environment is an externality that will depress the value of property.

F

feasibility study   an analysis of a specific real estate project or program to determine if it can actually be carried out successfully. It forms the basis for the developer's decision as to whether to proceed as well as the lender's decision whether or not to provide the necessary financing.

fee simple absolute   the most extensive interest in land recognized by law; absolute ownership but subject to the limitations of police power, taxation, and eminent domain; also known as a *fee simple* or *fee*.

fiduciary   one who the law regards as having a duty toward another by reason of a relationship of trust and confidence between them. An agent is generally considered under a fiduciary obligation to his principal.

finance charge the total costs imposed by a lender on the borrower in connection with the extension of credit, as defined under the Truth in Lending Act.

financial intermediary an institution that accepts deposits from individual savers and uses the funds to make loans to others (e.g., a savings and loan association).

financial risk in loan underwriting, the risk that a borrower may not be able to repay the loan as scheduled.

flexible payment mortgage (FPM) mortgage providing for payments during the first five years that are less than the payments during the balance of the loan; intended to make home ownership more available to young persons just starting out.

floor-to-ceiling loan a mortgage loan which is advanced in two separate portions. The initial portion (the *floor*) is advanced once certain conditions are met while the balance (the *ceiling*) is advanced when other conditions are met.

foreclosure the legal process by which a mortgagee, in case of default by a mortgagor, forces a sale of the mortgaged property in order to provide funds to pay off the loan.

FPM the acronym for flexible payment mortgage.

functional depreciation (obsolescence) the loss of value to improved real estate due to the fact that the improvements do not provide the same degree of use, or do so less efficiently, than would a new structure. Functional depreciation may be curable or incurable.

fungible goods of a given class or type, any unit of which is as acceptable as another and capable of satisfying an obligation expressed in terms of the class. For example, bushels of wheat are fungibles, whereas parcels of real estate are not.

G

gap financing financing provided by a second lender when the first lender advances only the floor portion of a floor-to-ceiling loan (i.e., the second loan fills the gap).

GC the acronym for general contractor.

GEI the acronym for gross effective income.

general agent an agent authorized to conduct all the business of the principal with stipulated limitations.

general contractor (GC) a person or firm that supervises a construction project under a contract with the owner; also known as the *prime contractor* (as distinguished from *subcontractors*).

GNP the acronym for gross national product.

going concern value the value of property on the assumption that it will continue to be utilized in an existing business. This value usually is greater than liquidation value.

government survey a method of land description which utilizes imaginary grid lines; used primarily in western United States.

GPI the acronym for gross possible income.

gross effective income (GEI)   gross possible income from an income property minus an allowance for vacancies and credit loss.

gross income multiplier (GIM) approach   a rule of thumb method for arriving at the value of an income property, which involves applying a multiplier to the gross rental receipts. Choice of the multiplier depends on the type of property, location, etc.

gross national product (GNP)   the sum of all final products of the economy, including both consumption goods and gross investment.

gross possible income (GPI)   gross rental receipts plus nonrental income (e.g., vending machine income).

gross rental receipts (GRR)   maximal rental income that a property would generate if it were fully occupied for the entire fiscal period.

ground rent   rent payable by a tenant to a landlord under a ground lease (i.e., a lease of vacant land).

GRR   the acronym for gross rental receipts.

H

hard-dollar costs   cash outlays which are not deductible and which, therefore, represent a true (or hard) cost to the developer.

heterogeneity   the quality of being unique. Every parcel of land is unique because its location cannot be duplicated.

highest and best use   the property use which at a given point of time is deemed likely to produce the greatest net return in the foreseeable future, whether or not such use is the current use of the property.

hospitality facility   a facility offering lodging accommodations to the general public and usually providing a wide range of additional services, including restaurants, meeting rooms and a swimming pool; a hotel or motel.

HUD   the acronym for the Department of Housing and Urban Development.

HVAC   the acronym for heating, ventilation, and air-conditioning.

I

ICSC   the acronym for the International Council of Shopping Centers.

ILSA   the acronym for the Interstate Land Sales Disclosure Act.

immobility   not capable of being moved from place to place. Land is both immobile and indestructible; while improvements placed on land can be moved, this is rarely done because of the difficulty and expense involved.

income approach   one of the three traditional appraisal methods. In this method, the appraiser seeks the present value of the future flow of income that can be expected from the property. This value is arrived at by projecting a stabilized annual income for the estimated future life of the property and applying an appropriate capitalization rate to that income.

income conduit   an entity, typically a partnership, which "passes through" profits and losses directly to the individual participants. This occurs because the entity itself is not subject to tax.

increasing and decreasing returns   an appraisal concept to the effect that the use of increasingly larger amounts of the factors of production will produce greater net income up to a certain point (*the law of increasing returns*) but thereafter further amounts will not produce a commensurate return (*the law of decreasing returns*).

industrial park   a large tract of improved land used for a variety of light industrial and manufacturing uses. Individual sites are either purchased or leased by users.

industrial real estate   improved real estate used for the purpose of manufacturing, processing, or warehousing goods.

in-fill incentives   public measures, such as tax abatement, that encourage the development of scattered vacant sites in a built-up section of a city.

inflation premium   the additional or incremental return that must be given to an investor to induce him to defer consumption during a period of inflation.

infrastructure   the services and facilities provided by a municipality, including roads and highways, water and sewer systems, fire and police protection, parks and recreation, etc.

input/output analysis   a method of analyzing the economy of a region that involves tabulating the data covering major industries in the region to show how an additional dollar spent in any one industry will affect sales in the others.

Institute of Real Estate Management (IREM)   an affiliate of the National Association of Realtors® whose purpose is to promote professionalism in the field of property management. IREM awards the professional designation of Certified Property Manager (CPM).

institutional lender   a savings bank, savings and loan association, commercial bank, or life insurance company that provides financing for real estate.

insurable value   the value of property for insurance purposes (i.e., the amount of insurance which an insurance company will agree to carry on property). This value is often different from market value.

insurance agent   one who acts as an intermediary between insurers and persons seeking insurance.

internal rate of return (IRR)   a method of analyzing return on investment which takes into consideration the time value of money. In essence, the method involves deriving a discount (interest) rate which causes the present worth of future cash outflows to be exactly equal to the present value of all cash inflows. The discount rate is the IRR.

International Council of Shopping Centers (ICSC)   a national trade association for owners, developers, and managers of shopping centers.

Interstate Land Sales Disclosure Act (ILSA)   a federal statute regulating the interstate sale of home sites and building lots in recreational developments. The basic purpose of the statute is to require full disclosure by the developer of all relevant information.

intestate   dying without leaving a will for the disposition of one's property.

investment credit   a credit against a taxpayer's tax liability equal to a percentage (up to 10 percent) of certain types of property.

IREM   the acronym for the Institute of Real Estate Management.

J

joint tenancy   a form of concurrent ownership which includes a right of survivorship (i.e., on the death of one joint tenant, title to his share passes automatically to the surviving joint tenants).

joint venture   an association of two or more persons or firms to carry on a single business enterprise for profit. Real estate projects frequently are carried on as joint ventures between a developer and a financing party.

L

land planner   one who specializes in the art of subdividing land in order to combine maximum utility with such desirable amenities as scenic views and winding roads.

land residual approach   an appraisal method used to find the value of land when the value of the improvement on it already is known.

land use regulation   local ordinances which deal with land development, the degree of building coverage of land, and requirements for open space; a broader term than *zoning regulation*.

leap-frogging   land development that skips close-in vacant space for outlying areas, usually because close-in land is too expensive.

lease concession   a benefit to a tenant to induce him to enter into a lease; usually takes the form of one or more month's free rent.

lease expiration schedule   schedule of leases in a building indicating the dates upon which they expire. If the percentage of short-term leases is high, there is less assurance of future cash flow but a greater opportunity to raise rentals in the near future if the market permits.

leasehold estate   the interest that a tenant holds in property by virtue of a lease; the right of a tenant to the use and occupancy of property pursuant to a lease.

legal capacity   the ability to enter into binding agreements. One who is an infant (in the legal sense) or is of unsound mind or is intoxicated lacks legal capacity to enter into a contract.

lessee   one who holds a leasehold estate; a tenant.

lessor   one who grants a leasehold estate; a landlord.

lien   the right to hold property as security until the debt which it secures is paid. A mortgage is one type of lien.

life insurance company   a primary source of permanent (long-term) financing for income properties, such as shopping centers, office buildings, and the like.

life tenant   one who has an estate for life in real property; the measuring life may be his own life or the life of a third party designated by the grantor of the life estate.

liquidation value   the net value realizable in the liquidation of a business or of a particular asset. Since liquidation is often distressed selling, liquidation value is ordinarily less than going concern value.

liquidity   the ability to convert assets into cash quickly without the need to mark the price down substantially below current market values. In general, real estate is not considered a liquid investment.

liquidity risk   risk associated with a slow convertibility of an asset to cash. Speeding up conversion may require discounting the price.

listing   an oral or written agreement whereby the owner of real estate authorizes a broker to sell or lease it in accordance with specified terms.

listing broker   a broker, particularly in a particular locality, whose listing automatically becomes available to other brokers in the area under an arrangement called a *multiple listing service*.

loan-to-value ratio (LTVR) the relationship between the amount of a mortgage loan and the value of the real estate securing it. For example, the loan-to-value ratio is 80 percent if an $8,000 loan is made on a property worth $10,000.

location effect an exogenous factor affecting the value of a particular parcel of property.

location quotient with respect to a particular industry, the relationship between the number of jobs in a particular region with the total number of jobs in the industry nationwide.

LTVR the acronym for loan-to-value ratio.

M

maintenance schedule a detailed listing of all maintenance procedures and the times when they are to be performed.

management contract a contract between the owner of real estate and an individual or firm that undertakes to manage it for a fee.

map a survey of a tract of land, prepared by a surveyor, showing boundaries of individual parcels, roads and highways, etc.; also known as a *plat.*

market in its broadest sense, the interaction of buying and selling interests in goods, services, or investments. Real estate markets traditionally have been a series of local markets since real estate is immobile and requires local management. However, this is gradually changing, with real estate becoming a national and even an international market.

marketable title a title to a parcel of real estate that is subject to no question about its validity; the type of title to which a purchaser of real estate is entitled unless the contract specifies otherwise.

market data approach one of the three appraisal methods; also known as the *comparison approach*. The underlying principle for this approach is that value is established by comparing the subject property with comparable properties which have recently been sold.

marketing study an analysis of various methods for the sale or lease of real estate (e.g., the use of newspaper advertising, outdoor billboards, etc.).

market rent the rent which space would command at any given time if not subject to lease. If market rent exceeds contract rent, the tenant has a bargain; if contract rent exceeds market rent, the landlord does.

market study the analysis of likely present or future market demand for a particular use on a specific site, and the existing and likely future supply of competitive space; also known as a *marketability study*.

market value the most probable price expressed in terms of money that a property would bring if exposed for sale in the open market in an arm's-length transaction between a willing seller and a willing buyer, both of whom are knowledgeable concerning the uses of the property.

mechanic's lien a claim that attaches to real estate to protect the right to compensation of one who performs labor or provides materials in connection with construction.

metes and bounds survey a method of describing land by identifying boundaries through terminal points and degrees of latitude and longitude.

miniwarehouse a one-story building subdivided into numerous small cubicles intended to be used as storage by families or small businesses.

MLS   the acronym for multiple listing service.

money market   in a broad sense, any market which matches the demand for and the supply of funds; in a technical sense, the market for short-term money instruments (those which mature within a year).

money risk   in loan underwriting, the risk that current interest rates may rise and thus adversely affect the current market price of a debt instrument which is valued primarily on a yield basis.

mortgage   instrument used in some states (rather than a deed of trust) to make real estate security for a debt. It is a two-party instrument between a mortgagor (borrower) and a mortgagee (lender).

mortgage banker   an individual or firm which primarily originates real estate loans and then sells them to institutional lenders and other investors.

mortgage constant   one of a series of periodic loan payments of equal amounts which is to be applied first to the payment of interest due on the loan since the last installment and second to principal reduction (amortization). The ratio of the total annual payments to the original loan principal is called the *mortgage constant percent.*

mortgagee   one to whom a mortgage is given as security for a loan, (i.e., the lender).

mortgagor   one who gives a mortgage to secure a loan (i.e., the borrower).

multiple listing service (MLS)   a selling technique frequently utilized by brokers in a particular locality whereby a listing with any one broker (the listing broker) automatically becomes available to all brokers participating in the service. If a sale is brought about by a broker (the selling broker) other than the listing broker, the commission is divided between the two.

mutual savings bank   a banking institution, found primarily in the Northeast, most of whose loans are in the form of home mortgages.

N

NAR®   the acronym for the National Association of Realtors®.

National Association of Realtors® (NAR®)   with a membership in excess of 700,000, the largest real estate organization in the country and probably in the world. Members are entitled to use the designation Realtor®, which is a trademarked term owned by the NAR®.

national income   the measure in dollars of the total annual production of goods and services in the economy. National income differs from gross national product in that national income is calculated after a provision for depreciation of capital goods.

national wealth   a term generally refering to the total real or tangible assets of a country (e.g., land, structures, equipment, inventories, etc.).

neighborhood   a segment of a city or town which is characterized by common features which distinguish it from adjoining areas.

negative cash flow   a cash deficit during a fiscal period, which requires the investor to raise additional cash either with equity or new debt.

net operating income (NOI)   the balance of cash remaining after deducting the operating expenses of a property from the gross income generated by the property.

net present value (NPV) the net present value of an investment is the sum of (1) the total present value of the annual after-tax equity cash flows during ownership plus (2) the present value of estimated proceeds from sale.

NPV the acronym for *net present value.*

NOI the acronym for net operating income.

nonpossessory interest an interest in land other than a fee or leasehold (i.e., an easement, license, or profit).

nuisance a property use or condition that unreasonably interferes with the rights of others to enjoy their property (e.g., establishing a motor cycle track in a residential neighborhood).

O

office building a building leased to tenants for the conduct of business or of a profession, as distinguished from residential, commercial, or retail buildings (although the lower floors of many office buildings are used for commercial purposes).

100 percent location the prime business location of a city and, consequently, the location where retail and office rentals are likely to be at their highest; usually the equivalent of the central business district.

open-end mortgage a mortgage which is written so as to permit the lender to make additional advances in the future. This eliminates the need for a new mortgage if the advances are made.

open listing the offering of a property for sale or lease through a real estate broker with the understanding that the broker has no exclusive agency or right of sale, thus permitting the owner to list the property with as many brokers as he wishes.

operating budget a budget, usually prepared a year in advance, listing projected costs of maintenance and repair for a building.

operating expenses expenses directly related to the operation and maintenance of the property, including real estate taxes, maintenance and repair expenses, insurance payments, payroll and management fees, supplies, and utility costs. They do not include debt service on mortgages or depreciation expense.

opportunity cost the return that might have been realized from alternative uses of capital that has been invested in a particular project. For example, capital invested in real estate incurs an opportunity cost equal to the return it might have earned had it been used to purchase corporate bonds or common stock.

option the right given by the owner of property (the optionor) to another (the optionee) to purchase or lease the property at a specific price within a set time. The option will be binding on the optionor when the optionee pays a consideration (usually cash).

ordinary income compensation, profits, dividends and all other income other than capital gain.

P

package mortgage a mortgage loan that packages what are normally two separate loans (e.g., a construction loan and a permanent loan).

participation mortgage a single mortgage loan made by several lenders, each putting up a portion of the total.

partnership an association of two or more persons for the purpose of carrying on an investment or business for profit and for the sharing of both profit and losses.

passive investor an investor who seeks no active role in construction or operation but merely seeks to invest funds in order to earn a return thereon. Institutional investors, such as pension funds, usually but not always are passive investors.

pension fund an institution that holds assets to be used for the payment of pensions to corporate and government employees, union members, and other groups.

percentage rental rental payable under a lease that is equal to a percentage of gross sales or gross revenues received by the tenant. Commonly used in shopping center leases, the percentage rental usually is joined with a minimum rental which the tenant must pay, regardless of the amount of sales volume.

permanent loan commitment an undertaking by a lender to make a long-term loan on real estate on specified conditions (e.g., the completion of construction of a building).

personal income tax the income tax levied against individuals, as distinguished from the income tax levied against corporations. Members of a partnership are subject to personal income taxes, but the partnership itself is not a taxable entity.

physical depreciation the loss of value suffered by improvements on lands resulting from wear and tear, disintegration, and the action of the elements. Physical depreciation may be curable (known as *deferred maintenance*) or incurable.

plat a survey of a tract of land prepared by a surveyor, showing boundaries of individual parcels, roads and highways, etc.; also known as a map.

police power the power of a state, which may be delegated to local governments, to enact and enforce laws protecting the public health, morals, safety, and general welfare. Zoning, taxation, subdivision regulation, and licensing of real estate sales persons are examples of the police power.

primary financial market a term used to describe the process whereby new capital is created by the sale of newly issued stock, bonds, and other investment instruments.

principal one who retains an agent to act for him; also, the amount of money loaned to another.

proceeds from sale the balance remaining to the seller after subtracting from the net sales price the amount of any loan repayment and any tax liability.

pro forma a financial statement that projects gross income, operating expenses, and net operating income for a future period (usually one year) based on certain specified assumptions.

progression an appraisal concept that an inferior property has its value enhanced by association with superior properties.

progressive income tax a tax, such as the federal income tax, under which the rate of tax increases in a series of steps as taxable income rises.

promisee one to whom a promise is made.

promisor one who makes a promise.

promissory note a written promise by a promisor to pay a sum of money to a promisee. It is a two-party instrument, as distinguished from an order to pay a sum of money, such as a draft or a check, which involves three parties.

property management the management of an individual real estate project building or development, including the functions of marketing, leasing, managing, and maintenance.

property manager a person or firm responsible for the operation of improved real estate. Management functions include leasing, managing, maintenance, etc.

property report an offering statement required to be given to purchasers of development lots regulated under the Interstate Land Sales Disclosure Act.

property residual approach a method of valuing and appraising improved real estate.

property tax a tax imposed on real estate by municipalities and other local government agencies.

psychic income nonmonetary benefits, such as the pride associated with home ownership.

"puffing" exaggerated claims or representations about property by the seller but sufficiently general in nature so that they do not amount to a fraudulent misstatement of fact.

purchase money mortgage a mortgage that is taken by a seller from a buyer in lieu of purchase money (i.e., the seller helps finance the purchase).

purchasing power risk in investment analysis, the risk of erosion and purchasing power of invested capital due to inflation; also known as the *inflation risk.*

Q

quantity survey method the most comprehensive method of estimating reproduction cost of improved real estate. It involves identifying the quantity and quality of all materials used in the improvement as well as the amount of labor involved and the application of unit cost figures to the results.

R

rate of return (ROR) the percentage relationahip between net operating income (or cash flow) and the total capital (or equity) invested. Cash flow of $1,000 from property in which an equity of $10,000 has been invested represents a 10 percent cash flow rate of return.

"ready, willing, and able" a phrase used in the absence of a specific agreement between the parties, whereby the traditional rule of law permits a broker to claim his commission as soon as he presents a buyer "ready, willing, and able" to buy on the terms offered by the seller.

real estate investment trust (REIT) an entity which pools capital for the purpose of investing in real estate or in mortgages and which need not pay federal income tax on earnings.

real estate licensing examination an examination given by a state to those who wish to become licensed real estate brokers or salespersons.

real estate market the interaction of buying and selling interests in real estate. Real estate markets traditionally have been a series of local markets since real estate is immobile and requires local management. However, this is gradually changing, with real estate becoming a national and even an international market.

real property   the rights, interests, and benefits inherent in the ownership of real estate; frequently thought of as a bundle of rights; often used synonymously with the term *real estate*.

real return   the return required by an investor to induce him to refrain from immediate consumption and utilize his capital for investment purposes.

recapture of depreciation   a provision of the tax law that causes gain realized on the sale of a capital asset to be treated as ordinary income (rather than capital gain) because of depreciation deductions taken during the period of ownership.

recapture premium   for any investment that will not produce income in perpetuity, the capital must be recouped over the life of the investment. The rate of such recoupment is the *recapture premium*.

redlining   the identification of a specific geographic area for the purpose of making loans or lending terms more difficult; a pattern of discriminatory lending. The name comes from the supposed practice of drawing a red line on a map to outline such an area.

recreational land development   a tract of land which has been divided into building lots and which may or may not be improved with buildings. Usually located in the South and Southwest, these developments often are marketed with "hard sell" tactics.

regional economics   the application of economic concepts in a regional context.

regression   an appraisal concept that the value of a superior property is affected adversely by association with inferior properties.

regressive income tax   a tax, such as the F.I.C.A. (social security) tax, which declines as a percentage of total income as income increases beyond a certain level.

REIT   the acronym for real estate investment trust.

release price   the amount of a mortgage loan that must be repaid in order to have a portion of the mortgaged premises released from the mortgage lien.

remainderman   one who will become entitled to an estate in property in the future, after the termination of an existing estate (e.g., one who is entitled to a fee simple interest in real estate after termination of an existing life estate).

rentable area   the measurement of leased space that excludes any space, such as elevator shafts, not actually available to the tenant.

rental achievement requirement   a condition in a floor-to-ceiling loan commitment that a specified portion of the building must be rented before the total loan is advanced.

replacement cost   the cost of creating a building or improvement in exact replica of an existing structure, on the basis of current prices, while using the same or closely similar materials.

replacement reserve   a fund which is set aside for making replacements of property and which is most important for property with short useful lives, such as furniture, carpeting, and refrigerators.

reproduction cost   the cost of creating a building or improvement having equivalent utility to an existing improvement, on the basis of current prices and using current standards of material and design.

rescission   the cancellation of an agreement, either by mutual consent of the parties or by judgment of a court.

resident manager   one who actually resides on the site of property which he manages.

restrictive covenant a limitation contained in a deed which restricts or regulates the use of the real property (e.g., a restriction that the land may be used for residential use only).

retainage a portion of the amount due under a construction contract that is withheld by the owner until the job is completed in accordance with plans and specifications; usually a percentage of the total contract price (e.g., 10 percent).

risk the possibility that returns on an investment or loan will not be as high as expected. The four main types of risk are business risk, financial risk, purchasing power risk, and liquidity risk.

risk aversion the tendency or desire of most persons to avoid risk. One's degree of risk aversion determines the risk premium that one will build into a required rate of return.

risk control techniques steps in the development or construction process at which the developer is able either to discontinue the operation or to modify it in light of new circumstances.

risk premium the return required by an investor to compensate him for the risk that he will be unable to recoup his capital over the life of the investment.

ROR the acronym for rate of return.

S

salesperson one who is employed by a real estate broker but who is licensed only as a salesperson. In most states, it is necessary to be a salesperson for a specified period of time before qualifying to be a broker.

sales tax a tax levied on purchases of goods and services. Despite its name, it is a tax paid by puchasers and not sellers.

S&L the acronym for a savings and loan association.

savings and loan association (S&L) a type of savings institution that is the primary source of financing for one to four family homes. Most S&Ls are mutual (nonstock) institutions.

scarcity one of the factors required for an object to have value, the others being desire for the object, its utility, and the effective purchasing power to acquire it.

secondary mortgage market the market in which existing mortgages are purchased (by investors seeking income) and sold (usually by lending institutions which originated the mortgages).

sector theory a theory that holds residential concentrations in an urban area develop according to cultural as well as economic factors.

security interest the legal interest in real estate represented by a mortgage (i.e., an interest created for the purpose of securing a loan).

self-liquidating loan a loan that will be completely repaid at maturity by reason of amortization payments during its life.

selling broker a broker other than a listing broker who brings about a sale and whose commission from the sale is divided with the listing broker.

sensitivity analysis a method for determining variations in the rate of return on an investment in accordance with changes in a single factor (e.g., how much will the rate of return change if operating expenses rise 10 percent?).

shift share a method of analyzing the economic growth in a particular region by comparing it with the economic growth of the nation.

shopping center integrated and self-contained shopping areas, mostly in the suburbs, that are generally considered the blue chips of real estate investment. The three main types are regional, community, and neighborhood (strip) centers.

sinking fund a fund of monies periodically set aside for the purpose of debt repayment together with the interest earned by such monies.

soft-dollar costs cash outlays which give rise to tax deductions and therefore are partially or wholly recoverable via tax savings.

sole proprietorship a business operated by an individual, as distinguished from a partnership or corporation.

special agent an agent authorized to perform one or more specific acts for the principal and no other acts. A real estate broker normally is a special agent.

special purpose property a property that has been developed for a special purpose or use (e.g., a motel, restaurant, etc.) and that is generally considered riskier than other real estate because it is not easily converted to other uses.

stabilized net operating income net operating income from property which differs from the actual historical income in that nonrecurring or unusual items of income and expense have been eliminated. The object is to show as closely as possible the true future earning power of the property.

standing loan a loan which calls for no amortization payments during its life (i.e., the entire loan will come due at maturity).

state board of equalization a state agency which adjusts the assessments from each separate tax district in the state to compensate for differences in fractions of full value that are utilized by different districts.

statute of frauds a type of statute in effect in every state that seeks to prevent frauds and perjuries by providing that certain types of contracts will not be enforceable in a court unless they are in writing. Included under the statutes are contracts for the sale of land.

straight line depreciation a method of depreciation whereby an equal amount is taken as a depreciation deduction each year over the useful life of the asset being depreciated.

subchapter S corporation a corporation that qualifies under subchapter S of the Internal Revenue Code and that is a small business corporation which can pass through profits and losses directly to its shareholders.

subcontractor an individual or company which performs a specific job for a construction project (e.g., electrical work) pursuant to an agreement with the general contractor.

subdivision ordinance a form of municipal ordinance that regulates the development and design of subdivisions, including such matters as the dedication (donation) of land for streets, parks and schools, provision of utility services, including water supply and sewage disposal, and requirements for building lines and lot size.

subject property the property being spoken about or for which a value is being sought.

substitution an appraisal concept to the effect that when several goods with substantially the same utility are available, the one with the lowest price attracts the greatest demand.

supply and demand an appraisal and economic concept that increasing the supply or decreasing the demand for a thing tends to affect its price adversely, while decreasing the supply or increasing the demand tends to increase the price.

surplus productivity in appraisal, the term given to the net real property income remaining after the costs of labor, capital, and coordination have been paid.

surveyor a real estate professional trained in the science of determining the precise location of a tract of land in relation to the surface of the earth.

syndicate a group of individuals who join together for the purpose of investment. The term syndicate has no specific legal significance.

T

takeout commitment the term used to describe the permanent loan commitment for a project to be constructed. The permanent commitment will provide the funds to "take out" the construction lender when the building is completed.

tax avoidance the legal right of a taxpayer to utilize all provisions of the tax statute in order to minimize tax liability. Tax evasion, by contrast, is the use of illegal means to reduce one's tax liability.

taxable gain the amount of gain realized on the sale of an asset that is subject to tax either as ordinary income or capital gain. In essence, the amount of gain is the excess of the net sales price over the seller's tax basis.

tax basis the amount of the seller's investment that may be deducted from the net sales price in order to determine the amount of gain or loss realized on the sale. Tax basis essentially is equal to original cost plus the amount of any capital expenditures during the period of ownership and minus the amount of accumulated depreciation taken for tax purposes.

taxable income income subject to tax after appropriate deductions and exemptions have been applied to the taxpayer's gross income.

tax conversion a form of tax avoidance that enables the taxpayer to convert ordinary income to more favorable taxed capital gain (e.g., the use of straight line depreciation).

tax deferral a form of tax avoidance by which the taxpayer is enabled to delay the payment of tax on income from a current year to a future year (e.g., the use of accelerated depreciation).

tax-free exchange a swap of investment or business real estate which permits the exchangor to defer the payment of tax on any appreciation in value of the property exchanged.

tax-preference income a certain type of income (e.g., the excess of accelerated over straight line depreciation) that is subject to the add-on minimum tax.

tax savings the dollar benefit to an investor as a result of deductions or losses realized for tax purposes. For example, each dollar of taxable loss is worth 70 cents to a taxpayer in the 70 percent tax bracket, and correspondingly less to a taxpayer in any lower bracket.

tax shelter in the broadest sense, any deduction or credit against income that is available only to a special category of taxpayer and that results in an increased cash flow to that taxpayer because of lower taxes. The primary source of tax shelter in real estate is the right to take depreciation deductions for improved property.

tenancy by the entirety   a form of concurrent ownership which can exist only between husband and wife and which includes the right of survivorship.

tenancy in common   a form of concurrent ownership under which each tenant in common may sell or devise his interest (i.e., no right of survivorship exists).

tenant allowance   a cash payment made by the developer to a tenant (usually in a shopping center) to enable the tenant, rather than the developer, to complete the interior work for the leased premises.

time sharing   the division of ownership or use of a resort unit or apartment on the basis of time periods (e.g., a resort unit may be divided into 25 time shares of two weeks each, with two weeks left open for maintenance).

time value of money   the idea that a dollar today is worth more than a dollar at some future date; the rationale behind compounding (for future value) or discounting (for present value).

title   evidence of ownership of real property; often used synonymously with the term *ownership* to indicated a person's right to possess, use, and dispose of property.

title company   a company which examines titles to real estate, which determines if they are valid and whether or not any limitations on the title exist, and which, for a premium, insures the validity of the title to the owner or a lender.

title examiner   one who is trained in the art of examining public land records in order to ascertain if the present owner of property has good title.

trade breakdown method   a method of estimating reproduction cost in which direct cost for labor and materials are added to indirect costs for financing, selling, insurance, etc., to arrive at the estimated reproduction cost new of the improvement on the site.

transient facility   hospitality facility (hotel or motel) which caters primarily to guests in transit from one location to another.

trust   an arrangement under which legal title to property is held by one person under an agreement to administer the property for the benefit of another (the beneficiary) who holds equitable title.

Truth in Lending Act   a federal law under which lenders are required to make advance disclosure to borrowers of the amount and type of finance charges incurred in connection with the loan.

two-part return   term which reflects the fact that the overall return to a real estate investor normally consists of (1) cash flows during the period of ownership and (2) proceeds from ultimate sale of the property.

U

unilateral contract   a contract involving the exchange of a promise for performance of an act (rather than for another promise) (e.g., *A* promises to pay *B* $10 if *B* walks five miles).

upside leverage   the method of increasing the return on equity (cash invested) by borrowing funds at a cost lower than the free and clear return from the property. Thus, the borrower is earning more on the borrowed funds than their interest cost.

upzoning   a change in the zoning classification of property from a lower use to a higher use (e.g., from heavy industrial use to light industrial use).

urban economics economic concepts applied in the context of a particular urban area.

useful life the period over which a business or investment asset is expected to have economic value and hence the period over which it must be depreciated.

utility one of the elements of value.

V

value in general, the amount of money that can be obtained in exchange for a thing. Value in this sense is also known as *market value* or *value in exchange.* A property may also have a value in use (i.e., it may be worth something to one who utilizes the property even though no identifiable market demand exists).

value in use assessment a method of real property taxation under which land is taxed on the basis of its existing use, rather than on the basis of its highest and best use; often used to prevent onerous taxation of farmland which would otherwise be taxed on the basis of its suitability for development.

variable rate mortgage (VRM) a mortgage which carries an interest rate which may move either up or down, depending on the movements of an outside standard (e.g., the Treasury bond rate) to which the interest rate is tied.

variance in general, the difference between expected results and actual results. Statistically, the term *variance* refers to the square of the standard deviation. Variation can be used as a definition of risk, especially on the downside.

VRM the acronym for variable rate mortgage.

W

warehouse a building which is used for the storage of goods or merchandise and which may either be owner-occupied or leased to one or more tenants.

wraparound mortgage a form of secondary financing in which the face amount of the second (wraparound) loan is equal to the balance of the first loan plus the amount of the new financing. Because the interest rate on the wraparound loan normally is greater than on the original first mortgage, upside leverage is achieved on the new lender's return.

Z

zoning ordinance the ordinance by which local governments assign land uses (e.g., residential, commercial, or industrial) to appropriate districts in accordance with a master plan. A zoning ordinance also regulates lot size and height and bulk of buildings.

INDEX